THE

WESTMINSTER ASSEMBLY'S

SHORTER CATECHISM

EXPLAINED,

BY WAY OF

QUESTION AND ANSWER.

PART I.

OF THE DUTY WHICH GOD REQUIRES OF MAN.

Hold fast the form of sound words."—2 Tim. i. 13.

Wipf & Stock
PUBLISHERS
Eugene, Oregon

Wipf and Stock Publishers
199 W 8th Ave, Suite 3
Eugene, OR 97401

The Westminster Assembly's Shorter Catechism
Explained by Way of Question and Answer, Part I and II
By Fisher, James
ISBN: 1-57910-791-5
Publication date 10/18/2001
Previously published by Presbyterian Board of Publication, 1765

PREFACE TO THE FIRST EDITION.

The *Shorter Catechism*, composed by the *Assembly* of *Divines* at *Westminster*, with assistance of *Commissioners* from the Church of *Scotland*, being approved by the General Assembly of the said church in 1648, and ratified by the Estates of Parliament in the year following, is above any recommendation of ours; having its praises already in all the churches of CHRIST, abroad and at home, among whom it has been justly admired as a *master-piece* of its kind, both for the fulness of its matter, and the compendious and perspicuous manner in which it is expressed.

Although it is only a human composure, yet being a *form of sound words*, agreeable unto, and founded on the word of GOD, it ought to be held fast, and earnestly contended for, by all the lovers of truth, in opposition to the contrary errors that are revived and raging in our day; and, in order hereto, it ought to be considered, that a divine faith is due to the words of the HOLY GHOST supporting it, as the evident *proofs* thereof.

Nothing tends more to the advantage and well-being of the church, than sound standards of doctrine, worship, and government; because, as they are a strong bulwark against contrary errors and opinions, so they tend to preserve truth in its purity, and the professors of it in unity and harmony among themselves. On the other hand, there is nothing more galling to the adversaries of truth, than such public standards, because they are a very severe check and curb upon their unbounded and licentious liberty, being directly levelled against their erroneous schemes and plainly discovering the harmonious chain of scripture truth, in opposition to them.

The *divine warrant* for such composures, is abundantly clear from 2 Tim. 1. 13, where we read of the *form of sound words* wherein Paul instructed Timothy; and Heb. v. 12, of *the first principles of the oracles of God;* and chap. vi. 1, of *the principles of the doctrine of Christ.* — Besides, there are several *summaries*, or compendious systems of divine truth, recorded in scripture; such as Exod. xx. 2—18; Matt. vi. 9—14; 1 Tim. iii. 16; and Tit. ii. 11—15, with many others, which are the examples, or patterns, upon which the Christian churches, both in ancient and latter times, have deduced, from the pure fountain of the word, the principal articles of their holy religion, as a test and standard of orthodoxy amongst them.

The *Shorter Catechism* sets forth the principles of Christianity in the most excellent method and order. It would be tedious to give a particular *analysis* or division of the several heads of divinity, according to the order of the *Catechism.* But, in general, the method of it may be taken up under these four comprehensive articles, namely, the *chief end,* the *only rule,* the *glorious object,* and the *great subject* of the Christian religion.

I. The *chief end* of the Christian religion, which is the glorifying of God, and the enjoying him for ever. Quest 1.

II. We have the *only rule* of the Christian religion; describe

1. In its *matter;* which is the *word* of God, contained in the scriptures of the Old and New Testaments. Quest. 2.

2. In its *principal parts;* which are, first, what man is to *believe* concerning God; and then the duty which God requires of man. Quest. 3.

III. The *glorious object* of the Christian religion; which is God; considered,

PREFACE.

1. *Essentially*, in his spiritual nature, infinite perfections, and in his most perfect unity and simplicity. Quest. 4, 5.

2. *Relatively* or *personally*; in the three distinct persons of the Godhead; and in the consubstantiality, and absolute equality of these persons. Quest. 6.

3. *Efficiently*, in his acts and operations, which are either immanent and essential, such as his decrees; or transient and external, such as his works of creation and providence, wherein he executes his decrees. Quest. 7—12.

IV. The *great subject* of the Christian religion, which is *man*; considered,

1st, In his state of *innocence*; where the covenant of works is opened. Quest. 12.

2dly, In his *state of nature*, together with the sinfulness and misery of that state. Quest. 13—20.

3dly, In his *state of grace*, or begun recovery; where the *Catechism* treats,

1. Of the *nature* of the covenant of grace. Quest. 20.

2. Of the *Mediator* of the covenant; who is described, in his person, offices, humiliation, exaltation, and in the application of his purchased redemption by the HOLY SPIRIT. Quest. 21—32.

3. Of the *benefits* of the covenant; in this life, at death, at the resurrection, and through all eternity. Quest. 32—39.

4. Of the *duties* by which we evidence our covenant relation and gratitude to GOD, in the *Ten Commandments*, as connected with their *Preface*. Quest. 39—82.

5. Of man's utter *inability* to obey the law in this life. Quest. 82.

6. Of the *aggravation* and *desert* of sin. Quest. 83, 84.

7. Of the *means* by which our salvation is carried on and perfected at death: the internal means, faith and repentance; the external means, the word, sacraments and prayer. Quest. 85, to the end.

PREFACE.

The *first part* of this catechetical treatise ends with Quest. 38. *What benefits do believers receive from Christ at the resurrection?* containing the doctrines we are to *believe* concerning God. The *second part* respects the *duty* which God requires of man.

The *materials* of the following Catechism are collected by several ministers, and it was recommended to *three* of their number, to revise what should be done by so many hands, that there might be a uniformity of style and method, and that repetitions might be prevented as much as possible. It has pleased the Lord to take home to himself *one*[*] of these three, who assisted in the composing and revising of this *first part;* but, though he be dead, he yet speaketh, and will be spoken of for his excellent works (which have already, or may hereafter see the light,) by all those who shall have any relish or taste for sound doctrine and experimental godliness.—Whatever loss the *second part* of this Catechism may sustain, by the removal of such an able and skilful hand, the *other two* make not the least doubt, but the Lord would carry on this work with as great, or greater advantage, though they were laid in the grave likewise.

Mean time, that what is here presented to public view may be blessed of God, for the edification of souls, is, in the name of our brethren, the earnest prayer of

February, 1753   EBEN. ERSKINE.
                              JAMES FISHER.

---

[*] The Rev. Mr. Ralph Erskine, of Dunfermline.

ADVERTISEMENT TO THE THIRD EDITION

'THE words of the Shorter Catechism, being advised with the greatest judgment, and with a peculiar view, both for establishing scripture-truth, and likewise for refuting contrary errors, they are therefore, in this edition, particularly taken notice of: and to distinguish them, they are enclosed within brackets, that the reader may the more easily discern how they are explained in this treatise.

As the Confession of Faith and Larger Catechism are granted to be the best interpreters of the Shorter, the latter is carefully explained by the former; and several of the following questions and answers framed from these standards, as will easily appear by the quotations taken from them, and the references made unto them.

In this edition, almost every answer is confirmed by the scriptures; many are added, where they were formerly wanting, and several exchanged, for those that are thought more apposite.—In the former impressions, the scripture-proofs were, mostly, subjoined to the end of the answer; but now, each scripture is immediately annexed to that part of the answer it is designed to confirm, that it may be consulted, with greater certainty, and less trouble, by those who incline to bring every position, here advanced, to the unerring rule and standard of the word. —Some of the longer answers are divided into two or more, for sake of the memory; and some additional questions are interspersed, through the whole, for illustration. A short Index is likewise annexed, of the most material things in both parts.

ADVERTISEMENT.

I have employed my spare time for several months, in studying to make this edition as correct and useful to the public as I could; and now I leave it in the hands of the *God of truth*, that he may use it for the purposes of his own glory, in *edifying the body of Christ, till* they *all come, in the unity of the faith, and of the knowledge of the Son of God, unto a perfect man, unto the measure of the stature of the fulness of Christ.*

JAMES FISHER.

GLASGOW, Jan. 14, 1765.

THE

SHORTER CATECHISM EXPLAINED

QUEST. 1. *What is the chief end of man?*
ANS. Man's chief end is to glorify God, and to enjoy him for ever.

Q. 1. What is meant by man's [*chief end?*]
A. That which ought to be man's chief aim and design; and that which he should seek after as his chief happiness.
Q. 2. What ought to be man's chief aim and design?
A. The glory of God. 1 Chron. xvi. 28, 29: "Give unto the Lord, ye kindreds of the people,—give unto the Lord the glory due unto his name."
Q. 3. What should he seek after as his chief happiness?
A. The enjoyment of God. Isa. xxvi. 8: " The desire of our soul is to thy name, and the remembrance of thee."
Q. 4. What connexion is there between the glorifying God, and the enjoyment of him?
A. They are connected by rich and sovereign grace, persuading and enabling the sinner to embrace Jesus Christ as the only way to God and glory. Eph. ii. 8: " By grace are ye saved, through faith, and that not of yourselves; it is the gift of God." John xvi. 6:—" I," says Christ, " am the way; no man cometh unto the Father, but by me."
Q. 5. Does the chief end exclude subordinate ends?
A. No: for, in aiming principally at the glory of God, men may use the supports of natural life for refreshing their bodies, 1 Cor. x. 31; and be diligent in their particular callings, that they may provide for themselves and their families, 1 Thess. iv. 11, 12; 1 Tim. v. 8.
Q. 6. Why ought the glory of God to be the chief end and design of man?
A. Because it is God's chief end in man's creation, preservation, redemption, and regeneration. Prov. xvi. 4: " The Lord hath made all things for himself;" and therefore it ought to be man's chief end likewise. 1 Cor. vi. 19, 20: " Ye are not your own; for ye are bought with a

price: therefore glorify God in your body, and in your spirit, which are God's."

Q. 7. How manifold is the glory of God?
A. Twofold; his essential and his declarative glory.
Q. 8. What is God's essential glory?
A. It is what he is absolutely in himself. Exod. iii. 14— I AM THAT I AM.
Q. 9. What is his declarative glory?
A. His showing, or making known his glory, to, in, and by his creatures, Isa. xliv. 23; 2 Thess. i. 10.
Q. 10. Can any creature whatsoever add any thing to God's essential glory?
A. No: for his essential glory is infinite, eternal, and unchangeable, Job xxxv. 7.
Q. 11. Do not the heavens and the earth, and all inferior creatures, glorify God?
A. Yes: in a *passive way*, all his works praise him; Psal. xix. 1, and cxlv. 10.
Q. 12. How ought man to [*glorify*] God?
A. Man being endued with a reasonable soul, ought to glorify God in an *active way*, Psal. lxiii. 4, by declaring his praise, Psal. ciii. 1, 2; and essaying to give him the glory due to his name, Psalm xcvi. 7.
Q. 13. How was man to glorify God in a state of innocence?
A. By a perfect, personal, and perpetual obedience to his law, Gen. i. 27; and by giving him the glory of all his works, chap. ii. 19.
Q. 14. Has man answered his chief end?
A. No: for, "all have sinned, and come short of the glory of God," Rom. iii. 23.
Q. 15. Has God then lost his end in making man?
A. No: for God will glorify his justice and power upon some, and his grace and mercy upon others of Adam's family, Rom. ix. 22, 23.
Q. 16. Was ever God glorified by a perfect obedience since Adam's fall?
A. Never, until CHRIST, the *second Adam*, appeared as a new covenant head, Isa. xlii. 21, and xlix. 3.
Q. 17. How did Christ, the second Adam, glorify God, as our surety and representative on earth?
A. By finishing the work the Father gave him to do John xvii. 4.
Q. 18. What was the work the Father gave him to do?
A. It was to assume a holy human nature, Luke i. 35; to yield a perfect sinless obedience to the whole law, Mat. iii. 15; and to give a complete satisfaction to justice, for man's sin, by his meritorious sufferings and death, Luke xxiv. 26.
Q. 19. How does Christ glorify God in heaven?

A. By appearing in the presence of God for us, Heb. ix. 24, and applying, by the power of his Spirit, that redemption which he purchased by the price of his blood on earth, Tit. iii. 5, 6.

Q. 20. When is it that a sinner begins uprightly to aim at the glory of God?

A. When, through a faith of God's operation, he believes in Christ: Acts viii. 37, 39.—"The eunuch answered and said, I believe that Jesus Christ is the son of God.—And he went on his way rejoicing."

Q. 21. Can no man glorify God acceptably, unless he first believe in Christ?

A. No: for, "Without faith it is impossible to please him." Heb. xi. 6; and, "Whatsoever is not of faith is sin," Rom. xiv. 23.

Q. 22. How is it that faith in Christ glorifies God?

A. As it sets its seal to the record of God, John iii. 33; and unites us to Christ, from whom only our fruit is found, Hos. xiv. 8.

Q. 23. Is not God glorified by the good works of believers?

A. Yes: "herein," says Christ, "is my Father glorified, that ye bear much fruit, John xv. 8.

Q. 24. What are these fruits brought forth by believers, by which God is glorified?

A. They may be summed up in faith working by love, Gal. v. 6; or, their aiming, in the strength of Christ, at universal obedience to the law, as the rule of duty. Phil. iv. 13: "I can do all things through Christ which strengtheneth me."

Q. 25. How should we glorify God in eating and drinking?

A. By taking a right to the supports of natural life, through the second Adam, the heir of all things, who has purchased a covenant right to temporal, as well as spiritual mercies, for his people, 1 Cor. iii. 21—23; and thankfully acknowledging God for the same, 1 Tim. iv. 4, 5.

Q. 26. How must we glorify God in our religious worship, and other acts of obedience?

A. By doing all that we do in the name of the Lord Jesus, Col. iii. 17; worshipping God in the Spirit, rejoicing in Christ Jesus, and having no confidence in the flesh, Phil. iii. 3.

Q. 27. What is it, next to the glory of God, we should aim at?

A. Next to God's glory, we should aim at the *enjoyment* of him, Ps. lxxiii. 25, 26.

Q. 28. Why should we aim at the enjoyment of God?

A. Because he is the chief good of the rational creature, Ps. cxvi. 7; and nothing else besides him, is either suitable to the nature, or satisfying to the desires of the immortal soul, Ps. cxliv. 15.

Q. 29. How may a finite creature [enjoy] an infinite God?

A. By taking and rejoicing in him, as its everlasting and upmaking portion, Ps. xvi. 5, 6, and xlviii. 14.

Q. 30. Did our first parents, in a state of innocence, enjoy God?

A. Yes: there was perfect friendship and fellowship between God and them; for, "God made man upright," Eccl. vii. 29.

Q. 31. What broke that blessed friendship and fellowship?

A. Sin: our iniquities have separated between us and our God, and our sins have hid his face from us, Isa. lix. 2.

Q. 32. Can a sinner, in a natural state, enjoy God, or have any fellowship with him?

A. No: for, "What communion hath light with darkness? and what concord hath Christ with Belial?" 2 Cor. vi. 14, 15.

Q. 33. How may a lost sinner recover the enjoyment of God, and fellowship with him?

A. As we lost it by our fall in the *first Adam*, so it can only be recovered by union with a *second Adam*, Rom. v. 18, 19; for there is no coming to God but by him, John xiv. 6.

Q. 34. When is it that a sinner begins to enjoy God?

A. When, having received Christ by faith, he rests upon him, and upon God in him, for righteousness and strength, Isa. xlv. 24; and out of his fulness receives, and grace for grace, John i. 16.

Q. 35. What are the external means by, or in which, we are to seek after the enjoyment of God?

A. In all the ordinances of his worship, public, private and secret; such as the word read and heard, the sacraments, prayer, meditation, fasting, thanksgiving, and the like.

Q. 36. Are the saints of God admitted to enjoy him in these?

A. Yes: they are the tristing places where his name is recorded, and to which he has promised to come and bless them, Ex. xx. 24—" In all places where I record my name, I will come unto thee, and I will bless thee."

Q. 37. What scripture-evidence have we, of their enjoying God in the duties and ordinances of his appointment?

A. We find them much employed in religious duties, Song iii. 1—3; and expressing the utmost regard for the ordinances of his grace, Ps. lxxxiv. 1, 2.

Q. 38. What satisfaction has the soul in the enjoyment of God?

A. Unspeakably more gladness than when corn, wine, and all earthly comforts, do most abound, Ps. iv. 7

Q. 39. Is there any difference between the enjoyment of God in this life, and that which the saints shall obtain in the life to come?

A. Not an *essential*, but a *gradual* difference, as to the *manner* and *measure* of it.

Q. 40. What is the difference as to the *manner* of the enjoyment here and hereafter?

A. Here, the enjoyment is *mediate*, by the intervention of means; hereafter, it will be *immediate*, without any use of these means: "Now we see through a glass darkly; but then FACE TO FACE," 1 Cor. xiii. 12.

Q. 41. What is the difference as to the *measure* of the enjoyment, in this life, and that which is to come?

A. In this life the enjoyment is only *partial*; in that which is to come, it will be *full* and complete, 1 John iii. 2—here, the enjoyment is only in the seed, or first fruits; there it will be in the full harvest, Ps. cxxvi. 5, 6.

Q. 42. Is the partial enjoyment of God in grace here, a sure pledge of the full enjoyment of him in glory hereafter?

A. It is both the pledge and earnest of it, Eph. i. 13, 14. Ps. lxxxiv. 11.

Q. 43. Does the gracious soul, in that state, fully receive its chief end?

A. Yes; in regard that then it shall be brimful of God, and celebrate his praises with high and uninterrupted *Hallelujahs* through all eternity, Ps. xvi. 11; Isa. xxxv. 10.

Q. 44. Why is the glorifying God made the leading part of man's chief end, and set before the enjoyment of him?

A. Because, as God's design in glorifying himself was the reason and foundation of his design in making man happy in the enjoyment of him, Rom. xi. 26; so he has made our aiming at his glory, as our chief end, to be the very way and means of our attaining to that enjoyment, Ps. l. 23.

Q. 45. Is our happiness, in the enjoyment of God, to be our chief end?

A. No: but the glory of God itself, Isa. xlii. 8; in our aiming at which *chiefly*, we cannot miss the enjoyment of him, Ps. cxi. 14, 15.

Q. 46. Is not our delighting in the glory of God, to be reckoned our chief end?

A. No: we must set the glory of God above our delight therein, otherwise, our delight is not chiefly in God, but in ourselves, Isa. ii. 11. Our subjective delighting in the glory of God belongs to the enjoyment of him, whose glory is above the heavens, and infinitely above our delight therein, Ps. cxiii. 4.

Q. 47. Whom does God dignify with the enjoyment of himself, in time and for ever?
A. Those whom he helps actively to glorify and honour him; for he has said, "Them that honour me, I will honour," 1 Sam. ii. 30.

Q. 48. Does any thing so much secure our happy enjoyment of God, as the concern that the glory of God has in it?
A. No: for as God cannot but reach the great end of his own glory, so, when he has promised us eternal life, in Christ, before the world began, Tit. i. 2, we cannot come short of it; because it stands upon the honour of his faithfulness to make it good, Heb. x. 23; "He is faithful that promised."

Q. 49. How does it appear, that the enjoyment of God, which is connected with the glorifying of him, shall be [*for ever?*]
A. Because he who is the object enjoyed, is the *everlasting God*, Isa. xl. 28; and the enjoyment of him is not transitory, like the passing enjoyments of time, but the eternal enjoyment of the eternal God, Ps. xlviii. 14.

———♦———

QUEST. 2. *What rule has God given to direct us how we may glorify and enjoy him?*

ANS. The word of God, which is contained in the scriptures of the Old and New Testaments, is the only rule to direct us, how we may glorify and enjoy him.

Q. 1. What necessity is there of a rule to direct us how to glorify and enjoy God?
A. It is necessary, because, since God will be glorified by the reasonable creature, nothing can be a perfect rule for that end, but his own revealed will, Rom. xii. 2.

Q. 2. Can man, by any wisdom or power of his own, ever attain to the glorifying of God, and the enjoyment of him, which he has come short of, by his fall in the *first Adam?*
A. No: his wisdom and knowledge in the things of God, are become folly and ignorance, Job xi. 12; and his power to do good is turned into utter impotency, John vi. 44.

Q. 3. Where has God revealed the way, in which man may recover and attain the end of his creation?
A. In [the word of God, which is contained in the scriptures of the Old and New Testaments,] John v. 39. *Search the scriptures, &c.*

Q. 4. How do you know the scriptures of the Old and New Testaments to be the *word of God?*
A. By the *print* of God that is evidently to be seen upon them: for, as none works like God, Isa. xliii. 13; so none speaks like him, John vii. 46.

Q. 5. What do you understand by the print or impress of God that is so discernible in the scriptures?
A. That majesty, holiness, light, life, and efficacy, which shine in the word itself, Rom. i. 16; Ps. xix. 7.

Q. 6. What may be said of those who do not see that print of God in the word, though they read it?
A. It may be said, " The god of this world hath blinded the minds of them that believe not," 2 Cor. iv. 4.

Q. 7. Since all men are spiritually blind by nature, is it not in vain for them to read the scriptures?
A. No: it is the will of God that they should read and search the scriptures, John v. 39; and the entrance of his word gives light and sight to them that are blind, Psalm cxix. 130.

Q. 8. What should a man do that the Bible may not remain a sealed book to him?
A. Whenever he looks into the word of God, he should look up to God, the author of it, saying, " Open thou mine eyes, that I may behold wondrous things out of thy law," Ps. cxix. 18. " O send out thy light and thy truth; let them lead me," Ps. xliii. 3.

Q. 9. By what arguments may we persuade men that are infidels, to receive the scriptures as the word of God?
A. We may deal with them by rational arguments drawn from their antiquity; the heavenliness of the matter; the majesty of the style; the harmony of all the parts, though written in different ages; the exact accomplishment of prophecies; the sublimity of the mysteries and matters contained in the word; the efficacy and power of it, in the conviction and conversion of multitudes; the scope of the whole, to guide men to attain their chief end, the glory of God in their own salvation; and the many miracles wrought for the confirmation of the truth of the doctrines contained in them.*

Q. 10. Can these or the like rational arguments, ever produce a divine faith?
A. No: for rational arguments can only produce a mere rational faith, founded on reason; but a divine and saving faith rests wholly upon the divine testimony inherent in the word itself; or upon a " Thus saith the Lord."

Q. 11. How is this inherent testimony discovered?
A. By the same Spirit of God that dictated the word, 2 Pet. i. 21; he being an "Interpreter, one among a thousand," John xvi. 13.

* See Confession of Faith, chap. i. § 5.

Q. 12. What is it that will fully persuade and assure a person that the scriptures are indeed the word of God?
A. "The Spirit of God bearing witness by, and with the scriptures in the heart of man, is alone able fully to persuade it, that they are the very word of God," John xvi. 13, 14. 1 John ii. 27.*

Q. 13. Whether does the authority of the scripture, for which it ought to be believed and obeyed, depend upon the testimony of the church, or wholly upon God?
A. "Wholly upon God, (who is truth itself,) the author thereof; and, therefore, it is to be received, because it is the word of God," 1 John v. 9. 1 Thess. ii. 13.†

Q. 14. Why cannot the authority of the scriptures depend upon the church?
A. Because the true church of Christ depends, in its very being, on the scriptures; and therefore the scriptures cannot depend upon it, as to their authority, Eph. ii. 20, 22.

Q. 15. Are not the light of nature, and the works of creation and providence, sufficient to direct us how we may glorify and enjoy God?
A. These "do so far manifest the goodness, wisdom, and power of God, as to leave men inexcusable, Rom. ii. 14, 15, and i. 19, 20; yet are they not sufficient to give that knowledge of God, and of his will, which is necessary unto salvation, 1 Cor. ii. 13, 14."‡

Q. 16. What makes a further revelation, than nature's light, necessary?
A. The glory of the Divine perfections, particularly his mercy, grace, love, and faithfulness, Ps. lxxxv. 8, 10, 11; the gross ignorance and degeneracy of mankind, 1 Cor. i. 20, 21; the sublimeness of the things revealed, which otherwise had never been known by men or angels, John i. 18: it is also necessary for trying the spirits and doctrines of men, and for unmasking the impostures of the devil, 1 John iv. 1—3.

Q. 17. How does it appear that the scriptures are not an imposition upon mankind?
A. If the penman of the scriptures had inclined to deceive, they would have accommodated themselves to the dispositions of the people with whom they conversed, and connived at their lusts; but, on the contrary, we find they faithfully exposed the errors and vices of men, and impartially set themselves against every thing that corrupt nature is fond of; and that, though they were laid open to the greatest hardships and sufferings for so doing, Acts v. 29, 30, 31—40, 41.

Q. 18. What is the meaning of the word [*scriptures?*]
A. It signifies *writings;* and the word of God is empha-

* Larger Cat. Q. 4.   † Confession, chap. i. § 4.
‡ Confession, chap. i. § 1.

OF THE HOLY SCRIPTURES. 17

tically so called, because God has therein *written* to us the great things of his law and covenant, Hos. viii. 12.

Q. 19. Why was the word of God committed to writing?

A. "For the better preserving and propagating of the truth; and for the more sure establishment and comfort of the church, against the corruption of the flesh, and the malice of Satan and of the world, Luke i. 3, 4. Prov. xxii. 20, 21."*

Q. 20. How was the will of God made known to the church, before it was committed to writing?

A. By immediate revelations, Gen. ii. 16, 17, and iii. 15; by frequent appearances of the Son of God, delighting, beforehand, to try on the human likeness, Gen. xviii. 2, compared with v. 3, Judg. xiii. 11, compared with verses 18, 19; by the ministry of the holy angels, Gen. xix. 1, 15, Heb. ii. 2, and of the patriarchs, Jude, ver. 14, 15. Heb. xi. 7.

Q. 21. Why are the scriptures of the Old and New Testament called [*the word of God?*]

A. Because " all scripture is given by inspiration of God," 2 Tim. iii. 16, being immediately indited by the Holy Ghost, 2 Pet. i. 21.

Q. 22. Why are they commonly called the BIBLE?

A. The word BIBLE signifying a book; the holy scriptures are so called by way of eminence, because they are incomparably the best of all books, as containing the invariable grounds of faith in Christ, for life eternal, John xx. 31: "These are written, that ye might believe that Jesus is the Christ, the Son of God, and that, believing, ye might have life through his name."

Q. 23. Why are the holy scriptures called a [*Testament?*]

A. Because they are the last will of the glorious Testator, first typically, and then actually confirmed by his death, concerning the vast legacies therein bequeathed to his spiritual seed: Heb. ix. 16, "Where a testament is, there must also of necessity be the death of the Testator."

Q. 24. Why are the writings of Moses and the prophets called the [*Old Testament?*]

A. Because the will of the Testator, Christ, was veiled, legally dispensed, and typically sealed by the blood of sacrificed beasts, upon which account it is called comparatively faulty, Heb. viii. 7, 8; and was therefore to vanish away, verse 13.

Q. 25. To whom were the oracles of God, under the Old Testament, committed?

A. To the church of the Jews, Rom. iii. 1, 2: "What advantage hath the Jew? Much every way: chiefly, because unto them were committed the oracles of God."

---

* Confession, chap. i. § 1.

OF THE HOLY SCRIPTURES.

Q. 26. Why are the scriptures from Matthew to the end of the Revelation, called the [*New Testament?*]

A. Because they contain the most clear and full revelation, and actual ratification of the covenant of promise, by the death of Christ the Testator, who is also the living Executor of his own testament, Rev. i. 18 : " I am he that liveth and was dead ; and behold, I am alive for evermore." John xiv. 19 : " Because I live, ye shall live also."

Q. 27. Will this New Testament dispensation of the grace of God ever undergo any other alteration?

A. No : it will remain new and unalterable, till the second coming of the Lord Jesus, Mat. xxvi. 29.

Q. 28. Do the scriptures of the Old Testament continue to be a rule of faith and practice to us who live under the New?

A. Yes : because they are the record of God concerning Christ, as well as the scriptures of the New Testament ; for all the prophets prophesied of him ; to him they did all bear witness, Acts x. 43 ; and Christ commands all to search them, because eternal life is to be found in them, and they testify of him, John v. 39.

Q. 29. How could the Old Testament be of force when it was not confirmed by the death of the Testator?

A. The death of Christ, the Testator, was typified in all the expiatory sacrifices of that dispensation ; hence is he called, " The Lamb slain from the foundation of the world," Rev. xiii. 8.

Q. 30. Is not that typical dispensation now quite abolished, under the New Testament?

A. Yes : for it was promised, that the Messiah should " cause the sacrifice and the oblation to cease ;" and accordingly, " Christ being come,—neither by the blood of goats nor calves, but by his own blood, he entered in once into the holy place, having obtained eternal redemption for us," Heb. ix. 11, 12.

Q. 31. Why was that ceremonial dispensation abolished?

A. Because it was only "a shadow of good things to come, and not the very image of the things ;" that is, not the very things themselves, Heb. x. 1.

Q. 32. Wherein does the New Testament excel the Old?

A. Amongst other things, it excels it in respect of evidence, worship, extent, gifts, and duration.

Q. 33. Wherein does the New Testament excel the Old in respect of *evidence?*

A. The Old Testament speaks of a Messiah to come, but the New presents him as already come, John i. 29, 41; The Old was dark and cloudy, but the New clear and perspicuous, 2 Cor. iii. 18.

Q. 34. How does it excel in respect of *worship?*

A. The worship of the Old Testament was a yoke of bondage; but the worship of the New is free, spiritual, and easy, Gal. v. 1.

Q. 35. How does the New Testament excel in respect of *extent* ?

A. The Old was confined to the Jews, Ps. cxlvii. 19, 20, and a few proselytes among the Gentiles, Ex. xii. 48; but the New extends to all the world, Mark xvi. 15; and its converts are vastly more numerous than under the old dispensation, Rev. vii. 9.

Q. 36. How does it excel in respect of *gifts* ?

A. The gifts of the Spirit are more plentiful, and more efficacious under the New, than under the Old, Acts ii. 17, 18.

Q. 37. How does the New Testament excel in respect of *duration* ?

A. The dispensation of the Old Testament, by types and sacrifices, was only for a time, Heb. viii. 13; but the dispensation of the New, is to continue unalterable to the end of the world, Matt. xxviii. 20.

Q. 38. Why are the scriptures said to be [*the* ONLY *rule*] to direct us, how we may glorify and enjoy God ?

A. Because none but God, the author of the scriptures, could, by them, show the way, how he himself is to be glorified and enjoyed by fallen sinners of mankind, Mic. vi. 6—9. Matt. xi. 25—28.

Q. 39. Although the light of nature, or natural reason, should not be *the only rule*, yet may it not be admitted as a *sufficient rule*, to direct us how to glorify and enjoy God ?

A. By no means; because of its utter incapacity to give the smallest discovery of Christ, the Mediator of the new covenant, 1 Cor. ii. 14, who is the only way of salvation for lost sinners of Adam's family, John xiv. 6.

Q. 40. Is it enough to assert, that the word of God is the *principal rule* to direct us ?

A. No: because this would leave room to conceive of *another* rule, beside the scriptures, which, though it might not be called the *principal one*, and *sufficient* for directing sinners to their chief end; which is false, and contrary to scripture, Luke xvi. 29, 31. Isa. viii. 20. Acts iv. 12.

Q. 41. Wherein consists the *perfection* of the scriptures ?

A. It consists in this, that, " the whole counsel of God, concerning all things necessary for his own glory, man's salvation, faith and life, is either expressly set down in scripture, or by good and necessary consequence may be deduced from scripture, 2 Tim. iii. 15—17. Gal. i. 8, 9." *

Q. 42. Are plain and necessary scripture consequences

* Confession, chap. i. § 6

OF THE HOLY SCRIPTURES.

to be admitted as a part of the rule, as well as express scriptures?

A. Yes: as is evident from the instance of our Lord, in proving the doctrine of the resurrection against the Sadducees, Matt. xxii. 31, 32. " As touching the resurrection of the dead, have ye not read that which was spoken unto you by God, saying, I am the God of Abraham, the God of Isaac, and the God of Jacob? God is not the God of the dead, but of the living."

Q. 43. Are the scriptures a clear and perspicuous rule?

A. All things necessary to be known, believed, and observed for salvation, are so clearly laid down in one place of scripture or another, that every one, in the due use of ordinary means, may attain to a sufficient understanding of them, Ps. cxix. 105, 130.*

Q. 44. Are human and unwritten traditions, how ancient soever, to be admitted as a part of the rule?

A. No: all human traditions are to be examined by the scriptures; and, "if they speak not according to this word, it is because there is no light in them," Isa. viii. 20.

Q. 45. Can the heathens, by all the helps they have, without revelation, attain to such a knowledge of God, and his will, as is necessary to salvation?

A. By no means: for they are declared to be "without God, and without hope in the world," Eph. ii. 12. "And where there is no vision, the people perish," Prov. xxix. 18; there being "no other name under heaven, given among men, whereby we must be saved," but that of Jesus, Acts iv. 12.

Q. 46. Is the light within men, or the Spirit without the word, which is pretended to by the Quakers, and other enthusiasts, to be used as any rule for our direction?

A. No: because whatever light or spirit is pretended to, without the word, it is but darkness, delusion, and a spirit of error, 1 John iv. 1, 6.

Q. 47. In what language were the scriptures originally written?

A. The Old Testament was written originally in *Hebrew*, and the New Testament in *Greek*.

Q. 48. Why ought the scriptures to be translated into the vulgar language of every nation where they come?

A. Because sinners of mankind have a right to, and interest in the scriptures, Prov. viii. 4,; and are commanded, in the fear of God, to read and search them, John v. 39.

Q. 49. Who is the supreme judge, in whose sentence we are to rest in determining all controversies of religion, and examining the decrees and doctrines of men?

* Confession, chap. i. § 7.

A. "No other but the Holy Spirit speaking in the scripture," Matt. xxii. 29. Acts xxviii. 25.*

Q. 50. Why are the books called the *Apocrypha* to be rejected as no part of the canon of scripture?

A. Because they were not written in the original language of the Old Testament; nor acknowledged for scripture by the Jews, to whom the oracles of God were committed; and have nothing of that impress of majesty, holiness, and efficacy, which shines so conspicuously in the scriptures of the Old and New Testaments; and because they were written after Malachi, whose book is called, *the end of the Prophets;* and contain many false things, contradictory and heretical.

Q. 51. Wherein consists the incomparable excellency and usefulness of the scriptures?

A. They are the well furnished dispensatory of all sovereign remedies, Ps. cvii. 20; the rich magazine of all true comfort, Rom. xv. 4; the complete armoury of all spiritual weapons, Eph. vi. 13—18; and the unerring compass to guide to the haven of glory, 2 Pet. i. 19.

QUEST. 3. *What do the scriptures principally teach?*

ANS. The scriptures principally teach, what man is to believe concerning God, and what duty God requires of man.

Q. 1. What is it [*to believe*] what the scriptures teach?

A. It is to assent and give credit to the truths thereof, because of the authority of God, whose word the scriptures are, John iii. 33. "He that hath received his testimony, hath set to his seal that God is true."

Q. 2. Are we to believe nothing in point of faith, and do nothing in point of duty, but what we are taught in the scripture?

A. No: because the scripture is the only book in the world of divine authority; and the revealed will and command of God therein, being so exceeding broad, nothing is incumbent on us to believe and do, but what is either directly, or consequentially prescribed in it, Isa. viii. 20.

Q. 3. Why are the scriptures said [*principally*] to teach matters of faith and practice?

A. Because though all things revealed in the scripture be equally true, yet every thing in it is not equally necessary to salvation, 1 Cor. vii. 12, 13.

* See Confession, chap. i. § 10.

OF THE SCOPE OF THE SCRIPTURES.

Q. 4. What is the order of doctrine laid down in this question?

A. Faith or believing is made the foundation of duty, or obedience; and not our obedience, or duty, the foundation of our faith, Tit. iii. 8.

Q. 5. Why are the things to be believed, set before the things to be practised?

A. To distinguish between the order of things in the covenant of grace, from what they were in innocency, in the covenant of works, Gal. iii. 12.

Q. 6. What was the order of things in the covenant of works?

A. Doing, or perfect obedience to the law, was the foundation of the promised privilege of life: "The man which doeth these things, shall live by them," Rom. x. 5.

Q. 7. Is this order inverted in the covenant of grace, or gospel revelation?

A. Yes: the promise is to be believed, and the promised privilege, namely, life, must be freely received; and upon this follows our obedience to the law, from gratitude and love, Jer. xxxi. 18, 19.

Q. 8. How does it appear that this is the order of gospel doctrine?

A. Because this is the order that God laid, in delivering the law at Mount Sinai; the foundation of faith is first laid in these words of the preface, "I am the Lord thy God," &c., which is the sum and substance of the covenant of grace; and then follow the *Ten Commandments*, which are, as it were, grafted upon this grant of sovereign grace and love, Ex. xx. 2—18.

Q. 9. Is this the order of doctrine laid down in the standards of the church of Scotland?

A. Yes: as appears from this *Answer* to that *Question* in the SHORTER CATECHISM, "What doth the preface to the ten commandments teach us?" The Answer is, "That because God is the Lord, and our God, and Redeemer; therefore we are bound to keep all his commandments."*

Q. 10. Are we then to keep the commandments, that God *may become* our God?

A. No: for this were to slide into a covenant of works; but we are to keep them, BECAUSE *he is our God*, according to the tenor of the covenant of grace; Ps. xlv. 11, in metre,—"Because he is thy Lord, do thou him worship reverently."

Q. 11. Why do men naturally think, that upon their doing certain acts, God will be their God?

A. Because of the natural bias of the heart of man, to the

* See also Confession, chap. xvi. § 2. Larger Catechism, Q. 101, 104.

order in the covenant of works, *do,* and *live,* Rom. ix. 32, and chap. x. 3.

Q. 12. Does not this order make void the law, or weaken our obligation to the duties of it?

A. By no means; but rather establishes the law, and settles our obligation to duty upon its proper foundation, Rom. iii. 31. "Do we then make void the law through faith? God forbid: yea, we establish the law."

Q. 13. How is this order of doctrine further evinced?

A. From the method of doctrine observed by the apostle Paul, who tells us, that all true gospel obedience is the obedience of *faith,* Rom. xvi. 26. And accordingly in his epistles, he first lays down the doctrine of faith to be believed; and, upon that foundation, proceeds to inculcate the duties that are to be practised.

Q. 14. Does gospel obedience interest us in God, as our God?

A. No: but it is a fruit and evidence of our interest in him, 1 John ii. 3, 5.

Q. 15. Is there any danger of inverting this order, and of making duty done by us, the foundation of believing the Lord to be our God?

A. There is exceedingly great danger; for it is the very soul of Popery. By inverting this order, they were led back to a covenant of works, and the doctrine of the merit of good works, which is the foundation of the whole Antichristian superstructure.

Q. 16. Do not we find frequently in scripture, a reward promised to good works, Ps. cxix. 1. "In keeping of thy commandments there is a great reward:" Ps. lviii. 11. "Verily there is a reward to the righteous?"

A. True; but this is a reward of grace, not of debt: the man that is rewarded, must be a believer in Christ, whose person is first accepted, through his union to Christ by faith, and the imputation of his righteousness, before any of his works or duties can be accepted, Eph. i. 6. Gen. iv. 4.

Q. 17. What may be said of the works of a man that has no faith?

A. They are dead works, and so cannot please a living God. An evil tree cannot bring forth good fruit, Matt. vii. 18: and without Christ, and union with him, we can do nothing, John xv. 4, 5.

Q. 18. What is to be thought of those who inculcate moral duties, without discovering the necessity of the new birth and union with Christ by faith, as the spring of all acceptable obedience?

A. They are foolish builders, laying their foundation on the sand, perverting the gospel of Christ; against whom the apostle denounces an awful doom, Gal. i. 9: "If any man preach any other gospel unto you than that ye have received, let him be accursed."

Quest. 4. *What is God?*

Ans. God is a Spirit, infinite, eternal, and unchangeable, in his being, wisdom, power, holiness, justice, goodness, and truth.

Of the Nature and Perfections of God in general.

Q. 1. What is the first fundamental truth to be believed, and upon which all other truths depend?

A. That God is; or that there is a God, Heb. ix. 6. "He that cometh unto God, must believe that he is."

Q. 2. Is this fundamental truth known by the light of natural reason?

A. Yes: as the apostle declares, Rom. i. 20. "The invisible things of God, from the creation of the world, are clearly seen, being understood by the things that are made; even his eternal power and Godhead."

Q. 3. In what *volumes* has God discovered the knowledge of himself to all mankind?

A. In the great volumes of *creation* and *providence;* which he opens to all the world.

Q. 4. What says the volume of *Creation* as to the *being* of a God?

A. All creatures in general, and every creature in particular, say that God "made us, and not we ourselves," Ps. c. 3.

Q. 5. What says the volume of *Providence?*

A. It says, that the same God who gave us being, upholds us therein; and governs us to the end for which he made us, Heb. i. 3.

Q. 6. Is not every man's *own being*, a convincing evidence that there is a God?

A. Yes: for, "in him we live, move, and have our being." No man can have any hand in his own formation in the womb, Ps. cxxxix. 15, 16; nor can he add a cubit unto his stature, or make one hair of his head either white or black, Matt. vi. 27; and v. 36.

Q. 7. Though the works of creation and providence declare *that* God is, can they also tell us *what* God is?

A. They afford us some dark glimpses of his eternal power, wisdom, greatness, and goodness; but it is only by and through the scriptures of truth, set home on the soul by his Spirit, that we can attain the saving knowledge of God, and of his perfections, John v. 39. 2 Pet. i. 19. Rom. xv. 4.

Q. 8. Who is it that reveals God to the sons of men in the word?

A. Christ, the eternal Son of God: "No man hath seen God at any time, the only begotten Son, which is in the bosom of the Father, he hath declared him,' John i. 18.

Q. 9. What account of himself, has God given us in the scriptures?

A. There are three short, but comprehensive descriptions which he has given of himself there; (1.) That God is light, 1 John i. 5. (2.) That God is love, 1 John iv. 8, 16. (3.) That God is a Spirit, John iv. 24.

Q. 10. Why is God said to be light?

A. Because of his infinite purity and omniscience, Hab. i. 13. Heb. iv. 13; and because he is the fountain and father of all light, whether material, natural, gracious, or glorious, James i. 17.

Q. 11. Why is God said to be love?

A. Because, according to the manifestation he has made of himself in Christ, love is the reigning excellency of his nature, which gives a dye or tincture to all his other perfections, in their egress, or exercise about the salvation of sinners, of mankind, John iii. 16. 1 John iv. 8—10.

Q. 12. Why is he said to be [*a Spirit?*]

A. Because he is necessarily and essentially a living intelligent substance; incorruptible, incorporeal, without flesh, or bones, or bodily parts, Luke xxiv. 39.

Q. 13. How far does God transcend all created spirits?

A. He is as infinitely above the being of all created spirits, as he is above the conception of all intelligent creatures. Job xxxvii. 23: "Touching the Almighty, we cannot find him out."

Q. 14. Since God is a most simple and pure Spirit, why are bodily parts, such as eyes, ears, hands, face, and the like, ascribed to him in scripture?

A. Such figurative expressions ought not to be understood in their literal sense, but according to the true scope and intent of them; which is to set forth some acts and perfections of the divine nature, to which these members of the body bear some faint resemblance. Thus, when eyes and ears are ascribed to God, they signify his omniscience; hands are designed to denote his power; and his face, the manifestation of his favour: and in this light, other metaphors of like nature, when applied to God, ought to be explained.

Q. 15. Is it lawful to form any external image of God with the hand, or any internal imaginary idea of him in the fancy?

A. It is absolutely unlawful and idolatrous; condemned in the second commandment, and other scriptures, Deut. iv. 12, 15. Rom. i. 23. Man cannot form an imaginary idea of his own soul or spirit, far less of Him who is the Father of spirits.

Q. 16. What may we learn from God's being a spirit?
A. To worship him in spirit and in truth, John iv. 24.

Q. 17. What is it to worship him in spirit and in truth?
A. It is to worship him, from a real and saving knowledge of what he is in Christ to lost sinners of mankind, John xvii. 3.

Q. 18. Is it possible for man to attain the real and saving knowledge of God?
A. Although neither men nor angels can have a comprehensive knowledge of God, Job xi. 7—9; yet, besides the speculative and merely rational knowledge of him, which men have, and may have much of, by the light of nature, a saving and satisfying knowledge of him is attainable, and is promised in the word, Jer. xxiv. 7. "I will give them a heart to know me, that I am the Lord." And John vi. 45. "It is written in the prophets, They shall be all taught of God."

Q. 19. Wherein consists the saving knowledge of God?
A. It is like the *white stone* and *new name*, which no man knows but he that receives it, Rev. ii. 17; and he that attains it, cannot make language of it, but silently admires what he cannot comprehend: only, there is no saving knowledge of God, but in and through Christ the Saviour 2 Cor. iv. 6.

Q. 20. What is the language of the soul that sees God, and knows him savingly in Christ?
A. It is like that of Moses, Ex. xv. 11: "Who is like unto thee, O Lord?—who is like unto thee, glorious in holiness, fearful in praises, doing wonders?" Or that of the Psalmist, Ps. xlviii. 14: "This God is our God for ever and ever: he will be our guide even unto death."

Q. 21. What are the rays of divine glory in the face of Jesus Christ, by which we come to know God savingly?
A. They are the attributes and perfections of his nature, by which he is pleased to manifest himself; such as, that he is [infinite, eternal, and unchangeable, in his being, wisdom, power, holiness, justice, goodness, and truth.]

Q. 22. Are these attributes of God, distinct things from God himself, or the divine essence?
A. By no means; for, *whatever is in God, is God himself;* and therefore the infinity of all perfection, is inseparable from the divine essence.

Q. 23. Are the divine attributes separable from one another, so as that which is infinite should not be eternal, and that which is infinite and eternal, should not be unchangeable, and so of the rest?

A. All perfections whatsoever being inseparable from God, must also be inseparable from one another; for though we, through weakness, must think and speak of them separately, yet all of them taken together, are, properly speaking, but the one infinite perfection of the divine nature, which cannot be separated from it, without granting that God is not infinitely perfect, which would be the height of blasphemy to suppose.

Q. 24. Why are the perfections of God called his attributes?

A. Because they are *attributed* or ascribed to him, as the essential properties of his nature, 1 Chron. xxix. 11.

Q. 25. How are the attributes of God commonly divided?

A. Into incommunicable and communicable.

Q. 26. What are the incommunicable attributes of God, mentioned in the *Answer?*

A. His infinity, eternity, and unchangeableness.

Q. 27. Why called incommunicable?

A. Because there is not the least resemblance of them to be found among the creatures.

Q. 28. What are the attributes that are called communicable?

A. They are being, wisdom, power, holiness, justice, goodness, and truth.

Q. 29. Why called communicable?

A. Because there is some faint resemblance or similitude of them to be found among the creatures, namely, angels, and saints: hence are they proposed in scripture for our imitation, Ps. xi. 6: " The righteous Lord loveth righteousness."—1 Pet. i. 16. " Be ye holy, for I am holy."

Q. 30. Can these communicable attributes be ascribed to any creature, as they are in God?

A. No: for they are in God, infinitely, eternally, and unchangeably; he is infinite, eternal, and unchangeable in his being; infinite, eternal, and unchangeable in his wisdom, and so on of the rest, which would be blasphemy to affirm of any creature: hence it is said, Matt. xix. 17, " There is none good but one, that is God:"—none infinitely, eternally, and unchangeably good, but he only.

OF GOD'S INFINITY.

Q. 1. What is it for God to be [*infinite?*]

A. It is to be absolutely without all bounds or limits in his being and perfections, Job xi. 7—9.

OF GOD'S INFINITY.

Q. 2. What does the infinity of God imply in it?
A. His incomprehensibleness, immensity, and omnipresence.

Q. 3. What is it for God to be incomprehensible?
A. It is infinitely to transcend the most enlarged capacity of men or angels, as to his being and perfections, Ps. cxlv. 3. Job xxxvi. 26.

Q. 4. What is the immensity of God?
A. As it includes his omnipresence, it is that perfection of his nature, by which he is every where present with all and every one of his creatures; and infinitely exceeds all their limits and boundaries, 1 Kings viii. 27.

Q. 5. What is the difference between the omnipresence and immensity of God?
A. The omnipresence of God is included in his immensity, and though not separable therefrom, yet may be conceived as having a respect to created substances, with every one of which he is intimately present; whereas his immensity extends infinitely beyond the boundaries of all created substance, 2 Chron. vi. 8.

Q. 6. Is God every where present only as to his knowledge and power?
A. He is every where present also as to his essence or being, as is evident from Jer. xxiii. 23, 24.

Q. 7. How may this be evinced also from reason?
A. Reason teaches us that no creature can subsist by itself, without the presence of God to uphold it in its being and operation. Acts xvii. 28: "In him we live, and move, and have our being."

Q. 8. How is God present with the church here on earth?
A. He is present, with the church visible, by the ordinances and symbols of his institution, Ex. xx. 24; and with the church invisible, or believers, by the inhabitation and operation of his Holy Spirit, Ezek. xxxvi. 27.

Q. 9. How is he present in heaven?
A. By the most bright and immediate displays of his glory; all the inhabitants of the upper sanctuary seeing him as he is, and enjoying him without interruption for ever, 1 John iii. 2. Ps. xvi. 11.

Q. 10. How is he present in hell?
A. In a way of tremendous power and justice, upholding the damned in their being, that they may lie under the strokes of his vindictive wrath for evermore, Ps. xc. 11. Matt. xxv. 46.

Q. 11. What may we learn from God's omnipresence?
A. That no affliction or temptation can befall the saints without his knowledge and sympathy, Isa. xliii. 2.

OF GOD'S ETERNITY.

Q. 1. What is the difference between time and eternity?
A. Time has a continual succession, the former time passing away, and another succeeding; but eternity is an infinite immutable duration.

Q. 2. What is it for God to be [*eternal?*]
A. It is that perfection of his nature, by which he continually exists, without any beginning, end, or succession of time.

Q. 3. How do you prove that God is without beginning?
A. From Ps. xc. 2, " Before the mountains were brought forth, or ever thou hadst formed the earth and the world, even from everlasting to everlasting thou art God;" that is, since thou didst exist before the mountains were brought forth, or before the beginning of time, thou art absolutely eternal.

Q. 4. How do you prove that God is without end?
A. From Ps. cii. 12, 27, " Thou, O Lord, shalt endure for ever,—and thy years shall have no end;" for that which had no beginning of duration, can never have an end of it, but must always necessarily exist.

Q. 5. How do you prove that he is without succession of time?
A. From Ps. xc. 4, " A thousand years are in thy sight but as yesterday when it is past:" and 2 Pet. iii. 8, " One day is with the Lord as a thousand years, and a thousand years as one day." He does not only always remain in being, but is always the same in that being, Ps. cii. 27.

Q. 6. What is the difference between God's eternity, and the eternity of angels and the souls of men?
A. God's eternity is essential, absolute, and independent, without beginning, as well as without end; but the eternity of angels, and of the souls of men, is quite of another nature; for, as they had a beginning, so their duration admits of a succession, as long as time lasts: and though they shall never have an end, yet this eternity of theirs is not necessary and essential to their nature, but flows from the will and power of God; who, if he pleased, could bring them to an end, as well as he gave them a beginning.

Q. 7. What use should the wicked make of God's eternity?
A. It should be matter of the greatest terror to them while they continue in their wickedness; for, in this case, God will be their eternal foe, and will punish them with everlasting destruction, 2 Thess. i. 9.

Q. 8. What use should the godly, or believers in Christ, make of it?

3 *

A. They should improve it as matter of unspeakable comfort; because their God, being the eternal God, will therefore be the strength of their heart, and their portion for ever, Ps. lxxiii. 26.

OF GOD'S UNCHANGEABLENESS.

Q. 1. What do you understand by God's being [*unchangeable?*]

A. His most perfect constancy, by which he is infinitely free from any actual or possible change, and is always the same.

Q. 2. How is God's unchangeableness proved from scripture?

A. From Mal. iii. 6, "I am the Lord, I change not;" and James i. 17—"The Father of lights, with whom is no variableness, neither shadow of turning."

Q. 3. How may it be proved from reason?

A. Reason teaches, that if God did change, it behoved either to be to the better, or to the worse; neither of which is consistent with his absolute perfection, Matt. v. 48.

Q. 4. Can any creature be unchangeable in its nature?

A. No: because every creature depends upon God for being and operation, Acts xvii. 28.

Q. 5. Are not holy angels, and glorified saints, unchangeable?

A. They are in a state of unchangeable happiness, Eph. i. 10; but this is owing to sovereign grace, and not to their own natures, Rom. vi. 23.

Q. 6. Did *creation* make any change in God?

A. It made a change in the creature, from nothing to being; but none in God, because his will and power to create were the same from eternity.

Q. 7. How is God unchangeable, when he is sometimes said in scripture to *repent*, as in Gen. vi. 6. Jonah iii. 10?

A. When, in these or the like places, he is said to repent, it imports only an alteration of his way, or outward conduct, according to his infallible foresight, but no change of his mind or will, Job xxiii. 13.

Q. 8. What may we learn from God's unchangeableness?

A. That he will accomplish his promise, Micah vii. 20; rest in his love, Zeph. iii. 17; and finish the good work which he has begun in the soul, Phil. i. 6.

Q. 9. In what is God infinite, eternal, and unchangeable?

A. [In his being, wisdom, power, holiness, justice, goodness, and truth.]

OF GOD'S BEING.

Q. 1. What is understood by God's [*being?*]
A. It is what is usually called his essence.
Q. 2. What is the divine essence?
A. It is the glorious and transcendent nature of God, by which he is infinitely blessed in himself, and comprehended by none beside himself.
Q. 3. What is the highest perfection of *being?*
A. That to which nothing can be added, and from which nothing can be taken, and which is independent of all things else, Job xxxv. 6—8.
Q. 4. Can *being* itself, or *being* in a proper and strict sense, be attributed to any, but God only?
A. No: for though the heavens and the earth, angels and men, have a being; yet there is no infinite, eternal, and unchangeable being, but God only. It is God alone that can say, I AM, Ex. iii. 14.
Q. 5. What is the import of that name, I AM?
A. It is of the same import with the name JEHOVAH: as if he had said, I am being itself, the author and fountain of all beings in heaven or earth.
Q. 6. What are all other beings, in comparison with the being of God?
A. All other beings are but created, contingent, and shadowy beings, if compared with his, who spoke them into being, Ps. xxxiii. 6, 9.
Q. 7. What says God concerning those that are taken up with created beings, without ever reflecting upon the supreme, infinite, and eternal Being?
A. That they are brutish among the people; fools, destitute of wisdom, Ps. xciv. 8; more brutish than the ox that knoweth his owner, Isa. i. 3.
Q. 8. Are not all created beings, with their perfections, originally in God, and from him?
A. Yes; as is evident from the unanswerable reasoning of the Spirit of God, Ps. xciv. 9, 10:—" He that planted the ear, shall he not hear? He that formed the eye, shall he not see?—He that teacheth man knowledge, shall not he know?"
Q. 9. What may we learn from God's *being?*
A. That as he gave being to all the creatures, so he will give being to all his promises, in their full accomplishment Ex. vi. 3

OF GOD'S WISDOM.

Q. 1. Is not omniscience, or infinite knowledge and understanding, inseparably connected with infinite [*wisdom?*]

A. Yes: "For the Lord is a God of knowledge, by him actions are weighed," 1 Sam. ii. 3.

Q. 2. What is God's omniscience?

A. It is that perfection of his nature, by which he knows all things most perfectly in himself, by one eternal act, Acts xv. 18.

Q. 3. How do you prove from scripture that he knows all things?

A. From 1 John iii. 20: "God is greater than our heart, and knoweth all things."

Q. 4. How does God's omniscience appear from reason?

A. He who made all things, cannot but know and comprehend his own workmanship, Ps. xciv. 9.

Q. 5. How does it appear that he has a perfect knowledge of intelligent creatures?

A. If he did not perfectly know them, and their actions, he could not be their supreme governor and judge, Heb. iv. 13.

Q. 6. What is the object of the divine knowledge or omniscience?

A. God himself, Matt. xi. 27, and all other things whatsoever, John xxi. 17.

Q. 7. How is it evident, that God has a most perfect knowledge of himself, and his own glorious excellencies?

A. Because otherwise his understanding would not be infinite, as it is asserted to be, Ps. cxlvii. 5, in regard all other objects, beside himself, are but finite.

Q. 8. Is the knowledge of God absolutely independent upon the creature?

A. It is so independent upon the creature, "as nothing is to him contingent or uncertain," Acts xv. 18. Ezek. xi. 5.*

Q. 9. How does it appear, that God has a certain and infallible knowledge of contingent actions, or of such things as seem casual and accidental to us?

A. It appears from this, that future events, which depend upon the freedom of man's will, or upon second causes, are expressly foretold in scripture, and, therefore, certainly foreknown by God; such as, Joseph's preferment, and Israel's oppression in Egypt; Ahab's death, though by an arrow shot at a venture; Cæsar's decree, that all the world should be taxed, bringing about Christ's birth at Bethlehem; and many other instances.

Q. 10. How does God know things that are only possible?

A. He knows them in his power, which could easily bring them to pass if he had so decreed, Matt. xix. 26.

Q. 11. How does he know things future, or such as actually come to pass in time?

---

* Confession, chap. ii. § 2.

OF GOD'S WISDOM. 33

A. He knows them not only in his power, as able to effect them; but in his will, as determining their futurition or after-existence, Gen. xvii. 21.

Q. 12. Is God's knowledge of things general or particular?

A. It is a particular knowledge of every individual creature, and every circumstance about it, Ps. cxxxix. 2. Matt. x. 29, 30.

Q. 13. Is there any succession in his knowledge, or does he know one thing before another?

A. As there is no succession in his essence, so there is none in his knowledge; he knows all things eternally, infallibly, and immutably, by one single act of his infinite understanding, Heb. iv. 13: "All things are naked and opened, unto the eyes of him with whom we have to do."

Q. 14. What conception may we have of the difference between the infinite knowledge and wisdom of God?

A. His infinite knowledge comprehends all things in heaven and earth, by one intuitive glance of his infinite mind; but his infinite wisdom directs these things to the proper ends, for which he gave them their being, Rom. xi. 36.

Q. 15. How does the wisdom of God appear in the work of creation?

A. It appears in the excellent order, beauty, and harmony that are to be seen in all parts of the creation, Ps. xix. 1—7; in the subserviency of one thing to another, Hos. ii. 21, 22; the tendency of the whole, to manifest the glory of God, Rev. iv. 11; and calculate also for the good of man as his peculiar favourite, Ps. cxv. 16.

Q. 16. How does the wisdom of God appear in the works of providence?

A. In adjusting the whole of his administrations according to the plan laid in his infinite mind from eternity; or his most judicious and regular putting his counsels into execution, Ps. xxxiii. 10, 11.

Q. 17. How does the wisdom of God shine in the work of redemption?

A. In making an honourable egress and vent for his mercy and love to sinners of mankind, in the way of satisfying his justice to the full, by the obedience and death of the blessed Surety, Rom. v. 21.

Q. 18. What encouragement ought we to take from the wisdom of God?

A. That he will make all things work together for our good, Rom. viii. 28; and that no plot can be so deeply laid for our ruin, but his wisdom can easily frustrate and disappoint, Job v. 13.

OF GOD'S POWER.

Q. 1. What is the [*power*] of God?

A. It is that essential perfection of his nature, by which he can do whatsoever he pleases, in heaven and earth, in the seas, and all deep places, Ps. cxxxv. 6.

Q. 2. What is the object of divine power, or to what does it extend?

A. To all things possible, though limited, by his will, to those things only which he has decreed to be done, Matt. xxvi. 53, 54.

Q. 3. Is it any impeachment of God's omnipotence, that he cannot lie, cannot deny himself?

A. By no means; for, on the contrary, God is therefore omnipotent, because it is impossible for him to do evil or depart from the infinite rectitude of his own will, 1 Sam. xv. 29: "The strength of Israel will not lie."

Q. 4. In what does God manifest his infinite power?

A. In creation, providence, and redemption.

Q. 5. How is the power of God manifested in creation?

A. In calling "those things that be not as though they were," Rom. iv. 7; without the assistance or instrumentality of any whosoever, Isa. xliv. 24.

Q. 6. How is it displayed in the conduct of providence?

A. In upholding and preserving all his creatures from sinking into their original nothing, Heb. i. 3; and, particularly, in protecting and defending his church, in midst of all the dangers and enemies, with which it is surrounded, Matt. xvi. 18.

Q. 7. How is the power of God illustrated in the glorious work of redemption?

A. By laying the chief corner-stone thereof, in the union of the human nature to the person of the Son of God; supporting him under the inconceivable load of divine wrath, for our sins, and spoiling principalities and powers in that very nature which Satan had vanquished at first; hence he is called "the power of God," 1 Cor. i. 24; "the arm of the Lord," Isa. liii. 1; and "the man of his right hand," Ps. lxxx. 17.

Q. 8. How is the power of God denied or abused by men?

A. By limiting it, as Israel did, Ps. lxxviii. 19; by trusting more to an arm of flesh, than to the arm of God, Jer. xvii. 5; and by fearing the wrath of man more than the displeasure of God, Isa. li. 12, 13.

Q. 9. What improvement may faith make of the power of a promising God?

A. It can fasten upon it, for the performance of his gracious word, Rom. iv. 20, 21: for resisting and conquering sin, Satan, and the world, saying, "If God be for us, who can be against us?" Rom. viii. 31; and for the practice of any commanded duty, however difficult, saying, "I can do all things through Christ who strengtheneth me," Phil. iv. 13.

OF GOD'S HOLINESS.

Q. 1. What is the [*holiness*] of God?
A. It is that essential rectitude or integrity of his nature, by which he infinitely delights in his own purity, and in every thing agreeable to his will, Hab. i. 13; and has a perfect hatred and abhorrence of every thing contrary to it, Jer. xliv. 4.

Q. 2. Is God necessarily holy?
A. Holiness is as necessary to him as his being: he is as necessarily holy, as he is necessarily God: "Who shall not fear thee, O Lord?—for thou only art holy," Rev. xv. 4.

Q. 3. What peculiar honour does God put upon his own holiness?
A. He singles it out as the attribute to swear by, for the accomplishment of his promises and threatenings, Ps. lxxxix. 35: "Once have I sworn by my holiness, that I will not lie unto David."

Q. 4. Are finite creatures able to behold the brightness of God's holiness?
A. No: for when the angels themselves view his infinite holiness, as manifested in Christ, they are represented as covering their faces with their wings, Isa. vi. 2.

Q. 5. How are sinners of mankind made partakers of his holiness?
A. By regenerating grace, and spiritual ingraftment into the *second Adam*, John xv. 4, 5; by faith's improvement of the great and precious promises, 2 Pet. i. 4; and by beholding the glory of this attribute, as it shines in the person and sufferings of the Son of God, presented to our view in the glass of the gospel revelation, 2 Cor. v. 21.

Q. 6. Does every thing pertaining to God, bear the stamp and impress of his holiness?
A. Yes: he is *holy in all his works*, Ps. cxlv. 17; his word is holy, Rom. i. 2; his covenant or promise is holy, Ps. cv. 42; his Sabbath is holy, Isa. lviii. 13; his people are holy, chap. lxii. 12; his ministering spirits are the holy angels, Rev. xiv. 10; and the place where he dwells, is the high and holy place, Isa. lvii. 15.

Q. 7. In what did the holiness of God appear in the creation of man?
A. In making him upright, Eccl. vii. 29, after his own image, Gen. i. 27; and writing a law upon his heart, which was the transcript of his holiness, Rom. vii. 12.

Q. 8. How has God discovered his holiness in his providential procedure?

A. In not sparing the angels who sinned; and in the visible and remarkable judgments, which he has inflicted upon notorious offenders in this life, 2 Pet. ii. 4—6.

Q. 9. What was the highest display of God's holiness, and detestation of sin?

A. His hiding his face from his own beloved Son, as bearing our iniquity, Matt. xxvii. 46.

Q. 10. What is the greatest opposite of the holiness of God?

A. Sin: therefore called that abominable thing which God hates, Jer. xliv. 4.

Q. 11. How does God hate sin?

A. He hates it necessarily, and with a "perfect hatred," Ps. v. 4—6.

Q. 12. Since God thus hates sin, how does his permission of it consist with his holiness?

A. It fully consists with it, because his permission of sin has no influence upon the commission of it, which entirely flows from the free will of the sinner, James i. 13, 14. Besides, God thereby takes occasion to give a brighter display of his holiness and detestation of sin, than though Adam had continued in innocence; when he spared not his own Son, but gave him unto death on account of it, Rom. viii. 32.

Q. 13. What improvement ought we to make of the holiness of God?

A. To "give thanks at the remembrance of his holiness," Ps. xxx. 4; to proclaim the glory of it, Ex. xv. 11; and to study holiness in all manner of conversation, 1 Pet. i. 15.

Q. 14. How may we know if we have suitable impressions of God's holiness?

A. If we stand in awe to offend him, Gen. xxxix. 9; and have an habitual desire after more conformity to him, 1 John iii. 3.

OF GOD'S JUSTICE.

Q. 1. What is the [*justice*] of God?

A. It is that essential attribute of his nature, by which he is infinitely righteous and equal in himself, and in all his ways towards his creatures, Deut. xxxii. 4.

Q. 2. How may the justice of God be considered?

A. Either as it relates to himself, or to rational creatures.

Q. 3. What is God's justice as it relates to himself?

A. It is his making his own glory the fixed and invariable rule of the whole of his procedure, Isa. xlii. 8.

Q. 4. What is God's justice in relation to rational creatures?

A. It is his righteous government of them, according to their nature, and the law he has given them, Rom. ii. 12, 14, 15.

Q. 5. How is it usually distinguished?

A. Into legislative and distributive justice.

Q. 6. What is *legislative* justice?

A. It is his giving most holy, just, and good laws to rational creatures, commanding and forbidding them, what is fit for them to do, or forbear, Isa. xxxiii. 22.

Q. 7. Has man a power to give obedience to these laws?

A. He once had power, but by the fall has lost it, Rom. iii. 23.

Q. 8. How does it consist with the justice of God to demand that obedience, which man has not power to give?

A. God cannot lose his right to demand obedience to his laws, though man has lost his power to give it; especially as man's inability was contracted by his own voluntary apostasy and rebellion, Eccl. vii. 29: "Lo, this only have I found, that God hath made man upright; but they have sought out many inventions."

Q. 9. What is God's *distributive* justice?

A. It is his constant will, to render to rational creatures their due, according to law, without respect to persons, Job xxxiv. 11. 1 Pet. i. 17.

Q. 10. What are the laws according to which God will distribute justice among men?

A. They are two: the law of *works*, and the law of *faith*.

Q. 11. Where are they mentioned?

A. In Rom. iii. 27: "Where is boasting, then? It is excluded. By what law? of works? Nay: but by the law of faith."

Q. 12. What is understood by the law of works, and the law of faith?

A. By the law of works, is understood the covenant of works; and by the law of faith, the covenant of grace.

Q. 13. What is due to the sinner, in justice, according to the law of works?

A. Death, and the curse; which include all wo and misery, in time, and through eternity, Rom. vi. 23. Gal. iii. 10.

Q. 14. What is the sinner's due according to the law of faith?

A. Acquittance and acceptance, on account of the surety-righteousness imputed to him, and apprehended by faith, Rom. iii. 24, and viii. 1.

Q. 15. Is God just in dealing thus with the ungodly sinner, who believes in Christ?

A. Yes: his righteousness is declared in so doing, Rom.

PART I.—4

OF GOD'S JUSTICE.

iii. 25, 26: "Whom God hath set forth for a propitiation through faith in his blood, to declare his righteousness,— that he might be just, and the justifier of him who believeth in Jesus."

Q. 16. Does God reward the sincere, though imperfect obedience of his people to the law, as a rule of life?

A. In keeping of his commandments there is indeed *great reward*, Ps. xix. 11; but then this reward is entirely of free grace, and not of debt, Rom. iv. 4, 5: it is not on account of any worth in their obedience, Ps. cxv. 1; but only on account of what Christ has *merited*, by his obedience to the death, 1 Pet. ii. 5.

Q. 17. How is this kind of justice called?

A. Remunerative or rewarding justice, Ps. lviii. 11: "Verily, there is a reward for the righteous."

Q. 18. Is not God's taking vengeance on transgressors, a righteous act of justice?

A. Yes; for "every transgression and disobedience receives a just recompense of reward," Heb. ii. 2. "It is a righteous thing to recompense tribulation to them that trouble you," 2 Thess. i. 6. Hence says the same apostle, Rom. iii. 5, 6,—"Is God unrighteous who taketh vengeance? God forbid: for then how shall God judge the world?"

Q. 19. How is this justice of God called?

A. Vindictive or punishing justice, Acts xxviii. 4.

Q. 20. What is *vindictive justice?*

A. It is God's inflicting the punishment upon sin, which is threatened in the law, Gen. ii. 17, Ezek. xviii. 4.

Q. 21. Could God, of his own free will, have pardoned sin without a satisfaction to his justice?

A. No: for he has declared, "that in forgiving iniquity, transgression and sin," he "will by no means clear the guilty;" namely, without a satisfaction, Ex. xxxiv. 7.

Q. 22. How do you prove, that vindictive, or punishing justice, is essential to God?

A. From the infinite holiness of God, who cannot but hate, and consequently punish sin, Hab. i. 12, 13; from his faithfulness in the threatening, Gen. ii. 17; Ps. xcv. 11; from the remarkable judgments that have been inflicted on sinners in this life, Jude, verse 5, 7; and from the sufferings and death of God's only begotten Son, whom he would surely have spared, if there had been any other possible way of pardoning sin, but through his satisfaction, Matt. xxvi. 42. 2 Cor. v. 21.

Q. 23. What improvement ought we to make of the justice of God, as glorified by the satisfactory death of his own Son?

A. To plead the perfect and full satisfaction of it by the Surety, as the honourable channel, in which we expect all mercy and grace to flow plentifully to us, as the Psalmist did, Ps. xxv. 11: "For thy name's sake, O Lord, pardon mine iniquity, for it is great."

OF GOD'S GOODNESS.

Q. 1. What is the [*goodness*] of God?
A. It is that essential property of his nature, by which he is infinitely good in himself, and the author and fountain of all good to others, Ps. cxix. 68.

Q. 2. How may the goodness of God be distinguished?
A. Into his absolute and relative goodness.

Q. 3. What is his *absolute* goodness?
A. It is the essential goodness of his nature, without considering it in relation to the creatures, Matt. xix. 17: "There is none good but one, that is, God."

Q. 4. What is his *relative* goodness?
A. It is the relation that his goodness bears to the creatures; both in the propensity of his nature to do them good, Ex. xxxiii. 19, and in the actual manifestation and communication of the blessings of his bounty to them, in creation, providence, and redemption, chap. xxxiv. 6, 7.

Q. 5. How is the goodness of God manifested in the work of creation in general?
A. In giving being to his creatures, when he stood in no need of them, being infinitely happy in himself, though no creature had ever been made, Ps. xvi. 2; and in making all things very good, Gen. i. 31.

Q. 6. How is the goodness of God displayed in the creation of man in particular?
A. In making him after his own image; furnishing the world with such a variety of creatures for his use; giving him dominion over them, Gen. i. 27, 28; and in entering into covenant with him, chap. ii. 16, 17.

Q. 7. How is the goodness of God manifested in his providence?
A. In preserving his creatures, and making bountiful provision for them, Ps. cxlv. 9, 15, 16.

Q. 8. How is this goodness distinguished?
A. Into common and special goodness.

Q. 9. What is his *common* goodness?
A. His dispensing the good things of this life, promiscuously among his creatures, Matt. v. 45: "He maketh his sun to rise on the evil and on the good, and sendeth rain on the just and on the unjust."

Q. 10. Is God good even to the wicked who are his enemies?
A. Yes; for he not only provides for them, "filling their

hearts with food and gladness," Acts xiv. 17; but exercises long-suffering patience towards them, Neh. ix. 17; and affords such of them as are within the visible church, the means of salvation, Acts xiii. 26.

Q. 11. What is the *special* goodness of God?

A. It is his distinguishing love to a certain number of mankind lost, manifested in their redemption through Christ, Rev. v. 9.

Q. 12. In what does the goodness of God appear in the work of redemption?

A. Both in the contrivance and execution of it.

Q. 13. How does the goodness of God appear in the *contrivance* of redemption?

A. In remembering us in our low state, Ps. cxxxvi. 23; laying our help on his own Son, the mighty One, Ps. lxxxix. 19; and in setting him up as a new covenant head from everlasting, Prov. viii. 23.

Q. 14. How does it appear in the *execution* of our redemption?

A. In sending his Son to assume our nature, and thus to fulfil all righteousness for us, John iii. 16, Jer. xxiii. 6; and on the foundation of that righteousness, giving us grace and glory, and every good thing, from a cup of cold water, to a seat with him on his throne, Ps. lxxxiv. 11. Rev. iii. 21.

Q. 15. What are the streams in which the special goodness of God flows out?

A. In the streams of love, grace and mercy, according to his name, Ex. xxxiv. 6,—" the Lord, the Lord God, merciful and gracious," &c.

Q. 16. What is the difference between the love, grace, and mercy of God?

A. They are much the same, only love considers the sinner simply as God's creature; grace views him as ill-deserving; and mercy, through a satisfaction, respects him as in misery.

Q. 17. Who are the objects of God's special goodness?

A. His chosen ones, Ps. cvi. 4, 5: " O visit me with thy salvation, that I may see the good of thy chosen."

Q. 18. Can this special goodness of God be expressed in words?

A. No; for " Eye hath not seen, nor ear heard, neither have entered into the heart of man, the things which God hath prepared for them that love him," 1 Cor. ii. 9. And Ps. xxxi. 19. " O! how great is thy goodness, which thou hast laid up for them that fear thee."

Q. 19. Where is this goodness of God *laid up*?

A. It is laid up in Christ, who has received the gifts of God's goodness for men, Ps. lxviii. 18: " When he ascended up on high, he—gave gifts unto men," Eph. iv. 8; and therefore, God has *made him most blessed for ever*, Ps. xxi. 6.

Q. 20. How is this goodness laid out and brought near to us?

A. It is laid out in the exceeding great and precious promises, 2 Pet. i. 4; and brought near in the full, free, and unhampered offer of the gospel, Mark xvi. 15.

Q. 21. How are we savingly interested in all this goodness?

A. By faith, receiving and resting upon Christ alone for salvation, as he is freely offered in the gospel, John i. 12. 1 Cor. iii. 22, 23.

Q. 22. What are the properties of this goodness?

A. It is seasonable goodness, Heb. iv. 16; it is soul-satisfying, Ps. cvii. 9; and it is immutable and everlasting, Ps. lii. 1.

Q. 23. What improvement ought we to make of the goodness of God?

A. We ought to "praise the Lord for his goodness, and for his wonderful works to the children of men," Ps. cvii. 8; to be influenced to repentance from the consideration of his goodness, Rom. ii. 4; and to imitate God in it, Heb. xiii. 16.

OF GOD'S TRUTH.

Q. 1. What is the [*truth*] of God?

A. It is that essential perfection of his nature, by which he cannot but fulfil and accomplish whatever he has spoken; or do as he has said, Num. xxiii. 19.

Q. 2. What is it that this perfection of God has a special relation to?

A. To the revelation of his will in his word: hence the whole scripture is infallible truth; "one jot, or one tittle, shall in no wise pass therefrom, till all be fulfilled," Matt. v. 18. For, "the word of the Lord endureth for ever," 1 Pet. i. 25.

Q. 3. What is God's truth, as respecting his word, commonly called?

A. His faithfulness, or veracity, Heb. x. 23: "He is faithful that promised."

Q. 4. To what is the truth or faithfulness of God opposed?

A. To all change of mind, Job xxiii. 13: "He is in one mind, and who can turn him?" and to all lying and dissimulation, Heb. vi. 18: "It is impossible for God to lie."

Q. 5. Can there be any inconsistency in his words?

A. No: for truth always hangs with itself, and he "keepeth truth for ever," Ps. cxlvi. 6.

Q. 6. Can he possibly forget what he has said?
A. No, surely; for "he will ever be mindful of his covenant," Ps. cxi. 5.

Q. 7. In what is the truth or faithfulness of God manifested?
A. In the exact accomplishment of his promises, Josh. xxiii. 14; and the certain execution of his threatenings, Zech. i. 6.

Q. 8. How do we give God the honour of his truth and faithfulness?
A. By faith, which sets to the seal that God is true, John iii. 33; and judges him faithful who hath promised, Heb. xi. 11.

Q. 9. By what sin is this attribute of God most dishonoured?
A. By the sin of *unbelief*, which makes God a liar, because it believes not "the record that God gave of his Son," 1 John v. 10.

Q. 10. What record does God give of his Son?
A. "This is the record, that God hath given to us eternal life, and this life is in his Son," 1 John v. 11.

Q. 11. To whom is this record given?
A. To all the hearers of the gospel, as a ground of faith. Mark xvi. 15: "Go ye into all the world, and preach the gospel to every creature:" Acts ii. 39: "The promise is unto you, and to your children, and to all that are afar off, even as many as the Lord our God shall call."

Q. 12. How does it appear that this record is given as a ground of faith, to all the hearers of the gospel?
A. If it were not so, it were impossible that unbelievers, under the gospel, could make God a liar; for if they have no concern in this record, and are not bound to believe it with application to themselves, their rejecting of it could not be their sin; because "where no law is, there is no transgression," Rom. iv. 15.

Q. 13. If the record, or promise of the God of truth, be made to every one of the hearers of the gospel, is he not, in that case, obliged to fulfil it to every one?
A. By no means: because the unbeliever wilfully rejects the promise, and will have no benefit by it, Ps. lxxxi. 10—13.

Q. 14. By what example, in scripture, may this be illustrated?
A. By the example of the promise of Canaan, made indefinitely to all Israel who came out of Egypt, Ex. vi. 6, 8; yet many of them "could not enter in because of unbelief," Heb. iii. 19: even so, the promise of eternal life is made to all the hearers of the gospel; yet many of them

come short of it, because "the word preached doth not profit them, not being mixed with faith in them that hear it," Heb. iv. 1, 2.

Q. 15. What then is the deplorable case of unbelievers under the gospel?

A. They are *condemned already*, and "the wrath of God abideth on them," John iii. 18, 36.

Q. 16. What improvement ought we to make of the truth and faithfulness of God?

A. We ought to choose the way of truth, Ps. cxix. 30; walk in it, 3 John, ver. 4; bear witness for it before the world, Heb. x. 23; praise God for his truth, Ps. cxxxviii. 2; and trust him on his word, without staggering at the promise through unbelief, Rom. iv. 20.

QUEST. 5. *Are there more Gods than one?*

ANS. There is but one only, the living and true God.

Q. 1. How does it appear from scripture, that there is but [*one*] God [*only?*]

A. From Deut. vi. 4: "Hear, O Israel, the Lord our God is one Lord:" Isa. xlv. 22: "I am God, and there is none else."

Q. 2. How does reason demonstrate this truth, that there is but one God?

A. Reason says, that there is but one first cause and ultimate end of all things: and that there cannot be two, or more, infinite, eternal, and unchangeable beings.

Q. 3. Why is God's omnipotence commonly adduced to prove, that he can be *but one only?*

A. Because he could not be omnipotent, or almighty, if any other could oppose or resist him, Job ix. 12.

Q. 4. How may it be proved from his government of the world?

A. There could not be a uniform governing of all things in the world, to one certain end, if the infinitely wise Governor, who is at the helm, were not one only.

Q. 5. How are some of the divine perfections expressed in scripture, for proving the unity of the essence?

A. They are expressed in the abstract; for instance God is said to be "light," 1 John i. 5; to be "love," ch. iv 8; to be "strength," 1 Sam. xv. 29; all which, and the like abstract properties, plainly denote that God is *one only*.

Q. 6. Is God compounded of the several perfections of his nature, as the Socinians speak?

A. By no means: for all the several attributes of God are only the one infinite perfection of his most simple and uncompounded nature; which infinite perfection, because of our weakness, is described by parts, according to the several objects about which it is conversant.

Q. 7. Is the vast variety of the divine decrees any argument against the divine unity?

A. No: because the decrees are various only with respect to the different objects and effects to which they extend, but not with respect to the act of the divine will, which is but one.

Q. 8. Are there not several in scripture who are called gods?

A. Yes: angels, magistrates, and the idols of the heathen nations.

Q. 9. Why are *angels* called gods? Ps. xcvii. 7.

A. Because of the excellency of their nature, power, and wisdom, Ps. ciii. 20.

Q. 10. Why are *magistrates* so called? Ex. xxii. 28.

A. Because they are God's deputies for government and justice among men, Rom. xiii. 4.

Q. 11. Why are the *idols* of the heathen nations called gods? 1 Chron. v. 25.

A. Because ignorant and brutish persons have honoured them as such; but there is no reason at all to be "afraid of them, for they cannot do evil, neither also is it in them to do good," Jer. x. 5.

Q. 12. Why is Satan called the god of this world? 2 Cor. iv. 4.

A. Because he reigns and rules over the greatest part of the world, as his servants and slaves; for he is "the spirit that now worketh in the children of disobedience," Eph. ii. 2.

Q. 13. Why are covetous men called idolaters? Eph. v. 4.

A. Because the world has that room in their heart which God should have.

Q. 14. What may we learn from God's being *one only*?

A. To beware of mistaken notions of him, as if he were partly in heaven and partly on earth; for he is so much one, that he is wholly every where present, Jer. xxiii. 24.

Q. 15. Why is this one only God said to be the [*living*] God?

A. Because he has life essentially in himself, John v. 26; and is the author and giver of that life that is in any living creature, Acts xvii. 28; and likewise in opposition to dead and dumb idols, Ps. cxv. 4—7.

Q. 16. Why is he called the [*true*] God?

A. In opposition to all false and imaginary gods, Jer. x. 10, 11.

Q. 17. Why are *living* and *true* put together in the answer?

A. Because they are inseparably conjoined in the infinitely perfect nature of God. He who is the living God is the only true God; and the true God, the only living God, 1 Thess. i. 9.

Q. 18. What may we learn from his being the living God?

A. To present our bodies a living sacrifice, holy, acceptable to God, which is our reasonable service, Rom. xii. 1.

Q. 19. What may we learn from his being the only true God?

A. To worship him in spirit and in truth, John iv. 24, because he desires truth in the inward parts, Ps. li. 6; and likewise to beware of setting up an idol, or regarding any iniquity in our hearts; otherwise he will not hear us, Ps. lxvi. 18.

QUEST. 6. *How many persons are there in the Godhead?*

ANS. There are three persons in the Godhead, the Father, the Son, and the Holy Ghost; and these three are one God, the same in substance, equal in power and glory.

Q. 1. Whence is it, that this article of our holy religion has been so much opposed by adversaries, in every period of the church?

A. The devil and his instruments have warmly opposed it because they know it is the primary object of our faith and worship; it not being enough for us to know *what* God *is*, as to his essential attributes, without knowing *who* he is, as to his personality, according as he has revealed himself in his word, to be Father, Son, and Holy Ghost, 1 John ii. 23,—" Whosoever denieth the Son, the same hath not the Father."

Q. 2. Is this doctrine of the Trinity, then, a *fundamental article*, upon the belief of which our salvation depends?

A. Beyond all doubt it is: because without the knowledge and belief of the Trinity of persons, we would remain ignorant of the love of the Father, the merit of the Son, and the sanctifying influences of the Holy Ghost, in the purchase and application of redemption; without which there could be no salvation, John xvii. 3,—" This is life eternal, that they might know thee the only true God, and Jesus Christ whom thou hast sent."

Q. 3. Can the Trinity of persons be proved from the *Old Testament?*

OF THE HOLY TRINITY.

A. Yes: not only from the history of man's creation, where God speaks of himself in the plural number, "Let us make man," Gen. i. 26; but likewise from such passages, as expressly restrict this plurality to three persons, such as, Ps. xxxiii. 6,—"By the word of the Lord, or JEHOVAH, were the heavens made; and all the host of them by the breath, or spirit, of his mouth;" where there is mention made of JEHOVAH, the Word, and the Spirit, as concurring in the creation of all things: accordingly, we are told that all things were made by the Word, John i. 3, and that the Spirit garnished the heavens, Job xxvi. 13. The same truth is also evident from Isa lxiii. 7, 9, 10; where we read of the loving-kindness of JEHOVAH; of the Angel of his presence saving them; and of their vexing his Holy Spirit. A plain discovery of a Trinity of persons.

Q. 4. What is the meaning of the word TRINITY, so commonly used in expressing this doctrine?

A. It signifies the same with TRI-UNITY, or *three in one;* that is, three distinct persons, in one and the same individual or numerical* essence, 1 John v. 7.

Q. 5. Is not a Trinity of persons, in the divine Essence, an unsearchable mystery?

A. Yes; and so is every perfection of God, which infinitely transcends our thoughts, and finite capacities, Col. ii. 2. Job xi. 6, 7.

Q. 6. Is it not unreasonable to require a belief of what we cannot understand?

A. It is not at all unreasonable in matters that are entirely supernatural; but, on the contrary, it is the highest reason we should believe what God says of himself, and of the manner of his own subsistence, John xx. 31: besides, it is the peculiar office of faith to subject our reason to divine revelation, Heb. xi. 1.

Q. 7. How has God revealed this mystery in his word?

A. He has in it told us, that "there are three that bear record in heaven, the Father, the Word, and the Holy Ghost; and these three are one," 1 John v. 7. Or, as our *Confession* expresses it, "In the unity of the Godhead there be three persons, of one substance, power, and eternity; God the Father, God the Son, and God the Holy Ghost," Matt. iii. 16, 17; and xxviii. 19. 2 Cor. xiii. 14.†

Q. 8. What is meant by the word [*Godhead?*]

A. The divine nature or essence; Rom. i. 20, compared with Gal. iv. 8.

Q. 9. What is meant by a [*person*] in the [*Godhead?*]

A. A complete, intelligent, and individual subsistence, which is neither a part of, nor sustained by any other;

---

* That is, *particular.* † Chap. ii. § 3.

but is distinguished by an incommunicable property in the same undivided essence.

Q. 10. Has each person then a distinct nature, or essence of his own?

A. No: but the same divine nature, or essence, is common to all the three glorious persons, 1 John v. 7,—" These three are one;" not only united in will and affection, but in one and the same common nature, or essence: it being the transcendent and incommunicable property of the divine nature, to reside in more persons than one.

Q. 11. What was the heresy of the Sabellians, and Tritheists, in opposition to this fundamental doctrine of the Trinity?

A. The Sabellians maintained that there is but one person in the Trinity under three different names; the Tritheists, that the three persons are three Gods.

Q. 12. Is the word PERSON, as applied to this mystery, made use of in scripture?

A. Yes; for the Son is said to be the "express image of the Father's person," Heb. i. 3.

Q. 13. How do you prove that there are [three persons] in the Godhead?

A. From the institution of baptism, Matt. xxviii. 19; from the apostolical blessing, 2 Cor. xiii. 14; from John's salutation to the seven churches, Rev. i. 4. 5; and from the baptism of Christ, Matt. iii. 16, 17; where the Father is manifested by a voice from heaven; the Son, by his bodily appearance on earth; and the Holy Ghost, by his lighting on him in the shape of a dove.

Q. 14. How is it farther evident that they are three distinct persons?

A. From the distinct capacities in which they are represented to act; for, in the work of redemption, we find in scripture, the Father "ordaining," the Son "purchasing," and the Holy Ghost "applying it," 1 Pet. i. 2.

Q. 15. How are the persons in the Godhead distinguished from each other?

A. By their personal properties, which are incommunicable to each other.

Q. 16. What is the personal property of the Father?

A. To beget the Son, and that from all eternity, Ps. ii. 7.

Q. 17. What is the personal property of the Son?

A. To be eternally begotten of the Father, John i. 14,— "We beheld his glory, the glory as of the only begotten of the Father."

Q. 18. What is the personal property of the Holy Ghost?

A. To proceed eternally from the Father and the Son John xv. 26: " When the Comforter is come, whom I will send unto you from the Father, even the Spirit of truth which proceedeth from the Father, he shall testify of me."

Q. 19. How does it appear that the Holy Ghost proceeds from the Son, as well as from the Father, when it is not expressly affirmed that he does so, in the above text?

A. Because he is called "the Spirit of the Son," Gal. iv. 6; "the Spirit of Christ," Rom. viii. 9; the Spirit is said to receive all things from Christ, John xvi. 14, 15; to be sent by him, John xv. 26; and the Father is said to send him in Christ's name, John xiv. 26; from all which, it may be safely gathered, that he proceeds from the Son, as well as from the Father.

Q. 20. What is the difference between a *personal* and an *essential* property?

A. A *personal* property is peculiar to one of the persons only, but an *essential* property is common to them all.

Q. 21. Why are the personal properties called *incommunicable*.

A. Because each of them is so proper to one of the persons in the Trinity, that it cannot be affirmed of any of the other two.

Q. 22. Is it the divine essence that begets, is begotten, or proceeds?

A. No: for these are not essential, but personal acts. It is the Father who begets the Son; the Son who is begotten of the Father; and the Holy Ghost, who proceeds from both.

Q. 23. Are the terms *necessary existence, supreme Deity,* and the title of the *only true God*, essential or personal properties?

A. They are essential properties of the divine nature, and so common to all the persons of the adorable Trinity, who have all the same essence, wholly, equally, and eternally.

Q. 24. May the above terms be taken, or are they, by sound authors, taken in a sense that includes the personal property of the Father, and so not belonging to the Son and Holy Ghost?

A. They may not be, and never are, by sound authors, taken in that sense; for this would be to make the Son and Holy Ghost inferior to, and dependent upon, the Father, for being or existence, which is the very soul of Arianism.

Q. 25. Does not the Father, being called the *first*; the Son, the *second*; and the Holy Ghost, the *third* person in the Godhead, imply an inequality, or preference of one person to another?

A. These are only terms of mere order, and imply no preference or priority, either of nature, excellency, or duration; and therefore we find in scripture, that sometimes the Son is named before the Father, as in 2 Cor. xiii. 14, Gal. i. 1; and sometimes the Spirit before the Son, as in Rev. i. 4, 5.

Q. 26. Is not each of these glorious persons truly and properly God?

A. Each of these persons is God, in the true and proper sense of the word; though none of them can be called the *Deity*, exclusively of the rest, in regard the *Deity*, being the same with the *divine nature*, or *essence*, is common to them all.

Q. 27. But does not our Lord say, that the Father is the "only true God," John xvii. 3: "This is life eternal, that they might know thee the only true God?"

A. Our Lord does not say, that the *Father only*, is the true God, exclusive of the other persons of the Trinity; but that *He* is the *only true God* (as each of the other persons is) in opposition to idols, or gods falsely so called.

Q. 28. How does it appear that the [*Father*] is God?

A. From his being expressly so called every where in scripture: particularly, 1 Cor. viii. 6; and xv. 24. Gal. i. 1, 3, &c.

Q. 29. Is it proper to say, that the Father is the *fountain of the Deity*?

A. The expression is dangerous, and now used by adversaries in an unsound sense, to exclude self-existence and independency from the Son and Holy Ghost, and therefore is to be avoided.

Q. 30. How does it appear from scripture, that Christ, the [*Son*,] is truly and properly the supreme God, equal with the Father?

A. From the same names, attributes, works, and worship being ascribed to him in scripture as are ascribed to the Father, and in as full and ample a sense.*

Q. 31. What are the names ascribed to Christ, that prove him to be equal with the Father?

A. He is expressly called "God," John i. 1; "the great God," Tit. ii. 13; "the mighty God," Isa. ix. 6; "the true God," 1 John v. 20; "the only wise God," Jude ver. 25; and JEHOVAH, which is a name never ascribed to any, in scripture, but the living and true God, Jer. xxiii. 6. Ps. lxxxiii. 18.

Q. 32. What are the *divine attributes* ascribed to Christ, that prove him to be the supreme God?

A. Eternity, in the strict and proper sense of the word, Mic. v. 2; unchangeableness, Heb. xiii. 8; omniscience,

---

* Larger Catechism, Q.11.

PART I.—5

John xxi. 17; omnipotence, for he calls himself "the Almighty," Rev. i. 8; omnipresence; "Lo," says he, "I am with you always, even unto the end of the world," Matt. xxviii. 20; and supremacy, Rom. ix. 5.

Q. 33. What are those *works* which manifest Christ to be the true God?

A. The creating and preserving of all things, Col. i. 16, 17; the obtaining eternal redemption for us, Heb. ix. 12; the working of miracles by his own power, Mark v. 41; the forgiving of sins, Mark ii. 5; the raising of the dead at the last day, John v. 28, 29; and his judging the world, Rom. xiv. 10.

Q. 34. What is that *worship* ascribed to Christ which proves him to be the supreme God?

A. The same divine worship and adoration that is given to the Father, John v. 33: we are commanded to believe in him equally with the Father, John xiv. 1; and we are baptized in his name, as well as in the name of the Father, Matt. xxviii. 19.

Q. 35. In what sense does Christ say, John xiv. 28, "My Father is greater than I?"

A. He does not speak in that place of his *nature*, as God, but of his *office*, as Mediator; in which respect he is the Father's *servant*, Isa. xlii. 1.

Q. 36. How do you prove the supreme Deity of the [*Holy Ghost?*]

A. From the same arguments, by which the Deity of the Son was proved; for, (1.) He is expressly called *God*, Acts v. 3, 4. (2.) Attributes, which are peculiar only to God, are ascribed to him, Heb. ix. 14. 1 Cor. ii. 10. Luke ii. 26. Ps. cxxxix. 7. (3.) Works which can be accomplished by none but God, are performed by him, Ps. xxxiii. 6. Job xxvi. 13. Luke i. 35. 2 Pet. i. 21. John xvi. 13. Rom. xv. 16. (4.) The same divine worship is paid to him, as to the Father and the Son, Matt. xxviii. 19. 2 Cor. xiii. 14.

Q. 37. Could the Trinity of persons, in the unity of essence, have been discovered by the light of nature?

A. By no means: for then it would be no mystery, seeing divine mysteries are such secrets, as the wisdom of man could never have found out, Matt. xi. 27. 1 Cor. ii. 9, 10, 14.

Q. 38. Is it lawful to explain this mystery by natural similitudes?

A. No; for there is no similitude amongst all the creatures, that has the remotest resemblance to this adorable mystery of the *three one* God. By making similes or comparisons of this kind, men have become vain in their imaginations, and their foolish minds have been darkened, Rom. i. 21—26; and therefore, as this doctrine is entirely a matter of faith, it becomes us to adore it, without prying curiously into what is not revealed.

Q. 39. Does the asserting of three persons in the Godhead, with distinct personal properties, infer any separation, or division, in the divine essence?

A. No; for the persons in the Godhead are not separated, but *distinguished* from one another, by their personal properties. As the unity of the essence does not confound the persons, so neither does the distinction of persons imply any division of the essence, 1 John v. 7.

Q. 40. Can any worship God aright, without the faith of this mystery of the Trinity?

A. No: "for he that cometh to God, must believe that he is," Heb. xi. 6; namely, that he is God, Father, Son, and Holy Ghost.

Q. 41. How is our worship to be directed to this *three one* God?

A. We are to worship the Father, in Christ the Son, by the Spirit; and thus, when we pray, we are to ask the Father, in the name of the Son, by the Holy Ghost, Eph. ii. 18; and v. 20.

Q. 42. Will not this mystery be more fully known and displayed in heaven?

A. Yes: for, says Christ, "at that day ye shall know, that I am in my Father," John xiv. 20. See also 1 Cor. xiii. 12. 1 John iii. 2.

Q. 43. What comfortable instruction may we learn from this doctrine of the Trinity?

A. That the gift of eternal life, in the promise and offer of the gospel, to sinners of mankind, is attested by the three famous witnesses in heaven, who are above all exception, 1 John v. 7, 11; and consequently, that a portion infinitely rich, is insured by the covenant of grace to all those who believe, when it makes over all the three persons to them, as their God, Jer. xxxi. 33.

Q. 44. What is the duty of the judicatures of the church with reference to Arians, Socinians, and Deists, who deny this fundamental doctrine of the Trinity?

A. It is their duty *after the first and second admonition*, to *reject* them as heretics, Tit. iii. 10.

QUEST. 7. *What are the decrees of God?*

ANS. The decrees of God are his eternal purpose, according to the counsel of his will, whereby, for his own glory, he hath fore-ordained whatsoever comes to pass.

Q. 1. What does the word [*counsel*] as ascribed to God import?

A. Not the receiving the knowledge of things from another, or in the way of study and advisement, as among men; but the eternity, wisdom, and immutability of his determinations, Ps. xxxiii. 11. Prov. xix. 21.

Q. 2. Does the scripture speak expressly of God's decrees?

A. Yes; in many places; such as, Ps. ii. 7. Job. xxviii. 26; and xxxviii. 10. Isa. x. 22. Jer. v. 22, &c.

Q. 3. Are we by [*the decrees of God*,] to understand the things decreed, or the act decreeing?

A. The act decreeing or discerning.

Q. 4. Is the decreeing act of God one simple act only?

A. Yes: because of the perfect oneness or simplicity of his nature, on account of which he could not but decree all things at once; because all things are naked and opened unto his omniscient eye, Heb. iv. 13; and because of his immutability, Mal. iii. 6.

Q. 5. Why then do we speak of the divine decrees as various, or many?

A. Because of the many objects which the decreeing act of God respects: the things decreed are many, but the act decreeing is but one only.

Q. 6. What are the properties of the divine decrees?

A. That they are eternal, most wise, absolute, and unchangeable.

Q. 7. How do you prove the decrees of God to be *eternal?*

A. The decrees of election, and publishing the gospel, are eternal, as is evident from Eph. i. 4; and 1 Cor. ii. 7; and therefore, all other decrees must be eternal likewise, because he decreed all things at once, by one simple act, Acts xv. 18.

Q. 8. In what does the *wisdom* of God's decrees appear?

A. In the beautiful order in which they are executed, Mark vii. 37: "He hath done all things well."

Q. 9. Why are the divine decrees said to be *absolute?*

A. Because they depend upon no condition without God himself, but entirely and solely upon his own sovereign will and pleasure, Eph. i. 11.

Q. 10. Are there not certain means by which the decrees of God are executed?

A. Yes: but these means are decreed as well as the end, 2 Thess. ii. 13.

Q. 11. How does it appear from scripture, that the means and the end are connected in the decree?

A. From the preservation of Paul, and those who were with him in the ship; God had decreed to preserve them all, Acts xxvii. 24; yet lawful means were to be used; the shipmen must not get leave to flee out of the ship, otherwise the rest cannot be saved, as Paul tells the centurion and the soldiers, ver. 31.

Q. 12. What is the difference between the means of execution, and decreeing conditionally?

A. The means of execution are stated in the decree; but to decree a thing conditionally, is to decree it upon an uncertain event, which may, or may never take place.

Q. 13. What is the absurdity of conditional decrees?

A. They make the will of God, which is the first cause, to depend upon the will of the creature: and they plainly suppose, that either God is ignorant of the event, or incapable to accomplish it; or that he has determined nothing certainly about it; all which are blasphemously absurd.

Q. 14. Are all the decrees of God then *unchangeable?*

A. Yes: "from all eternity he hath, for his own glory, unchangeably fore-ordained whatsoever comes to pass in time," Eph. i. 11.*

Q. 15. How do you prove the decrees of God to be unchangeable?

A. From scripture and from reason.

Q. 16. How is it proved from *scripture?*

A. From Job xxiii. 13: "He is in one mind, and who can turn him?" Isa. xlvi. 10: "My counsel shall stand, and I will do all my pleasure."

Q. 17. How do you prove from reason, that the divine decrees are unchangeable?

A. From this one argument—That there is in God no defect of wisdom, power, or faithfulness, from whence any change of his will may flow; as is the case among men, when they alter their resolutions.

Q. 18. Does the immutability of God's decree destroy the liberty of man's will, or the contingency of second causes?

A. No: there is in it no " violence offered to the will of the creature, nor is the liberty or contingency of second causes taken away, but rather established," Matt. xvii. 12. Acts ii. 23.†

Q. 19. Whence is it, that the absolute or unchangeable decree does not take away the liberty of the will?

A. Because God, in the execution of his decree, does not change the nature of things, but suffers rational agents to act freely and voluntarily, as being under no more constraint or compulsion, than though there had been no such decree.

Q. 20. How is this made clear from scripture?

A. By the instance of Pilate and the Jews, when they crucified the Lord of glory: what they did was with full

---

* Larger Catechism, Q. 12. † Confession chap. iii. § 1.

freedom of their will, and yet they did nothing but what God's " hand and counsel determined before to be done," Acts iv. 27, 28.

Q. 21. Does any thing come to pass in time, but what was decreed from eternity?

A. No: for the very reason why any thing comes to pass in time, is because God decreed it, Eph. i. 11. Acts xv. 18.

Q. 22. Are things that are casual or accidental, positively decreed?

A. Yes: as is evident from the instances of Joseph's advancement in Egypt; and the not breaking a bone of Christ; and many others.

Q. 23. What has the decree of God fixed with respect to man's continuance in this world?

A. It has immovably fixed the precise moment of every one's life and death, with every particular circumstance thereof.

Q. 24. How may it be proved that the precise moment of every one's death is unalterably fixed in the decree?

A. From express scripture testimony, Job xiv. 5; Ps. xxxix. 4; from the reason given why the Jews could not lay hands on Christ; namely, " because his hour was not yet come," John vii. 30; and from God's numbering the hairs of our head, Matt. x. 30; much more the days and moments of our life.

Q. 25. Were there not *fifteen* years added to Hezekiah's days, after the prophet said to him, " Set thine house in order; for thou shalt die, and not live?" Isa. xxxviii. 1, 5.

A. The sentence of death, by the prophet, was not an intimation of the decree of God, that Hezekiah was presently to die; but of the nature of his disease, which, according to the ordinary course of second causes, was mortal, if the power of God had not miraculously interposed.

Q. 26. How does the decree of God extend to things naturally and morally good?

A. Effectively: because God is the author and efficient cause of all good, Phil. ii. 13.

Q. 27. How does it extend to things morally evil?

A. Permissively and directively only, Acts xiv. 16.

Q. 28. Is the permissive decree a bare inactive permitting of evil?

A. No: it determines the event of the evil permitted, and overrules it to a good end, contrary to the intention both of the work and worker.

Q. 29. What scripture example is there of this?

A. God permits Joseph's brethren to sell him into Egypt, and Potiphar to throw him unjustly into prison, and yet overrules both these evils, and makes them means, contrary to the intention both of the work and workers, for executing the decree of his advancement to the greatest honour, Gen. xlv. 5—8; and l. 20: "Ye thought evil against me, (says Joseph to his brethren,) but God meant it unto good."

Q. 30. How can the decree of God be permissive and efficacious at the same time?

A. It is permissive, with respect to the *sinfulness* of the action as a moral evil; and efficacious, with respect to the *matter* of it as a natural act.

Q. 31. How do you prove that God cannot be the author of sin?

A. From the contrariety of it to his holy nature and law, and the indignation he has manifested against it, in what Christ suffered on account of it; for he can never be the author of that of which he is the avenger.

Q. 32. What is the great end of all God's decrees?

A. [His own glory,] Prov. xvi. 4: "The Lord hath made all things for himself;" and particularly the glory of his mercy and justice, Rom. ix. 22, 23, and, next to his own glory, the good of the elect, both here and hereafter, Rom. viii. 28.

Q. 33. Who are the special objects of God's decrees?

A. Angels and men.

Q. 34. What is God's decree concerning angels and men, commonly called?

A. His predestinating of them.

Q. 35. What is meant by *predestination*?

A. It is God's unchangeable purpose or decree, concerning the last end, and eternal state, of angels and men, 1 Tim. v. 21. Jude ver. 6. Ex. xxxiii. 19. Rom. ix. 11 13, 18.

Q. 36. Is the precise number of angels and men, thus predestinated, particularly and unchangeably defined?

A. Yes: "their number is so certain and definite, that it cannot be either increased or diminished," 2 Tim. ii. 19. John xiii. 18.*

Q. 37. How is the decree of predestination usually divided?

A. Into the decree of election and reprobation.

Q. 38. What is God's decree of *election*, as it respects men?

A. It is his choosing a certain number of mankind, in Christ, to eternal life, and the means of it, to the praise of his glorious grace, Eph. i. 4. 2 Thess. ii. 13, 14.

Q. 39. Was it the foresight of faith, or good works, or perseverance in either of them, or any other thing whatsoever in the creature, that moved God to make choice of some men, and not of others?

* Confession, chap. iii. § 4.

A. By no means; but his mere free grace and love Eph. i. 6, 12.

Q. 40. What is God's decree of *reprobation*, as it respects men?

A. It is his passing by, and ordaining all the rest of mankind whom he has not chosen, to dishonour and wrath, to be for their sins inflicted, to the praise of the glory of his justice, Rom. ix. 17, 18, 22. 1 Pet. ii. 8. Jude ver. 4.

Q. 41. Since God has appointed the elect to glory, has he not also fore-ordained all the means?

A. Yes; for "they who are elected, being fallen in Adam, are redeemed by Christ, 1 Thess. v. 9, 10;"* and free grace reigns, through his righteousness, to their eternal life, Rom. v. 21.

Q. 42. Do the decrees of election and reprobation import any partiality, or injustice in God?

A. No more than a potter is esteemed partial, or unjust, in making, out of the same lump, one vessel to honour, and another to dishonour, Rom. ix. 20. 21.

Q. 43. Is sin in the reprobate the cause of their damnation, or of their reprobation?

A. Their sin is indeed the cause of their damnation, Rom. vi. 23, "The wages of sin is death;" but the sovereign will and pleasure of God is the cause of their reprobation, Matt. xi. 25, 26. Rom. ix. 18.

Q. 44. Are the secret decrees of God, concerning the eternal state of men, the rule of faith and practice?

A. No: but the revealed will of God only, Deut. xxix. 29.

Q. 45. Does not this doctrine of particular election and reprobation limit the general call of the gospel?

A. No: for Christ commissions to go "into all the world, and preach the gospel to every creature," Mark xvi. 15; not as they are elect or reprobate, but as they are lost sinners of Adam's family, Matt. ix. 13; therefore, all that hear the gospel have an equal warrant to believe, 1 John iii. 23.

Q. 46. Has it a tendency to make men careless in the use of the means of salvation?

A. No: because God has chosen us to salvation, "through sanctification of the Spirit, and belief of the truth," 2 Thess. ii. 13.

Q. 47. Ought we then to improve the means of salvation, without regard to the decree?

A. We ought no more to regard the decree in the matter of believing to the salvation of our souls, than in eating, drinking, buying, selling, or any other common action of life; because "the secret things belong unto the

---

* Confession, chap. iii. § 6.

Lord our God, but those things which are revealed, belong unto us, and to our children for ever," Deut. xxix. 29.

Q. 48. What improvement ought we to make of the doctrine of absolute election?

A. We ought to be encouraged to believe in Christ: considering that electing love pitches on the chief of sinners, Ezek. xvi. 6; that it flows not from, nor is founded upon, any condition to be performed by men, Rom. ix. 11; and that it contains in it all things pertaining to life and godliness, 2 Pet. i. 3.

QUEST. 8. *How does God execute his decrees?*

ANS. God executes his decrees, in the works of creation and providence.

Q. 1. What is it for God to *execute* his decrees?

A. It is to bring them to pass; or, give an actual being in time, to what he purposed from eternity, Isa. xlvi. 10.

Q. 2. Does not God leave the execution of his decrees to second causes?

A. Whatever use God may make of second causes, in the execution of his decrees, yet they are merely tools in his over-ruling hand, to bring about his glorious designs; they are his servants, and must do all his pleasure, Acts iv. 27, 28.

Q. 3. What difference is there between the decree and the execution of it?

A. The decree is an *immanent* or inherent act in God, and is nothing else but *God decreeing*; but the execution is a *transient* or passing act of his infinite power, bringing the thing decreed into actual existence, 2 Pet. i. 3.

Q. 4. Is there an exact harmony, or correspondence, between God's decree and the execution of it?

A. When the thing decreed is brought actually into being, it exactly corresponds to the idea or platform of it in the infinite mind of God, Ps. cxxxix. 16; as the tabernacle of Moses answered the pattern given of it in the Mount, Ex. xxv. 40.

Q. 5. Can none of the decrees of God be defeated, or fail of execution?

A. By no means; the counsel of the Lord shall stand, and he will do all his pleasure, Isa. xlvi. 10. "Who hath resisted his will?" Rom. ix. 19. "None can stay his hand, or say unto him, What dost thou?" Dan. iv. 35.

Q. 6. What are the works of God, in which his decrees are executed?

A. They are [the works of creation and providence.]

Q. 7. To which of these works of God does *redemption* belong?

A. To the *providence* of God, as the most glorious part of it towards men.

Q. 8. What then is the first external work of God?

A It is creation: which is therefore called, " The beginning of his ways," Prov. viii. 22.

Q. 9. What is the difference between God's executing the work of creation, and that of providence?

A. He executed the work of creation entirely without means, by the word of his power; but he executes the work of providence, ordinarily, in the use of them.

Q. 10. What may we learn from God's executing his decrees?

A. That all his promises shall be punctually accomplished, and not one of them fall to the ground, Mark xiii. 31.

QUEST. 9. *What is the work of creation?*

ANS. The work of creation is, God's making all things of nothing, by the word of his power, in the space of six days, and all very good.

Q. 1. How do you know that the world had a beginning?

A. The light of nature teaches, that there must be a *first cause;* besides, "through faith we understand that the worlds were framed by the word of God," Heb. xi. 3.

Q. 2. Might not this world have existed from eternity?

A. No; it is impossible: this supposition is not only contrary to scripture, but to common sense and reason, which tells us, that what is created, and has a duration by succession of time, must have had a beginning.

Q. 3. From whom did this world receive its being and beginning?

A. From God only, who is being itself, and gives being to all things, Neh. ix. 6.

Q. 4. What is it for God to create?

A. It is his [making all things of nothing.]

Q. 5. When did God create this world?

A. In the beginning of time, Gen. i. 1.

Q. 6. Was there any pre-existent matter out of which God created the world?

A. No: for, by his powerful word, he called " those things which be not, as though they were," Rom. iv. 17; " so that things which are seen, were not made of things which do appear," that is. of any pre-existent matter, Heb. xi. 3.

OF CREATION IN GENERAL. 59

Q. 7. In what time did God create all things?
A. [In the space of six days,] Ex. xx. 11.
Q. 8. Could he not have created all things in a moment of time?
A. Yes: but he saw it more for his own glory, and the good of mankind, to set them an example of working six days, and resting the seventh.
Q. 9. On which of the six days, is it reckoned, that the angels were created?
A. It is probable they were created upon the first day, as would seem from Job xxxviii. 4, 7: " Where wast thou when I laid the foundations of the earth,—when the morning stars sang together, and all the sons of God shouted for joy?"
Q. 10. Can creating power be imparted to any creature?
A. No: it implies a contradiction for a creature to create, because this would vest a finite creature with infinite power, Isa. xiv. 12.
Q. 11. Is it not then a clear proof of the supreme Deity of the Son of God, that all things were made by him?
A. No doubt it is: for, none but he, who is truly and properly God, can command things that are not into being, Isa. xliv. 24.
Q. 12. Is creation a work common to all the persons of the Trinity?
A. Yes; for all the external works of God are common to each person; every one of the three adorable persons being the same in substance, equal in power and glory, 1 John v. 7: " These three are one."
Q. 13. For what end did God make all things?
A. He made all things for himself, or for the display of his matchless excellencies, Prov. xvi. 4.
Q. 14. What are those excellencies or perfections of God, which are more especially displayed in the work of creation?
A. His infinite power, extensive goodness, and manifold wisdom, Rom. i. 20.
Q. 15. How does the infinite power of God shine forth in creating the world?
A. In bringing all things, of a sudden, out of nothing, by his bare word, Ps. xxxiii. 6.
Q. 16. What was that bare word?
A. Let such a thing be, Gen. i. 3.
Q. 17. How is his manifold wisdom displayed in this work?
A. In the vast variety of creatures, great and small, which he has made; the order and harmony of them all; and their subserviency one to another, Ps. civ. 24.
Q. 18. Why is it said that he made all things [*very good?*]
A. Because God, upon a survey of his works, declared

them to be so, Gen. i. 31: "God saw all that he had made, and behold, it was very good."

Q. 19. In what consists the goodness of the creatures of God?

A. In the perfection of their nature, their being fit to answer the end of their creation; and their usefulness to man, being both profitable and pleasant to him.

Q. 20. Are not many creatures hurtful to man?

A. They were not so at their first creation, and while man continued in his allegiance to God: but through his sinning against God he has brought a curse on himself, and the whole creation, Gen. iii. 17: "Cursed is the ground for thy sake."

Q. 21. Is not God said to "create evil?" Isa. xlv. 7.

A. Not the evil of sin; but of punishment, as a just judge, Rom. iii. 5, 6. Amos iii. 6.

Q. 22. How then came sin and death into the world?

A. Man is the parent of sin, and sin opened the door to death: "By one man sin entered into the world, and death by sin," Rom. v. 12.

Q. 23. Upon what day did God rest from creating the world?

A. Upon the seventh day, Gen. ii. 2, 3; which was therefore appointed to be the weekly Sabbath, till the resurrection of Christ.

Q. 24. Does this resting, on the seventh day, say that he was weary with working?

A. No: "The everlasting God, the Creator of the ends of the earth, fainteth not, neither is weary," Isa. xl. 28.

Q. 25. What then is meant by his resting?

A. It is spoken after the manner of men; and the meaning is, that God ceased to create any other sorts of creatures than he had already made.

Q. 26. Is not the same power that created all things, exerted in sustaining them in their being?

A. Yes; for he, by whom the worlds were made, is said to uphold all things by the word of his power, Heb. i. 2, 3.

Q. 27. Do not the scriptures speak of a *new* creation, as well as of the old?

A. Yes: the Spirit of God, in scripture, speaks of a new world of grace, under the name of "new heavens" and a "new earth," Isa. lxvi. 22; Rev. xxi. 1.

Q. 28. What is to be understood by this new creation, or new world of grace?

A. The true church of Christ, particularly under the New Testament, not excluding the church triumphant in heaven.

Q. 29. By whom is this new world created?

A. By the same God that made the old world; "Behold, I create new heavens, and a new earth," Isa. lxv. 17.

OF THE CREATION OF MAN. 61

Q. 30. Who are the inhabitants of this new world?
A. They are all *new creatures*, taken out of the old world, 2 Cor. v. 17.

Q. 31. How came they out of this material, into that spiritual world?
A. By the new birth; for, except a man be born again, he cannot enter into it, John iii. 3: flesh and blood, or corrupted nature, continuing such, cannot inherit it, 1 Cor. xv. 50.

Q. 32. Is there any difference of nations, sexes, or persons, in this new world?
A. No; for "there is neither Greek nor Jew, circumcision, nor uncircumcision, Barbarian, Scythian, bond nor free; but Christ is all, and in all," Col. iii. 11.

Q. 33. By what door do men enter into this new world of grace?
A. Christ says, "I am the door; by me if any man enter in, he shall be saved, and shall go in and out, and find pasture," John x. 9, and chap. xiv. 6; "I am the way—no man cometh unto the Father, but by me."

Q. 34. In what lies the happiness of the inhabitants of this new world of grace?
A. None so happy as they, because they dwell in God, and God dwells in them as in a temple, 1 Cor. iii. 16; and walks in them as in his garden of pleasure, 2 Cor. vi. 16; and, at death, they are transported by the ministry of angels, to the world of glory above, Luke xvi. 22.

Q. 35. What may we learn from the doctrine of the creation?
A. That we ought to contemplate God in all his creatures, Ps. xix. 1; acknowledge him as the rightful proprietor and sovereign disposer of them all, 1 Chron. xxix. 11; and believe that the same almighty power of God, which was put forth in creating of all things, shall be exerted in defence and support of his church and people, in the time of their need, Ps. cxxi. 2.

QUEST. 10. *How did God create man?*

ANS. God created man, male and female, after his own image, in knowledge, righteousness, and holiness, with dominion over the creatures.

Q. 1. Upon which day of creation was [*man*] made?
A. Upon the *sixth* day, Gen. i. 26, and 31, compared.
Q. 2. Why was the creation of man delayed, or put off, to the sixth day?

PART I.—6

OF THE CREATION OF MAN.

A. To discover the great regard God had to man's happiness and welfare, in that he would first furnish the great house of the creation for him, before he brought him into it, Ps. viii. 6—8.

Q. 3. Was there any more solemnity observed in the creation of man, than in making the rest of the creatures?

A. Yes: for as to the rest of the creatures, he just commanded them into being; but when man is to be created, a council of the Trinity is held about his formation. Gen. i. 26, " Let us make man."

Q. 4. Why so much solemnity about man's formation beyond other creatures?

A. Because man was to be God's viceroy in this lower world, the only image of his Creator, in his formal perfections; and it was the purpose of God, though not then revealed, that the second person of the Godhead was to become man.

Q. 5. What is it that constitutes the human nature, or nature of man?

A. A true body and a reasonable soul united together.

Q. 6. Of what was the body of man formed?

A. "Of the dust of the ground," Gen. ii. 7; hence God is resembled to a *potter*, and man to the *clay*, and a *potsherd*, Isa. lxiv. 8, and xlv. 9.

Q. 7. What should this teach us?

A. To remember we are dust, Eccl. iii. 20; to admire the condescension of the son of God in coming into our tribe, and assuming a human body, 1 Tim. iii. 16; to consider that we are in God's hand, as the clay is in the hand of the potter, Jer. xviii. 6; and that, in this our fallen state, we are to return to the dust again, Gen. iii. 19.

Q. 8. How was the first woman formed?

A. Of a rib taken from the man's side, Gen ii. 21, 22.

Q. 9. Of what was this a figure?

A. Of Christ and the church, Eph. v. 31, 32.

Q. 10. In what respect was the formation of the woman a figure of these?

A. In as much as the church was, as it were, taken out of the pierced side of Christ, when the Lord God caused the deep sleep of death to fall upon him; first, *typically*, in the sacrifice; and then *actually*, in his decease which he accomplished at Jerusalem.

Q. 11. Why was marriage instituted of God before the fall?

A. To show that it belongs to the law of nature; and that mankind, as such, have a title to it. Heb. xiii. 4, "Marriage is honourable in all."

Q. 12. What is the other part of man's nature?

A. A reasonable soul.

Q. 13. How was the soul of man made?

A. God " breathed into his nostrils the breath of life, and he became a living soul," Gen. ii. 7.

Q. 14. Why is the creation of the soul of man thus expressed?

A. To show, that as the Lord is " the God of the spirits of all flesh," Num. xxvii. 16; who creates them immediately, and by himself, without the intervention of second causes, Zech. xii. 1; so he has an absolute dominion over them, and can call them back to himself when he pleases, Eccl. xii. 7.

Q. 15. In what does the soul of man differ from the body?

A. The body is a corporeal, but the soul is a spiritual and immaterial substance.

Q. 16. In what does the soul of man differ from the spirit or life of a beast?

A. The spirit or life of a beast goes downward to the earth, and perishes at its death, Eccl. iii. 21; but the soul of man, being rational and immortal, "returns to God who gave it," Eccl. xii. 7.

Q. 17. How do you prove the immortality of the soul of man?

A. (1.) From the great price paid for the redemption of the soul, which had ceased for ever, without a ransom of infinite value, Ps. xlix. 8. (2.) From the promises of eternal life, and the threatenings of eternal death, Mark xvi. 16. (3.) Christ tells us, that they who kill the body cannot kill the soul, Matt. x. 28. (4.) Christ, and his dying saints, commit their spirits, or souls, into the hand of God, Ps. xxxi. 5; Luke xxiii. 46; Acts vii. 59; and the soul of the thief went to paradise, with the soul of Christ, that day they died, Luke xxiii. 43. In a word, if the soul perishes with the body, the saints of God would be of all men the most miserable, 1 Cor. xv. 19.

Q. 18. What should this teach us?

A. To be more concerned for the salvation of our souls than for all things in the world: " For," says Christ, " what is a man profited, if he gain the whole world, and lose his own soul?" Matt. xvi. 26.

Q. 19. Why did God create man [*male and female?*]

A. For the propagation of mankind, Gen. i. 28; and mutual helpfulness to each other, chap. ii. 18.

Q. 20. Why were both the man and the woman called *Adam?* Gen. v. 2.

A. To intimate that their original was of the earth; that they were both of the same nature; that the promises and threatenings concerned them both equally, Rom. v. 12; and to teach us, that notwithstanding this, the man was the representing head of the covenant, 1 Cor. xv. 22.

Q. 21. After whose *image* did God create man?

A. [*After his own image,*] Gen. i. 26, 27.

Q. 22. Did this image of God lie in any outward shape of man's body?

A. By no means: for God is a pure Spirit, without all bodily parts, John iv. 24.

Q. 23. What then was the proper seat of it?

A. The soul of man was the painting table, on which this image of God was expressed and delineated, Gen. ii. 7; James iii. 9.

Q. 24. In what did the soul of man bear a likeness to God?

A. In its spiritual and immortal nature; and in the faculties of the understanding and the will, with which it was endued.

Q. 25. In what did the image of God, which was drawn on man's soul, chiefly consist?

A. [*In knowledge, righteousness, and holiness,*] Col. iii. 10; Eph. iv. 24.

Q. 26. What knowledge was man endued with at his creation?

A. A perfect knowledge of God, of his will, and works, so far as was necessary to render him happy, and fit for universal obedience.

Q. 27. What righteousness had man at his creation?

A. Not an imputed, but an inherent righteousness; which consisted in a perfect conformity of all the powers and faculties of his soul, to the pure nature of God, and the moral law written upon his heart, Eccl. vii. 29.

Q. 28. In what consisted his holiness?

A. In the lustre and beauty of his perfect knowledge and inherent righteousness, shining both in his heart and life.

Q. 29. Was the will of man, in a state of innocence, absolutely indifferent to good and evil?

A. No: God set man's will only towards good; yet it was movable to evil, and that only by man himself; to whom God gave a sufficient power to stand in his integrity, if he had pleased, Eccl. vii. 29.

Q. 30. What was the necessary consequence of this image of God drawn upon our first parents?

A. The immortality of the whole man, and [*dominion over the creatures.*]

Q. 31. Would they have been immortal if they had not sinned?

A. Yes; for it was only in case of sin that death was threatened, Gen. ii. 17.

Q. 32. How could their bodies have been immortal, when made of the dust?

A. The perfect purity or holiness of their souls, would

have preserved their bodies from sickness, death, and corruption, Rom. v. 12, and vi. 23.

Q. 33. In what did man's *dominion over the creatures* consist?

A. In his princely power over the inferior creatures, by which he could rule and use them as he pleased, for God's glory and his own good, without any injustice, Gen. i. 18, and ii. 19, 20.

Q. 34. Where did God put the man when he had formed him after his own image?

A. In the garden of Eden; a place eminent for pleasantness, wherein nothing was wanting, either for necessity or delight, Gen. ii. 8, 9.

Q. 35. What may we learn from the holy and happy state in which man was created?

A. The unspeakable difference between man's *former* and *present* condition: *formerly*, in a state of innocence, man's understanding was a lamp of light, his will lay straight with the will of God, and his affections were pure and holy, free from all disorder and distemper; but *now*, the very reverse: so that we may say, "How is the gold become dim! how is the most fine gold changed!" Lam. iv. 1. "The crown is fallen from our head! wo unto us that we have sinned!" chap. v. 16.

QUEST. 11. *What are God's works of providence?*

ANS. God's works of providence are, his most holy, wise, and powerful preserving and governing all his creatures, and all their actions.

Q. 1. How does it appear that there is a [*providence?*]

A. From scripture, and by reason.

Q. 2. How does the scripture evidence that there is a providence?

A. It tells us, that the Lord preserves man and beast, Ps. xxxiv. 6; that he gives "rain from heaven, and fruitful seasons, filling our hearts with food and gladness," Acts xiv. 17; that "he giveth to all, life, and breath, and all things," Acts xvii. 25.

Q. 3. How may providence be proved by reason?

A. The admirable order and harmony among such a vast variety of creatures in the world, continuing for so many ages, notwithstanding of their different and opposite natures; the accomplishment of future events, exactly according to the predictions of them long before; the revolutions of kingdoms; the orderly returns of seed-time and harvest; and the preservation of a church on earth, against the fury of hell and wicked men: all these plainly evince, to the rational world, that there is a providence.

Q. 4. Can providence be denied without denying the being of God?

A. No; for the same arguments that prove the one, prove the other: to deny that God governs the world, is to deny that God exists, Isa. xli. 23.

Q. 5. What is the *object* of God's providence, or to what does it extend?

A. To [*all his creatures, and all their actions.*]

Q. 6. What is God's providence towards the angels?

A. He permitted some of them to fall wilfully and irrecoverably into sin and damnation, Jude verse 6; and established the rest in holiness and happiness, 1 Tim. v. 21.

Q. 7. Are the smallest and meanest of the creatures the objects of God's providence, as well as the greatest and most considerable?

A. God's providence disdains not the meanest worm, more than the mightiest prince: he counts the hairs of our head, Matt. x. 30, as well as the number of the stars, Ps. cxlvii. 4.

Q. 8. Does it reflect any dishonour upon the providence of God to take care of the meanest creatures?

A. It can reflect no dishonour upon divine providence, to preserve what infinite wisdom saw meet to create, be it ever so mean in our view, Neh. ix. 6.

Q. 9. Does providence extend to all the [*actions*] of the creatures, as well as to the creatures themselves?

A. Yes: otherwise the creatures would be independent in their actions; and God would not be in all things the first cause, Gen. xlv. 7.

Q. 10. Are casual or contingent actions subject to divine providence?

A. What is casual to us, is ordained by God: nothing can be more casual than a *lot*, yet "the whole disposing thereof is of the Lord," Prov. xvi. 33.

Q. 11. Are voluntary or free actions subject to it likewise?

A. Yes; for, though "there are many devices in a man's heart, nevertheless the counsel of the Lord, that shall stand," Prov. xix. 21.

Q. 12. How is the providence of God conversant about good actions?

A. Not by compelling, but sweetly inclining and determining the will, both to the action and the right manner of performing it. Phil. ii. 13, "It is God who worketh in you, both to will and to do, of his good pleasure."

Q. 13. How is it conversant about sinful actions?

A. In permitting them to be done, Acts xiv. 16; and in limiting and directing them to good and holy ends, contrary both to the nature of sin, and the intention of the sinner, 2 Kings xix. 28.

Q. 14. What scripture instance may be given, of God's over-ruling the sinful actions of men to holy ends?

A. The worst action that ever was committed, the crucifying the Lord of glory, was ordered and directed by God, for bringing about the greatest mercy, the redemption of a lost world, Acts ii. 23, and iv. 28.

Q. 15. What are the [*works*] of providence about the creatures and their actions?

A. They are two; God's *preserving* them, and his *governing* them.

Q. 16. What is God's [*preserving*] work of providence?

A. It is his upholding all the creatures in their being and operation, by the same power by which he made them at first, Heb. i. 3—" Upholding all things, by the word of his power."

Q. 17. What would be the consequence of God's withholding from the creatures his preserving providence?

A. They would presently sink into their original nothing, Ps. civ. 29.

Q. 18. What is God's [*governing*] work of providence?

A. His directing and leading all his creatures to the proper ends, which he has prescribed and appointed, Prov. xvi. 9: "A man's heart deviseth his way, but the Lord directeth his steps."

Q. 19. How do you prove that God governs as well as preserves his creatures?

A. From their dependence upon him for operation, as well as for being; for in him they *live* and *move*, as well as have their *being*, Acts xvii. 28; and it is expressly said, that "God ruleth by his power for ever." Ps. lxvi. 7.

Q. 20. Does God's governing providence include in it his *immediate concurrence* with every action of the creature?

A. Yes: God not only efficaciously concurs in producing the action, as to the matter of it; but likewise predetermines the creature to such or such an action, and not to another, Isa. x. 6, 7; shutting up all other ways of acting, and leaving that only open, which he had determined to be done, Ezek. xxi. 21, 22.

Q. 21. How can God concur with the sinful actions of men, without sin, of which he cannot be the author?

A. Although God not only preserves and supports the faculties with which a man sins, but likewise previously, immediately, and efficaciously concurs to the substance, matter, or entity of the action, yet he by no means concurs to the sinfulness or wickedness of the act, Isa. x. 6, 7.

Q. 22. In what does the sinfulness of an action properly consist?

A. Not in the *matter* of the action, but in the *form* of it; that is, not in the action itself, considered as an act, but in the deficiency or swerving of that act from the rule of the law, 1 John iii. 4—" Sin is the transgression of the law."

Q. 23. How may the difference between the *matter* and *form* of an action be illustrated by an example?

A. In the stoning of Achan and Naboth; the *matter* of the action was the same, namely, the throwing of stones; but the *form* of the action, in point of conformity or disconformity to the law, was vastly different: the stoning of Achan, condemned by God, and all Israel, was an act of just punishment, agreeable to the law; but the stoning of Naboth, an innocent man, was an act of unjust murder, quite contrary to the law, Ex. xx. 13.

Q. 24. From whence then does the sinfulness or viciousness of actions proceed?

A. Although the power of acting be from God, yet the viciousness or malignity of the action is entirely from the inherent corruption of our own nature, James i. 13, 14.

Q. 25. Does not God present the object which is the occasion of sinning?

A. Sin does not arise from the object which God, in his providence, presents to us, but from our own inward depravity, called, "the corruption that is in the world through lust," 2 Pet. i. 4. God delivered Christ to the Jews; he presented him to them; but neither infused that malice in them, by which they crucified him, nor did excite it, but it was entirely of themselves, Acts ii. 23.

Q. 26. What are the properties of God's providence?

A. It is [*most holy, wise, and powerful.*]

Q. 27. Why is the providence of God called [*most holy?*]

A. Because of the infinite holiness and purity that shines in all his administrations, Ps. cxlv. 17.

Q. 28. In what does the holiness of God's providence appear?

A. In bringing glory to his mercy and justice out of sin.

Q. 29. How does he bring glory to his mercy out of sin?

A. In making the worst of sinners become the choicest of saints, as in the instance of Paul, 1 Tim. i. 12, 13, and others.

Q. 30. How does he bring glory to his justice out of sin?

A. By the judgments which he executes upon sinners, even in this life, Ps. ix. 16.

Q. 31. Why is the providence of God said to be [*wise?*]

A. Because it makes all things subservient to the end which God had fixed for himself, Rom. viii. 28.

Q. 32. How is the wisdom of providence manifested?

A. In the exact harmony of all the motions thereof with the word, Hos. xiv. 9.

Q. 33 Why is God's providence called [*powerful?*]

A. Because it cannot be resisted, Dan. iv. 35—" He doth according to his will, in the army of heaven, and among the inhabitants of the earth: none can stay his hand, or say unto him, what dost thou?"

Q. 34. How does the power of providence discover itself?

A. In bringing about great events, by small and apparently contemptible means: thus, he makes *worm Jacob* to thresh the mountains, Isa. xli. 15; and by the foolishness of preaching saves them that believe, 1 Cor. i. 21.

Q. 35. How is the providence of God usually distinguished?

A. Into ordinary and extraordinary, common and special.

Q. 36. What is the ordinary providence of God?

A. It is his observing the order of things, which he appointed from the beginning, Hos. ii. 21, 22.

Q. 37. What is the *extraordinary* providence of God?

A. It is his going beyond, or contrary to the natural order of things; and such events are called miraculous.

Q. 38. What is a *miracle*?

A. It is such an astonishing and surprising effect, contrary to the ordinary course of nature, as surpasses the power of all created beings, and can be produced by divine omnipotence only; such as, dividing the waters of the Red Sea and Jordan, making the sun to stand still, raising the dead, giving eye-sight to the born blind, curing all manner of diseases by a word, and the like.

Q. 39. What is *common* providence?

A. It is that which is exercised about all the creatures in general, Acts xviii. 28, called God's *natural* government

Q. 40. What is *special* providence?

A. It is that which is exercised about rational creatures in particular, Deut. xxx. 16—18, called his *moral* government.

Q. 41. What is the special providence which God exercises about his church and people?

A. His " eyes run to and fro throughout the whole earth, to show himself strong in behalf of them whose heart is perfect towards him," 2 Chron. xvi. 9; and he makes all things work together for their good, Rom. viii. 28.

Q. 42. Are not all the dispensations of providence, prosperous or adverse, to be carefully observed?

A. Yes; for "whoso is wise, and will observe these things, even they shall understand the loving-kindness of the Lord," Ps. cvii. 43.

Q. 43. How are the providences of God to be observed?

A. With humility and reverence, under a sense of our weakness to penetrate into them, Rom. xi. 34; and with gratitude and thankfulness, because there is always some mixture of mercy with judgment in this life, Ps. ci. 1.

Q. 44. Is it not dangerous to overlook the operations of divine providence?

A. Yes; for it is said, Ps. xxviii. 5, "Because they regard not the works of the Lord, nor the operation of his hands, he shall destroy them, and not build them up."

Q. 45. Are not some dispensations of providence very dark and mysterious?

A. Yes: his ways are many times in the sea, and his paths in the great waters, and his footsteps are not known, Ps. lxxvii. 19.

Q. 46. In what does the mystery of providence appear?

A. In the mysterious tract, and mysterious outward appearance of it.

Q. 47. How is providence mysterious in the *tract* of it?

A. In attaining its end by seemingly contrary means; such as making Joseph's imprisonment the step to his being *second* in the kingdom, and the casting of Daniel into the lions' den, the path to his higher preferment.

Q. 48. In what is providence mysterious in the *outward appearance* of it?

A. In that "all things come alike unto all;" there being *one event to the righteous and to the wicked:* and no man knowing love or hatred, by all that is before him in this life, Eccl. ix. 1, 2.

Q. 49. How do you prove that love or hatred cannot be known by the outward dispensations of providence in this life?

A. From the parable of the *rich man* and *Lazarus;* the *rich man*, in his lifetime, received good things, and *Lazarus* evil things; and yet, after death, *Lazarus* is comforted, and the other tormented, Luke xvi. 19—27.

Q. 50. Is this seemingly unequal appearance of providence in this life, any reflection upon the wisdom and righteousness of it?

A. No; for, though good men may be sometimes put to a stand by the outward prosperity of the wicked, and the straits and wants of the godly, as Jeremiah was, chap. xii. 1, "wherefore doth the way of the wicked prosper? wherefore are all they happy that deal very treacherously?" yet, if the enjoyments of the one, and wants of the other, are laid in the balance, it would be found, that a "little that the righteous man hath, is better than the riches of many wicked," Ps. xxxvii. 16.

Q. 51. What is our duty when providence seems to run contrary to the promise?

A. It is to believe the promise, and that providence is running in a direct line to the accomplishment of it, though we cannot see it at the time, as Abraham did, "who against hope believed in hope, and staggered not at the promise of God through unbelief," Rom. iv. 18, 20.

Q. 52. Will not dark providences be opened to the saints some time or other?
A. Yes: for, says Christ, "What I do thou knowest not now, but thou shalt know hereafter," John xiii. 7.

Q. 53. When will the mystery of providence be opened to the saints?
A. It shall be fully unveiled at the end of the day, when the mystery of it shall be finished, and all the labyrinths, in which the saints were led, fully unwinded, Rev. x. 6, 7.

Q. 54. What will be the language of the saints, when the whole mystery of providence shall be explained?
A. They will say, "He hath done all things well," Mark vii. 37: "Not one thing hath failed of all the good things which the Lord spake;—all are come to pass,—not one thing hath failed thereof," Josh. xxiii. 14.

Q. 55. What improvement ought we to make of this doctrine of providence?
A. To commit our way to the Lord; to "trust also in him, and he shall bring it to pass," Ps. xxxvii. 5.

QUEST. 12. *What special act of providence did God exercise towards man, in the estate wherein he was created?*

ANS. When God had created man, he entered into a covenant of life with him, upon condition of perfect obedience; forbidding him to eat of the tree of knowledge of good and evil, upon the pain of death.

Q. 1. Was there any thing special in God's government of man, when he was created, above the other creatures?
A. Yes; for God gave man a moral law, which the other creatures, not endued with reason, were not capable of: Job xxxv. 10, 11—"None saith, Where is God my maker?—Who teacheth us more than the beasts of the earth, and maketh us wiser than the fowls of heaven."

Q. 2. What call you a moral law?
A. A moral law signifies a law of right manners, or good and suitable behaviour towards God and man, and adapted to man's rational nature, Rom. vii. 12.

OF THE COVENANT OF WORKS.

Q. 3. How was this law first given to man?

A. It w.s written upon the table of his heart, the moment that *God created* him *in his own image*, Gen. i. 27.

Q. 4. What do you understand by God's writing the law upon the table of his heart?

A. God's inlaying a principle of obedience in his heart, disposing him to obey out of love to God, and a supreme regard to his authority, Eccl. vii. 29.

Q. 5. What was the peculiar favour which God manifested to man in a state of innocence, besides writing the law upon his heart?

A. The reducing that law to the form of a covenant, by which man became confederate with heaven.

Q. 6. What is a covenant?

A. A mutual free compact and agreement between two parties, upon express terms or conditions.

Q. 7. How many covenants are there, relating to the life and happiness of man?

A. Two; the covenant of works, and the covenant of grace, Gal. iv. 24—" These are the two covenants."

Q. 8. Which of these was the covenant which God entered into with man, when he was created?

A. The covenant of works, or of life.

Q. 9. Why called a covenant of *works*?

A. From the condition of it.

Q. 10. Why called [*a covenant of life?*]

A. From the promise of it.

Q. 11. How does it appear that God entered into a covenant with man in innocence?

A. From the condition and penalty that were in the first covenant, Gen. ii. 16, 17, and from express mention in scripture of Adam's breach of that covenant. Hos. vi. 7— " But they, like men, (margin, like *Adam*,) have transgressed the covenant."

Q. 12. How does it appear that Adam gave that consent, which was necessary in a mutual covenant?

A. His silent acquiescence to the will of his sovereign Creator, implied a consent; and his consent could not be withheld, by a creature made after the image of God, in knowledge, righteousness, and holiness.

Q. 13. What was the condition of the covenant of works?

A. [*Perfect obedience*] to the whole law of God, in heart and life.

Q. 14. What was the sum of that law, which was the rule of man's covenant obedience?

A. That man believe whatever God shall reveal, and do whatever he shall command, Rom. x. 5; and, in testimony of it, not to [*eat of the tree of knowledge of good and evil,*] Gen. ii. 17.

Q. 15. Was this prohibition, of not eating of the *tree of knowledge of good and evil*, a moral or a positive precept?
A. It was a positive precept, founded in the sovereign will of God.

Q. 16. Was it then a thing in itself indifferent to eat, or not to eat, of that tree?
A. There could be no moral evil in eating of that tree, more than any other, antecedently to the command of God forbidding it; but after that, it was no more indifferent, but highly sinful to do so.

Q. 17. Why did God extend the rule and matter of man's covenant obedience, to a thing in itself indifferent?
A. That man's obedience might turn upon the precise point of the will of God, which is the plainest evidence of true obedience, Ps. xl. 8.

Q. 18. Did man's life and death hang upon this positive precept about the forbidden fruit?
A. Not upon this only, but likewise on the whole law, Gal. iii. 10. "Cursed is every one that continueth not in all things written in the book of the law to do them."

Q. 19. Was there any mercy or favour in restricting man from eating of this tree?
A. Much every way; for this restriction taught him, that though he was lord of the creatures, yet he was God's subject: it was a beacon set up before him to beware of sin; and it pointed him away from the creatures to God himself for happiness.

Q. 20. What was the penalty in case of disobedience?
A. It was [*the pain of death:*]—"In the day that thou eatest thereof thou shalt surely die," Gen. ii. 17.

Q. 21. What kind of death was this which was threatened upon disobedience?
A. It was death temporal, spiritual, and eternal.

Q. 22. Did Adam die a *temporal* or natural death, that day he sinned?
A. No: but he became a dead man in law, and his body got its death-wound, and became mortal, Rom. v. 12.

Q. 23. Why was the immediate execution of natural death suspended?
A. Because of his posterity then in his loins; and because of another covenant that was prepared, Job xxxiii. 24.

Q. 24. What was the *spiritual* death threatened?
A. The loss of his original righteousness, and the favour of God, Gen. iii. 8, 10, 24.

Q. 25. What is meant by *eternal* death?
A. The enduring of the wrath of God, in soul and body, in a state of separation from him for ever, Matt. xxv. 46.

Q. 26. What was the promise in this covenant, in case of obedience?

A. It was life.

Q. 27. How does it appear that life was promised, when the promise of it is not expressly mentioned?

A. The promise of life is included in the threatening of death; "In the day that thou eatest thereof, thou shalt surely die:" which necessarily implies, If thou dost not eat thereof, thou shalt surely live, Gal. iii. 12.

Q. 28. What kind of life was it that was promised to man in the covenant of works?

A. The continuance of his natural life, consisting in the union of his soul and body; the continuance also of his spiritual life, consisting in the favour of God, Lev. xviii. 5; and his entering upon eternal life in heaven, after he had passed through the time of his trial upon earth, Rom. vii. 10.

Q. 29. How do you prove that eternal life, in heaven was included in the promise of this covenant?

A. From eternal death in hell being included in the threatening of it, as the natural wages of sin; and from Christ himself expounding the promise of the covenant of works of eternal life, Matt. xix. 16. When one puts the question to him, "What shall I do, that I may inherit eternal life?" he answers, ver. 17, "If thou wilt enter into life, (namely, eternal life, by doing,) keep the commandments."

Q. 30. Was there any proportion between Adam's obedience, though sinless, and the life that was promised?

A. There can be no proportion between the obedience of a finite creature, however perfect, and the enjoyment of the infinite God, Job xxii. 2, 3: "Can a man be profitable to God? Is it any pleasure to the Almighty, that thou art righteous? or, is it gain to him, that thou makest thy way perfect?"

Q. 31. Why could not Adam's perfect obedience be meritorious of eternal life?

A. Because perfect obedience was no more than what he was bound to, by virtue of his natural dependence on God, as a reasonable creature made after his image.

Q. 32. Could he have claimed the reward as a *debt*, in case he had continued in his obedience?

A. He could have claimed it only as a *pactional,* debt*, in virtue of the covenant promise, by which God became debtor to his own faithfulness, but not in virtue of any intrinsic merit of his obedience, Luke xvii. 10.

Q. 33. What then was the grace and condescension of God that shined in the covenant of works?

A. In that he entered into a covenant, at all, with his own creature; and promised eternal life as a reward of his work, though he had nothing to work with, but what he received from God, 1 Cor. iv. 7.

* By compact or agreement.

OF THE COVENANT OF WORKS.

Q. 34. Did the covenant of works oblige man to seek life upon the account of his obedience?
A. It left man to *expect* it upon his obedience, but did not oblige him to *seek* it on that score; but only on account of the faithfulness of God in his promise, graciously annexing life to man's sinless obedience, Matt. xix. 16.

Q. 35. Did the covenant of works oblige man to make his own life and happiness the chief end of his obedience?
A. By no means: the promise of life was an encouragement to his obedience, but the glory of God was to be the chief end in it; to which any view of his own happiness was to be subordinate, otherwise his obedience had not been perfect.

Q. 36. Was the covenant of works a law, as well as a covenant?
A. Yes; it was both the one and the other.

Q. 37. In what respect was it a law?
A. As it was not between equals, but enjoined by the sovereign Lawgiver.

Q. 38. In what respect was it a covenant?
A. As it contained a promise of reward, graciously annexed to the precept, Gal. iii. 12.

Q. 39. Is this covenant abrogated, or still in force?
A. It was never abrogated, but is still binding upon all that are under it, Matt. v. 18, and xix. 17.

Q. 40. Did not man's sin abrogate this covenant?
A. No: his sin bound him under the curse of it, Gal. iii. 10.

Q. 41. Did not Christ's doing and dying abrogate this covenant of works?
A. No: it fulfilled both the precept and penalty of it, Rom. x. 4.

Q. 42. Does not the law of faith abrogate the law of works?
A. No: "Do we make void the law through faith? God forbid; yea, we establish the law," Rom. iii. 31.

Q. 43. Are sinners, that live under the gospel dispensation, under the same obligation to obedience, as the condition of life, that Adam was under?
A. While they remain in unbelief, rejecting the surety of the *better testament*, they keep themselves under an obligation to do the whole law, and so are under the curse of it, Gal. v. 3, 4.

Q. 44. What may we learn from this doctrine?
A. It teaches us, that eternal death comes by the breach of the covenant of works in the *first Adam;* and that eternal life comes only by the fulfilling of the same covenant by the *second Adam*, Rom. v. 19.

QUEST. 13. *Did our first parents continue in the estate in which they were created?*

ANS. Our first parents, being left to the freedom of their own will, fell from the estate in which they were created, by sinning against God.

Q. 1. What mean you by the [*estate*] in which man was created?
A. His state of innocence, in which he had his standing under God, as his great Lord and Creator.

Q. 2. What standing had he under God in a state of innocence?
A. Perfect conformity to him; intimate fellowship and communion with him; and an ample dominion over all the work of his hands, in this lower world; the tree of knowledge of good and evil only excepted.

Q. 3. By what charter did man hold this state of his great Creator?
A. By the charter of the covenant of works.

Q. 4. What remarkable and significant circumstances appertained to this charter?
A. The tree of knowledge of good and evil, and the tree of life.

Q. 5. What did the *tree of knowledge of good and evil* signify?
A. It signified, that, as Adam knew much of his Creator's goodness, by what he had done for him, so he was to know much of his displeasure and indignation, if he tasted the fruit of that tree.

Q. 6. What did the *tree of life* signify to man?
A. That upon his fulfilling the condition of the covenant, by a course of obedience, he was to live forever.

Q. 7. What do you understand by the *course of obedience*, which Adam had to go through, in order to found his covenant title to eternal life?
A. A continuance in perfect obedience, during the time which God had appointed for *his state of probation*.

Q. 8. When was a *state of probation* only applicable to man?
A. It was only applicable to man while in innocence, before the breach of the covenant of works; and by no means applicable to man in any other state since the fall.

Q. 9. Why is it that no man, since the fall, can justly be said to be in a state of probation in this world?
A. Because the covenant of works being broken, all the children of men are either in a natural state, in the *first Adam*, or in a gracious state in the *second*; and conse-

quently under a dispensation either of divine justice or mercy.

Q. 10. Are not men to have rewards given them according to their good or evil works, and consequently may be said to be in a state of probation, as well as Adam was?

A. The consequence will not hold; because these rewards are of another kind than could have taken place under the covenant of works, though it had been fulfilled; for now, they are either rewards of impartial justice, for evil works, *the wages of sin* being *death*; or rewards of free mercy to the *doing persons*; not *for* their good works, but *according to them*, 2 Cor. v. 10.

Q. 11. What is it for God to dispense rewards of free mercy to his people, not *for* their good works, but *according* to them?

A. It is to bestow these rewards, not on account of any worth or merit that is in their good works, in themselves considered, but as they are evidences of union with Christ, *in whom* their persons and performances are accepted, and *through whom* the rewards of grace are freely conferred; for, "the gift of God is eternal life through Jesus Christ our Lord," Rom. vi. 23.

Q. 12. Is there any danger in asserting, that men are not now in a state of probation, as Adam was?

A. No: because though they cannot now be in that state, yet God still deals with them as rational creatures, under a moral government, and capable of rewards, whether of justice or mercy, of debt or grace, according to their state and works: hence men are judged at the great day, according to their state, as *sheep* or *goats*, separated from one another, and *then* according to their works, Matt. xxv. 32—46.

Q. 13. What then is the dangerous consequence of asserting, that fallen man is still in a state of probation in this life?

A. This dangerous consequence would follow, that mankind are hereby supposed to be still under a covenant of works that can justify the doer; or under a law that can give life, besides the *law of faith*, mentioned Rom. iii. 27, which is false: for, if there had been a law given, which could have given life, verily righteousness should have been by the law, Gal. iii. 21.

Q. 14. What improvement ought we to make of this doctrine respecting the state of probation?

A. To be restless in the use of all appointed means till we get in to Christ; that, in the way of believing and walking in him, we may share of the *sure reward*, promised, through grace. "to him that soweth righteousness," Prov. xi. 18.

Q. 15. How did our first parents fall from the state in which they were created?
A. [*By sinning against God,*] Gen. iii. 6, 7.
Q. 16. Were they not sufficiently furnished with every thing necessary, for yielding perfect obedience to the will of God?
A. Yes: for they had perfect knowledge in their understanding, freedom and inclination to good in their will, and spotless holiness in their hearts and affections, Eccl. vii. 29: "God made man upright."
Q. 17. How then did man's sin and apostasy come about?
A. Though he was a perfect, yet he was but a mutable creature, [*left to the freedom of his own will,*] which was subject to change.
Q. 18. In what did the freedom of man's will, in a state of innocence, consist?
A. In a perfect liberty and "power to will and to do that which is good and well pleasing to God; but yet mutable, so as that he might fall from it, Eccl. vii. 29. Gen. ii. 16, 17, and iii. 6."*
Q. 19. Why did *not* God make man immutable?
A. Because immutability, or unchangeableness of nature, is the essential property of God alone, Mal. iii. 6.—"I am the Lord, I change not," James i. 17.
Q. 20. Are not elect angels and saints made immutably good?
A. The elect angels are confirmed in a state of immutable happiness; and the saints, in virtue of union with Christ, are fixed in an unchangeable state of grace here, and glory hereafter; but the unchangeable state of the one and the other, is not owing to any thing in their own natures, but to the free love and favour of God, Eph. i. 10.
Q. 21. What freedom of will has man, since the fall, to any spiritual good?
A. He "has wholly lost all freedom and ability of will to any spiritual good accompanying salvation," so as that he can neither "convert himself, nor prepare himself thereunto," John vi. 44, 65.†
Q. 22. What freedom of will have they who are regenerated?
A. They are enabled by grace alone, freely to will and to do that which is spiritually good, Rom. vi. 18; yet so as that by reason of remaining corruption, they do not perfectly, and only, that which is good, but likewise frequently that which is evil, Rom. vii. 15, 19, 21.‡
Q. 23. When is the will of man made perfectly and immutably free to that only which is good?

Confession, chap ix. § 2.   † Ibid. chap. ix. § 3   ‡ Ibid. chap. ix. § 4

A. In the state of glory only, Eph. iv. 13. 1 John iii. 2.

Q. 24. What was it for man to be left to the freedom of his own will?

A. It was God's leaving him with a sufficient stock in his hand, without any promise of supernatural aid, or further assistance to improve the stock of grace already received.

Q. 25. How was he left to abuse the freedom of his will?

A. God did not incline him to abuse it, but only withheld that further grace, which he was no way obliged to give, for preventing his will from yielding to the temptation; and was pleased, according to his wise and holy counsel, to permit this abuse, having purposed to order it to his own glory, Rom. xi. 32.

Q. 26. At whose door then must the *fall* be laid?

A. Only at man's own door, who willingly yielded to the temptation of the devil, James i. 14.

Q. 27. What was the devil's agency in the fall of man?

A. He entered into a serpent, and therein, by seducing words, enticed the woman to take and eat the forbidden fruit; and she gave to her husband, and he did eat likewise, Gen. iii. 5, 6.

Q. 28. Why did Satan make use of the serpent, as his instrument to seduce the woman?

A. Because "the serpent was more subtle than any beast of the field," Gen. iii. 1, and so the most fit tool, of any other, to serve his subtle and murderous designs, John viii. 44.

Q. 29. Why was not Eve afraid to entertain converse with a serpent, lest it might be actuated by some evil spirit?

A. It is supposed, that Adam and Eve knew nothing as yet of the fall of the angels; and sin not having then entered into this lower world, they were not afraid of hurt from any of the good creatures of God.

Q. 30. Why was there no confirmatory clause annexed to the covenant of works, to secure man's standing in the state in which he was created?

A. Because it so pleased God; and, no doubt, infinite wisdom had another scene to open, through the occasion of man's fall, by his breaking the first covenant.

Q. 31. What was that scene?

A. A scene of redeeming love and grace, which will be matter of *hallelujahs*, or praises, to the Lord God and the Lamb for ever and ever, Rev. v. 8.

Q. 32. Was then the covenant of works a scaffold erected for carrying on a more glorious fabric?

A. Yes, it was; for God had said, and purposed from eternity, that mercy should be built up for ever, Ps. lxxxix. 2.

OF SIN IN GENERAL.

Q. 33. What improvement ought we to make of this doctrine of the fall of Adam?
A. To be persuaded that the best of creatures, if left to themselves, cannot be in safety one moment, Ps. xlix. 12; that since man could not be his own keeper, much less can he be his own saviour, 2 Cor. iii. 5: to see how dangerous it is to parley with sin and Satan; and how much we need an interest in the *second Adam*, to get the loss we sustained by the *first* repaired with advantage; for he has *restored that which he took not away*, Ps. lxix. 4.

QUEST. 14. *What is sin?*

ANS. Sin is any want of conformity unto, or transgression of, the law of God.

Q. 1. In what consisted man's apostasy from God?
A. In sinning against him, Lam. v. 16.
Q. 2. How does it appear that there is such a thing as sin in the world?
A. The God of truth declares, that all have sinned, Rom. iii. 23; the broken law cries for vengeance against transgressors, and by it is the knowledge of sin, Gal. iii. 10. Rom. iii. 20; conscience, God's deputy in every man's bosom, tells him he is guilty, Jer. xiv. 7; the reign of death, and the groans of the creatures round about us, Rom. viii. 22, all bear testimony that there is such a thing as sin in the world.
Q. 3. Can there be any sin, where there is no law?
A. No: "for where there is no law there is no transgression," Rom. iv. 15.
Q. 4. Of whose law is sin a transgression?
A. Of the law of God.
Q. 5. What may be understood by [*the law of God?*]
A. All the precepts, or commandments, God has given to man as a rule of his obedience.
Q. 6. Where is this law of God to be found?
A. There was a bright and fair copy of it written upon the heart of man in innocence; but that being, in a great measure, lost by the fall, God has written again to us the great things of his law, in the scriptures of truth, Ps. cxlvii. 19, 20.
Q. 7. Are all the laws of God mentioned in scripture, of binding force now under the New Testament?
A. No: the *ceremonial* law, which was a shadow of good things to come, is now abrogated since the coming of Christ in the flesh; and many of the *judicial* laws, in so far as they had a particular relation to the state of the Jewish

nation, are laid aside; but the *moral* law is perpetually binding on all mankind, in all ages and periods of the world, Ps. cxix. 160.

Q. 8. Does God require a perfect conformity to this law?

A. Yes; for there is a curse pronounced against every one that continues not in all things written in the book of the law to do them, Gal. iii. 10.

Q. 9. Why is the nature of sin expressed by a [*want of conformity*] to the law?

A. To let us know that our very natures, since the fall, are sinful, Isa. i. 5, 6; that we are now quite destitute of that original righteousness and holiness, which we had at our creation, Gen. vi. 5; and that every swerving from the holy law, even in omitting what it commands is sin, as well as in committing what it forbids, Isa. xliii. 22.

Q. 10. Why is sin called a [*transgression of the law?*]

A. Because the law is the boundary of all our actions; and whenever we sin, we break the boundary and limit that God has set us, and so are exposed to the curse of the law, Eccl. x. 8. Gal. iii. 10.

Q. 11. Does the law of God extend to the first motions of sin in the heart?

A. Yes; for, says the apostle, Rom. vii. 7—"I had not known lust, except the law had said, "Thou shalt not covet."

Q. 12. How many kinds of sin are there?

A. Two kinds; original and actual.

Q. 13. What do you understand by original sin?

A. The sin of our nature, which is called original sin, because we were "shapen in iniquity, and conceived in sin," Ps. li. 5; and because it was the first sin of man, and is the original and fountain of all actual sin, Matt xv. 19.

Q. 14. What do you understand by actual sin?

A. Every thing that is inconsistent with, and contrary to the law, in thought, word, or deed, 1 John iii. 4.

Q. 15. How are actual sins divided?

A. Into sins of omission and commission.

Q. 16. What is a sin of omission?

A. It is a neglecting, or forgetting to do that good which the law commands, James iv. 17.

Q. 17. What is a sin of commission?

A. It is a doing of what the law of God forbids, Ps. li. 4.

Q. 18. Is every sin mortal or deadly?

A. Yes: in its own nature, Rom. vi. 16, 21, 23; "The wages of sin is death." See also, 1 Cor. xv. 56. Gal iii. 10.

Q. 19. Are all sins pardonable through grace?

A. There is pardon through the blood of Christ, for all

sins, except one, namely, the *sin against the Holy Ghost* Matt. xii. 31, 32, Mark iii. 28, 29.

Q. 20. What is the sin against the Holy Ghost?

A. It is a wilful, malicious, and avowed rejection of Christ and salvation through him, by a blaspheming apostate, after manifest conviction of the truth of the gospel-report, and some kind of approbation of it, by the common influence or operation of the Spirit, Heb. vi. 4—6; and x. 26, 27. 1 John v. 16. Mark iii. 29, 30.

Q. 21. Why is this sin called blasphemy against the Holy Ghost, Matt. xii. 31?

A. Because it is an opprobrious and reproachful speaking of, and against the testimony of the Holy Ghost, in the word concerning Christ; with a direct intention to disparage his glory, and to disgrace his truth and way; hence called, "a putting him to an open shame," Heb. vi. 6.

Q. 22. What is the object of this sin, against which it is directly levelled?

A. It is Christ, and salvation through him, as held out in the gospel revelation; for, it is a "treading under foot the Son of God, and accounting the blood of the covenant, wherewith he was sanctified, an unholy thing," Heb. x. 29.

Q. 23. What are the acts of this dreadful sin?

A. A wilful rejecting, and obstinate opposing of the truth of the gospel: a spiteful scoffing at Christianity, and the professors of it, joined sometimes with a malicious persecution of them; and all these as fruits and concomitants of a total and final apostasy from the faith.

Q. 24. What are the aggravations of this sin?

A. Its being committed after a person has "received the knowledge of the truth, and tasted the good word of God, and the powers of the world to come," Heb. vi. 5, and x. 26.

Q. 25. Why is it said, that "the blasphemy against the Holy Ghost shall not be forgiven unto men?" Matt. xii. 31.

A. Not because it is above the virtue of the blood of Jesus to cleanse from it, but because it despises the only sacrifice for sin, and means of pardon; there being "no other name under heaven, given among men, by which we must be saved," but that of Jesus, Acts iv. 12, who is contemptuously rejected by it, Heb. ii. 2, 3.

Q. 26. How may a person be assured that he is not guilty of this sin?

A. He may well be assured that this sin is not charged on him, if he is afraid that he is guilty of it; or in the least concerned about his unbelief; or has any desire after salvation through Christ, and is content to be a debtor to the riches of his grace.

Q. 27. What may we learn from the nature of sin in general?

A. That it is exceedingly sinful, the greatest of all evils, Rom. vii. 13; and, consequently, that it must be the severest judgment in this world to be given up to it, Ezek. xxiv. 13, and the greatest mercy to be delivered from it, Matt. i. 21.

Quest. 15. *What was the sin whereby our first parents fell from the estate wherein they were created?*

Ans. The sin whereby our first parents fell from the estate wherein they were created, was their eating the forbidden fruit.

Q. 1. Why is the fruit called [*forbidden fruit?*]

A. Because the eating of it was forbidden, under the severest penalty, Gen. ii. 17: "But of the tree of the knowledge of good and evil, thou shalt not eat of it; for in the day that thou eatest thereof, thou shalt surely die."

Q. 2. Why did God forbid the eating of this fruit?

A. To try the obedience of our first parents, and to manifest his dominion over them as *Lord of all.*

Q. 3. Were not our first parents guilty of sin before eating of the forbidden fruit?

A. Yes: they were guilty in hearkening to the devil, and believing him, before they actually eat it.

Q. 4. Why then is their eating of it called their *first* sin?

A. Because it was the first sin *finished,* James i. 15, and an express violation of the positive precept, Gen. iii. 11.

Q. 5. Where was this first sin committed?

A. In *Paradise,* where God had placed the man, and created the woman, Gen. ii. 8, 22, and iii. 6.

Q. 6. Was there any aggravation of this sin, arising from the place where it was committed?

A. Yes; for, in Paradise, our first parents had abundance of other fruit, and of every thing necessary and delightful: and, that place being a type of heaven, should have even put them on their guard against this, and all other sins.

Q. 7. When did our first parents eat the forbidden fruit?

A. It is certain from Ps. xlix. 12, that it was done very soon after they were created: "Man being in honour, abideth not."

Q. 8. Why did the devil make such haste in tempting man to sin?

A. Because he did not know how soon man might be confirmed in a holy and happy state; and, in that case, become impregnable against all his temptations.

Q. 9. How did Satan lay his train for enticing our first parents to eat the forbidden fruit?

A. He attacked the woman, in the absence of her husband; endeavoured to make her doubt of the truth of God's threatening; presented the object, fruit pleasant to the eye; pretended a greater regard and concern for them, than God himself; and laboured to persuade them, that they should be like God, in the largeness of their knowledge, upon their eating: all which may be gathered from Gen. iii. 1—6.

Q. 10. Did the enemy prevail by this stratagem?

A. Yes: "the woman took of the fruit, and did eat: and gave also to her husband with her, and he did eat," Gen. iii. 6.

Q. 11. What was the nature of this first sin?

A. However light and trivial it may appear in the carnal eye, to eat of a little fruit; yet, if weighed in God's balance, it will be found to be a most heinous sin, and to incorporate many other sins, against the law of God, Hos. vi. 7: "They like Adam, (margin,) have transgressed the covenant."

Q. 12. How does that appear?

A. From our first parents being guilty of manifest unbelief, the highest ingratitude, the most intolerable pride and ambition, unaccountable inadvertency, most unnatural rebellion, and most cruel murder, in their eating the forbidden fruit.

Q. 13. How is *unbelief* included in that sin?

A. In their giving more credit to the devil, than to God, respecting the truth of the threatening, Gen. ii. 17. iii. 4.

Q. 14. How were they guilty of *ingratitude?*

A. In contradicting the orders of their bountiful Lord and Creator, who had allowed them the use of all the other trees of the garden besides, Gen. ii. 16.

Q. 15. What *pride* and *ambition* was there in the first sin?

A. In aspiring to equality with God in his inimitable attributes, particularly in infinite knowledge, Gen. iii. 5, 6: "Ye shall be as gods, knowing good and evil. And the woman saw that the tree was good,—and a tree to be desired to make one wise."

Q. 16. What *inadvertency* were our first parents guilty of in eating the forbidden fruit?

A. In entering into communication with a creature of

any kind, and however much disguised, about violating the express inhibition of their Creator.

Q. 17. How were they guilty of *rebellion* in the commission of this sin?

A. By entering into a confederacy with Satan against God, and thus virtually choosing him for their god and sovereign, instead of the true God, who made them, and all other creatures besides.

Q. 18. What *murder* were they guilty of in eating of this fruit?

A. They were guilty of their own death, and the death of all their posterity, Rom. v. 12.

Q. 19. How was this sin, of eating the forbidden fruit, aggravated?

A. In being committed when man had full light in his understanding; a clear copy of the law in his heart; when he had no vicious bias in his will, but enjoying perfect liberty; and when he had a sufficient stock of grace in his hand, to withstand the tempting enemy; in being committed after God had made a covenant of life with him, and given him express warning of the danger of eating this fruit.

Q. 20. What may we learn from our first parents being seduced by Satan to eat the forbidden fruit?

A. To resist the first motions of sin in the heart, and the temptations of Satan to it, Ps. lxvi. 18; James iv. 7; that since man, in innocence, fell before the temptation, how easy a prey must fallen man be, if not kept by the power of God, through faith, unto salvation! Ps. xxxix. 5, 1 Pet. i. 5; and therefore to be strong only "in the Lord, and in the power of his might," Eph. vi. 10.

QUEST. 16. *Did all mankind fall in Adam's first transgression?*

ANS. The covenant being made with Adam, not only for himself, but for his posterity; all mankind, descending from him by ordinary generation, sinned in him, and fell with him, in his first transgression.

Q. 1. How many public persons, representing mankind before God, do we read of in scripture?
A. Of two; the *first* and the *last Adam*, 1 Cor. xv. 45.
Q. 2. Of what *covenant* was the *first Adam* the head?
A. Of the covenant of works, Gen. ii. 16, 17.
Q. 3. Of what covenant was the *last Adam* the head?

A. Of the covenant of grace and promise. Ps. lxxxix. 3, 28.

Q. 4. Whom did the first Adam represent in the covenant of works?

A. He represented [*all mankind, descending from him by ordinary generation,*] Rom. v. 12, 14.

Q. 5. Whom did the last Adam represent in the covenant of grace?

A. All his spiritual seed given him of the Father, John xvii. 6.

Q. 6. Is there any similitude between the *first* and *last* Adam?

A. Yes: the first Adam was the "figure of him that was to come," Rom. v. 14.

Q. 7. In what did that figure, or similitude, consist?

A. It consisted chiefly in their being, each of them, a representing head of their respective seed, 1 Cor. xv. 22.

Q. 8. In what consists the dissimilarity, or disparity, between these two public persons?

A. It is infinitely great beyond all conception: The first Adam was made a living soul; the last Adam was made a quickening spirit: the first man is of the earth, earthy, a mere man; the second man is the Lord from heaven, Immanuel, God with us, 1 Cor. xv. 45, 47; Matt. i. 23: the first Adam, in his best estate, was only a mutable creature; the last Adam, is the unchangeable God, Heb. xiii. 8.

Q. 9. What relation has the first Adam to all mankind?

A. A twofold relation; that of a covenant head, and of a natural root.

Q. 10. How does it appear that he was a *covenant head;* or, that the covenant of works was made with him, [*not only for himself, but for his posterity?*]

A. From the imputation of his first sin to his posterity, Rom. v. 12; and the sentence of death passed upon all mankind on that account, ver. 17.

Q. 11. Was it reasonable, that Adam should represent his posterity in the covenant of works?

A. Nothing could be more reasonable, seeing he was to be the common parent of all mankind, and was created perfectly holy, with full power to fulfil the condition of the covenant, and thus to entail happiness upon himself and his posterity.

Q. 12. What happiness would Adam have entailed upon himself and his posterity, if he had stood?

A. Eternal life would have become due to him and them, by pactional debt.

Q. 13. Would not the title of every one of his posterity to life, in that case, have been founded upon their own perfect and personal obedience?

A. No: their title to eternal life would have been founded upon the perfect obedience of their covenant head; and their own personal obedience would have been the fruit of the promise of the covenant.

Q. 14. How does this appear?
A. Since Adam's disobedience is imputed to his posterity for their condemnation, Rom. v. 18, it necessarily follows, that his obedience would have been imputed to them for their justification and life.

Q. 15. Why is the first Adam called the *natural root* of his posterity.
A. Because all of them, descending from him by ordinary generation, are as so many branches sprung out of him, as their root and stock.

Q. 16. Did all Adam's natural offspring fall in his first sin?
A. Yes; "death passed upon all men, for that all have sinned," Rom. v. 12.

Q. 17. How could Adam's posterity, being then unborn, fall in his first sin?
A. Because they were considered as IN HIM, 1 Cor. xv. 22—"In Adam all die."

Q. 18. How were they *in him* when he first sinned?
A. They were in him *virtually*, as a natural root; and *representatively*, as a covenant head.

Q. 19. Why is it said, [*all mankind*, descending from him by ordinary generation, *sinned in him, and fell with him, in his first transgression?*]
A. That Christ might be excepted, who descended, as to his human body, from Adam; but not by *ordinary generation.*

Q. 20. What was there extraordinary in the generation of Christ's body?
A. It was conceived in the womb of a virgin, by the power of the Highest overshadowing her, Luke i. 35; on which account she is said to be "found with child of the Holy Ghost," Matt. i. 18.

Q. 21. What was the reason of this extraordinary generation?
A. That the human nature of Christ might not be stained or tainted with original sin which is conveyed from Adam to his posterity, by the way of ordinary generation; hence what was born of the virgin, is called "that holy thing," Luke i. 35.

Q. 22. Was ever the human nature of Christ represented in the first Adam as a federal head?
A. By no means: Christ's human nature was never in Adam as its representative, but he *derived it legally*, after Adam ceased to be a public person.

Q. 23. How did he derive it legally?

A. In virtue of his being considered as *one in law* with his spiritual seed, whom he represented as their surety, according to his undertaking from eternity, Prov. viii. 23; and therefore behoved to assume the same nature with them, Heb. ii. 11, 14.

Q. 24. Was ever any exempted from Adam's first sin, except Christ?

A. No; for all others descended from Adam by ordinary generation, and were represented by him, as their covenant head; and therefore sinned in him, and fell with him in his first transgression, Rom. v. 12. 1 Cor. xv. 22.

Q. 25. What may all this teach us?

A. That "as by one man's disobedience, many were made sinners; so by the obedience of one shall many be made righteous," Rom. v. 19; and that "as we have borne the image of the earthy, we shall also bear the image of the heavenly" *Adam*, 1 Cor. xv. 49.

QUEST. 17. *Into what estate did the fall bring mankind?*

ANS. The fall brought mankind into an estate of sin and misery.

Q. 1. Why is man's apostasy from God called [*the fall?*]

A. Because man is not now where God set him at his creation, but is *fallen* by his iniquity, Hos. xiv. 1.

Q. 2. Where did God set man at his creation?

A. Upon the high pinnacle of holiness and happiness, Eccl. vii 29.

Q. 3. Where is he now?

A. He is fallen into the depths of sin and misery, called in scripture, a *horrible pit, and miry clay*, Ps. xl. 2, and "the pit wherein is no water," Zech. ix. 11.

Q. 4. Why is man's state, by the fall, called an [*estate of sin?*]

A. Because he is now under the guilt of sin, Rom. iii. 19, which has dominion over him, chap. vi. 14.

Q. 5. Why is it called an [*estate of misery?*]

A. Because, according to the penalty of the law;-death and the curse involve him in all manner of misery, Rom. v. 12.

Q. 6. Why is the state of sin put before the state of misery?

A. Because there could be no misery, if there were no sin; sin being the procuring cause of all misery, Rom. vi. 23.

Q. 7. How came man into this state of sin and misery?
A. By the abuse of his free will; hence mankind sinners are called *self-destroyers*, Hos. xiii. 9: " O Israel, thou hast destroyed thyself."

Q. 8. How does the Spirit of God, in scripture, express man's state of sin and misery, into which he is fallen?
A. By a state of darkness, Eph. v. 8; a state of distance, Eph. ii. 13; a state of condemnation and wrath, John iii. 18, 36; a state of bondage, or captivity, Isa. xlix. 24, 25; and a state of death, both spiritual and legal, Eph. ii. 1.

Q. 9. Is man in any capacity to help himself out of this sinful and miserable state?
A. No more than a new-born infant, *cast out in the open field*, which, of all creatures, is the most helpless, Ezek. xvi. 4, 5.

Q. 10. Has he a desire and will to be helped out of a state of sin and misery, when help is offered?
A. No: his nature is become "enmity against God," and the way of salvation proposed in the gospel, Rom. viii. 7, Ps. lxxxi. 11; and therefore rejects the only help of God's appointment, John v. 40.

Q. 11. What may we learn from this?
A. That the whole world being guilty before God, every mouth had been for ever stopped, though he had left all mankind to perish eternally with the fallen angels, with whom they said, a *Confederacy*, Rom. iii. 19; and therefore to admire the infinite love of God, in sending his only begotten Son, to save us from sin, as the only way of being saved from misery, Heb. ii. 14, 16.

QUEST. 18. *Wherein consists the sinfulness of that estate whereinto man fell?*

ANS. The sinfulness of that estate whereinto man fell, consists in the guilt of Adam's first sin, the want of original righteousness, and the corruption of his whole nature, which is commonly called original sin, together with all actual transgressions which proceed from it.

Q. 1. What do you understand by [*original sin?*]
A. The sin we have from our original; that is, when the soul is united to the body, or the human nature completed, Ps. li. 5.

Q. 2. How is original sin usually distinguished?
A. Into original sin *imputed*, and original sin *inherent*.

Q. 3. What is original sin *imputed*?
A. [*The guilt of Adam's first sin.*]

Q. 4. What is original sin *inherent ?*
A. [*The want of original righteousness and the corruption of the whole nature.*]

Q. 5. What do you understand by the [*guilt*] of sin?
A. An obligation to punishment on account of sin, Rom. vi. 23.

Q. 6. How are all mankind guilty of Adam's [*first sin ?*]
A. By imputation, Rom. v. 19—" By one man's disobedience, many were made sinners."

Q. 7. Upon what account is Adam's first sin imputed to his posterity?
A. On account of the legal union between him and them, he being their legal head and representative, and the covenant made with him, not for himself only, but for *his* posterity likewise, 1 Cor. xv. 22—" In Adam all die."

Q. 8. Why was Adam's *first sin* imputed, and none of his after sins?
A. Because the covenant being broken by his first sin, his federal headship ceased; for being then legally dead, and his posterity in him and with him, he stood afterwards merely as a single person for himself, and no longer in the capacity of their public representative in that covenant of life, which, by that first sin, brought him and them under the sentence of death, Rom. v. 12, 13.

Q. 9. When Adam ceased to be the federal head, by breaking the covenant of works, did that covenant cease likewise?
A. No: that covenant, though broken, stands binding, so as the obligation to pay the debt of obedience to the precept, and satisfaction now to its penalty, remains upon every one of his posterity, while in a natural state, under the law as a covenant of works, Gal. iii. 10.

Q. 10. How does it appear from scripture, that all Adam's posterity had his first sin imputed to them?
A. From their being said to be "made sinners, by one man's disobedience," Rom. v. 19; and to have the judgment, or sentence, *by one to condemnation*, ver. 16; and surely there can be no condemnation, passed by a righteous judge, where there is no crime, Rom. iv. 15.

Q. 11. Is it not said, Ezek. xviii. 20, "The son shall not bear the iniquity of the father?"
A. The prophet is there speaking of particular private parents, not of Adam as a federal head; he is speaking of adult children, who were preserved from some grosser violations of the law, of which their parents were guilty, and who did not imitate them; not of the posterity of Adam in general, as exempting them from his first sin, with which the scriptures quoted in answer to the former question, plainly prove them chargeable.

MAN'S NATURAL STATE.

Q. 12. What is meant by the [*want of original righteousness?*]

A. The want of that rectitude and purity of nature, which Adam had at his creation; consisting in a perfect conformity of all the powers and faculties of his soul to the holy nature of God, and to the law which was written on his heart, Eccl. vii. 29.

Q. 13. How does it appear that all mankind are now destitute of this original righteousness?

A. From the express testimony of God, that among all Adam's race, there is none righteous, no, not one; and that by the deeds of the law there shall no flesh be justified in his sight, Rom. iii. 10—12, 20.

Q. 14. What follows upon this want of original righteousness?

A. That all mankind are naked before God; and that their fig-leaf coverings will stand them in no stead before his omniscient eye, nor answer the demands of his holy law, Rev. iii. 17. Isa. lxiv. 6.

Q. 15. Does the law of God demand original righteousness from mankind sinners, though they now want it?

A. Yes: their want of it can never derogate from the right of the law to demand it, because God endowed man with this part of his image, at his creation; and his want of it was owing to his own voluntary apostasy from God.

Q. 16. Under what penalty does the law demand this original righteousness?

A. Under the penalty of death and the curse, Rom. vi. 23. Gal. iii. 10.

Q. 17. Is there no help for a sinner in this deplorable state?

A. None in heaven or in earth, but in Christ, the *last Adam*, the Lord our righteousness, Jer. xxiii. 6, on whom our help is completely laid, Ps. lxxxix. 19.

Q. 18. Does original sin consist in a mere privation, or want of righteousness?

A. It consists also in the corruption of the whole nature, Tit. i. 15. Rom. iii. 10—19.

Q. 19. What is meant by [*the corruption of the whole nature?*]

A. The universal depravation both of soul and body, in all the faculties of the one, and members of the other, Isa. i. 5, 6.

Q. 20. How does this corruption of the whole nature appear?

A. In an utter impotency, and bitter enmity to what is spiritually good, Rom. viii. 7, and, in the strongest inclination and bias to what is evil, and to that *only and continually*, Gen. vi. 5.

Q. 21. How may we be certain that our [*whole nature*] is corrupted?

A. From the word of God, and from experience and observation.

Q. 22. How does the *word of God* assure us of the universal corruption of our nature?

A. It tells us, that the image after which man was at first *made*, and the image after which he is now *begotten*, are quite opposite the one to the other. Adam was at first made "in the likeness of God," but having fallen, he "begat a son in his own likeness, after his own image," Gen. v. 1, 3. The scripture assures us, that none "can bring a clean thing out of an unclean," Job xiv. 4; that we are shapen in iniquity, and that in sin did our mothers conceive us, Ps. li. 5; that "that which is born of the flesh is flesh," John iii. 6; and that we are by "nature children of wrath," Eph. ii. 3.

Q. 23. How may we know the corruption of our nature by the *experience* and *observation* of things without us?

A. The flood of miseries which overflow the world; the manifold gross out-breakings of sin in it; and the necessity of human laws, fenced with penalties, are clear outward evidences of the corruption of our nature.

Q. 24. What inward evidences may every one of us experience within ourselves, of the corruption of our nature?

A. Each of us may sadly experience a natural disposition to hearken to the instruction that causes us to err, Prov. xix. 27; a caring for the concerns of the body more than those of the soul, Matt. xvi. 26; a discontentment with some one thing or other in our lot in the present world, 2 Kings vi. 33; an aversion from being debtors to free grace, and an inclination to rest upon something in ourselves as the ground of our hope, Rom. x. 3; every one of which may be an evidence to ourselves, that our nature is wholly corrupted.

Q. 25. How is the corruption of nature propagated since the fall?

A. By natural generation, Job xv. 14: "What is man that he should be clean? and he that is born of a woman, that he should be righteous?"

Q. 26. How can this corruption be propagated to the soul, seeing it is created immediately by God, and not generated with the body?

A. As the creating and infusing of the soul are precisely at one and the same time, so the very moment the soul is united to the body, we become children of *fallen Adam*, not only as our natural, but as our federal head, Rom. v. 19.

Q. 27. What is the consequence of becoming the children of *fallen Adam*, as our federal head?

A. The consequence is, that, the moment we are so, his first sin is imputed to us, and we thus become legally and spiritually dead, under the curse; not only wanting original righteousness, but having our whole nature corrupted and depraved, 1 Cor. xv. 22: "In Adam all die."

Q. 28. Since, then, the soul of every one is a part of that person, which is cursed in Adam, does God, in the creating it, infuse any sin or impurity into it?

A. By no means; but only, as a righteous judge, in creating the soul, he denies or *withholds* that original righteousness which it once had in Adam; and this he does as a just punishment of Adam's first sin.

Q. 29. What follows upon God's withholding original righteousness from the soul, in its creation?

A. The soul being united to the body, in the moment of its creation, the universal corruption of the whole man follows as naturally upon that union, as darkness follows upon the setting of the sun.

Q. 30. Can it follow, then, from this doctrine, that *God is the author of our sin?*

A. So far from it, that, on the contrary, it evidently follows, that our *state*, both of sin and misery, is the bitter fruit of our own voluntary apostasy in the *first Adam*, as our covenant head, having sinned in him, and fallen with him in his first transgression.

Q. 31. Does the holiness of the parents prevent the propagation of original corruption to their children?

A. By no means: the saints are holy but in part, and that by grace, not by nature: wherefore, as after the purest grain is sown, we reap corn with the chaff; so the holiest parents beget unholy children, and cannot communicate their grace to them, as they do their nature, Gen. v. 3.

Q. 32. Has this poison of corruption run through the *whole man?*

A. Yes: "The whole head is sick, and the whole heart is faint; from the sole of the foot to the head, there is no soundness in it," &c. Isa. i. 5, 6.

Q. 33. How is the *understanding* corrupted?

A. With darkness and blindness, so that we cannot know and receive the things of the Spirit of God, 1 Cor. ii. 14.

Q. 34. How is the will corrupted?

A. With enmity and rebellion against God; with opposition to his law and gospel; with aversion from the chief good; and inclination to all evil, Rom. viii. 7.

Q. 35. How are the *affections* corrupted?

A. By being displaced and disordered, set upon trifling

vanities and sinful pleasures, instead of God the supreme good, Ps. v. 2, 6. Isa. lv. 2.

Q. 36. How is the *conscience* corrupted?

A. By not *discharging* its office faithfully according to the law, in accusing or excusing, but many times calling " evil good, and good evil," &c. Isa. v. 20.

Q. 37. How is the *memory* corrupted?

A. It is like the riddle, or sieve, that lets through the pure grain and keeps the refuse; it retains what is vain and unprofitable, and forgets what is spiritual and truly advantageous, Ps. cvi. 13, 21.

Q. 38. How is the *body* corrupted?

A. All the members of it are become *instruments*, or weapons of "unrighteousness unto sin," Rom. vi. 13.

Q. 39. Is original sin of its own nature damning?

A. Beyond all doubt it is; because it is in a state of sin and spiritual uncleanness we are born, Ps. li. 5. And "there shall in no wise enter into the heavenly Jerusalem, any thing that defileth," Rev. xxi. 27. The blood of Christ is necessary to cleanse from it, as well as from actual sin; for Christ is "the Lamb of God who taketh away the sin of the world," both original and actual, John i. 29.

Q. 40. How may we know the *being* of original sin, antecedently to the commission of any actual transgression?

A. From the severe troubles and distresses to which infants are liable, and from death passing upon them before they are capable of sinning, *after the similitude of Adam's transgression;* that is, of committing actual sin, Rom. v. 14.

Q. 41. What do you understand by [*actual transgression*] or sin?

A. Every deviation from the law of God in our *actions*, whether internal or external.

Q. 42. How may actual sin be distinguished from original?

A. As the *act* is distinguished from the *habit;* or a fault of the person, from a fault of the nature.

Q. 43. Is *omission* of what is required an actual sin, as well as the commission of what is forbidden?

A. Yes: because all omissions are either accompanied with some act of the will consenting, directly or indirectly, to it; or they flow from some antecedent act, which is either the cause, occasion, or impediment, of the duty omitted; as excess in eating and drinking is frequently the cause or occasion of omitting the public or private duties of God's worship.

Q. 44. From whence do all actual transgressions flow?

A. They all proceed from original sin, or the corruption of nature, as impure streams from a corrupt fountain, Eph. ii. 3. James iii. 11.

MAN'S NATURAL STATE. 95

Q. 45. What may we learn from the doctrine of original sin?
A. That it is no wonder the grave opens its devouring mouth for us, as soon as we come into the world, seeing we are all, in a spiritual sense, dead born, Eph. ii. 1; that as every thing acts agreeably to its own nature, so corrupt man acts corruptly, Matt. vii. 17, 18; and, consequently, we may learn the necessity of regeneration, and ingraftment in the second Adam, without which it is impossible we can enter into the kingdom of heaven, John iii. 3.

———

QUEST. 19. *What is the misery of that estate whereinto man fell?*

ANS. All mankind, by their fall, lost communion with God, are under his wrath and curse, and so made liable to all the miseries of this life, to death itself, and to the pains of hell forever.

Q. 1. What are the branches of man's misery expressed in this *answer*, as the effects of the fall?
A. They are these three, the happiness man has lost; the evil he lies presently under; and the future misery and punishment to which he is liable.
Q. 2. Is the *loss* which man has sustained by the fall great and grievous?
A. Yes: it is so great, that we have all reason to cry out with the church, "Wo unto us that we have sinned!" Lam. v. 16.—" How is the gold become dim! How is the most fine gold changed!" chap. iv. 1.
Q. 3. What is that great loss which man has sustained by the fall?
A. He has lost all that good which was promised him in the covenant of works, upon condition of his perfect obedience.
Q. 4. What was the good promised?
A. Life in its fullest latitude and extent; or all the happiness man was capable of, either in this world, or that which is to come.
Q. 5. What was man's chief happiness in that state in which he was created?
A. His chief happiness lay in his enjoyment of fellowship and [*communion with God.*]
Q. 6. In what did that fellowship and [*communion*] consist?
A. In the most agreeable intimacy and familiarity that

man had with God, in the uninterrupted enjoyment of his gracious presence.

Q. 7. How does it appear that man has [*lost*] this by the fall?

A. It appears from his being "without God in the world," Eph. ii. 12; and "alienated from the life of God," chap. iv. 18.

Q. 8. Did this breach of fellowship between God and man immediately follow upon the first sin?

A. Yes; for we find that our first parents immediately essayed to fly from the presence of God, and to hide themselves from him among the trees of the garden, Gen. iii. 8.

Q. 9. Upon what footing had man fellowship with God before the fall?

A. Upon a law footing, namely, his continuing in his integrity of nature, and yielding perfect obedience to the holy law.

Q. 10. Is that door of access to God, and fellowship with him, closed and shut against all mankind?

A. Yes: because "all have sinned and come short of the glory of God," Rom. iii. 23; the broken law, and its curse, stand as an insuperable bar in our way to God and glory, upon the footing of the first covenant, Gal. iii 10.

Q. 11. What is the second branch of man's misery?

A. His being under the [*wrath and curse*] of God.

Q. 12. What is it to be under the [*wrath*] of God?

A. It is to be under his anger, in the sad and dismal effects of it, whether in a more visible, or more secret way, Ps. xi. 6, and l. 21.

Q. 13. What is it to be under his [*curse?*]

A. It is to be under the sentence of his law, denouncing all evil upon the transgressor, Gal. iii. 10.

Q. 14. How does it appear that man is now under the wrath and curse of God?

A. From those passages of scripture, where God is said to be "angry with the wicked every day," Ps. vii. 11; that his "wrath is revealed from heaven against all unrighteousness and ungodliness of men," Rom. i. 18; that "he who believes not is condemned already, and the wrath of God abideth on him," John iii. 18, 36.

Q. 15. Is the wrath of an infinite God tolerable by a finite creature?

A. Oh! no: "Who shall dwell with devouring fire! who shall dwell with everlasting burnings!" Isa. xxxiii. 14. "Who knows the power of his anger!" Ps. xc. 11. It makes the whole creation groan, Rom. viii. 22; and when it lighted upon the Son of God for our iniquities, it crushed his human body down to the dust of death, and melted his soul like wax in the midst of his bowels, Ps. xxii. 14, 15.

Q. 16. Can any man hide himself from the presence of an angry God?

A. No: there is no flying from the presence of that God who is every where, Ps. cxxxix. 7—13.

Q. 17. What is the third branch of man's misery by the fall?

A. He is [*liable to all the miseries of this life, to death itself, and to the pains of hell for ever.*]

Q. 18. What are these miseries which man is liable to in [*this life?*]

A. They are such as extend both to his soul and body.

Q. 19. What are these soul miseries and maladies that sin has entailed upon us?

A. The precious soul is quite defaced, deformed, and debased, from its original beauty and excellency, being stricken with "blindness of mind, Eph. iv. 18; hardness of heart, Rom. ii. 5; a reprobate sense, Rom. i. 28; strong delusions, 2 Thess. ii. 11; horror of conscience, Isa. xxxiii. 14; vile affections, Rom. i. 26;"* and the thraldom and bondage of Satan, Eph. ii. 2.

Q. 20. Is there no medicine against these soul maladies and miseries?

A. Yes: there is "balm in Gilead, and a Physician there," Jer. viii. 22; who is "able to save to the uttermost," Heb. vii. 25; and who says, "Look unto me, and be ye saved, all the ends of the earth," Isa. xlv. 22.

Q. 21. What are those external miseries we are liable to in this life?

A. They are either more public, such as sword, famine, pestilence, desolation by fire and water, captivity, persecution, and the like, Ezek. v. 17; or more *private* and personal, such as diseases of all sorts, reproach and calumny, toil and labour, poverty, and crosses of all kinds. Deut. xxviii. 16, 17, &c.

Q. 22. Do not all these external miseries come alike to all, both godly and wicked?

A. Yes, as to the external conduct of providence, Eccl. ix. 2; but to the godly they are only fatherly chastisements, and work together for their good, Rom. viii. 28; whereas to the wicked, they come in a way of vindictive anger, and are but the beginnings of sorrows, unless the goodness of God do lead them to repentance, Rom. ii. 5.

Q. 23. Has sin any other retinue attending it than what has been already mentioned?

A. Yes: for like the *pale horse*, Rev. vi. 8, it has death, and then hell following after.

Q. 24. What [*death*] is here intended?

---

* Larger Catechism, Quest. 28.

A. A corporeal or bodily death, which lies in the separation of soul and body.

Q. 25. Is sin the cause of death?

A. It is both the cause of death, Rom. v. 12, and the sting of it, 1 Cor. xv. 55, 56.

Q. 26. Is the connexion between sin and death inseparable?

A. Yes; they are inseparable by the appointment of the righteous God, who has said, " The soul that sinneth, it shall die," Ezek. xviii. 4; and, " It is appointed unto men once to die," Heb. ix. 27.

Q. 27. How did this appointment of heaven hold, in the case of Enoch and Elijah?

A. They underwent what was equivalent to death in their translation to heaven; it fared with them as it will with the saints that shall be alive at Christ's second coming, concerning whom it is said, " We shall not all sleep, but we shall all be changed," 1 Cor. xv. 51.

Q. 28. What is the difference between the death of believers and the death of the wicked?

A. To the wicked it comes as standing under a covenant of works, but to believers as standing under a covenant of grace; to the one, in the hand of Christ, saying, " Death is yours;" to the other in the hand of Satan, as God's executioner, having the power of death: to the one without, but to the other as armed with a fearful sting: to the one as an everlasting and irreparable loss; to the other as eternal and unspeakable gain: to the one as a conqueror, dragging the sinner to the prison of hell; to the other as a vanquished enemy, paving the way to heaven and glory.

Q. 29. What will be the believer's language when he views death approaching in this light?

A. Faith will cry out, " O death! where is thy sting?" 1 Cor. xv. 55.

Q. 30. What will be the language of the wicked when they see death approaching as the king of terrors?

A. It will be like that of Ahab to Elijah, 1 Kings xxi. 20, —" Hast thou found me, O mine enemy!"

Q. 31. What misery has sin made us liable to after death?

A. [*To the pains of hell for ever.*]

Q. 32. What do you understand by [*hell?*]

A. A state and place of torment, prepared for the devil and his angels, Matt. xxv. 41.

Q. 33. If it was prepared for the devil and his angels, what concern have any of mankind with it?

A. Though it was prepared for the devil and his angels, yet the wicked of the world shall be turned into it also, and all the nations that forget God, Ps. ix. 17.

MAN'S NATURAL STATE.

Q. 34. Why must the wicked and ungodly world be turned into hell, with the devil and his angels?

A. Because they served and obeyed the devil as their god, and were in a confederacy with him against the living and true God, Isa. xxviii. 15; Eph. ii. 2.

Q. 35. How many fold are the punishments of the damned in hell?

A. Twofold; the punishment of loss, and the punishment of sense.

Q. 36. What *loss* shall the damned in hell sustain?

A. They shall lose God, the chief good, Matt. xxv. 41; they shall lose the vision and fruition of the glorious Immanuel, Matt. vii. 23; they shall lose their own souls, Matt. xvi. 26, and all the pleasures of sin and sense, in which they placed their happiness in this world, Luke xvi. 25.

Q. 37. What will be the punishment of *sense* which the wicked shall suffer in hell?

A. It is represented in scripture by their being shut up in outer darkness, Matt. viii. 12; in a lake of fire and brimstone, Rev. xx. 10, where the smoke of their torment shall ascend up for ever and ever, Rev. xiv. 11; which is called the *second death*, chap. xxi. 8, the worm that never dies, and the fire that shall never be quenched, Mark ix. 44.

Q. 38. How do you prove, from scripture, that [*the pains of hell*] shall be [*for ever*,] or everlasting?

A. The wicked are said to be "cast into everlasting fire," Matt. xviii. 8; to "go away into everlasting punishment," Matt. xxv. 46; to be "punished with everlasting destruction," 2 Thess. i. 9; to have the "mist of darkness" reserved for them *for ever*, 2 Pet. ii. 17; to be "tormented day and night, for ever and ever," Rev. xx. 10; and by several other expressions of the like nature.

Q. 39. Is eternity of punishment essential to the threatening, or penal sanction of the law?

A. No; else there never had been a satisfaction for sin.

Q. 40. Whence then arises the eternity of punishment?

A. From the nature of the creature, which being finite, can never be capable of enduring the uttermost of infinite wrath; Ps. xc. 11: "Who knoweth the power of thine anger?"

Q. 41. How can it consist with the justice of God, to inflict eternal punishment for temporal sinning?

A. Because sin, objectively considered, is an infinite evil, as being committed against an infinitely holy God; and therefore nothing can expiate it, but a satisfaction of infinite worth, which mere creatures can never yield, 1 Pet. i. 18, 19.

OF THE COVENANT OF GRACE.

Q. 42. What sort of sinners shall undergo the most dreadful degree of punishment in hell?
A. The despisers of Christ and the gospel: it will be more tolerable for Sodom and Gomorrah, for Tyre and Sidon, who never heard of Christ, than for Chorazin, Bethsaida, and Capernaum, and other cities, nations, and persons, to whom Christ, and his great salvation, have been offered, and yet rejected through unbelief, Matt. xi. 21—25; Heb. ii. 3.

Q. 43. What should all this teach us?
A. That however sweet sin be in the mouth, it will be bitter in the belly, even *lamentation, mourning, and wo;* in the latter end, Ezek. ii. 10; it should teach us to fly from the wrath to come, to the horns of the New Testament altar, the satisfaction and intercession of Christ; there being no name by which we can be saved from sin and wrath, except the name of Jesus only, Acts iv. 12.

QUEST. 20. *Did God leave all mankind to perish in the estate of sin and misery?*

ANS. God having out of his mere good pleasure, from all eternity, elected some to everlasting life, did enter into a covenant of grace, to deliver them out of the estate of sin and misery, and to bring them into an estate of salvation by a Redeemer.

Q. 1. What became of the angels that fell, by their sinning against God?
A. God left them without remedy, in that state of sin and misery into which they plunged themselves; and hath "delivered them into chains of darkness, to be reserved unto judgment," 2 Pet. ii. 4.

Q. 2. When man joined with the devil in a conspiracy against God, did God treat him the same way?
A. No; he had a purpose of grace and love towards some of Adam's race; and therefore, immediately after the fall, declares his fixed intention of assuming the human nature, in the person of the Son, that he might redeem lost man, and bruise the head of the old serpent, that had ruined him, Gen. iii. 15.

Q. 3. When did God's purpose of grace and love, towards any of Adam's family, commence or begin?
A. It never had a beginning; for he loved them from everlasting, Jer. xxxi. 3; Eph. i. 4.

OF THE COVENANT OF GRACE.

Q. 4. Can any reason be given why God has [*elected*] fallen man, rather than fallen angels, and why he elected [*some*] of Adam's race, and not others of them?

A. It is dangerous to search into the reasons of holy and adorable sovereignty; it becomes us to acquiesce in this, that God did it [*out of his mere good pleasure,*] Eph. i. 5; Matt. xi. 6.

Q. 5. To what happiness did God ordain his elect from among men?

A. He ordained them to [*everlasting life,*] Acts xiii. 48: "As many as were ordained to eternal life, believed."

Q. 6. Did God make choice of any to eternal life, because of their foreseen faith and holiness?

A. No; because faith and holiness are the fruits and effects, and therefore can never be the cause of election, Eph. i. 4—6.

Q. 7. Is Christ the cause of election?

A. No; the free love of God sent Christ to redeem the elect, and therefore he could not be the cause of electing love, John iii. 16.

Q. 8. Did not Christ procure God's love to an elect world?

A. No: the Father himself loved them, John xvi. 27.

Q. 9. If Christ is not the cause of election, why are the elect said to be chosen in him?

A. Because in one and the same decree of election, the love of God lighted both upon the head, and upon the members, considered as in him, Eph. i. 4.

Q. 10. By whom is it that God brings any of Adam's race to eternal life?

A. [*By a Redeemer,*] Rom. xi. 8.

Q. 11. How are sinners of mankind to be viewed in relation to a Redeemer?

A. As lawful captives, Isa. xlix. 24.

Q. 12. What is it to redeem the lawful captives?

A. It is to pay down a sufficient ransom to offended justice for their deliverance, and to rescue them by mere force and power out of the hands of Satan, Isa. xlix. 25.

Q. 13. What ransom is laid down to offended justice for their deliverance?

A. Nothing less than "the precious blood of Christ," or his obedience unto death, 1 Pet. i. 19.

Q. 14. What right and title has the Redeemer, to take the captives by force out of the hands of Satan?

A. The demands of law and justice being satisfied, he has a lawful right, both by donation and purchase, to rescue his captives out of the hands of Satan by his divine power, John xvii. 2.

Q. 15. Why did the Redeemer, in dealing with justice.

OF THE COVENANT OF GRACE.

lay down a price; but in dealing with Satan, act by way of power?

A. Because God, being the creditor, had a right to demand a price, but Satan being only the jailor, has no law-right to detain the prisoner, after the creditor is satisfied; and yet, refusing to quit hold of his captives, the Redeemer's power must be put forth for their deliverance. Luke xi. 22.

Q. 16. Was there a covenant transaction entered into for their deliverance, by price and power?

A. Yes; Ps. lxxxix. 3: "I have made a covenant with my Chosen."

Q. 17. How is that covenant called?

A. [*A covenant of grace.*]

Q. 18. Why called a covenant of grace?

A. Because it is a covenant of eternal life and salvation to sinners, to be given them in a way of free grace and mercy, Jer. xxxi. 33, 34.

Q. 19. Are not heaven and earth both concerned in this covenant?

A. Yes; because it is a covenant of peace between them, Isa. liv. 9, 10.

Q. 20. Who is the party contractor on Heaven's side?

A. It is God himself, the proposer of the covenant, and the offended party, Ps. lxxxix. 3.

Q. 21. Whether is it God essentially considered, or as in the person of the Father, that is the party-contractor on Heaven's side?

A. God essentially considered is the party-contractor on Heaven's side, in the person of the Father.

Q. 22. Who is the party-contractor on man's side?

A. It is Christ, *the chosen of God*, as he is called, Luke xxiii. 35.

Q. 23. In what does this covenant consist?

A. In the mutual agreement between God and his chosen One.

Q. 24. When was this covenant made?

A. From all eternity, or before the world began, Tit. i. 2.

Q. 25. "With whom was the covenant of grace made?"

A. "With Christ as the second [or *last*] *Adam;* and in him with all the elect as his seed, Gal. iii. 16."*

Q. 26. Why is Christ called the *last Adam?* 1 Cor. xv. 45.

A. Because as the *first Adam* was the federal head of all his natural offspring, in the covenant of works, so Christ is the *last Adam*, because he was the federal head of his

---

* Larger Catechism, Quest. 31.

spiritual seed in the covenant of grace; the last covenant that ever will be made about man's eternal happiness.

Q. 27. How was the covenant of grace made with Christ as the *second* or *last Adam?*

A. The Father purposed that a remnant of lost mankind should be the members of Christ's body, and gave them to him for that end; and Christ, standing as *second Adam,* accepted the gift, John xvii. 6; as also, the Father proposed to him, as the *last Adam,* the covenant of grace in the full tenor, condition, and promises of it, to which he consented; and thus the covenant of rich grace was concluded between them; Zech. vi. 13, " The counsel of peace shall be between them both."

Q. 28. How are we to conceive of the covenant of grace, in respect of order and being?

A. Although the covenant of grace was the *second* covenant, in respect of *order* and manifestation to the world, yet it was *first* in respect of *being,* because it was actually made with Christ from eternity, Tit. i. 2.

Q. 29. How do you prove from scripture, that there was such a covenant made with Christ?

A. From Isa. xlii. 6: " I will give thee for a covenant of the people ;" and Heb. viii. 6, where Christ is called " the Mediator of a better covenant;" and from Heb. xiii. 20, where we read of " the blood of the everlasting covenant."

Q. 30. What was the ancient usage in making of covenants?

A. It was to cut a beast in twain, and to pass between the parts of it, Jer. xxxiv. 18.

Q. 31. What does this usage import, as applied to God's making a covenant with his Chosen?

A. It imports, that it was a "covenant by sacrifice," Ps. l. 5.

Q. 32. What was the sacrifice in this covenant?

A. It was Christ himself, the party contractor on man's side, Heb. ix. 26.

Q. 33. What was the *sword* that cut this sacrifice asunder?

A. It was divine justice, Zech. xiii. 7.

Q. 34. How is Christ the party contractor on man's side, to be considered in this covenant?

A. He is to be considered as the head and representative of his spiritual seed, Isa lix. 21.

Q. 35. How does it appear that Christ is the head and representative of his spiritual seed in this covenant?

A. From the making of the promises originally to him and from his being the surety of the covenant.

Q. 36. When were the promises made to him?

A. Before the world began; which, in scripture style, it

the same as from eternity, Tit. i. 2, "In hope of eternal life, which God, that cannot lie, promised before the world began." And there was none before the world began, to whom the promise of eternal life could be made personally, but to Christ as the head and representative of his seed.

Q. 37. How do you prove, from scripture, that Christ was *surety* for his spiritual seed in this covenant?

A. From Heb. vii. 22: "By so much was Jesus made a surety of a better testament."

Q. 38. In what sense was he surety for them?

A. He was their surety in a way of satisfaction for all their debt of obedience and punishment, by taking it wholly on himself, as for persons utterly insolvent.

Q. 39. How is Christ's being the surety of the covenant, an evidence of its being made with him as the representative of his seed?

A. Because by his being surety for them, he became one with them in the eye of the law: hence is Christ said, not only to be *made sin for us*, but we are said to be "made the righteousness of God in him," 2 Cor. v. 21.

Q. 40. Why was the covenant of grace made with Christ as the head and representative of his spiritual seed?

A. That the love of God, and the covenant of grace, might be of the same eternal date; for, as the love of God is *an everlasting love*, Jer. xxxi. 3, so the covenant of grace is an *everlasting covenant*, Heb. xiii. 20.

Q. 41. Who is the party represented and contracted for in the covenant of grace?

A. The elect of mankind.

Q. 42. What do you understand by the elect of mankind?

A. A certain number of mankind chosen, from eternity, to everlasting life.

Q. 43. How does it appear, that the elect were the party represented and contracted for?

A. Because the party with whom the covenant was made is called God's CHOSEN, Ps. lxxxix. 3: "I have made a covenant with my Chosen;" that is, with Christ, as contracting for all the chosen, or elect of God.

Q. 44. Why are the elect called Christ's *seed?* Ps. lxxxix. 4.

A. Because he begets them with the word of truth, James i. 18; and they are born again to him in their regeneration, John iii. 3.

Q. 45. Why is Christ said to take on him the *seed of Abraham*, Heb. ii. 16, and not rather the *seed of Adam?*

A. To show that it was the elect only, whom he represented; in as much as the *seed of Abraham* are but a part of *Adam's seed*, which includes all mankind.

Q. 46. How are the elect of God to be considered in this covenant and federal representation?

A. They are to be considered as lost sinners, and as utterly unable to help themselves in whole or in part, Hos. xiii. 9; and yet withal as given to Christ by the Father, as objects of eternal, sovereign, and free love, John xvii. 6, 9.

Q. 47. How does the freedom of this electing love appear?

A. In pitching upon objects altogether unlovely, Ezek. xvi. 6.

Q. 48. How does the *sovereignty* of it appear?

A. In pitching on *some* such unlovely objects, and passing by others in the same condition, Rom. ix. 21.

Q. 49. Was it any disparagement to the federal representation of the *second Adam*, that he represented only *some* of mankind, whereas the *first Adam* represented the *whole* of his race?

A. No; because it was unspeakably more for Christ to undertake and contract for one sinner, than for Adam to contract for a *whole* righteous world.

Q. 50. Is what is called by some divines, the *covenant of redemption*, a distinct covenant from the covenant of grace?

A. Although Christ alone engaged from eternity to pay the price of our redemption, on which account the covenant is wholly of free grace to us; yet there is no warrant from scripture, to suppose a covenant of redemption distinct from the covenant of grace.

Q. 51. How many covenants are there for life and happiness to man in scripture reckoning?

A. They are but two in number: of which the covenant of works is one, and consequently the covenant of grace must be the other.

Q. 52. How do you prove from scripture, that there are only *two covenants*, of which the covenant of works is one?

A. From Gal. iv. 24, where it is said—" These are the two covenants, the one from mount Sinai, which gendereth to bondage."

Q. 53. How does it appear that the one from *Mount Sinai*, which gendereth to bondage, is the covenant of works?

A. Because the generating of bond children, excluded from the inheritance, Gal. iv. 30, is a distinguishing character of the covenant of works, which cannot agree to the covenant of grace under any dispensation of it.

Q. 54. Was then the covenant at Mount Sinai a covenant of works?

A. The covenant of works was only repeated at Mount

Sinai, together with the covenant of grace; to show to all Israel, that the clearing of both the principal and penalty of the covenant of works was laid on Christ, as the condition of the covenant of grace.

Q. 55. Does the scripture make mention of the blood of any more than one covenant?

A. The scripture makes mention of the blood of the *covenant*, in the singular number, four several times, namely, Ex. xxiv. 8; Zech. ix. 11; Heb. x. 29, and xiii. 20; but nowhere speaks of the blood of the *covenants*, in the plural number.

Q. 56. What is the native consequence of the scripture's mentioning the blood of the covenant, in the singular number, and not the blood of the covenants in the plural number?

A. The consequence is, that the covenant, the blood of which the scripture mentions, and upon which our salvation depends, is but ONE covenant, and not TWO.

Q. 57. What is the received doctrine in our standards upon this head?

A. Our standards make no distinction between a covenant of redemption, and a covenant of grace.*

Q. 58. Is the covenant of grace conditional, or absolutely free?

A. It was strictly conditional to the Surety, Isa. xlix. 3, but is absolutely free to the sinner, Jer. xxxi. 33, 34.

Q. 59. What is the proper *condition* of the covenant of grace?

A. It is Christ, as representative and surety, his *fulfilling all righteousness*, owing to God by his spiritual seed, in virtue of the broken covenant of works, Matt. iii. 15.

Q. 60. In what consists that *righteousness* which Christ had to fulfil, as the condition of the covenant of grace?

A. In the holiness of his human nature, perfect conformity to the law in his life, and satisfaction for sin in his death.

Q. 61. Why was *holiness of nature* necessary as a conditionary article of the covenant?

A. Because nothing being so opposite to God as an unholy nature, and yet the elect having their natures wholly corrupted, it was therefore necessary, that Christ, their representative, should have a human nature perfectly pure and holy, fully answering for them the holiness and perfection of nature required by the law, Heb. vii. 26.

---

* For proof of this, see *Larger Catechism, Quest.* 31, " With whom was the covenant of grace made? *Ans.* The covenant of grace was made with Christ, as the second Adam, and in him, with all the elect as his seed, Isa. liii. 10, 11; Rom. v 15, to the end, Gal. iii. 16."

Q. 62. Why was *righteousness of life*, or perfect conformity to the law, necessary as a conditionary article of the covenant?

A. Because Adam, as a public head, having failed in his obedience, there could be no entering into life for him, or any of his natural seed, without keeping the commandments by the Surety, Matt. xix. 17: "If thou wilt enter into life, keep the commandments."

Q. 63. Has Christ fulfilled this part of the condition?

A. Yes; for, "he became obedient unto death," Phil. ii. 8.

Q. 64. Was *satisfaction for sin* any part of the condition of Adam's covenant?

A. No: holiness of nature, and righteousness of life, were the sole condition of it.

Q. 65. How then came satisfaction for sin to be a conditionary article in the new covenant?

A. Because the covenant of works being broken, and the penalty of it incurred, the holiness, justice, and veracity of God insisted, that without shedding of blood, there should be no remission, Heb. ix. 22.

Q. 66. What was the conditionary article of the covenant relative to satisfaction for sin?

A. That all the sins of an elect world, being summed up as so many branches of the law, or covenant of works, Christ, as a public person, should satisfy publicly and completely for them all, Isa. liii. 5, 6.

Q. 67. How was he to make this satisfaction?

A. By suffering, Luke xxiv. 26: "Ought not Christ to have suffered these things?"

Q. 68. What was it that he had to suffer?

A. The very same punishment the elect would have undergone, for the breach of the covenant of works; that is, death, in its fullest latitude and extent, Gen. ii. 17, compared with 2 Cor. v. 14.

Q. 69. What is that death in the fullest latitude and extent which Christ had to endure, in satisfaction for sin?

A. It was both the *curse*, or *sentence*, of the broken law, binding him over, as the Surety, to suffer all that avenging wrath which sin deserved; and likewise the actual execution of this sentence upon him to the uttermost, for the full satisfaction of justice, Gal. iii. 10; Ezek. xviii. 4.

Q. 70. Has Christ fulfilled this part of the condition?

A. Yes; he was "made a curse for us," Gal. iii. 13; "and hath given himself for us, an offering and a sacrifice to God for a sweet-smelling savour," Eph. v. 2.

Q. 71. How does it appear, that this righteousness of Christ is the condition of the covenant of grace?

A. Because his fulfilling all righteousness is the only ground of a sinner's right and title to eternal life, Rom. v

21; and the sole foundation of his plea befor*e* God, Phil. iii. 8, 9.

Q. 72. Why may not *faith*, or believing, be the condition of the covenant of grace?

A. Because faith is promised in the covenant itself, Zech. xii. 10, and therefore cannot be the condition of it.

Q. 73. May not faith be the condition, when the scripture says, that Abraham's faith "was counted unto him for righteousness?" Rom. iv. 3.

A. It was the object upon which Abraham's faith terminated, namely, Christ and his righteousness, and not his faith itself, or his act of believing, that was counted to him for righteousness.

Q. 74. What place then has faith in the covenant?

A. It has the place of an *instrument and gift;* and is necessary, as such, savingly to interest us in Christ,* John i. 12; and to determine us to acquiesce in his fulfilling the condition of the covenant for us, Isa. xlv. 24.

Q. 75. What may we learn from the *conditionary part* of the covenant, as fulfilled by Christ?

A. That the redemption of the soul is precious, being ransomed at no less a sum than the holy birth, righteous life, and satisfactory death of the Son of God, 1 Pet. i. 19; and that the law is so far from being made void through faith, that it is established by it, Rom. iii. 31.

Q. 76. Seeing in every covenant there is a promise, what are the *promises* of the covenant of grace?

A. They are such as have either their direct and immediate effect upon Christ himself, as the Head; or such as have their direct and immediate effect on the elect, comprehended with him in the covenant.

Q. 77. What are these promises that have their direct and immediate effect on Christ himself, as the head of the covenant?

A. The promise of assistance in his work, Ps. lxxxix 21; of the acceptance of it, Isa. xlii. 21; and of a glorious reward to be conferred upon him, as the proper merit of his *work done*, Isa. lii. 13.

Q. 78. What are those promises that have their direct and immediate effect upon the elect?

A. They are all the promises pertaining to life and godliness; the promises of grace and glory, and of every good thing; which may all be comprehended in this one, to wit, the promise of *eternal life*, mentioned, Tit. i. 2: "In hope of eternal life, which God that cannot lie, hath promised before the world began;" and 1 John ii. 25: "This is the promise that he hath promised us, even eternal life."

Q. 79. What is meant by the promise of *eternal life?*

---

* Larger Catechism, Answer to Quest. 32.

A. It comprehends in it *all true happiness*, and its *everlasting continuance*.

Q. 80. How is it evident, that all true and eternal happiness is comprehended in the meaning of the promise of eternal life?

A. In as much as the death threatened in the covenant of works, included *all misery* in this world, and the world to come: so the *life* promised in the covenant of grace must needs comprehend *all happiness* in time and eternity, with all the means by which it is effected, Rom. vi. 23

Q. 81. To whom was this promise of eternal life made?

A. To Christ *primarily*, and to the elect *secondarily* in and through him: as is evident from Tit. i. 2, compared with 1 John ii. 25.

Q. 82. To whom are the promises of the covenant endorsed or directed?

A. To all who hear the gospel, with their seed, Acts ii. 39: "The promise is to you, and to your children."

Q. 83. What right to the promises have all the hearers of the gospel, by this general endorsement of them?

A. A right of *access* to the promises, and all the good that is in them, so as to be rendered inexcusable if they believe not, John iii. 18.

Q. 84. What right does *faith*, or believing, give to the promises?

A. A right of *possession*, in virtue of union with Christ, in whom all the promises are *yea, and amen;* John iii. 36: "He that believeth—HATH everlasting life."

Q. 85. What may we learn from the *promissory* part of the covenant?

A. That all the benefits of it are the free gifts of grace, running in the channel of the obedience and death of Christ; and are in him perfectly sure to the elect seed, Isa. lv. 3.

Q. 86. Was there any *penalty* in the covenant of grace, as there was in the covenant of works?

A. Although there was a penalty in the covenant of works, because Adam, with whom it was made was a *fallible* creature; yet there could be none in the covenant of grace, because Christ, the party contracting on man's side, was absolutely infallible, and could not fail, Isa. xiii. 4.

Q. 87. Are not the elect, the party contracted for, *fallible*, even after they are brought to believe?

A. It is certain, that believers are *fallible*, in respect of their *actions*, as long as they are in this world, Eccl. vii. 20, but not in respect of their state, Job xvii. 9; they can no more fall from their state of grace, than the saints in heaven can, John xiii. 1.

Q. 88. Can *fatherly chastisements* be called a penalty in the covenant of grace, with respect to believers?

A. No; because they are not vindictive, but *medicinaͷ*, and really belong to the *promissory part* of the covenant, as is evident from Ps. lxxxix. 30—35; Isa. xxvii. 9; Heb. xii. 6, 7.

Q. 89. What security have believers against any proper penalty in this covenant?

A. They have the security of Christ's performing the condition of it for them; and his doing so *legally* sustained in their favour, 2 Cor. v. 21.

Q. 90. On whom is the *administration* of the covenant of grace devolved?

A. On Christ the *second Adam*, alone, and that, as a reward of his work, Isa. xlix. 8.

Q. 91. What do you understand by the *administration of the covenant?*

A. The *entire management* of it, by which it may be rendered effectual to the end for which it was made, Ps. lxxxix. 28.

Q. 92. Who are the objects of this administration?

A. Sinners of mankind *indefinitely*, or *any* of the family of Adam, without exception, John iii. 14, 15.

Q. 93. How does he administer the covenant to sinners of mankind indefinitely?

A. In the *general offer* of the gospel, which is "*good tidings to* ALL PEOPLE," Luke ii. 10; in which all, without exception, are declared welcome, Prov. viii. 4; Mark xvi. 15.

Q. 94. What is the *foundation* of the unlimited administration of the covenant, in the gospel offer?

A. It is not founded on election, but on the *intrinsic sufficiency* of Christ's obedience and death for the salvation of all, John i. 29.

Q. 95. For what *end* does he thus administer the covenant to sinners of mankind?

A. [*To deliver them out of the estate of sin and misery, and to bring them into an estate of salvation,*] Gal. iii. 21, 22.

Q. 96. How does he bring them into a *state of salvation?*

A. By bringing them personally and savingly into the "bond of the covenant," Ezek. xx. 37, in the day of his power; when "one shall say, I am the Lord's—and another subscribe with his hand unto the Lord," Isa. xliv. 5.

Q. 97. How long will he continue to be the administrator of the covenant?

A. As he dispenses all the blessings of the covenant here, John iii. 35, so he will complete the happiness of the saints, in the other world, by a perfect accomplishment of all its promises to them, Eph. v. 27.

Q. 98. How does it appear that he will be the administrator of the covenant through eternity?

A. Because he is to remain the eternal *bond* of *union*, Heb. vii. 25, and *medium of communication*, between God and the saints for ever, Rev. vii. 17.

Q. 99. What is the *first* and *fundamental act* of his administration?

A. It is his *disposing* the *all things*, which he has in his hand, as the appointed *trustee* of the covenant, to poor sinners, by way of a TESTAMENT, Luke xxii. 29: "I appoint (or dispose) unto you a kingdom, as my Father hath appointed unto me."

Q. 100. What is the difference between a *federal* and a *testamentary disposition?*

A. A *federal* disposition is made upon a *weighty* cause, or proper condition; but a *testamentary* disposition is a deed, or conveyance, of grace and bounty, *without all conditions*, properly so called.

Q. 101. How is this applied to the Father's disposition and to Christ's?

A. The Father's federal disposition of all covenant-benefits to Christ, was on condition of his making "his soul an offering for sin," Isa. liii. 10; but Christ's testamentary disposition to sinners, who have nothing, is "without money and without price," chap. lv. 1.

Q. 102. Is Christ's *testament* of the same *date* with the *covenant* that was made with him?

A. The covenant of grace was made with him from eternity; but it is obvious, that his *commencing testator* of this covenant, being an act of his administration of it, could not take place till the covenant of works was broken.

Q. 103. At what *time*, then. did he make his testament?

A. The very day in which Adam fell—in the first promise, Gen. iii. 15.

Q. 104. How could his testament be of force, (according to Heb. ix. 17,) so long before his *actual* death?

A. He died typically, in all the sacrifices of the Old Testament; hence he is called, "The Lamb slain from the foundation of the world," Rev. xiii. 8.

Q. 105. Who are the *legatees*, or parties in whose favour the testament was made?

A. Since Christ is authorized by the Father, to administer the covenant to *mankind sinners indefinitely*, John vi. 37, none of these can be excepted out of his testament, as to the external revelation and exhibition of it, any more than they are out of his administration, Rev. xxii. 17.

Q. 106. Who is the *executor* of his testament?

A. Although in testaments among men, the *testator* and *executor* are always different persons, because the testator dying, cannot live again to see his will executed; yet here the testator, who *was dead*, is *alive for evermore*, as the executor of his own testament, by his Spirit, Rev. i. 18 Rom. iv. 25.

Q. 107. What are the *legacies* left in his testament?

A. They are all the benefits of the covenant, even HIM SELF, and ALL THINGS in and with him, Rom. viii. 32; Rev xxi. 7.

Q. 108. By what *means* is it that sinners are possessed of these rich legacies?

A. By faith, or believing on the Lord Jesus Christ, Acts xvi. 31.

Q. 109. Why is believing on Christ the appointed means of instating sinners in the covenant and legacies thereof?

A. Because the grace of the covenant is thus preserved entire, " to the end the promise might be sure to all the seed," Rom. iv. 16.

Q. 110. How may persons know, if they are savingly and personally within the covenant of grace?

A. If they have found themselves unable to dwell any longer within the boundaries of the covenant of works, and " have fled for refuge," from that covenant, " to lay hold upon the hope set before them," Heb. vi. 18.

Q. 111. In what respects do the covenants of *works* and *of grace* DIFFER from one another?

A. They *differ* in their nature, parties, contractors, properties, conditions, promises, the order of obedience, in their end and design, the manner of their administration, and in their effects.

Q. 112. How do these two covenants of works and grace differ in their *nature?*

A. The covenant of works was a covenant of *friendship*, and supposed the parties to be in a perfect amity; but the covenant of grace is a covenant of *reconciliation*, and supposes man to be at variance with God, and enmity against him, 2 Cor. v. 19.

Q. 113. How do they differ as to the *parties contractors?*

A. In the covenant of works, the parties contractors were, GOD and innocent *Adam*, representing all his *natural* seed; but in the covenant of grace, the parties are, GOD, and CHRIST the second *Adam*, representing all his *spiritual seed*, Ps. lxxxix. 3, 4.

Q. 114. How do they differ in their *properties?*

A. The covenant of works, as standing with the *first Adam*, was but *short-lived;* but the covenant of grace, which stands fast with the *second Adam*, is an *everlasting* covenant, Heb. xiii. 20: the covenant of works denounced nothing but wrath and curse upon the transgressor; but the covenant of grace is full of blessings to the sinner, in Christ, Eph. i. 3.

Q. 115. How do they differ in their *conditions?*

A. The condition of the covenant of works was only the perfect obedience of a *mere man*, bearing no proportion to the life promised; but the condition of the covenant of grace is the perfect righteousness of *God-man*, which is fully adequate to the promised reward, Jer. xxiii. 6.

Q. 116. How do they differ in their *promises*?

A. The promises of the covenant of works were strictly *conditional;* but the promises of the covenant of grace, as respecting us, are *absolutely free*, Jer. xxxi. 33, 34.

Q. 117. In what respect do they differ in the *order of obedience?*

A. In the covenant of works, duty, or obedience, was the foundation of privilege; acceptance first began at the work, and then went on to the person, if the work was perfectly right; but, in the covenant of grace, this order is quite inverted; for in it privilege is the foundation of duty; and acceptance first begins at the person, and then goes on to the work, because flowing from a principle of faith: Gen. iv. 4, compared with Heb. xi. 4.

Q. 118. How do they differ in their *end* and *design?*

A. The end of the covenant of works was to show man what he was to do towards God; but the end of the covenant of grace, is to show man what God is to do for him, and in him, Isa. xxvi. 12.

Q. 119. How do they differ in the *manner of their administration?*

A. The covenant of works was dispensed by God, *absolutely* considered; but the covenant of grace is dispensed by a *Mediator*, who is himself the ALL of the covenant, Isa. xlii. 6.

Q. 120. How do these two covenants differ in their *effects?*

A. The covenant of works wounds and terrifies a guilty sinner; but the covenant of grace heals and comforts a wounded soul, Isa. xlii. 3: the covenant of works shuts up to hell and wrath; but the covenant of grace casts open a door of escape, John x. 9; and xiv. 6.

Q. 121. What may we learn from this whole doctrine of the covenant of grace?

A. That it is our duty to believe that JESUS CHRIST is the *Saviour of the world*, and *our Saviour* in particular, by his Father's appointment, and his own offer; and that by the same appointment and offer, *his righteousness*, which is the condition of the covenant, and *eternal life*, which is the promise of it, are OURS in respect of *right* to it, so as that we may lawfully and warrantably take possession of the same, and *use* them as OUR OWN, to all the intents and purposes of salvation: John iv. 42, " We know that this is indeed the Christ, the SAVIOUR of the WORLD:" Luke i. 47 " My spirit hath rejoiced in GOD, MY SAVIOUR."

QUEST. 21. *Who is the Redeemer of God's elect?*

ANS. The only Redeemer of God's elect, is the Lord Jesus Christ, who, being the eternal Son of God, became man, and so was, and continues to be God and man, in two distinct natures, and one person, for ever.

Q. 1. What is the greatest *wonder* the world has ever beheld?
A. The incarnation of the Son of God, John i. 14; Jer. xxxi. 22.

Q. 2. What makes this the greatest wonder?
A. Because by it two natures, infinitely distant, are united in one person; hence called "a great mystery," 1 Tim. iii. 16.

Q. 3. Was this great event foretold before it came to pass?
A. Yes: God *spake* of it "by the mouth of his holy prophets, which have been since the world began," Luke i. 70.

Q. 4. By what *names* did they speak of his coming?
A. By a variety of names, such as *Shiloh*, Gen. xlix. 10; *Messiah*, Dan. ix. 25; *Immanuel*, Isa. vii. 14; *the Branch*, Zech. vi. 12; the *Messenger of the covenant*, Mal. iii. 1; and several others.

Q. 5. Is he *now* actually come into the world?
A. Yes, long since: and "it is a faithful saying, and worthy of all acceptation, that Christ Jesus came into the world," 1 Tim. i. 15, "not to condemn the world, but that the world through him might be saved," John iii. 17.

Q. 6. How do you prove, that our Lord Jesus Christ is the *true promised Messiah?*
A. By this one argument: that "all things which were written in the law of Moses, and in the prophets, and in the Psalms," concerning the Messiah, are literally fulfilled in Jesus of Nazareth, Luke xxiv. 44.

Q. 7. How does this appear?
A. By comparing every prophecy and promise concerning him in the Old Testament, with the exact accomplishment of it in the New, Acts iii. 18.

Q. 8. What *silencing questions* may be put to the *Jews*, who assert that the *Messiah* is not yet come in the flesh?
A. They may be asked, Where is the *sceptre* of civil government, which was not to *depart* from *Judah* until *Shiloh* came, according to Gen. xlix. 10? Where is the *second* temple, into which the *Messiah* was to come, and to make the glory of it *greater* than the glory of the *former*, by his personal appearance in it, according to Hag. ii. 9?

Where is the *sacrifice* and *oblation* now offered? has it not long since ceased, according to Dan. ix. 27? And where is the *family of David*, out of which Christ was to spring, according to Isa. xi. 1? is it not now quite extinct? They are utterly incapable of answering any of these.

Q. 9. What does the title of a [*Redeemer*] suppose with reference to the *redeemed*?

A. Bondage and captivity to sin, Satan, the world, death, and hell, through the breach of the first covenant; hence called *lawful captives*, Isa. xlix. 24.

Q. 10. Are all mankind, the elect of God as well as others, by nature under this bondage and captivity?

A. Yes; as is evident from Eph. ii. 1—3.

Q. 11. Why is Christ called the [*only*] *Redeemer of* God's elect?

A. Because there was none capable of the vast undertaking but himself, Isa. lxiii. 5.

Q. 12. How does Christ redeem the elect from their spiritual bondage and captivity?

A. By price and power; or by ransom, 1 Pet. i. 19, and conquest, Isa. xlix. 25.

Q. 13. What *ransom* or price did he lay down?

A. His own *life*, Matt. xx. 28, "The Son of man came—to give his life a ransom for many."

Q. 14. How does Christ redeem by *power* or *conquest?*

A. When, by his word and Spirit, he breaks the bonds of the captives, and says "to the prisoners, Go forth; and to them that sit in darkness, Show yourselves," Isa. xlix. 9; and thus spoils *principalities* and *powers*, Col. ii. 15.

Q. 15. Why is the Redeemer called [*Lord?*]

A. Because, as God, he "whose name alone is JEHOVAH, is most high over all the earth," Ps. lxxxiii. 18; and, as Mediator, "all power in heaven and earth is given unto him," Matt. xxviii. 18.

Q. 16. Why is he called [*Jesus?*]

A. Because he saves his people from their sins, Matt. i. 21.

Q. 17. Why is he called [*Christ?*]

A. CHRIST in the *Greek*, and MESSIAH in the *Hebrew* language, signify one and the same thing, John i. 41, to wit, the *Anointed*, Acts x. 38; which implies his designation to, and his being fully qualified for his mediatory office.

Q. 18. Upon what is Christ's sufficiency for the great work of our redemption founded?

A. Upon the infinite dignity of his person, as [*being the eternal Son of God,*] 1 John v. 20.

Q. 19. Is Christ the Son of God by *nature*, or only by *office?*

A. Christ is the eternal Son of God by *nature;* his *Son-*

ship is equally natural and necessary with the *Paternity* of the Father, Matt. xxviii. 19; 2 John ver. 3.

Q. 20. What would be the danger of asserting, that Christ is called the *Son of God* only with respect to his *mediatory office?*

A. This would make his personality depend upon the divine will and good pleasure, as it is certain his mediatory office did, John iii. 16; and, consequently, he would not be the self-existent God.

Q. 21. Might not the *Sonship* of Christ be the result of the *divine will*, though his *personality* is not?

A. No: because his *Sonship* is his *proper personality*, and therefore to make his Sonship the result of the divine will, is to overturn the *personal properties* of the Father and Son, and, consequently, to deny both, 1 John ii. 23.

Q. 22. How do you prove, from scripture, that Christ's Sonship is distinguished from his office?

A. From John vii. 29; where Christ, speaking of his Father, says, "I know him, for I am FROM him, and he hath SENT me." Where it is evident, that his being FROM the Father, as to his eternal generation, is distinguished from his being SENT by him, as to his office.

Q. 23. What did this glorious person, the eternal Son of God, *become*, that he might be our Redeemer?

A. He [*became* MAN,] John i. 14; Gal. iv. 4.

Q. 24. When he became man did he cease to be God?

A. No; but he became *Immanuel*, God-man, Matt. i. 23.

Q. 25. What is the import of the name *Immanuel?*

A. It imports, that God is in our nature; and that a God in our nature is not against us, but a God with us, and for us, to save us from the hands of all our enemies, Luke i. 71.

Q. 26. What moved God to become man, in the person of the Son?

A. Nothing but matchless and undeserved grace and love, 1 John iv. 10.

Q. 27. How many [*natures*] has Christ?

A. Two: namely, the nature of God, and the nature of man, 1 Tim. iii. 16.

Q. 28. Why are they called [*two distinct*] natures?

A. In opposition to the error of the Eutychians of old, who maintained, that the two natures were mixed or blended together, so as to make but one nature.

Q. 29. Why is he said to have but [*one person?*]

A. In opposition to the error of the Nestorians, who maintained, that each nature was a person; or, that he had two persons.

Q. 30. How does it appear, that the two natures of God and man are *united* in the person of the Son?

OF THE ONLY REDEEMER.

A. From Isa. ix. 6: "Unto us a child is born—and his name shall be called—The mighty God." It neither being possible nor true, that he who is the *child born*, could be the *mighty God*, except by union of the divine and human natures in one person, Rom. ix. 5; 1 Tim. iii. 16.

Q. 31. Will ever the union between the two natures be dissolved?

A. By no means: for he is, and will continue to be our *Kinsman, Priest*, and *Representative*, in both natures for ever, Heb. vii. 24, 25.

Q. 32. Does not each nature, notwithstanding of this union, still retain its own *essential properties?*

A. Yes: the divine nature is not made *finite*, subject to suffering or change; nor is the human nature rendered *omniscient, omnipresent* and *omnipotent*, as the Lutherans, contrary to scripture and reason, affirm.

Q. 33. Are not the acts and works of either of the two natures, to be ascribed to the person of Christ?

A. Yes: because all he did and suffered, or continues to do, as Mediator, must be considered as *personal acts*, and from thence they derive their value and efficacy, Acts xx. 28.

Q. 34. Why is the union of the two natures called a *hypostatical* or *personal* union?

A. Because the human nature is united to, and subsists in the person of the Son of God, Luke i. 35.

Q. 35. What is the difference between the hypostatical union, and the union that takes place among the persons of the adorable Trinity?

A. The union that takes place among the persons of the adorable Trinity, is a union of three persons in one and the same *numerical nature* and *essence;* but the hypostatical is a union of *two natures* in *one person*.

Q. 36. What is the difference between the hypostatical union, and the union that takes place between the soul and body?

A. Death dissolves the union that is between the soul and the body; but though the soul was separated from the body of Christ, when it was in the grave, yet both soul and body were, even then, united to the person of the Son as much as ever.

Q. 37. What is the difference between the hypostatical union, and the *mystical* union that is between Christ and believers?

A. Both natures in the hypostatical union are still but one person; whereas, though believers are said to be in Christ, and Christ in them, yet they are not *one person* with him.

Q. 38. Why was it requisite that our Redeemer should be [*man*?]

A. That being our *kinsman and blood relation*, the right of redemption might devolve upon him; and that he might be capable of obeying and suffering in our nature, Heb. ii. 14.*

Q. 39. Why was it requisite that our Mediator should be [*God?*]

A. That his obedience and sufferings in our nature and room, might be of infinite value for our redemption, Acts xx. 28; and that the human nature might be supported under the infinite load of divine wrath; which he had to bear for our sins, Rom. i. 4.†

Q. 40. "Why was it requisite that the Mediator should be God and man in one person?"

A. "That the proper works of each nature might be accepted of God for us, and relied on by us, as the works of the whole person, Heb. ix. 14. 1 Pet. ii. 6."‡

Q. 41. What may we learn from the indissoluble union of the two natures in the person of Christ?

A. That this union shall be an everlasting security for the *perpetuity* of the union between Christ and believers: that the one shall never be dissolved more than the other; for he has said, "Because I live ye shall live also," John xiv. 19.

QUEST. 22. *How did Christ, being the Son of God, become man?*

ANS. Christ, the Son of God, became man, by taking to himself a true body and a reasonable soul, being conceived by the power of the Holy Ghost, in the womb of the virgin Mary, and born of her, yet without sin.

Q. 1. Did Christ assume the *person* of a man?
A. No: he assumed the human nature, but not a human person, Heb. ii. 16.

Q. 2. Had ever the human nature of Christ a distinct personality of its own?
A. No: it never subsisted one moment by itself, Luke i. 35.

Q. 3. What is the reason that the human nature of Christ never subsisted by itself?
A. Because it was formed and assumed at once; for the moment the soul was united to the body, both soul and body subsisted in the person of the Son of God.

* Larger Cat. Q. 39.   † Ibid. Q. 38.   ‡ Ibid. Q. 40

Q. 4. How came the human nature to subsist in the person of the Son?

A. The whole Trinity adapted and fitted the human nature to him; but the *assumption* of it, into a personal subsistence with himself, was the peculiar act of the Son, Heb. ii. 14, 16.

Q. 5. Since the human nature of Christ has no personality of its own, is it not more imperfect than in other men, when all other men are human persons?

A. The human nature of Christ is so far from being imperfect, by the want of a personality of its own, that it is unspeakably more perfect and excellent than in all other men, because to *subsist in God*, or in a divine person, is incomparably more noble and excellent than to subsist by itself.

Q. 6. In what lies the matchless and peculiar dignity of the human nature of Christ?

A. That it subsists in the *second person* of the Godhead, by a personal and-indissoluble union.

Q. 7. What is the difference between the *human nature* and a *human person?*

A. A human person subsists by *itself;* but the human nature subsists *in a person.*

Q. 8. When Christ became man, did he become another *person* than he was before?

A. No: there was no change in his person; for he assumed our nature with his *former personality*, which he had from eternity.

Q. 9. What is the reason that the assumption of the human nature made no change in the divine person of the Son?

A. Because the human nature was assumed by Christ without a *human personality.*

Q. 10. Whether is it more proper to say, that the human nature subsists in the *divine nature*, or in the *divine person* of Christ?

A. It is more proper to say, that it subsists in the *divine person* of Christ, because the *natures* are DISTINCT, but the person is ONE; and it was the divine nature *only*, as it terminates in the *second person*, which assumed the human nature into personal union.

Q. 11. Can we not say, consistently with truth, that the *man Christ Jesus is God?*

A. We assuredly may; because in this case, we speak of the *person*, which includes the human nature.

Q. 12. But can we say, in consistency with truth, that Christ Jesus, *as man*, is God?

A. No: because in this case, we speak only of the *human nature*, which does not include his divine person.

Q. 13. What is the *human nature*, or in what does it consist?.

A. It consists in [*a true body and a reasonable soul*,] of which the first Adam, and every man and woman descending from him, are possessed.

Q. 14. Had our Redeemer *always* a true body and a reasonable soul, subsisting in his divine person?

A. No: until he came in the *fulness of time*, and then *took* to himself a true body and a reasonable soul.

Q. 15. How do you prove that he took this human nature to himself?

A. From Heb. ii. 14, 16: "Verily he took not on him the nature of angels; but he took on him the seed of Abraham."

Q. 16. Why is Christ said to take to himself a [*true body?*]

A. To show that he had real *flesh and bones*, as we have, Luke xxiv. 39; and that it was not, as some ancient heretics alleged, only the mere shape and appearance of a human body.

Q. 17. How does it appear that he had a true and real body, as other men have?

A. He is called *Man*, and the *Son of man*, Ps. lxxx. 27; he was conceived and born, Matt. i. 20, 25; he was subject to hunger, thirst, and weariness, like other men; he was crucified, dead, buried, and rose again: none of which could be affirmed of him, if he had not had a true body.

Q. 18. Had not he [*a reasonable soul*,] as well as a true body?

A. Yes: otherwise he had wanted the principal constituent part of the human nature: accordingly, we read, that his "soul was exceeding sorrowful, even unto death," Matt. xxvi. 38.

Q. 19. Why was not the human body created immediately out of *nothing*, or out of the *dust* of the earth, as Adam's body was?

A. Because, in that case, though he would have had a true body, yet it would not have been *akin* to us, *bone of our bone*, and *flesh of our flesh*.

Q. 20. Did Christ bring his human nature from *heaven* with him?

A. No; for he was the "seed of the woman," Gen. iii. 15.

Q. 21. How then is it said, 1 Cor. xv. 47, "The first man is of the earth, earthy; the second man, is the Lord from heaven?"

A. The plain meaning is, the *first man* had his origina. from the *earth*; but the *second man*, as to his divine nature, is the eternal, independent, and sovereign Lord of heaven and earth, equally with the Father; and as to his human nature, there was a more glorious concurrence of the adorable Trinity, in the formation of it, than in making of the *first Adam*.

Q. 22. What was the peculiar agency of each person of the adorable Trinity in this wonderful work?

A. The Father *prepares* a body, or human nature for him, Heb. x. 5; the Holy Ghost *forms* it, by his overshadowing power, out of the substance of the virgin, Luke i. 35; and the Son *assumes* the entire human nature to himself, Heb. ii. 14, 16.

Q. 23. Why was Christ born of a [*Virgin?*]

A. That the human nature might be found again in its primitive purity, and presented to God as spotless as it was at its creation, free from the contagion of original sin, which is conveyed to all Adam's posterity by natural generation.

Q. 24. Was it necessary that Christ should be [*conceived and born without sin?*]

A. It was absolutely necessary; both because the human nature was to subsist in union with the person of the Son of God, and likewise because it was to be a sacrifice for sin, and therefore behoved to be *without blemish*, Heb. vii. 26.

Q. 25. What benefit or advantage accrues to us by the spotless holiness of the human nature of Christ?

A. The spotless holiness of his human nature is imputed to us as a part of his righteousness, 1 Cor. i. 30; and it is a sure earnest of our perfect sanctification at last, Col. ii. 9, 10.

Q. 26. Was not the [*virgin Mary,*] the mother of our Lord, a sinner as well as others?

A. Yes; for she descended from Adam by ordinary generation; Christ rebuked her for going beyond her sphere, John ii. 4; and she needed a Saviour as much as others; and believed in him for salvation from sin, Luke i. 47.

Q. 27. What necessarily follows upon the union of the two natures?

A. A communication of the properties of each nature to the whole person.

Q. 28. How does the scripture apply this communication of properties to his person.

A. By ascribing *that* to his person, which properly belongs to one of his natures.

Q. 29. How is this illustrated in scripture?

A. It is illustrated thus: though it was only the human nature that suffered, yet God is said to purchase his church with *his own blood*, Acts xx. 28; and though it was only the human nature that ascended to heaven, yet, by reason of the personal union, God is said to go up *with a shout* Ps. xlvii. 5.

Q. 30. Can an *imaginary idea* of Christ, *as man*, be any way helpful to the faith of his being *God-man?*

A. So far is it from being any way *helpful*, that it is every way *hurtful;* because it diverts the mind from the *object* of *faith* to an *object* of *sense;* by means of which we cannot believe any truth whatever, divine or human; all faith being founded solely and entirely upon a testimony.

Q. 31. How then is the person of Christ, God-man, to be conceived of?

A. It can be conceived of no other way, than by faith and spiritual understanding; or, by "*the Spirit* of wisdom and revelation in the knowledge of him," Eph. i. 17.

Q. 32. What *improvement* ought we to make of Christ's incarnation?

A. To claim him as our own, in virtue of his wearing our nature, saying, "Unto us a Child is born, unto us a Son is given," Isa. ix. 6; or, which is the same thing, to follow the practice of Ruth, in lying down at the feet of our blessed Boaz, saying, *Spread thy skirt over me;* that is, take me, a poor bankrupt sinner, into a marriage relation with thee, "for thou art my near kinsman," Ruth iii. 9.

QUEST. 23. *What offices does Christ execute as our Redeemer?*

ANS. Christ, as our Redeemer, executes the offices of a prophet, of a priest, and of a king, both in his estate of humiliation and exaltation.

Q. 1. What is the *general office* of Christ, which respects the whole of his undertaking, and runs through the whole of the covenant made with him?

A. It is his being the *only Mediator* between God and man, 1 Tim. ii. 5: "There is one God, and one Mediator between God and men, the man Christ Jesus."

Q. 2. What does the office of a *Mediator* between God and men suppose?

A. It supposes a *breach* between them, occasioned by sin on man's part, Isa. lix. 2.

Q. 3. Could a mere verbal intercession make up this breach?

A. By no means; nothing less than a full reparation for all the damages which sin had done to the honour of God and his law, could do it away Isa. liii. 10.

Q. 4. Was none but Christ fit for being Mediator in this respect?

A. None else: because there was no other who stood related to the *two families* of heaven and earth, which were at variance, in such a manner as he did.

Q. 5. How did he stand related to these two families?

A. By being, from eternity, God equal with the Father, he stood *naturally* and *essentially* related to *heaven*, John x. 30; and by consenting to become man, he stood *voluntarily* and *freely* related to *earth*, Phil. ii. 6, 7.

Q. 6. What are the branches of Christ's mediatory office; or the *particular offices* included in it?

A. They are *three;* namely, his office of a [*Prophet,*] Deut. xviii. 15; of a [*Priest,*] Ps. cx. 4; and of a [*King,*] Ps. ii. 6.

Q. 7. Have each of these offices the *same relation* to the *covenant* of which he is the Mediator.

A. His *priestly* office, as to the *sacrificing* part of it, respecting the condition of the covenant, belongs to the MAKING of it; but his *prophetical* and *kingly* offices, with the intercessory part of his priestly office, respecting the promises of the covenant, belong to the ADMINISTRATION of it.

Q. 8. What respect have these offices to our misery by sin?

A. The prophetical office respects our ignorance; the priestly office our guilt; and the kingly office our pollution or defilement.

Q. 9. What is Christ *made of God to us*, in virtue of these offices, for the removal of these miseries?

A. As a Prophet, he is made of God to us *wisdom;* as a Priest, *righteousness;* and as a King, *sanctification;* and as vested with ALL these offices, he is made of God to us complete *redemption*, 1 Cor. i. 30.

Q. 10. Was he *ordained* or appointed to these offices?

A. Yes, from all eternity; 1 Pet. i. 20: "Who, verily, was foreordained before the foundation of the world."

Q. 11. What were the necessary consequences of this eternal designation?

A. His *mission* and *call*.

Q. 12. In what consisted his *mission?*

A. In his being promised, Isa. vii. 14, and typified under the Old Testament, John iii. 14; and in his being actually sent, in the fulness of time, to assume our nature, and finish the work which was given him to do, Gal. iv. 4, 5.

Q. 13. Was he formally *called* to his mediatory office?

A. Yes: he did nöt take *this honour unto himself*, but was *called of God, as was Aaron*, Heb. v. 4, 5.

Q. 14. Of what parts did his call consist?

A. Of his *unction* and *inauguration*.

OF CHRIST'S OFFICES IN GENERAL.

Q. 15. What do you understand by his *unction*?

A. The consecration of him to all his mediatory offices, John x. 36; and the giving of the Spirit, with all his gifts and graces, without measure to him, that he might be fully furnished for the execution of these offices, John iii. 34.

Q. 16. In which nature is Christ anointed with the Spirit?

A. The *person* of Christ was anointed in the *human nature*, which was the immediate *receptacle* of all gifts and graces, Ps. lxviii. 18:—" Thou hast received gifts for men :" Margin, *in the man;* that is, in the human nature.

Q. 17. When was he *inaugurated* into his mediatory offices?

A. Although, in virtue of his assuming the human nature, he was *born* to the execution of them, yet he was not solemnly *installed* into the public exercise of these offices, till his *baptism.*

Q. 18. What was the solemnity of his *inauguration* or *instalment* at that time?

A. "The heavens were opened, the Spirit of God *descended* like a dove, and *lighted* upon him: and lo, a voice from heaven, saying, This is my beloved Son, in whom I am well pleased," Matt. iii. 16, 17.

Q. 19. Why was Christ vested with this threefold office?

A. The nature of our salvation required that it should be *revealed* by him as a *Prophet; purchased* by him as a *Priest;* and *applied* by him as a *King.*

Q. 20. Did ever all these offices centre in any ONE person except *Christ alone?*

A. No; for, in order to set forth the vast importance of these offices, as united in the person of Christ, none of those who were typical of him under the Old Testament were ever clothed with *all the three:* this honour was reserved for himself, as his peculiar dignity and prerogative; John xiv. 6: "I am the way, and the truth, and the life;" that is, the WAY in my *death*, as a *Priest;* the TRUTH in my *word*, as a *Prophet;* and the LIFE in my Spirit, as a *King.*

Q. 21. In what states does Christ execute all these offices?

A. [*Both in his estate of humiliation*] on *earth*, and in his state of [*exaltation*] in *heaven.*

Q. 22. What do you understand by Christ's *executing* of his offices?

A. His doing or fulfilling what was incumbent upon him, in virtue of each of these offices, Matt. iii. 15.

Q. 23. Are the offices of Christ the *proper fountain* from whence the promises flow?

A. No: the proper fountain and spring of all the pro-

OF CHRIST'S OFFICES IN GENERAL.

mises, is the *sovereign will* and *good pleasure* of God: hence the *sovereign will* of God is set in the *front* of all the promises,—I WILL *put my law in their inward parts, and* I WILL *be their* God; I WILL *forgive their iniquity; and* I WILL *remember their sin no more,* Jer. xxxi. 33, 34; "I WILL take away the stony heart out of your flesh; and I will give you a heart of flesh," &c. Ezek. xxxvi. 26, 27.

Q. 24. What connexion then have the promises with the offices of Christ?

A. They are *revealed* to us by Christ as a *Prophet,* Heb. i. 2; *confirmed* by his blood, as a *Priest,* Heb. ix. 16; and effectually *applied* by his power, as a *King,* Ps. cx. 3.

Q. 25. Is the *order* in which the offices of Christ are *here* laid down, the very order in which they are *executed?*

A. Yes: for it is the order laid down in scripture, 1 Cor. i. 30.

Q. 26. By whom is this order *inverted?*

A. By the Arminians and other legalists, who make Christ's *kingly* office the *first* which he executes, in the application of redemption.

Q. 27. How do they make Christ's kingly office the *first* which he executes?

A. By alleging that Christ, as a King, has, in the gospel, given out a *new preceptive law,* of *faith* and *repentance,* by obedience to which we come to be entitled to Christ and his righteousness.

Q. 28. What is the *danger* of this scheme of doctrine?

A. It confounds the *law* and *gospel;* and brings *works* into the *matter* and *cause* of a sinner's justification before God, contrary to Rom. v. 19, and Gal. ii. 16.

Q. 29. When faith closes with Christ, does it not close with him in *all* his offices?

A. Yes; for Christ is never divided: we must have him *wholly* or *none* of him, John viii. 24.

Q. 30. Which of his offices does faith act upon for *justification?*

A. Upon his *priestly office* only: for the great thing a *guilty* sinner wants is *righteousness,* to answer the charge of the law; and the enlightened sinner sees that Christ, in his priestly office, is "the end of the law for righteousness," Rom. x. 4.

Q. 31. What may we learn for encouragement from Christ's being clothed with this three-fold office?

A. That since all these offices have a *relation* to us, we may warrantably employ him in every one of them; that in like manner as he is *made over* of God *unto us,* so we may actually have him for our "wisdom, righteousness, sanctification, and redemption," 1 Cor. i. 30.

QUEST. 24. *How does Christ execute the office of a Prophet?*

ANS. Christ executes the office of a Prophet, in revealing to us, by his word and Spirit, the will of God for our salvation.

Q. 1. Is Christ expressly called a [*Prophet*] in scripture?
A. Yes: as in Acts iii. 22; where Peter applies the words of Moses to him, "a prophet shall the Lord your God raise up unto you, of your brethren, like unto me," &c.

Q. 2. Why does he bear this name?
A. Because he has made a full revelation of the whole counsel of God, concerning the salvation of lost sinners of mankind, John xv. 15.

Q. 3. By what *other names* is Christ described, with relation to this office?
A. By the names of an *Apostle*, Heb. iii. 1; of a *Witness*, Isa. lv. 4; and of an *Interpreter*, Job xxxiii. 23.

Q. 4. Why is he called an *Apostle?*
A. Because he is the great *Ambassador* of Heaven, sent to declare the will of God to men, John iii. 34; hence called the Messenger of the covenant, Mal. iii. 1.

Q. 5. Why called a *Witness?*
A. Because being a son of Adam, Luke iii. 38, he was the more fit to attest the will of God to men; and being the eternal Son of God, was therefore liable to no error or mistake in his testimony: hence called the Amen, the faithful and true Witness, Rev. iii. 14.

Q. 6. Why is he called an *Interpreter?*
A. Because the mystery of godliness lies so far beyond the reach of our natural understanding, that we could never savingly comprehend it, unless "the Son of God gave us an understanding, that we may know him that is true," 1 John v. 20.

Q. 7. What was the *necessity* of his bearing this office of a Prophet?
A. Because there could be no knowledge of the things of the Spirit of God, without a revelation of them, 1 Cor. ii. 14; and there could be no revelation of these things, but through Christ, John i. 18.

Q. 8. By what *means* does Christ reveal to us the will of God?
A. He reveals it to us outwardly [*by his word,*] and inwardly, by his [*Spirit,*] 1 Pet. i. 11, 12.

Q. 9. To whom does he reveal the will of God outwardly in his word?

A. To his church, which, on this account, is called *the valley of vision*, Isa. xxii. 1.

Q. 10. Did he reveal the will of God to his church under the Old Testament?

A. Yes; for the Spirit of Christ was in the Old Testament prophets, 1 Pet. i. 11; he is said, in the days of Noah, to have preached unto the spirits [*now*] in prison, 1 Pet. iii. 19; and " to have spoken with Moses on Mount Sinai," Acts vii. 38.

Q. 11. Does he still continue, under the New Testament, to be the prophet and teacher of the church?

A. Yes; and is therefore said to speak from heaven, in his word and ordinances, Heb. xii. 25: "See that ye refuse not him that speaketh; for, if they escaped not, who refused him that spake on earth, much more shall not we escape, if we turn away from him that speaketh from heaven."

Q. 12. In what *manner* did he reveal the will of God under both Testaments?

A. Both *immediately*, in his own person; and *mediately*, by the intervention of others.

Q. 13. How did he reveal the will of God *immediately* in his own person?

A. By voices, visions, dreams, and *divers* other *manners*, under the Old Testament, Heb. i. 1: and by his own *personal ministry*, while here on earth, under the New, Heb. ii. 3.

Q. 14. How does he reveal the will of God *mediately*, or by the intervention of others?

A. By inspiring the prophets under the Old Testament, and his apostles under the New, to speak and write "as they were moved by the Holy Ghost," 2 Pet. i. 21; and by commissioning ordinary pastors to teach *all things whatsoever* he has *commanded*; and in so doing, promising to be with them, "alway, even unto the end of the world," Matt. xxviii. 20.

Q. 15. Wherein does Christ *excel* all other prophets and teachers whatsoever, whether ordinary or extraordinary?

A. They were all commissioned by him as the *original Prophet*, Eph. iv. 11: none of them had ever any gifts or furniture, except what they received from him, John xx. 22; and none of them could ever teach with such authority, power, and efficacy, as he does, John vii. 46.

Q. 16. What will become of those who will not hear this prophet?

A. "They shall be destroyed from among the people," Acts iii. 23.

Q. 17. May not a people enjoy a faithful ministry, have the word purely preached to them, and yet not profit by it?

A. Doubtless they may; as was the case of many of the Jews in Isaiah's time, Isa. liii. 1; and of Chorazin and Bethsaida, under the ministry of Christ himself, Matt. xi. 21.

Q. 18. What is the reason why the word purely preached does not always profit?

A. Because "it is not" always "mixed with faith in them that hear it," Heb. iv. 2.

Q. 19. What commonly follows upon people's not profiting by the word preached?

A. The word of the Lord *slays* them, Hos. vi. 5; and proves *the savour of death unto death* to them, 2 Cor. ii. 16.

Q. 20. Seeing the external dispensation of the word has so little influence upon the generality, what else is necessary to make it effectual?

A. The *inward* teaching of Christ by his *Spirit*, John vi. 63, and xiv. 26.

Q. 21. How does this great prophet teach *inwardly* by his Spirit?

A. He opens the understanding, and makes the *entrance* of his *words* to give such *light*, Ps. cxix. 130, that the soul is made to see a divine beauty and glory in the gospel-method of salvation, 1 Cor. ii. 10—12, and powerfully inclined to fall in with it, 1 Tim. i. 15.

Q. 22. Does Christ, as a prophet, make *all welcome* to come and be taught by him?

A. Yes; for, in the outward dispensation of the gospel, he opens the door to every man and woman, saying, "Come unto me—and learn of me, for I am meek and lowly in heart," Matt. xi. 28, 29.

Q. 23. At what *schools* does Christ, as a prophet, train up his *disciples?*

A. At the *school* of the *law*, the *school* of the *gospel*, and the *school* of *affliction*.

Q. 24. What does he teach them at the *school* of the *law?*

A. The nature and desert of sin; that by it they are "without Christ—having no hope, and without God in the world," Eph. ii. 12.

Q. 25. What does he teach them at the *school* of the *gospel?*

A. That he himself is the great doer of all for them, and in them, Mark x. 51; and that their business is to "take the cup of salvation, and call upon the name of the Lord," Ps. cxvi. 13.

Q. 26. What does he teach them at the *school* of *affliction?*

A. To justify God, Ezra ix. 13; to set their affections on things above, 2 Cor. iv. 17, 18; and to pray that their affliction may be rather sanctified, than removed without being so, Isa. xxvii. 9.

Q. 27. How may persons know if they have *profited* under this great Prophet and Teacher?

A. Such will *follow on to know* him more and more, Hos. vi. 3: they will delight in his company, Ps. xxvii. 4; grieve at his absence, Job xxiii. 3; and hide his word in their heart, Ps. cxix. 11.

QUEST. 25. *How does Christ execute the office of a Priest?*

ANS. Christ executes the office of a Priest, in his once offering up himself a sacrifice, to satisfy divine justice, and reconcile us to God; and in making continual intercession for us.

Q. 1. What do you understand by a [*priest?*]

A. A *priest* is a public person, who in the name of the guilty deals with an offended God, for reconciliation, by sacrifice, which he offers to God upon an altar, being thereto called of God, that he may be accepted, Heb. v. 1, 4.

Q. 2. What was the great event which the *priesthood* under the law, especially the office of *high priest,* typified and pointed at?

A. It was Christ's becoming a high priest, to appear before God, in the name of sinners, to make atonement and reconciliation for them, Heb. viii. 1—3.

Q. 3. Of whom was the high priest *a representative,* when bearing the names of the children of Israel upon his shoulders, and in the breast plate? Ex. xxviii. 12, 29.

A. He was the representative of all Israel; and so an illustrious type of Christ, as the representative of a whole elect world, Isa. xlix. 3.

Q. 4. Were not the ordinary priests, as well as the high priest, *types* of Christ?

A. Yes; because though the high priest was a more eminent type of him, yet the apostle, Heb. x. 11, 12, compares every priest, who offered sacrifices, with Christ, as a type with the antitype.

Q. 5. In what respect did Christ excel the priests after the *order of Aaron?*

A. In his person, manner of instalment, and in the efficacy and perfection of his sacrifice.

Q. 6. How does he excel them in his *person?*

A. They were only *mere men,* He, "the true God, and

eternal life," 1 John v. 20; they were *sinful* men, He "is holy, harmless, undefiled, and separate from sinners," Heb. vii. 26.

Q. 7. How did he excel them in the manner of his instalment?

A. "Those priests were made without an oath; but this with an oath, by him that said unto him, The Lord sware, and will not repent, Thou art a Priest for ever after the order of Melchizedek," Heb. vii. 21.

Q. 8. Why was Christ made a Priest with the solemnity of an *oath?*

A. Because, as the weight of the salvation of sinners lay upon his *call* to *this* office, so his Father's solemn investing of him in it by an oath, gave him access to offer himself *effectually,* even in such sort, as to fulfil the condition of the covenant, and thus to purchase eternal life for them, Heb. ix. 12.

Q. 9. In what respect did Christ excel the *Aaronical priests* in the *efficacy* and *perfection* of his sacrifice?

A. "It is not possible that the blood of bulls and of goats should take away sins:—But this man, after he had offered one sacrifice for sins, for ever sat down on the right hand of God," Heb. x. 4, 12.

Q. 10. After what order was Christ a priest?

A. After the order of Melchizedek, Ps. cx. 4.

Q. 11. What was the order of Melchizedek?

A. That being "made like unto the Son of God, *he* abideth a priest continually," Heb. vii. 3.

Q. 12. How could Melchizedek abide a priest continually, when he certainly died like other men?

A. The meaning is, he came not to his office by succession to any who went before him, and none succeeded him after his death.

Q. 13. Why then is Christ called a priest after the order of Melchizedek?

A. Because not succeeding to, or being succeeded by any other in his office, but "continuing ever, he hath an unchangeable priesthood;" *being made a priest,* "not after the law of a carnal commandment, but after the power of an endless life," Heb. vii. 16, 24.

Q. 14. What are the *parts* of Christ's priestly office?

A. His *satisfaction* on earth, Heb. xiii. 12, and his *intercession* in heaven, 1 John ii. 1.

Q. 15. Why behoved his satisfaction to be made upon *earth?*

A. Because this earth being the *theatre* of rebellion, where God's law was violated, and his authority trampled upon, it was meet that satisfaction should be made, where the offence was committed; hence, says Christ, John xvii. 4, *I have glorified thee on the earth.*

OF CHRIST AS A PRIEST.

Q. 16. How did Christ make satisfaction on the earth?
A. By sacrifice, 1 Cor. v. 7: "Even Christ our passover is sacrificed for us."

Q. 17. What was the [*sacrifice*] which he offered?
A. It was [*Himself*] Heb. ix. 26: "He appeared to put away sin by the sacrifice of himself."

Q. 18. What was essentially necessary to every sacrifice?
A. The shedding of blood unto death, Heb. ix. 22: 'Without shedding of blood is no remission."

Q. 19. Which of the two natures was the sacrifice?
A. The human nature, soul and body, Isa. liii. 10, Heb. x. 10, which were actually separated by death, John xix. 30.

Q. 20. What was necessary to the *acceptance* of every slain sacrifice?
A. That it be offered on such an altar as should sanctify the gift to its necessary value, and designed effect, Matt. xxiii. 19: "Whether is greater the gift, or the altar that sanctifieth the gift?"

Q. 21. What was the altar on which the sacrifice of the human nature was offered?
A. It was the divine nature.

Q. 22. How did this altar *sanctify the gift?*
A. It gave to it an infinite value and efficacy, because of the personal union, Heb. ix. 14.

Q. 23. Was Christ a sacrifice *only* while *on the cross?*
A. In the first moment of his incarnation, the sacrifice was laid on the altar, Heb. x. 5; *continued* thereon through the whole of his life, Isa. liii. 3; and was *completed* on the cross, and in the grave, John xix. 30. Isa. liii. 9.

Q. 24. Was there a necessity for a priest to offer this sacrifice?
A. Yes, surely; because a priest and sacrifice being inseparable, without a priest there could be no sacrifice at all to be accepted, and consequently no removal of sin, Heb. viii. 3.

Q. 25. Who was the *priest?*
A. As Christ himself was both the sacrifice and the altar, none else but himself could be the *priest*, Heb. v. 5.

Q. 26. Did Christ truly and properly offer himself a sacrifice, not for our good only, but in our room and stead?
A. Yes; as is evident from all those scriptures where Christ is said to have borne our sins, 1 Pet. ii. 24, to have died for us, Rom. v. 6, and to have redeemed us by his blood, Rev. v. 19.

Q. 27. How often did Christ offer up himself a sacrifice?
A. [ONCE] only, Heb. ix. 28, "Christ was ONCE offered to bear the sins of many."

Q. 28. Why could not this sacrifice be repeated?

A. Because as once dying was the penalty of the law, so once suffering unto death was the complete payment of it, in regard of the infinite dignity of the *sufferer*, Heb. ix. 27, 28.

Q. 29. For what *end* did Christ once offer up himself a sacrifice?

A. [*To satisfy divine justice*,] 1 Pet. iii. 18.

Q. 30. Was satisfaction to justice absolutely necessary?

A. Yes: since God freely purposed to save some of mankind, it was absolutely necessary that it should be done consistently with the honour of justice, Exod. xxxiv. 7.

Q. 31. What did the honour of justice require as a satisfaction?

A. That the *curse* of the broken law be fully executed, either upon the sinners themselves, Ezek. xviii. 4, or upon a sufficient substitute, Ps. lxxxix. 19.

Q. 32. What would have been the *effect* of executing the curse upon the *sinners themselves?*

A. The fire of divine wrath would have burned continually upon them, and yet there would be no satisfaction to avenging justice, Isa. xxxiii. 14.

Q. 33. Why could not avenging justice be ever satisfied?

A. Because they were not only *finite* creatures, whose most exquisite sufferings could never be a sufficient compensation for the injured honour of an *infinite* God; but they were *sinful* creatures likewise, who would still have remained sinful, even under their eternal sufferings, Rev. xiv. 11.

Q. 34. How could satisfaction be demanded from Christ, who was perfectly holy and innocent?

A. He voluntarily substituted himself in the room of sinners, Ps. xl. 7; their sins were imputed to him, Isa. liii. 5, 6; he had full power to dispose of his own life, John x. 18; and therefore it was most just to exact the full payment of him.

Q. 35. Has Christ *fully* and *perfectly* satisfied divine justice?

A. Yes; his "offering and sacrifice to God was for a sweet-smelling savour," Eph. v. 2; or a *savour of rest*, as it is said of Noah's typical sacrifice, Gen. viii. 21, margin.

Q. 36. Why is his sacrifice said to be for a sweet-smelling savour, or savour of rest?

A. Because it quite overcame the abominable savour arising from sin, and gave the avenging justice and wrath of God the calmest and profoundest rest.

Q. 37. How do you prove that Christ has *perfectly satisfied* the justice of God?
A. He said, "It is finished," John xix. 30; and evidenced that it was really so, by his *resurrection* from the dead, Rom. i. 4.

Q. 38. *For whom* did Christ satisfy justice?
A. For the *elect only*, John x. 15; and not for all mankind, Eph. v. 25.

Q. 39. How is it evident that Christ *satisfied* for the *elect only*, and not for all mankind?
A. From the satisfaction and intercession of Christ being of equal extent, so that the one reaches no further than the other; and he expressly affirms, that he intercedes for the elect only, and not for the whole world of mankind, John xvii. 9: "I pray not for the world, but for them which thou hast given me."

Q. 40. What is the blessed effect and consequence of Christ's perfectly satisfying the justice of God?
A. It is the *reconciling* us to God, Rom. v. 10.

Q. 41. How does the satisfaction of Christ [*reconcile us to God?*]
A. It discovers the *love* of God, in providing such a *ransom* for us; and this love, apprehended by faith, slays the natural enmity against God, 1 John iv. 10, 19.

Q. 42. When is it that the elect are actually reconciled to God?
A. When, in a day of power, they are determined to come to "Jesus the Mediator of the new covenant, and to the blood of sprinkling," Heb. xii. 24.

Q. 43. Why is the blood of *Jesus* called the *blood* of *sprinkling?*
A. To distinguish between the *shedding* and the application of his blood, Exod. xxiv. 8; and also to point out the necessity of the one, as well as the other, for reconciliation and pardon, Ezek. xxxvi. 25.

Q. 44. How may we know if we are reconciled to God?
A. If we are dead to the law as a covenant, Rom. vii. 4; and are content to be eternal debtors to rich and sovereign grace, Ps. cxv. 1.

Q. 45. What may we learn from the first part of Christ's priestly office, his satisfaction for sin?
A. The exceeding sinfulness of sin, Rom. vii. 13; the infinite love of God, John iii. 16; and the necessity of an interest in this satisfaction, Heb. x. 29.

Q. 46. What is the SECOND PART of Christ's priestly office?
A. It is his [*making continual intercession for us,*] Heb. vii. 25.

Q. 47. Had Christ's intercession any place in the making of a new covenant?

A. No: the love and grace of God made the motion for a new covenant freely, Ps. lxxxix. 3, 20.

Q. 48. Could the breach between God and sinners be made up by a simple intercession?

A. No: justice could not be satisfied with pleading, but by paying a ransom, Heb. ix. 22.

Q. 49. To what part of the covenant then does Christ's intercession belong?

A. As his *sacrificing* natively took its place in the *making*, and fulfilling the *condition* of, the covenant, so his *intercession* belongs to the *administration* of the covenant, and fulfilling the promises of it, Rom. viii. 34.

Q. 50. What occasion was there for an intercessor, or advocate with the Father, when the Father himself loveth us? John xvi. 27.

A. That through Christ's obedience unto death, as the honourable channel, his spiritual seed might have the blessed fruits and effects of the Father's everlasting love, flowing into their souls, in every time of need, Heb. iv. 14, 16.

Q. 51. What is the nature of Christ's intercession?

A. It is his WILLING, that the merit of his sacrifice be applied to all those in whose room and stead he died, according to the method laid down in the covenant in their favour, John xvii. 24—"Father, I WILL, that they whom thou hast given me, be with me, where I am," &c.

Q. 52. Who then are the *objects* of his intercession?

A. Those only whom he, as the second Adam, represented in the eternal transaction, John xvii. 9.

Q. 53. Is his intercession always prevalent on their behalf?

A. Yes, surely: for so he himself testifies, saying unto his Father, John xi. 42—"I know that thou hearest me always."

Q. 54. What is the first fruit of Christ's intercession with respect to the elect?

A. His effectually procuring the actual *in-bringing* of them into a covenant state of peace and favour with God at the time appointed, John xvii. 20, 21.

Q. 55. *Whence* is it that the intercession of Christ obtains peace between heaven and earth?

A. Because he purchased it for them by the blood of his sacrifice, Col. i. 20; and it was promised to him on that ground, Isa. liv. 13.

Q. 56. What does he by his intercession, in *consequence* of their being brought into a *covenant state?*

A. He appears for them; and, in their name, takes possession of heaven, and all the other blessings they have a right to, in virtue of that *covenant state*, Eph. ii. 6. Heb. vi. 20.

OF CHRIST AS A PRIEST. 135

Q. 57. Having brought the elect into a *state of peace*, does he leave it to themselves to maintain it?

A. No: if that were the case it would soon be at an end; but, by his intercession, he always prevents a rupture between heaven and them, Luke xxii. 32:—"I have prayed for thee, that thy faith fail not."

Q. 58. How does he maintain the peace between heaven and them?

A. Upon the ground of his satisfaction for them, he answers all accusations against them, and takes up all emerging differences between them and their covenanted God, 1 John ii. 1, 2.

Q. 59. Are not the saints on earth, being sinful, unfit to come into the presence of the King?

A. Yes; but the glorious *Advocate* introduces them, procuring them *access* by his interest in the court; "For through him we have an access, by one Spirit, unto the Father," Eph. ii. 18.

Q. 60. How are their prayers acceptable to God, when attended with so many blemishes?

A. Their *prayers* made in faith, though infected with the remains of corruption, yet being perfumed with the *incense* of his merit, are accepted in heaven, and have gracious returns made them, Rev. viii. 3.

Q. 61. What is the *last fruit* of Christ's intercession, on behalf of his elect, brought into a state of grace on this earth?

A. The obtaining their admittance into heaven, in due time; and continuing their state of perfect happiness there, for ever and ever, John xvii. 24.

Q. 62. Is not Christ a *Priest* for ever, according to Ps. cx. 4?

A. He is not a sacrificing priest for ever, "having, by one offering, perfected for ever them that are sanctified," Heb. x. 14; but he is, and ever will be, an interceding priest, Heb. vii. 27—" He ever liveth to make intercession."

Q. 63. What will be the *subject* of his intercession for ever, in behalf of the saints in heaven?

A. The everlasting *continuance* of their happy state, John xvii. 21, 22.

Q. 64. What is the *ground* of his *eternally willing* the everlasting *continuance* of their happy state?

A. He does it on the ground of the *eternal redemption* obtained for them, by the sacrificing of himself on this earth, Heb. ix. 12.

Q. 65. What then is the *everlasting security* that the saints in heaven have, for the uninterrupted continuance of their happiness?

A. That the infinite merit of Christ's sacrifice will be eternally presented before God in heaven itself, where, in their nature, he continually appears in the presence of God for them, Heb. ix. 24.

Q. 66. How will the happiness, issuing from the merit of Christ's sacrifice, *be communicated by him*, to the saints in heaven?

A. It will be communicated to them, by him, as their *Prophet* and their *King*.

Q. 67. Will not these offices be *laid aside* in heaven?

A. No; for as he is a Priest for ever, Ps. cx. 4, so of his kingdom there shall be no end, Luke i. 33; and the Lamb will be the light of the heavenly city, Rev. xxi. 23.

Q. 68. How will the saints' communion with God in heaven be for ever maintained?

A. It will be still in and through the Mediator, in a manner agreeable to their state of perfection, Rev. vii. 17— "The Lamb, which is in the midst of the throne, shall feed them, and shall lead them to living fountains of water."

Q. 69. What is the *difference* between the intercession of *Christ*, and the intercession of the *Spirit*, mentioned Rom. viii. 26?

A. Christ intercedes *without* us, by presenting the merit of his oblation for us, Heb. xii. 24; but the SPIRIT intercedes *within* us, by bringing the promise to our remembrance, John xiv. 26, and enabling us to importune a faithful God, to *do* as he has *said*, and not to let him go, except he bless us, Gen. xxxii. 26.

Q. 70. Are there any other *intercessors* for us in heaven *besides* Christ?

A. None at all: for there is only " one Mediator between God and men, the man Christ Jesus," 1 Tim. ii. 5. He who is the only "Advocate with the Father, is Jesus Christ, the righteous," 1 John ii. 1.

Q. 71. May we not apply to *saints* or angels to intercede for us, as the Papists do?

A. By no means; this would be gross idolatry: besides, they have no merit to plead, Rev. xxii. 9; nor do they know our cases and wants, Isa. lxiii. 16.

Q. 72. What may we learn from Christ's intercession?

A. That though the believer has nothing to pay for managing his cause at the court of heaven, yet it is impossible it can miscarry, seeing the *Advocate* is faithfulness itself, Rev. iii. 14; and pleads for nothing but what he has merited by his blood, John xvii. 4.

QUEST. 26. *How does Christ execute the office of a King?*

ANS. Christ executes the office of a King, in subduing

us to himself, in ruling and defending us, and in restraining and conquering all his and our enemies.

Q. 1. How does it appear that CHRIST is a KING?
A. From his Father's testimony, Ps. ii. 6, and his own, John xviii. 36, concerning this matter.

Q. 2. When was he *ordained* or *appointed* to his kingdom?
A. He " was set up from everlasting," Prov. viii. 23.

Q. 3. When was he publicly *proclaimed*?
A. At his birth, Matt. ii. 2, and at his death, John xix. 19.

Q. 4. Did he not actually exercise his kingly power before that time?
A. Yes: he commenced the exercise of his kingly power ever after the *first promise*, of his bruising the head of the serpent, Gen. iii. 15.

Q. 5. When was he solemnly *inaugurated* into his kingly office?
A. When he ascended, and " sat down on the right hand of the Majesty on high," Heb. i. 3.

Q. 6. Where stands the *throne* of this great Potentate?
A. His throne of glory is in heaven, Rev. vii. 17; his throne of grace is in the church, Heb. iv. 16; and his throne of judgment is to be erected in the ærial heavens at his second coming, 1 Thess. iv. 17.

Q. 7. What *sceptre* does he sway?
A. He has a *twofold sceptre:* one by which he gathers and governs his subjects, Ps. cx. 2; another by which he dashes his enemies in pieces like a potter's vessel, Ps. ii. 9.

Q. 8. What is that *sceptre* by which Christ gathers and governs his subjects?
A. It is the gospel of the grace of God, accompanied with the power of his Spirit, therefore called the *rod of his strength*, Ps. cx. 2.

Q. 9. What is that *rod of iron* by which he dashes his enemies in pieces?
A. It is the *power* of his *anger*, of which no finite creature can know the uttermost, Ps. xc. 11.

Q. 10. What *armies* does this King command and lead?
A. His name is the *Lord of hosts*, and all the armies in heaven, whether saints or angels, follow him as upon *white horses*, Rev. xix. 14.

Q. 11. What *other* armies does he command?
A. The devils in hell are the executioners of his wrath against the wicked of the world, who will not have him to rule over them: yea, he can levy armies of *lice, frogs, caterpillars, locusts*, to avenge his quarrel, as in the plagues of Egypt.

Q. 12. What *tribute* is paid to this mighty King?

OF CHRIST AS A KING.

A. He has the continual tribute of praise, honour, and glory paid him, by saints in the church militant, Ps. lxv. 1; and by both saints and angels in the church triumphant, Rev. v. 9, 13.

Q. 13. Does he levy a tribute also from among his *enemies*?

A. Yes; for the *wrath of man* shall praise him on this earth, Ps. lxxvi. 10; and he will, hereafter, erect monuments of praise to his justice, in their eternal destruction, Rom. ix. 22.

Q. 14. Who are the *ambassadors* of this king?

A. He has sometimes employed angels upon some particular embassies, Luke ii. 10: but because these are apt to terrify sinners of mankind, therefore, he ordinarily employs men of the same mould with themselves, even ministers of the gospel, whom he commissions and calls to that office, 2 Cor. xv. 18, 19.

Q. 15. May any man intrude himself into the office of an ambassador of Christ?

A. No man may lawfully take "this honour to himself, but he that is called of God, as was Aaron," Heb. v. 4.

Q. 16. What shall we think then of those who intrude themselves, or are intruded into the ministry, without a scriptural call?

A. Christ declares them to be thieves and robbers, or at best but hirelings, John x. 8, 12; that "they shall not profit the people at all, because he never sent them," Jer. xxxiii. 32; and that the leaders, and they that are led by them, shall both fall into the ditch, Matt. xv. 14.

Q. 17. How *many fold* is Christ's kingdom?

A. It is *twofold;* his *essential* and his *mediatorial* kingdom.

Q. 18. What is his *essential* kingdom?

A. It is that absolute and supreme power, which he has over all the creatures in heaven and earth, *essentially* and *naturally*, as God equal with the Father, Ps. ciii. 19 : "His kingdom ruleth over all."

Q. 19. What is his mediatorial kingdom?

A. It is that sovereign power and authority in and over the *church*, which is given him as Mediator, Eph. i. 22.

Q. 20. What is the nature of his mediatorial kingdom?

A. It is entirely spiritual, and not of this world, John xvii. 36.

Q. 21. Does the civil magistrate, then, hold his office of Christ as Mediator?

A. No: but of him as *God Creator*, otherwise all civil magistrates, Heathen, as well as Christian, would be church officers; which would be grossly Erastian.

Q. 22. What are the ACTS of Christ's kingly power?

A. They are such as have either a respect to his *elect*

people, John i. 49; or such as have a respect to his and their enemies, Ps. cx. 2.

Q. 23. What are the acts of his kingly administration, which have a respect to his *elect people?*

A. They are his [*subduing*] them [*to himself*,] Acts xv. 14; his [*ruling*] them, Isa. xxxiii. 22; and his [*defending*] them, Isa. xxxi. 2.

Q. 24. How does Christ SUBDUE his elect people to himself?

A. By the power of his *Spirit* so managing the *word* that he conquers their natural aversion and obstinacy, Ps. cx. 3; and makes them willing to embrace *a Saviour and a great one*, as freely offered in the gospel, Isa. xliv. 5.

Q. 25. In what condition does he find his elect ones, when he comes to subdue them to himself?

A. He finds them prisoners, and lawful captives, Isa. lxi. 1.

Q. 26. How does he loose their bonds?

A. By his *Spirit*, applying to them the whole of his satisfaction, by which all demands of law and justice are fully answered, John xvi. 8—12.

Q. 27. What is the consequence of answering the demands of law and justice, by the Spirit's applying the satisfaction of Christ?

A. The law being satisfied, the *strength of sin* is broken, and therefore the *sting of death* is taken away, 1 Cor. xv. 56, 57.

Q. 28. What follows upon taking away the *sting of death?*

A. Satan loses his power over them; and that being lost, the present evil world, which is his kingdom, can hold them no longer, Gal. i. 4.

Q. 29. What comes of them, when they are *separated* from the world that *lies in wickedness*?

A. The very moment they are delivered from the *power of darkness*, they are *translated into the kingdom* of God's *dear Son*, Col. i. 13.

Q. 30. Are they not in the world after this happy change?

A. Though *in* the world, yet they are not *of* it, but true and lively members of Christ's invisible kingdom; and, therefore, the objects of the world's hatred, John xv. 19.

Q. 31. When Christ as a king has subdued sinners to himself, what *other part* of his royal office does he exercise over them?

A. He RULES and *governs* them: hence he is called the "Ruler in Israel," Micah v. 2.

Q. 32. Does the rule and government of Christ dissolve the subjection of his people from the powers of the earth?

A. By no means: he paid *tribute* himself, Matt. xvii. 27;

and has strictly commanded that "every soul be subject to the higher powers, because there is no power but of God; and the powers that be, are ordained of God," Rom. xiii. 1.

Q. 33. In what things are the subjects of Christ's kingdom to obey the powers of the earth?

A. In every thing that is not forbidden by the law of God; but when the commands of men are opposite to the commands of God, in that case, God ought always to be obeyed, rather than men, Acts v. 29.

Q. 34. *How* does this glorious King *rule* his subjects?

A. By giving them the *laws*, Ps. cxlvii. 19, and administering to them the *discipline* of his kingdom, Heb. xii. 6.

Q. 35. What are the *laws* of Christ's kingdom?

A. They are no other than the laws of the *Ten Commandments*, originally given to Adam at his creation, and afterwards published from Mount Sinai. Ex. xx. 3—18.

Q. 36. How does Christ *sweeten this law* to his subjects?

A. Having fulfilled it as a *covenant*, he gives it out to his true and faithful subjects as a *rule of life*, to be obeyed in the strength of that grace which is secured in the promise, Ezek. xxxvi. 27.

Q. 37. Does he annex any *rewards* to the obedience of his true subjects?

A. Yes; in keeping of his commandments, *there is great reward*, Ps. xix. 11.

Q. 38. What are these rewards?

A. His special comforts and *love-tokens*, which he bestows for exciting to that holy and tender walk, which is the fruit of faith, John xiv. 21.

Q. 39. Why are these *comforts* called *rewards*?

A. Because they are given to a *working* saint, as a farther privilege on the performance of duty, Rev. iii. 10.

Q. 40. Is it the *order* of the new covenant, that *duty* should go *before privilege?*

A. No: the matter stands thus: the *leading privilege* is the *quickening Spirit*, then follows *duty;* and duty, performed in faith, is followed with *farther privilege*, till privilege and duty come both to *perfection* in heaven, not to be distinguished any more, 1 John iii. 2.

Q. 41. What is the *discipline* of Christ's kingdom?

A. *Fatherly chastisement;* which, being necessary for the welfare of his true subjects, is secured for them in the promise, Ps. lxxxix. 30—35.

Q. 42. To what *promise* of the covenant does *fatherly chastisement* belong?

A. To the promise of *sanctification*, being an appointed mean for advancing holiness in them, Heb. xii. 10. Isa. xxvii. 9.

Q. 43. What *other act* of kingly power does Christ exercise about his subjects, besides subduing them to himself, and ruling of them?

A. He DEFENDS them likewise, Ps. lxxxix. 18: "The Lord is our DEFENCE."

Q. 44. Against whom does he defend them?

A. Against all their enemies; sin, Satan, the world, and death, Luke, i. 71. 1 John iv. 4. Hos. xiii. 14.

Q. 45. Who are their worst enemies?

A. The remains of *corruption* within them, which are not expelled during this life, but left for their exercise and trial, Gal. v. 7.

Q. 46. How does he defend them against these *inward foes?*

A. By keeping alive in them the *spark* of *holy fire* in the midst of an *ocean* of corruption, and causing it to resist and overcome the same, until it is quite dried up, Rom. vii. 24, 25.

Q. 47. What are the *acts* of Christ's kingly office, with respect to his *people's enemies?*

A. His [*restraining and conquering*] them, 1 Cor. xv. 25: "He must reign till he hath put all his enemies under his feet."

Q. 48. Whence is it that this glorious King, and his subjects, have the *same enemies?*

A. He and they make up that *one body*, of which he is the *head* and they are the *members*, 1 Cor. xii. 12; and therefore they cannot but have *common* friends and foes, Zech. ii. 8.

Q. 49. What is it for Christ to *restrain* his and his people's enemies?

A. It is to overrule and disappoint their wicked purposes, Isa. xxxvii. 29; to set limits to their wrath, and to bring a revenue of glory to himself out of the same, Ps. lxxvi. 10.

Q. 50. What *restraints* does he put upon them?

A. He bounds them by his power, as to the kind, degree, and continuance of all their enterprises and attacks upon his people, Job i. 12, and ii. 6.

Q. 51. What is it for Christ to *conquer* all his and his people's enemies?

A. It is his taking away their power, that they cannot *hurt* the least of his *little ones*, with respect to their *spiritual state*, Luke x. 19.

Q. 52. How does he *conquer* them?

A. He has already conquered them in his *own person*, as the head of the new covenant, by the victory he obtained over them in his death, Col. ii. 15; and he conquers them daily in his *members*, when he enables them, by faith, to put their feet upon the neck of their vanquished foes, Rom. xvi. 20.

OF CHRIST'S HUMILIATION.

Q. 53. What may we *learn* from Christ's executing his kingly office?

A. That though believers, while in this world, are in the midst of their enemies, "as lambs among wolves," Luke x. 3; yet by this mighty King, as *the breaker*, going up before them, Mic. ii. 13, they shall be "more than conquerors through him that loved them," Rom. viii. 37.

QUEST. 27. *Wherein did Christ's humiliation consist?*

ANS. Christ's humiliation consisted in his being born, and that in a low condition, made under the law, undergoing the miseries of this life, the wrath of God, and the cursed death of the cross; in being buried, and continuing under the power of death for a time.

Q. 1. What do you understand by Christ's [*humiliation*] in *general?*

A. His condescending to have that glory, which he had with the Father, "before the world was," John xvii. 5, veiled for a time, by his coming to this lower world, to be "a man of sorrows, and acquainted with grief," Isa. liii. 3.

Q. 2. Was Christ's humiliation entirely *voluntary?*

A. It was voluntary in the highest degree; for, from eternity, he rejoiced "in the habitable part of the earth, and his delights were with the sons of men," Prov. viii. 31.

Q. 3. What was the spring and source of Christ's humiliation?

A. Nothing but his own and his Father's undeserved love to lost mankind, Rom. v. 6. 1 John iv. 10.

Q. 4. What are the several *steps* of Christ's humiliation, mentioned in the answer?

A. They are such as respect "his *conception* and *birth*, his *life*, his *death*," and what passed upon him, "*after his death*, until his resurrection." *

Q. 5. How did Christ humble himself in his conception and birth?

A. In that, being from all eternity the Son of God, "*in the bosom of the Father*, he was pleased, in the fulness of time, to become the Son of man, *made of a woman;* and to be born of her," in a very low condition, John i. 14, 18. Gal. iv. 4.†

Q. 6. What was the [*low condition*] in which he was born?

* Larger Cat. Q. 46 † Ibid, Q. 47.

A. He was born of a *poor woman*, though of *royal descent*, in *Bethlehem*, an obscure village; and there "laid in a manger, because there was no room for them in the inn," Luke ii. 4, 5, 7.

Q. 7. Why is the *pedigree* and *descent* of Christ, according to the flesh, so particularly described by the *evangelists?*

A. To evidence the faithfulness of God in his promise to Abraham, Gen. xxii. 18, and David, Ps. cxxxii. 11, that the *Messiah* should spring out of their seed.

Q. 8. Why was Christ born in such a low condition?

A. He stooped so low that he might lift up sinners of mankind out of the horrible pit and miry clay, into which they were plunged, Ps. xl. 2.

Q. 9. What *improvement* ought we to make of the incarnation and birth of Christ, in such circumstances of more than ordinary abasement?

A. To admire "the grace of our Lord Jesus Christ, that though he was rich, yet for our sakes he became poor, that we through his poverty might be rich," 2 Cor. viii. 9; and by faith to claim a relation to him as our kinsman, saying, "Unto us a child is born, unto us a Son is given," Isa. ix. 6.

Q. 10. How did Christ humble himself in his life?

A. In being [*made under the law, undergoing the miseries of this life, and the wrath of God.*]

Q. 11. What [*law*] was Christ made under as our Surety?

A. Although he gave obedience to all divine institutions, ceremonial and political, yet it was the *moral law*, properly, he was made under, as our Surety, Gal. iv. 4, 5.

Q. 12. How does it appear to have been the *moral law* he was *made under?*

A. Because this was the law given to Adam in his creation, and afterwards vested with the form of a covenant of works, when he was placed in *paradise;* by the breach of which law, as a covenant, all mankind are brought under the curse, Gal. iii. 10.

Q. 13. Was Christ made under the moral law, as a *covenant of works*, or only as a *rule of life?*

A. He was made under it as a covenant of works, demanding perfect obedience, as a condition of life, and full satisfaction because of man's transgression.

Q. 14. How do you prove this?

A. From Gal. iv. 4, 5: "God sent forth his Son—made under the law, to redeem them that were under the law:" where it is obvious, that Christ behoved to be made under the law, in the very same sense, in which his spiritual seed, whom he came to redeem, were under it; and they being all under it as a covenant, he behoved to be made under it as a covenant likewise, that he might redeem them from its curse, Gal. iii. 13.

Q. 15. What would be the absurdity of affirming that Christ was made under the law as a *rule*, and not as a *covenant?*

A. It would make the apostle's meaning, in the forecited passage, Gal. iv. 4, 5, to be, as if he had said, Christ was made under the law as a *rule* to redeem them that were under the law as a rule, from all subjection and obedience to it; which is the very soul of Antinomianism, and quite contrary to the great end of Christ's coming to the world, which was "not to destroy the law, but to fulfil it," Matt. v. 17.

Q. 16. Why is Christ's being made under the law, mentioned as a part of his humiliation?

A. Because it was most amazing condescension in the great Lord and Lawgiver of heaven and earth, to become subject to his own law, and that for this very end, that he might fulfil it in the room of those who were the transgressors of it, and had incurred its penalty, Matt. iii. 15.

Q. 17. What may we *learn* from Christ's being made under the law?

A. The misery of sinners out of Christ, who have to answer to God in their own persons, for their debt, both of obedience and punishment, Eph. ii. 12; and the happiness of believers, who have all their debt cleared, by Christ's being made under the law in their room, Rom. viii. 1.

Q. 18. What were [*the miseries of this life,*] which Christ endured in his state of humiliation?

A. Together with our nature, he took on him its sinless infirmities, such as hunger, thirst, weariness, grief, and the like, Rom. viii. 3; he submitted to poverty and want, Matt. viii. 20; and endured likewise the assaults and temptations of Satan, Heb. iv. 15; together with the contradiction, reproach, and persecution of a wicked world, Heb. xii. 3.

Q. 19. Why did he undergo all these?

A. That he might take the *sting* out of all the afflictions of his people, Rom. viii. 28; and *sympathize* with them in their troubles, Isa. lxiii. 9.

Q. 20. Were these the greatest miseries he experienced in this life?

A. No: he underwent [*the wrath of God*] also, Ps. cxvi. 3.

Q. 21. What was it for him to undergo the wrath of God?

A. It was to suffer the utmost effects of God's holy and righteous displeasure against sin, Ps. xc. 11.

Q. 22. What was it that made the human nature of

Christ capable of supporting the utmost effects of the wrath of God?

A. Its union with his divine person, by which it was impossible it could sink under the weight, Isa. l. 7.

Q. 23. How could Christ undergo the wrath of God, seeing he did "always the things that please him?"

A. He underwent it only as the *Surety* for his elect seed, on account of their sins which were imputed to him, Isa. liii. 6: " The Lord hath laid on him the iniquity of us all."

Q. 24. How did it appear that he underwent the wrath of God?

A. It appeared chiefly in his *agony*, in the *garden*, when he said, "My soul is exceeding sorrowful, even unto death," Matt. xxvi. 38; at which time, "his sweat was, as it were, great drops of blood, falling down to the ground," Luke xxii. 44; and again, on the *cross*, when he " cried with a loud voice, My God, my God, why hast thou forsaken me?" Matt. xxvii. 46.

Q. 25. Was not he the object of his Father's delight, even when undergoing his wrath on account of our sin?

A. Yes, surely: for though the *sin of the world*, which he was bearing, was the object of God's infinite hatred; yet the glorious person bearing it, was, even then, the object of his infinite love, Isa. liii. 10: "It pleased the Lord to bruise him."

Q. 26. What may we *learn* from Christ's undergoing the miseries of this life, and the wrath of God?

A. " That we must through much tribulation enter into the kingdom of God," Acts xiv. 22; and that he is "pacified towards us, for all that we have done," Ezek. xvi. 63.

Q. 27. How did Christ humble himself in his death?

A. By undergoing [*the cursed death of the cross,*] Phil. ii. 8.

Q. 28. Why is the death of the *cross* called a [*cursed death?*]

A. Because God, in testimony of his anger against breaking the first covenant, by eating the fruit of the forbidden tree, had said, "Cursed is every one that hangeth on a tree," Gal. iii. 13.

Q. 29. What evidences are there that Christ was made a curse for us in his death.

A. In as much as there was no pity, no sparing in his death; God spared him not, Rom. viii. 32; and wicked men were let loose upon him like *dogs* and *bulls*, Ps. xxii. 12, 16.

Q. 30. How does the scripture set forth the exquisite agony of his death?

PART I.—13

A. It tells us, that " they pierced his hands and his feet, that he was poured out like water; that all his bones were out of joint: his heart, like wax, melted in the midst of his bowels; his strength dried up like a potsherd; and his tongue made to cleave to his jaws," Ps. xxii. 14, 15.

Q. 31. How was Christ's death on the cross *typified* under the Old Testament?

A. By the *brazen serpent* lifted up in the wilderness, " For, as Moses lifted up the serpent in the wilderness, even so must the Son of man be lifted up," John iii. 14.

Q. 32. Were the soul and body of Christ actually separated by death on the cross?

A. Yes; for when " he had cried with a loud voice, he said, Father, into thy hands I commend my spirit: and having said this, he gave up the ghost," Luke xxiii. 46.

Q. 33. Was either soul or body separated from his divine person?

A. No; it is impossible they could be, because the union of the human nature to his divine person is absolutely inviolable, *Jesus* being " the same yesterday, and to-day, and for ever," Heb. xiii. 8.

Q. 34. What may we *learn* from Christ's dying the cursed death of the cross?

A. That " he hath redeemed us from the curse of the law, being made a curse for us," Gal. iii. 13.

Q. 35. How did Christ humble himself in what *passed upon him after his death?*

A. In being [*buried and continuing under the power of death for a time,*] 1 Cor. xv. 4.

Q. 36. What respect was paid to the dead body of Christ before its burial?

A. " Joseph of Arimathea bought fine linen," Mark xv. 43, 46, and " Nicodemus brought a mixture of myrrh and aloes, and they took the body of Jesus, and wound it in linen clothes, with the spices, as the manner of the Jews is to bury," John xix. 39, 40.

Q. 37. Where did they *bury* him?

A. In a " new sepulchre, wherein was never man yet laid," John xix. 41.

Q. 38. Why was it ordered in providence, that he should be laid in a new sepulchre?

A. That none might have it to say, that it was anothe , and not he, that rose from the dead, Acts iv. 10.

Q. 39. What do you understand by these words in the CREED, *He descended into Hell?*

A. Nothing else but his descent into the grave, to be under the power of death, as its prisoner, Ps. xvi. 10.

Q. 40. What was it that gave death power and dominion over Christ?

A. His being *made sin for us,* 2 Cor. v. 21.

OF CHRIST'S EXALTATION. 147

Q. 41. Were death and the grave able to maintain their dominion over him?
A. No: because of the complete payment of all demands made upon him as a Surety, Rom. vi. 9.

Q. 42. How long [*time*] did he continue under the power of death?
A. Till he rose on the *third day*, 1 Cor. xv. 4.

Q. 43. Why did he continue so long under the power of death?
A. To show that he was *really dead*, this being necessary to be believed, 1 Cor. xv. 3.

Q. 44. What *sign*, or *type*, was there of his continuing so long in the grave?
A. *The sign of the prophet Jonas*, Matt. xii. 40: "As Jonas was three days and three nights in the whale's belly, so shall the Son of man be three days and three nights in the heart of the earth."

Q. 45. Did he see corruption in the grave like other men?
A. No; being God's *Holy One*, absolutely free from sin, his body could see no corruption, Ps. xvi. 10.

Q. 46. What may we *learn* from Christ's being buried, and continuing under the power of death for a time?
A. That the grave being "the place where the Lord lay," Matt. xxviii. 6, it cannot but be sweet to a dying saint, to think that he is to lie down in the *same bed;* and that, in like manner, as "Jesus died and rose again, even so them also which sleep in Jesus, will God bring with him," 2 Thess. iv. 14.

———◆———

QUEST. 28. *Wherein consists Christ's exaltation?*

ANS. Christ's exaltation consists in his rising again from the dead on the third day, in ascending up into heaven, in sitting at the right hand of God the Father, and in coming to judge the world at the last day.

Q. 1. What do you understand by Christ's [*exaltation?*]
A. Not the conferring of any new glory upon his divine person, which is absolutely unchangeable; but a manifestation, in the human nature, (which had eclipsed it for awhile,) of the same glory, of which he was eternally possessed as the Son of God, John xvii. 5: "And now, O Father, glorify thou me with thine own self, with the glory which I had with thee before the world was."

Q. 2. Why does Christ's *exaltation* immediately follow his *humiliation?*

A. Because it is the proper reward of it, Phil. ii. 8, 9: "He humbled himself, and became obedient unto death, even the death of the cross; wherefore God also hath highly exalted him."

Q. 3. What is the consequence of Christ's exaltation with respect to *himself?*

A. That the ignominy of the cross is thus fully wiped off, Heb. xii. 2.

Q. 4. What is the design of it with respect to *us?*

A. "God raised him up from the dead, and gave him glory, that our faith and hope might be in God," 1 Pet. i. 21.

Q. 5. What are the several *steps* of Christ's exaltation mentioned in the *answer?*

A. They are, his *rising* again from the dead; his *ascending* up into heaven; his *sitting* at the right hand of God; and his coming to *judge* the world at the last day.

Q. 6. What is the FIRST STEP of Christ's exaltation?

A. [*His rising again from the dead on the third day,*] 1 Cor. xv. 4.

Q. 7. What day of the week did the [*third day*] fall upon?

A. Upon the *first day* of the week, which is ever since, called the *Lord's day*, Rev. i. 10; and is to be observed to the end of the world, as the *Christian Sabbath*, Acts xx. 7.

Q. 8. How can the day of Christ's resurrection be called the *third day*, when he was not two full days in the grave before?

A. It is usual in scripture to denominate the *whole day* from the *remarkable event* that happens in *any hour* of it: thus, Christ being crucified and buried on the *evening* before the *Jewish Sabbath*, and rising early in the *morning* after it, is said to rise again, "the third day according to the scriptures," 1 Cor. xv. 4.

Q. 9. How may the truth of Christ's resurrection be demonstrated?

A. From its being prefigured and foretold, and from its being attested by unquestionable witnesses and *infallible proofs*, Acts i. 3.

Q. 10. How was the resurrection of Christ *prefigured?*

A. By Abraham's receiving Isaac from the dead as a *figure* or representation of it, Heb. xi. 19.

Q. 11. Was his resurrection *foretold* in the scriptures of the Old Testament?

A. The apostle Paul expressly affirms that it was, Acts xiii. 32—38: "The promise," says he, "which was made unto the fathers, God hath fulfilled the same unto us their children, in that he hath raised up Jesus again; as it is also written, in the second Psalm, Thou art my Son, this day have I begotten thee; and that he raised him up from the dead, he said on this wise, I will give you the sure mercies of David," Isa. lv. 3. "Wherefore he saith in another Psalm, Thou shalt not suffer thine Holy One to see corruption," Ps. xvi. 10.

Q. 12. Did not Christ foretell his own resurrection before he died?

A. Yes; for he said, "Destroy this temple, and in three days I will raise it up," *meaning* the temple of his body, John ii. 19, 21; and directed his disciples, before his death, to meet him in Galilee, after his resurrection, Matt. xxvi. 32: "After I am risen, I will go before you into Galilee."

Q. 13. By whom was the resurrection of Christ, *attested?*

A. By angels, by the disciples, and many others who saw him alive after he was risen.

Q. 14. What testimony did the *angels* give to his resurrection?

A. They said to the women who came to the sepulchre, "He is not here, for he is risen, as he said," Matt. xxviii. 6.

Q. 15. How did the disciples attest the truth of his resurrection?

A. They unanimously declared, that "God raised him up the third day, and showed him openly, not to all the people, but unto the witnesses chosen before of God, even to us," says Peter, "who did eat and drink with him after he rose from the dead," Acts x. 40, 41.

Q. 16. Did Christ confirm the truth of his resurrection by frequent *bodily appearances* after it?

A. Yes; for on the very day he rose, "*he appeared first to Mary Magdalene,* Mark xvi. 9; then he appeared to her in company with *the other Mary,* Matt. xxviii. 1, 9; afterwards he showed himself to the *two disciples* going to Emmaus, Luke xxiv. 13, 15; then to Simon Peter alone, ver. 34; and "the same day at evening, being the first day of the week," he appeared to all the disciples, except Thomas, John xx. 19, 24; after eight days, he appeared to all the apostles, when Thomas was with them, ver. 26; "After these things Jesus showed himself again to his disciples, at the sea of Tiberias," John xxi. 1; then we read of his appearing to the *eleven disciples* on a *mountain* in Galilee, Matt. xxviii. 16; at which time, it is probable, he was seen of the *five hundred brethren at once,* mentioned, 1 Cor. xv. 6: *after that he was seen of James,* ver. 7; and, lastly, on the day of his *ascension,* he appeared to all the disciples on Mount Olivet, Acts i. 9, 12.

Q. 17. For how long *time* did Christ show himself *alive*, to his disciples, after his resurrection?

A. Forty days, Acts i. 3.

Q. 18. Why did he continue so long with them?

A. That they might be fully convinced of the truth of his resurrection, by his appearing frequently in their presence, and conversing familiarly with them, Acts x. 40, 41, and that they might be instructed in the nature and government of his kingdom, chap. i. 3.

Q. 19. How may we be sure, that the *testimony* of the *disciples,* who were *witnesses* of the resurrection of Christ, may be depended upon as an *infallible proof* of it?

A. Because they testified of his resurrection, as a thing of which they had certain and *personal* knowledge, and proclaimed it in a most *public* and *open manner,* in the *very place* where that remarkable event happened, Acts iii. 15, and that under the *outward disadvantages* of being imprisoned, beaten, Acts v. 18, 40, and persecuted to death itself, for publishing and defending such a doctrine, Acts xii. 2, 3.

Q. 20. By whose *power* did Christ rise from the dead?

A. Although the resurrection of Christ be frequently ascribed to the *Father,* as in Eph. i. 20; yet, in opposition to the Socinians, and other enemies of the *Deity* of Christ, it is to be maintained, that he rose also by *his own divine power,* as is evident from Rom. i. 4.

Q. 21. How may it further appear, that he rose by his own divine power?

A. He expressly affirms, that he would *raise up the temple of his body* on the *third* day, John ii. 19; and that he had power to *lay down* his life and to *take it again,* chap. x. 18.

Q. 22. In what *capacity* did he rise from the dead?

A. In the capacity of a *public person,* representing all nis spiritual seed; and as having their discharge in his hand, Rom. iv. 25.

Q. 23. What was the *necessity* of Christ's resurrection?

A. It was necessary in respect of God, in respect of Christ himself, and in respect of us.

Q. 24. Why was it necessary in respect of *God?*

A. Because, since he is the *God and Father of our Lord Jesus Christ,* it was necessary that he should not be the God of a *dead,* but of a *living* Redeemer: for he is "not the God of the dead, but of the living," Matt. xxii. 32.

Q. 25. Why was the resurrection of Christ necessary with respect to *himself?*

A. Because, having fully paid the debt for which he was incarcerated, justice required that he should be *taken from prison and from judgment,* Isa. liii. 8; and that, since he purchased a kingdom by his death, he should rise again to possess it, Rom. xiv. 9.

Q. 26. Why was it necessary with respect to *us?*

OF CHRIST'S EXALTATION. 151

A. Because, "if Christ be not risen, *our faith is vain, and we* are yet in our sins," 1 Cor. xv. 17.

Q. 27. Did Christ rise with the *self-same body* in which ne suffered?

A. Yes; for, says he to Thomas, "Reach hither thy finger, and behold my hands; and reach hither thy hand, and thrust it into my side: and be not faithless, but believing," John xx. 27.

Q. 28. What remarkable *circumstances* accompanied the resurrection of Christ?

A. It was accompanied with *a great earthquake*, the attendance of angels, and such terror upon the *keepers*, that they "did shake, and became as dead men," Matt. xxviii. 2, 4.

Q. 29. In what manner did the *high priest* and *elders* vainly attempt to smother the truth of his resurrection?

A. They bribed the soldiers to say, "his disciples came by night, and stole him away, while we slept," Matt. xxviii. 12, 13.

Q. 30. How does the *falsehood* of this *ill-made story* appear at first sight?

A. From this: that it is not to be supposed the whole company of soldiers, who guarded the sepulchre, would be all asleep at once, especially considering the great earthquake that accompanied the rolling away the stone, and the severity of the Roman military discipline, in like cases, Acts xii. 19; and if they were *really asleep*, how could they know that the disciples came and stole him away?

Q. 31. What does the doctrine of Christ's resurrection *teach us?*

A. That he must needs be a *God of peace*, who "brought again from the dead our Lord Jesus," Heb. xiii. 20; that death and the grave are *unstinged* and vanquished, 1 Cor. xv. 55; and that his resurrection is a certain pledge and earnest of the resurrection of his members at the last day, he having "become the first fruits of them that slept," ver. 20.

Q. 32. What is the SECOND STEP of Christ's exaltation?

A. [*His ascending up into heaven*,] Ps. lxviii. 18.

Q. 33. Does not Christ's [*ascending up into heaven*,] presuppose his descending thence?

A. Yes; for so argues the apostle; "Now that he ascended, what is it but that he also descended first into the lower parts of the earth," Eph. iv. 9.

Q. 34. Did Christ, when he is said to descend, bring a *human nature* from heaven with him?

A. By no means; for the human nature was *made of a woman*, on this earth, by the *overshadowing* power of the Holy Ghost, Luke i. 35; but his *descending* signifies his *amazing condescension*, in assuming our nature into personal union with himself, Phil. ii. 6, 7.

Q. 35. How is the ascension of Christ *expressed* in scripture?

A. By his going away, John xvi. 7; his being "received up into heaven," Mark xvi. 19; and his having "entered once into the holy place," Heb. ix. 12.

Q. 36. As to which of his two natures is he properly said to ascend?

A. Although Christ ascended *personally* into heaven, yet ascension is properly attributed to his human nature, as the divine nature is every where present, John iii. 13.

Q. 37. From what part of the earth did Christ ascend into heaven?

A. He ascended from Mount Olivet, which was nigh to Bethany, Luke xxiv. 50, compared with Acts i. 12.

Q. 38. What is worthy of consideration in this circumstance, that he ascended from *Mount Olivet?*

A. In the *Mount of Olives* was the place where his *soul was exceedingly sorrowful, even unto death;* and where he was in such an *agony*, that "his sweat was, as it were, great drops of blood falling down to the ground," Luke xxii. 39, 44; and therefore, in that very place, his *heart* is *made glad* by a triumphant ascension into that *fulness of joy*, and those *pleasures for evermore*, that are at God's *right hand*, Ps. xvi. 11.

Q. 39. Whither did Christ ascend, or to what *place?*

A. He ascended up [*into heaven,*] Acts i. 10, 11.

Q. 40. When did Christ ascend into heaven?

A. When *forty days* after his resurrection were elapsed, Acts i. 3.

Q. 41. Who were the *witnesses* of his ascension?

A. The *eleven disciples* were eye witnesses of it; for, "while they beheld, he was taken up, and a cloud received him out of their sight," Acts i. 9.

Q. 42. What was he doing when he parted from them?

A. He was *blessing* them, Luke xxiv. 51: "And it came to pass, while he blessed them, he was parted from them, and carried up into heaven."

Q. 43. What was his parting word?

A. "Lo! I am with you alway, even unto the end of the world," Matt. xxviii. 20.

Q. 44. In what *capacity* did Christ ascend?

A. In a public capacity, as representing his whole mystical body: hence he is called the *Forerunner*, who "is, for us, entered within the veil," Heb. vi. 20.

Q. 45. With what *solemnity* did he ascend?

A. With the solemnity of a glorious triumph: for, having vanquished sin, Satan, hell, and death, he ascended up on high, leading *captivity captive*, Eph. iv. 8.

Q. 46. Who went in his retinue?
A. *Thousands of angels*, sounding forth his praise, as a victorious conqueror, Ps. lxviii. 17.

Q. 47. What *evidence* did he give *from heaven*, of the reality of his ascension?
A. The extraordinary effusion of the Holy Ghost on the day of *Pentecost*, within a few days after it, Acts ii. 1, 3, 4.

Q. 48. Why was this remarkable down-pouring of the Spirit *delayed* till after Christ's ascension?
A. That he might evidence his bounty and liberality, upon his instalment into the kingdom, by giving "gifts unto men," Eph. iv. 8.

Q. 49. For what *end* did Christ ascend up into heaven?
A. That he might take possession of the *many mansions* there, and prepare them for his people, by carrying in the merit of his oblation thither, John xiv. 2, 3; and likewise, that he might make continual intercession for them, Heb. vii. 25.

Q. 50. What does the ascension of Christ *teach* us?
A. That he has brought in an everlasting righteousness, because he has gone to his Father, John xvi. 10; and to believe that he will come again to receive us to himself, that where he is, there we may be also, chap. xiv. 3.

Q. 51. What is the THIRD STEP of Christ's exaltation?
A. His [*sitting at the right hand of God the Father*,] Eph. i. 20.

Q. 52. What is meant by the [*right hand*] in scripture?
A. The place of the greatest honour and dignity, 1 Kings ii. 19.

Q. 53. What is meant by [*sitting?*]
A. It implies *rest* and *quietness*, Micah iv. 4: "They shall sit, every man under his vine, and under his fig-tree, and none shall make them afraid:" and likewise *power* and *authority*, Zech. vi. 13: "He shall sit and rule upon his throne."

Q. 54. What then are we to understand by Christ's [*sitting at the right hand of God the Father?*]
A. The quiet and peaceable possession of that matchless dignity, and fulness of power, with which he is vested, as the glorious King and Head of his church, Eph. i. 21, 22.

Q. 55. For what end does he sit at the right hand of the Father?
A. That he may there represent his people, and make his enemies his *footstool*.

Q. 56. How does it appear that he *represents* his people at the right hand of God?
A. Because they are said to "sit together in heavenly places in Christ Jesus," which can only be meant of their sitting *representatively* in him, as their glorious Head, Eph. ii. 6.

Q. 57. *How* are the enemies of Christ made his footstool?

A. By the triumphant victory which is obtained over them, Ps. lxxii. 9; and the extremity of shame, horror, and confusion, with which they shall be covered, Ps. cxxxii. 18.

Q. 58. *When* shall his enemies be made his *footstool?*

A. He has *already* triumphed over them in his *cross*, Col. ii. 15; but he will make his final conquest conspicuous to the whole world at the *last day*, Rev. xx. 10, 14.

Q. 59. How long *will Christ sit at the* right hand of God the Father?

A. For ever and ever, Ps. xlv. 6: "Thy throne, O God, is for ever and ever."

Q. 60. Will Christ's mediatory power and authority, at the right hand of God, be the *same* in the church *triumphant* in heaven, as it is in the church *militant* on earth?

A. It will be the same as to the *essence* or *substance* of it, but different as to the manner of its *administration*.

Q. 61. In what consists the *essence* of Christ's mediatory power and authority in heaven?

A. In the *relation* in which he stands to the members of his body: he will continue for ever to be the *King, Head,* and *Husband* of the church *triumphant,* the *fountain* of all blessing and happiness to them, and the *bond* of their perpetual fellowship and communion with God, Ps. xlviii. 14. Hos. ii. 19. Rev. vii. 17.

Q. 62. What is the *difference* between the manner of the administration of his mediatory power *here* and *hereafter?*

A. The administration of his kingdom on this *earth*, is, by the ministry of the word, the dispensation of the sacraments, and the exercise of ecclesiastical government and discipline: but in *heaven*, there will be no use for any of these, Rev. xxi. 22: "I saw no temple therein: for the Lord God Almighty, and the Lamb, are the temple of it."

Q. 63. What is meant then by Christ's delivering "up the kingdom to God, even the Father?" 1 Cor. xv. 24.

A. The meaning is, Christ having completed the salvation of his church, will present all and every one of them to his "Father, not having spot or wrinkle, or any such thing," Eph. v. 27, saying, "Behold! I, and the children which God hath given me," Heb. ii. 13.

Q. 64. What is meant by Christ's putting down *all rule, and all authority, and power,* in the above passage, 1 Cor. xv. 24?

A. The meaning is, he will have *no occasion* to exercise his power and authority, in *such sort* as he did *before ;* as there will be no more elect to save, and no more enemies to conquer, Rev. xix. 8, 20.

Q. 65. In what sense will the "Son also himself be sub

ject to him that put all things under him?" as it is said, ver. 28.

A. The Son, as Mediator, being the Father's servant in the great work of redemption, Isa. xlii. 1, shall then be "subject to him that put all things under him," in so far, as having finished his mediatorial service, in bringing all the elect to glory, he will render up his commission, as his Father's delegate, not to be executed any more, in the *former manner*, as ruling over his church in the midst of enemies; for he must reign, till he hath put all his enemies under his feet, 1 Cor. xv. 25.

Q. 66. In what respect is it said, that *God* shall *then* be *all in all?*

A. The glory of the Three-one God, Father, Son, and Holy Ghost, will *then* be most clearly displayed, and no more a seeing "through a glass darkly, but face to face," 1 Cor. xiii. 12, and a seeing him as he is, 1 John iii. 2.

Q. 67. What may we *learn* from Christ's sitting at the right hand of God?

A. That we ought to "seek those things which are above," where Christ is; and to "set our affections on things above, not on things on the earth," Col. iii. 1, 2.

Q. 68. What is the FOURTH STEP of Christ's exaltation?

A. His [*coming to judge the world at the last day,*] Rev. i. 7. John xii. 48.

Q. 69. How do you *prove* that there will be a *general judgment?*

A. The scripture expressly asserts it; and the justice and goodness of God necessarily require it.

Q. 70. Where is it *expressly asserted* in *scripture?*

A. In many places; particularly Acts xvii. 31: "He hath appointed a day in the which he will judge the world in righteousness, by that man whom he hath ordained," &c. See also 2 Cor. v. 10. Jude, ver. 6. Rev. xx. 11—13.

Q. 71. Why do the *justice* and *goodness* of God require a judgment?

A. Because they necessarily require that it be *well* with the righteous and *ill* with the wicked; that every man be rewarded according to his works, which not being done in this life, there must be a judgment to come: "Seeing it is a righteous thing with God to recompense tribulation to them that trouble you; and to you who are troubled, rest with us, when the Lord Jesus shall be revealed from heaven," 2 Thess. i. 6, 7.

Q. 72. Who is to be the *Judge?*

A. The Son of man, the man Christ Jesus, Matt. xxv. 31. Rom. xiv. 10.

Q. 73. How will Christ, as God-man, be Judge, when it is said, (Ps. l. 6,) that *God is Judge himself?*

A. The Three-one God, Father, Son, and Holy Ghost,

is Judge, in respect of judiciary authority, dominion, and power; but Christ, as God-man, Mediator, is the Judge, in respect of *dispensation* and special *exercise* of that power, John v. 22: " The Father—hath committed all judgment unto the Son."

Q. 74. Why is the judgment of the world committed to Christ as mediator?

A. Because it is a part of that exaltation, which is conferred upon him, in consequence of his voluntary humiliation, Phil. ii. 8—10.

Q. 75. *When* will Christ come to judge the world?

A. [*At the last day,*] John vi. 39, 40.

Q. 76. Why is it called the *last day?*

A. Because, after it time shall be no more; there will be no more a succession of days and nights, but one perpetual *day* of light, comfort, and joy, to the righteous, Rev. xxi. 23; and one perpetual *night of utter darkness*, misery, and wo, unto the wicked, Matt. xxiv. 30.

Q. 77. In what *manner* will Christ come to judge the world?

A. In a most splendid and glorious manner: "for he will come in the clouds of heaven, with power and great glory," Matt. xxiv. 30:—"In the glory of his Father, with the holy angels," Mark viii. 38.

Q. 78. Will the world be looking for him when he comes to judgment?

A. No: his coming will be a fearful surprise to the world; for "the day of the Lord shall come as a thief in the night," 2 Pet. iii. 10. See also Luke xvii. 26—31.

Q. 79. What is the *difference* between his *first* and *second* coming?

A. In his *first* coming, "he was made sin for us, though he knew no sin," 2 Cor. v. 21; but "he shall appear the second time without sin unto salvation," Heb. ix. 28.

Q. 80. Is the *precise time* of his second coming known to men or angels?

A. No: it is fixed in the counsel of God, but not revealed to us, Mark xiii. 32.

Q. 81. What will be the *forerunner* of his second coming?

A. The preaching of the gospel to all nations, Matt. xxiv. 14; the downfal of *Antichrist*, Rev. xviii. 21; the conversion of the *Jews*, Rev. xvi. 12; and yet, after all, a general decay of religion, and great security, Luke xviii. 8.

Q. 82. What are the *qualities* of the Judge?

A. He will be a visible Judge, "every eye shall see him," Rev. i. 7; an omniscient Judge, "all things will be naked and opened unto his eyes," Heb. iv. 13; a most just and righteous Judge, 2 Tim. iv. 8; and an omnipotent Judge, able to put his sentence into execution, Rev. vi. 17

OF CHRIST'S EXALTATION. 157

Q. 83. Who are the *parties* that shall appear?
A. All mankind, called *all nations*, Matt. xxv. 32; and likewise, "the angels which kept not their first estate," Jude, verse 6.

Q. 84. What *summons* will be given to the parties?
A. "The voice of the archangel and the trump of God," 1 Thess. iv. 16.

Q. 85. Will any of them be able to contemn the summons?
A. By no means: "all shall stand before the judgment seat of Christ; and every one shall give account of himself to God," Rom. xiv. 10, 12.

Q. 86. Where will be his *throne* of judgment?
A. In the *clouds*, or aerial heavens; for we read of being "caught up in the clouds, to meet the Lord in the air," 1 Thess. iv. 17.

Q. 87. *By whom* shall all mankind, great and small, be *gathered* to the bar of the Judge?
A. By the *angels*, who shall gather together all the *elect*, Mark xiii. 27, and likewise the *reprobate*, Matt. xiii. 41.

Q. 88. Will the elect and reprobate *stand together*, in one assembly, to be judged?
A. No: they shall be "separated one from another, as a shepherd divideth the sheep from the goats," Matt. xxv. 32.

Q. 89. How will they be *assorted* and *separated*, the one from the other?
A. The elect, who are called *the sheep*, being "caught up together in the clouds, to meet the Lord in the air," 1 Thess. iv. 17, shall be set on his right hand;" and the reprobate, being the *goats*, are left on the earth, (Matt. xxiv. 40,) upon the *judge's left hand*, Matt. xxv. 33.

Q. 90. What kind of a separation will this be?
A. It will be a *total* and *final* separation, never to meet or be fixed with one another any more, Matt. xxv. 46.

Q. 91. Will any man be a *mere spectator* of these two opposite companies?
A. No, surely: every man and woman must take their place in *one* of the *two;* and shall share with the company, whatever hand it be upon, Matt. xxv. 33.

Q. 92. What will be the *subject matter* of the trial?
A. Men's works, "for God shall bring every work into judgment," &c., Eccl. xii. 14; their words, "every idle word that men speak, they shall give account thereof in the day of judgment," Matt. xii. 36; and their thoughts, for he "will make manifest the counsels of the heart," 1 Cor. iv. 5.

Q. 93. Why are *books* said to be *opened* at this solemn trial? Rev. xx. 12.

PART I.—14

A. Not to prevent mistakes in any point of law or fact for the Judge has an infallible knowledge of all things but to show that his proceeding is most accurate, just, and well-grounded in every step of it, Gen. xviii. 25.

Q. 94. What are these books that shall be opened, and men "judged out of these things, which are written in the books?"

A. The book of God's remembrance, Mal. iii. 16; the book of conscience, Rom. ii. 15; the book of the law, Gal. iii. 10: and the book of life, Rev. xx. 12.

Q. 95. What is the *book of God's remembrance?*

A. It is the same with his *omniscience*, by which he knows exactly every man's state, thoughts, words, and deeds, whether good or bad, John xxi. 17: "Lord, thou knowest all things."

Q. 96. For what will this book *serve?*

A. It will serve for an *indictment* against the ungodly: but with respect to the saints, it will be a *memorial* of all the good they have ever done, Matt. xxv. 35—41.

Q. 97. What kind of a book is that of *conscience?*

A. It is just a duplicate of God's book of remembrance, so far as it relates to one's own state and case, Rom. ii. 15.

Q. 98. What is the *book of* the *law?*

A. It is the standard and rule of right and wrong, Rom. vii. 7: and likewise of the sentence that shall be passed upon those who are under it, Gal. iii. 10.

Q. 99. *Why* will this book be *opened?*

A. That all on the *left hand* may read their *sentence* in it, before it be pronounced, Ezek. xviii. 4.

Q. 100. By what law will the heathens be judged?

A. By the natural law, or the light of nature, which shows that they who commit such things (as they shall be convicted of) are worthy of death, Rom. i. 32.

Q. 101. By what law will *Jews* and *Christians* be judged?

A. By the *written* law, Rom. ii. 12: "As many as have sinned in the law," that is, under the written law, "shall be judged by the" written " law."

Q. 102. Whether will *Christians* or *Heathens* be most inexcusable?

A. Beyond all doubt, it will be *more tolerable for Tyre and Sidon* and other heathen countries, *at the day of judgment*, than for those who enjoyed the light of the gospel, and despised it, Matt. xi. 22, 24.

Q. 103. Will the book of the law be opened for the *sentence* of the *saints?*

A. No; for being, in this life, brought under a new covenant, they are no more *under the law, but under grace*, Rom. vi. 14; and therefore *another book* must be opened for their sentence.

OF CHRIST'S EXALTATION. 159

Q. 104. What is that *other book* out of which the saints shall be judged?

A. It is the *book of life*, Rev. xx. 12.

Q. 105. What is *registered* in this book?

A. The *names* of all the *elect*, Luke x. 20 : " Your names are written in heaven," Rev. iii. 5 : " I will not blot his name out of the book of life."

Q. 106. Why is it called the *book of life*?

A. Because it contains God's gracious and unchangeable purpose, to bring all the elect to salvation, or eternal life, " through sanctification of the Spirit, and belief of the truth," 2 Thess. ii. 13.

Q. 107. In whose hands is the book *lodged*?

A. In the hands of the Mediator, Christ Jesus, Deut. xxxiii. 3 : " All his saints are in thy hand."

Q. 108. What is the ground of the saints' acquittal, according to this book?

A. The book of life being opened, it will be known to all who are *elected*, and who not: Christ will, as it were, read out every man's and woman's name recorded in this book, Rev. iii. 5 : " I will confess his name before my Father, and before his angels."

Q. 109. Whether will the *cause* of the righteous or the wicked be *first discussed*?

A. As " the dead in Christ shall rise first," (1 Thess. iv. 16,) so it appears from Matt. xxv. 34, and 41, compared, that the judgment of the saints, on the *right hand*, will have the *preference*.

Q. 110. What is the *blessed sentence* that shall be pronounced upon the saints?

A. " Come, ye blessed of my Father, inherit the kingdom prepared for you from the foundation of the world," Matt. xxv. 34.

Q. 111. For what *reason* will this sentence be pronounced *first*?

A. Because the saints are to sit in judgment, as Christ's *assessors*, against wicked men and apostate angels, 1 Cor. vi. 3, 4.

Q. 112. Upon what *footing* or *foundation* will this sentence pass?

A. Upon the footing of *free grace* alone, reigning through the imputed righteousness of the Surety, unto eternal life, Rom. v. 21.

Q. 113. Is it not said, Rev. xx. 13, that they are " judged every man according to their works?"

A. The sentence passes upon the saints, ACCORDING *to their works*, as flowing from a heart renewed and sanctified; but neither for *their works*, nor for their *faith*, as if eternal life were in any way merited by them, Gal. iii. 18; for the *kingdom* is said to be prepared for them they inherit it as *children*, Rom. viii. 17; but do not procure it to themselves, as *servants* do their wages, Col. iv. 1.

Q. 114. Are not *good works* mentioned as the *ground* of the sentence, Matt. xxv. 35, 36: "I was a hungered, and ye gave me meat?" &c.

A. These good works are mentioned, not as grounds of their sentence, but as evidences of their union with Christ, and of their right and title to heaven in him, John xv. 5, 8; even as the apostle says in another case, of the unbelieving Jews, 1 Cor. x. 5: "With many of them God was not well pleased; for they were overthrown in the wilderness:" their overthrow in the wilderness, was not the ground of God's displeasure with them, but the *evidence* of it.

Q. 115. Will there be any mention made of the *sins* of the righteous?

A. It appears not; "In that time, the iniquity of Israel shall be sought for, and there shall be none: and the sins of Judah, and they shall not be found," Jer. v. 20. "Who shall lay any thing to the charge of God's elect? It is God that justifieth," &c. Rom. viii. 33, 34.

Q. 116. What will *follow* upon the saints' receiving their *sentence* of *absolution?*

A. They "shall judge the world," 1 Cor. vi. 2.

Q. 117. In what *way* and *manner* shall they judge the world?

A. As *assessors* to Christ the Judge, assenting to his judgment as just, Rev. xix. 2, and saying *Amen* to the doom pronounced against all the ungodly, Ps. cxlix. 6—9.

Q. 118. What will be the *sentence of damnation* that shall pass upon the ungodly?

A. "Depart from me, ye cursed, into everlasting fire, prepared for the devil and his angels," Matt. xxv. 41.

Q. 119. How is the *misery* of the wicked *aggravated*, by the pronouncing of this sentence?

A. In as much as they are *damned* by him who came to save sinners, Heb. ii. 3, and must undergo the *wrath of the Lamb*, from which they can make no escape, Rev. vi. 16, 17.

Q. 120. Is there any *injury* or *wrong* done them by this sentence?

A. By no means: for, says our Lord, "I was a hungered, and ye gave me no meat," &c. Matt. xxv. 42, 43.

Q. 121. Are these *evils* no more than *evidences* of their accursed state?

A. They are not only *evidences* of their ungodly state, but they are the proper *causes* and *grounds* of their condemnation: for, though good works do not merit salva-

OF CHRIST'S EXALTATION. 161

tion, yet evil works merit damnation, Rom. vi. 23: *The wages of sin is death.*

Q. 122. Why are only sins of *omission* mentioned in the above passage?

A. To show, that if men shall be condemned for sins of *omission,* James ii. 13, much more for those of *commission,* Rom. ii. 23, 24.

Q. 123. What will follow upon the sentence of condemnation against the wicked?

A. The immediate *execution* of it, without the least reprieve or delay, Matt. xxii. 13.

Q. 124. Will the *devils* also be judged?

A. Yes; they are "reserved unto the judgment of the great day," Jude verse 6.

Q. 125. How can they be said to be *reserved* unto the judgment of that day, when they are condemned already?

A. Though, from the first moment of their sinning, they were actually under the wrath of God, and ever since carry their hell about with them, yet their *final sentence* to further judgment is reserved for that day, 2 Pet. ii. 4.

Q. 126. What is the *final sentence,* or *further judgment,* to which they are *reserved?*

A. It will be a most dreadful addition, and accession to their present torments, not only by the holy triumph which the saints shall have over them, as vile, vanquished, and contemptible enemies; but likewise, by the *eternal restraint* that shall be laid upon them, from hurting the elect any more; and that, by their being shut up, and closely confined in the prison of hell, under the utmost extremity of anguish and horror for ever and ever, Rev. xx. 10.

Q. 127. Who will *keep the field* on that day?

A. Christ and his glorious company: they shall see the *backs* of all their enemies, for the DAMNED shall go off *first ;* as seems to be intimated in the *order* mentioned, Matt. xxv. 46: "These shall go away into everlasting punishment, but the righteous into life eternal."

Q. 128. What improvement ought we to make of Christ's coming to judge the world at the last day?

A. To be diligent that we be "found of him in peace at that day," 2 Pet. iii. 14, by closing with him in the offer of the gospel *now:* to be "looking for, and hasting unto the coming of the day of God," ver. 12, having our "loins girded about, and our lights burning," Luke xii. 35; that so, when he comes, whether at death or judgment, we may be able to say, with joy, "Lo! this is our God, we have waited for him," Isa. xxv. 9.

QUEST. 29. *How are we made partakers of the redemption purchased by Christ?*

ANS. We are made partakers of the redemption purchased by Christ, by the effectual application of it to us by his Holy Spirit.

Q. 1. What may we understand by [*redemption*] in this answer?
A. The whole of that salvation which is revealed and exhibited in the gospel, Ps. cxxx. 7, 8.

Q. 2. Why is redemption said to be [*purchased?*]
A. Because having brought ourselves into a state of bondage and servitude, Gal. iv. 24, we could not be ransomed, but at a *great price*, 1 Cor. vi. 20.

Q. 3. What was the *price* of our redemption?
A. The *precious blood of Christ*, 1 Pet. i. 19.

Q. 4. What is it to be [*partakers*] of this redemption?
A. It is to have a share in it, or to be entered upon the begun possession of it, 1 Cor. x. 17.

Q. 5. Can we *make ourselves* partakers of redemption?
A. No; we must be [*made*] partakers of it, Heb. iii. 14: *We are* MADE *partakers of Christ*, &c.

Q. 6. Why cannot we make ourselves partakers of it?
A. Because we are altogether *without strength*, Rom. v. 6; and utterly averse to all spiritual good, John v. 40.

Q. 7. How then are we made partakers of redemption?
A. [*By the application of it to us.*]

Q. 8. What is meant by the [*application*] of redemption [*to us?*]
A. The conferring all the benefits of it upon us, and making them our own, by way of free gift, John x. 28: "I give unto them eternal life."

Q. 9. How was the application of redemption *typified* under the Old Testament?
A. By *sprinkling* the *blood* of the *sacrifice* upon the *people*, Ex. xxiv. 8.

Q. 10. Does not the application of redemption *presuppose* the purchase of it?
A. Yes; if it were not *first* purchased, it could never be applied, Job xxxiii. 24.

Q. 11. How then could it be applied to the Old Testament saints, when it was not then actually purchased?
A. It was applied upon the *credit* of the *bond*, which the *Surety* gave from eternity, of making a meritorious purchase in the *fulness of time*, Prov. viii. 23, 31.

Q. 12. Can the purchase of redemption *avail* us, if it is not applied?

A. No more than meat can feed, clothes warm, or medicines heal us, if they are not used, John i. 12.

Q. 13. When may the application of redemption be said to be [*effectual?*]

A. When it produces the *saving effects* for which it is —designed.

Q. 14. What are these *saving effects?*

A. The opening of the eyes of sinners, and "turning them from darkness to light, and from the power of Satan to God," Acts xxvi. 18.

Q. 15. If the application of redemption be effectual, what *need* is there of any *after endeavours*, to grow in grace and holiness?

A. The giving us *all things that pertain to life and godliness* is the greatest encouragement and excitement to *add* to our *faith, virtue*, &c.; that is, to use all suitable endeavours, in the strength of grace, after spiritual growth, 2 Pet. i. 3, 5.

Q. 16. Is there any application of redemption that *is not* effectual?

A. Yes; there is an *outward* application of it in *baptism*, which is not, of itself, effectual, as is evident in the instance of Simon Magus, who was *baptized*, and yet remained in the "gall of bitterness, and in the bond of iniquity," Acts viii. 13, 23.

Q. 17. By whom is the redemption purchased by Christ effectually applied?

A. [*By his Holy Spirit,*] Tit. iii. 5, 6.

Q. 18. Why is the application of redemption ascribed to the [*Spirit?*]

A. To show that *each* of the three persons, in the adorable Trinity, is *equally hearty* and cordial in the work of man's redemption; the FATHER in *ordaining*, the SON in *purchasing*, and the SPIRIT in *applying* it, John vi. 57, 63.

Q. 19. Why is the Spirit, in this work, called the [*Holy Spirit?*]

A. Because, as he is *essentially* holy, Ps. li. 11; so he is holy in all his *works* and *operations*, Rom. xv. 16.

Q. 20. Why is redemption said to be applied by the Spirit of Christ, or [*His*] Holy Spirit?

A. Because the Spirit is sent for this work more immediately by Christ, and through his mediation, John xiv. 16, as the leading fruit of his purchase, John xiv. 7.

Q. 21. What is the *difference* between the *purchase* of redemption and the *application* of it?

A. The purchase of redemption is a work done *without* us, Isa. lxiii. 3; but the application of it takes place *within* us, Rom. viii. 26.

Q. 22. To whom is redemption effectually applied by the Spirit?

A. "To all those for whom Christ has purchased it," John x. 15, 16,* and to none else.

Q. 23. "Can they who have never heard the gospel, and so know not Jesus Christ, nor believe in him, be saved by their living according to the light of nature?"

A. "They—cannot be saved, John viii. 24, be they ever so diligent to frame their lives according to the light of nature, 1 Cor. i. 20, 21, or the laws of that religion which they profess, John iv. 22; neither is there salvation in any other but in Christ alone, Acts iv. 12, who is the Saviour only of his body the Church, Eph. v. 23."†

Q. 24. What *means* does the Spirit make use of in the application of redemption?

A. The Spirit of God makes use of the reading, 2 Tim. iii. 15, 16, but *especially* the preaching of the word, for this end, Rom. x. 17.

Q. 25. Are these means of *themselves* effectual?

A. Not without the power and efficacy of the Spirit accompanying them, 1 Thess. i. 5.

Q. 26. What is *incumbent* on us, in *way of duty*, that the redemption, purchased by Christ, may be effectually applied to us?

A. To search for the knowledge of Christ *as for hid treasure*, Prov. ii. 4, and to pray for the Spirit to *testify* of Christ, John xv. 26, in the faith of his own promise: "He shall glorify me; for he shall receive of mine, and shall show it unto you," chap. xvi. 14.

QUEST. 30. *How does the Spirit apply to us the redemption purchased by Christ?*

ANS. The Spirit applies to us the redemption purchased by Christ, by working faith in us, and thereby uniting us to Christ, in our effectual calling.

Q. 1. What is the *special* work of the Spirit in the *application* of redemption?

A. It is the [*uniting us to Christ,*] Rom. viii. 9, 11.

Q. 2. Can we have no *share* in the redemption purchased by Christ, without *union* to his person?

A. No; because all purchased blessings are lodged in his person, John iii. 35, and go along with it, 1 John v. 12.

Q. 3. What is it to be *united* to his person?

A. It is to be *joined* to, or made *one* with him, 1 Cor. vi. 17.

* Larger Catechism, Q. 59.   † Larger Catechism, Q. 60.

Q. 4. Is it then a *personal* union?
A. No; it is indeed a union of *persons*, but not a *personal* union: believers make not *one person* with Christ, but *one body* mystical, of which he is the head, 1 Cor. xii. 12, 27.

Q. 5. How can we be united to Christ, seeing he is in heaven, and we on earth?
A. Although the human nature of Christ be in heaven, yet his person is every where, Matt. xxviii. 20.

Q. 6. Where can he be found on earth, in order to our being united to him?
A. In the WORD, which is *nigh* to us, and Christ in it, Rom. x. 8, 9.

Q. 7. By what means are we united to Christ as brought nigh in the word?
A. By means of [*faith*] or believing, Eph. iii. 17: "That Christ may dwell in your hearts by faith."

Q. 8. Is it the indispensable duty of all who hear the word, to believe on Christ, or come to him by faith?
A. It certainly is; for, "This is his commandment, that we should believe on the name of his Son Jesus Christ," 1 John iii. 23.

Q. 9. Are any that hear the word able to believe of themselves?
A. No; faith is "not of ourselves, it is the gift of God," Eph. ii. 8.

Q. 10. How then come we by faith?
A. By the Spirit's [*working*] it [*in us:*] and therefore called the *Spirit of faith*, 2 Cor. iv. 13, because he is the principal and efficient cause of it.

Q. 11. Why can *no less a worker* than the Spirit of God produce this faith?
A. Because it is a work that requires almighty power, even the same power *which* was *wrought in Christ, when he* was *raised from the dead*, Eph. i. 19, 20.

Q. 12. What is the *end*, or design, of the Spirit in working faith in us?
A. It is the [*uniting us to Christ,*] Eph. iii. 17.

Q. 13. To whom are sinners united before union with Christ?
A. To the *first Adam*, Rom. v. 12.

Q. 14. By what *bond* are they united to the *first Adam?*
A. By the bond of the *covenant* of *works*, by which *Adam*, who was the *natural* root of his posterity, became their *moral* root also, bearing them as their *representative in* that covenant, Rom. v. 19.

Q. 15. How is this union dissolved?
A. By being "married to another, even *to* him who is raised from the dead," Rom. vii. 4.

Q. 16. Is Christ united to us before we become united to him?

A. The union is *mutual*, but it begins *first* on his side, 1 John iv. 19.

Q. 17. How does it *begin first* on his side?

A. By *unition*, which is before union.

Q. 18. What do you understand by *unition?*

A. It is the Spirit of Christ uniting himself first to us, according to the promise, "I will put my Spirit within you," Ezek. xxxvi. 27.

Q. 19. How does the Spirit of Christ unite himself first to us?

A. By *coming* into the soul, at the happy moment appointed for the spiritual marriage with Christ, and *quickening* it, so that it is no more *morally* dead, but *alive*, having new *spiritual* powers put into it, Eph. ii. 5: "Even when we were dead in sins, he hath quickened us."

Q. 20. Is the Spirit of Christ, upon his first entrance, *actively* or *passively received?*

A. The soul, *morally dead* in sin, can be no more than a mere *passive recipient*, Ezek. xxxvii. 14: "And shall put my Spirit in you, and ye shall live."

Q. 21. What is the *immediate effect* of quickening the dead soul, by the Spirit of Christ passively received?

A. The immediate effect of it is *actual believing:* Christ being *come in* by his Spirit, the dead soul is thereby quickened, and the immediate effect of this is, the embracing him by faith, by which the union is completed, John v. 25.

Q. 22. What are the *nature* and *properties* of this union?

A. It is a spiritual, mysterious, real, intimate, and indissoluble union.

Q. 23. In what respect is it a *spiritual* union?

A. In as much as the *one* Spirit of God dwells in the *head* and in the *members*, Rom. viii. 9.

Q. 24. Why is it called *mystical*, or mysterious? Eph. v. 32.

A. Because it is full of mysteries; Christ *in* the believer, John xvii. 23; *living* in him, Gal. ii. 20; *walking* in him, 2 Cor. vi. 16; and the believer *dwelling* in God, 1 John iv. 16; *putting on Christ*, Gal. iii. 27: "eating his flesh, and drinking his blood," John vi. 56.

Q. 25. Why is it called a *real* union?

A. Because believers are as really united to Christ, as the members of the natural body are to their head; "For we are members of his body, of his flesh, and of his bones," Eph. v. 30.

Q. 26. How *intimate* is this union?

A. It is so intimate, that believers are said to be *one* in the Father and the Son, as the Father is in Christ, and

Christ in the Father, John xvii. 21: "That they all may be one, as thou, Father, art in me, and I in thee; that they also may be one in us."

Q. 27. Can this union ever be *dissolved?*

A. By no means: "Neither death, nor life, &c., shall be able to separate us from the love of God which is in Christ Jesus our Lord," Rom. viii. 38, 39.

Q. 28. Is it a *legal* union that is between Christ and believers?

A. Though not a mere legal union, yet it is a union *sustained in law*, in so far, as that upon the union taking place, what Christ did and suffered for them, is reckoned in law as if they had done and suffered it themselves: hence they are said to be *crucified with Christ*, Gal. ii. 20; to be *buried with him*, Col. ii. 12; and to be *raised up together*, Eph. ii. 6.

Q. 29. What are the *bonds* of this union.

A. The *Spirit* on Christ's part, 1 John iii. 24, and *faith* on ours, Eph. iii. 7.

Q. 30. Is it the Spirit on Christ's part, or faith on ours, that unites the sinner to Christ?

A. They both concur in their order: Christ *first* apprehends the sinner by his Spirit, 1 Cor. xii. 13; and the sinner thus apprehended, apprehends Christ by faith, Phil. iii. 12.

Q. 31. How may persons *know* if they are *apprehended of Christ?*

A. If he has engaged their love and esteem, and dissolved the regard they had to other things that came in competition with him, 1 Pet. ii. 7.

Q. 32. Are the bonds of this union *inviolable?*

A. Yes; "I give unto them," says Christ, "eternal life, and they shall never perish; neither shall any pluck them out of my hand," John x. 28.

Q. 33. What makes the *Spirit* an inviolable bond of union?

A. Because he never departs from that soul into which he enters, but abides there for ever, John xiv. 16.

Q. 34. How can *faith* be an inviolable bond of union, when it is subject to *failing?*

A. Although the *actings* of faith may sometimes fail, yet neither the *habit* nor the *exercise* ever shall, in time of need, and that because of the prevalency of Christ's intercession, Luke xxii. 32: "I have prayed for thee, that thy faith fail not."

Q. 35. Are the *bodies* of the saints united to Christ, at the same time that their souls are?

A. Yes; their bodies are made "members of Christ, and temples of the Holy Ghost which is in them," 1 Cor vi. 15, 19.

Q. 36. Whether is it *sinners* or *saints*, that are united to Christ?

A. In the very moment of the union, sinners are made saints, 1 Cor. vi. 11.

Q. 37. To what is this union *compared* in scripture?

A. To the union between husband and wife, Rom. vii. 4; head and members, Col. i. 18; root and branches, John xv. 5; foundation and superstructure, 1 Pet. ii. 5, 6.

Q. 38. What are believers *entitled* to by their union with Christ?

A. To himself, and all the blessings of his purchase, 1 Cor. iii. 22, 23.

Q. 39. When does the Spirit work faith in us, and thereby unite us to Christ?

A. He does it [in our effectual calling,] 1 Cor. i. 9.*

Q. 40. What *improvement* ought both saints and sinners to make of the doctrine of *union with Christ?*

A. SAINTS ought to evidence that Christ is *in them*, by endeavouring that his image shine forth in their conversation, studying to "walk worthy of the Lord unto all pleasing," Col. i. 10; and SINNERS ought to seek after this happy relation to Christ, while he is yet *standing* at their *door* and *knocking*, Rev. iii. 20; and while the gates of the *city of refuge* are not yet closed, Zech. ix. 12.

QUEST. 31. *What is effectual calling?*

ANS. Effectual calling is the work of God's Spirit, whereby, convincing us of our sin and misery, enlightening our minds in the knowledge of Christ, and renewing our wills, he doth persuade and enable us to embrace Jesus Christ, freely offered to us in the gospel.

Q. 1. Why is *effectual calling* termed a [*work?*]

A. Because it is effected by various operations or workings of the Spirit of God upon the soul, therefore called "the seven Spirits which are before his throne," Rev. i. 4.

Q. 2. Why is it called a work of [*God's Spirit?*]

A. Because it relates to the application of redemption, which is the *special* work of God's Spirit, John xvi. 14:— "He," says Christ of the Spirit, "shall receive of mine, and shall show it unto you."

Q. 3. How *many fold* is the divine [*calling?*]

A. Twofold: *outward*, by the word; and *inward*, by the Spirit.

---

* Larger Catechism, Q. 66.

OF EFFECTUAL CALLING.

Q. 4. What is the *outward call* by the word?

A. It is the free and unlimited invitation given, in the dispensation of the gospel, to all the hearers of it, to receive Christ, and salvation with him, Isa. lv. 1. Rev. xxii. 17.

Q. 5. What is the *inward call* by the Spirit?

A. It is the Spirit's accompanying the outward call with power and efficacy upon the soul, John vi. 45.

Q. 6. Which of these is [*effectual*] in bringing sinners to Christ?

A. The inward call, by the Spirit: "for it is the Spirit that quickeneth," John vi. 63; the outward call, by the word, is of itself ineffectual; "for many are called, but few are chosen," Matt. xxii. 14.

Q. 7. What is meant by *few being chosen?*

A. That few are determined effectually to embrace the call; and therefore termed a *little flock*, Luke xxii. 32.

Q. 8. What is the *main* or *leading* work of the Spirit in effectual calling?

A. It is that by which [*he doth persuade and enable us to embrace Jesus Christ freely offered to us in the gospel,*] Phil. ii. 13.

Q. 9. What is it to [*embrace*] Christ?

A. It is, like Simeon, to *clasp* him in the arms of faith, with complacency and delight, Luke ii. 28.

Q. 10. *Where* is it that faith embraces him?

A. In the promises of the gospel, Heb. xi. 13.

Q. 11. What is the [*gospel?*]

A. It is good news, or glad tidings of life and salvation to lost sinners of mankind, through a "Saviour, who is Christ the Lord," Luke ii. 10, 11.

Q. 12. What warrant has faith to embrace him in the promise of the gospel?

A. His Father's *gift*, John iii. 16, and his own *offer* of himself in it, Isa. xlv. 22.

Q. 13. Can there be an embracing, or receiving, without a previous giving?

A. "A man can receive" [margin, *take unto himself*] "nothing, except it be given him from heaven," John iii. 27.

Q. 14. What is the *faith* of the gospel offer?

A. It is a *believing* that Jesus Christ, with his righteousness, and all his salvation is, by *himself*, offered to sinners, and to each of them in particular, Prov. viii. 4. John vii. 37.

Q. 15. When is the word of the gospel-offer savingly believed?

A. When it is powerfully applied by the Holy Spirit to the soul in particular, as the *word* and *voice* of Christ *himself*, and not of men, 1 Thess. i. 5, and ii. 13.

Q. 16. How can we believe it is the *voice of Christ him-*

self in the offer, when Christ is now in heaven, and we hear no voice from thence?

A. The voice of Christ in his written word, is *more sure* than a voice from heaven itself, 2 Pet. i. 18, 19; and it is *this* voice of Christ in the word, that is the stated ground of faith, Rom. i. 16, 17.

Q. 17. *How* is Christ offered in the gospel?

A. [*Freely,*] as well as *fully,* Rev. xxii. 17.

Q. 18. To whom is he offered?

A. [*To us*] sinners of mankind, as such, Prov. viii. 4.

Q. 19. Have we any *natural inclination* to embrace the gospel-offer?

A. No: the Spirit [*doth persuade*] us to it, 2 Cor. v. 11.

Q. 20. Will *moral suasion*, or arguments taken from the promises and threatenings of the word, persuade any to embrace Christ?

A. No: the *enticing words of man's wisdom* will not do; nothing less is sufficient, than the *demonstration of the Spirit,* that so our faith may not " stand in the wisdom of men, but in the power of God," 1 Cor. ii. 4, 5.

Q. 21. Have we any ability of our own to believe in Christ, or to embrace him?

A. No: the *Spirit of faith* [*doth enable us*] to do it, 2 Cor. iv. 13.

Q. 22. By what *means* does the Spirit persuade and enable us to embrace Christ?

A. By [*convincing us of our sin and misery, enlightening our minds in the knowledge of Christ, and renewing our wills.*]

Q. 23. What is the object of the [*convincing*] work of the Spirit; or of what does he convince us?

A. [*Of our sin and misery,*] Acts ii. 37.

Q. 24. Of what [*sin*] does the Spirit convince us?

A. Both of *original* and *actual* sin, Mark vii. 21, particularly of unbelief, John xvi. 9.

Q. 25. Of what [*misery*] does he convince us?

A. Of the misery of losing communion with God, 2 Cor. vi. 14, 15; and being under his wrath and curse, in time, and through eternity, Isa. xxxiii. 14.

Q. 26. How does the Spirit convince us of sin and misery?

A. By the *law*, Rom. iii. 20: " By the law is the knowledge of sin."

Q. 27. What knowledge of sin have we by the law?

A. By the *precept* of the law, we have the knowledge of the *evil nature* of sin, Rom. vii. 7, and by the *threatening*, the knowledge of the *guilt* and *desert* of it, Gal. iii. 10.

Q. 28. In what *capacity* does the Spirit convince us of sin by the law?

A. As a *spirit of bondage* working *fear*, Rom. viii. 15.

OF EFFECTUAL CALLING. 17.

Q. 29. Have all had an *equal measure* of this kind of conviction, who have been persuaded to embrace Christ?

A. No; some have had more, and some less, as in the instances of Paul and Lydia, Acts ix. 6, 9, compared with chap. xvi. 14.

Q. 30. What *measure* of conviction by the law, is requisite for such as are come to full ripeness of age?

A. Such a measure as to let them see, that they are sinners by nature, both in heart and life; that they are lost and undone under the curse of the law, and wrath of God; and that they are utterly incapable of recovering themselves, as being legally and spiritually dead, Rom. vii. 9.

Q. 31. Why is such a measure as this, of legal conviction, requisite in the adult?

A. Because, otherwise, they would never see the need they stand in of Christ as a Saviour, either from sin or wrath, Matt. ix. 12, 13.

Q. 32. Is this measure of conviction necessary as a *condition* of our *welcome* to Christ, or as a *qualification fitting* us to believe on him?

A. No; but merely as a *motive*, to excite us to make use of our privilege of free access to him, Hos. xiv. 1: "O Israel, return unto the Lord thy God; for thou hast fallen by thine iniquity."

Q. 33. Have not some been under deep legal convictions, and yet never effectually called?

A. Yes; Judas went to *hell* under a load of this kind of conviction, Matt. xxvii. 3—5.

Q. 34. Is not the [*enlightening our minds in the knowledge of Christ,*] a mean of persuading and enabling us to embrace him?

A. Yes; for, "how can they believe in him of whom they have not heard?" Rom. x. 14.

Q. 35. What is the subject of the Spirit's [*enlightening?*]

A. [*Our minds*] or understandings, which are the eyes of the soul, Eph. i. 18: "The eyes of your understanding being enlightened," &c.

Q. 36. What is the *object* of this *enlightening*, or in what are we enlightened?

A. It is [*in the knowledge of Christ,*] Phil. iii. 8.

Q. 37. Who is the *author* of saving illumination in the knowledge of Christ?

A. The Holy Spirit, who is therefore called, "the Spirit of wisdom and revelation in the knowledge of him," Eph. i. 17.

Q. 38. In what condition is the *mind*, before it is enlightened by the Spirit?

A. In gross darkness and ignorance, as to the "things of the Spirit of God," 1 Cor. ii. 14. Eph. v. 8.

Q. 39. *What* is it *in Christ* that the Spirit enlightens the mind in the knowledge of?
A. In the knowledge of his person, righteousness, offices, fulness, &c. John xv. 26, says Christ of the Spirit, "He shall testify of me."

Q. 40. What are the *distinguishing properties* of saving illumination?
A. It is of an humbling, Job. xlii. 5, 6, sanctifying, John xvii. 17, transforming, 2 Cor. iii. 18, and growing nature, Hos. vi. 3.

Q. 41. What is the *necessity* of this illumination, in order to the embracing of Christ?
A. Because, without it, there can be no discerning of his matchless excellency, inexhaustible sufficiency, and universal suitableness, the saving knowledge of which is necessary to the comfortable embracing of him, Ps. ix. 10: "They that know thy name, will put their trust in thee."

Q. 42. By what *means* does the Spirit enlighten the mind in the knowledge of Christ?
A. By means of the gospel, Rom. x. 17.

Q. 43. Does not the [*renewing our wills*] accompany the illumination of our minds?
A. Yes; when "the Lord shall send the rod of his strength out of Zion," there shall be a "willing people in the day of his power," Ps. cx. 2, 3.

Q. 44. In what *consists* the *renovation* of the *will?*
A. In working in it a new inclination or propensity to good, and a fixed aversion to whatever is evil, Ezek. xxxvi. 26.

Q. 45. Does the Spirit, in the renovation of the *will,* use any *violence* or *compulsion?*
A. No; he makes us *willing* in the day of his power, Ps. cx. 3.

Q. 46. What is the *natural disposition* of the *will* before it is renewed?
A. It is wicked and rebellious, full of enmity against Christ, and the way of salvation through him, John v. 40.

Q. 47. Can any man *change,* or *renew,* his own *will?*
A. No more than the "Ethiopian can change his skin, or the leopard his spots," Jer. xiii. 23.

Q. 48. What *necessity* is there for renewing the *will,* in order to the embracing of Christ?
A. Because till this be done, the natural *ill will* that is in sinners against Christ, *in all his offices,* will be retained, 2 Cor. v. 17.

Q. 49. In what appears the *ill will* which sinners bear to Christ as a *Prophet?*
A. In the conceit of their own wisdom, Prov. i. 22, and slighting the means of instruction, chap. xxvi. 12.

Q. 50. How do they manifest their aversion to him as a *Priest?*
A. "In going about to establish their own righteousness, and refusing to submit themselves unto the righteousness of God," Rom. x. 3.

Q. 51. How do they manifest their opposition to him as a *King?*
A. In their hatred of holiness, love to sin, and saying, in fact, concerning him, "We will not have this man to reign over us," Luke xix. 14.

Q. 52. Who are the only persons that are effectually called?
A. All the elect, and they only, Acts xiii. 48: "As many as were ordained to eternal life, believed."*

Q. 53. What may we learn from the doctrine of effectual calling?
A. That "the gifts and calling of God are without repentance," Rom. xi. 29; that "all things work together for good—to them that are the called according to his purpose," Rom. viii. 28; and that it is our duty to "walk worthy of God, who hath called us unto his kingdom and glory," 1 Thess. ii. 12.

QUEST. 32. *What benefits do they that are effectually called partake of in this life?*

ANS. They that are effectually called, do, in this life, partake of justification, adoption, sanctification, and the several benefits which, in this life, do either accompany or flow from them.

Q. 1. "What special [*benefits*] do the members of the invisible church (or such as are effectually called,) enjoy by Christ?"
A. They "enjoy union and communion with him, in grace and glory, Eph. ii. 5, 6." †

Q. 2. "What is the communion in grace, which the members of the invisible church have with Christ?'
A. It "is their partaking of the virtue of his mediation, in their justification, adoption, sanctification, and whatever else in this life manifests their union with him, 1 Cor. i. 30." ‡

Q. 3. How are all these benefits *connected* with effectual calling?

---

* Larger Catechism, Quest. 68. † Ibid, Quest. 65. ‡ Ibid, Quest. 69.

A. By a connexion established in the eternal purpose and counsel of God, in which all these blessings or benefits are sweetly linked together, Rom. viii. 30: "Whom he did predestinate, them he also called; and whom he called, them he also justified; and whom he justified, them he also glorified."

Q. 4. What is the *connexion* between *effectual calling* and *justification?*

A. In effectual calling, sinners, being united to Christ by faith, have thereby communion with him in his righteousness, for justification, Phil. iii. 9.

Q. 5. How is *adoption connected* with effectual calling?

A. In virtue of the union which takes place in effectual calling, believers stand related to Christ, as having a *new* kind of *interest* in God as *his Father*; and consequently *their Father* in him, according to John xx. 17: "I ascend to my Father, and your Father;" and Eph. i. 3: "Blessed be the God and Father of our Lord Jesus Christ."

Q. 6. What is the *blessed effect* of this new kind of interest, which Christ, as the head of the body, has in God as his Father?

A. That, by the Spirit of adoption, we may call God our Father, in the right of Jesus Christ, our elder brother, Rom. viii. 15: "Ye have received the Spirit of adoption, whereby we cry, Abba, Father."

Q. 7. How is effectual calling *connected* with *sanctification?*

A. In virtue of the union, which takes place in effectual calling, believers are related to Christ as the *Lord their strength*, their quickening, and influencing head, "who of God is made unto them—sanctification," I Cor. i. 30.

Q. 8. What is the connexion between effectual calling and a *blessed death?*

A. In effectual calling, believers are united to Christ, by a union that cannot be dissolved by death, Rom. viii. 38, 39.

Q. 9. What is the connexion between effectual calling and a *happy resurrection?*

A. In effectual calling, sinners are united to Christ, as a living and exalted head, and therefore their happy resurrection is absolutely secured in him, because he is "risen from the dead, and become the first fruits of them that slept," 1 Cor. xv. 20.

Q. 10. What *improvement* should we make of the sweet *connexion* that is between all these benefits of which the effectually called are partakers?

A. We ought, through grace, in the use of all the means and ordinances of God's appointment, to give all diligence to make our calling and election sure; that having the knowledge of our justification, and adoption, by our sanctification, we may have the comfortable prospect of a happy death, and glorious resurrection, 2 Pet. i. 10, 11.

QUEST. 33. *What is justification?*

ANS. Justification is an act of God's free grace; wherein he pardons all our sins, and accepts us as righteous in his sight, only for the righteousness of Christ, imputed to us, and received by faith alone.

Q. 1. From whence is the word [*justification*] borrowed?

A. Being a *law-word*, it is borrowed from courts of justice among men, when a person arraigned is *pronounced righteous*, and, in court, openly *absolved?*

Q. 2. How does it appear, that justification denotes an *act of jurisdiction*, and not an *inward change* upon the soul?

A. From its being opposed to *condemnation*, which all own to consist, not in the *infusing* of *wickedness* into a person, but in *passing sentence* upon him, according to the demerit of his crime, Ps. cix. 7.

Q. 3. What is it, then, to *justify* a person?

A. It is not to *make* him righteous, but to *declare* him to be so, upon a legal ground, and trial of a judge, Isa. xliii. 9, 26.

Q. 4. Who is the *author* or *efficient cause*, of our justification?

A. It is God himself; for, *it is God that justifieth*, Rom. viii. 33.

Q. 5. Is it God *essentially*, or *personally* considered?

A. God *essentially* considered, in the *person* of the *Father*, is the *justifier*, in respect of judiciary power and authority, Rom. iii. 26; and our Lord Jesus Christ, in respect of the dispensation, or exercise of that power, Acts v. 31.

Q. 6. In what respect is the *Spirit* said to justify? 1 Cor. vi. 11.

A. As the *applier* of the blood or righteousness of Christ, by which we are justified, Tit. iii. 5.

Q. 7. In what *state* is a sinner *before* justification?

A. In a state of sin and guilt, Rom. iii. 9, and, consequently, in a state of wrath and condemnation, Gal. iii. 10.

Q. 8. How can God justify the *ungodly?*

A. Every elect sinner, however ungodly in himself, yet, upon union with Christ, has communion with him in his righteousness, and on this account he is justified, Isa. xlv 25: "In the Lord shall all the seed of Israel be justified."

Q. 9. Why have elect sinners communion with Christ in his righteousness, upon their union with him?

A. Because their sins having been imputed to him from eternity, he became *legally one* with them, transferring their debt to himself, and undertaking to pay the same, Isa. liii. 6; wherefore, upon union with him by faith, his perfect satisfaction is imputed to them, as if they had made it themselves, 2 Cor. v. 21.

Q. 10. Why is justification called an [*act?*]

A. Because, like the sentence of a judge, it is *completed at once*, and not carried on gradually like a work of time, Deut. xxv. 1.

Q. 11. What is the *moving cause* of justification, or what *kind* of an act is it?

A. It is [*an act of God's free grace,*] Rom. iii. 24: "Being justified freely by his grace through the redemption that is in Christ Jesus."

Q. 12. How can *free grace* be the moving cause of our justification, when it is "through the redemption that is in Christ Jesus?"

A. Because the redemption that is in Christ, is the *channel* through which justifying grace runs *freely* to us, Eph. i. 7.

Q. 13. What are the *constituent parts* of justification?

A. They are *two;* that [*in which he pardons all our sins,*] Rom. vi. 7; and that, in which he [*accepts us as righteous in his sight,*] Eph. i. 6.

Q. 14. What is the *pardon* of sin?

A. It is God's absolving the sinner from the condemnation of the law, on account of Christ's satisfaction for sin, Rom. viii. 1.

Q. 15. Why is the pardon of sin *set before* the accepting us as righteous, in the *answer?*

A. Because, till the sentence of the broken law be dissolved by pardon, it is impossible that our persons can be accepted, or any blessing of the covenant conferred upon us. See Heb. viii. 10—13; where, after a great many other promised blessings, it is added, ver. 12: "FOR I will be merciful to their unrighteousness," &c., intimating that the pardon of sin led the way to other covenant blessings.

Q. 16. What is it *in sin* that pardon removes?

A. The *guilt* of it, which is a person's actual obligation or liability to eternal wrath, on account thereof, Eph. ii. 3.

Q. 17. Can the guilt of sin ever *recur* upon a pardoned person?

A. No: the obligation to punishment, being once taken off, can never recur again; because "there is no condemnation to them that are in Christ Jesus," Rom. viii. 1.

Q. 18. Will future sins *revoke* a former pardon?

A. No: future sins may provoke the Lord to withdraw the *sense* of former pardon, but can never revoke the pardon *itself;* because "The gifts and calling of God are without repentance," Rom. xi. 29.

Q. 19. *What sins* are pardoned in justification?

A. [*All our sins*] whatsoever, Ps. ciii. 3: "Who forgiveth ALL thine iniquities."

Q. 20. How are sins *past* and *present* pardoned?

A. By a *formal* remission of them, Ps. xxxii. 5: "Thou forgavest the iniquity of my sin."

Q. 21. How are sins *to come*, pardoned?

A. By securing the *non-imputation* of them, as to the guilt of eternal wrath, Rom. iv. 8: "Blessed is the man to whom the Lord will not impute sin."

Q. 22. If the *non-imputation* of eternal wrath, as to future sins, be *secured*, why do the saints *pray* for the *pardon* of them when committed?

A. Because the *guilt* or liability to *fatherly anger* is contracted by the commission of them; and, therefore, they *pray* for the removal of that guilt, Ps. li. 12: "Restore unto me the joy of thy salvation."

Q. 23. Is *repentance* a *condition* of pardon?

A. No; because this would bring in works into the matter of our justification before God, quite contrary to *scripture*, which tells us, that "a man is not justified by the works of the law, but by the faith of Jesus Christ," Gal. ii. 16.

Q. 24. How do you *prove*, that repentance has not the same *interest* as faith, in our justification?

A. From this, that in scripture we are frequently said to be *justified by faith*, but *never* said to be *justified by repentance*.

Q. 25. Is it not affirmed in our Confession, "that repentance is of such necessity to all sinners, that none may expect pardon without it?"*

A. The meaning is, that repentance is such an *inseparable concomitant* of pardon, that no *pardoned* person continues to be *impenitent*, 2 Sam. xii. 13. Matt. xxvi. 75.

Q. 26. If none can expect pardon, without expecting repentance along with it; will it not therefore follow, that repentance is a *condition* of pardon?

A. Not at all; for if repentance cannot so much as have the least *instrumentality* in pardon, it can never be the *condition* of it, nor have the smallest *influence* in *causing* it.†

---

* Confession, chap. xv. § 3.
† Confession chap. xv. § 3: "Repentance" is "not to be rested in, as any satisfaction for sin, or any cause of the pardon thereof."

Q. 27. How does it appear that repentance has not the least *instrumentality* in pardon?

A. It appears evidently from this, that *faith* is the *sole instrument* of receiving Christ and his righteousness; without receiving of which there can be no pardon, John viii. 24: "If ye believe not that I am he, ye shall die in your sins."

Q. 28. Does God do any more in justification than freely pardon all our sins?

A. Yes; he likewise [*accepts us as righteous in his sight,*] Eph. i. 6.

Q. 29. Why is the *accepting us as righteous* joined with *pardon*, in justification?

A. Because, though among men a criminal may be pardoned, and neither declared righteous nor received into favour, yet it is not so with God; for whom he forgives, he both accounts their persons righteous in his sight, and receives them into perpetual favour, Rom. v. 8—10.

Q. 30. How can a holy and righteous God, whose *judgment is according to truth,* accept sinners as *righteous* without a perfect righteousness?

A. He accepts them as *righteous* [*only for the righteousness of Christ,*] which is perfect, and becomes truly theirs through *faith*, Jer. xxiii. 6. Isa. xlv. 24.

Q. 31. By what *right* does the surety righteousness become *theirs?*

A. By the right of a free *gift received,* and the right of *communion* with Christ.

Q. 32. How does it become theirs by the right of a *gift received?*

A. In as much as Christ's righteousness being made over in the gospel, as God's gift to sinners, it is by faith actually claimed and received; hence called *the* GIFT *of righteousness*, Rom. v. 17.

Q. 33. How does Christ's surety righteousness become theirs by right of *communion with him?*

A. In as much as sinners being *united* to him by faith, have thus *communion* or a *common interest* with him in his *righteousness*, Phil. iii. 9.

Q. 34. When is it, then, that, according to truth, God accepts us as righteous in his sight?

A. When Christ's surety righteousness is actually *reckoned ours*, and we made *the righteousness of God* IN HIM, 2 Cor. v. 21: upon this account precisely, and no other, are we accepted of God as *righteous; the righteousness of GOD* being UPON *all them that believe*, Rom. iii. 22.

Q. 35 What is the *matter* of our justification, or that for which we are justified?

OF JUSTIFICATION. 179

A. The RIGHTEOUSNESS of Christ *only;* hence he is called "The Lord our Righteousness," Jer. xxiii. 6.

Q. 36. In what does [*the righteousness of Christ*] consist?

A. In the *holiness of* his *human nature*, his *righteous life*, and *satisfactory death*.*

Q. 37. Can law or justice reach the person who is under the covering of the surety righteousness?

A. By no means; for "Who shall lay any thing to the charge of God's elect?—It is Christ that died, yea, rather, that is risen again," Rom. viii. 33, 34.

Q. 38. Is the righteousness of Christ *meritorious* of our justification?

A. Yes; because of the infinite dignity of his person; for, though he "took upon him the form of a servant, yet, being in the form of God, he thought it no robbery to be equal with God," Phil ii. 6, 7.

Q. 39. How is the righteousness of Christ *commonly divided?*

A. Into his *active* and *passive* obedience.

Q. 40. What is his *active* obedience?

A. The holiness of his nature and righteousness of his life, in full and perfect conformity to the whole law, without the least failure, either of parts, or degrees of obedience to the end, Matt. v. 17, 18.

Q. 41. What is his *passive* obedience?

A. His *satisfaction for sin*, by enduring the *infinite execution* of the *curse*, upon him in his *death*, Gal. iii. 13, to the full compensation of all the injuries done to the honour of an *infinite* God, by all the sins of an elect world, Eph. v. 2.

Q. 42. Why does his satisfactory death, as well as his righteous life, get the name of *obedience?* Phil. ii. 8.

A. Because his sufferings and death were entirely voluntary, and in most profound submission to the commandment which he had received of his Father, John x. 18.

Q. 43. What is the *formal cause* of our justification, or that by which Christ's righteousness is made ours?

A. It is its being [*imputed to us,*] Rom. iv. 6.

Q. 44. What is it to *impute* Christ's righteousness to us?

A. It is God's *accounting* or *reckoning* it to us, as if we had obeyed the law, and satisfied justice in our own persons, and dealing with us accordingly, Rom. viii. 4. 2 Cor. v. 21.

Q. 45. Upon what *ground* or foundation is Christ's righteousness imputed to us?

A. Upon the ground of his *representing* us from eternity, and our union with him in time, Isa. liii 5.

---

* See these explained on Quest. 20, entitled, Of the Covenant of Grace.

Q. 46. What necessity is there for the *imputation* of Christ's *passive* obedience?

A. Because without the imputation of it, we could have no legal security from eternal death, Rom. v. 9.

Q. 47. What necessity is there for the *imputation* of Christ's *active* obedience?

A. Because without the imputation of it, we could have no legal *title to eternal life*, Rom. vi. 23.

Q. 48. If Christ, *as man*, gave obedience to the law for *himself*, how can his *active* obedience be *imputed* to us?

A. Though the *human nature, abstractly* considered, be a creature, yet never subsisting *by itself*, but in the person of the Son of God, the acts of obedience performed in it were never the acts of a *mere man*, but of him who is *God-man*, Mediator; and, consequently, acts of obedience, not for himself, but for us, Gal. iv. 4, 5.

Q. 49. If Christ's active obedience be *imputed* to us, are we not *released* from any *obligation* to yield obedience to the law in our *own persons?*

A. We are only released from an obligation to yield obedience to the law as *a covenant of works*, not released from obedience to it as a *rule of life*, Gal. ii. 19.

Q. 50. Is the righteousness of Christ, *itself*, imputed to us, or only *its effects?*

A. As the guilt *itself of Adam's first sin* is imputed to all his posterity, by which *judgment* comes *upon all men to condemnation*, so, the righteousness of Christ *itself* is imputed to all his spiritual seed, by which the *free gift* comes upon them *all unto justification of life*, Rom. v. 18.

Q. 51. What is the difference between the imputation of *our sins* to Christ, and the imputation of *his righteousness* to us?

A. Our sins were imputed to Christ as our Surety, only *for a time*, that he might *take them away;* but his righteousness is imputed to us to *abide with us for ever;* hence called an *everlasting righteousness*, Dan. ix. 24.

Q. 52. Why are we said to be pardoned and accepted [*only*] for the righteousness of Christ?

A. Because a sinner can have no *other* plea before God, for pardon and acceptance, but Christ's *fulfilling all righteousness*, as the only condition of the covenant, Isa. xlv. 24.

Q. 53. What is the *instrumental cause* of our justification?

A. It is *twofold;* namely, *external* and *internal*.

Q. 54. What is the *external instrumental cause?*

A. The GOSPEL; because the righteousness of God is revealed in it, and brought near to us as a free *gift*, Rom. i. 17, v. 17, and x. 8.

OF JUSTIFICATION.

Q. 55. What is the *internal instrumental cause* of our justification?

A. It is [FAITH,] Rom. x. 10.

Q. 56. Why is faith the *instrument* of our justification?

A. To show that our justification is wholly of grace; it being the nature of faith to take the *gift of righteousness* freely, *without money*, and *without price*; "therefore it is of faith, that it might be by grace," Rom. iv. 16.

Q. 57. What, then, is the *instrumentality* of faith in our justification?

A. It is merely the *hand* that *receives* and applies the righteousness of Christ, by which we are justified.*

Q. 58. Is the *grace of faith* or any act of it, imputed to a sinner for justification?

A. No; for, "To him that worketh not, but believeth on him that justifieth the ungodly, his faith is counted for righteousness," Rom. iv. 5.

Q. 59. What is the *difference* between *saving* faith, and *justifying* faith?

A. *Saving faith* receives and rests upon Christ in *all his offices*, as "of God made unto us wisdom, and righteousness, and sanctification, and redemption;" but *justifying faith* receives and rests upon him, more particularly, in his *priestly office*, for pardon and acceptance, on account of his meritorious righteousness, Phil. iii. 9: "And be found in him, not having mine own righteousness, which is of the law, but that which is through the faith of Christ, the righteousness which is of God by faith."

Q. 60. Why is the righteousness of Christ said to be received by *faith* [*alone?*]

A. That *works* may be wholly excluded from having any share in our justification, less or more, Rom. iii. 28: "Therefore we conclude, that a man is justified by faith, without the deeds of the law."

Q. 61. If good works have no influence upon our justification, of what use are they to the justified?

A. Though they cannot justify us before God, yet they are good "*evidences*" of our justification, being the fruits of a true and lively faith, James ii. 18: they "adorn the profession of the gospel, Tit. ii. 11, 12; stop the mouths of adversaries, 1 Pet. ii. 15; and glorify God, John xv. 8."†

Q. 62. If faith's *receiving* of Christ's righteousness justify us, does not *faith justify* as a *work*?

---

* Larger Catechism, Question 73: "Faith justifies a sinner in the sight of God, not because of those other graces which do always accompany it, or of good works that are the fruits of it, Gal. iii. 11; nor as if the grace of faith, or any act thereof, were imputed to him for his justification Rom. iv. 5; but only as it is an instrument, by which he receiveth and applieth Christ and his righteousness, John i. 12"

† Conf. chap. xvi. § 2.

OF ADOPTION.

A. It is not properly the *receiving*, or any other act of faith, that justifies us, but the *righteousness* of Christ RECEIVED, Rom. iii. 22; even as it is not the *hand* that nourishes us, but the *food* which we take by it.

Q. 63. If we are justified by faith alone, why is it said, James ii. 24, " That by works a man is justified, and not by faith only?"

A. This is to be understood of justifying, or evidencing the *reality* of our *faith before men*, and not of justifying our *versons before God*.

Q. 64. When is it that God justifies the ungodly?

A. " Though from eternity God *decreed* to justify all the elect," yet " they are not" *actually* "justified, until the Holy Spirit does, in due time, apply Christ," and his righteousness " unto them, Tit. iii. 5—7." *

Q. 65. How were believers, under the Old Testament, justified?

A. "Their justification was, in all respects, the *same* with the justification of believers, under the New Testament, Gal. iii. 9. Heb. xiii. 8." †

Q. 66. What may we *learn* from this *important* doctrine of *justification?*

A. That all ground of pride and boasting is taken away from the creature, Rom. iii. 27: that faith itself, by laying hold upon the surety righteousness without us, is nothing else than a *solemn declaration* of our poverty and nakedness; and that, therefore, it is our duty to glory only in Christ Jesus, saying, " Surely—in the Lord have we righteousness and strength," Isa. xlv. 24.

QUEST. 34. *What is adoption?*

ANS. Adoption is an act of God's free grace, whereby we are received into the number, and have a right to all the privileges of the sons of God.

Q. 1. What does the word [*adoption*] signify among men?

A. It signifies the taking of a *stranger* into a family, and dealing with him, as if he were a *child* or *heir*.

Q. 2. What is the *difference* between adoption, as it is an *act of God*, and as it is a *deed of men?*

A. Men generally adopt only *one* into their family, and they do it on account of some amiable properties, or qualifications, discerned in the adopted; but God adopts *many*

---

* Conf. chap. xi. § 4.   † Ibid. § 6.

into his family, and that, not upon account of any thing commendable in them, but merely out of his own free and unmerited love, Eph. i. 5.

Q. 3. Of how many *kinds* of adoption do the *scriptures* speak?

A. *Two* kinds; namely, *general* and *special*.

Q. 4. What is meant by *general* adoption?

A. It is the erecting of a certain indefinite number of mankind into a *visible church*, and entitling them to all the privileges of it, Rom. ix. 4.

Q. 5. What is the outward *seal*, or *badge*, of this general adoption?

A. It is *baptism*; which comes in the room of *circumcision* under the Old Testament, Eph. iv. 5.

Q. 6. What is to be understood by *special* adoption?

A. It is a sovereign and free translation of a sinner of mankind, from the family of *hell*, or *Satan*, into the family of *heaven*, or *household of God*, Eph. ii. 19; with an investiture into all the privileges of the sons of God, 1 John iii. 1.

Q. 7. By whose *act* and *authority* is this *translation* accomplished?

A. By the act and authority of God, Father, Son, and Holy Ghost.

Q. 8. What is the act of the *Father* in this matter?

A. He has "predestinated us unto the adoption of children to himself, according to the good pleasure of his will," Eph. i. 5.

Q. 9. What is the act of the *Son* in this special adoption?

A. In consequence of his purchasing the sinner by the price of his blood, he actually gives the power, right, or privilege, to become a child of God, in the day of believing, John i. 12.

Q. 10. What is the act of the *Holy Ghost?*

A. He comes in Christ's name, takes possession of the person, and dwells in him, as a *Spirit of adoption*, teaching him to cry, *Abba, Father*, Rom. viii. 15.

Q. 11. Why is this *translation* into the family of God, called [*an act?*]

A. Because it is done *at once*, Jer. iii. 19.

Q. 12. Why called an act of [*God's free grace?*]

A. Because the adoption of any of mankind into the household of God, flows entirely from his own *free love* and *favour*, Eph. i. 5, they being, all of them, *wretched, miserable, poor, blind, and naked*, Rev. iii. 17.

Q. 13. What is the *difference* between *good angels* being called the *sons of God*, Job xxxviii. 7, and *believers* being so called? 1 John iii. 1.

A. Good angels are called the sons of God, because they were *created immediately* by him; but *believers are so called,* because they are *adopted* by him into his family, Rom. viii. 15.

Q. 14. Why are we said, in adoption, to be [*received into the number of the sons of God?*]

A. Because the family of God, from among men, consists of a *certain definite number* of mankind, which can neither be augmented nor diminished, John xvii. 2, 9, 12, and vi. 39.

Q. 15. By what means or *instrument* does God receive any of mankind into his family?

A. By the means and instrumentality of *faith,* Gal. iii. 26: " Ye are all the children of God by faith in Christ Jesus."

Q. 16. What *connexion* is there between *faith in Christ Jesus,* and our being *the children of God?*

A. Faith unites us to Christ, and acquiesces in the redemption purchased by him, as the meritorious cause of our adoption, Gal. iv. 4, 5: "God sent forth his Son—to redeem them that were under the law, that we might receive the adoption of sons."

Q. 17. Since adoption is an act of translation, from the family of *Satan* to the family of *God,* to whom is it intimated?

A. To the angels in heaven; and sometimes to the *adopted themselves.*

Q. 18. How is it intimated to the *angels* in heaven?

A. It is probable that it is intimated to them by *immediate revelation,* Luke xv. 10: "There is joy in the presence of the angels of God, over one sinner that repenteth."

Q. 19. *How* is it intimated to the *adopted themselves?*

A. By the " Spirit itself bearing witness with their spirit that they are the children of God," Rom. viii. 16.

Q. 20. Is there any intimation of this made to *Satan?*

A. No; but he cannot miss to know, when he is spoiled of his goods, and the lawful captive delivered, Mark ix. 26.

Q. 21. When sinners of mankind are adopted, and enrolled into the family of heaven, is their NAME changed?

A. Yes: as the wife's name is sunk into her husband's, so the *former name* of the adopted is sunk into Christ's *new name,* Rev. iii. 12: " I will write upon him my new name."

Q. 22. What was the *former,* and what is the *present name* of the adopted children of God?

A. Their *former name* was, " strangers and foreigners;" their *present name* is, " fellow citizens with the saints, and of the household of God," Eph. ii. 19; their *former name* was, *guilty* and *condemned;* their *present name* is, "the Lord our righteousness," Jer. xxxiii. 16; their *former name* denoted, that they " were without Christ, having no hope, and without God in the world," Eph. ii. 12; their *present name* is *Jehovah Shamma,* The Lord is there, Ezek. xlviii. 35.

Q. 23. Why is Christ's name, put upon them, called his *new name?*

A. Because it is a name that shall never *wax old,* or *vanish away,* Heb. viii. 13.

Q. 24. *Whence come they* by this new name?

A. When Christ gives them the *white stone* of pardon he, at the same time, gives them, in that *stone,* the *new name* of being the *sons of God;* which name "no man knoweth, saving he that receiveth it," Rev. ii. 17.

Q. 25. What are the [*privileges*] with which the sons of God are invested?

A. Among others, they are invested with great dignity, glorious liberty, a title to the whole inheritance, boldness of access to God as a father, and his fatherly chastisement, or correction.*

Q. 26. What is the *great dignity* or *honour* to which they are advanced?

A. To the dignity of being "kings and priests unto God," Rev. i. 6, or "a royal priesthood," 1 Pet. ii. 9; to feast on Christ their *passover sacrificed* for them, 1 Cor. v. 7.

Q. 27. In what consists "the glorious liberty of the children of God," mentioned, Rom. viii. 21?

A. Not only in a freedom from the guilt and dominion of sin, the curse of the law, the tyranny of Satan, and sting of death, John viii. 36; but in a filial, and reverential *obedience,* flowing from a principle of faith and love inlaid in the soul, Gal. v. 6.

Q. 28. Upon what is their title to the inheritance founded?

A. Upon their being Christ's—"and heirs according to the promise," Gal. iii. 29.

Q. 29. What is the inheritance which the adopted children of God are heirs of "according to the promise?"

A. They are "HEIRS of the righteousness which is by faith," Heb. xi. 7; "heirs of the grace of life," 1 Pet. iii. 7; "heirs of salvation," Heb. i. 14; and, which comprehends all, they are "heirs of God, and joint heirs with Christ," Rom. viii. 17.

Q. 30. What does their boldness of access to God, as their Father, include in it?

A. A firm persuasion of the power, love, and faithfulness of a promising God, Rom. iv. 20, 21, and an assured expectation of relief from him: "And this is the confidence that we have in him, that if we ask any thing according to his will, he heareth us," 1 John v. 14.

* Confession of Faith, chap. xii.

OF SANCTIFICATION.

Q. 31. What are the *grounds* of this boldness?
A. The *righteousness* of Christ apprehended by faith, Ps. lxxxiv. 9, and his prevalent *intercession* within the veil, 1 John ii. 1.

Q. 32. *Why* is it that God *chastises* his adopted children?
A. Because he *loves* them, Heb. xii. 6: "Whom the Lord loveth, he chasteneth."

Q. 33. *With what* does he chastise them?
A. Sometimes with the rod of *outward affliction*, of various kinds, Ps. xxxiv. 19; and sometimes with the rod of *desertion*, Ps. xxx. 7.

Q. 34. For *what end* does he thus chastise them?
A. For their *profit*, that they may be "partakers of his holiness," Heb. xii. 10.

Q. 35. How ought the children to behave under the chastisement of their Father?
A. They ought neither to "despise the chastening of the Lord, nor faint when they are rebuked of him," Heb. xii. 5.

Q. 36. What are the *marks* or *evidences* of the adopted children of God?
A. They will resemble their Father, 1 John iii. 2; they know their Father's voice, John x. 4; delight in their Father's company, Rom. viii. 15; are deeply concerned for his absence, Job xxxiii. 3; and out of love to him that *begat*, they have great love to all them that are *begotten of him*, 1 John v. 1.

———

QUEST. 35. *What is sanctification?*

ANS. Sanctification is the work of God's free grace, whereby we are renewed in the whole man, after the image of God, and are enabled more and more to die unto sin, and live unto righteousness.

Q. 1. What is it for one to be SANCTIFIED?
A. It is to be made a *saint*, or a holy person set apart for a holy use, 1 Thess. v. 23.

Q. 2. Can any sinner *sanctify himself?*
A. No: we can defile, but cannot purify ourselves, Job xiv. 4.

Q. 3. *Whose work* is it to sanctify?
A. It is the special work of the Spirit of God, 2 Thess. ii. 13.

Q. 4. Do any of mankind sinners *deserve* that God should sanctify them?
A. No: there are none of them that can deserve any thing from God, but to be left to perish eternally in their

OF SANCTIFICATION. 187

sin and pollution, because "they are altogether become filthy; there is none of them that doeth good, no not one," Ps. xiv. 3.

Q. 5. What *moves* God to sanctify a sinner?
A. His own free grace and *good pleasure*, Phil. ii. 13.

Q. 6. Are not justification, adoption, and sanctification, *inseparably linked together?*
A. Yes; they that are justified, are adopted; and they that are justified and adopted, are sanctified and glorified, Rom. viii. 30.

Q. 7. In what respects are *justification* and *sanctification* inseparably joined and linked together?
A. In the decree of God, Rom. viii. 30; in the promise of God, Ps. cx. 3; in the end of Christ's death, Tit. ii. 14; in the offices of Christ, 1 Cor. i. 30; in the gospel-call and offer, 2 Tim. i. 9; 1 Thess. iv. 7; and in the experience of all believers, Phil. iii. 8, 12.

Q. 8. Though inseparably linked together, are they not carefully to be *distinguished?*
A. Yes; for the confounding of justification and sanctification lays the foundation of many errors, both in principle and practice; and the want of a clear understanding of the *difference* between these *two*, contributes to depress and encumber the believer in his exercise; whereas the distinct knowledge of it would free him from that bondage, John viii. 32.

Q. 9. In what do *justification* and *sanctification* DIFFER?
A. They *differ* in many respects; particularly in their *matter, kind, form, properties, subjects, order, extent, ingredients, evidences;* in their *relation* to the *law;* their relation to *Christ's offices;* and their *use to believers.*

Q. 10. In what do they differ in their *matter?*
A. The *matter* of *justification* is the *righteousness* of Christ; but the *matter of sanctification* is the *fulness* of Christ communicated, or grace imparted from him, out of whose *fulness* we receive, and *grace for grace*, John i. 16.

Q. 11. How do they differ as to their *kind?*
A. Justification makes a *relative*, sanctification a *real* change: the *first* changes a man's *state*, the *other* changes his *heart* and *life*, Ezek. xxxvi. 26.

Q. 12. How do they differ as to their *form*, or manner of *conveyance?*
A. Justification is effected by the *imputation* of Christ's righteousness to us; sanctification, by the *implantation* of his grace in us.

Q. 13. How do they differ in their *properties?*
A. Justification is *complete* and *perfect at first;* but sanctification is carried on *gradually*, from less to more, until the soul be ripe for glory; the righteousness of justification is strictly and properly *meritorious*, being the

righteousness of God, by which the *law* is not only fulfilled, but *magnified;* but the righteousness of sanctification is not so, being only the righteousness of a sinful creature, *imperfect* in degrees: justification is *equal* in all believers, but they are *not all equally* sanctified: hence, in God's family, there are *little children,* 1 John ii. 12: and in his garden, *trees of different tallness,* or *height,* Ps. xcii. 12, compared with Zech. i. 8.

Q. 14. How do they differ in their *subjects?*

A. Christ *himself,* and not the believer, is the subject of our justifying righteousness; it is *inherently* in him who wrought it out perfectly for us; but the believer *himself* is the *subject* of the righteousness of sanctification; it is *implanted* in him as a *new nature;* whereas his justifying righteousness is not *in him* as a *nature,* but *on him* as a *robe;* and hence it is said to *be* upon *all them that believe,* Rom. iii. 22.

Q. 15. How do they differ in their *order?*

A. Although, as to *time,* they are simultaneous; yet, as to the *order of nature,* justification goes *before* sanctification, as the *cause* before the *effect,* or as fire is before light and heat.

Q. 16. How do they differ as to their *extent?*

A. Although justification respects the *whole person,* yet, it immediately terminates upon *conscience,* God's deputy, purging it from dead works, and pacifying it with the sprinkling of the blood of Christ; nothing giving *true peace* to *conscience,* but that which gave *full satisfaction* to *justice:* but by sanctification we are *renewed* in the *whole man,* Eph. iv. 23, 24.

Q. 17. How do they differ as to their *ingredients?*

A. The main ingredient in justification is the *grace* and *love* of God *towards us,* manifested in pardoning and accepting us in Christ; whereas the main ingredient in sanctification is *our gratitude* and *love to God,* flowing from his love to us, and appearing in our obedience and keeping his commandments, by virtue of his " Spirit put within us, and causing us to walk in his statutes," Ezek. xxxvi. 27.

Q. 18. How do they differ as to *evidence?*

A. *Justification* is *evidenced* by our *sanctification;* for none can warrantably conclude they are justified by the righteousness of Christ, if not students of true holiness, and groaning under a body of sin and death: but sanctification *cannot be evidenced* by our justification; which being the hidden root of holiness under ground, does not appear, except in lively actings of justifying faith, and other graces, which are internal branches of sanctification, sometimes inwardly discerned by the believer, and sometimes outwardly discovered to others by works, James ii. 18.

Q. 19. How do they differ in their *relation* to the *law?*

A. Justification has relation to the law, *as a covenant,* and frees the soul from it, Rom. vii. 4; sanctification respects the law *as a rule*, and makes the soul breathe after conformity to it, and to delight in it after the inward man, Rom. vii. 22; hence justification is a *judicial sentence*, absolving us from *law-debt;* sanctification, a *spiritual change*, fitting us for *law-duty*.

Q. 20. How do they differ in their *relation* to the *offices* of *Christ?*

A. Justification springs from, and is grounded upon the *priestly office* of Christ, by which he satisfied law and justice, as our surety; but sanctification proceeds from his *kingly office*, by which he subdues us to his obedience, and writes his law in our hearts, Jer. xxxi. 33.

Q. 21. How do they differ in their *use* to *believers?*

A. Justification gives us a *title* to heaven and eternal life; sanctification gives a *meetness* for it: justification is God's *act*, pronouncing our persons righteous in Christ, and taking away the guilt of sin; sanctification is the Spirit's *work*, cleansing our nature, and taking away the filth of sin: by the *former*, we are instated into the favour of God; by the *latter*, adorned with the *image* of God.

Q. 22. How may the work of sanctification be *distinguished?*

A. Into *habitual* and *actual* sanctification.

Q. 23. What may be termed *habitual* sanctification?

A. It is that [*whereby we are renewed in the whole man, after the image of God,*] and so a renovation of the *nature*, Eph. iv. 24.

Q. 24. Can any have a *sanctified life*, who have not a *renewed nature?*

A. No; for *a corrupt tree* cannot *bring forth good fruit*, Matt. vii. 18.

Q. 25. What is to be understood by [*the whole man*] that must be renewed?

A. Both *soul* and *body;* in all the powers of the one, and members of the other, 2 Cor. vii. 1. 1 Thess. v. 23.

Q. 26. What is the *difference* between the renewing of the whole man in *sanctification*, and the *renewing* mentioned in *effectual calling?*

A. The renovation in effectual calling is only *begun;* but this of sanctification, is *carried on* by *degrees*, till *perfected* in glory, Phil. i. 6: *there*, the seed of grace is *sown; here*, it is *watered*, in order to growth: *there*, the *habit* is implanted, John i. 13; *here*, it is strengthened for exercise, Eph. ii. 10.

Q. 27. After *whose image* is the whole man renewed?

A. [*After the image of God:*] consisting in knowledge, righteousness, and holiness, Col. iii. 10. Eph. iv. 24.

OF SANCTIFICATION.

Q. 28. Whose image do we bear, *before* we are renewed in the whole man?

A. The image of the *first Adam* after the fall, having his nature corrupted, Gen. v. 3.

Q. 29. Can any be renewed in the whole man, without being *united* to the *second Adam?*

A. No; for we are not sanctified, except by *faith uniting* us to Christ, Acts xv. 9, and xxvi. 18. 1 Cor. i. 2,—*Sanctified in Christ Jesus.*

Q. 30. Though the believer be renewed [*in the whole man,*] yet is any part of the new creature WHOLLY renewed?

A. The *two* contrary principles, *grace* and *corruption,* are in the *sanctified;* being *together* in such sort, that in every *particular part,* where the one is, the other is *there* also *beside* it: for, what we have of this gracious work of sanctification upon us while here, is but *in part;* it is not *perfect,* 1 Cor. xiii. 9, 10.

Q. 31. What is the *tendency* of habitual sanctification?

A. The tendency of it is *to actual* sanctification, Eph. ii. 10.

Q. 32. In what consists ACTUAL sanctification?

A. In being [*enabled more and more to die unto sin, and live unto righteousness,*] Rom. vi. 4, 6.

Q. 33. In what does *habitual* sanctification differ from *actual?*

A. The *first* points at the renovation of our *nature;* the *second* at the renovation of our *life:* the *first* at the *habit;* the *second* at the *exercise* of grace, working inwardly in the *heart,* and outwardly in the *walk,* Eph. ii. 10.

Q. 34. What are the *parts* of *actual* sanctification, and how are they *commonly termed?*

A. *Mortification;* or, a *dying unto sin;* and *vivification;* or, a *living unto righteousness.*

Q. 35. Can any die to sin, and live to righteousness, without being [*enabled by grace?*]

A. No: "We are not sufficient of ourselves to think any thing as of ourselves, but our sufficiency is of God," 2 Cor. iii. 5. The strength of habitual grace will not be sufficient, without actual assistance.

Q. 36. How does the grace of God enable us to die to sin, and live to righteousness?

A. It enables us [*more and more,*] 1 Thess. iv. 2, or, by little and little, from time to time; for, "the path of the just is as a shining light, that shineth more and more unto the perfect day," Prov. iv. 18; and "they go from strength to strength," Ps. lxxxiv. 7.

Q. 37. Does the work of actual sanctification go on *constantly* without interruption?

A. The sanctified person is subject to backsliding

and decay; yet God never altogether takes his hand from the good work he has begun, but makes good use of backslidings for farther progress in it, Hos. xiv. 4, 7.

Q. 38. Why is not actual sanctification *perfected* in this life, but still a remainder of corruption left in God's people?

A. To make them know from experience, the strength of sin, the necessity of mortifying grace, and of the abundance of pardoning grace, 2 Cor. xii. 7—9; and to keep them exercised in prayer and humiliation, in the faith and hope of deliverance from a body of sin and death, through Christ, Rom. vii. 24, 25.

Q. 39. What is it to [*die to sin?*]

A. To have the power of sin, in our nature, so far destroyed as not to obey it, but to hate it in heart, and abstain from it in life, Rom. vi. 6.

Q. 40. What is it to [*live to righteousness?*]

A. To have our nature so quickened by the power of grace, as to love and obey the commands of righteousness in our life, Rom. vi. 13.

Q. 41. From whence is it that this death to sin, and life to righteousness spring?

A. They spring from the *virtue* that is in the *death* and *resurrection* of Christ, to render his mystical members *conformable* to him in *them;* "That, like as Christ was raised up from the dead, by the glory of the Father, even so we also should walk in newness of life; for, if we have been planted together in the likeness of his death, we shall be also in the likeness of his resurrection," Rom. vi. 4, 5.

Q. 42. Why have the death and resurrection of Christ such a *conforming virtue?*

A. Because he died and rose again as a *public* person, Eph. ii. 5, 6, and *merited* this *conformation* or fashioning of his mystical members to his own image, Phil. iii. 10.

Q. 43. In what consists the *excellency* of sanctification?

A. It is the end and design of our election, Eph. i. 4; of our effectual calling, 2 Tim. i. 9; of our justification and deliverance from the law as a covenant, Rom. vi. 14; and of our adoption, Eph. i. 4, 5: it is the end both of mercies and crosses, Rom. ii. 4, Isa. xxvii. 9; and, in a word, it is the end and design of all the precepts of the law, the promises of the gospel, and the operation of the Spirit of God.

Q. 44. Whence arises the necessity of holiness, or sanctification?

A. From the holy nature and will of God: for "it is written, Be ye holy, for I am holy," 1 Pet. i. 16; and "this is the will of God, even our sanctification," 1 Thess. iv. 3; and from the death of Christ, "who gave himself for us, that he might redeem us from all iniquity, and purify to himself a peculiar people, zealous of good works," Tit. ii. 14.

Q. 45. For what good *end* and *use* is sanctification necessary?

A. Not for justification before God; but for evidencing our justification and faith, James. ii. 18. It is necessary for glorifying God, Matt. v. 16, and showing forth his praise, 1 Pet. ii. 19; for adorning *the doctrine of God our Saviour*, Tit. ii. 10; for proving our union to Christ, John xv. 5, 6; for promoting inward peace and rejoicing, Ps. cxix. 165, 2 Cor. i. 12; for maintaining fellowship and communion with God, John xiv. 21, 23; for making us meet for heaven, because *without holiness no man shall see God*, Heb. xii. 14; for making us useful to men on earth, Tit. iii. 8; and for stopping the mouth of calumny when we are reproached as evil doers, 1 Pet. iii. 16.

Q. 46. What is the *meritorious* cause of our sanctification?

A. The blood of Christ, Heb. xiii. 12: "Wherefore Jesus also, that he might sanctify the people with his own blood, suffered without the gate."

Q. 47. Whence flows the *sanctifying* or *purifying virtue* of the blood of Christ?

A. From the *atoning* virtue of it, Heb. ix. 14.

Q. 48. What is the *instrumental* cause of our sanctification?

A. The faith of the operation of God, Acts xv. 9.

Q. 49. What is the *regulating* or *directing* cause?

A. The law of God, Isa. viii. 20.

Q. 50. What is the exemplary cause of sanctification?

A. The copy that Christ has set us by his obedience and sufferings, in so far as imitable by us, 1 Pet. ii. 21, 22.

Q. 51. What are the *marks* of sanctification?

A. A heart-respect to all God's commandments, and loving them because they are holy; a hatred of sin, and avoiding of all appearance of evil; a spirit of watchfulness and warfare against sin; a delight in doing good; a conversation becoming the gospel; and an habitual improvement of the blood of Christ, by faith and prayer, for cleansing from the filth of sin, and of the precious promises for that end, 2 Cor. vii. 1. 1 Pet. i. 4.

Q. 52. What are the chief *motives* and inducements to sanctification?

A. The will of God, commanding, 1 Pet. i. 15; the love of Christ constraining, 1 Cor. v. 14; the dignity of thus resembling God, Lev. xix. 2; and the indignity of resembling the devil by the want of it, John viii. 44.

Q. 53. What should we do to be sanctified?

A. We should fly to Christ by faith, touching the hem of his garment for healing and purification, for we "are sanctified in Christ Jesus," 1 Cor. i. 2; we should pray for the Spirit of sanctification, through whom alone the deeds of the body can be mortified, Rom. viii. 13; we should associate with saints, for "he that walketh with the wise, shall be wise," Prov. xiii. 20; association begets assimilation; and we should make a right use of God's word and rod, sabbaths and sacraments.

QUEST. 36. *What are the benefits which, in this life, do accompany or flow from justification, adoption, and sanctification?*

ANS, The benefits which, in this life, do accompany or flow from justification, adoption, and sanctification, are, assurance of God's love, peace of conscience, joy in the Holy Ghost, increase of grace, and perseverance therein to the end.

OF ASSURANCE.

Q. 1. Are not justification, adoption, and sanctification, *pregnant* with many blessings?

A. Yes; their name may well be called GAD, (Gen. xxx. 11,) for *troops* of blessings attend them; some in this life, some at death, but the best of all in the life to come.

Q. 2. What are the benefits which flow from them in *this life?*

A. There are *five* of them mentioned in the *answer;* namely, "assurance of God's love," Rom. v. 5; "peace of conscience," Rom. v. 1; "joy in the Holy Ghost," Rom. xiv. 17; "increase of grace," Prov. iv. 18; and "perseverance therein to the end," 1 Pet. i. 5.

Q. 3. Which of these benefits flow from a *sight* and *sense* of justification, adoption, and sanctification?

A. [*Assurance of God's love, peace of conscience, and joy in the Holy Ghost.*]

Q. 4. Which of them belong to the *being* of a justified, adopted, and sanctified state?

A. [*Increase of grace, and perseverance therein to the end.*]

Q. 5. Do *all* justified, adopted, and sanctified persons, enjoy assurance of God's love, peace of conscience, and joy in the Holy Ghost, *at all times?*

A. Though they have them *radically* in their justification, adoption, and sanctification, yet they are not always *sensible of the possession* of them, but are frequently filled with doubts and fears about their gracious state, Job xxiii. 8, 9. Isa. xlix. 14.

Q. 6. Whence is it that they who have assurance, peace, and joy in the *root*, have not always the *sensible possession* of these benefits?

A. This flows sometimes from a *sovereign cause* in God, to keep down a spirit of pride after special manifestations, 2 Cor. xii. 7; and sometimes from a *sinful cause* in believers; such as, untenderness in their walk, Isa. lix. 2; resting upon a manifestation, Luke ix. 33, 34; or quenching the gracious motions and operations of the Spirit, Eph. iv. 30.

Q. 7. Is it the assurance of *sense*, or the assurance of *faith*, that is mentioned in this *answer?*

A. It is the *assurance of sense,* or the sensible [*assurance of God's love.*]

Q. 8. What is the *difference* between the *assurance* of *faith*, and the *assurance of sense?*

A. The object of the assurance of *faith* is " Christ in the promise," James ii. 23; but the object of the assurance of sense is " Christ formed in the soul," 2 Tim. ii. 12; or, which is the same thing, the assurance of faith is founded on the *infallible word* of God, who *cannot lie;* but the assurance of sense upon the person's *present experience* of the communications of divine love.

Q. 9. How may assurance of God's love be said to [*accompany or flow from justification?*]

A. Because in it we see his love to us, in pardoning our sins, and receiving us into his favour, Ps. ciii. 3, 4.

Q. 10. How may it be said to *accompany* or *flow from* [*adoption?*]

A. Because we see in it his love to us, in bringing us into his family, and pitying us, " like as a father pitieth his children," Ps. ciii. 13.

Q. 11. How may it be said to *accompany* or *flow from* [*sanctification?*]

A. Because in it we see his love to us, in killing our corruptions, and quickening his graces, Rom. vi. 11, 14.

Q. 12. How do you *prove* that the sensible assurance of God's love is *attainable?*

A. From the command to *give diligence* to attain it, 2 Pet. i. 10; and from its being *actually attained,* by many of the saints; such as, Job, chap. xix, 25, 26. David, Ps. lxxiii. 26. Paul, 2 Tim. iv. 7, 8, and others.

Q. 13. How are the saints brought to this privilege?

A. Sometimes by a course of holy and self-denied diligence in the way of commanded duty, Isa. xxxii. 17; and sometimes by the *Spirit itself* bearing *witness* with their spirits, that they are the children of God, Rom. viii. 16.

Q. 14. What may afford *comfort* to a believer, when at any time he *loses* this assurance?
A. That the covenant stands fast with Christ, Ps. lxxxix. 28; that the love of God is invariably the same, Zeph. iii. 17; and that he will in his own time return with wonted loving-kindness, Isa. liv. 7, 8.

Q. 15. What is incumbent on believers for *recovering* the assurance of God's love when they have lost the present sense of it?
A. To be humbled for sin, as the procuring cause of the Lord's departure, Ps. xl. 12; to justify God, and to condemn themselves, Dan. ix. 7, 8; and to wait in the exercise of prayer and fasting, for the returns of his love, Isa. viii. 17.

Q. 16. Of what *advantage* to believers is the assurance of God's love?
A. It animates to the practice of every commanded duty, Ps. cxix. 32; it supports under all trials and afflictions, Ps. xxiii. 4; and it fills the soul with the love of God, "because he first loved us," 1 John iv. 19.

Q. 17. How may we *know* if we have the well-founded assurance of God's love?
A. If it flow from faith on Christ in the promise, Eph. i. 13; if it fill the soul with an humble and holy wondering at the condescending goodness of God, 2 Sam. vii. 18; and if it beget ardent desires after nearer conformity to God here, and the full enjoyment of him hereafter, 1 John iii. 2, 3.

Q. 18. What is the *difference* between a *true assurance* of God's love and a *false* and *presumptuous confidence?*
A. *True assurance* makes a man more humble and self-denied, Gal. ii. 19, 20; but *presumptuous confidence* puffs up with spiritual pride and self-conceit, 2 Kings x. 15, 16: the *one* excites to the practice of every commanded duty, Ps. cxix. 32; but the *other* encourages sloth and indolence, Luke xi. 21: the man who has *true assurance*, wants to be searched and tried as to the reality thereof, Ps. xxvi. 1, 2; but they who are stuffed with *presumptuous confidence* hate the light, "neither come to the light, lest their deeds should be reproved," John iii. 20.

OF PEACE OF CONSCIENCE.

Q. 1. What is [*peace of conscience?*]
A. It is the inward quiet and tranquillity of the mind arising from the faith of being justified before God, Rom v. 1.

Q. 2. Why is peace of conscience said to *accompany* or *flow* from justification, adoption, and sanctification?

A. Because none can have true peace of conscience who are not justified, adopted, and sanctified: there being "no peace to the wicked," Isa. lvii. 21.

Q. 3. When may we be said to have that peace of conscience which flows from *justification?*

A. When the conscience, being sprinkled with the blood of Christ, is set free from the fear of vindictive wrath, Heb. x. 22.

Q. 4. When have we that peace which flows from *adoption?*

A. When we have soul-quiet and composure, through the faith of God's being our friend and father in Christ, Jer. iii. 4, 19.

Q. 5. When have we that peace which accompanies or flows from *sanctification?*

A. When we have the Spirit of God shining on us, in the exercise of grace, and assisting us in the performance of duty, Ps. cxxxviii. 3.

Q. 6. Whether is the peace of sanctification, or that of justification, most *stable* and *permanent?*

A. The *peace of sanctification,* having many imperfections cleaving to it, is more fluctuating and unstable than the *peace of justification,* which is founded upon a *righteousness* that is *everlasting,* and always the same, Isa. xlv. 24, 25.

Q. 7. Have all believers peace in their consciences *at all times?*

A. They have *ground* of peace, being in a state of peace; but have not always the *sense* of it, Job vi. 4.

Q. 8. What is it that *hinders* or *mars* the *sense* of peace in those who are in a state of peace?

A. Their not improving the promises by faith, for promoting their sanctification, Isa. xl. 27, 28; their sitting down upon present or former attainments, Ps. xxx. 6, 7; and their giving way to the temptations of Satan, who is an enemy both to their grace and comfort, Isa. liv. 11.

Q. 9. What are the *marks* of *true peace* of conscience, which distinguish it from *carnal security?*

A. A continual warfare against all known sin, Ps. cxix. 104; and a sincere endeavour to please God, verse 165; with a constant fear of offending him, Gen. xxxix. 9.

OF JOY IN THE HOLY GHOST.

Q. 1. What is [*joy in the Holy Ghost?*]

A. It is that inward elevation and enlargement of soul which flows from the lively exercise of faith, feasting on

Christ in the promise, 1 Pet. i. 8: "Believing, ye rejoice, with joy unspeakable, and full of glory."

Q. 2. Why is this *joy* said to be [*in the Holy Ghost ?*]

A. Because the Holy Ghost is the *author* of it; as *personally inhabiting*, or residing in the believer, John xiv. 16, 17.

Q. 3. What is the *matter* or *ground* of this joy?

A. God in Christ as the everlasting portion of the believing soul, Ps. xvi. 5, 6.

Q. 4. What are the *properties* of it?

A. It is a hidden joy, Prov. xiv. 10; it is permanent, John xvi. 22; and it is unspeakable, 1 Pet. i. 8.

Q. 5. What are the peculiar *seasons* of this joy?

A. The time of special manifestations after a dark night of desertion, Isa. liv. 7, 8; the time of tribulation for Christ's sake, Acts xvi. 25; the time of God's remarkable appearance for his church, Ex. xv. 1; and sometimes in or about the time of death, Ps. xxiii. 4.

Q. 6. When may believers be said to have that joy in the Holy Ghost, which accompanies or flows from *justification?*

A. When they have "boldness to enter into the holiest by the blood of Jesus," Heb. x. 19.

Q. 7. When may they be said to have that joy which flows from *adoption?*

A. When the "Spirit itself beareth witness with *their* spirit, that *they* are the children of God;" and enables them to cry, *Abba, Father*, Rom. viii. 15, 16.

Q. 8. When may they be said to have the joy that flows from *sanctification?*

A. When they have the testimony of their conscience bearing witness to their sincerity, and to the uprightness of their aims and endeavours in all the duties of religion, 2 Cor. i. 12: "For our rejoicing is this, the testimony of our conscience, that in simplicity and godly sincerity, not with fleshly wisdom, but by the grace of God, we have had our conversation in the world."

Q. 9. What are the *signs* and *evidences* of joy in the Holy Ghost, which *distinguish* it from that joy which temporary believers, or hypocrites, may sometimes have in the word? Matt. xiii. 20.

A. Joy in the Holy Ghost has an enlivening, Neh. viii. 10; enlarging, Ps. xlv. 1; humbling, Job xlii. 5, 6; and sanctifying influence upon the soul, 2 Cor. iii. 18; whereas the joy of hypocrites has no such effects.

OF INCREASE OF GRACE.

Q. 1. What do you understand by [*increase of grace?*]

OF INCREASE OF GRACE.

A. The gradual advances which the saints are helped to make, in the exercise of grace, and experimental godliness, Ps. xcii. 12, 13.

Q. 2. To what is the increase of grace *compared* in scripture?

A. To "the shining light, that shineth more and more unto the perfect day," Prov. iv. 18.

Q. 3. What is the spring or cause of the believer's growth?

A. Union with Christ, John xv. 4; and participation of vital influences from him; Col. ii. 19.

Q. 4. Why is it ordered that believers shall grow in grace?

A. Because there is a particular *stature*, at which every member of the mystical body is appointed to arrive, even "the measure of the stature of the fulness of Christ," Eph. iv. 13.

Q. 5. How does growth in grace flow from *justification?*

A. In as much as the justified person is delivered from a *legal incapacity* to grow, Ps. cxvi. 16; and is made free and unfettered for the service of God, Gal. v. 1.

Q. 6. How does it flow from adoption?

A. In as much as *the sincere milk of the word is desired* by the *new-born babes, that they may grow thereby*, 1 Pet. ii. 2.

Q. 7. How does it flow from *sanctification?*

A. In as much as the image of God, drawn upon the soul, is in sanctification, carried on to a nearer conformity, till *we shall be* perfectly *like him*, when *we shall see him as he is*, 1 John iii. 2.

Q. 8. Do believers grow in grace at *all times?*

A. They have a *principle* of growth, the *seed* of God remaining in them, 1 John iii. 9; but they do not grow at *all times;* they have their *winters*, Song ii. 11, in which the influences of grace, necessary for growth, are *ceased*, chap. v. 2.

Q. 9. Whence is it that the believer's growth *ceases* at any time?

A. Faith being like the *pipe* that received the *oil* from the *bowl* to each *lamp* in the *candlestick*, Zech. iv. 2; if that *pipe* be stopped, or the saint's faith lie dormant and inactive, then all the rest of the graces will also languish and decay, Ps. xxvii. 13.

Q. 10. How is growth in grace *revived*, after the languishings and decays of it?

A. The *pipe* of faith remaining still at the fountain, as a bond of union between Christ and the soul, the Lord Jesus clears this mean of conveyance, and then the influences for growth *flow*, and the believer's graces look fresh and green again. Hos. xiv. 7: "They that dwell under his shadow shall return; they shall revive as the corn, and grow as the vine."

Q. 11. Since the *tares* have their growth, as well as the *wheat*, Matt. xiii. 26, how shall we distinguish between the growth of *hypocrites*, and the growth of the *true Christian*?

A. The distinction lies in the *nature* of the growth: the growth of the true Christian is *regular* and *proportionable* in all the parts of the *new man;* it is a *growing up into him in all things who is the head*, Eph. iv. 15; whereas, hypocrites when they get more knowledge into their *heads*, and no more holiness into their hearts, may be more taken up with the *externals* of religion than formerly, and yet as great strangers to the *power* of *godliness* as ever, 2 Tim. iii. 5.

Q. 12. What are the *several ways* in which believers grow *at once?*

A. They grow inwardly and outwardly; upward and downward, Isa. xxxvii. 31.

Q. 13. How do believers grow *inwardly?*

A. By uniting more closely to Christ, and cleaving more firmly to him as the head of influences, which is the spring of all other true Christian growth, Eph. iv. 15.

Q. 14. How do they grow *outwardly?*

A. By being fruitful in good works in their life and conversation, Tit. iii. 8.

Q. 15. How do they grow *upward?*

A. In heavenly-mindedness and contempt of the world, Phil. iii. 20: "Our conversation is in heaven?"

Q. 16. How do they grow *downward?*

A. In humility and self-abasement; the branches of the largest growth in Christ, are, in their own eyes, *less than the least of all saints*, Eph. iii. 8; yea, the *chief of sinners*, 1 Tim. i. 15; they see that they can *do nothing*, 2 Cor. iii. 5; that they *deserve nothing*, Gen. xxxii. 10; and that they *are nothing*, 2 Cor. xii. 11.

Q. 17. May not Christians mistake their case, by measuring their growth in one of these ways, exclusively of the rest of them?

A. Yes; if, for instance, they measure it *upwards*, and not at all *downwards;* for, though a Christian may want the sweet consolations and flashes of affection, which he has sometimes had, yet, if he be growing in humility, self-denial, and a sense of needy dependence on the Lord Jesus, he is a *growing Christian*, Hos. xiv. 5: "I will be as the dew unto Israel; he shall—cast forth his roots as Lebanon."

Q. 18. When believers cannot perceive their growth, how may they *know* if they have *true grace* at all, however *weak?*

A. If they have any measure of self-loathing on account of sin, Ezek. xxxvi. 31; if they have a desire for grace, Neh. i. 11; if they prize Christ above all things, Phil. iii. 8; and if they love his members for his sake, 1 John v. 1.

OF PERSEVERANCE.

Q. 1. What is meant by [*perseverance*] in grace?
A. A continuing still in the *state* of grace, and the habitual practice of godliness, to the end, John x. 28.
Q. 2. Can none who are justified, adopted, and sanctified, *fall totally* and *finally* from grace?
A. No: they can neither fall totally from *all grace* nor finally *without recovery;* for, "those that thou gavest me, says Christ, I have kept, and none of them is lost," John xvii. 12.
Q. 3. How is the perseverance of the saints *infallibly secured?*
A. By the immutability of electing love, Jer. xxxi. 3; by an indissoluble union with Christ, Rom. viii. 38, 39; by the merit of his purchase, 1 Pet. i. 18, 19; by the prevalency of his intercession, Luke xxii. 32; by the inhabitation of the Spirit, John xiv. 16; and by the power of a *promising* God, 1 Pet. i. 5.
Q. 4. What *promise*, among others, have believers for their perseverance in grace to the end?
A. They have that remarkable *promise*, in Jer. xxxii. 40: "I will not turn away from them to do them good; but I will put my fear in their hearts, that they shall not depart from me."
Q. 5. What *security* have believers by this promise?
A. They are secured on *every side;* both that God will never cast them off, and that they shall never depart from *him?*
Q. 6. What is the *ground, in law*, upon which believers are secured, that God will never cast them off, and that they shall never depart from him?
A. Christ's perseverance in obedience to the law for them, till the condition of the covenant was perfectly fulfilled, Phil. ii. 8, by which their perseverance was purchased, and infallibly secured, Tit. ii. 14.
Q. 7. Do all who make a zealous profession of religion persevere in it?
A. No: many of them afterwards *fall away*, John vi. 66.
Q. 8. What may we conclude about those who fall totally and finally from their profession?
A. That they were never in reality what they professed themselves to be, 1 John ii. 19: "They went out from us, but they were not of us; for if they had been of us, they

would no doubt have continued with us; but they went out, that they might be made manifest, that they were not all of us."

Q. 9. What are the *chief branches* of the promise of perseverance?

A. A promise of the *continued influence* of grace, Isa. xxvii. 3; and a promise of *continued pardon* for the sins of the believer's *daily walk,* Jer. xxxiii. 8.

Q. 10. Why is the promise of the *continued influences* of grace *necessary?*

A. Because the stock of inherent grace would soon fail: of itself, it would *wither* away, and *die* out, if it were not fed, John xv. 16.

Q. 11. Why is the promise of *continued pardon necessary* to the perseverance of saints already justified?

A. Not as if there were any need of *new pardons* with respect to their *state;* because none of their sins can bring them afterwards under the *guilt of eternal wrath,* Rom. viii. 1; but only with respect to the sins of their *daily walk,* which bring them under the *guilt of fatherly anger,* Ps. lxxxix. 30—32.

Q. 12. *How* is the pardon of the sins of their daily walk *granted* to believers?

A. Upon their renewed actings of faith in Jesus Christ, and of repentance towards God; yet not FOR their believing and repenting, but *for Christ's sake,* 1 John ii. 1, 2, even as the *first pardon* is given, chap. i. 7.

Q. 13. Does repentance then go before the pardon of sin?

A. Although *repentance* does not go before, but follows after the *pardon* of sin in *justification;* yet not only *faith* but *repentance* also, goes before the *pardons* given to those who are *already justified,* 1 John i. 9: "If we confess our sins, he is faithful and just to forgive us our sins."

Q. 14. How does the perseverance of the saints flow from their *justification?*

A. In as much as they who are *once* justified, and *accepted in the Beloved,* are *always* so; for "the gifts and calling of God are without repentance," Rom. xi. 29.

Q. 15. How does their perseverance flow from *adoption?*

A. In as much as he who has adopted them as his children, is their *everlasting Father,* Isa. ix. 6; and therefore they shall *abide* in his *house for ever,* John viii. 35.

Q. 16. How does it flow from their *sanctification?*

A. In as much as the *sanctifying Spirit* is given them to *abide with them for ever,* John xiv. 16; and to be in them *a well of water, springing up into everlasting life,* chap. v. 14.

Q. 17. What *improvement* should be made of this con-

nexion of the benefits and blessings that *accompany and flow from justification, adoption, and sanctification?*

A. It should excite in us a desire after the saving knowledge of the truth, *as it is in Jesus,* in whom all the lines of divine truth meet, as in their *centre,* Eph. iv. 21; and to admire the infinite goodness and wisdom of God, who has so linked all the blessings of the covenant *into one another,* that they who are possessed of *one,* are possessed of *all,* 1 Cor. iii. 22, 23.

Quest. 37. *What benefits do believers receive from Christ at death?*

Ans. The souls of believers are, at their death, made perfect in holiness, and do immediately pass into glory; and their bodies being still united to Christ, do rest in their graves till the resurrection.

Q. 1. Why are the persons spoken of in the *answer,* called [*believers?*]

A. Because they have been enabled, by grace, to credit the truth of God in his promise, and to embrace the good that is in it, Heb. xi. 13.

Q. 2. What is the *difference* between *believers,* and *others,* in their death?

A. *Believers* die in virtue of the *promise* of the *covenant of grace,* in which death is made over to them *unstinged,* as a part of Christ's legacy, 1 Cor. iii. 22; whereas all *others* die in virtue of the *threatening* of the *covenant of works,* Gen. ii. 17, having the *sting of death* sticking fast both in their souls and bodies.

Q. 3. What is *the sting of death?*

A. *The sting of death is sin,* 1 Cor. xv. 56; and the *curse* is the inseparable companion of sin, Gal. iii. 10.

Q. 4. What *security* in *law* have believers against the sting of death?

A. Christ's receiving it into his own soul and body, as their *Surety,* that they might be delivered from it: wherefore the promise of victory over death, made to him Isa. xxv. 8, secures the disarming of it to them, 1 Cor xv. 57.

Q. 5. How *many fold* are the benefits which believers receive from Christ at their death?

A. They are *twofold;* such as respect their souls, and such as respect their bodies.

Q. 6. How does it appear that [the *souls* of believers] *exist* in a *state* of *separation* from their bodies?

A. From the Lord's calling himself the "God of Abraham, the God of Isaac, and the God of Jacob," long after their death, as an evidence that their *souls* were *living;* for "God is not the God of the dead, but of the living," Matt. xxii. 32; and from the death of believers being called a *departure,* 2 Tim. iv. 6; intimating that the soul, upon its separation, *departs only* from *the earthly house of this tabernacle,* to *a house not made with hands, eternal in the heavens,* 2 Cor. v. 1.

Q. 7. Are the souls of men *absolutely* and *independently immortal?*

A. No: God only is so, 1 Tim. vi. 16: *Who only hath immortality.*

Q. 8. In what *sense* then are souls *immortal?*

A. In that, as to their *natural constitution,* they are *incorruptible,* having no inward principle of corruption, but remaining in a state of *activity* after the death of the body, Heb. xii. 23: "The spirits of just men made perfect."

Q. 9. How do you prove the *immortality* of the soul from the *nature* of it?

A. In its nature, it is a spiritual, immaterial, or incorporeal substance: and, therefore, where there is no *composition* of parts, there can be no *dissolution* of them, Luke xxiv. 39: "A spirit hath not flesh and bones."

Q. 10. How are we sure that the soul shall never be *annihilated?*

A. From the promise of *everlasting happiness* to the righteous; and the threatening of *everlasting misery* to the wicked, Matt. xxv. 46: "These shall go away into everlasting punishment; but the righteous into life eternal."

Q. 11. What are the *benefits* conferred upon the souls of believers, upon their separation from their bodies?

A. They are [*made perfect in holiness, and do immediately pass into glory,*] Heb. xii. 23. Phil. i. 23.

Q. 12. How does it appear, that the souls of believers are not made perfect in holiness, while united to their bodies in this life?

A. From the *remains* of corruption and indwelling sir which cleave to the best of the saints of God, while in ar *imbodied* state, Rom. vii. 23, 24.

Q. 13. In what consists that [*perfect holiness*] which it conferred upon the souls of believers at their separation.

A. Not only in a perfect freedom from all sin, as to the very *being* of it, Rev. xxi. 4, but in a perfect likeness and conformity to God, 1 John iii. 2.

Q. 14. What comfort may the believer have, in the *prospect* of the separation of his soul from his body?

A. That as *sin* made its *first entrance* into him at the *union* of his soul and body, so it shall be for ever *cast out* at their *separation;* in which respect, among many others, *death* is great *gain,* Phil. i. 21.

Q. 15. Why must the souls of believers be perfectly holy at their separation?

A. Because nothing that *defileth* can *enter* within the gates of the *heavenly Jerusalem,* Rev. xxi. 27.

Q. 16. What is the *necessary concomitant* of the soul's perfect holiness?

A.. Perfect and uninterrupted communion with God, 1 John iii. 2.

Q. 17. Where is this perfect and uninterrupted communion to be enjoyed?

A. In glory, 1 Cor. xiii. 12.

Q. 18. When do the souls of the saints [*pass into glory?*]

A. As they are made perfect in holiness *immediately* upon their separation, so do they likewise [*immediately*] pass into glory.

Q. 19. Why is it said in the *answer* that they pass [*immediately*] *into glory?*

A. To show that the fiction of a middle state, between heaven and hell, invented by the papists, has no manner of warrant, or foundation in scripture.

Q. 20. How do you prove from *scripture,* that the souls of believers, upon their separation from their bodies, *pass immediately into glory?*

A. The soul of that *certain beggar, named Lazarus,* was *immediately,* upon its separation, "carried by the angels into Abraham's bosom," Luke xvi. 22: in like manner the soul of the *thief* upon the cross was immediately glorified; for, says Christ to him, "To-day shalt thou be with me in paradise," Luke xxiii. 43; and *Stephen,* among his last words, prays, "Lord Jesus, receive my spirit," Acts vii. 59; plainly intimating, that he firmly believed his soul would be with Christ in glory *immediately* after death.

Q. 21 What is that [*glory*] into which the souls of believers immediately pass?

A. "Eye hath not seen, nor ear heard, neither have entered into the heart of man, the things which God hath prepared for them that love him," 1 Cor. ii. 9. However, since *naked* discoveries of the heavenly glory, divested of earthly resemblances, would be too bright for our weak eyes; such is the condescension of God, that he has been pleased to represent to us heaven's happiness, under similitudes taken from earthly things, glorious in the eyes of men.

Q. 22. What are the similitudes by which this glory, into which the souls of believers immediately pass, is held forth in scripture?

A. It is compared to a kingdom, Luke xii. 32; to a *house*

not made with hands, 2 Cor. v. 1; to *an inheritance incorruptible,* 1 Pet. i. 4; and to *a better country,* Heb. xi. 16.

Q. 23. Why is the heavenly glory compared to a *kingdom?*

A. Because of the fulness of all spiritual and eternal good, of which the saints are *there* possessed; and the glorious dignity to which they are advanced, Rev. i. 6: "And hath made us kings and priests unto God and his Father."

Q. 24. Why is it called a *house not made with hands?*

A. To signify the unspeakable excellency of the heavenly *mansions,* above the most stately palaces built by the hands of men.

Q. 25. Why is it said to be an *incorruptible inheritance?*

A. To intimate, that the *happiness* of the saints will be of an *unfading nature* for ever, 1 Pet. v. 4: "Ye shall receive a crown of glory that fadeth not away."

Q. 26. Why is it called a *better country?*

A. To show that there is no comparison between *the things which are seen,* and *are temporal.* and *the things which are not seen,* and *are eternal,* 2 Cor. iv. 18.

Q. 27. What *benefits* do believers receive from Christ, at death, with respect to their *bodies?*

A. [*Their bodies, being still united to Christ, do rest in their graves till the resurrection,*] Isa. lvii. 2. Job xix. 26.

Q. 28. How does it appear, that the [*bodies*] of believers in their [*graves,*], remain [*still united to Christ?*]

A. The union was with the *person* of believers, of which their bodies are a part; and this union being indissoluble, it must still subsist with their bodies in the grave, as well as with their souls in heaven, Isa. xxvi. 19.

Q. 29. How may believers be assured of this from the *union* between the *two natures* in the *person* of Christ?

A. Because, as at the death of Christ, though his soul was separated from his body, yet neither the one nor the other were separated from his divine person, but remained as firmly united to it as ever; so neither the soul nor body of the believer shall be separated from Christ by their separation from one another at death, but both of them remain indissolubly united to him for ever, Rom. viii. 38, 39.

Q. 30. What is the difference of the *grave* to the righteous and to the wicked?

A. To the one the grave is a *resting-place;* but to the other it is a *prison-house,* where they are kept in close custody for the judgment of the great day, Dan. xii. 2.

Q. 31. Why are the *bodies* of the saints said to [REST *in their graves?*]

A. Because their graves are like *beds of ease,* where

PART I—18

their bodies lie in safety, till they shall be awakened in the morning of the resurrection, Isa. lvii. 2.

Q. 32. How is their *resting in the grave* expressed in scripture?

A. By *sleeping in Jesus,* 1 Thess. iv. 14; intimating, that they *sleep in union* with Jesus, and that his Spirit keeps possession of every particle of their dust, which he will quicken and rebuild as his *temple* at the last day, Rom. viii. 11.

Q. 33. How long will they rest in their graves?

A. [*Till the resurrection*] of all the dead at the great day, John v. 29.

Q. 34. How may believers be assured of receiving these promised benefits from Christ at their death?

A. They may be assured of them, upon this ground, that the promises of these benefits to them are all ingrafted upon the promises made to him, as their glorious head, *before the world began,* 2 Tim. i. 9. Tit. i. 2.

Q. 35. Upon what promise made to Christ, is the promise of *disarming death,* to the dying believer, ingrafted; Hos. xiii. 14: "O death! I will be thy plagues?"

A. It is ingrafted upon the promise made to him, of complete victory over death, Isa. xxv. 8: "He will swallow up death in victory."

Q. 36. Upon what ground may believers be assured that their *souls,* at death, shall *immediately pass into glory?*

A. The promise of *transporting* their souls into heaven, immediately upon the separation from their bodies, (Luke xxiii. 43, "Jesus said unto him, Verily I say unto thee, To-day shalt thou be with me in paradise,") is ingrafted upon the promise made to Christ, that when he should make his soul an offering for sin, he should see his seed, Isa. liii. 10.

Q. 37. Upon what promise made to Christ is the promise of destroying death, to the dead believer, ingrafted; Hos. xiii. 14: "O grave! I will be thy destruction?"

A. It is ingrafted upon the promise made to him, of the resurrection of his mystical members, Isa. xxvi. 19: "Thy dead men shall live, together with my dead body shall they arise. Awake, and sing, ye that dwell in the dust."

QUEST 38. *What benefits do believers receive from Christ at the resurrection?*

ANS. At the resurrection, believers being raised up in glory, shall be openly acknowledged and acquitted in the day of judgment, and made perfectly blessed in the full enjoying of God to all eternity.

Q. 1. Will not all others of mankind be raised as well as [*believers?*]

A. Yes; "There shall be a resurrection of the dead, both of the just and unjust," Acts xxiv. 15.

Q. 2. How do you prove, that there will be a general resurrection of the dead?

A. From the *power* of God, which CAN raise them, and from the *scriptures*, which affirm that he WILL do it; by which two arguments, our Lord proves the doctrine of the resurrection, against the Sadducees, Matt. xxii. 29: "Jesus answered and said unto them, Ye do err; not knowing the scriptures, nor the power of God."

Q. 3. How does it appear that God CAN raise the dead?

A. Since his power was able to *speak* the world into *being* out of *nothing*, surely the same power can as easily raise up the bodies of men out of their former dust, and put them into order after their dissolution, Rom. iv. 17.

Q. 4. What *scripture instances* has God given of his *power* in raising the *dead?*

A. In the *Old Testament;* the son of the widow of *Sarepta* was raised, when he was but newly dead, 1 Kings xvii. 22; the *Shunamite's* son, when he had lain dead a considerable time, 2 Kings iv. 35; and the man cast into the sepulchre of Elisha, when they were burying him, chap. xiii. 21. In the *New Testament;* the daughter of *Jairus,* Mark v. 41, and *Dorcas,* Acts ix. 40, were both raised to life, when lately dead; the widow's son in *Nain,* when they were carrying him out to bury him, Luke vii. 12, 15; and *Lazarus,* when dead four days, John xi. 39, 44.

Q. 5. How can the dust of men's bodies be *distinguished* and *separated,* when the ashes of many generations are *mingled* together?

A. With men it is impossible, but not with God; for, whoever believes an infinite understanding, Ps. cxlvii. 5, must own, that no mass of dust can be so intermixed, but that God perfectly comprehends and infallibly knows how the most minute particle, and every one of them is to be matched; and therefore knows where the particles of each body are, and how to separate them one from another.

Q. 6. How is it evident from the *scriptures,* that God WILL *raise the dead?*

A. From several passages therein, which expressly affirm that he will do so, such as, Dan. xii. 2: "And many of them that sleep in the dust of the earth shall awake; some to everlasting life, and some to shame and everlasting contempt." John v. 28, 29: "All that are in their graves shall hear his voice, and shall come forth: they that have done good unto the resurrection of life, and they that have done evil unto the resurrection of damnation." See also Job xix. 26, 27. Acts xxiv. 15.

Q. 7. How did our Lord *prove* the resurrection against the *Sadducees,* who held only the *five books* of *Moses* as most authentic?

A. From Ex. iii. 6: "I am the God of Abraham, and the God of Isaac, and the God of Jacob." From whence he argues, Luke xx. 37, 38: "Now, that the dead are raised, even Moses showed at the bush, when he called the Lord, the God of Abraham, and the God of Isaac, and the God of Jacob: for he is not the God of the dead, but of the living."

Q. 8. What is the *force* of this argument for proving the resurrection?

A. It amounts to this: he is the God of their *persons,* and not the God of their *souls only;* and therefore, though their *souls,* in a separate state, love, worship, and praise him; yet their *bodies* must also be raised out of the dust, and be restored to life by the soul's resuming its possession, that they may, as *living persons,* or men, having soul and body *united,* love, serve, and adore him; and have the full enjoyment of all the blessings contained in his being *their God,* Heb. xi. 16.

Q. 9. Will the *self-same* body that dies be raised again?

A. Yes; it will be, for *substance,* the *same* body that will be raised, though endued with other *qualities.* The very notion of a resurrection implies as much; since nothing can be said to *rise* again, but that which *falls.*

Q. 10. How do you *prove* from *scripture,* that the self-same body that dies, shall be raised again?

A. Death, in scripture-language, is a *sleep,* and the resurrection, *an awakening* out of that sleep, Job xiv. 12; which shows the body rising up, to be the self-same that died; and the apostle tells us, that it is *this mortal,* which *must put on immortality,* 1 Cor. xv. 53; and that Christ shall "change our vile body, that it may be fashioned like unto his glorious body," Phil. iii. 21.

Q. 11. How do you *prove* this from the *equity* of the *divine procedure?*

A. Though the glorifying of the bodies of the saints cannot, in a strict sense, be said to be the reward of their services or sufferings on earth; yet it is not agreeable to the manner of the divine dispensation, that one body serve him, and another be glorified; that one *fight,* and another receive the *crown.*

OF BENEFITS AT THE RESURRECTION. 209

Q. 12. Will the *same* bodies of the *wicked*, which are laid in the dust, be also raised again?

A. Yes; that the same body which sinned may suffer: it being unsuitable, that one body be the instrument of sin here, and another suffer in hell for that sin.

Q. 13. By what *means* will the dead be raised?

A. " The Lord Jesus himself shall descend from heaven with a shout, with the voice of the archangel, and with the trump of God," 1 Thess. iv. 16; and at his alarming voice, which shall be heard all the world over, the scattered dust of all the dead shall be gathered together, dust to its dust; and likewise every soul shall come again to its own body, never more to be separated.

Q. 14. In what *order* will they be raised?

A. " The dead in Christ shall rise first," 2 Thess. iv. 16.

Q. 15. What will become of those who shall be found *alive* at the second coming of Christ?

A. They shall not die, and soon after be raised again; but they shall be *changed*, in some such manner as Christ's body was on the mount, when transfigured; and they shall become like those bodies of the saints which are raised out of their graves, 1 Cor. xv. 51.

Q. 16. In what *time* will the *dead* be raised, and the *living changed?*

A. " In a moment, in the twinkling of an eye, at the last trump," 1 Cor. xv. 52.

Q. 17. What will be the *difference* between the resurrection of the *godly*, and that of the *wicked?*

A. The *godly* shall be raised *by virtue of the* SPIRIT *of Christ*, the blessed bond of their union with him, Rom. viii. 11; and they shall come forth out of their graves with unspeakable joy, Isa. xxvi. 19: " Awake and sing, ye that dwell in the dust:" but the *wicked* shall be raised *by the power of Christ*, as a just Judge; and they shall come forth with unspeakable horror and consternation, as so many malefactors, " to be punished with everlasting destruction from the presence of the Lord, and from the glory of his power," 2 Thess. i. 9.

Q. 18. In what *state* and *condition* will the bodies of believers be raised?

A. They shall be [*raised up in glory*,] 1 Cor. xv. 43.

Q. 19. What is meant by the [*glory*] in which they shall be raised?

A. That they shall be incorruptible, glorious, powerful, and spiritual bodies, 1 Cor. xv. 42—44: " It is sown in corruption, it is raised in incorruption; it is sown in dishonour, it is raised in glory; it is sown in weakness, it is raised in power; it is sown a natural body, it is raised a spiritual body."

18*

Q. 20. What do you understand by the bodies of believers being raised *incorruptible?*

A. That they shall leave all the seeds of *corruption* behind them, in the grave; and be for ever incapable of any pain, sickness, or death: that they shall have an everlasting youth and vigour, no more subject to the decays which age produces in this life, Isa. xxxiii. 24.

Q. 21. Why are their bodies said to be *glorious?*

A. Because they shall "be fashioned like unto Christ's glorious body," Phil. iii. 21; not only beautiful, comely, and well proportioned, but full of splendour and brightness; for they shall "shine forth as the sun in the kingdom of their Father," Matt. xiii. 43.

Q. 22. Why are they said to be *powerful* or strong bodies?

A. Because they shall be able to bear up, under an "exceeding and eternal weight of glory," 2 Cor. iv. 17; and *rest not day and night,* but be, without intermission, for ever employed, in the heavenly temple, to sing and proclaim the praises of God, Rev. iv. 8; weariness being a weakness incompetent to an immortal body.

Q. 23. In what respect will they be *spiritual* bodies?

A. Not in respect of their being changed into *spirits,* (for they shall still retain the essential properties of bodies,) but in respect of their *spirit-like* qualities and endowments: they shall be nimble and active, and of a most refined constitution; for "they shall hunger no more, neither thirst any more;" and they shall never sleep, "but serve him day and night in his temple," Rev. vi. 15, 16.

Q. 24. What will follow immediately upon the resurrection of the dead?

A. [*The day of judgment,*] Rev. xx. 13.

Q. 25. What *kind* of a day will the *day of judgment* be?

A. It will be a day of wrath and vengeance to the wicked, 2 Thess. i. 8, 9, but a day of complete redemption to the godly, Luke xxi. 28.

Q. 26. What will be the *privilege* of believers in the day of judgment?

A. They [*shall be openly acknowledged and acquitted,*] Matt. xxv. 23.

Q. 27. What is it to be [*acknowledged*] by Christ in that day?

A. It is to be *owned* by him, as the blessed of his Father, for whom the kingdom of heaven is prepared, Matt. xxv. 34: "Then shall the King say to them on his right hand, Come, ye blessed of my Father, inherit the kingdom prepared for you from the foundation of the world."

Q. 28. What is it for believers to be [*acquitted*] in the day of judgment?

OF BENEFITS AT THE RESURRECTION.

A. It is not only to be vindicated from all calumny and false aspersions cast upon them here, 1 Cor. iv. 5, but to have all their sins *declaratively* pardoned, Acts iii. 19.

Q. 29. What is the *difference* between the acquitting of believers, when they are justified in *this life*, and the doing of it in the *day of judgment?*

A. In *this life*, believers are acquitted *secretly*, out of the sight of the world, and frequently without any intimation of it to themselves; but, *then*, the acquittal shall be pronounced in the most solemn and public manner.

Q. 30. Is not this what is meant by their being [*openly*] acknowledged and acquitted?

A. Yes; for it shall be done before God, angels, and men, Rev. iii. 5. Matt. xxv. 34—41.

Q. 31. *Why* will it be done so openly?

A. For the greater honour and comfort of the saints and the greater shame and confusion of their enemies, Isa. lxvi. 5: " Your brethren that hated you, and cast you out for my name's sake, said, Let the Lord be glorified; but he shall appear to your joy, and they shall be ashamed."

Q. 32. On what account shall they be acquitted in that day?

A. On the very same account they are justified *here;* namely, for Christ's righteousness' sake, imputed to them, and received by faith alone, Rom. iii. 24.

Q. 33. What benefits shall believers receive *after* the day of judgment in heaven?

A. They shall be [*made perfectly blessed in the full enjoying of God to all eternity*,] 1 Thess. iv. 17: " So shall we be ever with the Lord."

Q. 34. What is it to be [*perfectly blessed?*]

A. It is to be entirely free from all misery, and fully possessed of all happiness, Rev. xxi. 4, 7.

Q. 35. In what does the *highest pitch* of happiness consist?

A. [*In the full enjoying of God,*] the chief good, Ps. lxxiii. 25.

Q. 36. In what *way* and *manner* will God be fully enjoyed in heaven?

A. By such a perfect knowledge of him as shall have no measure set to it except what arises from the finite capacity of the creature, 1 Cor. xiii. 12; for otherwise a creature's comprehensive knowledge of an infinite being is impossible, Job xi. 7.

Q. 37. How *many ways* will God be perfectly and satisfactorily known?

A. *Two ways;* the one is by *sight*, which will satisfy the understanding; and the other is by *experience*, which will *satisfy* the will.

Q. 38. What is it that will give the greatest satisfaction to the *bodily eyes* in heaven?

A. A beholding that glorious and blessed body, which is united to the person of the Son of God, Job xix. 27.

Q. 39. Will not the glory of the *man Christ Jesus* be unspeakably *superior* to the glory of all the *saints?*

A. Yes, surely; for, though the saints *shall shine forth as the sun*, yet not they, but the *Lamb*, shall be the *light* of the heavenly city, Rev. xxi. 23.

Q. 40. What is it that will make the glory of the human nature of Christ, shine with a peculiar lustre, in the eyes of the saints?

A. It is the indissoluble subsistence of that nature in the person of the Son, as the everlasting bond of union between God and them, John xv. 23: "I in them, and thou in me, that they may be made perfect in one."

Q. 41. Is not the *blissful sight* of God in heaven, *something else* than the sight of that glory, which we will see with our bodily eyes, in the man Christ, or in the saints, or any other splendour and refulgence from the Godhead whatsoever?

A. Yes; for no created thing can be our chief good and happiness, nor fully satisfy our souls; and as these things are somewhat different from God himself, so the scriptures assure us, that we *shall see God*, Matt. v. 8, and *see him as he is*, 1 John iii. 2.

Q. 42. How will the saints see God, Father, Son, and Holy Ghost, in heaven?

A. Not with their *bodily eyes*, in respect of which, God is *invisible* 1 Tim. i. 17; but with the *eye* of the *understanding*, being blessed with the most perfect, full, and clear knowledge of God and divine things, of which the creature is capable, 1 Cor. xiii. 12.

Q. 43. What is the *difference* between believers seeing God *here*, and their seeing him *there?*

A. *Here* they have only a sight, as it were, of his *back parts:* but *there* they *shall see his face*, Rev. xxii. 4; it is but a *passing view* they can have of him *here*, but *there* they shall eternally, without interruption, feed the eyes of their souls upon him, Ps. xvii. 15: "As for me, I will behold thy face in righteousness: I shall be satisfied, when I awake, with thy likeness."

Q. 44. What will the eyes of the saints be eternally fed upon?

A. They will be for ever contemplating his *infinite love*, his *unchangeable truths*, and *wonderful works*, with the utmost complacency and delight, Ps. xvi. 11: "In thy presence is fulness of joy, at thy right hand there are pleasures for evermore."

Q. 45. How will the saints in heaven contemplate the infinite love of God towards them?

A. They shall be admitted to look into his heart, and there have a clear, distinct, and assured view of the love he bore to them from eternity, and will bear to them for evermore; for he has said, "I have loved thee with an everlasting love," Jer. xxxi. 3. " Enter thou into the joy of thy Lord," Matt. xxv. 23.

Q. 46. How will they contemplate God's *unchangeable truths?*

A. The *light of glory* will be a complete *commentary* on the *Bible,* and will disclose the whole *treasure* hid in that *field,* Ps. xxxvi. 9: " In thy light shall we see light."

Q. 47. Will there be any occasion for written or printed Bibles in heaven?

A. By no means, for the unchangeable truths of God, recorded in that holy book, will be indelibly stamped upon the minds of the redeemed company, as the subject of their everlasting song, Isa. lix. 21: " My words—shall not depart—out of the mouth of thy seed's seed, saith the Lord, from henceforth and for ever." 1 Pet. i. 25: " The word of the Lord endureth for ever."

Q. 48. What comprehension will they have of the *wonderful works* of God, particularly of *creation?*

A. Their knowledge of all the creatures will then be brought to perfection, and they will see, that *in wisdom* he has *made them all,* Ps. cxlv. 24.

Q. 49. What views will they have of adorable *providence?*

A. They will see the *checkered web* of providence spread out at its full length, and that there was a *necessity* for all the trials and troubles they met with in time, 1 Pet. i. 6.

Q. 50. How will the saints in heaven contemplate the *glorious work of redemption?*

A. It will be the matter of their eternal admiration; they shall for ever and alternately wonder and praise, and praise and wonder, at the mysteries of wisdom and love, goodness and holiness, mercy and justice, that shine through the whole of that glorious device, Rev. i. 5, 6.

Q. 51. What is the *experimental knowledge* the saints shall enjoy of God in heaven?

A. It is the participation of the divine goodness in full measure, accompanied with a most lively sense of it in the innermost part of their souls, Rev. vii. 17: " The Lamb shall lead them to living fountains of water;" which are no other than God himself, " the fountain of living waters,' who will *fully* and *freely* communicate himself to them.

Q. 52. In what respect will the communication of God to the *experience* of the saints in heaven, be *full?*

A. In as much as they shall not be limited to any measure, but the enjoyment shall go as far as their most enlarged capacities can reach, Ps. lxxxi. 10.

Q. 53. Will the *capacities* of the saints above be of *equal size?*

A. As there will be *different degrees* of glory, (the saints in heaven being compared to *stars*, which are of different magnitudes, Dan. xii. 3;) so, some capacities will contain more, and others less, yet all shall be filled, and have what they can hold, Ps. xvi. 11.

Q. 54. In what will consist the *freedom* of God's communicating himself to the *experience* of the saints in heaven?

A. In the unrestrained familiarity which he will *there* allow them with himself; he shall *walk in them*, 2 Cor. vi. 16; his fulness shall ever stand open to them, there being no veil between him and them, to be drawn aside, for they shall see him *face to face*, 1 Cor. xiii. 12.

Q. 55. What will be the *result* of the free communication, and full participation of the divine goodness in the upper sanctuary?

A. Perfect *likeness* to God, and unspeakable *joy:* hence says the Psalmist, "I shall be satisfied, when I awake, with thy likeness:—In thy presence is fulness of joy," Ps. xvii. 15, and xvi. 11.

Q. 56. *Why* will *perfect likeness* to God *follow* upon the beatific vision of him?

A. Because the seeing of God in all his matchless excellencies, no more "through a glass darkly, but face to face," cannot but be attended with a swallowing up of all the imperfections of the saints, into a glorious transformation to his blessed image, 1 John iii. 2: "We shall be like him, for we shall see him as he is."

Q. 57. Why is the communication, and participation of God in heaven, accompanied with unspeakable *joy?*

A. Because of the undoubted certainty, and full assurance which the saints have of the *eternal duration* of the same: the enjoyment of God being always *fresh* and *new* to them, through the ages of *eternity;* for they shall drink of *living fountains of waters* continually springing up in abundance, Rev. vii. 17.

Q. 58. Why will the saints in heaven have an *undoubted certainty* of their full enjoyment of God to all eternity?

A. Because the *everlasting GOD* himself will be their *eternal life* and *happiness*, 1 John v. 20: "This is the true God and eternal life." Isa. lx. 19: "The Lord shall be unto thee an everlasting light, and thy God thy glory." Hence it is said of heaven, that "the glory of God doth lighten it;" and that the Lamb *is the light thereof*, Rev. xxi. 23.

Q. 59. What *improvement* ought we to make of these *benefits* which believers receive from Christ at the resurrection?

A. We should "be diligent, that we may be found of him in peace, without spot, and blameless," 2 Pet. iii. 14; and *occupy* the *talents* he has given us, until he *come*, Luke xix. 13; we should "judge ourselves, that we may not be judged," 1 Cor. xi. 31; and because "the end of all things is at hand," we should "therefore be sober, and watch unto prayer," 2 Pet. iv. 17; yea, we should "hope to the end, for the grace that is to be brought unto us at the revelation of Jesus Christ," chap. i. 13.

END OF PART FIRST.

THE

WESTMINSTER ASSEMBLY'S

SHORTER CATECHISM

EXPLAINED,

BY WAY OF

QUESTION AND ANSWER.

PART II.

OF THE DUTY WHICH GOD REQUIRES OF MAN.

Hold fast the form of sound words."— 2 Tim. i. 13.

PREFACE.

This second part of the *Assembly's Shorter Catechism* explained, through various impediments, was not published, till about seven years after the first; which is the reason why there is an edition more of the first than of the second part.

In the *Preface* to the *first part* of this work, subscribed by the Rev. Mr. EBENEZER ERSKINE and ME, the usefulness of sound standards of public authority, together with the divine warrant for such composures, is briefly set forth; as likewise a short account of the *method*, which the *Westminster Assembly* most judiciously observe, in this compendious, and almost incomparable system of divinity, THE SHORTER CATECHISM.

Both these eminent lights, the Rev. Messrs. EBENEZER and RALPH ERSKINE, who assisted in composing and revising the *first part* of this *Catechism*, are some years ago removed to the upper sanctuary by death; the *first* soon after,* and the *second*, a little before the publishing of it :† so that the charge of this *second part* was, by a

---

* The Rev. Mr. Ebenezer Erskine, minister of the gospel, first at Portmoak, and then at Stirling, died June 2d, 1754, in the 74th year of his age, and fifty-first of his ministry.—There were what amounted to four octavo volumes of excellent sermons, published in his own lifetime, and a fifth after his death.

† The Rev. Mr. Ralph Erskine, minister of the gospel at Dunfermline, died Nov. 6th, 1752, in the 68 year of his age, and forty-second of his ministry in that place.

He published several polemical treatises on various subjects, but his practical works, both in prose and verse, were first collected into two large folio volumes, and elegantly printed. They are now

renewed recommendation of my brethren, laid upon me. They, indeed, promised to afford me materials, which some of them did; and I made all the use of them I could.

This performance, such as it is, was never *judicially* read and approved by any of our judicatories, (though several of my brethren had opportunity to peruse the most part of it, before the whole was issued ;) therefore, any imperfections or weaknesses that may be found therein, are not to be imputed to the body of ministers, with whom I am, in providence, connected, but to myself only.

As to mistakes in divinity, I dare not say there are none; but, if there are, I may be confident to affirm, there were none designed.

In this edition, there are several questions added which were not in the former; particularly, on the *ceremonial law*, which was the *typical gospel* of the Jews; and others are altered and corrected, in the plainest way I could devise.

The words of the *Shorter Catechism* from which the explicatory questions are formed, are enclosed within *brackets*, as is done in the first part, to distinguish them from quotations out of the *Confession* and *Larger Catechism*, of which there are several, in both parts of this treatise: and the scripture proofs are now ranged in such an order, as the reader may see, at first view, the branch of the answer each of them is designed to confirm.

It has been acknowledged in all ages, that the *catechetical* way of instructing is the most speedy and successful method of conveying the knowledge of divine things; because thereby the truths of God are brought level to the weakest capacity, being separately proposed one after

reprinted in ten handsome volumes octavo, with sundry additional sermons and discourses, not in the folio volumes; to which is prefixed an Account of the Author's Life and Writings; with an elegiac Poem on his death, not in the folio edition.

another, with plain and distinct answers to each. If people then would be at the pains carefully to peruse, particularly on Sabbath evenings, the helps that have been offered for understanding their Catechism, they would soon have the experience of attaining some tolerable insight into the leading principles of the Christian religion; and by that means hear the word preached with more spiritual benefit to their own souls; and likewise be capable to distinguish truth from error, in many of the practical books that are among their hands: for, *the first principles of the oracles of God* ought to be learned in the first place, and when the knowledge of these is once attained, a patent door will be opened to farther improvements; whereas, if the foundation is not laid, it is needless to dream of carrying up the fabric. And, indeed, herein lies the fatal mistake of the most part of people, that though they can scarce repeat, far less understand their Catechism, yet they imagine they may read any other divine subject that comes into their hands with advantage; while on the contrary, the understanding of their Catechism, in the *first place*, would be the most effectual and successful mean for their profiting by what they might read or hear, during the whole remainder of their life.

JAMES FISHER.

Glasgow,
May 3d, 1765.

THE

SHORTER CATECHISM EXPLAINED

PART SECOND.

QUEST. 39. *What is the duty which God requires of man?*
ANS. The duty which God requires of man, is obedience to his revealed will.

Q. 1. Why are the principles of faith, in the Shorter Catechism, treated of, before duties of obedience?
A. To show, that man's duty cannot be rightly performed, unless it flow from a belief of these principles, as the root and spring of it, Heb. xi. 6.

Q. 2. What do you understand by man's [duty?]
A. That which he owes to God, out of love and gratitude, Luke xvii. 10.

Q. 3. What is it that man thus owes to God?
A. Constant and universal [obedience,] 1 Sam. xv. 22.

Q. 4. From whence does our obligation of obedience to God arise?
A. From his universal supremacy, and sovereign authority over us, as rational creatures, Lev. xviii. 5, who depend entirely upon him, for our life, and breath, and all things, Acts xvii. 25.

Q. 5. What motive or excitement have Christians, above others, to the duties of obedience?
A. They have the revelation of God's free love, mercy, and grace in Christ, bringing salvation to them, which should teach them to live soberly, righteously, and godly, in this present world, Tit. ii. 11, 12.

Q. 6. What is the only rule and measure of our obedience?
A. The [revealed will] of God, Isa. viii. 20.

Q. 7. Why is our obedience limited to God's revealed will?
A. Because it is necessary that God should signify to us, in what instances he will be obeyed, and the manner how our obedience is to be performed; otherwise, it

would rather be a fulfilling of our own will than his, Mic. vi. 8.

Q. 8. Where has God revealed his will, as the rule and measure of our obedience?

A. In the scriptures of the Old and New Testament, 2 Tim. iii. 16.

Q. 9. What is the difference between God's secret and revealed will?

A. His secret will is reserved to himself, as the rule of his own procedure; but his revealed will is made known to us, as the rule of our faith and obedience, Deut. xxix. 29: "The secret things belong unto the Lord our God; but those things which are revealed belong unto us, and to our children for ever, that we may do all the words of this law."

Q. 10. Is it not agreeable to the revealed will of God that we give obedience to the just commands of our lawful superiors?

A. Yes; for thus we are commanded, 1 Pet. ii. 13: "Submit yourselves to every ordinance of man, for the Lord's sake."

Q. 11. What is the difference between the obedience we should yield to God, and that which we should give to our lawful superiors?

A. We should obey God for himself, or out of regard to his own authority, as the very ground and reason of our obedience; but we should obey our superiors, only in the Lord; or, as their commands are agreeable to his will, Eph. vi. 1: "Children, obey your parents in the Lord, for this is right."

Q. 12. What is our duty, when the commands of superiors are contrary to the commands of God?

A. In that case, we ought, without the least hesitation, to obey God rather than men, Acts v. 29. Dan. iii. 18.

Q. 13. Why ought God to be obeyed rather than men, when their commands are opposite?

A. Because, "God alone is the Lord of the conscience, James, iv. 12, and has left it free from the doctrines and commandments of men, which are in any thing contrary to his word," Acts iv. 19.*

Q. 14. What is the nature of that obedience which is acceptable to God?

A. It is such as flows from a vital union with Christ, and faith in him, as the principle of it, John xv. 4, 5; is performed in a due manner, Ps. v. 7; and aims at the glory of God, as its highest and ultimate end, 1 Cor. x. 31.

Q. 15. What encouragement does God give us to essay a universal obedience to his revealed will?

* Confession of Faith, chap. xx. § 2.

A. That he requires nothing of us in point of duty, but what he promises strength and furniture for the performance of, Ezek. xxxvi. 27: "I will—cause you to walk in my statutes, and ye shall keep my judgments, and do them."

QUEST. 40. *What did God at first reveal to man, for the rule of his obedience?*

ANS. The rule which God at first revealed to man for his obedience, was the moral law.

Q. 1. How are the laws of God distinguished?
A Into natural and positive.

Q. 2. What is the law of God natural, or the law of nature?
A. It is that necessary unalterable rule of right and wrong, founded in the infinitely holy and just nature of God, to which men, as reasonable creatures, cannot but be indispensably bound, Rom. ii. 14, 15.

Q. 3 What do you understand by positive laws?
A. Such institutions as depend only upon the sovereign will and pleasure of God, and which he might not have enjoined, and yet his nature remain the same; such as, the command about not eating the forbidden fruit, and all the ceremonial precepts under the old dispensation.

Q. 4. Where were the dictates of the law of nature originally inscribed?
A. A fair copy of them was originally written upon the heart or mind of man at his creation; because he was made after the image of God, Gen. i. 27.

Q. 5. Do these dictates become just and reasonable, because they are commanded; or, are they commanded, because they are just and reasonable in their own nature before?
A. They are commanded, because they are just and reasonable in their own nature, antecedently to any divine precept about them, being founded in the very holiness and wisdom of God, Ps. cxi. 7, 8.

Q. 6. Did the dictates of the law of nature undergo any change or alteration in the mind of man, after the fall?
A. The law of nature, being the natural instinct of the reasonable creature, implanted in the soul by God himself, can never be totally erased or obliterated, as to its common and general principles, and immediate conclusions flowing from them; though, with reference to such native consequences as are more remote, it is gro ily cor

rupted, and even altered and perverted, by the vicious and depraved nature of man, Rom. i. 21, 22.

Q. 7. What are the common and general principles of the law of nature, which are still engraved, in some measure, upon the minds of men, even where they have no written law?

A. They are such as these; that God is to be worshipped: parents to be honoured: none are to be injured: that we should not do to others, what we would not wish them to do to us; and the like.

Q. 8. How do you prove that these, and the like principles, are still ingrained in man's nature, even where there is no written law?

A. From Rom. ii. 14: "The gentiles, which have not the law," namely, the written law, "do by nature the things contained in the law."

Q. 9. How does it appear from men's own consciences, that they have innate principles of right and wrong implanted in their natures?

A. From their consciences excusing or accusing them, as they commit actions manifestly agreeable or disagreeable to these innate or inbred principles, Rom. ii. 15.

Q. 10. What are the horrid, though native, consequences, of denying innate principles of right and wrong?

A. The denial of this saps the foundation of all religion, natural and revealed; subverts all difference between moral good and evil; and, consequently, opens a wide door to gross and downright atheism.

Q. 11. Is there any difference between the law of nature and the moral law?

A. Although the same duties which are contained in the law of nature, are prescribed also in the moral law, yet there is this difference, that in the law of nature, there is nothing but what is moral; but in the moral law there is something also that is positive, namely, the means of worship, and circumscribing the particular day for the observance of the Sabbath.

Q. 12. What is the meaning of the word [moral,] when applied to the law?

A. Though the word literally has a respect to the manners of men, yet, when applied to the law, it signifies that which is perpetually binding, in opposition to that which is binding only for a time.

Q. 13. Was there any express revelation of the moral law made to Adam in his state of innocence?

A. He needed no express revelation of this, because it was interwoven with his very nature in his creation after the image of God, Eccl. vii. 9: God made man upright.

Q. 14. Why then is it said in the answer, that the moral law was [the rule which God at first revealed to man?]

A. Because it was so distinctly written in his heart, and impressed in his nature, that it was equal to an express revelation.

Q. 15. Is the moral law to be viewed only as the *rule* of our obedience?

A. It must be viewed also as the *reason* of it. We must not only do what is commanded, and avoid what is forbidden in the law; but we must also do good, for this very reason, that God requires it, and avoid evil, because he forbids it, Lev. xviii. 4, 5: "I am the Lord your God, ye shall THEREFORE keep my statutes, and my judgments."

Q. 16. Are the precepts of the moral law of immutable obligation, so as that they can be dispensed with in no case?

A. With respect to God, those precepts which do not flow absolutely and immediately from his own nature, may, in certain particular cases, be altered or changed, provided it be done by his own express appointment; but with respect to man, all the precepts of the moral law are of immutable obligation, and none of them can in any instance be dispensed with by him, Matt. v. 18.

Q. 17. Did not God dispense with the law against manslaughter, when he commanded Abraham to offer his only son Isaac for a burnt-offering, upon one of the mountains in the land of Moriah, which he was to tell him of? Gen. xxii. 2.

A. Though Abraham, it would seem, looked upon this mysterious command of his sovereign Lord, to be peremptory, in as much as he immediately took journey with his son, to put the divine order into execution; yet in the issue it proved only to be probatory, to discover to Abraham himself the reality of his faith, and the submissiveness of his obedience to God, as flowing from it, ver. 12, 16, 17.

Q. 18. Would Abraham have been guilty of murder, had he been permitted to sacrifice his son, on this occasion?

A. No; because he had the warrant of the most unquestionable authority, even the authority of the Lord, the Creator of the ends of the earth, for so doing, ver. 2.

Q. 19. Is the moral law a perfect rule of life and manners?

A. It is so perfect that nothing can be superadded to it, or corrected in it, Ps. xix. 7: "The law of the Lord is perfect."

Q. 20. Did Christ supply any defects of the law, or correct any mistakes in it?

A. No; he acted the part of an interpreter and defender of the law, but not of a new lawgiver; as is evident from his explaining the law, and vindicating it (Matt. chapters

v. vi. and vii.) from the corrupt glosses that were put upon it.

Q. 21. Did not Christ say, John xiii. 34, "A new commandment I give unto you, that ye love one another?"

A. This commandment was not new as to the substance of it, for it is the sum of the second table of the law, Matt. xxii. 39; and therefore called an old commandment, which we had from the beginning, 1 John ii. 7, 2 John ver. 5; but it is called *new*, because it was enforced with the new motive and example of Christ's unparalleled love to us, imported in the words immediately following: "As I have loved you, that ye also love one another."

Q. 22. Is the moral law abrogated under the New Testament?

A. By no means; for Christ came not to destroy the law, but to fulfil it, Matt. v. 17.

Q. 23. Can righteousness and life be attained by the moral law, since the fall?

A. No; for, "by the works of the law, shall no flesh be justified," Gal. ii. 16.

Q. 24. Of what use, then, is the law to men, since righteousness and life cannot be attained by it?

A. It is, notwithstanding, of much use, both to unregenerate sinners and to saints; "for the law is good, if a man use it lawfully," 1 Tim. i. 8; that is, in a suitableness to the state in which he is, either as a believer or unbeliever.

Q. 25. Of what use is the law, to unbelievers, or to unregenerate sinners?

A. It is useful to discover to them their utter impotence and inability to attain justification and salvation by the works of it; and thus it is a schoolmaster to bring them to Christ, that they may be justified by faith, Gal. iii. 24.*

Q. 26. How is the law a schoolmaster to bring sinners to Christ?

A. By requiring spotless holiness of nature; perfect, personal, and perpetual obedience in this life; and full satisfaction for sin: which none of mankind being capable of, they are thus shut up to see the need they stand in of Christ, who has done all these things for them; "for Christ is the end of the law for righteousness, to every one that believeth," Rom. x. 4.

Q. 27. Has the law this effect upon all the unregenerate?

A. No; the most part of them remain deaf to the dictates of the law, both as to their sin and danger, and are therefore rendered inexcusable, Rom. i. 20.

Q. 28. Of what use is the law to the regenerate, or to believers?

A. It is of use to excite them to express their gratitude

---

* Larger Catechism, Q. 96.

and thankfulness to Christ for his fulfilling it as a covenant, Rom. viii. 3, 4; by their studying conformity to it, both in their hearts and lives, as the *rule* of their obedience, Rom. vii. 22, and xii. 2.*

Q. 29. How can the moral law be the rule of obedience to believers, when it is said of them, Rom. vi. 14, that they are not under the law?

A. Though they are not under the law as a covenant of works, to be either justified or condemned by it, yet they are under it as a rule of duty, and account it their happiness and privilege to be so, 1 Cor. ix. 21.

Q. 30. What may we learn from the nature of the moral law in general?

A. That God having so clearly pointed out his own nature, and in a manner expressed his very image in it, Lev. xix. 2, we ought to loathe and abhor ourselves for our want of conformity to it, and our innumerable transgressions of it, Ps. xl. 12; and fly to the Lord Jesus, that by his righteousness imputed, the righteousness of the law may be fulfilled in us, Rom. viii. 3, 4.

Q. 31. What other laws did God give to the Jews, besides the moral law?

A. He gave them also the CEREMONIAL and JUDICIAL laws.

Q. 32. What was the CEREMONIAL law?

A. It was a system of positive precepts, respecting the external worship of God in the Old Testament church; chiefly designed to typify Christ, as then to come, and to lead them to the knowledge of the way of salvation through him, Heb. x. 1.

Q. 33. What were the principal ceremonies about which this law was conversant?

A. They were such as respected sacred persons, places, and things.

Q. 34. Who was the chief sacred person among the Jews?

A. The high priest, who was ordained for men in things pertaining to God, Heb. v. 1.

Q. 35. In what respect was he a type of Christ?

A. His being consecrated with a plentiful effusion of the holy anointing oil, typified the immeasurable communication of the Spirit to Christ, Ps. cxxxiii. 2, John iii. 34; and his bearing the names of the children of Israel upon his shoulder, and in the breast-plate, signified that Christ is the representative of all his spiritual seed, and has their concerns continually at heart, Isa. xlix. 3, 16.

Q. 36. Were not the other ordinary priests of Aaron's family likewise types of Christ?

* Larger Catechism, Q. 97.

A. Yes; for in as much as they daily offered sacrifices according to the law, Heb. x. 11, they were typical of him, who "now once in the end of the world, hath appeared to put away sin by the sacrifice of himself," chap. ix. 26.

Q. 37. What were the sacred places under the old dispensation?
A. The tabernacle and temple.

Q. 38. What was the tabernacle?
A. It was a movable and portable tent, secured from the injuries of the weather, by several coverings; the whole planned by God himself, and executed by Moses in the wilderness, precisely according to the pattern showed him on the mount, Heb. viii. 5.

Q. 39. How was it enclosed?
A. By a large or spacious court, open above, but hung round with curtains of fine twined linen, five cubits, or seven and a half feet high, Ex. xxvii. 18.

Q. 40. When and where was the temple built?
A. It was built by Solomon, at Jerusalem, on Mount Moriah, four hundred and eighty years after the children of Israel came out of Egypt; and, consequently, about the same number of years after the tabernacle was set up in the wilderness, 1 Kings vi. 1, compared with 2 Chron. iii. 1.

Q. 41. Was the plan of the temple the contrivance of human skill?
A. No; like the tabernacle, it was devised by God himself; for David gave to Solomon, his son, the pattern of the whole of it, as he had it, by the Spirit, 1 Chron. xxviii. 11, 12. And after enumerating several particular parts of the model, "All this, said David, the Lord made me understand in writing by his hand upon me, even all the works of this pattern," verse 19.

Q. 42. What did the tabernacle and temple typify?
A. Among other things, they both of them typified the human nature of Christ, which was assumed into union with his divine person, John ii. 19, 21.

Q. 43. How many apartments were there, in these sacred places?
A. Besides the large outward court, to which any of all Israel had access, who were not ceremonially unclean, there were, both in the tabernacle and temple, two sacred apartments; the first, called the holy, and the second, the most holy place, separated by an embroidered veil of cunning work, Ex. xxvi. 31—34.

Q. 44. What did these several apartments signify?
A. The outward court might signify the church visible, consisting in a mixture of saints and sinners; the holy place, the church invisible on earth, made up only of the

true members of Christ's mystical body; and the holiest of all represented heaven itself, or the church triumphant in glory.

Q. 45. What were the sacred things, in the outward court, which was before the tabernacle?
A. They were these three; the laver, the sacrifices, and the altar on which they were offered.

Q. 46. What was the laver?
A. It was a brazen vessel for holding water, made of the mirrors, or polished pieces of brass, presented by the women who assembled at the door of the tabernacle of the congregation, Ex. xxxviii. 8.

Q. 47. Where was it situated?
A. Between the tabernacle of the congregation and the altar, Ex. xxx. 18.

Q. 48. Why was it placed there?
A. That Aaron and his sons might wash their hands and their feet thereat, when they went into the tabernacle, or when they came near to the altar to minister, under no less penalty than death, verse 19—21.

Q. 49. Why was this ordinance of the priest's washing at the laver, enjoined under so severe a penalty?
A. To point out the absolute necessity of the application of the blood and Spirit of Christ to the soul, as that without which there can be no escaping of eternal death, 1 John i. 7, compared with Rom. vi. 23.

Q. 50. What was the subject matter of the sacrifices?
A. Such of the clean beasts and fowls, specified by God himself, as were perfectly free of any blemish or imperfection, Lev. xxii. 20.

Q. 51. What was signified by the sacrifices being without blemish?
A. The spotless holiness and purity of the human nature of Christ, which was sacrificed for us, 1 Pet. i. 19.

Q. 52. What were the instructive ceremonies that were used in expiatory sacrifices or burnt-offerings?
A. The sins of the offerers were to be typically laid upon the head of the sacrifice, Lev. i. 4; next, it was to be slain by blood-shedding, ver. 5; and then, it was to be consumed wholly, or in part, with fire upon the altar, ver. 9.

Q. 53. What was signified, by charging the sins of the offerers upon the head of the sacrifice?
A. That the sins of an elect world were laid on Christ, to be expiated by him, Isa. liii. 6.

Q. 54. What was typified, by shedding the blood of the sacrifice unto death?
A. That the blood of Christ was to be shed for many, for the remission of sins, Matt. xxvi. 28.

Q. 55. What was signified, by consuming the sacrifice with fire upon the altar?

A. That the whole of that infinite wrath, which was due to sinners, and would have been consuming them for ever was poured out upon the glorious Surety, and endured by him, Isa. liii. 10.

Q. 56. Upon what altar were the sacrifices offered and consumed?

A. Upon the brazen altar, or altar of burnt-offerings, which was placed without, before the door of the tabernacle of the congregation, Ex. xl. 6; intimating, that the sacrifice of Christ, was to be perfected on this earth, John xix. 30.

Q. 57. What was typified by this altar?

A. As the altar sanctifieth the gift, Matt. xxiii. 19, so this altar typified the divine nature of Christ, as giving infinite worth and value to the sacrifice of the human nature, because of the personal union, Heb. ix. 14.

Q. 58. From whence originally came the fire, which was kept burning on the altar of burnt-offering?

A. It came originally and immediately from God himself; for when Moses was dedicating the tabernacle in the wilderness, there came a fire out from before the Lord, and consumed, upon the altar, the burnt offering, and the fat, Lev. ix. 24. And afterwards at the dedication of Solomon's temple, when he had made an end of praying, the fire came down from heaven, and consumed the burnt-offering and the sacrifices, 2 Chron. vii. 1.

Q. 59. What was signified by this fire coming immediately from before the Lord, or from heaven?

A. It signified God's acceptance of, and acquiescence in, the obedience unto death of his own eternal Son, typified by all these expiatory sacrifices, Isa. xlii. 21.

Q. 60. Why was the fire never to go out, but to be kept ever burning upon the altar? Lev. vi. 13.

A. To show that it was not possible that the blood of bulls and goats could take away sin, Heb. x. 4; and therefore to teach the people, under that dispensation, to look to the atoning blood of the Messiah, as that only which could quench the flame of divine wrath against sin, and be an offering and sacrifice to God, for a sweet smelling savour, Eph. v. 2, in which he might eternally rest.

Q. 61. What were the sacred things in the holy place, called the first tabernacle? Heb. ix. 2.

A. They were the candlestick, the table with the shewbread, and the altar of incense.

Q. 62. What was typified by the *candlestick?*

A. That all true spiritual light is conveyed to the church only from Christ, John i. 9, 18; and that, as the branches were supplied with oil from the body of the candlestick, so all the members are supplied out of the fulness of Christ for God giveth not the Spirit by measure unto him, chap. iii. 34.

Q. 63. What was meant by the *shew-bread*, which was always set forth upon the table? Ex. xxv. 30.

A. That in Christ, who is the bread of life, there is food continually for starving sinners of mankind, John vi. 35; and that we may ever come to him for supply, because, "in him dwelleth all the fulness of the Godhead bodily," Col. ii. 9.

Q. 64. What was typified by the altar of *incense*, which was placed immediately before the veil? Ex. xxx. 6.

A. The incense which was continually burnt upon this altar, every morning and evening, Ex. xxx. 7, 8, (after the sacrifices were offered without, upon the altar of burnt-offering,) typified the prevalent intercession of Christ, founded upon his meritorious oblation, 1 John ii. 1, 2.

Q. 65. What were the sacred and significant things contained in the most holy place, or holiest of all, as it is called? Heb. ix. 3.

A. The apostle to the Hebrews says, that the tabernacle which is called the holiest of all,—had the golden censer, and the ark of the covenant, overlaid round about with gold, wherein was the golden pot that had manna, and Aaron's rod that budded, and the tables of the covenant; and over it the cherubims of glory, shadowing the mercy-seat, Heb. ix. 4, 5.

Q. 66. Did the golden censer, like other sacred utensils in the most holy place, remain in it perpetually?

A No; it remained no longer than the high priest continued within the veil, sprinkling the blood of the sin-offering upon the mercy seat, and before it, Lev. xvi. 14, during which time the cloud of incense, kindled with coals of fire from the altar of burnt-offering covered the mercy-seat, ver. 13, 14; and then, when the high priest retired from the most holy place, he carried off the golden censer with him to the altar of incense, where it lay till there was next occasion for it.

Q. 67. Why then was the holiest of all said to *have* the golden censer?

A. Because the principal use of it, was to carry in burning incense to the most holy place, along with the blood of the sacrifice on the great day of atonement, once every year, Lev. xvi. 12, 13.

Q. 68. What was typified by this cloud of incense carried in by the high priest to the most holy place, along with the blood of the sacrifice once a year?

A. The infallible prevalency of Christ's intercession, because of the infinite merit of his satisfaction, Heb. vii. 25.

OF THE CEREMONIAL LAW.

Q. 69. What was the most eminent pledge of the divine presence, in this most holy place?
A. The ark with the mercy-seat that covered it, Ex. xxv. 21, 22: "Thou shalt put the mercy-seat above upon the ark—and there will I meet with thee, and I will commune with thee."

Q. 70. What was put within the ark?
A. Nothing but the two tables of stone, on which the ten commandments were written by the finger of God at Mount Sinai, 1 Kings viii. 9. There was nothing in the ark, save the two tables of stone, which Moses put there at Horeb.

Q. 71. Were not the golden pot that had manna, and Aaron's rod that budded, put within the ark, as it would seem from Heb. ix. 4?
A. No: it is expressly said, that both these were appointed to be laid up before the testimony, not in it, Ex. xvi. 34, and Num. xvii. 10.

Q. 72. What did the golden pot that had manna signify?
A. The inexhaustible provision of all spiritual blessings laid up in Christ, for the members of his mystical body, John vi. 54, 55.

Q. 73. What was typified by Aaron's rod that budded?
A. The fixed choice that God had made of Christ, to the office of priesthood, he being called of God, as was Aaron, Heb. v. 4.

Q. 74. For what end was the ark of the covenant properly made?
A. It was for holding the two tables of the law, which are called the testimony, Ex. xxv. 16. Says God to Moses, "Thou shalt put into the ark the testimony which I shall give thee."

Q. 75. Why were the tables of the law called the two tables of testimony? Ex. xxxi. 18.
A. Because they testified the will of God to mankind as the unerring rule of duty, Isa. viii. 20.

Q. 76. Why were these tables put into the ark?
A. To signify that the law, which was broken by the first Adam, was put up, as fulfilled in the second, Isa. xlii. 21, that there might be "no condemnation to them which are in Christ Jesus," Rom. viii. 1.

Q. 77. Why were these tables called the tables of the covenant, and the ark containing them, the ark of the covenant? Heb. ix. 4.
A. Because the ten commandments, written on these tables, were the matter of the covenant of works made with Adam, as the head of his posterity, Rom. x. 5, and the fulfilment of them, both in point of doing and suffering, was the condition of the covenant of grace, made

with Christ, as the representative of his spiritual seed, Matt. iii. 15.

Q. 78. What was the mercy-seat?

A. It was a plate of solid gold, exactly fitted to the breadth and length of the ark, (Ex. xxv. ver. 10 and 17, compared,) so as to be a lid, or covering to the tables of the covenant, which were within it, ver. 21.

Q. 79. Why was it called the mercy-seat?

A. To intimate, that God is propitious and merciful to sinners, only through the meritorious satisfaction of Christ, Rom. v. 21.

Q. 80. What was signified by its being a lid, or covering, to the tables of the covenant?

A. That the broken law was so hid or covered by the glorious Surety, who answered all its demands, (Rom. viii. 33, 34,) that it could accuse none before God, who had "fled for refuge to lay hold upon the hope set before them," Heb. vi. 18.

Q. 81. What was it that peculiarly belonged to the mercy-seat?

A. The "cherubims of glory shadowing it," Heb. ix. 5.

Q. 82. What was represented by these cherubims?

A. They represented the ministry and service of the holy angels to Christ and his church, Heb. i. 14.

Q. 83. Why called cherubims of glory?

A. Because God manifested his glory from between them, Ex. xxv. 22, and gave gracious answers with respect to his church and people, Num. vii. 89.

Q. 84. How did they shadow the mercy-seat?

A. By stretching forth and spreading their wings over it, intimating their readiness to fly upon Christ's errands on all occasions, Ps. civ. 4.

Q. 85. In what posture were the faces of these cherubims?

A. They looked one to another, and towards the mercy-seat, Ex. xxv. 20.

Q. 86. What did this posture of their faces signify?

A. Their looking one to another, signified their perfect harmony in serving the interests of Christ's kingdom, Ezek. i. 20; and their looking towards the mercy-seat, signified their desire to look, with the most profound veneration and wonder, into the adorable mystery of redeeming love, 1 Pet. i. 12: "Which things the angels desire to look into."

Q. 87. Who was allowed to enter into this most holy place?

A. The high priest alone, without any to attend or assist him, Lev. xvi. 17; and in this he was an eminent type of Christ, who has the whole work of redemption laid upon his shoulders, "And of the people there was none with him," Isa. lxiii. 3.

Q. 88. When did the high priest enter into the holiest of all?

A. Only once every year; namely, on the great day of atonement, which was appointed to be a solemn anniversary fast, under that ceremonial dispensation, Lev xvi. 29, 30.

Q. 89. In what manner did the high priest enter within the veil?

A. He was expressly required to carry along with him the blood of the sacrifice, slain without the tabernacle, at the altar of burnt-offering, and the golden censer full of burning incense; without both which, he might by no means enter within the most holy place, Lev. xvi. 12—16.

Q. 90. What was typified by this solemnity?

A. It typified the perpetual efficacy of the blood of Christ in heaven, for all the blessings and benefits for which it was shed on earth, Heb. xii. 24.

Q. 91. Is the ceremonial law, or any part of it, obligatory now, under the New Testament?

A. Although the divine truths, couched and signified under the ceremonies of God's own institution, be unchangeably the same, yet the observance of the ceremonies themselves is abrogated by the death and satisfaction of Christ, in whom they had their full accomplishment, John i. 17.

Q. 92. How do you prove that the ceremonial law was abolished by the death and satisfaction of Christ?

A. From the utter destruction, many ages since, of the temple at Jerusalem, where only it was lawful to offer sacrifices; which adorable Providence would never have permitted, if these ceremonial institutions had been intended to subsist after the death of Christ, of whom it was foretold that he should "cause the sacrifice and the oblation to cease," Dan. ix. 27. See also Jer. iii. 16: "In those days, saith the Lord, they shall say no more, The ark of the covenant of the Lord; neither shall it come to mind, neither shall they remember it, neither shall they visit it, neither shall that be done any more."

Q. 93. What may we learn from the whole of this typical dispensation?

A. That as the ceremonial law was a shadow of good things to come, Heb. x. 1, so it is a perpetual evidence of the faithfulness and power of God, in the full accomplishment of all the blessings that were prefigured by it, John i. 17.

Q. 94. What was the JUDICIAL law?

A. It was that body of laws given by God, for the go

vernment of the Jews, partly founded in the law of nature, and partly respecting them, as they were a nation distinct from all others.

Q. 95. What were those laws which respected them as a people distinct from all others?

A. They were such as concerned the redemption of their mortgaged estates, Lev. xxv. 13; the resting of their land every seventh year, Ex. xxiii. 11; the appointment of cities of refuge for the manslayer, Num. xxxv. 15; the appearing of their males before the Lord at Jerusalem, three times in the year, Deut. xvi. 16; and the like.

Q. 96. Is this law abrogated, or is it still of binding force?

A. So far as it respects the peculiar constitution of the Jewish nation, it is entirely abrogated; but in so far as it contains any statute, founded in the law of nature, common to all nations, it is still of binding force.

QUEST. 41. *Wherein is the moral law summarily comprehended?*

ANS. The moral law is summarily comprehended in the ten commandments.

Q. 1. What is it to be [summarily comprehended?]

A. It is to be briefly summed up, in such few and well chosen words, as to take in a great deal more than what is expressed, Rom. xiii. 9.

Q. 2. Where is the moral law thus briefly summed up?

A. In the [ten commandments,] Deut. x. 4.

Q. 3. Where is the law more largely and fully set forth?

A. In the whole scriptures of the Old and New Testaments, Ps. cxix. 105.

Q. 4. By whom were the ten commandments first pronounced and promulgated?

A. By God himself, Exod. xx. 1; GOD spake all these words.

Q. 5. Whether was it God essentially considered, or God considered as in the person of the Son, who spake these words?

A. It was the three-one God considered as in the person of the Son, who was the speaker of them; as is evident from Acts vii. 37, 38, where the Prophet, whom the Lord was to raise up unto the Jews of their brethren, like unto Moses, is expressly called the angel which spake to him in Mount Sinai. See also Heb. xii. 25, 26.

Q. 6. What was the peculiar work of God about these

words, after he had spoken them with an audible voice, in the hearing of all Israel?

A. He wrote or engraved them with his own finger, on two tables of stone, Deut. ix. 10.

Q. 7. Was each of these tables written on both sides?

A. It is said expressly that they were, Ex. xxxii. 15. The tables were written on *both* their sides; on the one side, and on the other were they written.

Q. 8. What did this signify?

A. The tables being fully written on both sides, signified that nothing was to be added to the words of the law, or taken away from them, Deut. iv. 2; and likewise, that the whole man, soul, spirit, and body, must be sanctified wholly, 1 Thess. v. 23.

Q. 9. How often were the commandments written on tables of stone?

A. The first being broken by Moses, on occasion of the idolatry of Israel, Ex. xxxii. 19, the Lord condescended to write on two other tables, the very same words that were on the former, chap. xxxiv. 1.

Q. 10. Was there any difference between the first two tables and the second?

A. The first two, which were entirely the work of God, (the polishing as well as the engraving,) were broken beneath the mount, Ex. xxxii. 16, 19; but the second, which were hewed by Moses, the typical mediator, were put into the ark, Deut. x. 3, 5.

Q. 11. What spiritual mystery was represented by this?

A. That though the covenant of works, made with the first Adam, was broken and violated by him, yet it was fulfilled in every respect by Christ the true Mediator, who "restored that which he took not away," Ps. lxix. 4.

Q. 12. Why were the ten commandments written on tables of stone?

A. To intimate the perpetuity, and everlasting obligation of the moral law, Ps. cxi. 8.

Q. 13. What was signified by their being written with the finger of God?

A. That it is the work of God, alone, to put his laws into the mind of sinners, and to write them in their hearts, Heb. viii. 10.

Q. 14. Where was the law of the ten commandments thus expressly revealed?

A. At Mount Sinai, which is also called Horeb, Deut. v. 2.

Q. 15. In what form was the law of the ten commandments given out at Mount Sinai?

A. In the form of a *covenant*, Deut. v. 2: The Lord our God made a covenant with us in Horeb. Accordingly, the ten commandments are called the words of the covenant, Ex. xxxiv. 28; and the tables of stone are termed the tables of the covenant, Deut. ix. 9.

Q. 16. Was the Sinai transaction in the form of the covenant of works, or in the form of the covenant of grace?

A. There was, on that solemn occasion, a repetition of *both* those covenants.

Q. 17. In what order were these two covenants repeated on Mount Sinai?

A. The covenant of grace was first promulgated, and then the covenant of works was displayed, as subservient to it.

Q. 18. How does it appear that the covenant of *grace* was first promulgated?

A. From these words in the preface, prefixed to the commands, I am the Lord thy God, spoken to a select people, the natural seed of Abraham, as typical of his whole spiritual seed, Gal. iii. 16, 17.

Q. 19. How are the ten commandments to be viewed, as they stand annexed to this promulgation of the covenant of grace on Mount Sinai?

A. They are to be viewed as the law of Christ, or as a rule of life, given by Christ the Mediator to his spiritual seed, in virtue of his having engaged to fulfil the law, as a covenant, in their room, Rom. vii. 4.

Q. 20. How does it appear that the covenant of *works* was likewise displayed on Mount Sinai?

A. From the thunderings and lightnings, and the voice of the living God, speaking (the words of the ten commandments) out of the midst of the fire, Ex. xx. 18. Deut. v. 22, 26.

Q. 21. What was signified by the thunderings and lightnings, and the voice of God, speaking out of the midst of the fire?

A. These awful emblems represented that infinite avenging wrath, which was due to all of Adam's family, for the breach of the covenant of works, by which the whole of God's holy law was violated and infringed, Gal. iii. 10.

Q. 22. Why did God make a display of the covenant of works in such an awful and tremendous manner?

A. That sinners of mankind might be deterred from the most remote thought of attempting obedience to the law as a condition of life; and be persuaded to fly to, and acquiesce in the undertaking of Christ, who engaged his heart to approach to God, as Surety in the room of an elect world, Jer. xxx. 21.

Q. 23. If both covenants, of grace and works, were exhibited on Mount Sinai, were not the Israelites, in that case, under both these covenants at one and the same time?

A. They could not be under both covenants in the same

respects, at the same time; and therefore they must be considered either as believers or unbelievers, both as to their outward church state and inward soul frame.

Q. 24. In what respects were the believing Israelites, in the Sinaitic transaction, under both covenants?

A. They were internally and really under the covenant of grace, as all believers are, Rom. vi. 14, and only externally, under the above awful display of the covenant of works, as it was subordinate and subservient to that of grace, in pointing out the necessity of the Surety righteousness, Gal. iii. 24.

Q. 25. In what respects were unbelievers among them, under these two covenants of works and grace?

A. They were only externally, and by profession, in respect of their visible church state, under the covenant of grace, Rom. ix. 4; but internally, and really, in respect of the state of their souls, before the Lord, they were under the covenant of works, chap. iv. 14, 15.

Q. 26. Which of the two covenants was the principal part of the Sinai transaction?

A. The covenant of grace was both in itself, and in God's intention, the principal part of it; nevertheless, the covenant of works was the more conspicuous part of it, and lay most obvious to the view of the people; for they *saw* the thunderings and the lightnings, and the noise of the trumpet, and the mountain smoking, Ex. xx. 18. And so terrible was the sight, that Moses said, I exceedingly fear and quake, Heb. xii. 21.

Q. 27. What effect had this tremendous display of the covenant of works upon the Israelites?

A. It tended to beat them off, in some measure, from that self-confidence which they had expressed before the publication of the law, Ex. xix. 8; and to discover the necessity of a Mediator, and of faith in him as the sole foundation of all acceptable obedience, Rom. xvi. 25, 26.

Q. 28. How does it appear that it had this effect?

A. From their own words to Moses, after the terrible sight which they saw, Deut. v. 27: "Speak thou unto us all that the Lord our God shall speak unto thee; and we will *hear* [that is, believe] and *do*." On which account the Lord commends them, ver. 28: "They have well said all that they have spoken: O that there were such a heart in them!"

Q. 29. In what respect had they said well in what they had spoken?

A. In as much as they had made faith, or believing, the source and spring of acceptable doing; for, "whatsoever is not of faith is sin," Rom. xiv. 23.

Q. 30. How many commandments are commonly allotted to each of these two tables of the law?

A. Four to the first table, containing our duty to God; and six to the second, containing our duty to man.

Q. 31. How are the precepts, which are naturally moral, distinguished from those that are but positively so?

A. The precepts which are naturally moral have, in them, an innate rectitude and holiness, which is inseparable from them; but the precepts which are positively moral, have their rectitude, not from their own nature, but from the positive command of God.

Q. 32. What example may be given of this for illustration?

A. The fourth commandment, as it requires God to be worshipped, is naturally moral, founded in the very nature of God; but as it enjoins, that he be worshipped on such a particular day of the week, it is positively moral, founded entirely in the will of God.

Q. 33. What is the difference between the commands that are expressed in affirmative, and those that are expressed in negative terms?

A. "What God forbids is at no time to be done, Rom. iii. 8; what he commands is always our duty, Deut. iv. 8, 9; and yet every particular duty is not to be done at all times, Matt. xii. 7."*

Q. 34. Why are negative precepts binding at all times?

A. Because what is forbidden is at all times sinful; and ought never to be done, on any pretext whatsoever, Gen. xxxix. 9.

Q. 35. What are the peculiar properties of the law of the ten commandments?

A. That it is perfect, Ps. xix. 7; spiritual, Rom. vii. 14; and exceedingly broad, or most extensive, Ps. cxix. 96.

Q. 36. What rule is to be observed for the right understanding of the perfection of the law?

A. "That it binds every one to full conformity in the whole man, unto the righteousness thereof, and to entire obedience for ever; so as to require the utmost perfection in every duty and to forbid the least degree of every sin, Matt. v. 21, to the end, James ii. 10."†

Q. 37. What rule is to be observed for understanding the spirituality of the law?

A. That it reaches to the thoughts and motions of the heart, as well as to the words and actions of the life, Deut. vi. 5.‡

Q. 38. What rule is to be observed for the right understanding of the breadth or extent of the law?

A. That, as where a duty is commanded, the contrary sin is forbidden, Isa. lviii. 13; and where a sin is forbidden, the contrary duty is commanded, Eph. iv. 28: so, when

* Larger Catechism, Q. 99. Rule 5.   † Ibid. Rule 1.   ‡ Ibid. Rule 2.

OF THE SUM OF THE TEN COMMANDMENTS.

any duty is commanded, all the causes and means of it are commanded also, Heb. x. 24, 25; and when any sin is forbidden, all occasions and temptations to it, are likewise forbidden, Gal. v. 26.*

———

QUEST. 42. *What is the sum of the ten commandments?*

ANS. The sum of the ten commandments is, To love the Lord our God with all our heart, with all our soul, with all our strength, and with all our mind; and our neighbour as ourselves.

Q. 1. How is the sum of the ten commandments divided in this answer?

A. Into the sum of the four commandments in the first table, which contain our duty to God; and into the sum of the six commandments in the second table, which contain our duty to man.

Q. 2. What is the sum of the four commandments in the first table, which contain our duty to God?

A. It is [to love the Lord our God, with all our heart, with all our soul, with all our strength, and with all our mind,] Luke x. 27.

Q. 3. Why is this called "the first and great commandment?" Matt. xxii. 38.

A. Because the duties of the first table have a more direct relation to God, as being the immediate object of them, or, because love to our neighbour should flow from love to God, as the proper fountain and principle of it, 1 John v. 1.

Q. 4. What is meant by the [*sum*] of the commandments?

A. The comprehensive duty of the law, which includes all other duties in the bosom of it, Rom. xiii. 9.

Q. 5. What is the comprehensive duty of the law?

A. It is *love*; for "love is the fulfilling of the law," Rom. xiii. 10.

Q. 6. What is the nature of that love which is the comprehensive duty of the law?

A. It is such as flows from faith, as the source and fountain of it; for "faith worketh by love," Gal. v. 6.

Q. 7. What ought to be the supreme object of our love?

A. [The *Lord*,] or *Jehovah* himself, as he is *our God*, Deut. xxx. 6.

Q. 8. How many ways may the Lord be said to be [our God?]

---

* Larger Catechism, Rules 4, 6.

A. Two ways; either by external revelation and offer; or, by special property and possession.

Q. 9. To whom does he make the external revelation and offer of himself, as their God?

A. To all such of mankind, without exception, as have the word of this salvation sent to them, Prov. viii. 4. Heb. viii. 10.

Q. 10. When is he our God by special property and possession?

A. When by faith we are united to Christ, 1 Cor. iii. 23, in whom mercy and truth are met together, righteousness and peace have kissed each other, Ps. lxxxv. 10.

Q. 11. What is it to love the Lord our God [with all our heart?]

A. It is to love him unfeignedly, without hypocrisy or dissimulation, Rom. xii. 9.

Q. 12. What is it to love him [with all our soul, and mind?]

A. It is to have an intelligent, cordial, and affectionate love to God; expressed in all the duties, in which any power or faculty of the soul can be exercised, Isa. xxvi. 8, 9.

Q. 13. What is it to love the Lord our God [with all our strength?]

A. It is to love nothing so much as God, Matt. x. 37; and nothing but in subordination to him, Luke xiv. 26.

Q. 14. How may we know, if we have such a supreme love to the Lord our God?

A. If we love him purely for himself, and his own matchless excellency, as shining in the face of Jesus, Song i. 3; if we account all things but loss in comparison of him, Phil. iii. 8; and if we centre in him as the only resting-place of our souls for ever, Ps. lxxiii. 25, 26.

Q. 15. What is the sum of the six commandments in the second table, which contain our duty to man?

A. It is to love [our neighbour as ourselves,] Matt. xxii. 39: "The second is like unto it, Thou shalt love thy neighbour as thyself."

Q. 16. Why is the sum of the second table said to be like unto the sum of the first?

A. Because the duties of the second table are enjoined by the same authority as those of the first, James ii. 10.

Q. 17. In which of the two tables is the lawful love of ourselves contained, seeing it is not expressly mentioned in either of them?

A. It is fairly implied and supposed in both tables, particularly in the second, where love to ourselves is made the example and pattern, according to which we should love others, Luke x. 27: "Thou shalt love—thy neighbour as thyself."

Q. 18. What is lawful self-love?

A. It is an aiming at our own happiness, in subordination to the glory of God, which ought to be our chief and ultimate end, 1 Cor. x. 31.

Q. 19. Whom are we to understand by [our neighbour?]

A. All of mankind to whom we have any way access to be useful, either as to their temporal or spiritual good Luke x. 36, 37.

Q. 20. What is it to love our neighbour [as ourselves?]

A. It is to love him as truly and sincerely as we do our selves, Eph. v. 29: "No man ever hated his own flesh, but nourisheth and cherisheth it."

Q. 21. Should our love to our neighbour be as great as it is to ourselves?

A. It is not required that it be as great in degree, but only that it be as sincere, and free of hypocrisy, as it is to ourselves. Rom. xii. 9.

Q. 22. What is the rule according to which our love to our neighbour should be regulated?

A. That we do to others what we would have them do to us, Matt. vii. 12.

Q. 23. How is this rule to be explained for preventing the abuse of it?

A. That we do as we would be done to, from a well-informed judgment; and by such as place themselves in the same relations, and in the same circumstances with us.

Q. 24. Why are we enjoined to esteem others better than ourselves? Phil. ii. 3.

A. Because the more of the grace of God we have in our hearts, we will the more clearly see that we ourselves are the chief of sinners, 1 Tim. i. 14, 15, and have the seed of all sin in us, which would soon spring up into the worst of actions, if not restrained, Rom. vii. 23.

Q. 25. What is the difference between the love we should have to all in general, and the love we should have to the saints in particular?

A. We should love all men in general, with a love of benevolence, and likewise of beneficence according to our ability, Gal. vi. 10; but we should love the saints with a love of complacency and delight, Ps. xvi. 3.

Q. 26. How ought our love to extend itself to our enemies?

A. By forgiving them, and praying for them, Matt. v 44. Acts vii. 60.

Q. 27. What may we learn from the sum of the commandments?

A. That charity, or love, which is the end of the commandment, ought to flow from a pure heart, and a good conscience, and faith unfeigned, 1 Tim. i. 5.

QUEST. 43. *What is the preface to the ten commandments?*

ANS. The preface to the ten commandments is in these words: *I am the Lord thy God, which have brought thee out of the land of Egypt, out of the house of bondage.*

QUEST. 44. *What does the preface to the ten commandments teach us?*

ANS. The preface to the ten commandments teaches us, That because God is the Lord, and our God, and Redeemer, therefore we are bound to keep all his commandments.

Q. 1. What is a [preface?]
A. It is something spoken before, or a preparatory introduction to the following discourse.

Q. 2. Are these words, [I am the Lord thy God,] &c. to be understood as a preface to all the commandments, or to the first only?
A. They are to be understood as a preface to them all, though they stand immediately connected with the first, as being the ground of the particular applicatory faith in a redeeming God, which is enjoined in it.

Q. 3. Why are the above words prefixed as a preface to all the commandments?
A. Because they are designed as so many reasons and arguments to enforce our obedience to them.

Q. 4. Why does God give reasons to enforce obedience to his commands, when his will is the supreme law?
A. To manifest his amazing condescension, in dealing with us in a suitableness to our natures as rational creatures, Hos. xi. 4.

Q. 5. How many reasons or arguments are there in this preface, by which God enforces obedience to his law?
A. Three; the first is, because he is *the Lord,* or *Jehovah;* the second, because he is *our God;* and the third, because he is our *Redeemer.*

Q. 6. Which of these three is the formal reason of obedience?
A. The first, namely, God's essential greatness, as he is *" Jehovah,* the Most High over all the earth," Ps. lxxxiii. 18; though, at the same time, his relative goodness, as our God, and the deliverance he has accomplished as our Re-

OF THE PREFACE TO THE COMMANDMENTS.

deemer, are invincible arguments and motives to obey him, Lev. xix. 36, 37.

Q. 7. What is the strength of the first argument for obedience, taken from God's being [*the Lord?*]

A. The strength of it lies in this, That because God is *Jehovah*, " the eternal, immutable, and almighty God, having his being in and of himself, and giving being to all his words and works:"* therefore, all obedience and subjection is due to him, Lev. xx. 8.

Q. 8. In what lies the strength of the second argument for obedience to God's law, taken from his being [*our God?*]

A. It lies in this, That because he makes himself over to sinners of mankind, by a new covenant grant, in the word of divine revelation; therefore, this ought to sweeten all his commands, and powerfully excite us to the obedience of them, Lev. xx. 7.

Q. 9. What does God make over to us in the word, when he makes a grant of himself in it to be our God?

A. He makes over to us whatever he is, Hos. xiii. 4, and whatever he has, Ps. lxxxiv. 11, as God, to be ours freely and eternally.

Q. 10. What does he make over to us when he makes a grant of whatever *he is?*

A. He makes over to us both what he is essentially, and what he is personally.

Q. 11. What does he make over to us when he makes a grant of what he is essentially?

A. All his glorious attributes and excellencies to be ours, Ex. xxxiv. 6; his infinity, to be the extent of our inheritance, Rev. xxi. 7; his eternity, to be the date of our happiness, John xiv. 19; his unchangeableness, to be the rock of our rest, Mal. iii. 6; his wisdom, to direct us, Ps. lxxiii. 24; his power, to protect us, 2 Chron. xvi. 9; his holiness, to sanctify us, Ezek. xvi. 14; his justice, to justify and preserve us, Rom. iii. 26; his goodness, to reward us in the way of grace, not of debt, 1 John ii. 25; and his truth, to secure us in the accomplishment of all his promises, Heb. x. 23.

Q. 12. What does he make over to us, when he makes a grant of what he is personally?

A. He makes over himself in the person of the Father, to be our God and Father in Christ, 1 Pet. i. 3; in the person of the Son, to be our Redeemer and Saviour, Isa. xlviii. 17; and in the person of the Holy Ghost, to be our Sanctifier and Comforter, John xiv. 16.

Q. 13. What is it that he makes over to us, when he makes a grant of whatever *he has?*

---

* Larger Catechism, Quest. 101.

A. As he has all the good things we can possibly need in time, or through eternity, so he makes them all freely over to us in the promise;—" All things are yours," 1 Cor iii. 21: for instance, he has life, for the quickening of us who are dead in trespasses and sins, Eph. ii. 1; righteousness, for the justifying of us who are guilty, Isa. xlv. 25; and redemption for delivering us who are lawful captives, chap. xlix. 24, 25. In a word, " Eye hath not seen, nor ear heard, neither have entered into the heart of man, the things which God hath prepared for them that love him,' 1 Cor. ii. 9.

Q. 14. Is this grant that God makes of himself to us in the word, to be our God, no more than a mere argument, or motive to enforce our obedience?

A. It also strengthens and enables us to obey God, Ezek. xxxvi. 27, 28.

Q. 15. How does the revelation of God's being our God, strengthen and enable us to obedience?

A. In as much as by the revelation of this, the Holy Ghost is conveyed as the immediate efficient of holiness, Gal. iii. 2; and faith is produced in the soul, as the spring and fountain of it, chap. v. 6.

Q. 16. Why does God front his law with this grant of himself as the Lord our God?

A. Because it comprehends all the promises of the covenant, and all the blessings that are wrapt up in them, and therefore is the best encouragement to the obedience of faith; for, because he is our God, he will give us one heart, and one way; he will not turn away from us to do us good, but will put his fear in our hearts, that we shall not depart from him, Jer. xxxii. 38—40.

Q. 17. Why does God make this declaration of his grace in the present time [I am] and not in the future, I *will* be thy God?

A. To show that God's covenant of promise is always a solid ground and foundation for the present actings of faith, in every case and circumstance in which we can be situated, James ii. 23.

Q. 18. Why does God, in this grant, address the sinner in the singular number, I am [*thy*] God?

A. That every individual sinner, to whom the revelation of his grace may come, should believe it with a particular applicatory faith, Zech. xiii. 9: " I will say, It is my people; and they shall say, The Lord is *my God.*"

Q. 19. How may we know, if ever we have, by faith, received the offer and grant that God makes of himself in the word?

A. By our love and esteem of him, Ex. xv. 2; by our reposing entire trust and confidence in him, Ps. xviii. 2; by our likeness and conformity to him, 1 John iii. 3; and by our longing after the full fruition and enjoyment of him, Ps. lxxiii. 25.

Q. 20. What is the *third argument*, in the Preface, for enforcing our obedience?

A. It is in these words: [which have brought thee out of the land of Egypt, out of the house of bondage.]

Q. 21. How are these words explained in our Catechism?

A. Of our spiritual redemption by Jesus Christ; for, [the preface to the ten commandments teaches us, That because God is the Lord, and our God, and *Redeemer*, therefore we are bound to keep all his commandments.]

Q. 22. In what lies the strength of this argument, for enforcing our obedience to the commands of God?

A. It lies in this, that as he brought Israel of old out of their bondage in Egypt, so he delivered us out of our spiritual thraldom; and therefore we should " serve him without fear, in holiness and righteousness before him, all the days of our life," Luke i. 74, 75.

Q. 23. In what respects did the deliverance of Israel out of Egypt resemble our spiritual redemption by Christ?

A. The Israelites were made to serve the Egyptians with rigour, Ex. i. 14; so sinners, by nature, are under the most cruel bondage and servitude to sin and Satan, 2 Pet. ii. 19; the Israelites were not able of themselves to shake off the Egyptian yoke, Ex. ii. 23; no more are sinners of mankind capable of extricating themselves from a state of spiritual slavery in which they are naturally inthralled, Rom. v. 6: the Israelites were brought out of Egypt, with a strong hand and a stretched out arm, Ps. cxxxvi. 12; so are we, out of our spiritual thraldom, by the mighty power of God, Ps. cx. 2, 3: the Egyptians were destroyed, when Israel were delivered, Ex. xiv. 28; so principalities and powers were spoiled, Col. ii. 15, transgression finished, Dan. ix. 24, and death unstinged, 1 Cor. xv. 55, when our redemption was accomplished, ver. 57.

Q. 24. Seeing the deliverance of Israel, which was typical of our spiritual deliverance, was brought about by divine power, without the payment of a price, will it follow, that our spiritual redemption was also without a price?

A. By no means; unless the similitude between the type and the antitype held in every respect, which it cannot possibly do; for, though there be a resemblance between them in some things, yet there is always a disparity in others; as might be made evident in every one of the scriptural types and metaphors, to which divine things are compared: for instance, Jonah was alive in the whale's belly, whereas Christ was actually dead in the grave.

Q. 25. Since God brought all the Israelites, without exception, out of Egypt, does it not from thence follow, that Christ redeemed all mankind from their spiritual bondage?

A. No; because the Israelites did not typify and represent all mankind, but the elect only, Ps. cxxxv. 4.

Q. 26. How do you prove that the elect only, and not all mankind, were redeemed by Christ?

A. From the Father's gift of them to him from eternity, John xvii. 6; from his representing them in his death, John x. 11: and from his intercession within the veil for them only, John xvii. 9: "I pray for them; I pray not for the world, but for them which thou hast given me."

Q. 27. Are the purchase and intercession of Christ precisely of the same extent?

A. Surely they are; for, his intercession being founded on his purchase, and consisting in a presentation of the merit of it before the throne, Heb. ix. 24, it clearly follows, that the one can be no more extensive than the other, John xvii. 24: "Father, I will that they also whom thou hast given me, be with me where I am."

Q. 28. How then are those scriptures to be explained, which seem to speak of a universal purchase of all mankind; such as, that Christ died for all, 2 Cor. v. 15; that he tasted death for every man, Heb. ii. 9; that he is the propitiation also for the sins of the whole world, 1 John ii. 2; and the like?

A. They are to be explained in a limited sense, of some only, and not of every individual of mankind; as the like general terms are undoubtedly to be understood in other places of scripture; such as Col. i. 6, and Rev. xiii. 3; for, if it is alleged, that the above scripture expressions prove a universal purchase, it may be said, with the same parity of reason, that they prove a universal application of it, which few will assert.

Q. 29. Does not the universal offer of Christ prove the universal redemption of all, at least within the visible church?

A. No: it only proves the unquestionable duty of all to believe, upon the call and command of God, 1 John iii. 23; and the infinite intrinsic worth of the satisfaction of Christ for the salvation of all, had it been so designed, chap. iv. 14.

Q. 30. Does the redemption purchased by Christ bring any benefit or advantage to the reprobate world?

A. It is owing to it that the gospel is sent among them, John iv. 4; that temporal judgments are shortened, Mark xiii. 20; and it is on account of the elect, who are to spring of them, that they are preserved for awhile in this world, Rom xi. 30; but then these, or the like benefits, are not to be considered as the fruit of Christ's purchase to the reprobate themselves, but to the elect only, who are living among them, 2 Cor. iv. 15, or who are to descend from them, Isa. vi. 13.

Q. 31. In what consists the spiritual bondage we are naturally under, and redeemed from by Christ?

A. It consists in our being under the wrath of God, John iii. 18; the guilt, power, and pollution of sin, Rom. viii. 7; the tyranny of Satan, Eph. ii. 2; the snares and temptations of the world, 1 John ii. 16; and in our liability to the pains of hell for ever, Matt. xxv. 46.

Q. 32. What right had Christ to be our Redeemer from this state of spiritual bondage?

A. He had a right of property, and a right of propinquity.

Q. 33. How had he a right of property?

A. As God, he is the original owner, Rom. ix. 21; and as Mediator, he has the elect given to him by his Father, John xvii. 6.

Q. 34. How has he a right of propinquity?

A. He has it by the legal union which subsisted between him and us from eternity, in virtue of his being "made a surety of a better testament," Heb. vii. 22; and by the assumption of our nature in time, by which he became our kinsman, and is not ashamed to call us brethren, Heb. ii. 11, 12.

Q. 35. What does God's delivering Israel out of the land of Egypt teach us, with respect to his church and people in general?

A. It teaches us, that as affliction is the lot of the Lord's people, in this present evil world, so deliverance from it is secured in due time, Ps. xxxiv. 19: "Many are the afflictions of the righteous, but the Lord delivereth him out of them all."

Q. 36. What is the difference between the afflictions of the godly, and those of the wicked?

A. The afflictions of the godly are the chastisements of a gracious Father, flowing from love, and designed for their profit, Heb. xii. 6, 10; but the afflictions of the wicked are the punishments of an avenging Judge, flowing from wrath, and designed for their ruin and destruction, Eccl. v. 17.

Q. 37. What improvement ought we to make of our spiritual redemption?

A. It should excite us to "stand fast in the liberty wherewith Christ hath made us free, and not to be entangled again with the yoke of bondage," Gal. v. 1; to ascribe all the praise of our spiritual liberty to our glorious Deliverer, Rev. i. 5, 6; and to testify our gratitude and thankfulness to him, by a conversation becoming the gospel, Phil. i. 27.

OF THE FIRST COMMANDMENT.

QUEST. 45. *Which is the first commandment?*

ANS. The first commandment is, *Thou shalt have no other gods before me.*

QUEST. 46. *What is required in the first commandment?*

ANS. The first commandment requireth us to know and acknowledge God to be the only true God, and our God; and to worship and glorify him accordingly.

Q. 1. Why are most part of the commands of the law delivered in negative terms?
A. Because negative precepts are of the strictest obligation, binding always, and at all times.

Q. 2. Why is the first commandment, in particular, so expressed?
A. Because of the perpetual propensity of our nature, since the fall, to depart from the living God; "through an evil heart of unbelief," Heb. iii. 12.

Q. 3. Why is this commandment set in front of all the rest?
A. To teach us, that the having *Jehovah* to be our God, is the leading and fundamental duty of the law, Ex. xv. 2, which sweetly and powerfully influences obedience to all the other commands of it, Ps. cxviii. 28.

Q. 4. What influence has obedience to the first, upon obedience to the other precepts of the law?
A. As obedience to the first commandment, is to believe that God is our God, upon the gift of himself to us, in these words, [I am the Lord thy God;] so, without believing this it is impossible we can do any thing else that will please him, Heb. xi. 6; for whatsoever is not of faith is sin, Rom. xiv. 23

Q. 5. Why do this, and other commands, run in the second person singular, *thou*, and not in the plural, *you*, or *ye?*
A. To signify, that God would have us to take his commandments, as spoken to éach of us in particular, as if we were mentioned by name.

Q. 6. What is the connexion between the preface and the first commandment?
A. The preface reveals and exhibits the object of faith, and the first commandment enjoins the duty of believing on that object: the one makes a grant of grace, and the other warrants us to lay hold on it.

Q. 7. Are the preface and first commandment of equal extent?

A. Yes; every one to whom the promise in the preface is revealed, is obliged, by the command, to believe it, with application, John iii. 18.

Q. 8. Can the obligation of the law be in the least weakened by the grace of the gospel, published in the preface?

A. So far from it, that it is impossible for any man to share of the grace of the gospel, published in the preface, but in a way of believing, enjoined in the first command of the law, Rom. iii. 31: "Do we make void the law through faith? God forbid."

Q. 9. What are the chief duties required in the first commandment, as thus connected with the preface?

A. [To know and acknowledge God, to be the only true God, and our God; and to worship and glorify him accordingly.]

Q. 10. What *knowledge* of God does the first commandment require?

A. It requires us to know that God is; and that he is such a God as he has manifested himself to be in his word, Heb. xi. 6.

Q. 11. What has God manifested himself to be in his word?

A. He has manifested himself to be, "The Lord, the Lord God merciful and gracious, long-suffering, and abundant in goodness and truth, keeping mercy for thousands, forgiving iniquity, transgression, and sin, and that will by no means clear the guilty;" namely, without a satisfaction, Ex. xxxiv. 6, 7; or, he has manifested himself to be in Christ, reconciling the world to himself, 2 Cor. v. 19.

Q. 12. What is it to [know] God as he is in Christ?

A. It is to know that he is well pleased for Christ's righteousness' sake, because he has magnified the law, and made it honourable, Isa. xlii. 21.

Q. 13. How is the knowledge of God usually distinguished?

A. Into speculative or common, and practical or saving knowledge.

Q. 14 What is the speculative or common knowledge of God?

A. It is only a floating knowledge of him in the head, without any saving influence or efficacy upon the heart and practice; as is to be found in ungodly persons or hypocrites, who may "profess that they know God, but in works they deny him," Tit. i. 16.

Q. 15. What is it to have a saving and practical knowledge of God?

A. It is to have such a lively apprehension of his relation to us as our God in Christ, as is accompanied with an habitual conformity to his will, in heart and life, 1 John ii. 3, 4.

Q. 16. What are the evidences of true saving knowledge?

A. It is an experimental, Col. i. 6, interesting, Ps. xli. 11, sanctifying, 2 Pet. i. 8, and humbling knowledge, Job xl. 4, 5.

Q. 17. What is it to [acknowledge] God?

A. It is to own, avouch, and confess him, both in secret, and before the world, Rom. x. 10,—" With the mouth confession is made unto salvation."

Q. 18. Why are the knowing and acknowledging of God joined together?

A. Because wherever the saving knowledge of God is implanted in the heart, there will be always some evidences of it, either to ourselves, or others, discovered in the life, Dan. xi. 32: " The people that do know their God, shall be strong, and do exploits."

Q. 19. What should we know and acknowledge God to be?

A. We should know and acknowledge him to be [the only true God, and our God.]

Q. 20. What is it to know and acknowledge God to be [the only true God.]

A. It is to believe and profess, that he alone, and none else, is possessed of all infinite perfection, and that the perfections of the divine nature are most eminently displayed and manifested in the person of Christ, our only Saviour and Redeemer, Hos. xiii. 4: " Thou shalt know no God but me: for there is no Saviour besides me."

Q. 21. What is it to know and acknowledge God to be [our God?]

A. It is to profess our relation to him, as his people, upon the faith of the grant that he makes of himself to us as ours, in the word; Deut. xxvi. 17, 18. Ps. xlviii. 14.

Q. 22. Can we know and acknowledge God to be our God, (as required in this commandment) unless we believe in Christ?

A. No; for " no man cometh unto the Father but by me," says Christ—" He that hath seen me hath seen the Father," John xiv. 6, 9.

Q. 23. Is not faith, or believing in Christ, a gospel precept only, and not required in the law?

A. By no means; for, in the gospel, strictly and properly taken, as it is contra-distinct from the law, there can be no precept; because the gospel, in this strict sense, is nothing else than a promise, or glad tidings of a Saviour, with grace, mercy, and salvation in him, for lost sinners of Adam's family; according to the following scriptures, Gen. iii. 15, Isa. lxi. 1—3, Luke ii. 10, 11.

Q. 24. Since faith and repentance are duties consequently to the entrance of sin, and the revelation of the gospel, must they not therefore be new precepts, not given to Adam in innocence?

A. Though there was no occasion for the exercise of these duties in an innocent state; yet Adam being bound by the law of creation, (particularly the ten commandments, given him in the form of a covenant of works,) to believe whatever God should reveal, and obey whatever he should command.; no sooner was the gospel revelation made, than the very same law, which bound him, while in innocence, to believe in God as his Creator, obliged him, when fallen, to believe in God as his Redeemer, now revealed and made known to him; and likewise to turn from sin to God, Rom. iii. 31.

Q. 25. Whence is it that the obligation of the law is so extensive, as to bind to the belief of whatever God shall reveal?

A. This arises from the absolute perfection of the law, which being a complete rule of all obedience, cannot but fasten the duty, the same moment that the object is revealed, Ps. cxix. 96: Thy commandment is exceeding broad.

Q. 26. What is the absurdity of making faith and repentance new gospel precepts?

A. The absurdity is, that by this another righteousness is introduced in our own persons, than the righteousness of Christ, as the immediate ground of our pardon and acceptance before God.

Q. 27. How does this absurdity necessarily follow from the aforesaid doctrine?

A. If Christ, as our surety, has fulfilled the precept, and endured the penalty of the moral law, according to Gal. iv. 4, 5, then it cannot but follow, that this law of faith and repentance, not being fulfilled by him, must be fulfilled by ourselves, in our own persons, as our righteousness before God: and thus another ground of justification is established, besides the Surety righteousness, contrary to Gal. ii. 16, and iii. 21.

Q. 28. What is the doctrine of our Larger Catechism on this head?

A. That believing and trusting in God (which is the same with faith,) " being careful in all things to please him," and " sorrowful when in any thing he is offended," (which is the same with repentance,) are among " the duties required in the first commandment:" and that " unbelief—distrust—incorrigibleness—and hardness of heart, or impenitency, (according to Rom. ii. 5, there quoted,) are among the sins forbidden in it."*

Q. 29. What does God require of us in this commandment, as the evidence of our knowing and acknowledging him to be the only true God, and our God?

A. That we [worship and glorify him accordingly,] Matt. iv. 10: "Thou shalt worship the Lord thy God, and him only shalt thou serve."

Q. 30. What is it to [worship] God?

A. It is to make him the supreme object of our esteem, Ps. lxxi. 19, desire, Ps. lxxiii. 25, and delight, Ps. cxlii. 5, and that not only in our secret devotions, but likewise when joining with others in any religious exercise, Ps. cxi. 1.

Q. 31. What is it to [glorify] him?

A. It is to ascribe all possible glory and perfection to him, Ex. xv. 11, and, in all our actions, to aim at the advancement of his honour and glory in the world, 1 Cor. x. 31.

Q. 32. What is imported in our being required to worship and glorify him [accordingly?]

A. It imports, that since God commands us to know and acknowledge him, not only to be the true God, but our own God, in virtue of the covenant grant he makes of himself in the word; it becomes us, in all our actions, religious and civil, to behave towards him, as standing in such a near and intimate relation to us, Ps. xlv. 11. 1 Cor. vi. 20.

Q. 33. Can we glorify God aright, unless we acknowledge him to be our God in Christ?

A. No; for, unless we acknowledge a God in Christ, as our God, we make him a liar, in saying, I am the Lord thy God, and rebel against his authority in the first commandment, which is, Thou shalt have no other gods before me.

Q. 34. Is believing the promise, then, the foundation of all acceptable worship and obedience?

A. Yes; for all true obedience, is "the obedience of faith," Rom. vi. 26, and "without faith it is impossible to please God," Heb. xi. 6.

Q. 35. In what manner are we required to worship and glorify God?

A. Both inwardly in our hearts, John iv. 24, and outwardly in our lives, Matt. v. 16.

Q. 36. How are we to worship God inwardly in our hearts?

A. By trusting, Isa. xxvi. 4; hoping, Ps. cxxx. 5, and delighting in him, Ps. xxxvii. 4; by thinking and meditating upon him, Mal. iii. 16, Ps. lxiii. 6; devoting ourselves

* See Larger Catechism, Quest. 104, 105

to him, Isa. xlv. 5; and by being filled with grief, when he is offended by ourselves or others, Ps. xxxviii. 18, and cxix. 136.

Q. 37. How are we to worship and glorify him outwardly in our lives?

A. By praying to him, and praising him with our lips, Ps. cxlii. 1, and cxlv. 21; by being zealous for his glory, Ps. lxix. 9; careful to please him, Col. i. 10; and by walking humbly before him, Mic. vi. 8.

Q. 38. What improvement ought we to make of the covenant grant in the preface, [I am the Lord thy God;] and the precept enjoining the belief of this, [Thou shalt have no other gods before me!]

A. That it is the duty of every one of us, without waiting till we find gracious qualifications wrought in us, instantly to lay claim to a God in Christ, as our God, Ps. xcv. 7; this being what he requires in the first place, as the foundation of all other acts of obedience, 2 Chron. xx. 20.

Q. 39. If it is an external federal relation to the visible church, which God asserts in the preface, when he says, I am the Lord thy God, how can the first commandment warrant the faith of a special relation?

A. As the command always warrants a particular application of every general promise, so the external federal relation which God bears to the visible church, becomes a special one, the moment that the promise is believed with a particular applicatory faith, Jer. iii. 22.

QUEST. 47. *What is forbidden in the first commandment?*

ANS. The first commandment forbiddeth the denying, or not worshipping and glorifying the true God, as God and our God; and the giving that worship and glory to any other which is due to him alone.

Q. 1. To what general heads may the sins forbidden, in the first commandment, be reduced?
A. To these two: atheism and idolatry.
Q. 2. What is *Atheism?*
A. It is the [denying,] or not having a God.
Q. 3. How is atheism commonly distinguished?
A. Into speculative and practical.
Q. 4. How is speculative atheism again subdivided?
A. Into that which is directly, and that which is interpretatively such.

Q. 5. What is direct speculative atheism?
A. It is a fixed persuasion in the heart, and an open profession with the mouth, that there is no God.

Q. 6. What is speculative atheism, interpretatively, or by necessary consequence?
A. It is the rejection of any of those truths which are necessarily connected with the being of a God; such as the denial of providence, or any of the essential perfections of God: because from thence it would necessarily follow, that there is no God.

Q. 7. Why would it necessarily follow, from the denial of providence, or any of the divine perfections, that there is no God?
A. Because it is impossible to conceive that there is a God, without conceiving, at the same time, that he preserves and governs the world, Isa. xli. 23; and it is impossible to conceive his being or existence, without conceiving him to be possessed of all infinite perfection, 1 John i. 5.

Q. 8. Can there be such a person among men, as a direct speculative atheist?
A. No: there can be none of mankind, who has, at all times, such a fixed and constant persuasion that there is no God, as at no time whatsoever to have the least fear or doubt of the contrary, Dan. v. 6, 9.

Q. 9. How does it appear that there can be no such person as a downright speculative atheist?
A. From universal experience, which attests, that the knowledge and impression of the being of a God, is so natural to man, that he can no more divest himself of it at all times, than he can strip himself of his reason, or shake off his own existence, Rom. i. 19: " That which may be known of God is manifest in them; for God hath showed it unto them :" that is, ingrained it in their natures.

Q. 10. Would it not seem, that there may be a downright speculative atheist, from Ps. xiv. 1: " The fool hath said in his heart, there is no God?"
A. The words do not import a fixed and permanent persuasion, but rather a secret wish: accordingly, the expression is not, The fool hath believed, or is persuaded in his heart, but hath said: that is, would fain have harboured such a secret desire.

Q. 11. Why do wicked men wish there were no God?
A. To be free of any check or restraint upon their lusts, and that they may work all uncleanness with greediness, Eph. iv. 19.

Q. 12. Who are they that are interpretatively atheists?
A. Not only they who deny the providence of God, or any essential attribute of his nature, but likewise all deists, who reject supernatural revelation; and all openly wicked

and profane persons, who live as if there was no God, Ps. x. 4, 11, 13.

Q. 13. Is it speculative or practical atheism, that is chiefly levelled against, in this commandment?

A. Both: but especially practical atheism, as being universally prevalent, Rom. iii. 11.

Q. 14. What is practical atheism?

A. It is a denial of God, in our practice, Tit. i. 16: "They profess that they know God, but in works they deny him."

Q. 15. How does practical atheism evidence itself?

A. In omitting the duties required in this commandment; namely, not knowing and acknowledging God to be what he really is, and neglecting to worship and glorify him accordingly.

Q. 16. Who are guilty of not knowing God?

A. Not only heathens, who walk contrary to nature's light, Rom. i. 21; but likewise Christians, who being privileged with the means of knowing God, as in Christ, yet slight and neglect the same; John xv. 22: "If I had not come and spoken unto them, they had not had sin; but now they have no cloak for their sin."

Q. 17. Who are they that are guilty of not acknowledging God?

A. They who rush upon the actions of life, without asking his counsel about them, Josh. ix. 15: "The men took of their victuals, and asked not counsel at the mouth of the Lord."

Q. 18. Who are guilty of [not worshipping] God?

A. They who live in the habitual neglect of the public, private, and secret exercises of his worship, Isa. xliii. 22: "Thou hast not called upon me, O Jacob; thou hast been weary of me, O Israel."

Q. 19. Who are guilty of [not glorifying] God?

A. They who set up themselves as their own rule, Ps. xii. 4, and make themselves their own end and happiness, in opposition to God, Phil. ii. 21.

Q. 20. When are men chargeable with this piece of practical atheism; namely, of setting themselves up as their own rule?

A. When they perform any action, religious or civil, more because it is agreeable to self, than as it is pleasing to God, Zech. vii. 5, 6; when they envy the gifts and prosperity of others, Ps. lxxiii. 3: and when they would model or frame God himself according to their own fancy, imagining him to be altogether such a one as themselves, Ps. l. 21.

Q. 21. When do men make themselves their own end and happiness in opposition to God?

A. When they ascribe the glory of what they have or

do, to themselves, and not to God, Dan. iv. 20; when they are more troubled for what disgraces themselves, than for what dishonours God, 1 Sam. xv. 30; and when they prefer the pleasures and profits of this world, to the glorifying and enjoying of God, Matt. xix. 22.

Q. 22. When may we be said to worship the true God, and yet not [*as* God ?]

A. When we draw nigh to him with the mouth, and honour him with our lips, but our hearts are far from him, Matt. xv. 8.

Q. 23. When are we guilty of not worshipping and glorifying him, as [*our* God ?]

A. When, in the course or tenor of our behaviour and deportment towards him, we want the habitual exercise of the faith of our federal relation to him, Ps. lxxxi. 10, 11.

Q. 24. May not the saints themselves be chargeable with some degree of practical atheism ?

A. No doubt they may; when they entertain unbecoming thoughts of God in their mind, or speak unadvisedly to him with their lips. Thus Job is censured by Elihu, for charging God with injustice, chap. xxxiii. 10, 11; and Jonah speaks most rashly to God, when he says, "I do well to be angry, even unto death," chap. iv. 9.

Q. 25. How may a person know when blasphemous thoughts, and atheistical expressions, are not inconsistent with a state of grace ?

A. When a blasphemous thought is so far from being indulged, that it is treated with abhorrence; and when an atheistical expression (uttered through surprise, and the hurry and violence of temptation) is deeply regretted and lamented, Ps. lxxiii. 21, 22.

Q. 26. What is the other general and comprehensive sin forbidden in this commandment?

A. *Idolatry.*

Q. 27. What is idolatry?

A. It is [the giving that worship and glory to any other, which is due to God alone.]

Q. 28. How is idolatry commonly distinguished?

A. Into that which is gross and external, and that which is more refined and internal?

Q. 29. What is the idolatry which is gross and external?

A. It is an ascription of the ordinary signs of worship, or religious homage, to any person or thing, besides the true God, Lev. xxvi. 1.

Q. 30. Who are they that are guilty of this grosser kind of idolatry?

A. *Heathens* and *Papists.*

Q. 31. What was the nature of the idolatry of the Heathens?

A. They made gods of the sun, moon, and stars, and of

almost every other creature; yea, of devils themselves, as the apostle witnesses, 1 Cor. x. 20. But that which was most frequent among them, was their making images or idols in the shape of some sort of living creatures, or of a mixture of them, and then worshipping them as if they were gods, Ps. cxxxv. 15—19.

Q. 32. How did Heathenish idolatry take its rise in the world?

A. By men becoming "vain in their imaginations, whereby they changed the glory of the incorruptible God into an image made like to corruptible man, and to birds, and four-footed beasts, and creeping things," Rom. i. 21. 23.

Q. 33. How does it appear that the Papists are guilty of this grosser kind of idolatry?

A. By their bowing to images and altars; giving divine honour to the consecrated bread in the sacrament; adoring the crucifix; praying to angels; invoking the saints, especially the virgin Mary, whom they supplicate much more frequently than they do Christ himself. By all which it appears, that Popish idolatry succeeds in the room of the Heathenish; and is more inexcusable than theirs, because those who practise it have the benefit of divine revelation, which the heathens have not.

Q. 34. How do you prove, that the paying religious homage to such things is gross idolatry?

A. From the nature of idolatry itself; the very essence of which consists in giving divine worship and honour to any creature whatsoever, whether in heaven or earth; for it is written, "Thou shalt worship the Lord thy God, and him only shalt thou serve," Matt. iv. 10.

Q. 35. What is the idolatry which is more refined and internal?

A. It is a setting up of idols in the heart, Ezek. xiv. 4; or giving that room in our esteem and affection to any thing else, which God alone ought to possess, Luke xiv. 26.

Q. 36. To whom is this kind of idolatry incident?

A. To all mankind naturally; and even believers themselves are cautioned and warned against it, 1 John v. 21: "Little children, keep yourselves from idols."

Q. 37. What are these idols which have a seat in every man's and woman's heart by nature?

A. Among many others, there are these two, which are worshipped and served by the generality, even of the visible church, namely, self and the world.

Q. 38. How does it appear that self is an idol which naturally reigns in the heart of every one?

A. From the very first lesson in the school of Christianity, which is, to deny self, Matt. xvi. 24: " Then said Jesus unto his disciples, If any man will come after me, let him deny himself."

Q. 39. What is it for a man to deny himself?

A. It is to give up with his self-wisdom, his self-will, and his self-righteousness.

Q. 40. When do we give up with the idol of self-wisdom?

A. When we are made to see our own depraved reason to be but folly, when compared with the wisdom of God revealed in his word; "for the wisdom of this world is foolishness with God," 1 Cor. iii. 9.

Q. 41. When is the idol of self-will dethroned?

A. When God's will of precept becomes the sole rule of our heart and life, Ps. cxix. 105; and his will of providence is cheerfully acquiesced in, as the best for us, Rom. viii. 28.

Q. 42. When do we part with the idol of self-righteousness?

A. When we submit to the righteousness of God, or found our plea, for eternal life, wholly and entirely upon the meritorious obedience and satisfaction of Christ, as our Surety, in our room and stead, Phil. iii. 8, 9.

Q. 43. How does it appear that the *world* is an idol seated in every man's heart by nature?

A. From the habitual turn of our thoughts and affections to things temporal, Matt. vi. 31; the eager pursuit of them, and ardent desire after them, in preference to those that are spiritual and eternal, chap. xvi. 26.

Q. 44. What are the things of this world which we naturally incline to idolize?

A. Some make an idol of their worldly riches; making gold their hope, and saying "to the fine gold, Thou art my confidence," Job xxxi. 24; some, of their worldly pleasures, being "lovers of pleasures, more than lovers of God," 2 Tim. iii. 4; some make an idol of their worldly credit and reputation, receiving "honour one of another," and not seeking "the honour that cometh from God only," John v. 44; some, of their worldly relations bestowing more of their love upon them, than upon God, Matt. x. 37; and some make an idol of their worldly helps and confidences, trusting more to these than to God, Isa. xxxi. 1. Jer. xvii. 5.

Q. 45. What is the verdict of the Spirit of God concerning those who make the world their idol?

A. It is this, that "if any man love the world, the love of the Father is not in him," 1 John ii. 15.

Q. 46. How may Satan be said to be even idolized, by those who profess to bear him an implacable hatred?

A. When his suggestions are regarded, more than the dictates of the Spirit of God in his word, Isa. xl. 27. xlix. 14.

Q. 47. How may the suggestions of Satan be distinguished from the dictates of the Spirit of God?

A. The tendency of all Satan's suggestions is to set up, in the soul, some one thing or other in Christ's room, 2 Cor. iv. 4; but the dictates of the Spirit of God are wholly calculated for giving Christ in all things the pre-eminence, John xvi. 14.

Q. 48. Why is Satan called the God of this world? 2 Cor. iv. 4.

A. Because he is "the spirit that worketh in the children of disobedience," Eph. ii. 2, till "the prey be taken from the mighty, and the lawful captive delivered," Isa. xlix. 24, 25.

Q. 49. Who are they that explicitly acknowledge the devil as their God?

A. They are such as use sorcery, divination, witchcraft, charms, and other diabolical arts and practices, condemned in Deut. xviii. 10—12.

Q. 50. Was Joseph's cup an instrument of divination, or did he himself use this unlawful art, when he says, Gen. xliv. 15—"Wot ye not that such a man as I can certainly divine?"

A. By no means; for the word translated *divine*, is on the margin, rendered, make trial, or inquiry; and so the meaning is, Know ye not that such a man as I, who am so diligent and industrious in other matters, would soon miss the cup in which I usually drink, and make inquiry after the person who had stolen it?

Q. 51. What improvement ought we to make of the first commandment, as it stands connected with the preface?

A. That as God warrants and commands us to believe in him, as our God and Redeemer, Ps. xlv. 11; so it is our duty to carry along with us the faith of this relation, in all our approaches to his presence, Heb. xi. 6.

QUEST. 48. *What are we especially taught by these words* [BEFORE ME] *in the first commandment?*

ANS. These words [BEFORE ME] in the first commandment, teach us, That God, who seeth all things, taketh notice of, and is much displeased with, the sin of having any other god.

Q. 1. What is the strength of the argument implied in these words [*before me*?]

A. That the sin of having any other god, is committed in the presence of him, [who seeth all things,] Heb. iv. 13.

Q. 2. What is it for God to see all things?
A. It is to have a most intimate, perfect, and comprehensive knowledge of them, Ps. cxlvii. 5: "His understanding is infinite."

Q. 3. In what consists the infinity of God's knowledge?
A. Not so much in the perfect and comprehensive knowledge of the creatures, which are finite; as in the perfect and comprehensive knowledge of himself, and his own excellencies and perfections, which are infinite. 1 Cor. ii. 11.

Q. 4. How is it that God sees, or knows all things?
A. He sees all things at once in his own essence, distinctly, infallibly, and immutably, 1 John i. 5.

Q. 5. How do you prove that God has such a comprehensive sight and knowledge of all things?
A. Because otherwise he could not be the Creator, Governor, and Judge of the world, 1 Cor. iv. 5.

Q. 6. In what light does God see or know evil actions?
A. As they are opposite to his nature, Jer. xliv. 4, and contrary to his law, 1 John iii. 4, which is the sole and unerring standard of all rectitude, Rom. vii. 12.

Q. 7. What is that sin which strikes more immediately and directly against the authority of God in this commandment?
A. It is [the sin of having any other god.]

Q. 8. What is it to have another god?
A. It is to have our minds, wills, and affections carried out after other objects, as much, or more than after God himself, Isa. xlvi. 9, compared with Ezek. xiv. 4.

Q. 9. What [notice] does God take of this sin?
A. He threatens to resent it with the highest marks of displeasure, and that even in this life, as well as in the world to come, Deut. xxix. 24—29.

Q. 10. Why is God so [much displeased] with the sin of having any other God?
A. Because it sets up a rival or competitor in his room, and that in his very sight and presence, Jer. xxxii. 30.

Q. 11. What influence ought the presence of an all-seeing God to have upon us in all our actions?
A. The consideration of this ought to quicken and animate us to every duty, Gen. v. 22, 24; and affright and deter us from every sin, as being an affronting of him to his face, who is our witness, and ere long will be our judge, Gen. xxxix. 9.

QUEST. 49. *Which is the second commandment?*

ANS. The second commandment is, *Thou shalt not make unto thee any graven image, or any likeness of any thing that is in heaven above, or that is in the earth beneath, or that is in the water under the earth. Thou shalt not bow down thyself to them, nor serve them; for I the Lord thy God am a jealous God, visiting the iniquity of the fathers upon the children, unto the third and fourth generation of them that hate me; and showing mercy unto thousands of them that love me and keep my commandments.*

QUEST. 50. *What is required in the second commandment?*

ANS. The second commandment requireth the receiving, observing, and keeping pure and entire, all such religious worship and ordinances as God hath appointed in his word.

Q. 1. What is the opinion of the Papists respecting this commandment?

A They allege that it is not a distinct precept from the first, but only an appendix, or supplement to it, by way of illustration.

Q. 2. What is their practice, in consequence of this opinion?

A. They constantly leave it out in their mass books and other liturgies of their church, lest the people should observe the manifest contrariety of their image worship, to what is here so expressly forbidden.

Q. 3. In what then does the second commandment differ from the first?

A. The first commandment respects the object, and requires that we worship the true God, for our God, and no other: the second respects the means of worship, and requires that the true God be worshipped in such a way only, and by such ordinances as he has appointed in his word, in opposition to all human inventions.

Q. 4. What is meant by [religious worship?]

A. That homage and respect we owe to a gracious God, as a God of infinite perfection; by which we profess subjection to, and confidence in him, as our God in Christ, for the supply of all our wants; and ascribe the praise and glory that is due to him, as our chief good, and only happiness, Ps. xcv. 6, 7.

Q. 5. What are these religious [ordinances,] which God has appointed in his word?

A. They are "prayer and thanksgiving in the name of Christ; the reading, preaching, and hearing of the word, the administration and receiving of the sacraments; church government and discipline; the ministry and maintenance thereof; religious fasting; swearing by the name of God; and vowing to him."*

Q. 6. Is prayer a moral duty founded in the law of nature?

A. It certainly is; the necessary dependence of the rational creature upon its Creator, plainly proves it to be so. Hence we find the very Heathens practising it, when reduced to straits, Jonah i. 14.

Q. 7. How does it appear to be an instituted means of worship?

A. From a variety of scripture texts enjoining the practice of it, in all cases and circumstances, Ps. l. 15. Phil. iv. 6. 1 Thess. v. 17.

Q. 8. What is acceptable prayer?

A. It is an asking in Christ's name, what God has promised to give, John xiv. 13; with a full persuasion that he hears, and will answer, Mark xi. 24, James i. 6.

Q. 9. How many fold is religious thanksgiving?

A. *Twofold;* stated and occasional.

Q. 10. What is stated thanksgiving?

A. It is not only the thankful acknowledgment of mercies daily received, which is a branch of prayer; but likewise the singing the praises of God with the voice, which is a stated act of worship, distinct from prayer, though ejaculatory prayer ought always to be joined with it, Ps. lvii. 7.

Q. 11. How do you prove that singing with the voice is a stated act of worship appointed under the New Testament?

A. From the example of Christ and his apostles, who, after the first supper, sang a hymn, [or psalm, as on the margin,] Matt. xxvi. 30; and from the injunction laid upon all Christians to be employed in this exercise, as a stated duty, Eph. v. 18, 19. James v. 13.

Q. 12. What should be the subject matter of our praises to God?

---

* See larger Catechism, Quest. 108.

† It is scarcely necessary to say that the Presbyterian Church in the United States, under the sanction of the General Assembly, celebrate the praises of God in hymns of human composure, expressing evangelical sentiments, and there are convincing arguments in favour of this practice and against the restricted one recommended in the following answer.

PART II.—5.

A. The psalms, hymns, and spiritual songs, which are dictated by the Spirit of God in scripture; and not any human composure whatever, Eph. v. 19.

Q. 13. In what manner should these be sung?

A. With grace in our hearts to the Lord, Col. iii. 16.

Q. 14. What is it to sing with grace in our hearts to the Lord?

A. It is to have our hearts going along with our voice, in suitable acts of faith, and elevated affections, Ps. lvii. 7.

Q. 15. Are not the Psalms of David, as we sing them in our language, of human composure?

A. The translation in metre is human, but the sense and meaning are the same as the original.

Q. 16. What is occasional thanksgiving?

A. It is the setting some time apart for giving thanks to God, on account of some remarkable mercy and deliverance, respecting either churches and nations in general, Neh. xii. 27; or ourselves and families in particular, Eph. v. 20.

Q. 17. How ought we to engage in this duty?

A. With an humble sense of our utter unworthiness of the least of all God's favours, 2 Sam. vii. 18.

Q. 18. Are reading, hearing, and preaching of the word, acts of worship?

A. Although they are not acts of such immediate worship as prayer and praise, in which God is immediately addressed; yet being the instituted and ordinary means of salvation, they ought to be practised and attended with that reverence and regard which is due to the great God our Saviour, who is present in them, Matt. xxviii. 20. Acts x. 33.

Q. 19. How are the administration and receiving of the sacraments acts of worship?

A. As in them, by the sensible signs of divine appointment, Christ, and his benefits, are represented, sealed, and applied to believers, Gal. iii. 27. 1 Cor. xi. 26.

Q. 20. In what sense are church government and discipline to be ranked among the ordinances of divine worship?

A. In as far as they are exercised in the name of the Lord Jesus, the alone head of the church, according to the rule of his word, by church judicatories lawfully constituted, Matt. xviii. 20.

Q. 21. Why are the ministry and the maintenance of it placed among religious ordinances?

A. Because, as a standing ministry in the church, till the end of time, is of express divine institution, Eph. iv. 11—13; so the suitable and comfortable maintenance of it, is as expressly appointed, not only in the Old Testament, Num. xviii. 21, 24, but likewise in the New, 1 Cor. ix. 13,

14: "Do ye not know, that they which minister about holy things, live of the things of the temple? and they which wait at the altar, are partakers with the altar? Even so hath the Lord ordained, that they which preach the gospel should live of the gospel."

Q. 22. What is religious fasting?

A. "A religious fast requires total abstinence, not only from all food, (unless bodily weakness do manifestly disable from holding out, till the fast be ended,) but also from all worldly labour, discourses, and thoughts, and from all bodily delights."*—Josh. vii. 6. Judges xx. 26.

Q. 23. Is bodily fasting, or bare abstinence from food, any part of religious worship?

A. Not properly in itself; but as it is a mean of divine appointment, for fitting and disposing us for more spiritual and solemn exercises.

Q. 24. How does fasting appear to be a mean of divine appointment?

A. From the practice of the saints under the Old Testament, Esth. iv. 16; Dan. x. 2, 3; from the testimony of Christ, Matt. vi. 17, 18, and xvii. 21; and the example of his apostles under the New, Acts xiii. 3; and xiv. 23.

Q. 25. What are those spiritual and solemn exercises for which fasting is designed to dispose us?

A. Deep humiliation of soul before the Lord on account of sin, Ezra ix. 6; free confession of it, Dan. ix. 20, and turning from it, Joel ii. 12, as the genuine fruits of our taking hold of God's covenant, Jer. l. 4, 5; together with an importunate requesting of our gracious God, for that which is the particular occasion of the fast, Ps. xxxv. 13.

Q. 26. Is religious fasting an occasional or a stated duty?

A. It is merely occasional and extraordinary, to be observed as the call of Providence may require and direct.

Q. 27. What are the occurrences in providence, which are a call to this extraordinary duty?

A. "When some great and notable judgments are either inflicted upon a people," Dan. ix. 3, 12—14, " or apparently imminent," 2 Chron. xx. 2—4; "or, by some extraordinary provocations notoriously deserved," 1 Sam. vii. 3, 6; "as also when some special blessing is to be sought and obtained," * ver. 5, 8, 10.

Q. 28. Is swearing by the name of God an act of immediate and instituted worship?

A. It is undoubtedly: and that either when we devote ourselves to God in a covenant of duties, Deut. vi. 13, or declare the truth upon oath, when called thereto: because, in both cases the name of God is solemnly interposed and invoked, Jer. iv. 2.

* Directory for the public worship of God, in the article, Concerning public solemn Fasting.

Q. 29. To whom are vows to be made?

A. To God alone, as the only party and witness in the making and performing of them, Ps. lxxvi. 11: Vow and pay unto the *Lord* your *God.*

Q. 30. What should be the subject matter of our vows to God?

A. Nothing except what may tend either to promote the practice of commanded duty, Ps. cxix. 57, or prevent the commission of any sin to which we are more ordinarily inclined and addicted, verse 106.

Q. 31. What does this commandment require, with respect to all those ordinances, and parts of worship, which God has appointed in his word?

A. The receiving and observing them; and keeping them pure and entire.

Q. 32. What is it to [receive] God's ordinances?

A. It is to approve of, and embrace them, as bearing the stamp of his authority upon them, Ps. lxxxiv. 1, 2.

Q. 33. What is it to [observe] them?

A. It is to set about the practice of them, or to be actually employed in them, Ps. lv. 17, and cxix. 164. Luke ii. 33.

Q. 34. What is it to keep the ordinances of God [pure?]

A. It is to contribute our utmost endeavour to preserve them from all mixture of human invention, Deut. xii. 32.

Q. 35. What is it to keep them [entire?]

A. It is, in the exercise of faith, to attend upon each of them in its proper season, so as that one duty may not justle out another, Luke i. 6.

Q. 36. What does God require of us in this command, with reference to all false worship?

A. He requires "the disapproving, detesting, opposing all false worship, Ps. xvi. 4; and according to each one's place and calling, removing it, and all monuments of idolatry, Deut. vii. 5." *

QUEST. 51. *What is forbidden in the second commandment?*

ANS. The second commandment forbiddeth the worshipping of God by images, or any other way not appointed in his word.

Q. 1. What are the leading sins forbidden in this commandment?

A. Idolatry and will-worship.

* Larger Catechism, Quest. 108.

Q. 2. What is the idolatry here condemned?
A. [The worshipping of God by images:] "Thou shalt not make unto thee any graven image," &c.

Q. 3. What is an image?
A. It is a statue, picture, or likeness of any creature whatever.

Q. 4. Is it lawful to have images or pictures of mere creatures?
A. Yes, provided they be only for ornament; or the design be merely historical, to transmit the memory of persons and their actions to posterity.

Q. 5. Can any image or representation be made of God?
A. No; it is absolutely impossible; he being an infinite, incomprehensible Spirit, Isa. xl. 18: "To whom will ye liken God? or, what likeness will ye compare unto him?" If we cannot delineate our own souls, much less the infinite God; Acts xvii. 29: "We ought not to think that the Godhead is like unto gold, or silver, or stone, graven by art and man's device."

Q. 6. What judgment should we form of those who have devised images of God, or of the persons of the adorable Trinity?
A. We should adjudge their practice to be both unlawful and abominable.

Q. 7. Why unlawful?
A. Because directly contrary to the express letter of the law in this commandment, and many other scriptures; such as, Jer. x. 14, 15; Hos. xiii. 2, and particularly Deut. iv. 15—19, 23: "Take ye therefore good heed unto yourselves, (for ye saw *no manner* of similitude on the day that the Lord spake unto you in Horeb, out of the midst of the fire,) lest ye corrupt yourselves, and make you a graven image, the similitude of any figure, the likeness of male or female," &c.

Q. 8. How is it abominable?
A. As debasing the Creator of heaven and earth to the rank of his own creatures; and a practical denial of all his infinite perfections, Ps. l. 21.

Q. 9. May we not have a picture of *Christ*, who has a true body?
A. By no means; because, though he has a true body and a reasonable soul, John i. 14, yet his human nature subsists in his divine person, which no picture can represent, Ps. xlv. 2.

Q. 10. Why ought all pictures of Christ, to be abominated by Christians?
A. Because they are downright lies, representing no more than the picture of a mere man: whereas, the true Christ is God-man; "Immanuel, God with us," 1 Tim. iii. 16. Matt. i. 23.

Q. 11. Is it lawful to form any inward representation of God, or of Christ, upon our fancy, bearing a resemblance to any creature whatever?

A. By no means; because this is the very inlet to gross outward idolatry: for, when once the Heathens "became vain in their imaginations, they presently changed the glory of the incorruptible God into an image made like to corruptible man, and to birds, and four-footed beasts, and creeping things," Rom. i. 21, 23.

Q. 12. What is it to worship God by images, according to the idolatrous practice of Papists?

A. It is either to make use of images, as pretended helps to devotion; or, to worship God before the images of saints, as intercessors with him.

Q. 13. Can any feigned image of God, or of Christ, be helpful in devotion?

A. No: it is the Spirit only who helpeth our infirmities in all acts of spiritual devotion, Rom. viii. 26; and that faith which is necessary for acceptance in duty, fixes upon the word of the living God, as its sole foundation, and not upon dead images, Luke xvi. 31.

Q. 14. Will it excuse any from the charge of idolatry, that they pretend to worship the true God before images, or by them, as means of worship, and not the very images themselves?

A. Not at all; because this is a mean of worship expressly forbidden in this commandment, which prohibits all bowing down before images, upon whatever pretext it be: "Thou shalt not *bow down* thyself to them, nor serve them."

Q. 15. Do they worship images who bow down before them, even though it be the true God they intend to worship by them?

A. In scripture reckoning they do; Isa. ii. 8, 9: "Their land is full of idols: they worship the work of their own hands. The mean man boweth down, and the great man humbleth himself."

Q. 16. Was it the ultimate intention of the Israelites in the wilderness to pay divine worship to the golden calf itself; or, to *Jehovah*, by it, and before it?

A. It was undoubtedly their ultimate intention to worship *Jehovah*, the true God, before that image; as appears from Ex. xxxii. 5: "When Aaron saw it, he built an altar *before it;*—and said, "To-morrow is a feast to the *Lord*," (or *Jehovah*, as it is in the original.) And yet, because they did this, so directly contrary to the very letter of this commandment, they are charged with worshipping the image itself, verse 8:—" They have made them a golden calf, and have worshipped *it*," &c.

Q. 17. Do not they who honour the picture of a prince, honour the prince himself?

A. If the prince forbid the making of his picture, it is a contempt of his authority to have it. God has strictly prohibited all images for religious purposes, and therefore it is impious to have or use them for these ends, Lev. xxvi 1, 30.

Q. 18. May images be worshipped at all, upon their own account?

A. No: because they are the work of man's hands: far inferior in dignity to man himself, Isa. xliv. 9—18.

Q. 19. May they be worshipped on account of their *originals;* or those whom they are designed to represent?

A. They may not; whether designed to represent *God*, or the saints.

Q. 20. Why may they not be worshipped as they are designed to represent God?

A. Because he never put his name in them; but declares his greatest hatred and detestation of them, Jer. xliv. 2—9.

Q. 21. Why may they not be worshipped as they are designed to represent eminent saints?

A. Because saints, however eminent, are only mere creatures; and therefore cannot be the objects of worship, either in themselves, or by their images, Acts xiv. 14, 15.

Q. 22. Can saints in heaven be intercessors for sinners on earth?

A. No: because intercession being founded on satisfaction, none but Christ can be the intercessor, as none but he is the propitiation for our sins, 1 John ii. 1, 2.

Q. 23. Is it lawful, as some plead, to have images or pictures in churches, though not for worship, yet for instruction, and raising the affections?

A. No: because God has expressly prohibited not only the worshipping but the making of any image whatever on a religious account; and the setting them up in churches, cannot but have a natural tendency to beget a sacred veneration for them; and therefore ought to be abstained from, as having, at least, the appearance of evil, 1 Thess. v. 22.

Q. 24. May they not be placed in churches for beauty and ornament?

A. No: the proper ornament of churches is the sound preaching of the gospel, and the pure dispensation of the sacraments, and other ordinances of divine institution.

Q. 25. Were not the images of the cherubim placed in the tabernacle and temple, by the command of God himself?

A. Yes; but out of all hazard of any abuse, being placed in the holy of holies, where none of the people ever came:

they were instituted by God himself, which images aie not; and they belonged to the typical and ceremonial worship, which is now quite abolished.

Q. 26. What do you understand by will-worship, the other leading sin forbidden in this command?
A. It is the worshipping God in [any other way not appointed in his word.]

Q. 27. Should there be an express appointment in the word for every part of divine worship in which we engage?
A. Undoubtedly there should; otherwise we are guilty of innovating upon the worship of God, and prescribing rules to the Almighty, which is both displeasing to him, and unprofitable to ourselves, Matt. xv. 9.

Q. 28. Who are they that are guilty of innovating upon the worship of God?
A. All they who presumptuously annex their own superstitious inventions to the divine institutions, under pretence of their being teaching significant ceremonies; as they of the Popish and Episcopal persuasions do.

Q. 29. What are these significant ceremonies which they add to the instituted ordinances of God's worship?
A. The sign of the cross in baptism; kneeling at receiving the sacrament of the supper; erecting altars in churches; and bowing at the name of *Jesus*, are a few of many.

Q. 30. Why may not such ceremonies be used, when they are designed for exciting devotion, and beautifying the worship of God?
A. Because God has expressly forbidden the least addition to or abatement from the order and directions he himself has given in his word concerning his own worship; Deut. xii. 30—32: "What thing soever I command you, observe to do it: thou shalt not *add* thereunto, nor *diminish* from it."

Q. 31. Were there not significant ceremonies in the Jewish worship, under the Old Testament?
A. Yes; but they were of express divine appointment; and by the same appointment abolished in the death and resurrection of Christ, Heb. ix. 1—15.

Q. 32. May not significant ceremonies be founded on 1 Cor. xiv. 40: "Let all things be done decently and in order?"
A. No: because that text speaks only of the decent and orderly observance of the ordinances of God already instituted, and not in the least of any thing new to be added as a part of worship.

Q. 33. How may we be further guilty of a breach of this commandment, than by idolatry and will-worship?
A. When we neglect, Heb. x. 25, contemn, Matt. xxii. 5,

hinder, chap. xxiii. 13, or oppose the worship and ordinances which God has appointed in his word, 1 Thess. ii. 16.

QUEST. 52. *What are the reasons annexed to the second commandment?*

ANS. The reasons annexed to the second commandment, are, God's sovereignty over us, his propriety in us and the zeal he hath to his own worship.

Q. 1. Why does our Catechism make mention of *Reasons annexed* to this and the three following commandments?
A. Because God himself has been pleased to subjoin to each of these precepts, the reasons, arguments, or motives, that should influence our obedience to them.

Q. 2. How many reasons are annexed to this second commandment?
A. *Three;* contained in these words, "I the Lord thy God am a jealous God."

Q. 3. Which is the first of these reasons?
A. It is [God's sovereignty over us,] in these words, *I the Lord*; or, *I Jehovah.*

Q. 4. What do you understand by God's sovereignty over us?
A. It is his absolute supreme power, or right of dominion over us, as his creatures, Rom. ix. 20, 21, by which he can dispose of, ver. 22, 23, and prescribe to us as seems to him good, Deut. vi. 17.

Q. 5. In what lies the strength of this first reason for worshipping God by means of his own appointment?
A. It lies in this, that being our sovereign Lord, it must be his sole prerogative to prescribe to us the means of his own worship; and, consequently, that it must be our duty to make his pleasure in this, both the rule and reason of our punctual observance of what he enjoins, Ps. xcv. 2, 3.

Q. 6. What is the *second* reason annexed to this commandment?
A. It is [his propriety in us,] in these words, *Thy God.*

Q. 7. What other propriety has God in us than by right of creation?
A. He has a propriety likewise by right of redemption, intimated in the preface to the commands, "I am the Lord *Thy God,* which have brought thee out of the land of Egypt, out of the house of bondage," Ex. xx. 2.

Q. 8. Is it his propriety by right of creation, or by right

of redemption, that constitutes the federal relation between him and us?

A. It is his propriety by right of redemption, Isa. xliii. 1: "I have redeemed thee; I have called thee by thy name: thou art *Mine.*"

Q. 9. What influence should his propriety in us, as his people, have upon our receiving and observing the ordinances of his worship?

A. If we are his people, we are ransomed by the blood of his only begotten Son, and so under the strongest ties of duty and gratitude, to cleave to the precise manner of worship prescribed in his word, rejecting all other modes and forms whatever, Josh. xxiv. 24.

Q. 10. What is the *third* reason annexed to this commandment?

A. It is [the zeal he hath to his own worship,] in these words,—*I am a jealous God.*

Q. 11. In what sense is God said to be a jealous God?

A. Jealousy is ascribed to him (after the manner of men,) to denote that he puts no confidence in his creatures, Deut. v. 29; that he has his eye upon them; and is highly offended when they slight him, and bestow that love upon any other, which is due to him alone, chap. xxii. 15—26.

Q. 12. What is it for God to have [zeal] for his own worship?

A. It is to have such a regard for the ordinances of his own institution, as highly to resent or revenge any addition to, or alteration of them; of which there is an awful instance in Nadab and Abihu, who offered strange fire before the Lord, Lev. x. 1—4.

Q. 13. In what does God manifest his zeal for his worship?

A. Both by way of threatening, and by way of promise.

Q. 14. What does God threaten as a testimony of his zeal for his worship?

A. To visit the iniquity of the fathers upon the children, to the third and fourth generation of them that hate him.

Q. 15. What is it to visit the iniquity of the fathers upon the children?

A. It is to inflict punishment upon the children for the faults and offences of their fathers.

Q. 16. Are there any scripture examples of God's doing so?

A. As to temporal punishments there are:—Seven of Saul's sons were hanged before the Lord, for his offence in slaying the Gibeonites, 2 Sam. xxi. 8, 9; and for the sins of Jeroboam, his whole house was utterly extinguished, 1 Kings xv. 29, 30.

Q. 17 Whether are temporal judgments only, or **spi-**

ritual and eternal plagues also, intended in this threatening?

A. Spiritual and eternal plagues are also intended, Matt. xxv. 41.

Q. 18. How does it appear that spiritual and eternal judgments are included in this threatening?

A. It appears from this, that the punishment threatened should bear some proportion to the mercy promised; so that if the mercy promised be of a spiritual and eternal nature, the judgments threatened must be of the same kind.

Q. 19. How does the scripture illustrate this?

A. By the issue of the final sentence at the great day, which is, that the wicked "go away into everlasting punishment, but the righteous into life eternal," Matt. xxv. 46.

Q. 20. How does it consist with the justice of God, to inflict spiritual and eternal judgments upon children for the sins of their parents?

A. It is entirely consistent with it; because the children punished with spiritual and eternal judgments, are only such as have shown themselves heirs to their fathers' sins, either by copying them over, Jer. xxxi. 29, 30, or not dis approving of, and mourning for them; by which means their fathers' sins become their own, Ps. xlix. 13.

Q. 21. How can the visiting the iniquity of the fathers upon the children, be reconciled with Ezek. xviii. 20: "The son shall not bear the iniquity of the father?"

A. This passage in Ezekiel is to be understood of the son who does not tread in the steps of his wicked father; as is evident from ver. 14, 17: "If he beget a son that seeth all his father's sins, and doth not such like, he shall not die for the iniquity of his father, he shall surely live;" whereas the threatening in this commandment respects wicked children, who copy after the example of their graceless parents, as Nadab the son of Jeroboam did, who "walked in the way of his father, and in his sin wherewith he made Israel to sin," 1 Kings xv. 26.

Q. 22. How does it appear from the threatening itself, that this is the meaning?

A. Because the children on whom God visits the iniquity of their fathers are expressly said to be "the third and fourth generation of them that *hate* him."

Q. 23. Why does God threaten to visit the iniquity of the fathers upon the children, to the third and fourth generation only, of them that hate him; and not to all succeeding generations of such children?

A. Not but that the haters of God to all generations shall meet with deserved punishment; but the threatening is limited to the third and fourth generation, for a greater judgment upon wicked parents, some of whom may live to see their posterity of these generations, and to read their own sin in the punishment of their offspring whom they have seduced; as Zedekiah, for his wickedness, saw his sons, and the princes of Judah, slain before his eyes, Jer. lii. 3, 10.

Q. 24. What if such wicked parents should die, before they see their third and fourth generations?

A. In that case, if their consciences are not quite seared, they will die under the dread and fear of the judgments here threatened, befalling their children, Hos. ii. 4; as well as of the fiery indignation which shall devour themselves, Heb. x. 27.

Q. 25. May not God sometimes visit the iniquities of the breakers of this commandment upon their godly children?

A. He will never visit the iniquities of the fathers upon their godly children with spiritual and eternal judgments, though sometimes he may do it with temporal calamities: as no doubt many pious Israelites were carried captive to Babylon for the sins of their fathers, Lam. v. 7; which, nevertheless, was for their real good, Jer. xxiv. 5.

Q. 26. What may we learn from this threatening to visit the iniquity of the fathers upon the children?

A. That as nothing can be more cruel than for parents to set a bad example before their children, Jer. ix. 14, 15; so the example of forefathers will not vindicate their posterity in the way of sin, particularly in the practice of any corrupt or false worship, Ezek. xx. 18, 21.

Q. 27. What is it, on the other hand, that God promises as an evidence of his zeal for his worship?

A. To show mercy to thousands of them that love him, and keep his commandments.

Q. 28. Who are they that truly love God?

A. They who, from a faith of his own operation, have complacency and delight in him as their own God and portion, Ps. v. 11.

Q. 29. What is it to keep his commandments?

A. It is to essay a uniform and self-denied obedience to the law as a rule, because Christ has fulfilled it as a covenant, Rom. vii. 4.

Q. 30. What mercy does God show to them that love him, and keep his commandments?

A. He shows strengthening, Ps. xciv. 18, comforting, Ps. xxxi. 7, directing, Ex. xv. 13, and persevering mercy to them, 2 Sam. vii. 15.

Q. 31. Does God show mercy to children, because they are the offspring of godly parents?

A. No; but merely because so it pleases him, Rom. ix. 15: "I will have mercy on whom I will have mercy."

Q. 32. What benefit then have the children of godly parents beyond others?
A. They have the privilege of a religious education, Gen. xviii. 19; are the children of many prayers, Job i. 5; and may plead the promise, I *will* be a God to thee, and to thy seed after thee, Gen. xvii. 7.

Q. 33. Why does the threatening run only to the third and fourth generation of them that hate him, and yet the promise to thousands of them that love him?
A. To show that God has far greater pleasure in the exercise of mercy, than in the venting of wrath, Ezek. xxxiii. 11; and likewise for an encouragement, both to parents and children, to aim at " walking in all the commandments and ordinances of the Lord blameless," Luke i. 6.

QUEST. 53. *Which is the third commandment?*

ANS. The third commandment is, *Thou shalt not take the name of the Lord thy God in vain: for the Lord will not hold him guiltless that taketh his name in vain.*

QUEST. 54. *What is required in the third commandment?*

ANS. The third commandment requireth the holy and reverend use of God's names, titles, attributes, ordinances, word, and works.

Q. 1. What does this commandment require in general?
A. That the instituted means of God's worship be used in a right manner, becoming the majesty of him with whom we have to do, Ps. v. 7.

Q. 2. What is the duty directly opposite to the sin of taking God's name in vain?
A. It is the sanctifying of his name, Isa. viii. 13: "Sanctify the Lord of hosts himself, and let him be your fear and your dread."

Q. 3. What do you understand by the *name* of God?
A. Every thing by which he is pleased to make himself known.

Q. 4. By what does God make himself known
A. By his [names, titles, attributes, ordinances, word, and works.]

Q. 5. Does God need any name to distinguish him from all others?
A. No; because he is a most singular Being, quite well

distinguished from all others, by the infinity and absolute perfection of his nature, Isa. xliv. 6.

Q. 6. Why then are [names] ascribed to him in scripture?

A. That some knowledge of his nature and perfections may be conveyed to us, Acts ix. 15.

Q. 7. What are the names by which he conveys the knowledge of himself to us?

A. He conveys the knowledge of his absolute, eternal, and immutable essence by the names of *Jehovah*, Ex. vi. 3, *Jah*, Ps. lxviii. 4, and, I AM, Ex. iii. 14; the knowledge of his excellency and sovereignty, by the names *God* and *Lord*, Deut. vi. 4; and the knowledge of the essential relation of the three divine persons among themselves, by the names of *Father*, *Son*, and *Holy Ghost*, Matt. xxviii. 19.

Q. 8. Is there any difference between God's names and his titles?

A. His names set forth what he is in himself; his titles, what he is to others.

Q. 9. How are God's [titles] commonly distinguished?

A. Into those that belong to him as the God of nature, and those which are ascribed to him as the God of grace.

Q. 10. What are the titles that belong to him as the God of nature?

A. They are such as these, The Creator of the ends of the earth, Isa. xl. 28; the Preserver of men, Job vii. 20; King of nations, Jer. x. 7, and Lord of hosts, Isa. i. 9.

Q. 11. What are the titles that are ascribed to him as the God of grace?

A. They are the following among others: The God of Abraham, Isaac, and Jacob, Ex. iii. 6; the Holy One of Israel, Isa. xlviii. 17; King of saints, Rev. xv. 3; the Father of mercies, 2 Cor. i. 3; the hearer of prayer, Ps. lxv. 2; and the God of salvation, Ps. lxviii. 20.

Q. 12. Which is the most common and ordinary title ascribed to God under the New Testament?

A. It is the infinitely amiable and encouraging title of "the God and Father of our Lord Jesus Christ," Eph. i. 3. 1 Pet. i. 3.

Q. 13. What comfortable views may we take of God, as he is the God and Father of our Lord Jesus Christ?

A. In this light we may view him as a reconciled God, 2 Cor. v. 19; a pardoning and accepting God through Christ, Eph. i. 6, 7; and as our God and Father in him, John xx. 17,—"I ascend unto my Father and your Father, and to my God and your God."

Q. 14. What is to be understood by God's [attributes?]

A. The perfections and excellencies which are ascribed to him as the essential properties of his nature. *

* See the divine attributes explained in the 4th Quest. What is God?

Q. 15. What are God's [ordinances?]

A. The reading, preaching, and hearing of the word; the administration of the sacraments; prayer and praise; religious fasting and thanksgiving.*

Q. 16. What are the ordinances in which the name of God is more immediately interposed?

A. The name of God is more immediately interposed in oaths, vows, and lots.

Q. 17. What is an oath?

A. It is an act of religious worship, in which God is solemnly invoked, or called upon, as a witness for the confirmation of some matter in doubt.

Q. 18. Why is it said to be an act of religious worship?

A. Because there is, or ought to be, in every formal oath, a solemn invocation of the name of God, Deut. vi. 13: "Thou shalt fear the Lord thy God—and shalt swear by his name."

Q. 19. What is imported in calling upon God as a witness in an oath?

A. It imports, that we acknowledge him to be the infallible searcher of our hearts; the powerful avenger of all perjury and falsehood; and at the same time to be infinitely superior to us; "for men verily swear by the greater," Heb. vi. 16.

Q. 20. In what cases should an oath be required?

A. Only in cases that are doubtful, when the truth of things cannot be known with certainty any other way.

Q. 21. What is the end of an oath in a lawful judicature?

A. It is for confirmation of the truth formerly doubtful; and for terminating strife and contradiction among men. "An oath for confirmation is to them an end of all strife," Heb. vi. 16.

Q. 22. What are the necessary qualifications of a lawful oath?

A. That we swear—"in truth, in judgment, and in righteousness," Jer. iv. 2.

Q. 23. What is it to swear in truth?

A. It is to take special care, that what is sworn be strictly agreeable to truth; and that there be an exact agreement between the sentiments of our minds, and the words of our mouth, without the least equivocation, or mental reservation.

Q. 24. What is it to equivocate, or dissemble in an oath?

A. It is to have an inward reserved meaning and sense of words, contrary to the common and ordinary acceptation of them, and that with a design to deceive.

---

* See all these explained in Quest. 50. What is required in the second commandment?

Q. 25. In what consists the evil and sinfulness of this practice?

A. It destroys the nature and end of an oath, which is to bring forth nothing but the truth: it opens a wide door to all falsehood and lying, contrary to Eph. iv. 25; "Wherefore putting away lying, speak every man truth with his neighbour;" and it unhinges the firmest bonds of society, that none can put confidence in another.

Q. 26. What is it to swear in judgment?

A. It is to swear with knowledge and deliberation; seriously pondering in our mind, what it is we are about to swear, and the solemn appeal we make to God in the oath, together with the dangerous risk we run, if we swear either falsely or ignorantly.

Q. 27. What is it to swear in righteousness?

A. It is to give our oath only in things lawful, or such as are consistent with piety towards God, and equity towards man; and likewise to give it on a lawful occasion.

Q. 28. When is a civil oath taken upon a lawful occasion?

A. When it is required by a lawful magistrate, for the ending of strife and debate, and the impartial administration of justice.

Q. 29. How do you prove that it is warrantable for Christians under the New Testament, to declare the truth upon oath, when called to it?

A. From this, that an oath, being no part of the ceremonial law, there can be no reason given, why it was lawful to swear under the Old Testament, which will not apply in the like circumstances *now;* especially as there are approved examples of the use of an oath under the New Testament, 2 Cor. i. 23. Rev. x. 6. Heb. vi. 16.

Q. 30. Does not our Lord say, Matt. v. 34,—Swear not at all; and the apostle James, chap. v. 12, Above all things, swear not?

A. These texts manifestly condemn profane swearing in ordinary conversation, and not lawful swearing in judgment, when called to do it; as appears from the injunction subjoined in both places, "Let your communication be, Yea, yea; Nay, nay."

Q. 31. What is the ordinary outward form or sign, in scripture, of appealing to God in an oath?

A. It is the lifting up of the hand; as appears from Gen. xiv. 22. Dan. xii. 7. Rev. x. 5, 6.

Q. 32. What are we to think of that mode of swearing, by touching and kissing the gospel?

A. It is evidently superstitious, if not idolatrous, and borrowed from the heathens, who worshipped their idols in this manner, Job xxxi. 27. Hos. xiii. 2.

IN THE THIRD COMMANDMENT.

Q. 33. How are oaths commonly distinguished as to their *kinds?*
A. Into assertory and promissory oaths.

Q. 34. What is an assertory oath?
A. It is an invoking God as a witness to the truth of what we declare about things past or present.

Q. 35. Why called assertory?
A. Because the party swearing, without any promise for the future, only asserts the things to have been, or to be at present, as he then swears.

Q. 36. What is the chief use of assertory oaths?
A. It is to determine suits and processes in human courts about matters of fact.

Q. 37. What is a promissory oath?
A. It is the invoking God as a witness to the performance of a thing for the time to come, either absolutely or conditionally.

Q. 38. Why called promissory?
A. Because the party swearing promises or engages to do something hereafter.

Q. 39. What should be the subject matter of assertory oaths?
A. Such things as are both true and weighty, and which we know to be so.

Q. 40. What should be the subject matter of promissory oaths?
A. Such things as to our knowledge, are lawful, possible, and in our power to perform.

Q. 41. How may promissory oaths be subdivided?
A. Into civil and religious.

Q. 42. To what has a civil promissory oath a respect?
A. To contracts and engagements among men, whether of a more private or public nature.

Q. 43. May not the supreme magistrate require an allegiance of his subjects, or an oath of fidelity to obey his just and lawful commands?
A. It appears evidently from scripture that he may, Eccl. viii. 2: "I counsel thee to keep the king's commandment, and that in regard of the oath of God," 1 Chron. xxix. 24.

Q. 44. To what has a religious promissory oath a respect?
A. It respects the duties and services we owe more immediately to God, and the interests of religion.*

Q. 45. In what lies the obligation of an oath?
A. In the strong tie or bond that the party swearing

---

* Of religious promissory oaths, see afterwards on this same Question under the head of vows.

comes under, to the performance of some duty engaged to.

Q. 46. How many fold is the obligation of a promissory oath?

A. *Two-fold:* one to the person to whom the oath is made, as a party; the other to God, by whom the oath is made, as a witness and avenger.

Q. 47. What is the difference between the obligation of a promise, and the obligation of an oath?

A. A man is bound to perform his promise as well as his oath: but an oath being an immediate invocation of the name of God as a witness and judge, it is, on this account, of a stronger obligation, and the breach of it a more heinous sin, than the breach of a simple promise.

Q. 48. Does not all obligation to duty respect a future time in which it is to be performed?

A. It necessarily does so, in the nature of the thing; although, in some cases, the time of performance may be very short after the obligation is contracted.

Q. 49. Under what obligation does a person come in an assertory oath, which respects the time past or present?

A. He comes under an obligation to declare the truth, and nothing but the truth, in what he is about to say; or, that his words shall exactly agree with his mind.

Q. 50. Under what obligation does a person come in a promissory oath, which respects the time to come?

A. He comes under an obligation to endeavour, as far as in him lies, to fulfil that which he has sworn; or, to perform all that he has promised by oath, Num. xxx. 2: "If a man vow a vow unto the Lord, or swear an oath to bind his soul with a bond; he shall not break his word; he shall do according to all that proceedeth out of his mouth."

Q. 51. Is an oath about a thing lawful and possible obligatory, even though it be extorted by force or fear?

A. Undoubtedly it is: because of the reverence due to God, by whom the oath is made as a witness and judge, Lev. xix. 12: "Ye shall not swear by my name falsely; neither shalt thou profane the name of thy God: I am the Lord." Matt. v. 33: "Thou shalt not forswear thyself, but shalt perform unto the Lord thine oaths."

Q. 52. Is a person bound to pay such a sum to a robber as he has promised by his oath, for the ransom of his life?

A. He is certainly bound to pay it; because, of two *penal* evils, he voluntarily made choice of the least; to part with his money, rather than his life; accordingly, the righteous man sweareth to his own *hurt*, and changeth not, Ps. xv. 4.

Q. 53. Is an oath, which is lawful as to the matter of it,

though sinful as to the manner, and even obtained by deceit, or rashly made, binding and obligatory upon the person who has sworn it?

A. Yes: as is evident from the instance of the Gibeonites, who deceived Israel into a league with them by oath, and yet their oath was binding, Josh. ix. 14—20.

Q. 54. Are oaths and contracts to be kept with Heathens and heretics?

A. No doubt they should, as well as with others.—Zedekiah, king of Judah, was severely punished for his breach of oath to the king of Babylon, 2 Chron. xxxvi. 13. Ezek. xvii. 16. Besides, if infidelity and heresy do not nullify the marriage oath, neither ought they to make void any other lawful contract.

Q. 55. What is a vow?

A. It is a voluntary and deliberate engagement to God only as party, and that respecting matters of a sacred or religious character, Ps. cxxxii. 2—6.

Q. 56. What is the difference between an oath and a vow?

A. In an oath, man is generally the party, and God is brought in as the witness: but in a vow, God himself is always the sole party, besides his being a witness, Ps. l. 14. Isa. xix. 21.

Q. 57. What is the subject matter of vows?

A. Only things religious; or such as relate immediately to the glory of God, and the salvation of our souls.

Q. 58. How ought vows to be entered into?

A. In the exercise of faith; or, in the strength of the grace that is in Christ Jesus, John xv. 5; without which there can be no performance, Phil. iv. 13.

Q. 59. How many kinds of vows are there?

A. Two; personal and social.

Q. 60. What is a personal vow?

A. It is the act of an individual, or single person, taking hold of God's covenant of grace, or acquiescing in it as made with Christ, who is the all of it; and thus engaging to be the Lord's, and to essay the practice of all duty in his strength, Isa. xliv. 5: "One shall say, I am the Lord's," Ps. cxix. 106: "I have sworn, and will perform it, that I will keep thy righteous judgments."*

Q. 61. What is a social vow?

A. It is the joint concurrence of several individuals in the same exercise as in a personal one, openly avouching

---

* This is what is commonly called Personal Covenanting. Whoever wants to be instructed in the true nature and right manner of setting about this necessary duty, let him carefully peruse Mr. Boston's Memorial concerning personal and family fasting, subjoined to his View of the covenant of grace, chap. II. sect. iii. direction 8.

the Lord to be their God, Deut. xxvi. 17; where Moses, speaking of all Israel, says, "Thou hast avouched the Lord this day to be thy God, to walk in his ways," &c.

Q. 62. Is our obligation to moral duties increased, by our vowing or engaging to perform them?

A. Although it is impossible that our obligation to moral duty can be increased by any deed of ours, beyond what it is already by the law of God, which is of the highest authority; yet by reason of our own voluntary and superadded engagement, this obligation from the law may make a deeper impression than before, Ps. xliv. 17, 18, and our sins receive a higher aggravation, if we either omit the duty engaged to, or commit the evil opposite to it, Deut. xxiii. 21, 22.

Q. 63. What is a *lot*, or lotting?

A. It is the laying aside the use of all means or second causes, and appealing directly to God, that he may, by his immediate providence, give a present decision respecting any matter in question; "for the lot is cast into the lap; but the whole disposing thereof is of the Lord," Prov. xvi. 33.

Q. 64. Why are lots said to be an appeal to God?

A. Because, by casting of lots between two or more persons, or things, we, as it were, require him immediately to declare his mind by the event, which way the decision shall go, Acts i. 24, 26: "Show whether of these two thou hast chosen. And the lot fell on Matthias."

Q. 65. In what cases may a decision be put upon the event of a lot?

A. Only in cases of great weight and absolute necessity, Josh. vii. 13, 14.

Q. 66. Why should a lot be used only in cases of great weight and moment?

A. Because a lot being a material or implicit invoking of God to give a decision, it would be a wicked profanation of his name, to call him to determine in trifles, or things of little or no value.

Q. 67. Why should it be used only in cases of absolute necessity?

A. Because, where human prudence can determine, it would be a tempting of God, to require his decision.

Q. 68. What then is the end of lots?

A. It is the same as of oaths, to determine finally in momentous controversies, that which can be decided in no other way, Prov. xviii. 18: "The lot causeth contention to cease, and parteth between the mighty."

Q. 69. In what manner ought lots to be used?

A. In a most reverential manner, as in the presence of God, who pronounces the sentence; and in whose deci-

IN THE THIRD COMMANDMENT.

sion all parties ought cheerfully to acquiesce, Acts i. 24, 26. "And they prayed—and gave forth their lots."

Q. 70. What is the [word] in which the name of God is declared?

A. The scriptures of the Old and New Testament.

Q. 71. What is meant by God's [works] in this answer?

A. His works of creation and providence; which last includes redemption.

Q. 72. What does this commandment *require*, with reference to God's names, titles, attributes, ordinances, word, and works?

A. [The holy and reverend use of] them.

Q. 73. What is it to make a holy and reverend use of these?

A. It is, in all our meditations, speeches, and writings, to have the most profound respect and regard for every thing, by which God manifests his name and glory, Deut. xxviii. 58.

Q. 74. When do we essay to make a reverend use of God's names, titles, and attributes?

A. When we view them as in Christ, and in this light draw virtue from them, for the increase of our faith and holiness, Ex. xxiii. 20, 21: Obey his voice—for my name is in him.

Q. 75. When do we endeavour a holy and reverend use of the ordinances?

A. When we view God as present in them, Matt. xxviii. 20; and attend or perform them with a single eye to his glory, Ps. lxxxvi. 9.

Q. 76. When do we use the word in a holy and reverend manner?

A. When we search and believe the scriptures, as testifying of Christ, John v. 39; and are directed by them as a lamp to our feet, and a light to our path, Ps. cxix. 105.

Q. 77. When do we essay to make a holy and reverend use of the works of God?

A. When we are enabled to make suitable improvement of the bright displays he has made of his glorious excellencies, in creation, providence, and redemption, so as to walk humbly and thankfully before him, Rev. xv. 3, 4: "Great and marvellous are thy works, Lord God Almighty; just and true are thy ways, thou King of saints. Who shall not fear thee, O Lord! and glorify thy name for thou only art holy."

Quest. 55. *What is forbidden in the third commandment?*

Ans. The third commandment forbiddeth all profaning or abusing of any thing whereby God maketh himself known.

Q. 1. What do you understand by [profaning or abusing of any thing whereby God makes himself known?]

A. It is the using of his names, titles, attributes, ordinances, word, and works, in a rash, irreverent, and unbecoming manner.

Q. 2. How are God's names, titles, and attributes, profaned or abused by men?

A. Many ways: particularly, "by blasphemy, perjury, sinful cursings, oaths, vows, and lots." *

Q. 3. What is blasphemy?

A. It is speaking in a reproachful, reviling, and undervaluing manner of God, Isa. xxxvi. 20; of his word, Acts xiii. 45; or of any of his providential dispensations, Ezek. xviii. 25.

Q. 4. What is the aggravation of this sin?

A. It is an atheistical contempt of the most high God;— the greatest affront that can be done him by his creatures, Ex. v. 2.

Q. 5. May not persons be guilty of blasphemy in their hearts, though never uttered in words?

A. Yes, undoubtedly they may; either when atheistical thoughts of him are harboured, Ps. xiv. 1; or, disparaging and unbecoming conceptions of him entertained, Ps. x. 11 and l. 21.

Q. 6. What was the punishment of blasphemy, at the hand of man, by the law of God?

A. It was death, Lev. xxiv. 16: "He that blasphemeth the name of the Lord, he shall surely be put to death."

Q. 7. What is perjury?

A. It is a breach or violation of any solemn oath or vow, we have entered into, or come under, Matt. v. 33: "Thou shalt not forswear thyself."

Q. 8. When are persons guilty of perjury in assertory oaths?

A. When they assert such a thing, upon oath to be true, which yet they know to be false, like the witness against Naboth, 1 Kings xxi. 13; or even when they are doubtful and uncertain about the truth of what they are swearing;

* Larger Catechism, Quest. 113.

like the witnesses against Christ, whose witnessing did not agree together, Mark xiv. 58, 59.

Q. 9. When are persons guilty of perjury in promissory oaths?

A. When they promise upon oath what they have no mind to perform; or when, without any insuperable impediment laid in their way, or any just and relevant excuse, they fail in the performance: as in the perjury of Zedekiah king of Judah, who broke his oath to the king of Babylon, Ezek. xvii. 16.

Q. 10. Is a person guilty of perjury, if he swears to do a thing impossible or unlawful?

A. Surely he is: for, if he swear to a thing impossible, he swears to a manifest lie; if he swear to do a thing unlawful, he is doubly perjured; both in making such an oath, and in fulfilling it, as was the case with Herod, Matt. xiv. 9, 10.

Q. 11. What is the aggravation of the sin of perjury?

A. It not only breaks all the bonds of society among men, but impeaches the omniscience of God himself, calling him to attest what conscience knows to be an untruth; and therefore God threatens, that his "curse shall enter into the house of him that sweareth falsely—and shall consume it, with the timber thereof, and the stones thereof," Zech. v. 3, 4.

Q. 12. How is God's name profaned by sinful cursings?

A. When God's wrath and vengeance are imprecated upon ourselves or others; or when the devil is in any manner invoked for harm.

Q. 13. For what do wicked persons wish, when they imprecate the wrath and vengeance of God upon themselves?

A. They do, in effect, pray, that God would hasten their everlasting destruction, and that their damnation may not slumber, but be speedily inflicted, 2 Pet. ii. 3.

Q. 14. Do the devils themselves venture to wish for this?

A. No: they believe that there is farther wrath awaiting them at the judgment of the great day; and they tremble at the forethoughts of it, James ii. 19. Jude verse 6.

Q. 15. What is the evil of imprecating divine vengeance upon others?

A. It is a piece of the most profane, presumptuous, and impudent freedom with the Majesty of heaven; as if he were bound to empty the vials of his wrath upon our fellow creatures, at our pleasure, and that in order to gratify our passionate revenge upon them, 2 Sam. xvi. 5, 8.

Q. 16. Is it not a most horrid and abominable wickedness to call or invoke the devil to *take* ourselves or others?

A. Surely it is; for it is a putting the devil in God's stead, or an employing of him to do God's work for him, even when he is delaying to do it himself; which is no less than devil-worship, and we ought not to have fellowship with devils, 1 Cor. x. 20.

Q. 17. How is the name of God abused by sinful oaths?

A. When men take unlawful oaths that may be imposed upon them, and when, in their ordinary conversation, they swear by God, or by any thing by which he makes himself known; contrary to Matt. v. 37: "Let your communications be, Yea, yea; Nay, nay: for whatsoever is more than these, cometh of evil:" or of the evil one.

Q. 18. In what lies the heinousness of swearing in common discourse?

A. It is a most heaven-daring wickedness, even an insulting of the great God, our maker, to his face; a crime, which we dare not, without danger, be guilty of against our fellow creatures; and which is neither attended with the allurements of pleasure nor temptations of profit.

Q. 19. Is it a taking of God's name in vain, to swear by the creatures; such as, by heaven, by our life, soul, conscience, or the like?

A. Yes: because swearing by any of his creatures, is interpretatively a swearing by God the Creator and Preserver of all things, Matt. xxiii. 2: "He that sweareth by *Heaven*, sweareth by the throne of God, and by him that sitteth thereon."

Q. 20. Did not Joseph, who was a good man, swear repeatedly by the life of Pharaoh? Gen. xlii. 15, 16.

A. The goodness of the man did not excuse the sinfulness of the action: we are not to do evil, that good may come, Rom. iii. 8. For, though it may be alleged, that to say, By the life of Pharaoh, is no more than to say, As sure as Pharaoh lives; yet the words themselves being in the form of an unlawful oath, which it would seem was commonly used by the Egyptians, they ought not, for this reason, to have been uttered.

Q. 21. Is swearing by faith, or troth, a formal profaning of God's name?

A. No doubt it is; for when a person swears in this manner, he tacitly invokes God to bear witness, that he is speaking faithfully and truly, and to punish him, if he is doing otherwise; which, in ordinary conversation, is undoubtedly sinful, and a falling into condemnation, James v. 12.

Q. 22. Will a habit or custom of swearing in common discourse, be an excuse for it?

A. By no means; any more than a habit or custom of killing men, can be an excuse for wilful murder.

Q. 23. How is the name of God profaned by sinful vows?

A. Either when we solemnly enter into a resolution to do what is absolutely unlawful, as Jezebel did, 1 Kings

xix. 2; or when we come under engagements to duty, and against sin, in our own strength, without a due dependence on the grace of God, as the greater part of the Israelites did, Deut. v. 27, 29; or, when we vow, and are not resolved to perform, as Johanan and his confederates did, Jer. xlii. 5, compared with verse 20.

Q. 24. When is the name of God profaned or abused by lots?

A. When God is appealed to by way of diversion, as in playing at cards, and dice, where the great God is most presumptuously invoked to determine who shall be the gainer. Lots are also unlawful, when there is an appeal by them to God in matters of small moment, which might be otherwise easily decided; this being too like the practice of the soldiers, who, after they had crucified Christ, did cast lots for his vesture, John xix. 23, 24.

Q. 25. How do men profane the name of God in their outward walk?

A. By making profession of religion in hypocrisy, and backsliding from it, Heb. vi. 6; or, by committing such enormities and immoralities, as reflect dishonour upon it, and make the name of God to be evil spoken of, Rom. ii. 24.

Q. 26. How are the ordinances of God profaned and abused?

A. Either when they are quite neglected, Acts vii. 42, 43, or when they are attended in a formal, superficial, and customary manner, without seeking to meet with God in them, or to have spiritual food and nourishment to our souls by them, Isa. xxix. 13, 14.

Q. 27. How is the word profaned and abused?

A. "By misinterpreting, misapplying, or perverting any part of it, to profane jests, curious and unprofitable questions, vain janglings, or the maintaining of false doctrines; abusing it,—or any thing, contained under the name of God, to charms,—or any way opposing God's truth, grace, and ways."*

Q. 28. How are the works of God abused?

A. When "the creatures" are prostituted to "sinful lusts and practices; and when there is a murmuring and quarreling at God's providences."†

QUEST. 56. *What is the reason annexed to the third commandment?*

ANS. The reason annexed to the third commandment

* Larger Catechism, Quest. 113. † Ibid.

is, That however the breakers of this commandment may escape punishment from men, yet the Lord our God wil. not suffer them to escape his righteous judgment.

Q. 1. Are there any arguments against taking God's name in vain, couched in the preceptive part of this commandment?

A. Yes; he whose name we are forbidden to take in vain, is the *Lord our God;* " Thou shalt not take the name of the *Lord thy God* in vain."

Q. 2. What is the force of the argument taken from his being [the Lord] or *Jehovah?*

A. That his infinite essential glory and excellency should fill us with the greatest reverence and humility, when we think or speak of any thing by which he makes himself known, Ps. lxxxiii. 18.

Q. 3. What is the force of the argument taken from his being [our God?]

A. That his making himself over to us in the covenant of promise, as our reconciled God and Father in Christ, should lay us under the strongest obligation to a holy and reverential use of his name, Ex. xv. 2.

Q. 4. What is the particular reason expressly subjoined or annexed to this commandment?

A. It is in these words, by way of threatening: For the Lord will not hold him guiltless that taketh his name in vain.

Q. 5. What is the import of the threatening, the Lord will not hold him guiltless?"

A. It imports, that he will surely hold him guilty in a peculiar manner, who presumes to profane or abuse his name, so that divine vengeance shall be infallibly certain against him, Zech. v. 3.

Q. 6. In what light does the scripture represent those who take God's name in vain?

A. It represents them as his open and avowed enemies, Ps. cxxxix. 20: Thine *enemies* take thy name in vain.

Q. 7. How does it appear that divine vengeance is infallibly certain against the profaners of God's name?

A. It appears from the very terms of the threatening, The Lord *will not* hold him guiltless; that is, as sure as there will be a judgment seat, before which sinners must appear; so sure it is, that this sin shall then be taken particular notice of, as a main article of the indictment, Mal. iii. 5.

Q. 8. Why do [the breakers of this commandment escape punishment from men?]

A. Because many of those to whom the administration of justice is committed, being themselves guilty, do therefore show no concern for vindicating the honour of God's name in punishing the profaners of it.

Q. 9. Why will not the Lord our God [suffer them to escape his righteous judgment?]

A. Because, if heathens are highly punishable for this crime, as contrary to one of the first dictates of nature's light, Rom. i. 32, much more, among Christians; the manifestation of God's name in Christ being the greatest blessing, John xv. 22, their profaning or abusing of it, must be the greatest sin, Amos iii. 2.

QUEST. 57. *Which is the fourth commandment?*

ANS. The fourth commandment is, *Remember the Sabbath day, to keep it holy. Six days shalt thou labour and do all thy work. But the seventh day is the Sabbath of the Lord thy God: in it thou shalt not do any work, thou, nor thy son, nor thy daughter, thy manservant, nor thy maid-servant, nor thy cattle, nor thy stranger that is within thy gates. For, in six days the Lord made heaven and earth, the sea, and all that in them is, and rested the seventh day; wherefore the Lord blessed the Sabbath day, and hallowed it.*

QUEST. 58. *What is required in the fourth commandment?*

ANS. The fourth commandment requireth the keeping holy to God such set times as he hath appointed in his word; expressly one whole day in seven, to be a holy Sabbath unto himself.

Q. 1. To what about the worship of God has this command a reference?

A. It refers to the special *time* of God's worship.

Q. 2. Is the *time* of God's worship left arbitrary to the will of man?

A. No: we are to keep [holy to God such set times as he hath appointed in his word.]

Q. 3. Why should [such set times] be kept holy, and no other?

A. Because God is the sovereign Lord of our time, and has the sole power and authority to direct how it should be improved.

Q. 4. What is meant by the set times mentioned in the answer?

A. The stated feasts, and holy convocations for religious worship, instituted under the ceremonial law, which the church of the Jews was obliged to observe during that dispensation, Lev. xxiii.

Q. 5. Is there any warrant for anniversary, or stated holidays, now, under the New Testament?

A. No: these under the Old, being abrogated by the death and resurrection of Christ, there is neither precept nor example in scripture, for any of the yearly holidays observed by Papists, and others: on the contrary, all such days are condemned, Gal. iv. 10, Col. ii. 16, 17.

Q. 6. What crimes does the observance of them import?

A. The observance of them imports no less than an impeachment of the institutions of God, concerning his worship, as if they were imperfect; and an encroachment upon the liberty wherewith Christ has made his church and people free, Col. ii. 20.

Q. 7. What is the special and stated time, which God has [expressly,] appointed in his word, to be kept holy?

A. [One whole day in seven, to be a holy Sabbath to himself.]

Q. 8. What is meant by a [whole day?]

A. A whole natural day, consisting of twenty-four hours.

Q. 9. What do you understand by one whole day [in seven?]

A. A seventh part of our weekly time; or one complete day, either after or before six days' labour.

Q. 10. When should we begin and end this day?

A. We should measure it just as we do other days, from midnight to midnight, without alienating any part of it to our own works.

Q. 11. Are not sleeping and eating on the Sabbath day our own works?

A. If these refreshments of nature are in moderation, and to the glory of God on the Sabbath, they are not properly our own works, because they are necessary to strengthen our bodies for religious exercises.

Q. 12. What is the signification of the word [Sabbath?]

A. It is a Hebrew word, signifying *rest*; as it is interpreted, Heb. iv. 9: " There remaineth therefore a *rest*," [margin, keeping of a Sabbath] " to the people of God."

Q. 13. Is Sunday a proper or fit name for this day?

A. Although it cannot charitably be supposed that many who use this term have any knowledge of, or pay the smallest regard to the idolatrous rise of this name, or the names assigned to the other days of the week; yet it were to be wished, that all Christians would call this holy-day by one or other of its scripture designations.

Q. 14. May it not continue to be called Sabbath *now*, as well as under the Old Testament?

A. Yes; in regard our Lord himself calls it by this name, Matt. xxiv. 20: "Pray ye that your flight be not in the winter, neither on the Sabbath day."

Q. 15. But is not our Lord speaking there of the Jewish, not of the Christian Sabbath?

A. He evidently means the Christian Sabbath only; for he is speaking of the flight which should happen at the destruction of Jerusalem; which did not take place till about forty years after the Jewish Sabbath was abolished, and the Christian Sabbath had come in its room.

Q. 16. Why is it called a [holy] Sabbath?

A. Because it was consecrated and set apart by God himself, for his own worship and service.

Q. 17. Is there any other day holy beside the Sabbath?

A. Other days may be occasionally employed in the worship of God, according to providential calls to it; yet there is no other day, except the Sabbath, morally and perpetually holy.

Q. 18. Is the Sabbath instrumentally holy, or is the time itself of the Sabbath an instrument and means (as the word and sacraments are) of conveying spiritual grace?

A. Not at all: for the time of the Sabbath is only a holy *season*, in which God is pleased to bless his people, more ordinarily than at other times, John xx. 19, 24; still reserving to himself the prerogative of communicating his grace at other times likewise, as he shall see meet, chap. xxi. 15—18.

Q. 19. Is the fourth commandment founded on the light of nature, or upon positive institution?

A. It is founded partly on both.

Q. 20. What part of this commandment is it, that is founded entirely on nature's light; or is what they call moral-natural?

A. The substance of it; namely, that as God is to be worshipped, so some stated time should be set apart for that end.

Q. 21. What part of it is founded on positive institution: or is what they call moral-positive?

A. That one proportion of time should be observed for God's worship and service rather than another; namely, that it should be a seventh, rather than a third, fourth, fifth, or sixth part of our weekly time.

Q. 22. Why do you call this a *positive* institution?

A. Because the observance of one day in seven, for a Sabbath, flows from the sovereign will of God in appointing it; and could never have been observed, more than any other part of time, merely by the force of nature's light.

Q. 23. Why do you call it *moral*-positive?

A. Because, though the law appointing the precise time of the Sabbath be positive, yet the reason of the law (plainly implied in the law itself, namely, that divine wisdom saw it most equal and meet, that man having six, God should have a seventh day to himself) is *moral*.

Q. 24. In what, then, consists the morality of the fourth commandment?

A. In keeping holy to God any seventh day he shall be pleased to appoint.

Q. 25. What is meant by [the seventh day] mentioned in the command?

A. Not only the seventh in order from the creation, but any other seventh part of our weekly time, as God shall determine.

Q. 26. How does this appear from the words of the command itself?

A. In the beginning of the commandment, it is not said, Remember the seventh day, (namely, in order from the creation,) but Remember the Sabbath-day, to keep it holy. Just so, in the end of this command, the words are not, The Lord blessed the seventh-day; but, the Lord blessed the Sabbath day, and hallowed it.

Q. 27. How do you prove the observance of [one whole day in seven] for a holy Sabbath to the Lord, to be of moral and perpetual obligation?

A. From the time of the first institution of the Sabbath; from its being placed in the *decalogue*, or summary of moral precepts; and from there being nothing originally ceremonial, or typical, in the scope or substance of it.

Q. 28. When was the Sabbath first instituted?

A. The will of God, that some stated time should be set apart for his worship was written, with the rest of the commandments, upon man's heart at his first creation; and God's resting from all his works on the first seventh day, his blessing and sanctifying it, Gen. ii. 1—3, were sufficient evidences of his will to mankind, that they should observe every seventh day thereafter, till God should be pleased to alter it.

Q. 29. How is the morality of the Sabbath evinced from the first institution of it?

A. Being instituted while Adam was in innocence, and consequently before all types and ceremonies respecting an atonement for sin; and being appointed him upon a moral ground, without any particular reference to an innocent state, more than any other, it must therefore be of perpetual obligation.

Q. 30. What was the moral ground upon which the Sabbath was appointed to Adam?

A. It was this, that infinite wisdom saw it meet, for God's glory, and needful for man's good, that man have one day in the week for more immediate and special converse with God.

Q. 31. What need was there for Adam in innocence, being perfectly holy, to have one day set apart from the others, for more immediate converse with God?

A. That in this respect he might be like God, who set him an example of holy working six days, and of a holy resting on the seventh.

Q. 32. Could Adam's mind be equally intent upon the immediate worship of God, when about his ordinary employment in dressing the garden, as on a day set apart for that purpose?

A. No; for though there could be no interruption of his happiness and fellowship with God, when dressing the garden, as he was a perfect creature; yet being at the same time a finite creature, his mind, while he was about that employment, could not be so intent upon the immediate worship of God, as it would be on a day set apart for that purpose; therefore it was fit he should have such a day, that he might thus have an uninterrupted freedom in the immediate contemplation and enjoyment of his Maker, without any avocation from worldly things.

Q. 33. What may be inferred from this, in favour of the morality of the Sabbath?

A. That if Adam in innocence needed a Sabbath, for the more immediate service and solemn worship of God, much more do we, who are sinful creatures, and so immersed in worldly cares, need such a day.

Q. 34. Did the religious observance of the Sabbath take place immediately after the creation, or not till the publishing of the law at Mount Sinai?

A. It took place at, and from the first seventh day after the creation; for God's blessing and sanctifying of the Sabbath is related as a thing actually done at that time, and not as a thing to be done upwards of two thousand years afterwards, Gen. ii. 3.

Q. 35. How can the observance of the Sabbath be said to have taken place immediately after the creation, when the scripture is wholly silent about the observance of it till the time of Moses?

A. It might as well be argued, that the Sabbath was not observed after Moses' time, during the government of the Judges, which, according to Acts xiii. 20, was about the space of four hundred and fifty years, there being no mention of the church observing a Sabbath during the whole of that long period: and yet it cannot be supposed, that such godly men as the Judges were, would suffer the observance of the Sabbath to go into entire disuse.

Q. 36. Is there any evidence from scripture, that the Israelites knew the observance of the Sabbath to be a moral duty, before the publication of the law, from Mount Sinai?

A. Yes; for when the manna was first given them, before they came to Mount Sinai, Moses speaks of the Sabbath, as a day well known to them, Ex. xvi. 23: "To-morrow is the rest of the holy Sabbath unto the Lord."

Q. 37. How may the morality of the Sabbath be demonstrated from its *situation* in the decalogue, or ten commandments?

A. It is placed in the midst of moral precepts, and must therefore be of the same nature and kind with them. It has the same dignity and honour put upon it, that the other nine commandments have; for it was, with them, proclaimed by the mouth of God, in the hearing of all Israel; twice written upon tables of stone, by the finger of God; and with them lodged within the ark: none of which privileges were conferred upon the ceremonial law: and, consequently, the fourth commandment must be of the same perpetual obligation as the other moral precepts, James ii. 10.

Q. 38. Was there any thing *typical* of Christ in the original institution of the Sabbath?

A. It is impossible there could: for Adam, in innocence, being under a covenant of works, had no need of Christ, or the revelation of him by types; no, not to confirm him in that covenant, Gal. iii. 12.

Q. 39. What would have been the consequence, if the Sabbath had been originally and essentially typical?

A. If so, then it would have been abolished, upon the death of Christ, and there would be no more remembrance of it than of the new moons and jubilees: which is, indeed, what they who argue against the morality of the Sabbath seem much to desire.

Q. 40. Were not the Israelites commanded to keep the Sabbath day in memory of their deliverance out of Egypt, which was typical of our redemption by Christ?

A. Yes: their deliverance out of Egypt was annexed, at Mount Sinai, as a superadded ground for the observance of that particular seventh day, which God appointed to be kept immediately after the creation, Deut. v. 15. For which reason, this particular seventh day was abolished at the resurrection of Christ: but still the seventh part of weekly time fixed by God at the beginning, as the substance of this commandment, remained unchangeably moral

Q. 41. Will it follow that the substance of this commandment is ceremonial, because it is said of Christ, Matt. xii. 8, that he is "Lord even of the Sabbath day?"

A. By no means: the very contrary will follow; namely, that such a seventh part of weekly time, as is now observed, is moral, because he who is the Lord of the Sabbath, has appointed it to be so; and, consequently, has power to order the work of it for his own service.

Q. 42. Is it any argument against the morality of the Sabbath, that it " was made for man, and not man for the Sabbath?"

A. No; but rather an argument for it: the meaning doubtless is, that resting on the Sabbath was appointed for man's good, that it might be a mean to a further and better end, even the true sanctification of it, in the exercise of the duties of piety and mercy required on the day.

QUEST. 59. *Which day of the seven hath God appointed to be the weekly Sabbath?*

ANS. From the beginning of the world, to the resurrection of Christ, God appointed the seventh day of the week to be the weekly Sabbath; and the first day of the week, ever since, to continue to the end of the world, which is the Christian Sabbath.

Q. 1. When did God appoint the seventh day of the week to be the weekly Sabbath?

A. [From the beginning of the world,] Gen. ii. 2, 3.

Q. 2. Why is it said to be from the beginning of the world, when it was not done till after man was created on the sixth day?

A. Because the world as to its perfection of parts, did not properly begin, till the creation was completely finished; which was not till man was made, who was to have dominion over all the earth, Gen. i. 26.

Q. 3. How long was this seventh or last day of the week appointed to be the weekly Sabbath?

A. [To the resurrection of Christ,] Matt. xxviii. 1.

Q. 4. Which day of the week did God appoint for the Sabbath [ever since] that time?

A. [The first day of the week,] Acts xx. 7.

Q. 5. For how long time is the first day of the week appointed to be the weekly Sabbath?

A. [To the end of the world.]

Q. 6. How are we sure that it is appointed to [continue to the end of the world?]

A. Because the canon of scripture is concluded, and therefore no new revelations and institutions are to be expected, Rev. xxii. 18, 19.

Q. 7. Why is the first day of the week called [the Christian Sabbath?]

A. Because it was instituted by *Christ*, and uniformly observed by Christians ever since his resurrection.

Q. 8. Are not all divine institutions observed in virtue of some moral precept?

A. Yes; otherwise the law of the Lord would not be perfect, as it is declared to be, Ps. xix. 7.

Q. 9. In virtue of what moral precept has the first day of the week been observed by Christians?

A. In virtue of the fourth commandment; even as the means of worship, instituted under the New Testament, have been observed in virtue of the second.

Q. 10. How can the first day of the week be observed in virtue of the fourth commandment, when it is not in it particularly mentioned?

A. The morality of the Sabbath does not lie in observing the seventh day in order from the creation; but in observing such a seventh day as is determined and appointed by God; which may be either the first or last of the seven days, as he shall see meet.

Q. 11. Under what name or designation is the Christian Sabbath foretold in the Old Testament?

A. Under the name of the eighth day, Ezek. xliii. 27: "And when these days are expired, it shall be that upon the eighth day, and so forward, the priests shall make your burnt offerings upon the altar, and your peace offerings: and I will accept you, saith the Lord."

Q. 12. Why called the eighth day?

A. Because the first day of the week now, is the eighth in order from the creation.

Q. 13. What is the efficient cause of the change of the Sabbath?

A. The sovereign will and pleasure of him who is Lord of the Sabbath, Mark ii. 28.

Q. 14. What is the moving cause of this change?

A. The resurrection of Christ from the dead, which was early on the first day of the week, Mark xvi. 9.

Q. 15. Why is the day of Christ's resurrection appointed to be the Sabbath?

A. Because his resurrection was a demonstrative evidence that he had completely finished the glorious work of redemption, Rom. i. 4; and therefore it was his *Resting Day*, Heb. iv. 10: "He that is entered into his rest, he also hath ceased from his own works, as God did from his."

Q. 16. Why might not the day of Christ's incarnation

or the day of his passion, have been consecrated to be our Sabbath day?

A. Because they were both of them days of Christ's labour and sorrow, which he had to go through before he came to his rest, Luke xxiv. 26. In his incarnation, and birth, he entered upon his work, Gal. iv. 4, 5. In his passion, he was under the sorest part of his labour, even the exquisite and unspeakable agonies of his soul, Matt. xxvi. 38.

Q. 17. Why might not the day of his ascension be made the Sabbath, as well as the day of his resurrection?

A. Because on the day of his ascension he entered only into his *Place* of rest, the third heavens; whereas he had entered before into his *State* of rest on the day of his resurrection; and the place is but a circumstance, when compared with the state.

Q. 18. Why did God change his day of rest?

A. Because his rest in the work of creation was marred and spoiled by man's sin, Gen. vi. 6; whereas his rest in the work of redemption, entered into at the resurrection of Christ, is that in which he will have eternal and unchangeable pleasure, John xvii. 23. Besides, redemption is a far greater and more excellent work than even that of creation.

Q. 19. How may the change of the Sabbath from the last to the first day of the week be evinced from scripture?

A. If our Lord Jesus, after his resurrection, met ordinarily with his disciples on the first day of the week; if, after his ascension, he poured out his Spirit in an extraordinary manner on that day; if, by the example and practice of the apostles and primitive Christians, recorded in the New Testament, the first day of the week was honoured above any other for the public exercises of God's worship; if, by apostolic precept, the observance of this day, rather than any other, was enjoined for Sabbath services; and if this day is peculiarly dignified with the title of the *Lord's Day*—then it must undoubtedly be the Christian Sabbath by divine institution.

Q. 20. How does it appear that our *Lord*, after his resurrection, met ordinarily with his disciples on the first day of the week?

A. From two instances of it, expressly recorded, John xx. 19, 26; where it is affirmed, that he met with them on the evening of the same day on which he arose from the dead, being the first day of the week: and that Thomas was not with them when Jesus came, ver. 24. Likewise, on that same day, eight days, he appeared to them again, when they were within, and Thomas was with them, ver. 26. From whence it would seem, that he met with them ordinarily on that day, during his forty days' abode on the earth, after his resurrection.

Q. 21. How is it evident that Christ, after his ascension, poured out his Spirit in an extraordinary manner on this day?

A. From Acts ii. 1—5: "And when the day of Pentecost was fully come, they were all with one accord, in one place; and suddenly there came a sound from heaven,— and they were all filled with the Holy Ghost," &c.

Q. 22. What was the day of Pentecost?

A. It was the fiftieth day after the passover, when the new meat offering was brought unto the Lord, Num. xxviii. 26.

Q. 23. How do you prove that this was the first day of the week?

A. From Lev. xxiii. 16; where it is said, that the morrow after the seventh Sabbath is the fiftieth day, (or Pentecost.) And it is certain that the morrow after the Jewish Sabbath must be the first day of the week.

Q. 24. How does it appear, from the example and practice of the apostles and primitive Christians, that the first day of the week was honoured above any other, for the public exercise of God's worship?

A. From Acts xx. 7: "And on the first day of the week, when the disciples came together to break bread, Paul preached unto them:" where it is obvious that the disciples met ordinarily upon the first day of the week, to hear the word, and celebrate the sacrament of the supper: for it is not said, the apostle called them, but that they *came* together to break bread; and Paul, on that occasion, preached unto them.

Q. 25. How may it be proved from the context, that the disciples met ordinarily for the public exercises of God's worship, on the first day of the week?

A. That they did so may be proved from this, that Paul abode with them seven days, as is evident from ver. 6, and yet upon none of the seven did they meet for communicating, or breaking of bread, but on the first day of the week only: which plainly says that they held it for the Christian Sabbath, and not the seventh or last day, which is not even mentioned.

Q. 26. But do we not read, Acts xiii. 14, that Paul preached in a synagogue on the Sabbath day, which certainly behoved to be the Jewish Sabbath or last day of the week?

A. He only preached occasionally on the Jewish Sabbath, as the fittest time, when the Jews were assembled together, to dispense gospel truth among them; but did not honour this day as a stated time for public worship.

Q. 27. What apostolic precept is there, for the observ

ence of the first day of the week, rather than any other, for Sabbath services?

A. It is in 1 Cor. xvi. 1, 2: "Now, concerning the collection for the saints, as I have given order to the churches of Galatia, even so do ye. Upon the first day of the week, let every one of you lay by him in store, as God hath prospered him."

Q. 28. What is the argument from this text, to prove an apostolic precept, for observing the first day of the week as the Christian Sabbath?

A. It may run thus: That if collections for the poor are expressly commanded to be made on the first day of the week, it plainly follows, that Christians must meet together on that day, for this and other Sabbath services.

Q. 29. But may not this be a temporary precept, binding, for a time, upon the church of Corinth only?

A. As the words of the text expressly affirm that it was binding also upon the churches of Galatia, so the apostle directs his epistle not to the church of Corinth only, but to all that in every place call upon the name of Jesus Christ, chap. i. 2; and consequently it must be binding upon all the churches to the end of the world.

Q. 30. In what place of the New Testament is there mention made of a day dignified with the title of the Lord's day?

A. In Rev. i. 10: I was in the Spirit, says John, on the Lord's day.

Q. 31. How may it be proved, that what is here called the Lord's day, is the first day of the week?

A. By these two arguments: That no other day of the week but the first can justly be called the Lord's day; and that the first day of the week is so called in virtue of Christ's sanctifying it, above any other day, for his own honour and service.

Q. 32. Why can no other day of the week, but the first, be justly called the Lord's day?

A. Because there is no action or work of Christ (save healing on the Sabbath) mentioned or recorded as done upon any one day of the week by another, except that of his resurrection, which is unanimously affirmed by the evangelists, to be on the first day of the week.

Q. 33. How does it appear that the first day of the week is called the Lord's day, in virtue of his sanctifying it for his own honour and service?

A. As the seventh day Sabbath was called the Sabbath of the Lord, because instituted by him as God-creator; so the first day of the week is called the Lord's day, because instituted by him as God-redeemer; or, as the sacrament of bread and wine is called the Lord's table, and the Lord's supper, 1 Cor. x. 21, and xi. 20, because it is an ordinance of his institution; so, the first day of the week is called the Lord's day, for the very same reason.

Q. 34. Would the apostles have observed and recommended the first day of the week for the Christian Sabbath, if they had not been particularly instructed in this by Christ himself?

A. No, surely: for, after his passion, he spoke of the things pertaining to the kingdom of God, Acts i. 3; among which the change of the Sabbath from the last to the first day of the week, was none of the least; and it is certain, that the apostles delivered nothing to the churches, as a rule of faith or practice, but what they received of the Lord, 1 Cor. xi. 23.

Quest. 60. *How is the Sabbath to be sanctified?*

Ans. The Sabbath is to be sanctified, by a holy resting all that day, even from such worldly employments and recreations as are lawful on other days; and spending the whole time in the public and private exercises of God's worship, except so much as is to be taken up in the works of necessity and mercy.

Q. 1. In what sense is the Sabbath to be [sanctified?]

A. As it is dedicated by God, for man's sake and use that he may keep it holy to God.

Q. 2. In what manner should he keep it holy to God?

A. By [a holy resting,] and by holy exercises.

Q. 3. What should we rest from on the Sabbath?

A. [Even from such worldly employments and recreations as are lawful on other days;] or, which is the same thing, from all servile work, Neh. xiii. 15—23.

Q. 4. What is it that makes a work servile?

A. If it is done for our worldly gain, profit, and livelihood; or if, by prudent management, it might have been done the week before; or, if it be of such a kind as may be delayed till after the Sabbath, Ex. xxxiv. 21: Six days thou shalt work, but on the seventh thou shalt rest: in earing time,* and in harvest thou shalt rest.

Q. 5. Why does God enjoin rest on the Sabbath so peremptorily and particularly, in the time of ploughing and harvest?

A. Because in these seasons men are most keenly set upon their labour; and may be in the greatest hazard of grudging the time of the Sabbath for rest.

---

* Ploughing-time, or Seed-time.

Q. 6. If the weather is unseasonable through the week, do not reaping and ingathering, in that case, become works of necessity on the Sabbath?

A. By no means; because any unseasonableness of the weather that may happen, being common and general, proceeds only from the course of God's ordinary providence, which we ought not to distrust, in regard of his promise, that, "While the earth remaineth, seed-time and harvest—shall not cease," Gen. viii. 22.

Q. 7. If a field of corn is in hazard of being carried away by the unexpected inundation of a river, is it lawful to endeavour the preservation of them upon the Sabbath?

A. Yes: because the dispensation is extraordinary; the case not common nor general; and the damage likewise, in an ordinary way, irrecoverable.

Q. 8. Are Christians, under the New Testament, obliged to as strict an abstinence from worldly labour, as the Jews were under the Old?

A. Yes, surely; for moral duties being of unchangeable obligation, Christians must be bound to as strict a performance of them now, as the Jews were then, Ps. xix. 9.

Q. 9. Were not the Jews prohibited to dress meat on the Sabbath? Ex. xvi. 23.

A. They were prohibited such servile work as was requisite in preparing manna for food: such as the grinding of it in mills, beating it in mortars, and baking it in pans, Num. xi. 8; but not all dressing of meat, for the comfortable nourishment of their bodies, any more than we.

Q. 10. How does it appear that they were allowed to dress meat on the Sabbath, for the comfortable nourishment of their bodies?

A. From our Lord's being present at a meal on the Sabbath day, to which there were several guests bidden, and consequently meat behoved to be prepared and dressed for their entertainment, Luke xiv. 1, 7.

Q. 11. Were not the Jews forbidden to kindle fire in their habitations upon the Sabbath day? Ex. xxxv. 3.

A. Yes, for any servile work, though it were even making materials for the tabernacle, (which is the work spoken of through the following part of that chapter;) but they were not forbidden to kindle fires for works of necessity or mercy, any more than Christians are.

Q. 12. Were they not ordered to abide every man in his place, and not to go out of his place on the seventh day? Ex. xvi. 29.

A. The prohibition only respects their going abroad about the unnecessary and servile work of gathering manna upon the Sabbath; otherwise, they were allowed to go out about works of necessity and mercy: and it appears from Acts i. 12, that they were allowed to travel a Sabbath day's journey.

Q. 13. What was a Sabbath day's journey?

A. Whatever was the tradition of the Pharisees about it, it appears to have been the distance of their respective dwellings, from the place where they ordinarily attended public ordinances, 2 Kings iv. 23.

Q. 14. Are we not to rest on the Lord's day from lawful recreations, as well as from lawful worldly employments?

A. Yes; because we are expressly required, on this holy day, to abstain from doing our own ways, finding our own pleasure, and speaking our own words, Isa. lviii. 13.

Q. 15. What are these recreations that are lawful on other days?

A. Innocent pastimes, visiting friends, walking in the fields, talking of the news, or common affairs, and the like.

Q. 16. Why are these recreations unlawful on the Lord's day?

A. Because they tend to divert the mind from the duties of the Sabbath, as much as, if not more than, worldly employments.

Q. 17. Is not the Sabbath a festival, or feast day; and consequently may not our conversation on it be cheerful and diverting?

A. It is, indeed, properly a feast day, but of a spiritual, not of a carnal nature: we may refresh our bodies moderately, but not sumptuously; and our conversation ought to turn wholly upon spiritual and heavenly subjects, or such as have that tendency, after the example of our Lord, Luke xiv. 1—25.

Q. 18. What should be the principal end of our six days' labour?

A. That it be so managed, as in no way to discompose or unfit us for a holy resting on the Sabbath, or meeting with God on his own day.

Q. 19. What is a [holy resting?]

A. Not only an abstaining from our own work, or labour, but an entering by faith, (in the use of appointed means,) into the presence and enjoyment of God in Christ, as the only rest of our souls, Heb. iv. 3; that having no work of our own to mind or do, we may be wholly taken up with the works of God.

Q. 20. Why called a [holy] resting?

A. Because we should rest from worldly labour, in order to be employed in the holy exercises, which the Lord requires on this day; otherwise, as to bare cessation, our cattle rest from outward labour, as well as we.

Q. 21. What are the holy *exercises*, in which we ought to be employed on the Lord's day?

A. [In the public and private exercises of God's worship.]

Q. 22. What are the [public exercises] of God's worship in which we should be employed?

A. Hearing the word preached, Rom. x. 17; joining in public prayers and praises, Luke xxiv. 53; and partaking of the sacraments, Acts xx. 7.

Q. 23. What is included under the [private] exercises of God's worship?

A. Family and secret duties.

Q. 24. What are the duties incumbent on us in a family capacity on the Lord's day?

A. Family worship, and family catechizing, together with Christian conference, as there is occasion, Lev. xxiii. 3: "It is the Sabbath of the Lord in all your *dwellings*, or private families; and therefore God is to be worshipped in them on that day.

Q. 25. What is family worship?

A. It is the daily joining of all that are united in a domestic relation, or who are dwelling together in the same house and family, in singing God's praises, Acts ii. 47 reading his word, Deut. vi. 7, and praying to him, Jer. x. 25.

Q. 26. How do you prove family worship to be a duty daily incumbent upon those who have families?

A. From scripture precept, and from scripture example.

Q. 27. How is family worship evinced from scripture precept?

A. Besides that this commandment enjoins every master of a family to sanctify the Sabbath within his gates, that is, to worship God in his family; there are also other scriptures, inculcating the same thing, by necessary consequence; such as, Eph. vi. 18, "Praying always, with all prayer and supplication," 1 Tim. ii. 8; "I will therefore that men pray every where." If with all prayer, then surely with family prayer; if every where, then certainly in our families.

Q. 28. What are the examples of family worship recorded in scripture for our imitation?

A. Among others, there are the examples of Abraham, Gen. xviii. 19; of Joshua, chap. xxiv. 15: "As for me and my house, we will serve the Lord;" of David, 2 Sam. vi. 20; of Cornelius, Acts x. 2; and especially the example of our blessed Lord, whom we find singing psalms, Matt. xxvi. 30, and praying with his disciples, who were his family, Luke ix. 18.

Q. 29. What should be the subject matter of family catechizing?

A. What they have been hearing through the day, together with the principles of our religion, as laid out in the Shorter Catechism, with the helps that are published upon the same, which masters of families ought to use for their assistance in this work.

Q. 30. What are the proper seasons of Christian conference on the Sabbath?

A. At meals, and in the interval of duties: our speech should be always, but especially on the Lord's day, seasoned with salt, Col. iv. 6.

Q. 31. What are the secret duties in which we ought to be exercised on the Lord's day?

A. Secret prayer, reading the scriptures, and other soul-edifying books, meditation upon divine subjects, and self-examination.

Q. 32. With what frame and disposition of soul should we engage in the public and private exercises of God's worship?

A. With a spiritual frame and disposition, Rev. i. 10: I was *in the Spirit* on the Lord's day.

Q. 33. What is it to be in the Spirit on the Lord's day?

A. It is not only to have the actual inhabitation of the Spirit, which is the privilege of believers every day, Ezek. xxxvi. 27; but to have the influences and operations of the Spirit more liberally let out, Luke iv. 31, 32, and his graces in more lively exercise, than at other times, Acts ii. 41.

Q. 34. What moral argument have we from the ceremonial law, for offering a greater plenty of spiritual sacrifices to God on the Sabbath, than upon other days?

A. The daily sacrifice, or continual burnt offering, was to be doubled on the Sabbath, Num. xxviii. 9; intimating, that they were bound to double their devotions on that day, which was consecrated to God to be spent in his service.

Q. 35. How much of the Sabbath is to be spent in the public and private exercises of God's worship?

A. The *whole* of it, from the ordinary time of rising on other days, to the ordinary time of going to rest; [except so much as is to be taken up in the works of necessity and mercy.]

Q. 36. What is to be understood by works of [necessity?]

A. Such as could not be foreseen, nor provided against the day before, nor delayed till the day after the Sabbath.

Q. 37. What instances may be given of such works of necessity on the Lord's day?

A. Flying from, and defending ourselves against an enemy; quenching of fire, accidentally or wilfully kindled; standing by the helm, or working a ship at sea, (provided they do not weigh anchor, nor hoist sail from harbours or friths, on the Lord's day,) and the like.

Q. 38. What are the works of [mercy] which may be done on the Sabbath?

A. The moderate refreshment of our bodies, Luke vi. 1; visiting the sick, preparing and administering remedies to them, Luke xiii. 16; feeding our cattle, ver. 15; and preserving their lives, if in danger, chap. xiv. 5; and making collections for the poor, 1 Cor. xvi. 2.

Q. 39. What cautions are requisite about works of necessity and mercy?

A. That these works be real, and not pretended; that we spend as little time about them as possible; and that we endeavour to attain a holy frame of spirit while about them.

Q. 40. How does it appear that works of necessity and mercy are lawful on the Lord's day?

A. Because, though God rested from his work of creation on the seventh day, yet he did not rest on it, from preserving what he had made.

Q. 41. "Why is the charge of keeping the Sabbath more especially directed to governors of families, and other superiors?"

A. "—Because they are bound not only to keep it themselves, but to see that it be observed by all those that are under their charge: and because they are prone oftentimes to hinder them by employments of their own." *

Q. 42. Ought not magistrates to punish those who are guilty of the open and presumptuous breach of the Sabbath?

A. Undoubtedly they should; and they have the example of Nehemiah for a precedent, worthy of their imitation in this matter, chap. xiii. 21.

Q. 43. What is the most effectual way for the civil magistrate to suppress Sabbath profanation?

A. To be impartial in the execution of the laws against Sabbath breaking, especially upon those who are of a more eminent rank and station, because they ought to be exemplary to others, Neh. xiii. 17: "Then I contended with the *nobles* of Judah; and said unto them, What evil thing is this that ye do, and profane the Sabbath day?"

Q. 44. "Why is the word *remember* set in the beginning of the fourth commandment?"

A. "Partly, because we are very ready to forget it: and partly, because in keeping it, we are helped better to keep all the rest of the commandments."†

---

* Larger Catechism, Q. 118.   † Ibid. Q. 121.

QUEST. 61. *What is forbidden in the fourth commandment?*

ANS. The fourth commandment forbiddeth the omission, or careless performance, of the duties required, and the profaning the day by idleness, or doing that which is in itself sinful, or by unnecessary thoughts, words, or works, about our worldly employments and recreations.

Q. 1. How are the sins ranked that are forbidden in this commandment?
A. They are ranked into sins of omission, and sins of commission.*

Q. 2. What are the sins of [omission] here forbidden?
A. Both the total neglect of the duties required, and the neglect of the careful performance of them, when essayed.

Q. 3. Of what is the total neglect of the duties required on the Sabbath an evidence?
A. It is a plain evidence of the neglect of all religious duties through the week; and, consequently, an evidence of atheism, profaneness, and apostasy.

Q. 4. When are persons guilty of the [careless performance] of the duties required on the Sabbath?
A. When they go about them in a partial, formal and lifeless way, Matt. xv. 8.

Q. 5. What is it to go about duties in a partial way?
A. It is to perform some of them, and omit others equally necessary; such as, attending the public, and neglecting the private exercises of God's worship; or the contrary.

Q. 6. What is formality in duty?
A. It is the bare outward performance of it, without regarding the manner in which it ought to be done, or the vital principle from whence it should flow, 2 Tim. iii. 5.

Q. 7. What are the ordinary causes of the dead and lifeless performance of religious duties?
A. Wandering thoughts, weariness, and drowsiness, are among none of the least.

Q. 8. What is the best antidote against wandering thoughts?
A. Faith in exercise: for this will fix the attention to what we are presently engaged in, whether hearing, praying, or praising, Ps. lvii. 7.

Q. 9. Whence arises weariness in duty?
A. From the natural bias of the heart and affections to worldly things, rather than religious exercises, Amos viii.

---

* See both these explained, Part I. on the head, Of sin in general.

5: "When will the new moon be gone, that we may sell corn? and the Sabbath, that we may set forth wheat?"

Q. 10. What is the evil of drowsiness, particularly in hearing the word, or joining in prayer and praise?

A. If it be voluntary and customary, it is a manifest contempt of the word and presence of the great God, and paying less regard to him, than we even do to our fellow-creatures.

Q. 11. What are the sins of *commission* forbidden in this commandment?

A. [The profaning the day by idleness, or doing that which is in itself sinful, or by unnecessary thoughts, words, or works, about our worldly employments and recreations.]

Q. 12. What is the idleness here prohibited?

A. It is a loitering away the Sabbath, in a slothful, indolent, and inactive manner, without any real benefit or advantage, either to soul or body, Matt. xx. 3.

Q. 13. Why is there a prohibition of [doing that which is in itself sinful,] on the Lord's day, when it is unlawful on every other day?

A. Because whatever the sinful action be, there is a greater aggravation of guilt in committing it on the Sabbath, which ought to be kept holy to God, than upon any other day, Jer. xvii. 27.

Q. 14. What are these [thoughts, words, or works,] that are here called [unnecessary?]

A. They are such as are [about our worldly employments and recreations;] or, they are all such thoughts, words, or works, as are not inevitably used about the works of necessity and mercy, which are lawful on this day.

Q. 15. Why is the day said to be profaned by the sins here forbidden?

A. Because these sins are each of them the reverse of that holiness, which should shine in all our duties, public and private, on the Lord's day, Isa. lviii. 13, 14.

QUEST. 62. *What are the reasons annexed to the fourth commandment?*

ANS. The reasons annexed to the fourth commandment are God's allowing us six days of the week for our own employments, his challenging a special propriety in the seventh, his own example, and his blessing the Sabbath day.

Q. 1. How many reasons are there annexed to this commandment?

A. *Four;* which are more than to any of the rest.

Q. 2. Why are more reasons annexed to this command than to any of the rest?

A. Because of the proneness of men to break it; and likewise that the violation of it may be rendered the more inexcusable.

Q. 3. Which is the first reason?

A. It is [God's allowing us six days of the week for our own employments;] in these words, Six days shalt thou labour and do all thy work.

Q. 4. In what lies the strength of this reason?

A. It lies in this, that it would be most highly unreasonable and ungrateful to grudge a seventh part of our time, in the more immediate service and worship of God; when he has been so liberal as to allow us six parts of it, for our own secular and worldly affairs.

Q. 5. What similar instance of ingratitude may be given for the illustration of this?

A. The sin of our first parents, in refusing to abstain from one tree, when they were allowed the free use of all the rest of the garden, Gen. iii. 2, 3, 6.

Q. 6. Is working six days in our own employments a precept properly belonging to this commandment?

A. No: it is properly a branch of the eighth commandment, but it is brought in here incidentally, to enforce the sacred observance of a seventh day, when God has been so bountiful as to allow us six for our own occasions.

Q. 7. Which is the second reason annexed to this commandment?

A. It is [his challenging a special propriety in the seventh;] in these words, "but the seventh day is the Sabbath of the Lord thy God."

Q. 8. What is the force of this reason?

A. The force of it is this;—As that gracious God, who makes a grant of himself to us in the covenant of promise, claims this day as his own, so it is our greatest privilege or happiness to have access to, and communion with him on it, Isa. lviii. 14.

Q. 9. In what lies the privilege or happiness of communion with God on his own day?

A. In having a foretaste in grace here of what shall be more fully enjoyed in glory hereafter, 1 Cor. xiii. 12.

Q. 10. Which is the third reason?

A. It is [his own example;] in these words, "For in six days the Lord made heaven and earth, the sea, and all that in them is, and rested the seventh day."

Q. 11. Could not God have made heaven and earth, the

sea, and all that in them is, in less time than the space of six days!

A. No doubt, he could have made all things, in the same beauty and perfection, in which ever they appeared, in an instant of time, if he had pleased.

Q. 12. Why then did he take six days?

A. To fix the morality of six days for worldly labour, and of a seventh for holy rest; and both these by his own example.

Q. 13. But does not the example of God's resting the seventh day, oblige us still to observe the seventh day, in order from the creation, as a Sabbath?

A. No; because, though moral examples bind always to the kind of action, yet not always to every particular circumstance of it.

Q. 14. What is the kind of action to which God's example binds us?

A. It is to observe one day in seven as a holy rest, either the last or first, as he shall appoint.

Q. 15. How can God's example of resting on the seventh day be an argument for our resting on the first?

A. Though the observance of a particular day in seven be *mutable*; yet the duty of observing a seventh part of weekly time is *moral*, both by God's precept and example.

Q. 16. Which is the fourth reason annexed to this commandment?

A. It is [his blessing the Sabbath day;] in these words: " Wherefore, the Lord blessed the Sabbath day, and hallowed it."

Q. 17. In what sense may the Sabbath be said to be blessed?

A. Not only by God's consecrating the day itself to a holy use; but by his blessing it to the true observers of it, and by his blessing them in it.

Q. 18. How does God bless the Sabbath to the true observers of it?

A. By ordering it so in his providence, that the religious observance of the Sabbath shall be no detriment to, but rather a furtherance of their lawful employments through the week; even as the profanation of it draws a train of all miseries and woes after it, Neh. xiii. 18.

Q. 19. How does he bless them in it, or upon it?

A. By making it the happy season of a more plenteous communication of all spiritual blessings to them, Isa. lviii. 14.

Q. 20. What does the illative particle *Wherefore* teach us?

A. That God's resting on the Sabbath was the great reason of his setting it apart to be a day of holy rest to us, that we might contemplate the works of God, both of creation and redemption, upon it.

QUEST. 63. *Which is the fifth commandment?*

ANS. The fifth commandment is, *Honour thy father and thy mother; that thy days may be long upon the land which the Lord thy God giveth thee.*

QUEST. 64. *What is required in the fifth commandment?*

ANS. The fifth commandment requireth the preserving the honour, and performing the duties, belonging to every one in their several places and relations, as superiors, inferiors, or equals.

Q. 1. "Who are meant by father and mother in the fifth commandment?"
A. "Not only natural parents, but all superiors in age and gifts; and especially such as, by God's ordinance, are over us in place of authority, whether in family, church, or commonwealth." *

Q. 2. "Why are superiors styled father and mother?"
A. "To teach them in all duties towards their inferiors, like natural parents, to express love and tenderness to them according to their several relations; and to work inferiors to a greater willingness and cheerfulness, in performing their duties to their superiors, as to their parents." †

Q. 3. "What is the general scope of the fifth commandment?"
A. It "is the performance of those duties we mutually owe in our several relations."‡

Q. 4. What are the *relations* in which we stand to each other?
A. All mankind stand related to each other, either [as superiors, inferiors, or equals.]

Q. 5. Who are our [superiors?]
A. All that are above us in office, place, or dignity.

Q. 6. Who are meant by [inferiors?]
A. Such as are subject to others, or below them in station or gifts.

Q. 7. Whom do you understand by [equals?]
A. Such as are of like age and condition in the world.

* Larger Catechism, Q. 124   † Ibid. Q. 125.   ‡ Ibid. Q. 126.

Q. 8. What is the general duty required in this commandment?
A. It is *honour:* Honour thy father and thy mother.
Q. 9. What is meant by the honour here required?
A. All inward regard and esteem, manifested by outward tokens of respect, Rom. xiii. 10, reverence, chap. xiii. 7, and obedience, Heb. xiii. 17.
Q. 10. What is the rule and measure of that obedience and submission, which is due from inferiors to their superiors?
A. The law of God; for, when any thing is enjoined contrary to it, the fixed rule is, to obey God rather than men, Acts iv. 19, and v. 29.
Q. 11. What is it that procures honour from one person to another?
A. It is something of eminence, excellency, or worth, that is discernible in them, Acts x. 25.
Q. 12. Are there not different degrees of external honour due to some beyond others?
A. Yes: according to the different office and stations in which God places them in the world, 1 Tim. v. 1, 2.
Q. 13. What is that degree of honour which the meanest and lowest part of mankind are entitled to, from the greatest and highest?
A. It is to be esteemed and regarded by them, in proportion as they are necessary and useful, Eph. vi. 9.
Q. 14. Why are we commanded to honour all men? 1 Pet. ii. 17.
A. Because there are few or none, in whom we may not observe some gift or other, in which they are superior to us, if we were to judge ourselves humbly and impartially, Phil. ii. 3.
Q. 15. Are men to be honoured according to their riches?
A. No; but according as they employ their riches, in some measure, for the good of others, either in the church or commonwealth, 1 Tim. vi. 17, 18.
Q. 16. What are the several relations in which duties are mutually to be performed, according to this commandment?
A. They are such as subsist between parents and children; magistrates and subjects; ministers and people; husbands and wives; masters and servants; and likewise between those who have a greater or less degree of gifts and graces.
Q. 17. Who are they that have the first and natural right to honour and respect?
A. *Natural Parents;* fathers and mothers.
Q. 18. Is equal honour and regard due from children to their mother as to their father?

A. Yes, surely; and therefore, to prevent any difference, in respect of esteem, reverence, and obedience, she is named before the father, in Lev. xix. 3: "Ye shall fear every man his mother and his father."

Q. 19. What are the duties of parents to their children?

A. To train them up for God, Prov. xxii. 6, in the knowledge and profession of the true religion, Deut. vi. 7; to teach them by example, as well as precept, Ps. ci. 2, 3; to be careful in applying suitable and seasonable correction to their faults, Prov. xiii. 24, and xix. 18, and xxiii. 13, 14; to provide for them according to their ability, 2 Cor. xii. 14; and to be earnest in prayer to God for a blessing upon them, Gen. xlviii. 15, 16.

Q. 20. What are the duties of children to their parents?

A. To love them dearly, Gen. xlvi. 29; to esteem and think highly of them in their minds, Lev. xix. 3, Mal. i. 6; to hearken to their counsels, Prov. iv. 1, and obey their lawful commands, Eph. vi. 1; to submit patiently to their corrections, Heb. xii. 9; and to succour and relieve them in case of poverty and want, Gen. xlvii. 12, especially in old age, Ruth iv. 15.

Q. 21. May children dispose of themselves in marriage without the knowledge or consent of their parents?

A. No; as appears from the charge given by Abraham, concerning his son Isaac, Gen. xxiv. 3, 4, and that of Isaac to Jacob, chap. xxviii. 1, 2; but if children should dispose of themselves without the knowledge and consent of their parents, they act contrary to the honour, deference, and gratitude they owe to them, as Esau did, Gen. xxvi. 34, 35.

Q. 22. What are the duties of magistrates towards their subjects?

A. To establish good laws, 2 Kings xviii. 4, and see them impartially executed, Rom. xiii. 3, 4; to protect their subjects in their religion, lives, and liberties, 1 Pet. ii. 14; and to be nursing fathers to the church, Isa. xlix. 23.

Q. 23. What are the duties of subjects towards their magistrates?

A. To honour and reverence them, 2 Sam. ix. 6; to obey their just laws, Eccl. viii. 2; to pay them the tribute that is due to them, Rom. xiii. 7; to pray for them, 1 Tim. ii. 1, 2; and to support and defend their persons and authority, 1 Sam. xxvi. 15, 16. Esth. vi. 2.

Q. 24. Are subjects bound to be obsequious to the lawful commands of magistrates, who are of a different religion from them?

A. "Infidelity, or difference in religion, doth not make void the magistrate's just and legal authority, nor free the people from their due obedience to him."*

* Confession, chap. xxiii. § 4.

Q. 25. What are the duties of ministers to their people

A. Diligently to study, 1 Tim. iv. 15; and faithfully to preach the gospel, 2 Tim. iv. 2; not shunning to declare to them all the counsel of God, Acts xx. 27; to evidence their own belief of their doctrine, by a holy and exemplary walk, 1 Tim. iv. 12; to watch for their souls as they that must give account, Heb. xiii. 17; and to pray much for them, Rom. i. 9: all which duties require their ordinary residence among them, 1 Pet. v. 2.

Q. 26. What are the duties of people to their ministers?

A. To esteem them very highly in love for their work's sake, 1 Thess. v. 13; to strive together in their prayers to God for them, Rom. xv. 30, that they may be enabled to give them their portion of meat in due season, Luke xii 42; to attend diligently upon the ordinances dispensed by them, Heb. x. 25; to defend their character and doctrine against unjust calumnies and reproaches, 1 Tim. v. 19; and to make a competent and comfortable provision for them, Gal. vi. 6.

Q. 27. What are the duties mutually incumbent upon husband and wife?

A. The most tender and affectionate love, on both sides, Eph. v. 28, 33; the strictest fidelity to the marriage-bed and covenant, Matt. v. 28; and the promoting the temporal and spiritual welfare of each other, 1 Tim. v. 8. 1 Pet. iii. 7.

Q. 28. What are the duties of masters to their servants?

A. To be meek and gentle towards them, forbearing threatening, Eph. vi. 9; to instruct them in the principles of religion, Gen. xviii. 19; to see to their external observance of the Sabbath, Ex. xx. 10; and to pay them punctually their wages, Deut. xxiv. 15.

Q. 29. What are the duties of servants to their masters?

A. To be diligent and faithful in their master's work, "not with eye-service, as men-pleasers, but—with good will, doing service as to the Lord, and not to men," Eph. vi. 6, 7; to obey in all things their masters according to the flesh, Col. iii. 22; and to please them well in all things, not answering again, Tit. ii. 9.

Q. 30. Are masters and servants on earth, subject to one common Lord and Master in heaven?

A. Yes; and therefore they ought to behave towards one another, as in his sight; for there is no respect of persons with him, Eph. vi. 9.

Q. 31. What are the duties of those who have a larger measure of gifts and graces conferred upon them, towards such as have a less share of the same?

A. To be exemplary in humility and self-denial, Gen. xxxiii. 10, as having nothing but what they have received, 1 Cor. iv. 7; to be communicative of what the Lord has freely given them, Matt. x. 8; and improve their talents for the benefit of themselves and others, chap. xxv. 16.

Q. 32. What are the duties of such as are weaker in gifts and graces, towards those that are stronger?

A. To be followers of them in so far as they are of Christ, 1 Cor. xi. 1; to be willing to learn from their experiences, Heb. vi. 12; and to covet earnestly the best gifts, 1 Cor. xii. 31.

Q. 33. What is the duty of the younger towards the aged?

A. To honour and respect them, especially if the hoary head be found in the way of righteousness, Prov. xvi. 31: "Thou shalt rise up before the hoary head, and honour the face of the old man," Lev. xix. 32.

Q. 34. What are the duties of equals to one another?

A. To provoke each other unto love and good works, Heb. x. 24; "to be kindly affectioned one to another, in honour preferring one another," Rom. xii. 10.

Q. 35. What is the fruit and consequence of the conscientious performance of these relative duties?

A. Hereby outward peace and concord will be better maintained between man and man, 1 Pet. iii. 10, 11; and likewise the members of Christ's body will be knit more closely to one another in love, 1 John. iv. 7.

QUEST. 65. *What is forbidden in the fifth commandment?*

ANS. The fifth commandment forbiddeth the neglecting of, or doing any thing against, the honour and duty, which belong to every one in their several places and relations.

Q. 1. What is it to neglect the honour and duty which belong to every one in their several places and relations?

A. It is not only to omit the performance of such relative duties altogether, but even when they are performed, to do them without any regard to the command and authority of God enjoining them, Isa. xxix. 13.

Q. 2. What is it to do any thing against the honour and duty which belong to every one?

A. It is to commit those sins which are the very opposite of the relative duties incumbent on us, Rom. ii. 22.

Q. 3. "What are the sins of inferiors against their superiors?"

A. "Envying at, contempt of, and rebellion against their persons and places, in their lawful counsels, commands, and corrections."*

* Larger Catechism, Quest. 128.

Q. 4. "What are the sins of superiors?"
A. "— Commanding things unlawful, or not in the power of inferiors to perform; counselling, encouraging, or favouring them in that which is evil;" and "dissuading, discouraging, or discountenancing them in that which is good—"*

Q. 5. "What are the sins of equals?"
A. "— Envying the gifts, grieving at the advancement or prosperity one of another, and usurping the pre-eminence one over another." †

Q. 6. What punishment did the law of Moses inflict upon children, for smiting or cursing their parents?
A. *Death*, Ex. xxi. 15: "He that smiteth his father, or his mother, shall surely be put to *death.*" And verse 17: "He that curseth his father, or his mother, shall surely be put to *death.*"

Q. 7. Why was so severe a punishment inflicted for these crimes?
A. Because either beating or cursing of parents is a sin directly opposite to the light and law of nature, and a pregnant evidence, not only of the worst kind of ingratitude, but of incurable disobedience; and therefore the equity of this punishment seems to be approved by our Lord under the New Testament, Matt. xv. 4.

QUEST. 66. *What is the reason annexed to the fifth commandment?*

ANS. The reason annexed to the fifth commandment is a promise of long life and prosperity (as far as it shall serve for God's glory, and their own good) to all such as keep this commandment.

Q. 1. Does the [promise] annexed to this commandment, respect temporal or spiritual good?
A. It respects temporal good, to show that "godliness is profitable unto all things, having the promise of the life that now is, as well as of that which is to come," 1 Tim. iv. 8.

Q. 2. What is the temporal good here promised?
A. It is [long life;] in these words, That thy days may be long upon the land which the Lord thy God giveth thee.

Q. 3. Is it long life merely that is promised, without any thing else?
A. No; it is long life [and prosperity,] or the blessings

* Larger Catechism, Quest 130. † Ibid. Q. 132.

and comforts of life; without which, long life would be a grievous burden, Rev. ix. 6.

Q. 4. Has not this promise a particular reference to obedient children among the Jews, their living long in the land of Judea, which God gave to them?

A. Any reference it had to them, is not exclusive of a reference or relation to children that shall honour their parents, in any other part of the earth, to the end of the world; for so the apostle explains it, Eph. vi. 2, 3: "Honour thy father and thy mother—that it may be well with thee, and that thou mayest live long on the earth."

Q. 5. What is the difference between the promise of long life in this commandment, and the promise of mercy in the second?

A. The promise of showing mercy, in the second commandment, extends to all such as love God, and keep his commandments in general; but the promise of long life here, extends only to the keepers of this commandment in particular.

Q. 6. Has this promise always a literal accomplishment; or, do godly and obedient children always live long on earth?

A. If any of them are removed by death, in their younger years, it is either to take them away from the evil to come, Isa. lvii. 1; or to transplant them, so much sooner, to a better country, that is, a heavenly, Heb. xi. 16.

Q. 7. What are the things which tend to make a long life a happy and comfortable one?

A. They are these three, among others; growth in grace and holiness, in proportion to our advancing in years, Ps. xcii. 13, 14; retaining the entire exercise of reason, and some vigour of body, in old age, Deut. xxxiv. 7; and continuing useful to others, in our generation, to the end, Josh. xxiv. 25, compared with ver. 29.

Q. 8. Why is the fifth commandment called the first commandment with promise? Eph. vi. 2.

A. Because it is the first commandment of the second table, and the only commandment in it, that has an express promise annexed to it.

Q. 9. Why is there a special and express promise annexed to this commandment, when it is so strongly enforced by the light of nature?

A. To show the great regard that God has to the lawful authority of parents, Deut. xxi. 18—22; and to engage children to behave dutifully and obsequiously towards them, Prov. iv. 10.

Q. 10. Is the promise of long life, in this commandment, absolute or limited?

A. It is limited, and that in the most comfortable manner.

Q. 11. What is the comfortable limitation?
A. Long life, with prosperity, is promised [as far as it shall serve for God's glory and their own good.]

Q. 12. Could any wish for long life and prosperity upon other terms?
A. No child of God will desire any temporal blessing, but as it is for God's glory and their good, Prov. xxx. 8.

Q. 13. What advantage have the godly, with respect to temporal blessings, above the wicked?
A. They are warranted by promise, which the wicked are not, to expect as many temporal good things, as are needful and necessary for them, Ps. xxxiv. 10, Isa. xxxiii. 16: and God's blessing upon what they enjoy, however small their portion of temporal comforts may be, Ps. xxxvii. 16: "A little that a righteous man hath, is better than the riches of many wicked."

QUEST. 67. *Which is the sixth commandment?*

ANS. The sixth commandment is, *Thou shalt not kill.*

QUEST. 68. *What is required in the sixth commandment?*

ANS. The sixth commandment requireth all lawful endeavours to preserve our own life, and the life of others.

Q. 1. What does this commandment chiefly respect?
A. The [*life*] of man, which is the nearest and most valuable of all his temporal concerns, Job ii. 4: Skin for skin ; yea, all that a man hath will he give for his life.

Q. 2. What makes the life of man valuable?
A. His being made in the image of God, Gen. ix. 6.

Q. 3. What does this commandment require with reference to man's life?
A. [All lawful endeavours to preserve] it, in ourselves and others.

Q. 4. What lawful endeavours should we use for the preservation of [our own] life?
A. The "just defence thereof against violence;—a sober use of meat, drink, physic, sleep, labour, and recreation." *

Q. 5. By what means should we endeavour to preserve [the life of others?]
A. "By resisting all thoughts and purposes, subduing all passions and avoiding all occasions, temptations, and practices, which tend to the unjust taking away the life of any."†

* Larger Catechism, Question 135.   † Ibid

104 DUTIES REQUIRED IN THE SIXTH COMMANDMENT.

Q. 6. Why are we restricted by the answer to [lawful endeavours?]

A. To caution and guard us against the unlawful means which some have used, for the preservation of their lives.

Q. 7. What are the unlawful means which some have used for this end?

A. Denying the truth, 1 Tim. i. 19, 20, and lying, Gen. xii. 12, 13.

Q. 8. What will be the consequence of denying the truth, for preserving of natural life?

A. The losing of a better life than that which we thus intend to preserve, Matt. xvi. 25, 26.

Q. 9. May not a lie be told at a time, for preserving life, especially if its preservation be for the public good?

A. At no time, and on no occasion whatever, are we to do evil that good may come, Rom. iii. 8.

Q. 10. Are we restricted, by this commandment, to the preservation of bodily life only?

A. No; we are also required to consult the welfare of our own souls, and the souls of others.

Q. 11. What is required of us for the welfare of our own souls?

A. A careful avoiding of all sin, Prov. xi. 19; and a diligent use of all the means of grace, 1 Pet. ii. 2.

Q. 12. What is required of us for promoting the welfare of the souls of others?

A. That we be communicative of our knowledge and experiences to them as occasion offers, Ps. lxvi. 16; that we pray for them, James v. 16; and that we set an example of holy walking before them, Matt. v. 16.

Q. 13. What are those Christian virtues or graces which this commandment requires, in order to the preservation of life?

A. It requires for this end, "love, compassion, meekness, gentleness, kindness—and comforting, and succouring the distressed."*

Q. 14. Why should we bear a love to mankind in general?

A. Because they are partakers of the same nature, and possessed of the same rational faculties with us, Acts xvii. 26, 28.

Q. 15. How does love contribute to the preservation of life?

A. It covers all those infirmities, and buries all those quarrels which tend to raise strife and variance among men, Prov. x. 12.

Q. 16. What influence has compassion, upon the duty here required?

* Larger Catechism, Q. 135.

A. It affects us so deeply with the calamities and miseries of our fellow creatures, that it inclines us to relieve them according to our ability, Luke x. 33, 34.

Q. 17. How does meekness tend to preserve life?

A. As it governs our passions, Prov. xiv. 29, and prevents our being easily disturbed at the unkind and unmannerly treatment of others, Col. iii. 13.

Q. 18. How does gentleness contribute to the duty here mentioned?

A. As it excites to an affable and courteous behaviour towards all with whom we are conversant, 1 Pet. iii. 8, and disposes us to put the most favourable construction upon any of their actions that may appear doubtful, 1 Cor. xiii. 5.

Q. 19. What influence has kindness upon preserving life?

A. As it excites us to the performance of all good offices in our power, both to the souls and bodies of men, Rom. xii. 10, 12.

Q. 20. What should engage us to comfort and succour the distressed?

A. A desire to honour the Lord with our substance, Prov. iii. 9; and to lend to him, who will surely pay us again, chap. xix. 17.

Quest. 69. *What is forbidden in the sixth commandment?*

Ans. The sixth commandment forbiddeth the taking away of our own life or the life of our neighbour unjustly, and whatsoever tendeth thereunto.

Q. 1. Does this precept [thou shalt not kill] prohibit the killing of beasts?

A. No: God made a grant of them to man for food, and other uses, Gen. ix. 3, and iii. 21: nevertheless, the exercising cruelty upon beasts (as Balaam did, Num. xxii. 29,) is very unbecoming all sober men; for a righteous man regardeth the life of his beast, Prov. xii. 10.

Q. 2. Were not the Jews prohibited to seethe a kid in his mother's milk, Deut. xiv. 21, and to kill the dam when they took the young? chap. xxii. 6, 7.

A. As the doing either of these was an evidence of the savage disposition and temper of some men; so the reason of the prohibition, was to curb and restrain all cruelty to the brute creatures, in order to prevent any inlet to the horrid sin of murder, or the barbarous usage of one another.

Q. 3. What are the general sins here forbidden?

A. [The taking away of our own life, or the life of our neighbour unjustly,] or whatever has a tendency to either of the two.

Q. 4. Is it lawful, in any case, to take away [our own life?]

A. No: it is absolutely unlawful, in any case whatever, to desert our station, or leave the world, without the permission and allowance of the sovereign Lord of our life, Job xiv. 14.

Q. 5. Is there any instance in scripture of a good man being suffered to lay violent hands on himself?

A. No: any instances the scripture gives of self-murder, are in men of the most infamous character; such as Saul, Ahithophel, Judas, and others of the like stamp.

Q. 6. Was not Samson (who was a good man, Heb. xi. 32,) guilty of this heinous crime? Judges xvi. 30.

A. When Samson pulled down the house upon himself, and upon all the lords of the Philistines, with about three thousand men and women that were in it, he did not intend his own death any farther than as an inevitable consequence of destroying so many of the church's enemies, to which he was called and strengthened in an extraordinary manner by God, as the Lord of life and death, whom he also supplicated for this extraordinary strength, Judges xvi. 28: and herein he was an eminent type of Christ, "who, through death, destroyed him that had the power of death, that is, the devil," Heb. ii. 14.

Q. 7. What are the aggravations of the crime of self murder?

A. It is directly opposed to the natural principle of self-preservation implanted in us, Job ii. 4; it argues the highest impatience, and rooted discontent with our lot in the present world, ver. 19: it is an impious invasion of the prerogative of God, as the sole author and disposer of life, 1 Sam. ii. 6; and a most daring and presumptuous rushing upon death, and an awful eternity, chap. xxxi. 4, 5.

Q. 8. What is meant in the answer, by taking away [the life of our neighbour unjustly?]

A. The taking it away in any event, "except in case of public justice, lawful war, or necessary defence." *

Q. 9. What is it to take away life in case of public justice?

A. It is to inflict capital punishment upon notorious criminals, by a lawful magistrate, who is ordained of God for that purpose, Rom. xiii. 2, 4.

* Larger Catechism, Quest. 136.

Q. 10. What warrant has the civil magistrate to take away the life of a wilful murderer?
A. The express command of God, Gen. ix. 6: "Whoso sheddeth man's blood, by man shall his blood be shed."
Q. 11. Is it lawful to wage war under the New Testament?
A. Yes: as appears from John the Baptist's prescribing rules for a military life, Luke iii. 14; and Christ's commending the faith of the centurion, and finding no fault with his office, Matt. viii. 10.
Q. 12. What makes war lawful, and the shedding of blood in it warrantable?
A. When it is undertaken in defence of civil or religious liberties, after all due means have been rejected, for obtaining redress of the unjust invasions made upon them, Judges xi. 12—34.
Q. 13. When is the killing of another to be sustained, as done in necessary defence?
A. When there is no way of flying from the aggressor, (which is rather to be chosen, if it can be done with safety,) but we must either lose our own life, or take away his, Ex. xxii. 2.
Q. 14. What if one kill another at unawares, or unwillingly?
A. If it is not through any culpable neglect, or careless oversight, it is not reputed murder, either by the law of God or man, and therefore cities of refuge were of old appointed for such, Josh. xx. 9.
Q. 15. How are men lavish and prodigal of their lives on points of honour?
A. By duelling.
Q. 16. What is a duel?
A. It is a combat or fight between two private persons, upon a challenge given and accepted; in which each party aims at the life or maiming of the other.
Q. 17. In what lies the sinfulness of such a practice?
A. It flows from passion, pride, and insatiable revenge, as the springs of it; and is a bold invasion of God's right of vengeance, together with a desperate contempt of death, judgment, and eternity, Rom. xii. 19.
Q. 18. Did not David fight a duel with Goliath?
A. No; he fought by a peculiar divine impulse, under the sanction of lawful authority, for the public good, and not from any private or personal revenge, 1 Sam. xvii. 37—53.
Q. 19. Who was the first murderer of souls?
A. The devil, who is therefore called a murderer from the beginning, John viii. 44.
Q. 20. Who was the first murderer of the body?
A. Cain, who slew his brother, Gen. iv. 8.

Q. 21. Wherefore did he slay him?.
A. Because his own works were evil, and his brother's righteous, 1 John iii. 12.

Q. 22. Why was he not put to death?
A. Because God set a peculiar mark of his displeasure upon him, Gen. iv. 15, (worse, in some sort, than natural death,) by protracting his miserable life, to be a fugitive, and a vagabond in the earth, and a visible monument of an intolerable load of guilt, and hopeless despair, ver. 11, 12.

Q. 23. What is the dismal effect of this sin upon murderers themselves, even though they escape capital punishment from men?
A. God frequently gives them up to the terror of a guilty conscience, which is their continual tormentor, Gen. iv. 13, 14.

Q. 24. How has God testified his displeasure against this sin?
A. Ordinarily, by shortening the lives of murderers, Ps. lv. 23: Bloody and deceitful men shall not live out half their days: and sometimes by transmitting temporal judgments to their posterity; as Saul's murder of the Gibeonites was punished in the death of seven of his sons, 2 Sam. xxi. 6, 8, 9.

Q. 25. How may murder be aggravated?
A. If committed under pretence of religion, as Jezebel murdered Naboth, 1 Kings xxi. 9, 10; and as the Papists perpetrate their massacres; or, if done under the disguise and mask of friendship, as Joab killed Amasa, 2 Sam. xx. 9, 10; or, which is unspeakably worse, as Judas betrayed our Lord, Matt. xxvi. 48, 49.

Q. 26. Does this command forbid only the taking away of our own life, and the life of our neighbour unjustly?
A. It forbids also [whatsoever tends thereto.]

Q. 27. What are those things which tend to the taking away of our own life?
A. "Neglecting or withdrawing the lawful and necessary means of preserving it;—all excessive passions, distracting cares, and immoderate use of meat, drink, labour, and recreation." *

Q. 28. How may we be guilty before God, of taking away the life of our neighbour, though we do not actually imbrue our hands in his blood?
A. We may be guilty this way in our hearts, with our tongues, and by our actions.

Q. 29. How may we be guilty of murder in our hearts?
A. By harbouring "sinful anger, hatred, envy, and a desire of revenge."†

---

* Larger Catechism, Quest. 136, with the scriptures quoted.   † Ibid

Q. 30. May there be anger which is not sinful?

A. Yes: when there is a detestation of the sin, and yet no dislike of the person; in which sense the apostle says, "Be ye angry and sin not," Eph. iv. 26.

Q. 31. What is the hazard of sinful anger?

A. "Whosoever is angry with his brother, without a cause, shall be in danger of the judgment," Matt. v. 22.

Q. 32. What is it to be in danger of the judgment?

A. It is to be in danger of eternal punishment in the other world, for the breach of this commandment, if rich and sovereign grace prevent it not, Prov. xix. 19.

Q. 33. How does hatred tend to take away the life of our neighbour?

A. It has such a tendency to it, that whosoever hateth his brother is accounted a murderer, 1 John iii. 15.

Q. 34. What tendency has envy to the taking away of life?

A. As it is grieved at the good of another, or takes a secret pleasure in his death, Prov. xxvii. 4.

Q. 35. How does desire of revenge tend to take away life?

A. As it is accompanied with an inward habitual imprecation of some visible or remarkable judgment upon the person who is the object of it, quite contrary to the command of God, Rom. xii. 19: "Avenge not yourselves; —for it is written, Vengeance is mine; I will repay, saith the Lord."

Q. 36. How may we be guilty of what tends to take away the life of our neighbour with our tongues?

A. By bitter and provoking words, Prov. xii. 18; or threatening, reviling and deriding speeches, Matt. v. 22.

Q. 37. How may we be guilty, this way, by our actions?

A. By oppression, Ezek. xviii. 18; quarrelling, Gal. v. 15; striking or wounding, Num. xxxv. 21, and the like.

Q. 38. What may we learn from this commandment?

A. That however innocent we may be of the actual blood-shedding of others, yet we are still chargeable with the worst kind of murder, even that of our own souls, while we will not come to Christ, that we might have life, John v. 40, he being the only living and true way, chap. xiv. 6; and "no other name under heaven given among men whereby we must be saved," Acts iv. 12.

QUEST. 70. *What is the seventh commandment?*

ANS. The seventh commandment is, *Thou shalt not commit adultery.*

QUEST. 71. *What is required in the seventh commandment?*

ANS. The seventh commandment requireth the preservation of our own and our neighbour's chastity, in heart, speech, and behaviour.

Q. 1. What is [chastity?]
A. It is an abhorrence of all uncleanness, whether in the body, or in the mind and affections, Job xxxi. 1.

Q. 2. What does this commandment require with reference to such chastity?
A. [The preservation] of it, both in ourselves, and in our neighbours.

Q. 3. What is the best means for preserving our own and our neighbour's chastity?
A. The cherishing in our minds and consciences a continual regard, reverence, and awe of the divine Majesty, and a fear of displeasing him, Prov. v. 20, 21.

Q. 4. What influence will this have upon the preservation of chastity?
A. It will make us boldly resist all assaults or attacks that may be made upon it; as in the instance of Joseph, when solicited by his master's wife to lie with her, he refused; and said—"How can I do this great wickedness, and sin against God?" Gen. xxxix. 7—9.

Q. 5. Wherein are we to preserve [our own and our neighbour's chastity?]
A. [In heart, speech, and behaviour.]

Q. 6. How ought we [in heart] to preserve our own chastity?
A. By resisting the very first emotions of lust in the soul, Prov. iv. 23; by repelling all wanton imaginations, Matt. v. 28; and by essaying both these in the way of praying to God that he would turn away our hearts and eyes from beholding vanity, Ps. cxix. 37.

Q. 7. How ought we to preserve our [neighbour's chastity] in our hearts?
A. Not only by ardently desiring the preservation of it, but by loving one another with a pure heart fervently, 1 Pet. i. 22.

Q. 8. How ought we to preserve our own and our neighbour's chastity in our [speech?]
A. By "letting no corrupt communication proceed out of our mouth, but that which is good, to the use of edifying, that it may minister grace unto the hearers," Eph. iv. 29.

Q. 9. How should we do this in our [behaviour?]

A. By such a uniform modesty in our conduct and deportment, as may evidence that every one of us possesses his vessel, (that is, his body,) in sanctification and honour, 1 Thess. iv. 4.

Q. 10. Why should we be so careful to preserve our chastity?

A. Because we should study to have our bodies to be the temples of the Holy Ghost, and therefore should keep them free from those pollutions which are so provoking to a holy God, 1 Cor. vi. 19.

Q. 11. What is the ordinary mean of divine appointment for the preservation of chastity?

A. Lawful wedlock or marriage, 1 Cor. vii. 2: "Nevertheless, to avoid fornication, let every man have his own wife, and let every woman have her own husband."

Q. 12. When was marriage first instituted?

A. Before the fall, in paradise, Gen. ii. 24.

Q. 13. For what end was it instituted?

A. "For the mutual help of husband and wife, Gen. ii. 18; for the increase of mankind with a legitimate issue, and of the church with a holy seed, Mal. ii. 15; and for preventing of uncleanness," 1 Cor. vii. 2.*

Q. 14. What is necessary to constitute marriage?

A. The voluntary and mutual consent of both parties, Gen. xxiv. 58, 67.

Q. 15. Who may be lawfully married?

A. "All sorts of people, who are able, with judgment, to give their consent," Heb. xiii. 4: "Marriage is honourable in all." †

Q. 16. What is the duty of Christians with reference to marriage?

A. It is to marry only in the Lord, 1 Cor. vii. 39.

Q. 17. What is the native import of marrying "only in the Lord?"

A. It plainly imports, that "such as profess the true reformed religion should not marry with infidels, Papists, or other idolaters: neither should such as are godly be unequally yoked, by marrying with such as are notoriously wicked in their life, or maintain damnable heresies." ‡

Q. 18. What is an incestuous marriage?

A. It is that which is within the degrees of consanguinity, or affinity, forbidden in the word, Lev. xviii. 6—18.

Q. 19. What is the meaning of the words consanguinity and affinity?

A. *Consanguinity* is a relation by blood, being between persons descended from the same family: *Affinity* is an alliance by marriage, between persons who were not blood relations before.

---

* Confession, chap. xxiv. § 2.   † Ibid. § 3.
‡ Confession of Faith, chap. xxiv. § 3, with the scripture proofs.

Q. 20. What is the general rule for preventing incestuous marriages?

A. "The man may not marry any of his wife's kindred nearer in blood than he may of his own: nor the woman of her husband's kindred nearer in blood than of her own."*

Q. 21. Is it proper to call marriage a *holy* state?

A. No; because they who are without the visible church, such as heathens, Turks, and Jews, may marry as well as the professed members of it, Heb. xiii. 4.

Q. 22. Was marriage instituted to signify the "mystical union that is between Christ and his church," as the Book of Common Prayer affirms?

A. No; because this borders too near upon making marriage a sacrament, as the Papists do; in as much as an outward visible sign, of divine institution, and a spiritual benefit signified by it, would make it partake of the nature of a sacrament.

Q. 23. Does not the apostle make it a significant sign, when he says, "Husbands, love your wives, even as Christ loved the church?" Eph. v. 25.

A. He exhorts husbands to have such a love to their wives, as may bear a faint resemblance in some respects, to the love of Christ; but does not make the one a sign significant of the other.

Q. 24. Is not marriage called a great mystery? ver. 32.

A. It is not marriage that is called a great mystery, but the union that is between Christ and the members of his mystical body; as will appear by reading the whole verse, "This is a great mystery; but I speak concerning *Christ* and the *Church*."

QUEST. 72. *What is forbidden in the seventh commandment?*

ANS. The seventh commandment forbiddeth all unchaste thoughts, words, and actions.

Q. 1. What is forbidden in this commandment under the name of *Adultery?*

A. All sorts of unchastity or uncleanness, of what kind, or in what manner soever committed, Eph. v. 3.

Q. 2. In what respects may persons be guilty of unchastity or uncleanness?

A. They may be guilty this way, in their [thoughts, words, and actions.]

* Confession of Faith, § 4.

IN THE SEVENTH COMMANDMENT.

Q. 3. When are persons chargeable before God with unchaste [thoughts?]

A. When lustful desires are entertained and gratified in the mind; and, as it were, acted in the imagination, Prov. vi. 18, Matt. v. 28.

Q. 4. What are the usual incentives to unchaste thoughts?

A. "Lascivious songs, books, pictures, dancings, stageplays, and the like."*

Q. 5. What influence have stage-plays upon fomenting unchaste thoughts?

A. They are generally stuffed with such amorous adventures, many of them of a most criminal nature, that they have a native tendency to debauch and defile the mind. If no corrupt communication is to proceed out of our mouth, according to Eph. iv. 29, neither ought we to listen to it with our ears, as is done by those who attend the profane diversions of the stage.

Q. 6. What is meant by unchaste [words?]

A. All filthy, obscene, or smutty discourse; than which, nothing can be more grating and disagreeable to modest ears, Eph. v. 4.

Q. 7. What are the unchaste [actions] that are forbidden in this commandment?

A. Besides several others, that ought not to be named among Heathens, far less Christians, there are these following: polygamy, unjust divorce, fornication, and adultery, properly so called.

Q. 8. What is *Polygamy*?

A. It is the having more wives or husbands than one at the same time, Mal. ii. 14.

Q. 9. Is this a sin contrary to the law of nature?

A. Yes; for it is contrary to the first institution of marriage; God having created but one woman, as a help meet for man; Gen. ii. 22—25, compared with Matt. xix. 5, 6.

Q. 10. Is it a sin prohibited in scripture?

A. Yes; Lev. xviii. 18: "Thou shalt not take a wife to her sister, to vex her—in her lifetime."

Q. 11. What is the meaning of taking a wife to her sister?

A. The meaning is, (according to the marginal reading,) Thou shalt not take one wife to another; that is, thou shalt not have more wives than one at a time.

Q. 12. But may not this be a prohibition of incest, namely, of marrying the wife's sister?

A. No; because it is said, Thou shalt not do it in her lifetime; whereas it would be incestuous in a man to marry his sister-in-law, after his wife's death, as well as to do it in her lifetime; so that the meaning is, Thou shalt not take

---

* Larger Catechism, Question 139

another wife to her whom thou hast married, by which means they would become sisters.

Q. 13. Who was the first polygamist we read of in scripture?

A. Lamech, of the posterity of Cain, who had two wives, Gen. iv. 19.

Q. 14. Were not several of the godly likewise guilty in this matter, as Abraham, Jacob, David, Solomon, and others?

A. Yes; but though these and other bad actions of good men are recorded in scripture, they are not approved of, nor proposed for our imitation; but rather set up as beacons, to prevent our making shipwreck on the same rocks.

Q. 15. Has not God even testified his displeasure at the sin of polygamy, in the godly, though we do not read of his reproving them for it in express words?

A. Yes: he has testified his displeasure in the course of his providence, by the emulations, quarrels, and disturbances, that were thus occasioned in their families; as in the instances of Sarah and Hagar, in Abraham's family, Gen. xxi. 10, 11; of Leah and Rachel, in Jacob's, Gen. xxx. 1, 15; and of Hannah and Peninnah, in Elkanah's family, 1 Sam. i. 6.

Q. 16. Does not God seem to approve of polygamy, when he says to David, "I gave thee thy master's wives into thy bosom?" 2 Sam. xii. 8.

A. It being the custom of those times, for succeeding kings to take possession of all that belonged to their predecessors, the meaning is, I have made thee king, in room of Saul, and have given thee the property of all that appertained to him: but we do not read of David taking any of Saul's wives into his bed.

Q. 17. What is an unjust *divorce?*

A. It is the prosecuting and obtaining a dissolution of marriage, upon other grounds than such as are warranted in the word of God, and by right reason.

Q. 18. What are the grounds upon which a divorce may be sued for, and obtained, according to the word of God and right reason?

A. "Although the corruption of man be such as is apt to study arguments, unduly to put asunder those whom God hath joined together in marriage; yet nothing but adultery, or such wilful desertion, as can no way be remedied by the church or civil magistrate, is cause sufficient of dissolving the bond of marriage, Matt. xix. 8, 9. 1 Cor. vii. 15."*

Q. 19. Did not Moses suffer the Israelites to put away their wives, upon slighter grounds than that of adultery as may be alleged from Deut. xxiv. 1?

* Confession of Faith, chap. xxiv. § 6.

A. Moses, in the text cited, gives no positive command about divorces in such cases; but only, in order to restrain the licentious freedom of the Israelites, in turning off their wives, at their own hand, upon every trivial occasion, he enjoins that none put away his wife, but upon a legal process or a bill of divorce, obtained in the ordinary course of law; which is the true meaning of the place.

Q. 20. Why then does our Lord tell the Pharisees, Matt. xix. 8, "Moses, because of the hardness of your hearts, suffered you to put away your wives?"

A. The meaning is, Moses, because of the wicked and malicious disposition of the Jews, and in order to prevent a greater evil, namely, the ill usage, or even killing of their hated wives, (if they could not be separated from them) permitted processes of divorce to be legally commenced.

Q. 21. Why is it added, "but from the beginning it was not so?"

A. Because, according to the original institution of marriage, nothing could dissolve it but the death of one of the parties, Matt. xix. 6: "Wherefore they are no more twain, but one flesh. What, therefore, God hath joined together, let no man put asunder."

Q. 22. Is it lawful to marry after a divorce is obtained?

A. "It is lawful for the innocent party to sue out a divorce; and after the divorce, to marry another, as if the offending party were dead." *

Q. 23. Is the innocent party obliged, from Matt. v. 32, to sue for a divorce?

A. No: divorces are not enjoined as a precept, but allowed as a privilege, which the innocent party may claim, or not, as they please.

Q. 24. What if the adultery be on both sides?

A. In that case the right of divorce seems to be taken away from each of them.

Q. 25. What is *fornication?*

A. It is uncleanness committed between a man and a woman, both of them being unmarried; as it would seem Shechem and Dinah were, when guilty this way, Gen. xxxiv. 2.

Q. 26. Was this esteemed a sin among the Heathens?

A. No: they made light of it, (as too many professed Christians have always done:) hence the synod of Jerusalem enjoined the converted Gentiles to abstain from fornication, Acts xv. 29.

Q. 27. In what lies the evil of this sin?

A. It defiles the body, 1 Cor. vi. 18; stupefies the conscience, Hos. iv. 11; and exposes to eternal wrath and damnation, 1 Cor. vi. 9.

* Confession of Faith, chap. xxiv. section 5.

Q. 28. What is *adultery* properly so called?
A. It is uncleanness committed between a man and a woman, either both or one of them at least, in a married relation.

Q. 29. What is it commonly called when both the guilty persons are married?
A. It is called double adultery, as was the case between David and Bathsheba, 2 Sam. xi. 3, 4.

Q. 30. Whether are the consequences to families worse, when the man is married and the woman free; or when the woman is married and the man free?
A. The consequences to families seem to be worse when the woman is married; because a man's offspring is thus corrupted, and his inheritance is alienated to a spurious issue.

Q. 31. What are the aggravations of this heinous sin?
A. It is a breach of the marriage oath, Mal. ii. 14; an involving of two at once in the same guilt, 1 Cor. vi. 16; and is a crime committed after obtaining the remedy which God has provided against it, chap. vii. 2.

Q. 32. What are the fatal effects of adultery in this life?
A. It consumes the body, Prov. v. 11; wastes a man's estate, bringing him to a piece of bread, chap. vi. 26; and leaves an indelible blot upon his name: His reproach shall not be wiped away, ver. 33.

Q. 33. What will be the effect of it in the life to come?
A. Eternal wrath and damnation, if rich mercy and grace prevent it not, Eph. v. 5.

Q. 34. How does God testify his abhorrence of this sin?
A. By declaring that he will reserve the punishment of it, in his own hand, to be inflicted in a very peculiar manner, upon such as are guilty of it, Heb. xiii. 4: Whoremongers and adulterers God will judge.

Q. 35. What are the usual incentives to this and other acts of uncleanness?
A. Drunkenness, Gen. xix. 33; fulness of bread, and abundance of idleness, Ezek. xvi. 49.

Q. 36. What is the evil of idleness?
A. It is a deliberate wasting of precious time, to the manifest detriment both of soul and body, Eccl. x. 18; and is a fit season for temptations to lust, Prov. vii. 7, 8.

Q. 37. In what consists the evil of gluttony?
A. It indisposes for all duty, both religious and civil, Prov. xxiii. 21; and is making a god of our belly, Phil. iii. 19.

Q. 38. What is the evil of drunkenness?
A. It deforms the image of God in the soul, by divesting a man of the right use of his reason; and leaves him defenceless against all temptations, Prov. xxiii. 29, 30.

Q. 39. What are the proper remedies against lust, and all the incentives to it?
A. A serious reflection upon the all-seeing eye of an infinitely holy God, Gen. xxxix. 9; walking in the Spirit, which will preserve us from fulfilling the lusts of the flesh, Gal. v. 16; keeping a strict watch over our hearts, Prov. iv. 23; studying to shun all occasions of this sin by the external senses, Job xxxi. 1; and fervent prayer to God to be kept from it, and all temptations to it, Ps. cxix. 37.

QUEST. 73. *Which is the eighth commandment?*

ANS. The eighth commandment is *Thou shalt not steal.*

QUEST. 74. *What is required in the eighth commandment?*

ANS. The eighth commandment requireth the lawful procuring and furthering the wealth and outward estate of ourselves and others.

Q. 1. What is the subject matter of this commandment?
A. [The wealth and outward estate of ourselves and others.]
Q. 2. What does it require with reference to these?
A. [The procuring and furthering] of them.
Q. 3. In what manner does it enjoin us to procure and further them?
A. Only in a [lawful] manner; for it requires the *lawful* procuring and furthering of them.
Q. 4. Whose wealth is it we should procure and further?
A. Our own wealth, and that of others.
Q. 5. By what lawful means should we procure and further *our own* wealth?
A. By labour and industry in some honest calling, Eph. iv. 28.
Q. 6. What is included in the labour and industry we should exercise in our respective stations and callings?
A. Frugality in managing the affairs of our calling, and a moderate endeavour to recover our own when wrongfully detained from us.
Q. 7. What is to be understood by frugality in managing the affairs of our calling?
A. Prudence and moderation in our expenses, so as to be sure always to spend within our incomes, Prov. xxxi. 16.

Q. 8. Is it warrantable to go to law, for recovering our own, when wrongfully detained?

A. Yes, surely; provided other means have been previously tried without success.

Q. 9. How do you prove that it is warrantable for Christians to go to law with one another, when urged by necessity?

A. From the lawfulness of magistracy, which is the ordinance of God, Rom. xiii. 2, for the punishment of evil doers, and for the praise of them that do well, 1 Pet. ii. 14.

Q. 10. Does not our Lord find fault with this method, when he says, "If any man will sue thee at the law, and take away thy coat, let him have thy cloak also?" Matt. v. 40.

A. The meaning is, that we should rather part with a little of our right, than run ourselves into unnecessary charges at law, perhaps vastly beyond the value of what we are seeking to regain; and thus discover a contentious and quarrelsome spirit, unbecoming Christianity.

Q. 11. Does not the apostle also blame Christians for this practice, when he says, "Ye go to law one with another; why do ye not rather take wrong?" 1 Cor. vi. 7.

A. The apostle is there speaking of bringing pleas unnecessarily before Heathen magistrates; and his meaning is, that Christians should make up differences among themselves, by submitting to arbitration; or even by suffering some wrong, rather than by vexatious law-suits, (especially about lesser matters) thus bringing a scandal upon the religion which they profess.

Q. 12. How is the necessity of labouring in an honest calling enforced in scripture?

A. From the necessity of eating: the apostle argues from the natural necessity of the one, to the moral necessity of the other, 2 Thess. iii. 10: "This we commanded you, that if any would not work, neither should he eat."

Q. 13. Can we procure and further our wealth and outward estate, merely by our own labour and industry?

A. Our own industry is necessary; but without the Lord's blessing upon it, it will not be successful; for it is the blessing of the Lord that maketh rich, Prov. x. 22.

Q. 14. What ends should we propose to ourselves, in endeavouring to further, or increase, our own outward estate?

A. That we may honour the Lord, with our substance, Prov. iii. 9; live comfortably ourselves, Eccl. v. 19; and be useful to others, Eph. iv. 28.

Q. 15. By what means should we procure and further the wealth and outward estate of others?

A. By exercising justice and righteousness towards all,

Ps. xv. 2; and by relieving the wants and necessities of those who stand in need of our charity, 1 John iii. 17.

Q. 16. What is the rule and standard of that justice and righteousness we should exercise towards all men?

A. That we so deal with others, as we would have them deal with us, if we were in their place or condition; or, that we should never do that to another, which, if we were in the other's place or circumstances, we would reckon to be unjust, Matt. vii. 12.

Q. 17. In what cases is this rule to be particularly applied, according to the scope of this commandment?

A. In all contracts, or matters of traffic and commerce between man and man; and likewise in making satisfaction for injuries.

Q. 18. How is it to be applied in contracts, or matters of traffic between man and man?

A. It is to be applied thus: that in buying and selling, there be always a just proportion between the price and the thing sold; or, that the sale be according to the worth or value of the goods, without taking the advantage of ignorance or poverty on either side, Gen. xxiii. 15, 16.

Q. 19. How may the worth and value of goods be known?

A. By this general maxim, That every thing is worth as much as it may be currently sold for.

Q. 20. May not the price of the same commodity vary and change at different times?

A. Yes; according to the plenty or scarcity of the commodity at the time of sale.

Q. 21. What satisfaction should be made to others, for taking or detaining what belongs to them, or in any manner defrauding them?

A. No other satisfaction is agreeable to God's will of precept, or will gain the approbation of men, but restitution, if the injuring party is ever capable to make it, Lev. vi. 2—6. 1 Sam. xii. 3.

Q. 22. What if the person to whom the restitution should be made, or his nearest of kin, cannot be found?

A. In that case, what has been unjustly detained ought to be given to the poor, or some pious use, Num. v. 8.

Q. 23. Is relieving the necessities of the poor a duty required in this commandment?

A. Yes; because it is a furthering the outward estate of our neighbour who is in want.

Q. 24. Why should we relieve the necessities of the poor?

A. Because, "He that hath pity upon the poor, lendeth to the Lord; and that which he hath given, will he pay him again," Prov. xix. 17.

Q. 25. Who are the proper objects of charity?

OF THE SINS FORBIDDEN

A. All who are in real poverty and want, and are not able to work; especially those who are of the household of faith, Gal. vi. 10.

Q. 26. How should our acts of charity be managed?

A. They should be conducted with prudence, namely, as our own circumstances will permit, and the necessity of the object requires, 1 John iii. 17.

Q. 27. When should we perform acts of charity?

A. Presently, if the necessities of those whom we are bound to relieve, call for present assistance, Prov. iii. 28.

Q. 28. What should we shun or avoid, in our acts of charity?

A. All ostentation, or a desire to be seen of men, and commended by them, Matt. vi. 2—5.

QUEST. 75. *What is forbidden in the eighth commandment?*

ANS. The eighth commandment forbiddeth whatsoever doth or may unjustly hinder our own or our neighbour's wealth or outward estate.

Q. 1. What does the forbidding of *Theft* necessarily suppose?

A. That there are distinct rights and properties among men, which cannot be justly invaded or encroached upon, Lev. vi. 4,

Q. 2. What would be the necessary consequences of a community of goods among men?

A. It would destroy traffic and commerce; abolish all acts of charity; encourage sloth and idleness; and if there were no right and property there could be no encroachment upon it by theft or stealing.

Q. 3. From whom are we forbidden to steal?

A. Both from ourselves and others.

Q. 4. How may we be said to steal from *ourselves?*

A. By idleness niggardliness, and prodigality.

Q. 5. How do we steal from ourselves, or impair our own estates, by idleness?

A. When we either live without a lawful calling, Prov. xix. 15; or neglect it, if we have any, chap. xviii. 9.

Q. 6. How may a person be said to steal from himself by niggardliness?

A. When he defrauds himself of the due use and comfort of that estate which God has given him, Eccl. vi. 2.

Q. 7. How do persons on the other hand, steal from themselves, by prodigality?

A. By being lavish and profuse in spending above their income, Prov. xxiii. 20, 21.

Q. 8. What is the sin which is more directly pointed at in this commandment?

A. It is stealing from *others;* or laying hands upon, and taking away unjustly, that which is the right and property of another.

Q. 9. How many ways may persons be said to steal from others, or [unjustly hinder their neighbour's wealth or outward estate?]

A. Several ways; particularly, by theft, robbery, resetting, defrauding, monopolizing, and taking unlawful usury.

Q. 10. What is theft?

A. It is the taking away clandestinely, or privily from another, that which is his, Lev. xix. 11.

Q. 11. How is theft commonly distinguished?

A. Into private and public.

Q. 12. What is private theft?

A. It is the taking away less or more of any private person's property, without their knowledge or consent, Obadiah ver. 5.

Q. 13. Against whom is public theft committed?

A. Both against the church and commonwealth.

Q. 14. How is public theft called, as committed against the church?

A. Either Simony or sacrilege.

Q. 15. What is Simony?

A. It is the buying and selling of ecclesiastical places and offices for money, or other good deeds; so called, from the wicked practice of Simon Magus, who offered the apostles "money, saying, Give me also this power, that on whomsoever I lay hands, he may receive the Holy Ghost," Acts viii. 18, 19.

Q. 16. What is sacrilege?

A. It is the taking away or alienating of any thing which has been dedicated to a sacred use, Prov. xx. 25, Mal. iii. 8.

Q. 17. Why are these called public theft, when, for the most part, they are privately committed?

A. Because they very much affect the public interest and welfare of the church; nothing having a greater tendency to her ruin, than Simoniacal compacts and sacrilegious usurpations.

Q. 18. In what consists public theft, as committed against the commonwealth?

A. In embezzling the current coin, or doing detriment to the public for private advantage, Rom. xiii. 7. Phil. ii. 4.

Q. 19. What is robbery or rapine?

A. It is the taking away the goods of another by violence and open force, Job xx. 19.

Q. 20. In what lies the aggravation of this crime?

A. In its being an avowed pillaging or plundering of our neighbour; and in being ordinarily accompanied with a threatening to take away his life, if ne ventures to make the least resistance, Judges ix. 25.

Q. 21. What is the evil of resetting, or receiving of what is taken away, whether by stealth or violence?

A. It is a manifest encouragement of, and participation with thieves and robbers in their sins, Ps. l. 18; and consequently, a coming under the same guilt and condemnation with them, Prov. xxix. 24.

Q. 22. How do men commonly defraud one another?

A. In buying, selling and borrowing.

Q. 23. How do they defraud in buying?

A. By depreciating and vilifying what they intend to buy, that they may have it cheaper than the value, Prov. xx. 14.

Q. 24. How do they defraud one another in selling?

A. By taking an unreasonable price, 1 Thess. iv. 6; or, cheating by false weights and measures, Deut. xxv. 13—15.

Q. 25. How do they defraud in borrowing?

A. When they borrow what they know they can never be able, in the ordinary course of providence, to pay, Ps. xxxvii. 21.

Q. 26. If a man's creditors compound with him for less than he owes, is he therefore discharged of the whole debt?

A. Though his creditors, for fear of losing all, may compound and discharge for a part, so that there can be no action in law for the remainder; yet, in the court of conscience, and before God, he is bound, if ever he is able, to pay every farthing: and, if he is an honest man, he will never reckon his substance his own, till he do it, Rom. xiii. 8.

Q. 27. How may servants defraud their masters?

A. By wasting their masters' goods, which they may have in their hands; and not working faithfully for their wages, Tit. ii. 9, 10.

Q. 28. How may masters defraud their servants?

A. By detaining from, or tricking them out of their wages, Lev. xix. 13; or by exacting of them too rigorous labour, Ex. v. 9.

Q. 29. What is it to monopolize?

A. It is to engross commodities, in order to enhance the price of them.

Q. 30. What is the worst kind of monopolizing or forestalling?

A. It is the buying up grain, or other provisions, in large quantities, in order to exact a higher price for them afterwards.

Q. 31. In what consists the evil of this sin?

A They who are guilty of it enrich themselves upon

the spoils of others, Ezek. xxii. 29; they grind the faces of the poor, Isa. iii. 15; and bring upon themselves the curse of the people, Prov. xi. 26: "He that withholdeth corn, the people shall *curse* him; but blessings shall be upon the head of him that selleth it."

Q. 32. What is it to take *usury*, according to the proper signification of the word?

A. It is to take gain, profit, or interest, for the loan of money.

Q. 33. What kind of usury or interest is lawful?

A. That which is moderate, easy, and no way oppressive, Deut. xxiii. 20, compared with Ex. xxii. 21.

Q. 34. How do you prove that moderate usury is lawful?

A. From the very light of nature, which teaches, that since the borrower proposes to gain by the loan, the lender should have a reasonable share of his profit, as a recompense for the use of his money, which he might otherwise have disposed of to his own advantage, 1 Cor. viii. 13.

Q. 35. What is the usury condemned in scripture, and by right reason?

A. It is the exacting of more interest or gain for the loan of money, than is settled by universal consent, and the laws of the land, Prov. xxviii. 8: "He that by usury, and unjust gain, increaseth his substance, shall gather it for him that will pity the poor."

Q. 36. How do you prove from scripture, that moderate usury, or common interest, is not oppression in itself?

A. From the express command laid upon the Israelites not to oppress a stranger, Ex. xxiii. 9; and yet their being allowed to take usury from him, Deut. xxiii. 20; which they would not have been permitted to do, if there had been an intrinsic evil in the thing itself.

Q. 37. Is it warrantable to take interest from the poor?

A. By no means; for, if such as are honest, and in needy circumstances, borrow a small sum towards a livelihood, and repay it in due time, it is all that can be expected of them; and therefore the demanding of any profit or interest, or even taking any of their necessaries of life in pledge, for the sum, seems to be plainly contrary to the law of charity, Ex. xxii. 25—28. Ps. xv. 5.

Q. 38. Were not the Israelites forbidden to take usury from their brethren, whether poor or rich? Deut. xxiii. 19: "Thou shalt not lend upon usury to thy brother."

A. This text is to be restricted to their poor brethren, as it is explained, Ex. xxii. 25, and Lev. xxv. 35, 36; or, if it respects the Israelites indifferently, then it is one of the judicial laws peculiar to that people, and of no binding force now.

Q. 39. What is the spring of all these different ways by

which men defraud and injure one another in their outward estate?

A. Covetousness, Luke xii. 15, or an inordinate prizing and loving of worldly goods, Ps. lxii. 10.

Q. 40. What should affright and deter every one from such wicked practices?

A. The consideration of the curse that shall enter into the house of the thief, Zech. v. 3, 4; and of the vengeance that shall light upon such as go beyond and defraud their neighbour: for, the Lord is the avenger of all such, 1 Thess. iv. 6.

QUEST. 76. *Which is the ninth commandment?*

ANS. The ninth commandment is, *Thou shalt not bear false witness against thy neighbour.*

QUEST. 77. *What is required in the ninth commandment?*

ANS. The ninth commandment requireth the maintaining and promoting of truth between man and man, and of our own and our neighbour's good name, especially in witness-bearing.

Q. 1. In what does the ninth commandment differ from the three preceding ones?

A. The three commands immediately preceding, have a respect to the injuries that may be done to ourselves or others by deeds or actions; but the ninth has a reference to wrongs done by words.

Q. 2. What is the general duty required in this commandment?

A. It is [the maintaining and promoting of truth between man and man.]

Q. 3. What is the *truth*, between man and man, we are required to maintain and promote?

A. It is the strict veracity of our words or speeches, in whatever we assert or deny; whether in our ordinary conversation, or in our oaths, promises, bargains, and contracts, Zech. viii. 16: "Speak ye every man the truth to his neighbour."

Q. 4. In what consists the strict veracity that ought to be in our words and speeches?

A. In uttering things as they really are in themselves, according to our belief of them; that is, that there be an exact agreement and harmony between our thoughts, words, and the things themselves, Ps. xv. 1, 2: "Who shall dwell in thy holy hill? He that—speaketh truth in his heart."

Q. 5. Why will God have nothing to be uttered but strict truth?

A. Because he is "a God of truth, and without iniquity; just and right is he," Deut. xxxii. 4.

Q. 6. Is it lawful at any time to conceal part of the truth?

A. Yes; when neither the glory of God, nor our own, or our neighbour's good requires that the whole of it be told; only no untruth must be uttered in concealing it, 1 Sam. xvi. 2, 5.

Q. 7. What is the chief end for which the tongue or gift of speech is conferred upon us?

A. That we may thus glorify God by praying to, Ps. l. 15, and praising him, verse 23; and by contending earnestly for, Jude verse 3, and confessing his truth, Rom. x. 10; hence is the tongue called our glory, Ps. xxx. 12: "To the end that my *glory* [that is, my tongue, as on the margin] may sing praise unto thee, and not be silent."

Q. 8. What is the subordinate end of it?

A. The edification and profit of our fellow-creatures, Eph. iv. 29: "Let no corrupt communication proceed out of your mouth, but that which is good, to the use of edifying;" margin, to edify profitably, in opposition to the insipid and vain talk which is in the mouths of most men.

Q. 9. What is the particular duty required in the ninth commandment?

A. That we maintain and promote [our own and our neighbour's good name, especially in witness-bearing.]

Q. 10. What is a [good name?]

A. It is the having of reputation and esteem, especially among the sober and religious, Ps. xvi. 3, and ci. 6.

Q. 11. How may a good name be obtained?

A. By being useful in the world, in the several stations and relations in which adorable providence has placed us, Ps. cxii. 9.

Q. 12. Is self-commendation a fit mean to obtain a good name?

A. No: it is ordinarily the highway to procure scorn and contempt, 2 Cor. x. 12.

Q. 13. Does not the apostle commend himself, when he says, "In nothing am I behind the very chiefest apostles?" 2 Cor. xii. 11.

A. He only magnifies and exalts his office, and at the same time lessens and disparages himself; for, although he says, In nothing am I behind the very chiefest apostles, yet he immediately subjoins, "though I be nothing;" and I

Cor. xv. 9: "I am the least of the apostles, who am not meet to be called an apostle, because I persecuted the church of God."

Q. 14. May we not commend the grace of God in us?

A. To be sure we may; for, whatever is spoken to the commendation of free grace, is for the abasement of self, 1 Cor. xv. 10: "By the grace of God I am what I am."

Q. 15. How ought we to maintain and promote [our own] good name?

A. Not only by a blameless walk and conversation before the world, Phil. ii. 15; but likewise by vindicating ourselves from the calumnies and aspersions that may be injuriously cast upon us, Acts xxiv. 12, 13.

Q. 16. With what frame of spirit ought the lawful vindication of ourselves to be managed?

A. With moderation, meekness, and readiness to forgive those who have reproached and injured us, Col. iii. 12, 13.

Q. 17. Who ought, in a special manner, to maintain and promote their own good name?

A. This is especially incumbent on professors of religion, Matt. v. 16; and such as are in places of public trust, Tit. ii. 7, 8.

Q. 18. Why should professors be careful to maintain their good name?

A. Because the loss of it tends to reflect dishonour on religion, by which the enemies of it take occasion to blaspheme, 2 Sam. xii. 14.

Q. 19. What is the advantage of a good name?

A. A good name procures mutual love to, and confidence in one another; and, consequently, tends to promote the interests both of sacred and civil society; on which account a good name is said to be better than precious ointment, Eccl. vii. 1; and rather to be chosen than great riches, Prov. xxii. 1.

Q. 20. What does this command require in reference to [our neighbour's good name?]

A. The maintaining and promoting it, as we would do our own, Phil. ii. 4; and that both in his presence and in his absence.

Q. 21. How should we behave in the presence of our neighbour, for maintaining and promoting of his good name?

A. When we observe any thing faulty in him, which deserves present notice, we should reprove it with meekness and love, Lev. xix. 17; and what is really commendable we should prudently encourage and applaud, Rom. i. 8.

Q. 22. How should we maintain and promote the good name of others in their absence?

A. By commending what is praise-worthy in them, 3 ohn ver. 12; vindicating their character when unjustly attacked, Prov. xxv. 23; and by covering their infirmities and blemishes, so far as can be done in a consistency with truth, and the credit of religion, 1 Pet. iv. 8.

Q. 23. Why is the word [*especially*] subjoined to witness-bearing?

A. Because, as we should give testimony to truth on all occasions, so, in a special manner, when called by lawful authority to declare the matter of fact upon oath, Jer. iv. 2.

Q. 24. What special obligation lies upon us, to declare the true matter of fact, between man and man, when called to do it upon oath?

A. In an oath, God is appealed to, that we will declare nothing but the truth, as we shall answer to him at the great day; and therefore, our doing otherwise, either out of hatred, or favour, is laying ourselves open to his immediate wrath and displeasure, according to Mal. iii. 5: "I will be a swift witness—against false swearers,—saith the Lord of hosts."

Quest. 78. *What is forbidden in the ninth commandment?*

Ans. The ninth commandment forbiddeth whatsoever is prejudicial to truth, or injurious to our own or our neighbour's good name.

Q. 1. What does this command forbid in general?
A. [Whatsoever is prejudicial to truth.]

Q. 2. What are we to understand by that which is [prejudicial to truth?]
A. All falsehood and lying of whatever kind, James iii. 14: Lie not against the truth.

Q. 3. What is the formal nature and meaning of a *lie*?
A. It is voluntarily to speak or express what we know to be false, as the old prophet at Bethel did to the man of God, 1 Kings xiii. 18.

Q. 4. How is a lie aggravated?
A. When it is uttered with a design to deceive, and to harm others by it; like the devil, when he said, "Ye shall not surely die.—Ye shall be as gods, knowing good and evil," Gen. iii. 4, 5.

Q. 5. May not persons utter what is untrue or false, and yet not be guilty of a lie?
A. Yes; and that either through ignorance or misinformation.

Q. 6. When may they be said to utter what is false through ignorance, and yet not be guilty of lying?

A. When they speak rashly, according to their present conception of things, without due examination; as the barbarians, when they saw the venomous beast hang on Paul's hand, said among themselves, No doubt this man is a murderer, &c., Acts xxviii. 4.

Q. 7. When may we utter what is false through misinformation, and not be guilty of a lie?

A. When we speak according to the report we have had from others, without any suspicion of being imposed upon; as Jacob did, when, by the imposition of his sons, (who had sold Joseph into Egypt, and dipped his coat in the blood of a kid) he said, "It is my son's coat; an evil beast hath devoured him: Joseph is without doubt rent in pieces," Gen. xxxvii. 33.

Q. 8. How many sorts of lies are there?

A. They are commonly ranked into three sorts; namely, ludicrous, pernicious, and officious lies.

Q. 9. What is a ludicrous or jocose lie?

A. It is when persons relate things they know to be false, with a design to make a jest or diversion to others.

Q. 10. What is it to be guilty of a pernicious lie?

A. It is to contrive or spread some malicious report we know or suspect to be false, on purpose to bring about some hurt or damage to another, as Ziba did against Mephibosheth, 2 Sam. xvi. 3.

Q. 11. What is the aggravation of a pernicious lie?

A. It is the very worst sort of lying, being both a contempt of the omniscient God, who is witness to the falsehood; and a deliberate intention to do injury to our neighbour, though in our conscience we believe him innocent of what we lay to his charge.

Q. 12. What is it for a person to make an officious lie?

A. It is to tell a downright untruth, for their own, or their neighbour's safety and security in time of danger, as Rahab did who hid the spies in the roof of her house, and yet alleged they were gone out of the city, and that she knew not where they went, Josh. ii. 4—6.

Q. 13. Does not the apostle ascribe this action of hers to her faith, when he says, Heb. xi. 31: "By faith Rahab, the harlot, perished not with them that believed not, when she had received the spies with peace?"

A. No; what he ascribes to her faith is, her having received the spies with peace, that is, her having consulted their safety and preservation with the greatest care and diligence; but not the lie she invented in order to conceal them. Her protecting the spies is commended, but not the manner in which she did it.

Q. 14. Who are they that plead in favour of officious lies?

A. The Papists, Socinians, and most of our modern moralists.

Q. 15. What arguments do they allege in defence of this sort of lying?

A. That it has been practised by saints in scripture; and that it is so far from being hurtful to any, that it has been beneficial to some in certain cases.

Q. 16. What answer is to be given to the practice of the saints in this matter?

A. That their sinful failures, in this and other instances, are not recorded in scripture for imitation, but for caution and warning, that we fall not into the same snares.

Q. 17. How do you answer the other argument for officious lying, "That it is so far from being hurtful to any, that it has been beneficial and advantageous to some, in certain cases, particularly in saving the life of a dear friend, or useful member of society, which might otherwise have been manifestly endangered?"

A. It is answered thus, that in no case are we to do evil that good may come, Rom. iii. 8. If we are not to speak wickedly for God, nor talk deceitfully for him, according to Job xiii. 7, neither are we to do so, though it were for the benefit of all mankind, or the best among them.

Q. 18. How do you prove lying to be sinful, or unlawful, in itself?

A. From this, that lying of all sorts, without exception, is condemned in scripture, as hateful and abominable to God, Prov. vi. 17, 19, and xii. 22, Col. iii. 9.

Q. 19. Who is the author and father of lies?

A. The devil, John viii. 44: "When he speaketh a lie, he speaketh of his own;. for he is a liar, and the father of it."

Q. 20. How does God testify his displeasure against lying of all kinds?

A. By declaring, that he who speaketh lies shall perish, Prov. xix. 9; accordingly it is said, *All* liars shall have their part in the lake which burneth with fire and brimstone, Rev. xxi. 8.

Q. 21. What is more particularly forbidden in this commandment, according to the answer?

A. Whatever is [injurious to our own or our neighbour's good name.]

Q. 22. How may we injure our own good name?

A. By a vain-glorious commendation of ourselves, Prov. xii. 15; by despising of others who ought justly to be esteemed, chap. xxiii. 9; or by doing any thing scandalous and offensive in the eye of the world, 1 Sam. ii. 17, 30.

Q. 23. In what may we be injurious to our neighbour's good name?

A. By flattering him to his face, Prov. xxviii. 4; by defaming him behind his back, Ps. l. 20; or by bearing false witness against him in public judicature, Ezek. xxii. 9.

Q. 24. What is the evil of flattering our neighbour to his face?

A. It tends to foster and foment his pride, and thus to bring on his ruin, Prov. xxvi. 28: A flattering mouth worketh ruin.

Q. 25. What is the evil of defaming him behind his back?

A. Nothing can be more devilish and malicious, than to fix calumny and reproach upon one, when he is not present to vindicate and defend himself: hence the same original word, which is rendered slanderer, 1 Tim. iii. 11, is used also to signify the devil, 1 Pet. v. 8.

Q. 26. Who are they that may be guilty of bearing false witness against their neighbour in public judicature?

A. The prosecutor, defendant, witness, advocate, and judge, may each of them be guilty in this way.

Q. 27. How may the prosecutor be guilty?

A. In making an unjust demand upon the defendant, Acts xxiv. 5; or laying to his charge that of which he believes him to be innocent, chap. xxv. 7.

Q. 28. How is the defendant, upon the other hand, chargeable with guilt in this matter?

A. By artful and dilatory evasions, by which the plaintiff is put to needless trouble and charge in the obtaining of justice.

Q. 29. How may witnesses, in public judicature, be injurious to their neighbour's good name?

A. Not only by the heinous sin of bearing testimony to a downright falsehood, but likewise by denying, mincing, or keeping back the truth, or any part of it.

Q. 30. When are advocates or attorneys guilty in this way?

A. When they take in hand to plead and maintain a bad cause, looking on it as a part of their profession to be as warm and zealous in defending what is wrong, as what is just and right.

Q. 31. How may the judge be guilty of bearing false witness?

A. By a rash, partial, and iniquitous sentence; thus perverting justice, and injuring the innocent, like Pilate, Matt. xxvii. 24, 26.

Q. 32. What is the evil of injuring our neighbour in his good name?

A. It robs him of a most valuable treasure; for, if once his good name or character is sunk, his further usefulness in the world is, to all appearance, irrecoverably gone.

Q. 33. What should affright and deter us from the sins of the tongue, forbidden in this commandment?

A. That we are to answer, in the last and great day

for our words, as well as our actions, Matt. xii. 36, 37: " Every idle word that men shall speak, they shall give account thereof in the day of judgment; for, by thy words thou shalt be justified, and by thy words thou shalt be condemned."

QUEST. 79. *Which is the tenth commandment?*

ANS. The tenth commandment is, *Thou shalt not covet thy neighbour's house, thou shalt not covet thy neighbour's wife, nor his man-servant, nor his maid-servant, nor his ox, nor his ass, nor any thing that is thy neighbour's.*

QUEST. 80. *What is required in the tenth commandment?*

ANS. The tenth commandment requireth full contentment with our own condition, with a right and charitable frame of spirit toward our neighbour, and all that is his.

Q. 1. What is the practice of the Papists with reference to the tenth commandment?

A. They have, (in some of their formularies,) erased the second commandment, because contrary to their image worship; therefore, in order to keep up the number *ten*, they split *this* into two, making these words, Thou shalt not covet thy neighbour's house, to be the ninth; and, Thou shalt not covet thy neighbour's wife, &c. to be the tenth.

Q. 2. How are they confuted?

A. By the words of this commandment (as they are here inserted from Ex. xx. 17,) being transposed into a different order in Deut. v. 21; where desiring our neighbour's wife is put before coveting of his house; which is a plain evidence, that what the Papists make two, is but one undivided precept; otherwise what, according to them, is the ninth in the one place, will be the tenth in the other.

Q. 3. What is the general duty required in this commandment?

A. It is an inward disposition and inclination of the whole soul, to perform all the duties contained in the law, particularly in the second table, which this commandment more immediately respects; and that out of love to God, and a desire to please him, Ps. cxix. 5, 47.

Q. 4. How do you prove this to be the general duty required?

A. From the general sin forbidden; namely, *Covetousness*, which includes the motion or stirring of corruption against all the commands of the law, because of their holiness and contrariety to depraved nature, Rom. vii. 7, 8.

Q. 5. What inward disposition of soul does this commandment require with reference to ourselves in particular?

A. It requires, with reference to ourselves, [full contentment with our own condition,] 1 Tim. vi. 6.

Q. 6. What do you understand by full contentment with our own condition?

A. A cheerful acquiescence in the lot which God, in his holy and wise providence, is pleased to carve out for us in this world, Heb. xiii. 5: Be content with such things as ye have.

Q. 7. Is full contentment with our own condition attainable in this life?

A. Though the perfection of no grace is attainable in this life, yet a great measure, and eminent degrees of grace, particularly this of contentment, may be, and has been, attained by the saints in this world, Phil. iv. 11: "I have learned, in whatever state I am, therewith to be content."

Q. 8. Is contentment, in a prosperous condition, an easy attainment?

A. No; without grace it cannot be attained; because, naturally, our ambitious and covetous desires increase in proportion to our riches; as is evident in the instance of Ahab, whom a kingdom could not satisfy without Naboth's vineyard, 1 Kings xxi. 4.

Q. 9. How is true contentment attained under prosperous circumstances?

A. By looking above all the enjoyments of time as transitory and vain, to God himself, as our chief good and eternal inheritance, Ps. lxii. 10, and xvi. 5, 6.

Q. 10. Is contentment likewise required under cross dispensations of providence; such as, poverty, reproach, bodily afflictions, and loss of near relations?

A. Though it be a grievous sin to be stupidly insensible and unconcerned under these or the like circumstances, Hos. vii. 9; yet a contentment of submission, or such as is without repining and murmuring, is, undoubtedly, required under the severest troubles that can befall us in this life, Lam. iii. 39: "Wherefore doth a living man complain?"

Q. 11. What ground of contentment have we under outward poverty and want?

A. That though we be the poor of this world, yet we may be rich in faith, and heirs of the kingdom, James ii. 5.

Q. 12. Why should we bear reproach without murmuring?

A. Because whatever reproach is cast upon us for Christ's sake, he will wipe it clean off at his second appearing, Luke xxii. 28, 29. Matt. xxv. 34.

Q. 13. What reason for contentment have we under bodily afflictions?

A. That they are only of short duration, 2 Cor. iv. 17; mixed with mercy, Lam. iii. 32; consistent with love, John xi. 3; and designed for our profit, that we might be partakers of his holiness, Heb. xii. 10.

Q. 14. What should content and comfort us under the loss of near and dear relations?

A. That the Lord Jesus, who stands in every amiable relation to us, is always at hand, being the same yesterday, to-day, and for ever, Heb. xiii. 8.

Q. 15. Are we required to be content under divine desertion, or the want of the sense of the love of God?

A. Though we have no reason to quarrel with God, for withdrawing the light of his countenance, which we never deserved; yet it is impossible for any gracious soul to be easy and content under the hidings of his face, but it must needs earnestly long for, and ardently breathe after the returns of his love; as is evident from the example and practice of the saints, in the following texts, Job xxiii. 3, and xxix. 2, 3, Ps. xiii. 1, xlii. 1, 2, and lxxxiv. 2.

Q. 16. What inward frame or disposition of soul does the tenth commandment require with reference to our neighbour?

A. It requires [a right and charitable frame of spirit toward him, and all that is his,] Rom. xii. 16.

Q. 17. When may we be said to have this [right and charitable frame of spirit] here required?

A. When our inward motions and affections are influenced by grace, to sway and determine us to promote and rejoice in the welfare of our neighbour, both as to his spiritual and temporal concerns, 1 Cor. xiii. 4—8.

Q. 18. When may it be evident to ourselves, that we have a right and charitable frame of spirit towards those who excel us in gifts and graces?

A. When, under an humbling sense of our own defects, we are thankful for the honour that is brought to God, by the shining of his gifts or graces in others, Gal. i. 23, 24.

Q. 19. What should induce us to a right and charitable frame of spirit towards those that are in more prosperous circumstances than ourselves; or whose condition in the world is better than our own?

A. The considering that a flourishing condition in the

world is not always the best, Ps. xxxviii. 16; that if we enjoy communion with God, it is infinitely preferable to all outward prosperity, without it, Ps. xvi. 5, 6.

Q. 20. How may such a right and charitable frame of spirit be attained?

A. Only by the implantation of faith, as the root of this and all other motions of the soul that are acceptable to God, Heb. xi. 6. Rom. xiv. 23.

QUEST. 81. *What is forbidden in the tenth commandment?*

ANS. The tenth commandment forbiddeth all discontentment with our own estate, envying or grieving at the good of our neighbour, and all inordinate motions and affections to any thing that is his.

Q. 1. What is the leading sin forbidden in this commandment?

A. It is *Covetousness:* Thou shalt not *covet.*

Q. 2. What is covetousness?

A. It is an excessive and irregular desire after those worldly goods which we have not, Prov. i. 19, and which God, in his providence, does not see meet that we should have, Ps. lxxv. 6, 7.

Q. 3. How does the excess of an avaricious mind discover itself?

A. By such an insatiable thirst after worldly gain, as can never be satisfied, Prov. xxx. 15.

Q. 4. In what consists the irregularity of covetousness?

A. In the desire of worldly goods which are in the possession of our neighbour, and even sometimes as they are his, 1 Kings xxi. 2.

Q. 5. How does the covetousness of the heart discover itself?

A. By [discontentment with our own estate,] and [envying or grieving at the good of our neighbour.]

Q. 6. What is [discontentment with our own estate?]

A. It is to murmur and fret at our present condition in the world, as being worse than we think should fall to our share, or than we are expecting and looking for, 2 Kings vi. 33.

Q. 7. What is the aggravation of this sin?

A. It argues an unwillingness to be at God's disposal, Ps. xii. 4; an esteeming ourselves more competent judges than he, of what is best for us, 1 Kings i. 5; and it is, in effect, usurping the throne of God, and taking his government into our own hands, Ex. v. 2.

Q. 8. What are the proper remedies against it?

A. The only sovereign remedy, is to give Christ the pre-eminence in our hearts, Ps. lxxiii. 25; for then we will undervalue all temporal things, in comparison of him, Ps. lxxvi. 4.

Q. 9. What is [envying or grieving at the good of our neighbour?]

A. It is to repine and grudge at his prosperous circumstances, Neh. ii. 10, or any superior endowment or privilege he is possessed of above ourselves, Ps. cxii. 9, 10.

Q. 10. What is the evil of this sin?

A. It wastes and consumes the body, Prov. xiv. 39; Envy is the rottenness of the bones; and it is fertile of confusion, and every evil work, James iii. 16.

Q. 11. What is the source or spring of covetousness?

A. The [inordinate motions and affections] that are in our souls.

Q. 12. What do you understand by the [inordinate motions and affections] here forbidden?

A. Not only the unlawful purposes, intentions, and desires, that are actually formed in the heart, but even the first risings and stirrings of corruption in the soul, which are antecedent to the consent of the will, Gen. vi. 5.

Q. 13. Are not the vicious lusts and desires that are formed and assented to in the heart, forbidden in other commandments of the second table, as well as in this?

A. Yes; as appears from our Saviour's exposition of the seventh commandment, Matt. v. 28: "But I say unto you, Whosoever looketh on a woman to lust after her, hath committed adultery with her already in his heart."

Q. 14. How then is this commandment distinguished from others, which forbid heart sins equally with it?

A. This commandment is levelled particularly at the root of all sin, namely, habitual lust, or corruption of nature, together with its very first motions, and especially as these are contrary to the love of our neighbour; whereas, other commandments chiefly respect such secret and heart sins as are actually committed, though not known to the world.

Q. 15. How does it appear that this commandment is levelled particularly at habitual lust, or at the root of all sin?

A. Because, since other commandments chiefly forbid heart sins actually formed, this commandment must forbid the very rise of them, or the least bias and inclination to evil; otherwise it would not be distinct from the rest, nor would the law be absolutely perfect.

Q. 16. Does not the apostle James distinguish between

136 SINS FORBIDDEN IN THE TENTH COMMANDMENT.

lust and sin, chap. i. 15: When lust hath conceived it bringeth forth sin; and will it not from thence follow, that lust, or corruption of nature, is not properly sin, and consequently not forbidden in this commandment?

A. The apostle distinguishes between lust and sin merely as a corrupt principle and the act which it produces; both which are hateful to God, and contrary to his law.

Q. 17. If lust, or corruption of nature, cannot be remedied, or extirpated by any prescription in the divine law, why is it at all prohibited?

A. It is nevertheless prohibited, both because contrary to the nature of God, and as a mean to reprove and humble us for it, Rom. vii. 9.

Q. 18. What is the difference between human and divine laws on this head?

A. Human laws respect only overt or open acts of sin, but divine laws respect likewise the internal inclination and disposition which persons have to commit it, Ps. lxvi. 18.

Q. 19. What is the opinion of the Papists concerning the prohibition of habitual lust?

A. They pretend that the law of God respects only the corruption of our actions, but not the habit or principle from whence they proceed.

Q. 20. How are they refuted?

A. From the spirituality of the law, which extends to the motions of the heart, as well as the actions of the life, Rom. vii. 14, 23.

Q. 21. If the first motions of corruption are not entertained, but immediately curbed and restrained, why are they prohibited as sinful?

A. Because, however soon they are curbed or restrained, yet having once been in the soul, they cannot but leave a stain and pollution behind them, contrary to the holiness and purity required in the law, James i. 14.

Q. 22. Who are they that are sensible of these inordinate motions and affections of the heart, and are humbled for the same?

A. None properly but the regenerate; as is evident from the instance of the apostle, who says of himself, after his conversion, "I had not known lust, except the law had said, Thou shalt not covet," Rom. vii. 7.

Q. 23. What is the apostle's meaning in these words?

A. It is, as if he had said, I had not known this strong propensity that is in my heart to all manner of sin, even before it be consented to, or deliberately committed; unless the Spirit of God had discovered it to me, in this precept of the law forbidding the same.

Q. 24. How does this propensity to sin evidence itself?

OF MAN'S INABILITY TO KEEP THE LAW. 137

A. In that no sooner is the object presented, than instantly there is an inordinate motion and affection of the heart after it. The combustible matter within catches fire at the very first spark of temptation, Josh. vii. 21.

Q. 25. What may we learn from the general scope of this, and all the other commandments?

A. That though we could forbear the evil, and do the good contained in every commandment, it would not be sufficient, except we did it for the Lord's sake, out of love to him, and regard to his authority, Ezek. xx. 19.

QUEST. 82. *Is any man able perfectly to keep the commandments of God?*

ANS. No mere man, since the fall, is able, in this life perfectly to keep the commandments of God, but doth daily break them, in thought, word, and deed.

Q. 1. What is it [perfectly to keep the commandments of God?]

A. It is, from a nature perfectly holy, to yield constant and uninterrupted obedience to them, both in heart and life, Matt. xxii. 37, 39.

Q. 2. Was ever any man, in this world, able to keep the commandments of God in this manner?

A. Yes; Adam, before his fall, was able to give perfect obedience to them all, Eccl. vii. 29: God made man upright.

Q. 3. Whether was Adam's ability to keep the commandments of God, concreated with him, or, was it a superadded gift?

A. It was concreated with him, as being made after the image of God, Gen. i. 27.

Q. 4. Has none, since the fall, been able to keep them perfectly?

A. [No mere man] has ever been able to do it, since that time, Rom. iii. 9, 10.

Q. 5. What do you understand by a [mere man?]

A. One who is no more than a man; and all Adam's family, descending from him by ordinary generation, are only mere men, Acts xvii. 26.

Q. 6. Why is the limitation of no mere man inserted in the answer?

A. That *Christ* might be excepted, who is infinitely more than a man, being *Immanuel*, God with us, Matt. i. 23.

Q. 7. Why should he be excepted?

12 *

A. Because he not only yielded perfect obedience to the law in our nature, but an obedience meritorious of life, for all his spiritual seed, Matt. iii. 15. Rom. v. 17, 19.

Q. 8. Do not the saints, in this life, keep the commandments of God perfectly?

A. No; for there is not a just man upon earth, that doeth good, and sinneth not, Eccl. vii. 20.

Q. 9. Will they ever be capable of doing it?

A. Yes; when they come to heaven, where they are made perfect, Heb. xii. 23; and where the former things are passed away, Rev. xxi. 4.

Q. 10. Why are they not able perfectly to keep them [in this life?]

A. Because of the remains of corruption cleaving to every one of them, while in this world, Rom. vii. 23; and from which they long to be delivered, verse 24.

Q. 11. But may not grace received, in this life, enable them to keep the commandments of God perfectly?

A. There is no promise of any such grace, nor would it be consistent with the gradual nature of spiritual growth, as the saints do not arrive at their full stature till they come to glory, 1 Thess. iii. 13.

Q. 12. How does it appear from scripture, that the saints cannot attain perfection in this life?

A. The scripture expressly affirms, that in many things they offend all, James iii. 2: and it records the failings and infirmities of the most eminent of them that ever lived; such as Abraham, Gen. xx. 2; Moses, Ps. cvi. 33; David, 2 Sam. xi. 4, 15; Peter, Matt. xxvi. 72, 74; and many others.

Q. 13. Do not the saints themselves ingenuously acknowledge, that they cannot attain perfection while here?

A. Yes; Job ix. 20: "If I say, I am perfect, it shall also prove me perverse." Paul, likewise, Phil. iii. 12: "Not as though I had already attained, or were already perfect."

Q. 14. But is it not said that Noah, Gen. vi. 9, Hezekiah, Isa. xxxviii. 3, and Job, chap. i. 8, were each of them perfect?

A. The perfection ascribed to them, is only comparative; that is, they were more holy and circumspect than many others; but it cannot be understood of absolute perfection, as their sins and blemishes stand also upon record: Noah, for drunkenness, Gen. ix. 21; Hezekiah, for ingratitude, 2 Chron. xxxii. 25; and Job, for some degree of impatience under the rod, chap. iii.

Q. 15. If the saints cannot attain perfection in this life, why is it said, that they do not commit sin? 1 John iii. 9: "Whosoever is born of God, doth not commit sin."

A. The meaning is, they do not take pleasure and de-

..ight in sin, nor make a trade of it, as unregenerate persons do, who are therefore called the workers of iniquity, Ps. cxxv. 5.

Q. 16. Is not the perfection of sincerity attainable by the saints?

A. They may attain to a very high and eminent degree of sincerity in this world, Ps. xviii. 23, 2 Cor. i. 12; but the absolute perfection of this, or any other grace, is not to be expected by them, till they come to heaven, 1 Cor. xiii. 12.

Q. 17. Will they not be accepted upon such sincerity as they can attain to, though short of the perfection required in the law?

A. Their acceptance before God is not founded on their sincerity, or any other branch of their sanctification; but solely in their justification, by which the righteousness of the law is fulfilled in them, in virtue of the surety righteousness imputed to them, Rom. viii. 4; and thus they are accepted in the Beloved, Eph. i. 6.

Q. 18. Since none of mankind are able, in this life, perfectly to keep the commandments of God, how often does the answer say that they break them?

A. It says that they break them [daily] or continually, Gen. vi. 5.

Q. 19. In what do they daily break them?

A. They do it [in thought, word, and deed.]

Q. 20. Is there any other possible way of breaking the commandments of God?

A. No; there is no other way of breaking any of them, (as to actual transgression,) than either in our thoughts, words, or deeds; and our doing so, in all these respects, shows the justice of that charge which the Lord has against every one of us, Jer. iii. 5: "Behold, thou hast spoken and done evil things as thou couldst."

Q. 21. How do we break the commandments of God in our *thoughts?*

A. When our thoughts are sinfully employed either with reference to God, ourselves, or our neighbours.

Q. 22. When are our thoughts sinfully employed about God?

A. When they are entertaining unworthy and unbecoming notions and conceptions of him, Ps. l. 21, and xciv. 7, such as reflect dishonour upon his perfections and providence, Zeph. i. 12; or such as are inconsistent with the discovery he has made of himself, as being " in Christ reconciling the world to himself," 2 Cor. v. 19.

Q. 23. When are our thoughts sinfully exercised about ourselves?

A. When they are gratifying our pride, Obadiah ver. 3 ambition, Isa. xiv. 13, 14, and self-applause, Rom. xii. 3.

Q. 24. When are they sinfully employed about our neighbours?

A. When they are meditating and indulging envy, Gen. iv. 15; reproach, Jer. xx. 10; or revenge against them, Gen. xxvii. 41.

Q. 25. What is the aggravating evil and malignity of sinful thoughts?

A. The evil and malignity of them consists in this, that they are the immediate source and spring from whence all our sinful words and deeds flow; "for out of the abundance of the heart the mouth speaketh," Matt. xii. 34.

Q. 26. What is the proper remedy and antidote against sinful thoughts?

A. The Spirit's taking the things of Christ, and showing them unto us, John xvi. 14, by which they will become the subject matter of our meditation and highest esteem: for where the treasure is, there will be the heart also, Matt. vi. 21.

Q. 27. How do men break the commandments of God by their *words*?

A. When, besides idle and unprofitable words, Matt. xii. 36, they utter such as are more directly dishonouring to God, Ps. xxiii. 9, 11, and hurtful and prejudicial to themselves and others, Ps. cxl. 3.

Q. 28. How do they break them by their *deeds*?

A. When those sins are committed, which have been conceived in the thought, and uttered by the tongue; being inconceivably more than can be condescended upon, "for, innumerable evils have compassed us about," Ps. xl. 12.

Q. 29. What may we learn from man's inability to keep the commandments perfectly in this life?

A. That we must be wholly indebted to the free grace of God, for salvation and eternal life, Tit. iii. 5, and not to any thing in ourselves, who are, at best, but unprofitable servants, Luke xvii. 10.

QUEST. 83. *Are all transgressions of the law equally heinous?*

ANS. Some sins in themselves, and by reason of several aggravations, are more heinous in the sight of God than others.

Q. 1. What do you understand by some sins being [more heinous] than others?

A. That they are more abominable, hateful, and offensive to God than others are, Ezek. viii. 6, 13, 15.

OF SIN IN ITS AGGRAVATIONS.

Q. 2. Are not all sins hateful, and offensive to God?
A. Yes: but not equally so, Matt. vii 3: "Why beholdest thou the *mote* that is in thy brother's eye, but considerest not the *beam* that is in thine own eye?"

Q. 3. How does it appear that all sins are not equally offensive to God?
A. From the different degrees of punishment that shall be inflicted in the other world, Matt. xi. 22: "But I say unto you, it shall be more tolerable for Tyre and Sidon in the day of judgment than for you." See also Luke xii. 47, 48.

Q. 4. In whose sight are some sins more heinous than others?
A. [In the sight of God,] who is the best judge of the heinousness of sins, Job xxxvi. 9.

Q. 5. In what respects are some sins more heinous in the sight of God than others?
A. Some are more heinous [in themselves,] and some are so [by reason of several aggravations.]

Q. 6. What is it for sins to be heinous [in themselves?]
A. It is to be heinous in their own nature, though no other aggravating circumstances should attend them.

Q. 7. How are these sins, that are in their own nature more heinous than others, commonly ranked?
A. Sins committed more immediately against God, or the first table of his law, are more heinous in their own nature, than sins committed more immediately against man, or any precept of the second table. Likewise, some sins against the second table, are more heinous in themselves, than other sins against the said table.

Q. 8. What examples are usually given of both these?
A. Blasphemy against God, is more heinous in its own nature, than defaming, or speaking evil of our neighbour, 1 Sam. ii. 25; and adultery is more heinous than theft, Prov. vi. 33, to the end of the chapter.

Q. 9. "What are those [aggravations] that make some sins more heinous than others?"
A. Sins "receive their aggravation, 1. From the persons offending. 2. From the parties offended. 3. From the nature and quality of the offence. 4. From the circumstances of time and place." *

Q. 10. How may the persons *offending* be viewed?
A. They may be viewed, either as to their age, gifts, or office.

Q. 11. What aggravation arises from the age of the persons offending?
A. If persons are advanced in years, by which they may be supposed to have more experience, their sins are more highly aggravated than if committed by children, or such as are raw and inexperienced, Job xxxii. 7.

* Larger Catechism, Q. 151.

Q. 12. How are sins aggravated from the gifts of the persons offending?

A. If the offenders have been eminent for their profession, 2 Sam. xii. 14, or have had a larger measure of gifts, 1 Kings xi. 9, or grace, James iv. 17, conferred upon them, their sins will be proportionably aggravated beyond others, who have not been so privileged.

Q. 13. How are sins aggravated from the office, or station, in which persons offending may be placed?

A. If the persons who give the offence be in an eminent station in the world, or vested with any office in the church, Jer. xxiii. 11, 14, or in the state, 1 Kings xiv. 16; their sins cannot but be of a deeper tincture and dye, because their example is more likely to be followed by others, Jer. xxiii. 14.

Q. 14. How do sins receive their aggravation from the parties *offended*?

A. If committed "immediately against God, his attributes and worship; against Christ and his grace; against the Holy Spirit, his witness and working; against superiors, and such as we stand especially related and engaged unto; against any of the saints, particularly weak brethren;—and the common good of all, or many."*

Q. 15. On what account is sin aggravated as being committed immediately against God, his attributes and worship?

A. In as much as it is doing evil in his sight, Ps. li. 4; is despising the riches of his goodness, Rom. ii. 4; and undervaluing his ordinances, Mal. i. 8, and the glory he has stamped upon them, verse 14.

Q. 16. In what consists the heinousness of sin, as being against Christ and his grace?

A. In its being a slighting and contemning the only remedy which infinite wisdom has provided for our malady, Acts iv. 12; and surely there can be no escape, if we neglect so great salvation, Heb. ii. 3.

Q. 17. How is sin aggravated by its being committed against the Holy Spirit, his witness and working?

A. In as much as it is a rejection of his testimony without us, in the word, John xv. 26, and a quenching his motions and operations within us, 1 Thess. v. 19.

Q. 18. What aggravation does sin receive, as being committed against superiors, and such as we stand especially related and engaged to?

A. In so far as sin is committed against any of these, it is a violation of the most sacred bonds, both of nature, Prov. xxx. 17, and gratitude, Ps. lv. 12, 13.

Q. 19. How is it aggravated, as being committed against the saints, particularly weak brethren?

* Larger Catechism, Question 151, § 2.

A. As being committed against the saints, it is a contempt of the image of God in them, Luke x. 16; and as against weak brethren, it is laying a stumbling-block before them, by which they may be insnared and fall, 1 Cor. viii. 12.

Q. 20. Who are they that sin against the common good of all men, or many of them?

A. They are such as do what in them lies to hinder the propagation of the gospel where it is not, and to mar the success of it where it is, 1 Thess. ii. 15, 16; there being nothing that tends more to the common good of all men, than the word of this salvation being sent among them, Acts xiii. 26.

Q. 21. What is the aggravation of this sin?

A. It makes those who are guilty of it bear the nearest resemblance they can to the devil, who aims at nothing more than the ruin and destruction of mankind, 1 Pet. v. 8.

Q. 22. How are sins aggravated from the *nature* and *quality* of the offence?

A. They are much aggravated, if the offence be against the express letter of the law; break many commandments; —if it break forth in words and actions;—admit of no reparation; if against conviction of conscience—if done deliberately—obstinately, and with delight.*

Q. 23. Why is the offence said to be aggravated from being committed against the express letter of the law?

A. Because in this case there can remain no manner of doubt about the sinfulness of the action; and therefore it must be sinning with the greatest boldness and presumption, Rom. i. 32.

Q. 24. What aggravation is there in breaking many commandments at once?

A. The sin thus becomes a complicated offence, containing many crimes in the bosom of it; like David's sin in the matter of Uriah, 2 Sam. xii. 9.

Q. 25. How is sin aggravated by breaking forth in words and actions?

A. Sinful words and actions reflect a more public dishonour on God, Matt. v. 22, and do greater injury to men, Mic. ii. 1, than if they were latent only in the thought.

Q. 26. What aggravation is there in those sins which admit of no reparation?

A. Their admitting of no reparation, cannot fail to aggravate them in the very nature of things; thus murder or adultery cannot but be more heinous than theft, because there may be restitution of one kind or other for theft, Lev. vi. 4, 5; but nothing can compensate the taking away of

---

* See more particulars on this head, Larger Catechism, Q. 151, § 3

the life of another, Num. xxxv. 31, or the violation of the marriage-bed and covenant, Prov. vi. 35.

Q. 27. What is the aggravation of sinning against convictions of conscience?

A. This kind of sinning offers violence to ourselves, contrary to the checks of that judge and reprover which every one has in his own breast, Rom. i. 32.

Q. 28. What is the evil of sinning deliberately, obstinately, and with delight?

A. It argues the giving a kind of defiance to the Almighty, Ex. v. 2; a rooted hatred of him, Rom. viii. 7; and is a strong evidence of judicial blindness and hardness of heart, Zech. vii. 11, 12.

Q. 29. What aggravation do sins receive from the circumstance of *time*?

A. They are more heinous if committed on the Lord's day, Jer. xvii. 27, or on days occasionally set apart for fasting or thanksgiving, Isa. xxii. 12, 13, than at other times.

Q. 30. How are sins aggravated from the circumstance of the *place* in which they are committed?

A. An offence is more heinous, if it be done in a land of gospel light, Isa. xxvi. 10; or if committed in public, or in the presence of others, who are thereby likely to be provoked or defiled, 2 Sam. xvi. 22.*

Q. 31. What improvement should we make of this doctrine of sin in its aggravations?

A. To be more humbled and abased before the Lord, under a sense of our sins thus aggravated, Ezra ix. 6; and likewise so much the more to admire the riches of pardoning mercy, as extended to the very chief of sinners, 1 Tim. i. 13, 15.

QUEST. 84. *What doth every sin deserve?*

ANS. Every sin deserves God's wrath and curse, both in this life, and that which is to come.

Q. 1. What do you understand by the desert or demerit of sin?

A. It is that in the nature of sin, which of itself deserves all that wrath and curse, which God, in his infinite justice, has entailed upon it, Gal. iii. 10.

Q. 2. What is it in the nature of sin, which, of itself, deserves this wrath and curse?

A. It is the opposition, and contrariety of it to the holiness of God expressed in his law, Hab. i. 13; which is the

* Larger Catechism, Quest. 151, § 4.

very thing tnat constitutes the enormity, or heinousness of it, Jer. xliv. 4.

Q. 3. Can wrath be ascribed to God as it is a passion?

A. No; for all passions, properly speaking, are inconsistent with God's absolute unchangeableness, Mal. iii. 6, and independence, Acts xiv. 15.

Q. 4. What then is to be understood by [God's wrath?]

A. That most pure and undisturbed act of his will, which produces most dreadful effects against the sinner, Isa. xxxiii. 14.

Q. 5. What are these dreadful effects, which the wrath of God produces against the sinner?

A. All the miseries of this life, death itself, and the pains of hell for ever. *

Q. 6. Is the desert of sin separable from the nature of it?

A. No; as sin is the very opposite of God's holy nature and righteous law, it cannot but deserve his wrath and curse, Rom. vi. 23.

Q. 7. If every sin deserves God's wrath and curse, must not the sins of believers deserve the same likewise?

A. Whatever be the desert of their sin, their persons can never be exposed, or liable to God's vindictive wrath, either in this life, or that which is to come, Zeph. iii. 17. Hos. xiii. 14.

Q. 8. Why cannot the persons of believers be liable to the wrath and curse of God?

A. Because of their union with Christ, Rom. viii. 1, who has fulfilled all righteousness for them, ver. 33, 34; or answered all the demands of law and justice in their room, chap. iv. 25.

Q. 9. What do the Papists mean by venial sins?

A. Such sins as are in their own nature so small and trivial, that they do not deserve eternal punishment.

Q. 10. Are there any sins in this sense venial?

A. By no means; for the least sin, being committed against a God of infinite perfection, must, on that account, be objectively infinite, and consequently deserve an infinite punishment, 2 Thess. i. 9.

Q. 11. May not smaller offences be atoned for, by human satisfaction or penances?

A. "Even the least sin—cannot be expiated, but by the blood of Christ," Heb. xi. 22. 1 Pet. i. 18, 19. †

Q. 12. What may we learn from the desert of sin?

A. The amazing love of God, in transferring the guilt and punishment of sin, to the glorious Surety, making 'him to be sin for us, who knew no sin, that we might be made the righteousness of God in him," 2 Cor. v. 21.

---
* All which see explained, Part I, On the misery of man's natural state.
† Larger Catechism, Quest. 152. See the necessity of satisfaction proved, Part I. On Christ's priestly office.

QUEST. 85. *What doth God require of us that we may escape his wrath and curse, due to us for sin?*

ANS. To escape the wrath and curse of God, due to us for sin, God requireth of us faith in Jesus Christ, repentance unto life, with the diligent use of all the outward means whereby Christ communicateth to us the benefits of redemption.

Q. 1. What weighty argument or motive (among many others,) does the scripture afford, for essaying the practice of what [God requires of us?]

A. That though we are enjoined, to work out our own salvation with fear and trembling; yet, we are at the same time assured, that it is God which worketh in us, both to will and to do, of his good pleasure, Phil. ii. 12, 13.

Q. 2. Does God require any thing of us in point of duty, without promising suitable furniture, for the performance of it?

A. No; for he has said, "I will—cause you to walk in my statutes, and ye shall keep my judgments, and do them," Ezek. xxxvi. 27.

Q. 3. Can we [escape the wrath and curse of God, due to us for sin,] by any thing we can do of ourselves?

A. No, surely; for "all our righteousnesses are as filthy rags," Isa. lxiv. 6; and, " by the works of the law, shall no flesh be justified," Gal. ii. 16.

Q. 4. Why then does the answer say, that to escape the wrath and curse of God, due to us for sin, [God requires of us, faith in Jesus Christ, repentance unto life, and a diligent use of all the outward means?]

A. Because, though these duties, as performed by us, can neither give a title to, nor possession of eternal life; yet God appoints and requires them, both as they are *means* of conveying and improving the salvation purchased, 1 Cor. i. 21, and likewise, as they are *evidences* of our interest in it, when conveyed, John vi. 47.

Q. 5. Why does God require [faith in Jesus Christ] as the sovereign means of escaping his wrath and curse?

A. Because there is salvation in no other; there being " none other name under heaven, given among men, whereby we must be saved," Acts iv. 12.

Q. 6. What encouragement have we to essay believing in Jesus Christ?

A. There cannot be a greater encouragement than this, that faith is the gift of God, Eph. ii. 8; and accordingly the promise runs, "I will say, It is my people, and they shall say, The Lord is my God," Zech. xiii. 9.

SALVATION IN GENERAL. 147

Q. 7. Why is [repentance unto life] required?
A. Because it is the inseparable fruit and effect of faith or believing, Zech. xii. 10: "They shall look upon me whom they have pierced, and they shall mourn for him."

Q. 8. What encouragement have sinners of mankind, privileged with gospel light, to look for, or expect this blessing of repentance unto life, which God requires of them?
A. They are warranted to expect it on this ground, that as Christ has received gifts for men, Ps. lxviii. 18, so "him hath God exalted with his right hand to be a Prince and a Saviour, to give repentance to Israel," Acts v. 31.

Q. 9. Why does God require of us [the diligent use of all the outward means whereby Christ communicates to us the benefits of redemption?]
A. Because a neglect or contempt of the means of divine appointment, for communicating the benefits of redemption, is, in the sight of God, the same thing as a neglect or contempt of these inestimable benefits themselves, Luke x. 16: "He that despiseth you, despiseth me; and he that despiseth me, despiseth him that sent me."

Q. 10. Can our believing, repenting, and diligent use of means, as they are acts of ours, be the procuring cause of our escaping wrath, or found our title to life and salvation?
A. No; for, "by the deeds of the law, there shall no flesh be justified in his sight," Rom. iii. 20. Our security from wrath and title to heaven, are founded on the imputation of the surety righteousness alone, Isa. xlv. 25.

Q. 11. What would be the consequence of making our faith, repentance, and good works, the procuring cause of our escaping the wrath and curse of God due to us for sin?
A. This would be setting aside the satisfaction of Christ, and making a saviour of our duties, than which nothing could nail us more effectually down under the curse, Gal. iii. 10: "As many as are of the works of the law, are under the curse."

Q. 12. Have unbelieving and impenitent sinners any warrant to conclude, that they have escaped the wrath and curse of God, due to them for sin?
A. No, surely; for "he that believeth not, is condemned already," John iii. 18; and our Lord says, "Except ye repent, ye shall all likewise perish," Luke xiii. 3.

Q. 13. Is our escaping the wrath and curse of God suspended on the condition of our faith, repentance, and diligent use of the outward means?
A. No; for, if any promised blessing were suspended upon the condition of our personal obedience, it would be the very form of the covenant of works, Rom. x. 5: "Moses describeth the righteousness which is of the law, that the man which doth these things, shall live by them."

Q. 14. When do carnal and unregenerate men turn the

dispensation of the covenant of grace into the form of the covenant of works?

A. When they separate the duties of faith, repentance, and the diligent use of the means, from the promises of the covenant, and hope to make themselves accepted with God by their personal performance of these duties, Rom. x. 3.

Q. 15. What *connexion* have faith, repentance, and the use of outward means, with salvation?

A. They have the connexion of appointed means prescribed by God himself, which, by his blessing, are subservient for such a valuable end; being themselves a part of salvation, and evidences of it, 2 Thess. ii. 13.

Q. 16. How are the means of salvation usually distinguished?

A. Into internal and external.

Q. 17. What are the internal means?

A. Faith and repentance, with the other graces that accompany or flow from them.

Q. 18. Why called internal, or inward?

A. Because they are wrought in the hearts of the elect, by the Spirit of God, as the fruits and effects of Christ's purchase and mediation, Zech. xii. 10.

Q. 19. What are the external or outward means?

A. They are the ordinances of divine institution, and appointment; such as, the word, sacraments, and prayer.

Q. 20. How is faith in Jesus Christ connected with salvation?

A. As it is the hand that receives Christ and his righteousness, as the all of our salvation, Ps. lxviii. 31. John. i. 12.

Q. 21. How is repentance unto life connected with salvation?

A. As it consists in that godly sorrow for sin, flowing from faith, which is both the exercise and ornament (in some measure) of all the travellers Zion-ward, while in this world, Jer. l. 4. 2 Cor. vii. 11.

Q. 22. How is the diligent use of outward means connected with salvation?

A. As it is by them that [Christ communicates to us the benefits of redemption,] Prov. ii. 1—16.

Q. 23. Could he not communicate the benefits of redemption, without the outward means?

A. Whatever he could do, yet his ordinary method is to honour his own ordinances, as the means of communicating these benefits to us, which we are not to expect but in the use of them, Prov. viii. 34. Rom. x. 17.

Q. 24. What *use* does God require us to make of the outward means?

A. He requires us to make [a diligent use] of them.

Q. 25. What is a diligent use of the outward means?

A. It is an embracing every opportunity offered in providence, for attending upon God in them, looking earnestly for his blessing upon them, by which alone they become efficacious for our spiritual benefit, 1 Cor. iii. 6, 7.

QUEST. 86. *What is faith in Jesus Christ?*

ANS. Faith in Jesus Christ is a saving grace, whereby we receive and rest upon him alone for salvation, as he is offered to us in the gospel.

Q. 1. What are the several kinds of faith mentioned in scripture?
A. They are these four: historical, temporary, the faith of miracles, and saving faith.

Q. 2. What is historical faith?
A. It is a bare assent to the truth of what is revealed in the word, without any real affection or regard to the things revealed in it. Such a faith as this may be found in devils, James ii. 19; and in wicked men, Acts viii. 13.

Q. 3. Why called historical?
A. Not merely because it believes only the histories of the Bible; but because it assents to the truths revealed in it, as being little or no way concerned in them, or without any particular application of them to the soul, Acts xxviii. 26.

Q. 4. What is temporary faith?
A. It is such as, together with an assent to the truth of divine revelation, is also accompanied with some slight and transient motion upon the affections; which may endure for awhile, and then vanishes, Matt. xiii. 20, 21.

Q. 5. Has this kind of faith any influence upon the practice?
A. It may be, for a time, accompanied with an external reformation from some grosser sins, 2 Pet. ii. 20.

Q. 6. What is the faith of miracles?
A. It is that peculiar gift, by which a person believes, that, by the power of God, something shall be effected by him which is quite above the power of all natural causes, 1 Cor. xiii. 2.

Q. 7. On what occasion has God bestowed upon any this faith?
A. For the confirmation of some extraordinary mission, or of some important article of revealed religion; as the miracles of Moses under the Old Testament; and of the apostles under the New.

Q. 8. Was not the faith of miracles, in the days of our Saviour and his apostles, conferred upon some who were not in a state of salvation?

OF FAITH IN JESUS CHRIST.

A. Yes; both the extraordinary gift of the faith of miracles, and the ordinary and common gifts of the Spirit, were conferred upon some, who, we are assured, will be utterly rejected of God, Matt. vii. 22, 23 : "Many will say unto me in that day, Lord, Lord, have we not *prophesied* in thy name? and in thy name have *cast out devils?* and in thy name done many *wonderful works?* And then will I profess unto them, I never *knew* you: depart from me ye that work iniquity."

Q. 9. What is saving and justifying faith?

A. It is that faith in Jesus Christ, which is described in the answer, "whereby we receive and rest upon him alone for salvation," &c.

Q. 10. Why is this faith, described in the answer, called a [*grace?*]

A. Because it is the gift of God, freely bestowed upon the sinner, Eph. ii. 8, who has no antecedent worth, value, or good qualification, of which he can boast, 1 Cor. iv. 7.

Q. 11. Why a [*saving*] grace?

A. Because wherever true faith is, there salvation is already begun, which shall certainly be consummated in due time, John iii. 36.

Q. 12. Where is the connexion established between faith and salvation?

A. Faith being the gifted hand that is stretched out to receive Christ in the promise, Ps. lxviii. 31, cannot but be inseparably connected with salvation; because Christ, whom faith receives, is the *all* of our salvation, Col. iii. 11 : hence is that promise, Mark xvi. 16, He that believeth— shall be saved.

Q. 13. Why is it called faith [in Jesus Christ?]

A. Because Christ is the main, or principal object of saving faith, Acts xvi. 31.

Q. 14. Why do you call him the main or principal object of faith?

A. Because nothing can fill the eye or hand of faith, but Christ only, or God in him, Ps. lxxiii. 25.

Q. 15. How is faith in Jesus Christ denominated in the answer?

A. It is called a [receiving,] John i. 12, and [resting] on him, Ps. xxxvii. 7.

Q. 16. Are there not other denominations of faith in Christ of the same divine authority with those mentioned?

A. Yes; such as eating, drinking, flying, entering, and many others.

Q. 17. From whence are these various denominations of faith derived?

A. From the different views in which Christ is represented in the word.

Q. 18. How may the above denominations of faith be

applied to the different views in which Christ is represented in the word?

A. When the flesh and blood of Christ (or his incarnation and satisfaction) are exhibited as meat indeed, and drink indeed; faith, in conformity to this, is called eating and drinking of the same, John vi. 55, 56; when Christ is held forth as a refuge, faith is a flying to him for safety, Heb. vi. 18; and when he is represented as a door, faith is an entering in by him, John x. 9.

Q. 19. Why is faith, in the answer, expressed by [receiving?]

A. Because Christ, the glorious object of it, is revealed in scripture, under the notion of a gift, 2 Cor. ix. 15, presented to such as are quite poor, and have nothing of their own, Rom. iii. 17, 18.

Q. 20. Can there be a receiving of Christ, without a previous giving of him?

A. No: there may indeed be a giving, where there is no receiving, because the gift may be refused; but there can be no such thing as a receiving of Christ, without a giving of him before; for a man can receive nothing except it be given him from heaven, John iii. 27.

Q. 21. Why is faith called a [resting] on Christ?

A. Because he is revealed in the word as a firm foundation, Isa. xxviii. 16, on which we may lay the weight of our everlasting concerns, with the greatest confidence and satisfaction, Ps. cxvi. 7.

Q. 22. To what other scripture expression is resting on Christ equivalent?

A. It is the same with trusting in him, Isa. xxvi. 4; or relying on his righteousness and fulness, as laid out in the word, for our unanswerable plea, and inexhaustible treasure, chap. xlv. 24.

Q. 23. For what end do we receive Christ and rest upon him?

A. [For salvation,] Acts xv. 11.

Q. 24. What is the [salvation] for which we receive and rest upon Christ?

A. It is salvation from sin, Matt. i. 21, as well as from wrath, 1 Thess. i. 10; consisting in a life of holiness here, as well as of happiness hereafter. It is salvation begun in this life, and consummated in glory, Rev. iii. 21.

Q. 25. Why are we said to receive and rest upon Christ [alone] for this salvation?

A. To exclude every thing else except Christ himself, and his righteousness, as the ground of our confidence before God, and title to eternal life, Acts iv. 12.

Q. 26. What else do men ordinarily rest upon for salvation?

A. Upon the general mercy of God; the works of the

law; or a mixture of their own works with the righteousness of Christ.

Q. 27. Who are they that rest on the general mercy of God?

A. They who never saw the necessity of a satisfaction to law and justice, in order to the honourable exercise of mercy, according to Ex. xxxiv. 7.

Q. 28. Who are they who rest on the works of the law, as the ground of their confidence?

A. Such as have never been convinced, that the demands of the law are utterly above their reach, Gal. iii. 12.

Q. 29. Who are they that are for blending or mixing their own works with the righteousness of Christ, as the ground of their hope?

A. Such as foolishly imagine they can supply what is defective in their own obedience, by what Christ has done for them, Rom. ix. 31, 32.

Q. 30. To what does our Lord resemble this practice?

A. To the putting a piece of new cloth into an old garment, by which the rent is made worse, Matt. ix. 16.

Q. 31. Are not the very expressions of receiving and resting on Christ, designed to exclude the works of the law, from being any part of the ground of our hope of salvation?

A. Yes; for, when a poor man receives his alms, or a weary man sits down, and rests himself; neither of them can, in any propriety of speech, be said to work.

Q. 32. Upon what warrant do we receive and rest upon him for salvation?

A. Upon the warrant of his being offered.

Q. 33. To whom is he offered?

A. He is offered [to us,] men and women of Adam's family, in contradistinction to the angels that fell, Heb. ii. 16.

Q. 34. Where is the offer made?

A. [In the gospel.]

Q. 35. What is the [gospel] as containing this offer?

A. It is good tidings, Luke ii. 10; or the promise of eternal life, 1 John ii. 25, to sinners of mankind, as such, through Jesus Christ our Lord, Prov. viii. 4.

Q. 36. Though the offer of Christ to us be last mentioned, in the answer, yet is it not the first thing to be believed?

A. Surely it is; for unless one believe that Christ is offered to him as a Saviour, he will never receive and rest upon him for salvation, Rom. x. 14.

Q. 37. Who offers Christ to us in the gospel?

A. God, essentially considered in the person of the Father, makes the original or authentic gospel offer of him, John

vi. 32: "My Father *giveth* you the true bread from heaven."

Q. 38. In what form or tenor does this authentic offer run?

A. In the form of a deed of gift, or grant, in which he makes over his Son, Jesus Christ, to mankind lost, that whosoever of them all shall receive this gift, shall not perish, but have eternal life.

Q. 39. In what text of scripture (amongst others) is this grant, or authentic gospel offer, contained?

A. It is expressed in so many words, John iii. 16: "God so loved the world, that he gave his only begotten Son, that whosoever believeth on him should not perish, but have everlasting life."

Q. 40. Who are they that offer Christ to sinners in subordination to God?

A. Ministers of the gospel, who have a commission from him so to do, 2 Cor. v. 19, 20.

Q. 41. What is the ministerial offer?

A. It is the publishing or proclaiming of Heaven's gift, or grant, to sinners of mankind, without exception, as the foundation of their faith or warrant to believe, 1 John v. 11.

Q. 42. What would be the consequence, if there were any exception in the authentic gospel offer?

A. The consequence would be, that no ministerial offer of Christ could be made to the party excepted, more than to the fallen angels.

Q. 43. Does the universality of Heaven's grant, and of the ministerial offer founded on it, infer a universal redemption as to purchase?

A. By no means; it only infers a universal warrant to believe.

Q. 44. How do you prove that it infers a universal warrant to believe?

A. From this, that if there were not such a gift and grant of Christ as warranted all to receive him, the unbelieving world could not be condemned for rejecting him, as we find they are, John iii. 18: "He that believeth not is condemned already."

Q. 45. Is there any analogy, or proportion, between our receiving and resting on Christ, and the offer that is made of him in the gospel?

A. Yes: we receive and rest upon him [*as*] he is offered in it, 1 Cor. xv. 11: So we preach, and so ye believed.

Q. 46. How is he offered in the gospel?

A. He is offered freely, wholly, and particularly.

Q. 47. How do you prove, that he is offered, and should be received freely?

A. From Isa. lv. 1: "Ho, every one that thirsteth, come ye to the waters, and he that hath no money; come ye buy and eat; yea, come, buy wine and milk, without money and without price, Rev. xxii. 17: Whosoever will, let him take the water of life freely."

Q. 48. Why is Christ to be received freely?

A. Because God, out of his sovereign and matchless love, makes a free gift of him to mankind sinners, John iii. 16, as being infinitely above all price, Job xxviii. 13—24.

Q. 49. What do the proud and legal hearts of sinners bring as a price for Christ, who is absolutely inestimable?

A. Their duties, their good qualifications, their honest aims, their sincere endeavours, and the like.

Q. 50. Why do they presume to bring such things as these?

A. Because they know not that they are wretched, and miserable, and poor, and blind, and naked, Rev. iii. 17.

Q. 51. What is it to receive Christ wholly?

A. It is to receive him in his person, as vested with all his relative offices, of prophet, priest, and king.

Q. 52. Why must he be received wholly?

A. Because there is nothing of Christ we can possibly do without: standing in absolute need of him, as a prophet for instruction; as a priest, for righteousness; and as a king, for sanctification, 1 Cor. i. 30.

Q. 53. What is it for a person to receive Christ particularly?

A. It is to be verily persuaded that Christ is his, upon the grant and offer of him, in the word, to him in particular, John vii. 37, and ix. 35.

Q. 54. Is it not sufficient that a man believe, that the grant and offer of Christ is to sinners of mankind in general?

A. No: there can be no benefit by a belief of the general offer, without a particular application, or appropriation of it to the person himself, 1 Tim. i. 15.

Q. 55. How is this illustrated by an example?

A. It is commonly illustrated thus: If a king makes a proclamation of pardon and indemnity to all the rebels within his kingdom, it is plain, that every individual rebel must either believe the pardon of his own crime of rebellion in particular, or else reject the king's proclamation of grace, and continue in his rebellious practices: there is no medium.

Q. 56. Is not believing that an indemnity is offered to rebels in general, a medium between the two?

A. No: because loyal subjects, who need no pardon, may believe that a general indemnity is offered to rebels; and this even rebels themselves may believe, who yet may reject the benefit of that indemnity, and continue in their rebellion, John v. 40.

Q. 57. Is a belief and persuasion of the mercy of God in

Christ, and of Christ's ability and willingness to save al. that come to him, all that is necessary to constitute justifying faith?

A. No: because there being no appropriation, or particular application in this persuasion, it can be no more than such a faith as devils and reprobates may have; or such as Papists and Arminians may subscribe to, consistently with their other errors and heresies.

Q. 58. What is that appropriating persuasion, in the nature of faith, which is necessary to answer the call and offer of the gospel?

A. It is not a persuasion that Christ is mine in possession, or that I am already in a state of grace: but a persuasion that Christ is mine in the gift of God, and offer of the gospel, Zech. xiii. 9: "I will say, It is my people; and they shall say, The Lord is my God: and therefore I appropriate to myself the common salvation, Acts xv. 11; or what did lie before me in common, in the gospel offer, I take home to my own soul in particular, Gal. ii. 20, "Who loved me, and gave himself for me:" believing that I shall have life and salvation by Christ; and that whatever he did, for the redemption of sinners, he did it for me.

Q. 59. Why is an appropriating persuasion (or, a man's being persuaded that Christ is his in particular) necessary to the nature of saving and justifying faith?

A. Because nothing can relieve the sinner from the curse of the law, accusing and condemning him in particular, but faith's application of an offered Saviour, as made a curse for him in particular, to deliver him from that law-curse, Gal. iii. 10, 13.

Q. 60. How do you prove, that a particular application of Christ is the effectual relief from the curse of the law, denounced against the sinner in particular?

A. From this, that the free gift is as full to justification, as the offence, through the law, was to condemnation; for, "as by the offence of one, judgment came upon all men to condemnation; even so, by the righteousness of one, the free gift came upon all men to justification of life," Rom. v. 18.

Q. 61. Since an appropriating persuasion is necessary to the nature of faith, has every one that has true faith, always an assurance of his being in a gracious state?

A. No; for though a believer be persuaded that Christ is his in the promise and offer of the gospel: yet, through the prevalency of remaining corruption, he may frequently doubt of his being in a state of grace, or of his present title to eternal life, Isa. xlix. 14.

Q. 62. Is doubting, then, in the nature of faith, because it is incident to the believer?

A. Doubting can no more be said to be in the nature of

faith, because, through the prevalence of unbelief and corruption, it sometimes takes place in the believer, than darkness can be said to be in the nature of the sun, because it is sometimes eclipsed; for faith and doubting are, in their own nature, opposite, Matt. xxi. 21 : "If ye have faith, and doubt not."

Q. 63. Have all true believers the same measure of saving faith?

A. No; some are but of little faith, Matt. xiv. 31; whereas others are "strong in faith; giving glory to God," Rom. iv. 20. Howbeit the lowest measure of true and saving faith is infallibly connected with glory, Matt. xii. 20.

Q. 64. What are the evidences of a strong faith?

A. Trusting to the bare word of a faithful and powerful God, even when the outward course of providence seems to run against the performance of the promise, Rom. iv. 19; a fixed resolution to wait on the Lord, for the promised good which we want, even after seeming repulses and refusals, Matt. xv. 22—29; and a sedate reposing ourselves on an unchangeable God, under all the vicissitudes of time, Ps. cxii. 7.

Q. 65. How may the weakness of faith be discerned?

A. The more easily a person can suspect the love and favour of God, Isa. xl. 27; the more impatient under delays of answering requests, chap. xxxviii. 14; and the more addicted to a life of sense, John xx. 25, the weaker is the faith.

Q. 66. How may the truth and reality of saving faith be known, though it be in the weakest and lowest degree?

A. If we bear an inward enmity to all sins, because offensive to God, Ps. li. 4; if we can say, that it is the desire of our souls to love Christ above all things, John xxi. 17; and to be eternal debtors to free grace, reigning through his righteousness, Rom. v. 20, 21; then we may warrantably conclude, that our faith, however weak, is yet of a saving nature.

Q. 67. To what is true faith opposed in scripture?

A. It is opposed to a staggering at the promise, Rom. iv 20; to wavering, James i. 6; to doubting, Matt. xxi. 21; and, in a word, to unbelief, Mark ix. 24.

Q. 68. Who are they who will not be charged with the sin of unbelief?

A. The Heathen world, who are not privileged with the light of gospel revelation, Rom. x. 14: "How shall they believe in him of whom they have not heard?"

Q. 69. What is the evil of this sin, in those who are favoured with gospel light?

A. It makes God a liar, 1 John v. 10; treads "under foot the Son of God;" and does "despite unto the Spirit of grace," Heb. x. 29.

Q. 70. What is the proper seat of faith?
A. The *heart:* for with the heart man believeth unto righteousness, Rom. x. 10; though faith be radically in the understanding, yet it operates upon the will, which embraces the object with particular application, Heb. xi. 13.

Q. 71. Is knowledge necessary to saving faith?
A. It is so necessary that there can be no saving faith without it, 1 John iv. 16: " We have known and believed the love that God hath to us."

Q. 72. What is the difference between the knowledge of faith, and speculative knowledge?
A. The knowledge of faith is humbling, 1 Cor. viii. 2; transforming, Acts xxvi. 18; affectionate, 1 John iv. 8; and progressive, Hos. vi. 3: whereas, common or speculative knowledge has none of these properties, nor effects.

Q. 73. In what consists the harmony or agreement between faith, love, and hope?
A. By faith, we get a sight of an unseen good, and believe it, Heb. xi. 27; by love we desire and seek after it, Isa. xxvi. 8; and by hope, we confidently expect, and patiently wait for it, Rom. viii. 25.

Q. 74. How does faith view and consider its objects?
A. It views them, as certain, suitable, and invisible.

Q. 75. Why does it view them as certain?
A. Because of the unquestionable veracity of God who reveals them, John vi. 69: " We believe, and are *sure*, that thou art that Christ, the Son of the living God."

Q. 76. Why does it consider them as suitable?
A. Because they are exactly adapted to the state and circumstance of the soul, whatever they are, 1 Cor. i. 30. 1 Tim. i. 15.

Q. 77. Why does faith view its objects as invisible?
A. Because it acts and goes forth toward them, upon the bare testimony of God; not only without the concurrence of sense and carnal reason, John xx. 29, but oftentimes contrary to them, Rom. iv. 18, 19.

Q. 78. Is faith any part of our justifying righteousness?
A. No: we acknowledge no other righteousness, for pardon and acceptance, but the righteousness of Christ alone, Phil. iii. 9.

Q. 79. Why then are we said to be justified by faith? Rom. v. 1.
A. Because it is faith which lays hold upon, and receives that righteousness by which we are justified, Rom. iii. 22.

Q. 80. Is not faith necessary to interest us in Christ, and the benefits of his purchase?
A. Yes; for though the endorsement of the promise to us, gives us a right of access, Acts ii. 39; yet it is faith, that gives the right of possession, John vi. 47: "He that believeth on me *hath* everlasting life."

OF REPENTANCE UNTO LIFE.

QUEST. 87. *What is repentance unto life?*

ANS. Repentance unto life is a saving grace, whereby a sinner, out of a true sense of his sin, and apprehension of the mercy of God in Christ, doth, with grief and hatred of his sin, turn from it unto God, with full purpose of, and endeavour after, new obedience.

Q. 1. Why is the repentance, described in the answer called [repentance unto life?] Acts xi. 18.

A. Because being a saving grace, it is inseparably connected with salvation, of which it is a part; and likewise to distinguish it from the sorrow of the world, which worketh death, 2 Cor. vii. 10.

Q. 2. What is meant by the sorrow of the world working death?

A. The meaning is, that the legal sorrow, or horror of conscience, which the men of the world may have, from a dread of God, as a vindictive judge, ready to pour out the vials of his wrath and vengeance upon them, without any conception or belief of his mercy through Christ, is nothing else but the beginning of eternal death, and inconceivable misery; as was the case with Cain, Judas, and others.

Q. 3. Whether is repentance a transient action or an abiding principle?

A. It is an abiding principle, continually disposing the person to mourn for sin, and to turn from it all the days of his life, Isa. xxxviii. 14, 15.

Q. 4. Is repentance then to be considered as a thing that is over with the first days of one's religion?

A. No; but it is to be viewed as a permanent grace, an habitual frame of soul, inclining those who are privileged with it, to mourn daily for sin, till "God shall wipe away all tears from their eyes," in heaven, Rev. xxi. 4.

Q. 5. Who is the proper subject of repentance?

A. None but a [sinner] can be the subject capable of it: for just or righteous persons need no repentance, Luke xv. 7.

Q. 6. By whom is it wrought in the heart of a sinner?

A. "By the Spirit of God, Zech. xii. 10." *

Q. 7. What is the instrument or means, by which the Spirit works this grace?

A. "The word of God, Acts, xi. 18, 20, 21."†

Q. 8. What is the instrumentality of the word, in the hand of the Spirit, for working repentance?

A. In the word there is a display of the holiness of the

---

* Larger Catechism, Quest. 76. † Ibid.

divine nature and law, to which we ought to be conformed, Lev. xix. 2; the word also discovers the necessity of union with Christ, and the imputation of his righteousness, as the foundation of true holiness, 1 Cor. i. 30; together with the inevitable ruin of all who go on in their trespasses, Ps. lxviii. 21, and all these powerfully set home, by the Spirit, upon the conscience of the sinner.

Q. 9. In what consists [a true sense of sin?]

A. In a "sight and sense, not only of the danger, but also of the filthiness and odiousness of sin, Ezek. xxxvi. 31,"* as contrary to the holiness of God, and, consequently, as highly offensive to him, Ps. li. 4.

Q. 10. How is a true sense of sin begotten in the soul?

A. By faith, or an [apprehension of the mercy of God in Christ.]

Q. 11. May there not be a sense of sin without this apprehension of the mercy of God in Christ?

A. Yes; but not a [true] sense; there may be a sense of sin as hurtful to the person, Gen. iv. 13; but not as hateful to God, Hab. i. 13.

Q. 12. Why is the mercy of God said to be apprehended [in Christ?]

A. Because though God is essentially merciful, yet his mercy can have no egress towards any sinner of mankind, consistently with the honour of his justice and holiness, except through the obedience and satisfaction of Christ, Ex. xxxiv. 6, 7.

Q. 13. What is it to *apprehend* the mercy of God in Christ?

A. It is the same with faith, or believing; it being by faith only, that we can lay hold upon his mercy, Ps. xiii. 5.

Q. 14. Is it from faith then that repentance flows, as the proper source of it?

A. Yes; for though faith and repentance are graces given together, and at once in respect of time; yet, in the order of nature, the acting of faith goes before the exercise of repentance, Zech. xii. 10.

Q. 15. How does it appear, from scripture, that faith goes before repentance, in the order of nature?

A. The scriptures set forth the blessed object of faith, and the promises of rich grace, as powerful motives and inducements to repentance, Jer. iii. 14, Joel ii. 13; by which it is evident that it must be by a believing application of this glorious object, brought nigh in the promise, that a sinner is enabled to exercise true repentance, Acts xi. 21: "And a great number believed, and turned unto the Lord."

Q. 16. How may the precedency of faith be evinced from the nature of repentance itself?

* Larger Catechism, Question 76.

A. Repentance is turning from sin unto God; but there can be no turning to God, but through Christ, John xiv. 6; and no coming to Christ except by faith, chap. vi. 35.

Q. 17. Is not repentance placed before faith in scripture, Mark i. 15, Repent ye, and believe the gospel?

A. The reason is, repentance being the end, and faith the means to that end; though the end be first in one's intention, yet the means are first in practice. Thus, in the text quoted, Christ commands sinners to repent; but then in order to their repenting, he commands them to believe the gospel, as the only way to do it.

Q. 18. How are we sure, that where repentance is named before faith in scripture, it is to be understood of repentance as the end, and of faith as the only way and means?

A. From Acts xx. 21: Testifying—"repentance toward God, and faith toward our Lord Jesus Christ:" where it is obvious, that if faith toward our Lord Jesus Christ is not the means of repentance toward God, that fundamental truth would be destroyed, that Christ is the only way to the Father, as he himself affirms, John xiv. 6: "No man cometh unto the Father but by me."

Q. 19. Is repentance to be separated from faith?

A. No: though these graces are to be distinguished, yet they are never to be separated from one another, being conjoined in the same promise, Zech. xii. 10: "They shall *look* upon me whom they have pierced, and they shall *mourn* for him."

Q. 20. What is the evil of maintaining, that none but true penitents have a warrant to embrace Christ by faith?

A. It sets sinners upon spinning repentance out of their own bowels, that they may fetch it with them, as a price in their hand to Christ, instead of coming to him by faith, to obtain it from him, as his gift, Acts v. 31.

Q. 21. What are the constituent parts, or ingredients, of true repentance, as flowing from faith?

A. [Grief and hatred of sin; turning from it unto God; with full purpose of, and endeavour after, new obedience.]

Q. 22. What is that [grief] which is an ingredient of true repentance?

A. It is a real, inward and abiding sorrow for sin, as offensive and dishonouring to a holy and gracious God, Job xl. 4, 5.

Q. 23. What is that [hatred] of sin, which accompanies true repentance?

A. It is not only a loathing and abhorring of our sin, but of ourselves, on account of it, Isa. vi. 5.

Q. 24. What are the qualities of this hatred?

A. It is universal, against all sin, Ps. cxix. 104; and irreconcilable to any known sin, Ps. ci. 3.

Q. 25. What is the formal nature of evangelical repentance, or that which properly completes it?

A. It is when a sinner doth, with grief and hatred of his sin, [turn from it unto God.]

Q. 26. From what does the sinner turn in repentance?

A. He turns from sin; because a continuance in the practice of sin is inconsistent with repentance, Ezek. xiv. 6: "Repent and turn—from your idols, and turn away your faces from all your abominations."

Q. 27. How can penitents be said to turn from sin, when it remains in them, and they are daily offending while in this life?

A. Though they cannot shake themselves loose of the being and remains of sin, yet they turn from it, not only in their life and conversation, but likewise in their heart and affection.

Q. 28. How do they evidence that they turn from it in their life and conversation?

A. By resisting the outbreakings of sin, and all temptations to it, Ps. xviii. 23; by watching against all occasions of it, Prov. iv. 14, 15; and endeavouring to "have always a conscience void of offence toward God, and toward men," Acts xxiv. 16.

Q. 29. How do they manifest their turning from sin in heart and affection?

A. In as much as though sin cleaves to them, they do not cleave to it, as formerly, but hate and loathe it, Ps. cxix. 104, 113.

Q. 30. To what does the sinner turn in repentance?

A. He turns [unto God,] Hos. vi. 1: Come, and let us return unto the Lord.

Q. 31. Do not many turn from one sin to another, and never to God?

A. Yes: "They return, but not to the Most High," Hos. vii. 16.

Q. 32. What is the true cause of the sinner's turning to God?

A. It is his being turned unto God first, Jer. xxxi. 19: "Surely, after that I was turned, I repented."

Q. 33. How is the sinner turned unto God first?

A. By the Spirit's working faith in him, whereby he receives and rests on Christ for salvation, of which remission of sin, and repentance, are a part, Acts v. 31.

Q. 34. In what does the sinner's turning to God consist?

A. It consists in his turning to the loving of God, as his Lord and Master, Isa. xxvi. 13; and to his duty to him as such, Acts ix. 6.

Q. 35. How does the returning sinner express his love to God, as his Lord and Master?

OF REPENTANCE UNTO LIFE.

A. By a voluntary choice of him as his only Lord, Hos. ii. 7; and by looking upon his service as the greatest freedom and happiness, Ps. lxxxiv. 4.

Q. 36. How does he testify his returning to his duty to God, as his Lord and Master?

A. By a [full purpose of, and endeavour after new obedience.]

Q. 37. What is the nature of this [purpose] of duty to God, into which the true penitent enters?

A. It is a purpose or resolution to return to the practice of every known duty, Ps. cxix. 106, and to spirituality in it, Phil. iii. 3.

Q. 38. Why called a [*full*] purpose?

A. Because it is not only a resolution of what a person will do hereafter, but a resolution which is immediately put in execution, without delay, Ps. cxix. 60: "I made haste, and delayed not to keep thy commandments;" like the prodigal, who says, I will arise, and go to my father; and immediately he arose and went, Luke xv. 18, 20.

Q. 39. What is the inseparable concomitant of this full purpose in all true penitents?

A. An [endeavour after new obedience.]

Q. 40. Why is a full purpose of new obedience connected with an endeavour after it?

A. Because purposes, without endeavours, are but like blossoms without fruit, which can never prove one to be a true penitent, Matt. xxi. 30.

Q. 41. Why called an [endeavour] after new obedience?

A. Because, though the penitent is sensible he cannot perform this kind of obedience in his own strength, yet he aims at it, and at no less than perfection in it, Phil. iii. 14: "I press toward the mark, for the prize of the high calling of God in Christ Jesus."

Q. 42. Why is the obedience which the true penitent purposes and endeavours after, called [new obedience?]

A. Because it is such an obedience as flows from a new principle, is influenced by new motives, performed in a new manner, and is aimed at a new end.

Q. 43. What is the new principle from which this obedience flows?

A. A principle of faith, Rom. xiv. 23, and a principle of love, John xiv. 15.

Q. 44. What are the new motives by which this new obedience is influenced?

A. The grace of God, Tit. ii. 11, 12; and the love of Christ, 2 Cor. v. 14, 15.

Q. 45. What are the motives by which men, in a natural state, are influenced to duties?

A. The dictates of a natural conscience, Rom. ii. 15; their own interest and reputation, Matt. vi. 5, a mercenary hope of heaven, Micah vi. 6, 7, or a slavish fear of hell, Isa. xxxiii. 14.

Q. 46. What is the new manner in which new obedience is performed?

A. It is performed in the strength of Christ, Phil. iv. 13; or in a dependence on the furniture secured in the promise, 2 Cor. xii. 9; it is done with delight, Isa. lxiv. 5; and with the whole heart, Ps. cxix. 69.

Q. 47. What is the new end at which it aims?

A. The glory of God is the ultimate end of it, 1 Cor. x. 31.

Q. 48. What is the difference between legal and gospel repentance?

A. Legal repentance flows from a dread of God's wrath, Matt. xxvii. 3, 5, 6; but gospel repentance from the faith of his mercy, Ps. cxxx. 4; in legal repentance, the sinner is taken up mostly with the fatal consequences of sin, Isa. lxix. 9—12; in gospel repentance, he is chiefly affected with the evil nature of it, as contrary to the holy nature and law of God, Luke xv. 21.

Q. 49. What are the motives that should produce repentance?

A. The command of God, Acts xvii. 30; the sufferings of Christ, Zech. xii. 10; and the certain danger of impenitency, Luke xiii. 5.

Q. 50. What are the evidences of true repentance?

A. The very same that are mentioned by the apostle, 2 Cor. vii. 11: "For behold, the self-same thing that ye sorrowed after a godly sort, what carefulness it wrought in you; yea, what clearing of yourselves; yea, what indignation; yea, what fear; yea, what vehement desire; yea, what zeal; yea, what revenge!"

Q. 51. What is that carefulness which is a mark of the true penitent?

A. It is carefulness about the one thing needful, that good part which shall not be taken away, Luke x. 42.

Q. 52. Upon what ground will the true penitent clear himself?

A. Only upon the ground of the surety righteousness imputed to him, Isa. xlv. 24.

Q. 53. What is the principal object of his indignation?

A. It is sin, as striking immediately against God, Ps. li. 4, compared with Ps. cxix. 104.

Q. 54. What is that fear, which is an evidence of true repentance?

A. It is a filial and reverential fear of God, or a standing in awe to offend him, Gen. xxxix. 9.

Q. 55. What is that vehement desire, with which a true penitent is privileged?

A. It is an earnest and ardent desire after conformity to God, and fellowship with him, Ps. xxvii. 4.

Q. 56. What kind of zeal is it, that is evidential of gospel repentance?

A. It is zeal for the glory of God, and the interest of Christ in the world, Ps. cxxxvii. 5, 6.

Q. 57. What is that revenge, which is competent to a true penitent?

A. It is such a revenge against sin, as aims at its utter ruin and extirpation, Rom. vii. 24.

Q. 58. In what respects is repentance necessary?

A. It is necessary in respect of the command of God, Acts xvii. 30, and as evidential of the reality of faith, of which it is the native fruit, and effect, Zech. xii. 10.

Q. 59. May not this duty be delayed or put off for a while?

A. No; because of the uncertainty of time, Luke xii. 19, 20, and of the continuance of the Spirit's striving, Gen. vi. 3.

Q. 60. When should the Lord's people apply to him, for the exercise of this grace of repentance, in a more especial and particular manner?

A. After great falls, 2 Sam. xii. 13; when under severe trials, or deep affliction, 2 Sam. xv. 26, 30; and when they are to ask of God some singular favour or mercy, Dan. ix. 8, compared with verses 18, 19.

Q. 61. By what means may the lively exercise of repentance be attained?

A. By looking on it as the gift of Christ, Acts v. 31; and by viewing our sins as laid on him, who was pierced for them, Zech. xii. 10; together with searching and trying our ways, Lam. iii. 40.

QUEST. 88. *What are the outward and ordinary means whereby Christ communicateth to us the benefits of redemption?*

ANS. The outward and ordinary means whereby Christ communicateth to us the benefits of redemption, are his ordinances, especially the word, sacraments, and prayer all which are made effectual to the elect for salvation.

Q. 1. What do you understand by [the benefits of redemption?]

A. All the blessings of Christ's purchase, which may be summed up in grace here, and glory hereafter, Ps. lxxxiv. 11.

Q. 2. Who [communicateth] these benefits or blessings to us?

A. [*Christ*] himself, who has them wholly at his disposal, Luke xxii. 29: I appoint unto you a kingdom.

Q. 3. How comes Christ to have the disposal of them wholly in his hands?

A. By his Father's gift, John iii. 35: "The Father loveth the Son, and hath *given* all things into his hand;" and by his own purchase of them; hence called a purchased possession, Eph. i. 14.

Q. 4. What is it for Christ to communicate the benefits of redemption?

A. It is not to give away the property of them from himself, but to make us sharers with him in them all; that is, to make us heirs of God, and joint heirs with Christ, Rom. viii. 17.

Q. 5. Does Christ communicate them in a mediate or immediate way?

A. In a mediate way, through the intervention of ordinances, Eph. iv. 11—14.

Q. 6. What are the [ordinances] by which Christ communicates to us the benefits of redemption?

A. They are " prayer and thanksgiving, in the name of Christ; the reading, preaching, and hearing of the word; the administering, and receiving the sacraments; church government and discipline; the ministry and maintenance thereof; religious fasting; swearing by the name of God, and vowing unto him." *

Q. 7. Why are these called [*His*] ordinances?

A. Because they are all of them instituted and prescribed by him in his word, as the alone King and Head of his church, to be observed in it to the end of the world, Matt. xxviii. 20.

Q. 8. Have we any reason to expect, that the benefits of redemption will be communicated by ordinances of man's invention and appointment?

A. No; for all such ordinances, having no higher sanction than the commandments of men, are declared to be *in vain*, Matt. xv. 9: they are condemned as will-worship, Col. ii. 23; and the observers of them severely threatened, Mic. vi. 16.

Q. 9. Why is it said, [especially the word, sacraments, and prayer?]

A. Because, though the other ordinances above mentioned are not to be excluded, as being all of them useful in their own place; yet the word, sacraments, and prayer, are the chief or principal outward means for communicating the benefits of redemption, Acts ii. 42.

---

* Larger Catechism, Quest. 108. See them all explained, on the Duties required in the Second Commandment.

Q. 10. What is the special usefulness of the [word] for communicating the benefits of redemption?

A. In the word these benefits are exhibited and offered to sinners of mankind, as the ground of their faith, that, believing they may be possessed of them all, John xx. 31.

Q. 11. What is the special usefulness of the [sacraments] for communicating these benefits?

A. The sacraments represent to our senses, 1 Cor. x. 16, what the word does to our faith, and are designed for the confirmation of it, Rom. iv. 11.

Q. 12. What is the special usefulness of [prayer] for the above purpose?

A. The prayer of faith fetches home to the soul all the good that is wrapped up both in the word and in the sacraments, Mark xi. 24: "What things soever ye desire when ye pray, believe that ye receive them, and ye shall have them."

Q. 13. Why are the word, sacraments, and prayer, called [means,] by which Christ communicates to us the benefits of redemption?

A. Because he is pleased to begin and carry on the work of grace in the soul, by and under these ordinances, Acts ii. 41, 42.

Q. 14. Why called the [outward] means?

A. To distinguish them from faith, repentance, and other inward means; and particularly to distinguish them from the inward and powerful influences of the Holy Spirit, which are necessary to accompany the outward means in order to salvation, Zech. iv. 6.

Q. 15. Why called [ordinary] means?

A. Because they are the stated and ordinary way and method, by which Christ communicates the benefits of redemption to sinners of mankind, Rom. x. 14—18. Ezek. xxxvii. 28.

Q. 16. Are there any extraordinary means without the word, by which Christ communicates the benefits of redemption to adult persons?

A. No; for whatever providences God may make use of, when he is beginning or carrying on his work of grace in the soul, Acts ix. 3—7; yet these dispensations are always to be considered in a subserviency to the word, chap. xvi. 25—33, or as occasions of the Spirit's working in concurrence with it, 2 Pet. i. 18, 19.

Q. 17. Are the ordinances, of themselves, effectual for communicating the benefits of redemption?

A. No; they are [made effectual,] Rom. i. 16.

Q. 18. To whom are they made effectual?

A. To the [elect] only, Acts xiii. 48.

Q. 19. For what end are they made effectual to the elect?

A. For [salvation,] Heb. x. 39

Q. 20. What is meant by salvation?

A. Not only a begun deliverance from all sin and misery, and a begun possession of all happiness and blessedness in this life, John iii. 15; but likewise a total freedom from the one, and a full and uninterrupted enjoyment of the other, in the life to come, Rev. xxi. 4.

Q. 21. If the ordinances are made effectual to the elect only for salvation, why have others, in the visible church, the benefit of them?

A. To show the infinite intrinsic sufficiency of the satisfaction of Christ, 1 John iv. 14; and, at the same time, to render those who slight such valuable privileges the more inexcusable, John xv. 22.

Q. 22. What may we learn from Christ's instituting his ordinances to be the outward and ordinary means of salvation?

A. We may from thence learn the difference between the church militant, which sees but through a glass darkly, and the church triumphant, which sees face to face, 1 Cor. xiii. 12.

QUEST. 89. *How is the word made effectual to salvation?*

ANS. The Spirit of God maketh the reading, but especially the preaching of the word, an effectual means of convincing and converting sinners, and of building them up in holiness and comfort, through faith, unto salvation.

Q. 1. What is meant by [the word] in this answer?

A. The whole of divine revelation, contained in the scriptures of the Old and New Testament.

Q. 2. What has God appointed with reference to his word, that it may be effectual to salvation?

A. He has appointed [the reading,] John v. 39; but especially the preaching thereof, 2 Tim. iv. 2.

Q. 3. "Is the word of God to be read by all?"

A. "Although all are not permitted to read the word publicly to the congregation, Deut. xxxi. 9, 11, yet all sorts of people are bound to read it apart by themselves, chap. xvii. 19, and with their families, chap. vi. 7." *

Q. 4. What is the meaning of these words in our Larger Catechism, "all are not permitted to read the word publicly to the congregation?"

A. The meaning is not, as if there were an order of men

* Larger Catechism, Question. 156.

appointed by Christ, to be *readers* in the church, distinct from ministers; but only, that none ought to read publicly to the congregation, except those whose office it is, not only to read the word of God, but to explain it to the edification of others, Neh. viii. 8: "So they read in the book of the law of God distinctly, and gave the *sense*, and caused them (namely, the people,) to understand the reading."

Q. 5. Why is the reading of the scriptures apart by ourselves necessary for every one?

A. Because the scriptures are a sword for defence, Eph. vi. 17; a lamp for direction, Ps. cxix. 105; and food for nourishment, Jer. xv. 16: in all which respects they are necessary for every Christian travelling Zion-ward, 2 Tim. iii. 16, 17.

Q. 6. May not the reading of the scriptures in our families, supersede the reading of them apart by ourselves?

A. No; the doing of the one ought by no means to justle out the other.

Q. 7. What is essentially requisite in order to capacitate the unlearned to read the scriptures?

A. That they be "translated out of the original into vulgar languages, 1 Cor. xiv. 11."*

Q. 8. How is the word of God to be read?

A. "The holy scriptures are to be read with a high and reverend esteem of them, Neh. viii. 5; with a firm persuasion that they are the very word of God, 2 Pet. i. 21; and that he only can enable us to understand them, Luke xxiv. 45."†

Q. 9. Why should we read the scriptures with a high and reverend esteem of them?

A. Because they are dictated by the Holy Ghost, and "are able to make us wise unto salvation," 2 Tim. iii. 15.

Q. 10. Why should we read them with a firm persuasion that they are the very word of God?

A. Because without this we can never build our hope on them, as containing the words of eternal life, 1 Thess. ii. 13.

Q. 11. Why should we read them with a persuasion that God only can enable us to understand them?

A. Because, without this, we cannot exercise a dependence upon him, for that spiritual and internal illumination, which is necessary to a saving and experimental knowledge of them, 1 Cor. ii. 10.

Q. 12. "By whom is the word of God to be preached?"

A. "Only by such as are sufficiently gifted, Mal. ii. 7, and also duly approved and called to that office, Rom. x. 15. 1 Tim. iv. 14." ‡

* Larger Catechism Quest. 156. † Ibid. Quest. 157. ‡ Ibid. Quest. 158.

Q. 13. Who are they that are sufficiently gifted?
A. They are such as are not only of a blameless moral walk, and have a good report of them that are without, 1 Tim. iii. 7: but likewise such as have a competent stock of human literature, Tit. i. 9; and are, in the judgment of charity, reputed to be pious and religious men, 2 Tim. i. 5.

Q. 14. What is it to be duly approved and called to that office?
A. It is not only to be approved by the presbytery, who have the sole power of trying the ministerial qualifications, and of ordination to that office, 1 Tim. iv. 14; but likewise to have the call and consent of the people, who are to be under the pastoral inspection and charge, Acts i. 23, and xiv. 23.

Q. 15. "How is the word of God to be preached by those that are called thereunto?"
A. They are to preach "sound doctrine diligently, plainly, faithfully, wisely, zealously, and sincerely."*

Q. 16. What are we to understand by sound doctrine?
A. The whole system of divine truth, contained in the holy scriptures, or evidently deducible from it; particularly whatever has the greatest tendency to depreciate self, and to exalt Christ, who ought to be the main and leading subject of all gospel preaching, 2 Cor. iv. 5.

Q. 17. What is it to preach sound doctrine diligently?
A. It is to be "instant in season, and out of season, 2 Tim. iv. 2:" † embracing every opportunity of doing good to souls; and watching for them, as they that must give account, Heb. xiii. 17.

Q. 18. What is it to preach plainly?
A. It is to essay it, "not in enticing words of man's wisdom, but in demonstration of the Spirit, and of power, 1 Cor. ii. 4."‡

Q. 19. What is it to preach the word faithfully?
A. It is a "making known the whole counsel of God," (or at least a not shunning to do so,) Acts xx. 27. §

Q. 20. When may ministers be said to preach wisely?
A. When in studying, or preaching, they are wholly taken up in "applying themselves to the necessities and capacities of the hearers," ‖ Luke xii. 42. 1 Cor. iii. 2.

Q. 21. When do they preach the word zealously?
A. When they do it "with fervent love to God, and the souls of his people, ¶ 2 Cor. v. 14, and xii. 15."

Q. 22. How is the word preached sincerely?
A. When there is an "aiming at God's glory," and his people's "conversion, edification, and salvation, 1 Thess. ii. 4. 1 Cor. ix. 22. 1 Tim. iv. 16."**

* Larger Catechism, Quest. 159. † Ibid. ‡ Ibid. § Ibid.
‖ Ibid. ¶ Ibid. ** Ibid.

Q. 23. Who is it that makes the reading and preaching of the word effectual to salvation?

A. [*The Spirit of God,*] 1 Cor. ii. 11: The things of God knoweth no man, but the *Spirit* of God.

Q. 24. How does he make them effectual?

A. By accompanying them with his divine power upon the soul, Rom. i. 16.

Q. 25. Of what is it that the Spirit of God makes the reading and preaching of the word an effectual means?

A. He makes them an effectual means [of convincing and converting sinners, and of building them up in holiness and comfort, through faith, unto salvation.]

Q. 26. Does the Spirit make more frequent and ordinary use of the reading, or of the preaching of the word, for these valuable ends?

A. He makes more frequent and ordinary use of the [preaching] of the word; and therefore there is an [*especially*] prefixed to it in the answer.

Q. 27. How do you prove, that the preaching of the word is honoured as the most ordinary means?

A. From express scripture testimony to this purpose, Acts iv. 4: "Many of them which heard the word believed;" chap. xi. 20, 21: "And some of them—spake unto the Grecians, preaching the Lord Jesus. And the hand of the Lord was with them: and a great number believed, and turned unto the Lord." *

Q. 28. May not people be more edified in reading good sermons at home, than in hearing from the pulpit, such as are not perhaps, so well digested?

A. If they are in health, and not necessarily detained from the public ordinances, they have no ground to expect any real and saving benefit to their souls in the neglect of hearing the word preached: because it pleases "God, by the foolishness of preaching, to save them that believe," 1 Cor. i. 21; and "faith cometh by *hearing*," Rom. x. 17.

Q. 29. What use does the Spirit make of the reading, but especially of the preaching of the word, with reference to [sinners] in a natural state?

A. He makes use of them as an effectual means of [convincing and converting] them, 1 Cor. xiv. 24. Acts xxvi. 18.

Q. 30. What does the Spirit convince sinners of by the word?

A. Of their sin and misery.†

Q. 31. Is it by the word of the law, or the word of the gospel, that the Spirit convinces of sin?

A. It is ordinarily by the word of the law, Rom. iii. 20 —" By the *law* is the knowledge of sin."

---

* See Acts ii. 37, vi. 7. † Part I, On Effectual Calling.

Q. 32. What of sin does the Spirit convince sinners by the law?
A. Both of the nature and desert of sin.
Q. 33. In what consists the nature of sin?
A. In the want of conformity to, and transgression of, the law of God.*
Q. 34. What is the desert of sin?
A. The wrath and curse of God, both in this life and that which is to come.†
Q. 35. How does the Spirit convince men effectually, by the word, that they are sinners?
A. By convincing them, from it, that they are unbelievers, John xvi. 8, 9: He [the Spirit] will reprove [or convince] the world of sin, because they believe not on me, says our Lord.
Q. 36. What influence has a conviction of unbelief, upon convincing a person that he is indeed a sinner?
A. Were a person once convinced, that unbelief is a rejection of the only method of salvation, devised in infinite wisdom, or treating of God's unspeakable gift, offered in the word, with the utmost contempt, he could not but conclude himself, on this account, to be the greatest of sinners, and that he deserved the severest of punishments, Heb. x. 29.
Q. 37. How does the Spirit make the word an effectual means of converting sinners?
A. By making use of it to open their eyes, and to turn them from darkness to light, and from the power of Satan to God, Acts xxvi. 18.
Q. 38. Do all convictions of sin issue in conversion?
A. Far from it: many may be very deeply convinced of sin by the law, and yet never have a thorough change wrought upon their hearts; as in the instances of Cain, Judas, and others.
Q. 39. What is conversion?
A. It is the spiritual motion of the whole man toward God in Christ, as the immediate effect of the real and supernatural change, that is wrought in regeneration, Jer. iii. 21.
Q. 40. Is there any difference between conversion and regeneration?
A. They are as inseparably conjoined, as the effect is to its cause. Regeneration, or the formation of the new creature (in which we are wholly passive,) is the cause; and conversion, or the motion of the soul to God, is the effect, which infallibly follows, Hos. vi. 2.
Q. 41. Cannot man be the author of his own regeneration?

---

* Part I. On sin in general.   † See above, On the desert of sin.

A. No: he can neither prepare himself for it, nor co-operate with God in it.

Q. 42. Why can he not prepare himself for it?

A. Because the carnal mind is enmity against God, and remains so until regenerating grace take place in the soul, Rom. viii. 7, 8.

Q. 43. Why cannot man co-operate with God in this work?

A. Because there can be no acting, without a principle of action. Regeneration, being the infusing of spiritual life into the soul, it is impossible the creature can co-operate or concur with God in it, any more than Lazarus in the grave could concur in his own resurrection, till the powerful voice of Christ infused life and strength into him.

Q. 44. What would be the consequence if man could co-operate with God in regeneration?

A. The consequence would be, that God would not be so much the author of grace, as he is of nature; nor have such a revenue of glory from the one, as from the other.

Q. 45. How are regeneration and conversion denominated in scripture, to prove that God alone can be the author of them?

A. They are called a creation, Eph. ii. 10, and a resurrection, chap. v. 14.

Q. 46. Why called a creation?

A. Because there is nothing in the heart of man, out of which the new creature can be formed; every imagination of the thoughts of his heart being only evil continually, Gen. vi. 5.

Q. 47. Why called a resurrection?

A. Because it is God only "who quickeneth the dead, and calleth things which be not, as though they were," Rom. iv. 17.

Q. 48. What influence has the word upon the conversion of sinners?

A. It has no physical or natural influence of itself, but only as it is an instituted means, in the hand of the Spirit of God to that end, John vi. 63.

Q. 49. What is the efficacy of the word, in the work of conversion, compared to in scripture?

A. It is compared to a fire, to a hammer, Jer. xxiii. 29; to rain, Deut. xxxii. 2; and to light, Ps. cxix. 105.

Q. 50. Why compared to fire?

A. Because as fire purifies the metal, separating the dross; so the word, in the hand of the Spirit, purifies the heart, purging away the dross of sin and corruption that is there, Isa. iv. 4.

Q. 51. Why compared to a hammer?

A. As a hammer breaketh the rock in pieces, (Jer. xxiii. 29,) and thus fits it for the building; so the Spirit of God, by the word, breaks the hard heart of man, and fits it for being built on the foundation God has laid in Zion, Prov. xvi. 1.

Q. 52. Why compared to rain?
A. Because as the rain falls irresistibly, so there is no withstanding the efficacy of the word in the hand of the Spirit, Isa. lv. 11.

Q. 53. Why compared to light?
A. Because as light discovers things that were indiscernible in the dark; so the Spirit, by the word, discovers the latent wickedness of the heart, 1 Cor. xiv 25, and the matchless glory and excellency of Christ, as *Immanuel*, God with us, John xvi. 14.

Q. 54. What use does the Spirit make of the reading, but especially the preaching of the word, with reference to *saints*, who are brought into a state of grace?
A. He makes use of it as an effectual means [of building them up in holiness and comfort, through faith unto salvation,] Acts xx. 32. Rom. xv. 4.

Q. 55. Is [holiness] necessary in order to our justification before God?
A. It is necessary in the justified, but not in order to their justification; because this would found their justification upon works, contrary to Rom. iii. 20: "By the deeds of the law shall no flesh be justified in his sight."*

Q. 56. Is it necessary as the ground of our title to heaven?
A. It is necessary to clear our title; but our title itself can be founded only in our union with Christ, and the imputation of his righteousness, 1 Cor. iii. 22, 23: "All are yours, and ye are Christ's:" compared with Rom. viii. 30 —"Whom he justified, them he also glorified."

Q. 57. Why are the saints said to be built up in holiness?
A. Because the work of sanctification, like a building, is gradually carried on towards perfection until death, Prov. iv. 18.

Q. 58. How does the Spirit make the reading and preaching of the word, an effectual means of building up the saints in holiness?
A. By giving them, in the glass of the word, such clear and repeated discoveries of the glory of Christ, as to transform them more and more into the same image with him, 2 Cor. iii. 18.

Q. 59. How does he, by means of these ordinances, build them up in [comfort?]
A. By conveying with power to their souls, the great and precious promises, which contain all the grounds of real and lasting comfort, Gal. iii. 29, and iv. 28.

---

* See Part I. On Sanctification, Quest. 45.

OF THE MANNER OF READING THE WORD.

Q. 60. Through what instrument is it, that the Spirit makes these means effectual, for building up the saints in holiness and comfort?
A. It is [through faith,] 1 Thess. ii. 13.

Q. 61. What instrumentality has faith, in the hand of the Spirit, for building up the saints, in holiness and comfort?
A. It rests upon God's faithful word for the promotion of both, Ps. cxxxviii. 8: "The Lord will perfect that which concerneth me."

Q. 62. To what end does the Spirit, by means of the word, build them up in holiness, and comfort through faith?
A. It is unto their complete and eternal [salvation,] Rom. i. 16.

Q. 63. What may we learn from the Spirit's making the means effectual to salvation?
A. That as no special blessing can be expected from God, in the wilful neglect of the ordinances, Prov. xxviii. 9; so we may sit all our days under a pure dispensation of the gospel, without reaping any spiritual profit, unless divine supernatural agency concur, 1 Cor. iii. 6.

QUEST. 90. *How is the word to be read and heard, that it may become effectual to salvation?*

ANS. That the word may become effectual to salvation, we must attend thereunto with diligence, preparation, and prayer; receive it with faith and love; lay it up in our hearts, and practise it in our lives.

Q. 1 What has God enjoined upon us, in order to our reading and hearing his word in a right manner?
A. That we [attend thereunto;] that we [receive it;] and that we [lay it up in our hearts, and practise it in our lives.]

Q. 2. What is it to [attend] to the reading and hearing of the word?
A. It is to make the reading and hearing of it the main business of our life; to have it mostly at heart, because the word contains "that good part which shall not be taken away," Luke x. 42.

Q. 3. How ought we to attend to, or set about the reading and hearing of the word?
A. [With diligence, preparation, and prayer.]

Q. 4. What do you understand by attending to the word with diligence?
A. A careful observing and embracing every seasonable

opportunity, that may offer in providence, for reading and hearing the same, Prov. viii. 34.

Q. 5. What [preparation] should we make for reading and hearing the word?

A. We should consider, that the word has the authority of God stamped upon it, 2 Tim. iii. 16; that it is he himself who speaks to us in it, Heb. xii. 25; that it is his ordinance for our salvation, John v. 39; and will be the savour either of life or death to us, 2 Cor. ii. 16.

Q. 6. Why is [prayer] requisite for reading and hearing the word in a right manner?

A. Because as it is God alone, and none else, who can dispose our hearts for the right performance of those religious exercises, so he ought always to be addressed and supplicated for that end, Ps. cxix. 18.

Q. 7. What should we pray for, when setting about the reading and hearing of the word?

A. That it may be "the power of God unto our salvation," Rom. i. 16; or an effectual means in his hand for convincing, converting, and edifying our souls, John vi. 63.

Q. 8. What is our immediate duty, when we are actually engaged in reading or hearing of the word?

A. Our immediate duty, in that case, is to [receive it.]

Q. 9. What is it to receive the word?

A. It is, with all readiness of mind, to take it in, as the dictates of the Holy Ghost to our souls, Acts xvii. 11.

Q. 10. Why is the right improvement of the word, in time of reading and hearing of it, called a receiving it?

A. Because we can reap no real benefit to our souls, by the offer and exhibition of all the blessings that are brought nigh to us in it, unless we receive them as God's free gift to us, John iii. 27.

Q. 11. How are we to receive the word, and all the good that is in it?

A. [With faith and love.]

Q. 12. When is the word received [with faith,] in time of reading and hearing of it?

A. When there is an application of it to the soul in particular, in a suitableness to the state and case of the person, and the nature of the word, whether in a way of promise, Lam. iii. 24, or threatening, Ps. cxix. 120.

Q. 13. How may a person know if he receives the word with faith?

A. By the quickening, Ps. cxix. 50, enlightening, ver. 130, sanctifying, ver. 9, and strengthening effect of it, Dan. x. 19

Q. 14. What is the native consequence of receiving the word with faith?

A. A receiving it also with [love;] for faith worketh by love, Gal. v. 6.

Q. 15. How may our receiving the word with love be discerned?

A. When our affections are drawn out to the blessed truths and objects revealed in it; so as to esteem them more than thousands of gold and silver, Ps. cxix. 72, or even than our necessary food, Job xxiii. 12.

Q. 16. What improvement ought we to make of the word after reading or hearing of it?

A. We should [lay it up in our hearts, and practise it in our lives.]

Q. 17. What do you understand by the heart, where the word should be laid up?

A. The soul, with all its faculties, Prov. xxiii. 26; the understanding, to know the word; the will, to comply with it; the affections, to love it; and the memory, to retain it.

Q. 18. What is implied in laying up the word in our hearts?

A. That we account it the most valuable treasure, Ps. cxix. 127; that we keep it with the utmost care, ver. 11; and that we resolve to use it in all the future exigencies of our souls, ver. 24.

Q. 19. How may we know if the word is really laid up in our hearts?

A. By our delighting to meditate upon it, Ps. cxix. 97; by the Spirit's bringing it to our remembrance, John xiv. 26; and by our habitual desire of farther conformity and subjection unto it, Ps. cxix. 5.

Q. 20. For what end should we lay up the word in our hearts?

A. That we may [practise it in our lives.]

Q. 21. What is it to practise the word in our lives?

A. It is to have a conversation becoming the gospel, Phil. i. 27; or to have both the outward and inward man regulated according to the unerring rule of the word, Ps. cxix. 105.

Q. 22. What does the right manner of reading and hearing of the word teach us?

A. That the bare outward performance of duty will not be acceptable to God, unless the heart is engaged in it. Isa. xxix. 13.

Quest. 91. *How do the sacraments become effectual means of salvation?*

Ans. The sacraments become effectual means of salvation, not from any virtue in them, or in him that doth administer them; but only by the blessing of Christ, and the working of his Spirit, in them that by faith receive them.

OF THE SACRAMENTS AS EFFECTUAL MEANS. 177

Q. 1. What is meant by [effectual means of salvation?]
A. Such means as, by the blessing of God, do fully attain the end for which they are appointed, 1 Thess. ii. 13.

Q. 2. What is the meaning of these words, in the answer [not from any virtue in them?]
A. The meaning is, that the sacraments have not any virtue or efficacy, in themselves, to confer salvation; being only among the outward and ordinary means of grace, which can have no more efficacy of themselves to confer any saving benefit, than the rainbow, of itself, has to prevent a deluge.

Q. 3. Who are they who maintain, that the sacraments have a virtue or power, in themselves, to confer grace?
A. The Papists, who affirm, that the sacraments of the New Testament are the true, proper, and immediate causes of grace; and that the efficacy of them flows from the sacramental action of receiving the external elements.

Q. 4. How do you prove that the sacraments have not any innate, or intrinsic virtue in themselves, to confer grace, or salvation?
A. From this one argument, that if the sacraments had any such virtue, then grace, or salvation, would be infallibly connected with the external use of them: but it is obvious from scripture, that after Simon Magus was baptized, he remained still in the gall of bitterness, and bond of iniquity, Acts viii. 13, 23.

Q. 5. Why is it said in the answer, that the sacraments become effectual means of salvation, not from any virtue [in him that doth administer them?]
A. It is so said in opposition to the Papists, who maintain, that the efficacy of the sacraments depends upon the intention of the priest; so that any benefit by them, is conferred, or withheld, according to them, just as the secret will of the administrator would have it.

Q. 6. How is this error refuted?
A. If the efficacy of the sacraments depended upon the intention of the administrator, then there could be no certainty about the efficacy of them at all; because no mortal can be absolutely certain about the intention of another; the secrets of the heart being known to God only, Acts i. 24.

Q. 7. From whence, then, have the sacraments their efficacy and virtue?
A. [Only] from [the blessing of Christ, and the working of his Spirit.]

Q. 8. What do you understand by [the blessing of Christ?]
A. That divine power and life, with which he is pleased to accompany the sacraments and other ordinances; and

without which they would be utterly ineffectual, Rom. i. 16.

Q. 9. What is [the working of his Spirit,] which is necessary to make the sacraments effectual means of salvation?

A. Not only the planting of grace in the soul at first, but the drawing of it out into suitable exercise on all sacramental occasions, Zech. iv. 6.

Q. 10. Why is the working of the Spirit necessary to the efficacy of the sacraments?

A. Because we are utterly impotent of ourselves for any thing that is spiritually good, John xv. 5.

Q. 11. In whom are the sacraments [by the blessing of Christ, and the working of his Spirit,] effectual means of salvation?

A. [In them that by faith receive them.]

Q. 12. What is it to [receive] the sacraments [by faith?]

A. It is to apply Christ, and the benefits of his purchase, as represented, and exhibited to us in them, Luke xxii. 19, 20.

Q. 13. What may we learn from the necessity of Christ's blessing, and of the Spirit's working, in order to the efficacy of the sacraments?

A. It teaches us, that our whole dependence for the blessing, whether upon ourselves, when we partake of the sacrament of the supper, or upon our children, when we are sponsors for them in baptism, should be only on Christ alone, and the saving influences and operations of his Spirit, held forth in the promise, to accompany his own institutions; and therefore our partaking of these solemn ordinances, dispensed by some ministers, to the slighting of them as dispensed by others, equally sound and faithful, though perhaps in our esteem somewhat inferior in outward gifts, says upon the matter, that the efficacy of the sacraments depends, somehow, upon the administrator, and not upon the blessing of Christ alone: quite contrary to the mind of the Spirit of God, 1 Cor. iii. 7: "So, then, neither is he that planteth any thing, neither he that watereth; but God that giveth the increase."

QUEST. 92. *What is a sacrament?*

ANS. A sacrament is a holy ordinance instituted by Christ, wherein, by sensible signs, Christ, and the benefits of the new covenant, are represented, sealed, and applied to believers.

SACRAMENTS IN GENERAL.

Q. 1. From whence is the word [sacrament] derived?
A. It is of Latin origin, being anciently used, by the Romans, to signify their military oath; or that oath which their soldiers took to be true and faithful to their prince, and that they would not desert his standard.

Q. 2. How is it used by the church?
A. Not only to signify something that is sacred, but likewise a solemn engagement to be the Lord's.

Q. 3. What is the general nature of a sacrament?
A. It is [a holy ordinance, instituted by Christ.]

Q. 4. Why is a sacrament called [a holy ordinance?]
A. Because it is appointed not only for holy ends and uses, but likewise for persons federally holy.

Q. 5. Is it necessary that a sacrament be [instituted by Christ?]
A. Yes: it is essentially necessary that it have his express and immediate warrant and institution, otherwise it does not deserve the name, 1 Cor. xi. 23: "For I have received of the Lord, that which also I delivered unto you," &c.

Q. 6. Why must sacraments be expressly or immediately instituted by Christ?
A. Because he alone is the head of the church; and has the sole power and authority to institute sacraments and other ordinances in it, Eph. i. 22, 23.

Q. 7. "What are the parts of a sacrament?"
A. "Two; the one, an outward and sensible sign, used according to Christ's own appointment; the other, an inward and spiritual grace, thereby signified, Matt. iii. 11. 1 Pet. iii. 21."*

Q. 8. What are the outward [signs] in sacraments?
A. They are the sacramental elements, and the sacramental actions; but chiefly the elements, because it is about these that the sacramental actions are exercised.

Q. 9. Why called [sensible] signs?
A. Because they are obvious to the outward senses of seeing, tasting, feeling, &c.

Q. 10. What kind of signs are sensible signs in a sacrament?
A. They are not natural, nor merely speculative, but voluntary and practical signs.

Q. 11. Why are they not natural signs?
A. Because natural signs always signify the self-same thing, as smoke is always a sign of fire, and the morning light a sign of the approaching sun; whereas the signs in a sacrament never signify what they represent in that holy ordinance, but when sacramentally used.

Q. 12. Why are they practical, and not merely speculative signs?

---

* Larger Catechism, Quest. 163.

A. Because they are designed not only to represent the spiritual grace signified by them; but likewise to seal and apply the same.

Q. 13. Why are the signs in a sacrament called voluntary signs?

A. Because they depend entirely upon the divine institution to make them signs; yet so as there is some analogy or resemblance between the sign and the thing signified.

Q. 14. When are sacramental signs used according to Christ's own appointment?

A. When they are dispensed with the words of institution annexed to them, Matt. xxviii. 19. 1 Cor. xi. 23—25.

Q. 15. What do the words of institution imply or contain in them?

A. They contain, "together with a precept authorizing the use" of them, "a promise of benefit to the worthy receivers, Matt. xxviii. 20."*

Q. 16. What is the inward and spiritual grace signified by the sensible signs in a sacrament?

A. [Christ and the benefits of the new covenant.]

Q. 17. Why is the covenant of grace called [the new covenant?]

A. Because it is always to remain in its prime and vigour, without the least change or alteration; for that which decayeth and waxeth old, is ready to vanish away, Heb. viii. 13.

Q. 18. What are the [benefits] of the new covenant?

A. They are all the blessings contained in the promises of it, which may be summed up in grace here, and glory hereafter, Ps. lxxxiv. 11.

Q. 19. Are Christ, and the benefits of the new covenant, separable from one another?

A. No; for, "he that hath the Son, hath life," 1 John v. 12; whoever has Christ, has all things along with him; "all are yours, and ye are Christ's," 1 Cor. iii. 22, 23.

Q. 20. What is the intention and design of sensible signs in a sacrament, with reference to Christ and the benefits of the new covenant?

A. The design of them is, that Christ and his benefits may be [represented, sealed, and applied] by them.

Q. 21. Why are Christ and his benefits said to be represented by the signs in a sacrament?

A. Because as sacramental signs are of divine institution, so there is a resemblance or similitude between the signs and the things signified.

Q. 22. Why are Christ and his benefits said to be sealed by these signs?

A. Because, by the sacramental signs, Christ and his

* Confession of Faith, chap. xxvii. § 3.

benefits are confirmed to the believer, even as a seal is a confirmation of a bond or deed, Rom. iv. 11.

Q. 23. Why said to be applied?

A. Because, by the right and lawful use of the sacramental signs, Christ and his benefits are really communicated, conveyed, and made over to the worthy receiver, 1 Cor. xi. 24: " Take, eat; this is my body, which is broken for you."

Q. 24. To whom do the sacramental signs represent, seal, and apply Christ and his benefits?

A. Not to all who use them, but to [believers] only.

Q. 25. Why to believers only?

A. Because nothing but true faith can discern, and apply the spiritual grace, which is represented and exhibited by sensible signs in the sacrament, Gal. iii. 26, 27.

Q. 26. In what consists the form of a sacrament?

A. In "a spiritual relation, or sacramental union, between the sign and the thing signified." *

Q. 27. What is the consequence of this sacramental union between the sign and the thing signified?

A. The consequence is, "that the names and effects of the one are attributed to the other." † Thus Christ is called our passover, 1 Cor. v. 7; and the bread in the supper is called Christ's body—" This is my body," 1 Cor. xi. 24.

Q. 28. When are the signs, and the things signified, united, in those who partake of the sacraments?

A. When, together with the signs, (in virtue of Christ's institution) the blessings signified are received by faith, Gal. iii. 27.

Q. 29. How may this be illustrated by an example?

A. A little earth and stone put into a man's hand at random, signify nothing; but when this is done in a regular manner, according to the forms of law, to give a proprietor possession of his lands, from whence these symbols were taken, it is of great importance to corroborate his right: so bread and wine in the sacrament, are of little value in themselves abstractly considered; yet when received in faith, as the instituted memorials of the death of Christ, by which his testament was ratified and sealed, the believer's right to all the blessings of his purchase is by it most comfortably confirmed, 1 Cor. xi. 24: " This is my body, which is broken *for you.*"

Q. 30. Are the sacraments necessary for the confirmation of the word?

A. No; the word being of divine and infallible authority, needs no confirmation without itself: but they are necessary on *our* account, for helping our infirmity, and confirming and strengthening our faith, Rom. iv. 11.

*Confession of Faith, chap. xxvii. § 2. † Ibid.

Q. 31. What is the difference between the word and the sacraments?

A. The word may be profitable to the adult, without the sacraments; but the sacraments cannot profit them without the word, Gal. v. 6.

Q. 32. What is the end of the sacraments?

A. It is "to represent Christ and his benefits; and to confirm our interest in him: as also to put a visible difference between those that belong unto the church, and the rest of the world; and solemnly to engage them to the service of God in Christ, according to his word."*

Q. 33. Who are they that have a right to the sacraments?

A. They "that are within the covenant of grace, Rom xv. 8." †

Q. 34. Who are to be reckoned within the covenant of grace, in the sight of men?

A. They who "profess their faith in Christ, and obedience to him, Acts ii. 38;" and "infants descending from parents, either both or but one of them professing faith in Christ, and obedience to him, are, in that respect, within the covenant, Rom. xi. 16." ‡

Q. 35. What may we learn from the nature of the sacraments in general?

A. The amazing love of the Lord Jesus, in giving us not only the word as the instrument in the hand of the Spirit, for begetting faith, and all other graces, Eph. i. 13; but likewise the sacraments for strengthening and increasing the same, as well as for cherishing our love and communion with one another, 1 Cor. xii. 13.

Quest. 93. *What are the sacraments of the New Testament?*

Ans. The sacraments of the New Testament are, baptism and the Lord's supper.

Q. 1. What were the ordinary sacraments under the Old Testament?

A. They were two: *circumcision* and the *passover*.

Q. 2. When was circumcision first instituted?

A. In the ninety-ninth year of Abraham's age, Gen. xvii. 24; at which time, both he, and all the men of his house, were circumcised, verse 26, 27.

---

* Confession of Faith, chap. xxvii. § 1.
† Larger Catechism, Question 162.   ‡ Ibid. Q. 166.

OF THE NUMBER OF THE SACRAMENTS.

Q. 3. At what age were the male children afterwards to be circumcised?
A. Precisely on the eighth day after they were born, Gen. xvii. 12.

Q. 4. What was the spiritual meaning of this sacramental ceremony?
A. It signified the impurity and corruption of nature, Jer. iv. 4; the necessity of regeneration, or being cut off from the first Adam, as a federal head, Rom. ii. 28, 29; and of being implanted in Christ, in order to partake of the benefits of his mediation, chap. viii. 1; together with a solemn virtual engagement to be the Lord's, Gen. xvii. 11.

Q. 5. What was the other sacrament of the Old Testament?
A. The passover.

Q. 6. When was it instituted?
A. At the departure of the children of Israel out of Egypt, Ex. chapter xii.

Q. 7. Why called the passover?
A. Because the destroying angel passed over the houses of the Israelites, in the night when he smote the first-born with death, in every house or family of the Egyptians, Ex. xii. 27.

Q. 8. On what account did the angel pass over the houses of the Israelites?
A. Because, according to the express command of God, the blood of the passover-lamb was stricken upon the lintels and side posts of their doors, as a signal to the destroying angel to pass over them, Ex. xii. 22, 23.

Q. 9. What was meant by striking the blood upon their lintels and door posts?
A. It signified, that it is only in virtue of the blood or satisfaction of Christ, that the curse and sentence of the law (which is the wrath of God) is not executed upon the sinner, Rom. v. 9.

Q. 10. What were the significant ceremonies of divine institution that were to be observed in this sacrament?
A. The passover-lamb was to be without blemish, Ex. xii. 5; it was to be slain, verse 6; it was to be roasted with fire, verse 9; and it was to be eaten, and that wholly and entirely, verse 10.

Q. 11. Why was it necessary that the passover-lamb should be without blemish?
A. To signify, that though our sins were imputed to Christ, yet he was in himself holy, harmless, undefiled, Heb. vii. 26; and therefore called a Lamb without blemish and without spot, 1 Pet. i. 19.

Q. 12. Why must the lamb be slain, or killed by blood shedding?
A. To denote, that the death of Christ was necessary,

for satisfying justice, and reconciling us to God, Luke xxiv. 26: "Ought not Christ to have suffered these things?"

Q. 13. Why was it to be roasted with fire?

A. To intimate, that Christ's sufferings, as our Surety, were exquisitely and inconceivably great, without the least abatement of any of that wrath which was due to our sins, Isa. liii. 10: "It pleased the Lord to bruise him;" Rom. viii. 32, "God spared not his own Son."

Q. 14. Why was it to be eaten wholly and entirely, and none of it to be left?

A. To signify, that Christ was to be wholly applied, in a way of believing, as being, " of God, made unto us wisdom and righteousness, and sanctification, and redemption," 1 Cor. i. 30.

Q. 15. Why were all the families of Israel to eat the passover, at one and the same time? Ex. xii. 8.

A. To signify that there is enough in Christ to satisfy the need of all his people at once; "for in him dwelleth all the fulness of the Godhead bodily," Col. ii. 9.

Q. 16. Why was it to be eaten the very same evening in which it was slain? ver. 6, 8.

A. To signify, that Christ ought to be applied and appropriated by faith speedily, without delay: Behold, *now* is the accepted time, 2 Cor. vi. 2.

Q. 17. "How many sacraments hath Christ instituted in his church under the New Testament?

A. "Under the New Testament, Christ hath instituted in his church only two sacraments; baptism and the Lord's supper." *

Q. 18. How do these two sacraments come in the place of those under the Old Testament?

A. Baptism comes in the place of circumcision; and the Lord's supper in the place of the passover.

Q. 19. Were the sacraments of the Old Testament no more than shadows of that grace, which is actually conferred by the sacraments under the New, as the Papists would have it?

A. By no means; for "the sacraments of the Old Testament, in regard of the spiritual things thereby signified and exhibited, were, for substance, the same with those of the New, 1 Cor. x. 1—5." †

Q. 20. In what do they differ?

A. The sacraments of the Old Testament represented Christ as yet to come; whereas those of the New hold him forth as already come, and as having finished the work of our redemption, as to the purchase of it, Eph. v. 2.

Q. 21. Is there any difference between them as to clearness and perspicuity?

Larger Catechism, Q. 164. † Confession of Faith, chap. xxvii \ 6.

A. The words annexed to the outward signs in the sacraments of the New Testament, make the things signified appear vastly more plain and perspicuous, than in the sacraments of the Old.

Q. 22. What other sacraments do the Papists add to baptism and the Lord's supper?

A. They boldly venture to add other five; namely, confirmation, penance, orders, marriage, and extreme unction.

Q. 23. How may it appear, in a word, that all these are false and spurious sacraments?

A. In regard that none of them have sacramental signs of divine institution, signifying any inward and spiritual grace; and, consequently, none of them can be appointed seals of God's covenant.

Q. 24. Who may lawfully dispense the sacraments of the New Testament?

A. "Neither of them may be dispensed by any, but a minister of the word, lawfully ordained, 1 Cor. iv. 1." *

QUEST. 94. *What is baptism?*

ANS. Baptism is a sacrament, wherein the washing with water, in the name of the Father, and of the Son, and of the Holy Ghost, doth signify and seal our ingrafting into Christ, and partaking of the benefits of the covenant of grace, and our engagement to be the Lord's.

Q. 1. What is the proper signification of the word [baptism?]

A. It is of Greek origin, and properly signifies a washing, sprinkling, or pouring out, in order to cleansing, Mark. i. 8: "I indeed baptize you with water, but he shall baptize you with the Holy Ghost;" that is, he shall pour his Spirit upon you, according to the promise, Isa. xliv. 3: "I will pour my Spirit upon thy seed, and my blessing upon thine offspring."

Q. 2. Who is the author of baptism?

A. The Lord Jesus Christ, the Mediator and Head of the church.

Q. 3. When did he institute and appoint it, as a sacrament of the New Testament?

A. A little before his ascension into heaven, when he gave his apostles that solemn charge, Matt. xxviii. 19: "Go ye, therefore, and teach all nations, baptizing them in

---

* Confession of Faith, chap. xxvii. § 5.

the name of the Father, and of the Son, and of the Holy Ghost."

Q. 4. Was not baptism used before that time?

A. It was used long before by the Jews, in receiving their proselytes, but not by divine institution.

Q. 5. When came baptism to have a divine warrant and institution?

A. When God sent John the Baptist to baptize with water, John i. 33.

Q. 6. Was there any difference between the baptism of John, and the baptism dispensed by the apostles after Christ's ascension?

A. There was no essential difference between them; for both of them had the same visible sign, and the same blessings signified by it. The difference was only circumstantial, in respect of time, and the objects of administration.

Q. 7. How did they differ in respect of time?

A. The baptism of John was dispensed before Christ had finished the work which his Father gave him to do; but the baptism of the apostles was mostly after Christ had suffered, and had entered into his glory.

Q. 8. How did they differ as to the objects of administration?

A. The baptism of John was confined to Judea only; but the baptism of the apostles extended to all nations, to whom the gospel was preached, Matt. xxviii. 19.

Q. 9. Why did Christ, who had no need of it, condescend to be baptized by John?

A. He gives the reason himself; It becometh us, says he, to fulfil all righteousness, Matt. iii. 15.

Q. 10. Did Christ himself baptize any?

A. No: "Jesus himself baptized not, but his disciples," John iv. 2.

Q. 11. Why did not Christ baptize any himself?

A. That he might commend the ministry of men of like passions with ourselves; and to show that the efficacy of the ordinance did not depend upon the administrator, but upon the divine blessing; even as the words spoken by him on earth, when they were efficacious, were so, not merely as spoken or uttered from his lips, but as accompanied with his own almighty power, Luke v. 17.

Q. 12. What is the visible sign, or outward element in baptism?

A. Only [water,] pure and unmixed, Acts x. 47.

Q. 13. How is water to be applied to the body in baptism?

A. "Dipping of the person into the water is not necessary, but baptism is rightly administered by pouring or sprinkling water upon the person."*

* Confession of Faith, chap. xxviii. § 3.

Q. 14. How does it appear from scripture, that baptism is rightly administered by pouring or sprinkling water upon the person?

A. From repeated instances of the administration of baptism by the apostles in this manner; particularly when three thousand were baptized by them, Acts ii. 41, water must have been sprinkled upon them, as the apostles could not have time, in a part only of one day, to take them one by one, and plunge them into it. Nor is it probable that the jailor, Acts xvi. 33, had such store of water, in the night season, as was sufficient for himself and whole family to be dipped into; or that they went abroad in quest of some river for that purpose; it is much more reasonable to infer, that in both the above instances, they were baptized by sprinkling. The same may be said of Paul's baptism, Acts ix. 18; and of the baptism of Cornelius and his friends, Acts x. 47, 48.

Q. 15. Why is it most expedient to sprinkle water upon the face in baptism?

A. Because the face is the principal part of the body, and the whole person is represented by it, Ex. x. 29.

Q. 16. What is signified by water in baptism?

A. The cleansing virtue of the blood of Christ, Rev. i. 5, and Spirit of Christ, Tit. iii. 5.

Q. 17. What is the difference between cleansing by the blood, and cleansing by the Spirit, of Christ?

A. The blood of Christ cleanseth meritoriously, 1 John i. 7; the Spirit of Christ efficaciously, Ezek. xxxvi. 27. By the former, the guilt of sin is, at once, taken away in justification; by the latter, the blot and stain of it is gradually carried off in sanctification.

Q. 18. What is signified by sprinkling of water upon the body?

A. The application of the blood of Christ to the soul, by the Spirit of God, Tit. iii. 5, 6.

Q. 19. What is the analogy, or resemblance, between the sign in baptism, and the thing signified?

A. Water makes clean, what before was foul; so the blood and Spirit of Christ purify from the guilt and pollution of sin, Zech. xiii. 1: water is open and free to all; so Christ and his benefits are freely offered to all the hearers of the gospel, Rev. xxii. 17.

Q. 20. In whose name are we baptized?

A. [In the name of the Father, and of the Son, and of the Holy Ghost,] Matt. xxviii. 19.

Q. 21. What is it to be baptized in the name of the Father, and of the Son, and of the Holy Ghost?

A. It is not only to be baptized by the will, command, and authority of the Three-one God; but likewise to be, by baptism, solemnly dedicated and devoted to the Father, the Son, and the Holy Ghost, as our God and portion for ever, Isa. xliv. 5.

Q. 22. What is it to be baptized by the command and authority of the Father, Son, and Holy Ghost?

A. It intimates that the Trinity of persons do not only authorize and appoint baptism to be a sacrament of the New Testament; but that they become jointly engaged to make good all the blessings of the covenant, signified and sealed by that ordinance, Jer. xxxi. 33: "I will be their God, and they shall be my people."

Q. 23. What is included in our being, by baptism, solemnly dedicated and devoted to the Father, Son, and Holy Ghost, as our God and portion for ever?

A. It includes a solemn profession, that these three adorable persons have the sole right to all our religious worship, Ps. v. 7; that all our hope of salvation is from them, Ps. lxii. 1, 5, and that we should be wholly and for ever the Lord's, Ps. xlviii. 14.

Q. 24. Is it necessary that baptism be dispensed in these express words, "In the name of the Father, and of the Son, and of the Holy Ghost?"

A. Yes; because ministers are peremptorily commanded by Christ, to baptize in this very form, Matt. xxviii. 19: "Go ye, therefore, and teach all nations; baptizing them in the name of the Father, and of the Son, and of the Holy Ghost."

Q. 25. Did not the apostles baptize in another form, when they baptized in the name of the Lord Jesus? Acts viii. 16.

A. It is not to be supposed, that the apostles would alter the form, so expressly delivered to them by their glorious Master; and therefore, when any are said to be baptized in the name of the Lord Jesus, it is not designed by this to notify to us in what form of words they were baptized; but only that they were baptized by the authority of Christ, who appointed this sacrament; and to faith in him, and communion with him.

Q. 26. How ought the mentioning of the holy Trinity to be introduced in baptism?

A. It is proper that it be introduced by words in the first person, expressing the present act of administration; and likewise setting forth the authority that a minister, lawfully called, has to dispense this sacrament; such as, "I baptize thee, in the name," &c.*

Q. 27. What are the ends and uses of baptism?

A. They are to [signify and seal our ingrafting into Christ, and partaking of the benefits of the covenant of grace.]

---

* See the Directory for Public Worship, on the head of Baptism.

OF THE NATURE OF BAPTISM.

Q. 28. What is it to signify and seal [our ingrafting into Christ?]

A. It is to signify and seal our union with him, and consequently the imputation of his righteousness to us, Gal. iii. 27: "As many of you as have been baptized into Christ, have put on Christ."

Q. 29. What are the [benefits of the covenant of grace,] the partaking of which is signified and sealed in baptism?

A. They are "remission of sins by the blood of Christ; regeneration by his Spirit, adoption, and resurrection unto everlasting life." *

Q. 30. What is the consequence of its being signified and sealed to us in baptism, that we partake of such great and glorious benefits?

A. The consequence is, that on this account "we enter into an open and professed engagement to be — the Lord's." †

Q. 31. What is included in our engagement to be the Lord's?

A. That we shall be his "wholly and only." ‡

Q. 32. What is it to be his wholly?

A. It is to be his, in all that we are, soul, spirit, and body, 1 Cor. vi. 19, 20; and in all that we have, whether gifts, graces, or worldly comforts, 1 Chron. xxix. 14.

Q. 33. What is it to be the Lord's only?

A. It is to be his in opposition to all his rivals and competitors, every one of whom we profess to renounce in baptism, Hos. xiv. 8.

Q. 34. Who are these rivals and competitors with God, whom we profess to renounce in baptism?

A. They are sin, Rom. vi. 6, Satan, Acts xxvi. 18, and the world, John xvii. 14.

Q. 35. Does baptism make or constitute persons church-members?

A. No: they are supposed to be church-members before they are baptized, and if they are children of professing parents, they are born members of the visible church, 1 Cor. vii. 14.

Q. 36. Why must they be church-members before they are baptized?

A. Because the seals of the covenant can never be applied to any, but such as are supposed to be in the covenant; nor can the privileges of the church be confirmed to any that are without the church.

Q. 37. Why then do our Confession,§ and Larger Catechism,‖ say that "the parties baptized are solemnly admitted into the visible church?"

---
* Larger Catechism, Quest. 163. See all these explained, Part I. On Justification, sanctification, adoption, and resurrection.
† Larger Catechism. Q. 165. ‡ Ibid. § Chap. xxviii. § 3.
‖ Larger Catechism, Q. 165.

A. Because there is a vast difference between making a person a church-member, who was none before; and the solemnity of the admission of one, who is already a member. All that our Confession and Catechism affirm, is, that, by baptism, we are solemnly admitted into the visible church; that is, by baptism we are publicly declared to be church-members before, and thus have our membership solemnly sealed to us: "For by one Spirit we are all baptized into one body," 1 Cor. xii. 13.

Q. 38. Is it warrantable to call the baptizing of any, the Christening of them?

A. No: because this is an encouraging of the superstitious Popish notion, that baptism makes even those who are born within the visible church, to become Christians; and that by the want of it, they remain infidels, and are left to uncovenanted mercy.

Q. 39. What are the extremes about the necessity of baptism?

A. The Socinians and Quakers deny that it is necessary at all; on the other hand, the Papists, and some others, maintain that it is so absolutely necessary, that no salvation can be expected without it.

Q. 40. What is the doctrine of our Confession of Faith, on this head?

A. That "although it be a great sin to contemn or neglect this ordinance, yet grace and salvation are not so inseparably annexed unto it, as that no person can be regenerated and saved without it; or that all who are baptized are undoubtedly regenerated."*

Q. 41. In what consists the greatness of the sin of contemning and slighting this ordinance?

A. It consists in despising an express and positive institution of Christ, appointed to be administered in his church to the end of the world, Matt. xxviii. 19, 20; and in slighting all the great and glorious benefits and privileges signified and sealed by it, Luke vii. 30.

Q. 42. How does it appear that grace and salvation are not inseparably annexed to baptism?

A. From the instance of Abraham, who had the righteousness of faith before he was circumcised, Rom. iv. 11; of Cornelius, who feared God, and was accepted of him, before he was baptized, Acts x. 2, 4; and from the instance of the thief on the cross, who was saved without being baptized at all, Luke xxiii. 43.

Q. 43. How does the scripture evince, that all who are baptized are not regenerated and saved?

A. From the instance of Simon Magus, who was baptized, and yet, after baptism, remained in the gall of bitterness, and in the bond of iniquity,† Acts viii. 13, 23.

* Confession of Faith, chap. xxviii. § 5. † Ibid.

Q. 44. Does baptism give a right to covenant-blessings; or, is it only a declarative sign and seal of them?
A. It is only a declarative sign and seal of them, as circumcision was, Rom. iv. 11.

Q. 45. What, then, gives a right?
A. The promise of the covenant, which is endorsed to the children, as well as to the parents, Acts ii. 39: "The promise is unto you, and to your children."

Q. 46. Is baptism designed to make the covenant more sure, or our faith stronger?
A. It is designed only to make our faith stronger; for the sureness of the covenant flows from the faithfulness of God, which is inviolable and unchangeable, Ps. lxxxix. 33, 34. Isa. liv. 10.

Q. 47. In what consists the efficacy of baptism?
A. It consists in sealing and ratifying the right to covenant-blessings, which persons have from the promise, so infallibly, that they shall certainly be put in possession of them, Eph. v. 25, 26. For, according to the doctrine of our Confession, " the grace promised is not only offered, but really exhibited and conferred, by the Holy Ghost, to such (whether of age, or infants,) as that grace belongeth unto, according to the counsel of God's own will, in his appointed time."*

Q. 48. Is baptism efficacious at the time of its administration?
A. Not always: "the efficacy of baptism is not tied to that moment of time wherein it is administered,"† but may take place afterwards, as God in his sovereignty has fixed it; for the wind bloweth where it listeth, &c. John iii. 8.

Q. 49. What may we learn from the nature of baptism?
A. The infinite goodness of God, in appointing an initiating ordinance, irreversibly sealing all the blessings of the covenant to the elect seed, Gen. xvii. 7.

QUEST. 95. *To whom is baptism to be administered?*

ANS. Baptism is not to be administered to any that are out of the visible church, till they profess their faith in Christ, and obedience to him: but the infants of such as are members of the visible church are to be baptized.

Q. 1. Who may administer the sacrament of baptism?
A. Neither of the two sacraments "may be dispensed by any, but by a minister of the word, lawfully ordained."‡

* Confession of Faith, chap. xxviii. § 6. † Ibid. ‡ Ibid. chap. xxvii. § 4.

Q. 2. How do you prove, that ordination by presbyters is lawful and valid, without a diocesan bishop?

A. From express scripture testimony, asserting the validity of ordination to the ministry, by the laying on of the hands of the *Presbytery*, 1 Tim. iv. 14.

Q. 3. Why should ministers lawfully ordained, and no other persons whatsoever, dispense the sacraments of the New Testament?

A. Because they only are the stewards of the mysteries of God, 1 Cor. iv. 1; and have the sole commission and authority from Christ to preach and baptize, Matt. xxviii. 19: Go ye, therefore, and *teach* all nations, *baptizing* them, &c.

Q. 4. Is public prayer requisite before the administration of baptism?

A. It is evident, that our Lord, at the first institution of the supper, and his apostles, afterwards, according to his example, prayed for the divine blessing to attend the dispensation of that solemn ordinance, 1 Cor. xi. 24; and therefore, by parity of reasoning, ministers ought to pray, and the people to join in it, for the same blessing upon the administration of the sacrament of baptism.

Q. 5. Ought not teaching, or preaching of the word, to go before baptism?

A. Yes; because our Lord has joined them together, Matt. xxviii. 19: "Go ye, therefore, and teach all nations, baptizing them," &c. And accordingly it was the uniform practice of the apostles to preach when they baptized, Acts ii. 38, 41; viii. 35, 38, and xvi. 32, 33.

Q. 6. Is naming of children necessary at baptism?

A. No; baptism dispensed by sprinkling of water, together with the words of institution, is every way valid and complete, though the person baptized is not named at all.

Q. 7. But was not the naming of children, at circumcision, an ancient practice among the Jews? Luke i. 59.

A. It was so; and the names of children may be published at baptism still, provided it is not looked upon as essential to that solemn ordinance; for it is the parent, and not the minister, who gives the name.

Q. 8. May baptism be administered in private?

A. It is more agreeable to the nature of this ordinance, when the Lord gives his people peace and opportunity for their public assemblies, that it be administered wherever the congregation is orderly called together, to wait on the dispensing of the word, Acts ii. 41.*

Q. 9. What if the child should be removed by death, before such a regular opportunity can be had?

* See Act X. Assembly, 1690.

OF THE SUBJECTS OF BAPTISM.

A. Then the parents may comfort themselves in this, that they were neither guilty of an unnecessary delay, nor of contemning the ordinance; and that, in these circumstances, the want of it cannot harm the child, 2 Sam. xii. 18, 23.

Q. 10. With what frame and disposition of mind ought this sacrament to be dispensed and witnessed?

A. With a firm persuasion that it is an ordinance of God; with a filial and reverential fear of him on our spirits; and with gratitude and thankfulness for the inestimable benefits that are signified and sealed in it.

Q. 11. How often is baptism to be administered to any person?

A. But once only, Acts xix. 4, 5.

Q. 12. Why but once only?

A. Because when our ingrafting into Christ (which is the comprehensive benefit signified and sealed in baptism) once takes place, it is never repeated, but remains firm and inviolable for ever, John xvii. 23.

Q. 13. To whom is baptism not to be administered?

A. [Baptism is not to be administered to any that are out of the visible church.]

Q. 14. Whom do you understand by those [that are out of the visible church?]

A. All infidels, or such as are Jews, or Heathens, and their children.

Q. 15. Why may not these be baptized?

A. Because being strangers from the covenant of promise, they can have no right to the seals of it, Eph. ii. 12.

Q. 16. May infidels in no event be baptized?

A. Yes, they may, so soon as [they profess their faith in Christ, and obedience to him.]

Q. 17. What is it to [profess faith in Christ?]

A. It is to profess a belief of the whole doctrines of the Christian religion, Acts viii. 37.

Q. 18. What is it to profess [obedience to him?]

A. It is to yield an external subjection to all the ordinances and institutions of Christ, Acts ii. 46.

Q. 19. Whom does such a profession respect?

A. It respects only the adult, or such as are grown up to ripeness of age.

Q. 20. Have not *infants* (who can make no such profession) a right to baptism?

A. Yes: [The infants of such as are members of the visible church are to be baptized.]

Q. 21. Who are [the members of the visible church?]

A. They "are all such as profess the true religion, and their children." *

* Larger Catechism, Quest. 62.

Q. 22. What are we to understand by the true religion?

A. We are to understand by it the whole of those doctrines deduced from the holy scriptures, which are contained in our Confession of Faith, and Catechisms, as agreeing, in the main, with the Confessions of other reformed churches, 2 Tim. i. 13: "Hold fast the form of sound words."

Q. 23. What is it to profess the true religion?

A. It is openly to acknowledge, on all proper occasions, a steadfast adherence to the whole of divine truth, without espousing or countenancing any opposite error, Ps. cxix. 1, 5. Rom. x. 10.

Q. 24. Is a bare profession of the true religion sufficient?

A. No; for "faith without works is dead." James ii. 26.

Q. 25. Upon what ground have the infants of such as are members of the visible church a right to baptism?

A. Upon the ground of the grace and goodness of God in the promise, including them in the same covenant with their parents; as in the promise made to Abraham, Gen. xvii. 7: "I will establish my covenant between me and thee, and thy seed after thee—to be a God unto thee, and to thy seed after thee."

Q. 26. But what if this promise of including the seed in the same covenant with the parents have a respect only to the natural offspring of Abraham, and to none else?

A. The apostle Peter plainly affirms, that it is a promise of the covenant of grace, extending to the Gentiles, as wel. as to the Jews; and, at the same time, that it is the foundation of church-membership, and consequently, of baptism, when he says, Acts ii. 38, 39, "Repent, and be baptized, every one of you;—for the promise is unto you, and to your children, and to all that are afar off, even as many as the Lord our God shall call."

Q. 27. How does it appear from the text, that the promise of assuming the children into the same covenant with their parents, extends to the Gentile nations?

A. Because the apostle says, that the promise is unto "all that are *afar off*, even as many as the Lord our God shall call;" namely, by the external call of the word, which is appointed to be published to every creature, Mark xvi. 15.

Q. 28. How does it appear, that this promise is the foundation of church-membership, and consequently of baptism?

A. It appears from this, that the apostle enforces his exhortation to repent, and be baptized, upon the adult persons to whom he is speaking, from this powerful and encouraging motive, that then their children should have a right and title to the privileges of the same covenant of promise, and the seal of which they themselves were to receive in their baptism; Repent, says he, and be baptized; —for the promise is unto you and to your children.

Q. 29. To what promise does the apostle here point?

A. He points at the promise made to Abraham, Gen. xvii. 7: "I will be a God unto thee, and to thy seed after thee."

Q. 30. What seal was annexed to this promise, or promulgation of the covenant of grace, made to Abraham?

A. The seal of circumcision, ver. 10: "This is my covenant, which ye shall keep between me and you;—Every man-child among you shall be circumcised." And ver. 12: "He that is eight days old shall be circumcised among you."

Q. 31. What connexion is there between circumcising the seed of Abraham on the eighth day, under the Old Testament, and baptizing the children of professing parents under the New?

A. The connexion is, that though circumcision and baptism be different signs, yet they are both of them seals of the same covenant of grace; and since the infant-seed of Abraham received the seal of circumcision under the Old Testament, by parity of reason, the infant children of professing parents should receive the seal of baptism under the New; especially as baptism is now come in the room of circumcision.

Q. 32. How do you prove, from scripture, that baptism is come in the room of circumcision?

A. From Col. ii. 10—12: "Ye are complete in him—in whom, also, ye are circumcised with the circumcision made *without* hands:—buried with him in baptism, wherein also ye are risen with him."

Q. 33. How does it appear, from this text, that baptism is now come in the room of circumcision?

A. From the plain and obvious scope of it, which is to show, that there is no need now of that circumcision which was outward in the flesh, as we have all the blessed fruits and effects of Christ's death and resurrection more clearly, and, at the same time, more extensively, represented and sealed in baptism; which is dispensed equally to both sexes.

Q. 34. What would be the consequence, if the infants of professing parents, under the New Testament, were not admitted to the initiating seal of the covenant, as well as the infants of the Jews under the Old?

A. The consequence would be, that the privileges of the New Testament church would be more abridged and lessened, than those of the Old, whereas they are rather increased and enlarged, Isa. liv. 2, 3.

Q. 35. How can infants be baptized, when they are incapable of making a profession of their faith, which seems to be required in order to baptism? Acts viii. 37.

A. An explicit or formal profession of faith, is required only of them that are adult, or come to age, when they are to be baptized: but not of infants now, any more than when they were circumcised of old, on the eighth day after their birth.

Q. 36. Are infants capable of the blessings signified and sealed in baptism?

A. Undoubtedly they are; for some of them have been filled with the Holy Ghost even from their mother's womb, Luke i. 15; and, consequently, by grace capable of regeneration, pardon, and eternal life; wherefore the sign and seal of these blessings ought not to be withheld.

Q. 37. How are children of professing parents designated in scripture?

A. If any one of the parents be a visible believer, or regular church-member, the children, on that account, are called holy, 1 Cor. vii. 14: " The unbelieving husband is sanctified by the wife; and the unbelieving wife is sanctified by the husband; else were your children unclean, but now are they holy."

Q. 38. What holiness is here meant?

A. Federal holiness, or being admitted to church membership, together with their believing or professing parent.

Q. 39. May not this holiness be understood of legitimacy, or being lawfully begotten?

A. No: because marriage being an ordinance of the law of nature, the children of married parents, though both of them be infidels, are as lawfully begotten as those of professing Christians.

Q. 40. How does federal holiness entitle an infant to baptism?

A. Federal holiness necessarily supposes a being within the covenant, in virtue of the credible profession of the parent; and, consequently, a right to the initiatory seal of it.

Q. 41. Is there any express precept in the New Testament for baptizing the infants of visible believers?

A. The privilege of the infant seed of visible church members, having been settled ever since Abraham's time, and never reversed, there was no need of any more than the general precept, "Go and baptize," Matt. xxviii. 19.

Q. 42. Why is there need of no precept more express than this general one?

A. Because the infants' privilege of being assumed into the same covenant with their parents, is declared to be continued in New Testament times, Acts ii. 39: " The promise is unto you, and to your children."

Q. 43. Have we any scripture example for infant baptism?

A. Yes: the apostles baptized whole households or families at once; such as the household of Lydia, Acts xvi. 15; all the jailor's family, ver. 33; and the household of Stephanas, 1 Cor. i. 16.

Q. 44. But there is no mention of their baptizing infants in those families.

A. Neither is there mention of their baptizing adult persons in them; only, since they baptized the whole, it may be inferred that there were some infants, or young ones, among them.

Q. 45. "How is our baptism to be improved by us?"

A. "By serious and thankful consideration of the nature of it, and of the ends for which Christ instituted it;—by being humbled for our sinful defilement, our falling short of, and walking contrary to our engagements;—and by endeavouring to live by faith, to have our conversation in holiness and righteousness, as those that have therein given up their names to Christ, and to walk in brotherly love, as being baptized by the same Spirit into one body."*

Q. 46. When should we thus improve our baptism?

A. "All our life long, especially in the time of temptation, and when we are present at the administration of it to others." †

QUEST. 96. *What is the Lord's supper?*

ANS. The Lord's supper is a sacrament, wherein, by giving and receiving bread and wine, according to Christ's appointment, his death is showed forth; and the worthy receivers are, not after a corporal and carnal manner, but by faith, made partakers of his body and blood, with all his benefits, to their spiritual nourishment, and growth in grace.

Q. 1. Why is this sacrament compared to a [supper?]

A. Because it was instituted immediately after eating the passover, (Matt. xxvi. 26,) which was always at night, Ex. xii. 6, 8.

Q. 2. Why is it called [the Lord's supper?]

A. Because the Lord Jesus was the sole author of it, 1 Cor. xi. 23; and it is highly requisite it should be so.

Q. 3. Why was it highly requisite that the Lord Jesus should be the sole author of this holy ordinance?

---

* Larger Catechism, Question 167. † Ibid.

A. Because all the grace that is held forth in it, is treasured up wholly in him; and is conveyed and applied by him to the soul, John i. 16.

Q. 4. When did Christ institute and appoint this sacrament?

A. "The same night in which he was betrayed," 1 Cor. xi. 23.

Q. 5. What night was that?

A. It was the very last night before his death, Matt. xxvi. 47, 48, compared with chap. xxvii. 1, 35, 46, 50.

Q. 6. What is implied in his instituting this sacrament the same night in which he was betrayed?

A. It implies his infinite goodness, and inviolable attachment to mankind lost, whom he represented; that in the immediate prospect of his greatest sufferings and soul agonies in their stead, he should have their salvation and comfort so much at heart, as to leave this memorial and pledge of his dying love among them, till he come again, Matt. xxvi. 29.

Q. 7. Are Christians under any obligation to celebrate this ordinance at night, as our Lord and his disciples did at the first institution of it?

A. No; the substitution of this sacrament in the room of the passover, [which was eaten immediately before,] was the occasion of its being first administered at night; and that particular occasion can never recur again.

Q. 8. In what posture should the Lord's supper be received?

A. This sacrament being called the Lord's table, 1 Cor. x. 21, a table posture, which is sitting, seems to be most agreeable to the practice of our Lord, and his disciples, at the first supper, Matt. xxvi. 20, 26.

Q. 9. From whence did the practice of kneeling at the sacrament take its rise?

A. From the church of Rome, who maintain that the consecrated bread, or wafer, is changed into the real body of Christ, and therefore to be worshipped.

Q. 10. What are the outward *elements*, appointed by Christ, in this sacrament?

A. They are [bread and wine,] Mark xiv. 22, 23.

Q. 11. What sort of bread and wine is proper to be used?

A. Just such as is ordinarily used in entertainments among men.

Q. 12. Is the sacrament of the supper to be received, by every partaker, in both elements?

A. Certainly it ought; for our Lord gave both elements to his disciples; and the apostle appoints both the elements to be dispensed to communicants, 1 Cor. xi. 28: "Let a man examine himself, and so let him eat of that *bread*, and drink of that cup." And therefore the withholding of the cup from the people, as is done by the church of Rome, is both sacrilegious and impious.

Q. 13. What is signified by the bread and the wine?

A. The [body] and [blood] of Christ, 1 Cor. xi. 24, 25.

Q. 14. What is to be understood by Christ's body and blood?

A. His incarnation and satisfaction, for the complete accomplishment of our redemption, John vi. 51: "The bread that I will give is my flesh, which I will give for the life of the world."

Q. 15. What is the analogy, or resemblance, between the bread and wine, and what is signified and represented by these elements?

A. As bread and wine make a sufficient entertainment for the nourishment of the body; so the righteousness and fulness of Christ, are a full and satisfying feast for the refreshment of the soul, John vi. 55: "My flesh is meat indeed, and my blood is drink indeed."

Q. 16. What are the sacramental actions with reference to these elements?

A. They are all of them comprehended in the answer, under [giving and receiving bread and wine, according to Christ's appointment.]

Q. 17. Whom do these sacramental actions respect?

A. Some of them respect the administrator, and some the partakers in this holy ordinance.

Q. 18. Who are the administrators of this sacrament?

A. *Christ* himself was the first administrator of it; and after him, ministers of the word, lawfully called and set apart to that office.

Q. 19. What were the actions of Christ, the first administrator, which ministers are to imitate, in dispensing this sacrament?

A. After his example, they take the bread, and the cup; they bless these elements; they break the bread, and give both the bread and the wine to be distributed among the communicants.

Q. 20. What is meant by taking the bread and the cup?

A. Christ's voluntarily assuming the human nature into union with his divine person, Heb. ii. 16, that in it he might be a sacrifice of infinite value in our stead, Eph. v. 2.

Q. 21. What is implied in blessing the elements?

A. That Christ has appointed the bread and the wine in this sacrament, to be the visible signs or symbols of his body and blood; and likewise, by his example, has warranted ministers to set apart, by solemn prayer, so much of these elements, as shall be used in this sacrament, from a common, to a holy use.

Q. 22. Why is Christ's blessing the elements called his giving thanks? 1 Cor. xi. 24.

A. Because so inconceivably great was his love to lost sinners of mankind, that he was thankful he had all their debt to pay, Ps. xl. 7, 8; and that he was able to do it to the uttermost, Heb. vii. 25.

Q. 23. What is to be understood by breaking the bread?

A. The most exquisite sufferings of the Son of God, Ps. xxii. 14, 15, and the necessity of them, as the channel, in which mercy was to be vented to the sinner, Rom. v. 21.

Q. 24. What is intimated to us by [giving] the bread and [giving] the cup? Matt. xxvi. 26, 27.

A. It intimates, that Christ is the free gift of God to sinners of mankind, for salvation and eternal life, John iii. 16.

Q. 25. What are the sacramental actions of the partakers in this sacrament, included in their [receiving] of bread and wine?

A. They take the bread and the cup: they eat the bread, and drink a part of the wine in the cup.

Q. 26. What is imported in their taking the bread and the cup?

A. It imports, that our receiving of Christ, is founded on the gift and grant that is made of him in the word; for, "a man can receive nothing, except it be given him from heaven," John iii. 27.

Q. 27. What is included in their eating the bread, and drinking the wine?

A. It includes, that there ought to be an application of Christ to the soul in particular, in virtue of the particular endorsement of the promise, to every one that hears the gospel: For the promise, says the apostle Peter, is unto you, (that is, unto every one of you,) and to your children, Acts ii. 39.

Q. 28. For what end did Christ institute these sacramental elements and actions?

A. That thereby [his death,] might be [showed forth,] 1 Cor. xi. 26, and the remembrance of it kept up, Luke xxii. 19.

Q. 29. What is it to show forth the death of Christ?

A. It is to profess, by partaking of the sacrament, that we believe his death, in our room, to have been most acceptable to God, Eph. v. 2; and that we acquiesce in it, together with his obedience, as the sole ground of our hope of salvation, Rom. iv. 25.

Q. 30. How does it appear, that his death, in our room, was most acceptable to God?

A. By his resurrection from the dead, 1 Thess. i. 10, and his entrance into glory, Luke xxiv. 26.

Q. 31. How may we know if we acquiesce in the obedience and death of Christ, as the sole ground of our hope of salvation?

A. If we are renouncing all other confidences, Hos. xiv.

3, and are convinced that the meritorious obedience unto death of the Son of God as our Surety, is the sole payment of the debt we owed to law and justice, Jer. xxiii. 6 " This is his name whereby he shall be called, *The Lord our righteousness.*"

Q. 32. Why has Christ appointed this sacrament to be observed in remembrance of him, Luke xxii. 19: "This do in remembrance of me?"

A. Because though his incarnation and satisfaction are the greatest events that ever happened in the world, and the most interesting to us, yet we are apt to forget them; or at least not to have the solid and lively impression of them habitually upon our spirits, Ps. cvi. 13: "They soon forgat his works."

Q. 33. What is it about the death of Christ which we ought to remember in this sacrament?

A. The truth of it, the necessity of it, and the sufficiency of it.

Q. 34. What is it to remember the truth of Christ's death?

A. It is by a true and saving faith, to believe that Christ really did and suffered all these things for us, that are recorded of him in scripture, 1 Cor. xv. 3, 4.

Q. 35. What is it to remember the necessity of his death, Luke xxiv. 26: "Ought not Christ to have suffered these things?"

A. It is to believe, that we had certainly gone down to the pit, unless God had found a ransom, or an atonement, Job xxxiii. 24.

Q. 36. What is it to remember the sufficiency of it?

A. It is to believe that it is infinitely valuable; and, therefore, could have procured the salvation of thousands of worlds, had it been so ordained, it being the death and blood of him, who is the supreme God, Acts xx. 28: "Feed the church of God, which he hath purchased with his own blood."

Q. 37. In what *manner* should we show forth and remember the death of Christ in this sacrament?

A. We ought to do it fiducially, humbly, mournfully, and thankfully.

Q. 38. Why ought we to remember his death fiducially?

A. Because as he " was delivered for our offences," Rom. iv. 25, so "God raised him up from the dead, and gave him glory, that our faith and hope might be in God," 1 Pet. i. 21.

Q. 39. Why ought we to remember it humbly?

A. Because when we are unworthy of the least of all God's mercies, Gen. xxxii. 10, we are much more so of the greatest that can be conferred, John iii. 16: "God so loved the world " &c.

Q. 40. Why mournfully?

A. Because our sins were the procuring cause of his sufferings, Isa. liii. 5, 6: "He was wounded for *our* transgressions, he was bruised for *our* iniquities:—The Lord hath laid on him the iniquities of us all." *

Q. 41. Why should the death of Christ be remembered thankfully?

A. Because his death was in our room, Tit. ii. 14; and was the finishing stroke of the work which his Father gave him to do, John xix. 30.

Q. 42. How often should the death of Christ be remembered, by partaking of this sacrament?

A. The scripture has not precisely determined how often; but it would appear that it ought frequently to be done.

Q. 43. How does it appear that the death of Christ should be frequently remembered in the supper?

A. From the words of our Lord, 1 Cor. xi. 25, 26: "This do ye, as oft as ye drink it, in remembrance of me; for, as often as ye eat this bread," &c., plainly implying, that it ought *often* to be done.

Q. 44. When will the death of Christ be remembered perpetually, without interruption?

A. In heaven, though not in a sacramental way, Rev. xxi. 22: "I saw no temple there."

Q. 45. How may it be proved, that it will be perpetually remembered in heaven?

A. From the song of the redeemed there, recorded, Rev. i. 5, 6: "Unto him that loved us, and washed us from our sins in his own blood—to him be glory." And chap. v. 9—14: "And they sung a new song, saying—Thou wast slain, and hast redeemed us to God by thy blood," &c.

Q. 46. Who are called [worthy receivers,] in the answer?

A. None are worthy receivers of this sacrament, but true believers; and even they, in order to their partaking worthily and comfortably, ought to have grace in exercise, as well as in the habit, Song i. 12.

Q. 47. Why are true believers called *worthy* receivers?

A. Not on account of any worthiness in themselves, for they have nothing of their own of which they can boast; but because they are united to Christ, and have all that grace from him, which enables them to partake in a suitable and becoming manner, 2 Cor. iii. 5.

Q. 48. What are the worthy receivers [made partakers of] in this sacrament?

A. They are [made partakers of Christ's body and blood, with all his benefits.]

Q. 49. What is it to be partakers of Christ's body and blood?

---

* *Marg.* Hath made the iniquities of us all to meet in him.

A. It is to be entertained, in the sacrament upon all that was transacted upon the person of Christ, as God-man, Mediator: this being the only proper and suitable food of the soul, John vi. 51, 53.

Q. 50. In what respect is it, that the worthy receivers are *not* made partakers of his body and blood?

A. They are not made partakers [after a corporal and carnal manner.]

Q. 51. Why are these words inserted in the answer, [not after a corporal and carnal manner?]

A. They are inserted in opposition to the Popish doctrine of transubstantiation, "which maintains a change of the substance of bread and wine, into the substance of Christ's body and blood, by consecration of a priest."*

Q. 52. What is the absurdity of this doctrine?

A. It is "repugnant not to scripture alone, but even to common sense and reason; overthroweth the nature of the sacrament; and hath been and is the cause of manifold superstitions, yea, of gross idolatries." †

Q. 53. How is it repugnant to scripture?

A. The scripture expressly affirms, that Christ gave the very same bread and cup to his disciples, after consecration, that he had taken into his hands before, Matt. xxvi. 26, 27. Whereas the doctrine of transubstantiation maintains, that the elements, after consecration, are no more the same, having only the form, colour, taste, and smell of bread and wine, wanting the substance of either; being turned into the substance of Christ's body and blood; in opposition to which, the apostle calls the elements, after consecration, by the same names they had before it, to intimate, that there was no change of their substance, 1 Cor. xi. 26—28: "As often as ye eat this *bread*, and drink this cup," &c.

Q. 54. How is transubstantiation repugnant to common sense and reason?

A. Common sense and reason tell us, that a body occupies but one place, and cannot be in divers places at one and the same time; whereas they who defend transubstantiation must allow, that the body of Christ may be in a thousand places at once, even as many places as there are consecrated wafers.

Q. 55. How does transubstantiation overthrow the nature of the sacrament?

A. By destroying the spiritual or sacramental relation, that is between the sign and the thing signified; for if the sign be turned into the thing signified, then all relation and similitude between them cease. Besides, the sacrament being a commemoration of what was done and suffered

---

* Confession of Faith, chap. xxix. § 6.   † Ibid.

in the human nature of Christ, it supposes his body to be absent, whereas transubstantiation supposes it present.

Q. 56. How is it the cause of manifold superstitions and gross idolatries?

A. In as much as strange and surprising effects are ascribed to the host, or consecrated wafer, even when not used sacramentally; and the alleged change of the bread and wine, into the substance of Christ's body and blood in the sacrament, is the very pretence, why they pay religious worship and adoration to the elements themselves; which is gross superstition and idolatry.

Q. 57. What is the difference between the Papists and Lutherans on this head?

A. The Papists maintain, that the bread and wine lose their own natural substance, and are turned into the substance of Christ's body and blood; but the Lutherans affirm, that the bread and wine retain their own natural substance still, and, at the same time, that the substance of Christ's body and blood is in, with, or under, these elements.

Q. 58. Are not both opinions equally absurd?

A. Yes: for transubstantiation supposes, that one body may be in many places at the same time; and consubstantiation takes it for granted, that two bodies may be together in the very same place, or that they may both occupy the same individual space at the same time.

Q. 59. Is Christ offered up, in this sacrament, as a sacrifice for the remission of sins?

A. No: there is in it "only a commemoration of that one offering up of himself, by himself, upon the cross, once for all; and a spiritual oblation of all possible praise unto God for the same. *

Q. 60. Why does our Confession say, that Christ's once offering up of himself was done *by himself?*

A. In opposition to the unbloody sacrifice of the mass, which is offered up daily by the Popish priests, for remission of the sins both of the quick and the dead.

Q. 61. What does our Confession of Faith affirm concerning this Popish "sacrifice of the mass," as they call it?

A. It affirms, that it is "most abominably injurious to Christ's one only sacrifice, the alone propitiation for all the sins of the elect, Heb. vii. 27." †

Q. 62. Is not Christ really present in the sacrament of the supper?

A. He is "as really, but spiritually, present to the faith of believers in that ordinance, as the elements themselves are to their outward senses, 1 Cor. xi. 29." ‡

Q. 63. If Christ be really present in the sacrament only

---

* Confession of Faith, chap. xxix. § 2.   † Ibid.   ‡ Ibid. § 7.

in a spiritual sense, and not corporally, why does he say of the bread, This is my body?

A. The plain and obvious meaning is, This bread is the sign or symbol of my body: so that the words are to be understood in the figurative, not in the literal sense.

Q. 64. How do you prove, that these words, This is my body, are to be understood in the figurative, and not in the literal and proper sense?

A. From this known rule in all language, that when the strict literal sense involves a manifest absurdity, or contradiction, we must of necessity have recourse to the figurative sense; as when the apostle says, 1 Cor. x. 4, "That rock was Christ," it cannot be understood literally, as if that rock, materially considered, was really Christ; but, figuratively, that rock signified Christ; and so of a great many other scripture expressions.

Q. 65. Since the worthy receivers are not made partakers of Christ's body and blood after a corporal and carnal manner, how do they partake of the same?

A. They partake of his body and blood, in this sacrament, only [by faith.]

Q. 66. What is it for the worthy receivers to partake of his body and blood by faith?

A. It is to apply and appropriate himself and his righteousness, [with all his benefits,] to themselves, Ps. xvi. 5, 6.

Q. 67. What are these [benefits].. which faith, in this sacrament, applies together with Christ himself?

A. Among many others, there are these three comprehensive ones; namely, an ample indemnity of all sin, Micah vii. 19; an unquestionable security for the progress of sanctification, Job xvii. 9; and an undoubted title to eternal life, John x. 28.

Q. 68. Why are these, and the like, called [his] benefits?

A. Because he is the purchaser, Tit. ii. 14, proprietor, John iii. 35, and dispenser of them, Eph. iv. 8.

Q. 69. Why are worthy receivers said to be made partakers of [all] his benefits?

A. Because where himself is received, all good things go along with him, 1 Cor. iii. 22, 23:—all are yours; and ye are Christ's.

Q. 70. What is the fruit and effect of their being, by faith, made partakers of Christ, and all his benefits?

A. The fruit and effect of it is, [their spiritual nourishment, and growth in grace.]

Q. 71. What does [their spiritual nourishment] imply in it?

A. That this sacrament is not a converting, but a nourishing ordinance.

OF THE WORTHY RECEIVING

Q. 72. What does their [growth in grace] imply?
A. That the worthy receivers are already in a state of grace.

Q. 73. How may spiritual nourishment and growth in grace be discerned?
A. If there is a more enlarged desire after the sincere milk of the word, 1 Pet. ii. 2; if there is more living by faith, and not by sense, 2 Cor. v. 7; and if there is more inward opposition to sin, Ps. lxvi. 18, and outward tenderness in the walk, Ps. xxxix. 1.

———◆———

QUEST. 97. *What is required to the worthy receiving of the Lord's supper?*

ANS. It is required of them that would worthily partake of the Lord's supper, that they examine themselves of their knowledge to discern the Lord's body, of their faith to feed upon him, of their repentance, love, and new obedience; lest, coming unworthily, they eat and drink judgment to themselves.

Q. 1. What preparatory duty is here required of those that would partake of the Lord's supper?
A. It is, [that they examine themselves,] 1 Cor. xi. 28: "But let a man examine himself, and so let him eat of that bread, and drink of that cup."

Q. 2. What is it for persons to [examine themselves?]
A. It is to make a strict inquiry into, and to pass an impartial judgment upon their spiritual state and frame, by the rule of the word, Ps. lxxvii. 6, and cxix. 105.

Q. 3. What is the best and most successful way of essaying this duty?
A. It is to put it into the hand of the Spirit of God to manage it for us, Ps. cxxxix. 23, 24: "Search me, O God, and know my heart," &c.

Q. 4. Why is self-examination necessary before receiving the Lord's supper?
A. Because it is peremptorily commanded, in order to discover whether we be in a gracious state; or, if we have grace in any measure of exercise; without either of which there can be no comfortable participation of this ordinance: "Let a man examine himself, and so let him eat."

Q. 5. Is this the duty of every man, or of some only?
A. It is unquestionably the duty of every man: Let a man examine himself; that is, every man and woman,

without exception, whether they think themselves gracious or graceless.

Q. 6. Why should a gracious man examine himself?

A. Because "there is not a just man upon earth, that doeth good and sinneth not," Eccl. vii. 20.

Q. 7. Why should they, who think they are graceless, examine themselves?

A. Because "they that be whole need not a physician, but they that are sick," Matt. ix. 12. They thus come to see more clearly their absolute need of Christ.

Q. 8. Is self-examination the duty of those only who are to partake for the first time?

A. It is the duty of persons every time they venture to partake of this ordinance, as the words of the precept evidently bear, "*so* let him eat;" that is, let none approach this holy table at any time without first essaying this duty.

Q. 9. Is self-examination to be practised only about the time of communion?

A. It ought to be practised daily or habitually, 2 Cor. xiii. 5; and especially in the view of such a solemn approach to the Lord at his table.

Q. 10. What are those things, about which they that would worthily partake of the Lord's supper are required to examine themselves?

A. They are required to examine themselves [of their knowledge—of their faith—of their repentance, love, and new obedience.]

Q. 11. What are they to try or examine about their [knowledge?]

A. If they have a competent measure of it; and if the measure they have, be of a saving kind.

Q. 12. What is that competent measure of knowledge, which is requisite to the worthy receiving of the Lord's supper?

A. That there be some understanding of the person, offices, and righteousness of Christ; of the fulness, freedom, and stability of the covenant of grace; of the nature, use, and end, of the sacrament of the supper; and likewise of our own manifold sins and wants.

Q. 13. Why is such a knowledge necessary?

A. It is necessary [to discern the Lord's body.]

Q. 14. What is it to discern the Lord's body in this sacrament?

A. It is to view the meritorious atonement, made by the Son of God in our nature, through the symbols of bread and wine, which are designed to signify and represent the same.

Q. 15. Who are they who are guilty of not discerning the Lord's body?

A. They who rest in partaking of the outward elements,

without a firm belief of the mysteries that are wrapped up in them.

Q. 16. How may we know if the measure of knowledge we have attained, be of a saving kind?

A. If we think we know nothing yet, as we ought to know, 1 Cor. viii. 2; if we are following on to know the Lord more and more, Hos. vi. 3; and if our knowledge influences our practice, John xiii. 17: "If ye know these things, happy are ye if ye do them."

Q. 17. Why is [faith] necessary to the worthy partaking of the Lord's supper?

A. It is necessary in order [to feed upon him.]

Q. 18. What is it to feed upon Christ in the sacrament of the supper?

A. It is to receive into our souls, from his fulness, all that spiritual good which is exhibited to us in the promise, John i. 16.

Q. 19. What is it of Christ that faith feeds upon in the sacrament?

A. It feeds upon all those discoveries of him that are made in the word; such as, his person, offices, mediatorial character, and relations, John vi. 57.

Q. 20. How may we know if we have that faith which feeds on Christ in the word and sacrament?

A. Where this true and saving faith is, it is of an appetizing nature, whetting the spiritual appetite after more and more of him, Isa. xxvi. 8, 9; it purifies the heart, Acts xv. 9; accounts all things but loss for Christ, Phil. iii. 8; and is careful to maintain good works, Tit. iii. 8.

Q. 21. What is the use of [repentance] in this sacrament?

A. Without repentance there can be no mourning for sin, which is an inseparable concomitant of faith's looking to, or improving a crucified Saviour in this ordinance, Zech. xii. 10: "They shall look upon me whom they have pierced, and they shall mourn for him."

Q. 22. How may we know if our repentance be genuine or of a right kind?

A. It is true and genuine, if we are grieved for sin as it is offensive to God, Ps. li. 4; if we are forsaking, and turning from it both in heart and life, Hos. xiv. 1; and, particularly, if we are deeply affected with the sin of unbelief, John xvi. 9.

Q. 23. What necessity is there for the exercise of the grace of [love] in partaking of the Lord's supper?

A. Without love to Christ, there can be no communion with him in this, or any other ordinance, John xiv. 21: "He that loveth me, shall be loved of my Father, and I will love him, and I will manifest myself to him."

Q. 24. How may we know if our love to Christ be sincere and unfeigned?

A. If it put us upon essaying the most difficult duties he may call us to, Ps. xxiii. 4; if it engage us to put a favourable construction upon the afflicting providences we meet with in our lot, Heb. xii. 10, and if we love his members out of love to himself, or because they are begotten of him, 1 John v. 1.

Q. 25. Why is the obedience required of worthy receivers called [new obedience?]

A. Because it flows from a new principle of faith and love, Gal. v. 6; it is performed in a new manner, namely, in the strength of the grace that is in Christ Jesus, 2 Tim. ii. 1, and is directed to a new end, even the glory of God, 1 Cor. x. 31.

Q. 26. How may we know if our obedience is indeed new obedience?

A. If we are conscientiously diligent in the practice of every duty, and at the same time look on ourselves as unprofitable servants, Luke xvii. 10, and lean wholly to the surety righteousness as the sole ground of our acceptance, Isa. xlv. 24.

Q. 27. What risk do they run who omit to examine themselves as to the above graces, before they come to the Lord's table?

A. They run the risk of [coming unworthily.]

Q. 28. What is it to come unworthily?

A. It is to come without any real sense, or consciousness of the need that we stand in of Christ, as "of God made unto us wisdom, righteousness, sanctification, and redemption," 1 Cor. i. 30.

Q. 29. What danger do they incur who thus come unworthily?

A. [They eat and drink judgment to themselves,] 1 Cor. xi. 29.

Q. 30. In what sense can they who come unworthily, be said to eat and drink judgment to themselves?

A. In so far as by their eating and drinking unworthily, they do that which renders them obnoxious to the righteous judgment of God.

Q. 31. To what [judgment] do they render themselves obnoxious?

A. To temporal judgments, or afflictions of various kinds, in the present life; and to eternal judgment, or condemnation (if mercy prevent not,) in the life to come, 1 Cor. xi. 30, 32.

Q. 32. "May not one who doubteth of his being in Christ, or of his due preparation, come to the Lord's supper?

A. "—If he be duly affected with the apprehension of the want of an interest in Christ, and unfeignedly desires to be found in him, and to depart from iniquity:" in that case, "he is to bewail his unbelief, and labour to have his doubts resolved; and, in so doing, he may and ought to come to the Lord's supper, that he may be further strengthened." *

Q. 33. When may a person be said to be duly affected with the apprehension of his want of an interest in Christ?

A. When he is filled with a restless uneasiness, and can take no comfort in any outward enjoyment, while he thinks himself destitute of an interest in Christ; and, at the same time, is active and diligent in the use of all the ordinary means, in which Christ is usually to be found, Song iii. 1—5.

Q. 34. "May any who profess their faith, and desire to come to the Lord's supper, be kept from it?"

A. "Such as are found to be ignorant or scandalous, notwithstanding their profession of the faith, and desire to come to the Lord's supper, may and ought to be kept from that sacrament, by the power which Christ hath left in his church; until they receive instruction, and manifest their reformation." †

Q. 35. Why ought the ignorant to be kept back?

A. Because they cannot discern the Lord's body, nor comprehend the end and design of this sacrament; and, therefore, will but eat and drink judgment to themselves, 1 Cor. xi. 29.

Q. 36. Why ought the scandalous to be kept back from this sacrament?

A. Because, by the habitual immorality of their practice, they manifest themselves to be under the dominion of the prince of darkness; and, therefore, while in that state, can have no right to the privileges which belong only to the members of Christ's family, 1 Cor. x. 21.

Q. 37. "What is required of them that receive the sacrament of the Lord's supper, in the time of the administration of it?"

A. "It is required of them, that they—heedfully discern the Lord's body, and affectionately meditate on his death and sufferings, and thereby stir up themselves to a vigorous exercise of their graces; in sorrowing for sin, hungering and thirsting after Christ, feeding on him by faith—and in renewing their covenant with God, and love to all the saints." ‡

Q. 38. What is it for the Lord's people to renew their covenant with him at his table?

A. It is to acquiesce anew in the covenant of grace, as made with Christ, Isa. xliv. 5; and, in so doing, to surrender themselves to the Lord, to be wholly his, trusting that he will keep them by his power, through faith unto salvation, 1 Pet. i. 5.

* Larger Catechism. Quest. 172. † Ibid. Q. 173. ‡ Ibid. Q. 174.

Q. 39. What is it for them to renew their love to all the saints on that occasion?

A. It is to embrace the opportunity of being at the Lord's table, to breathe out the secret and habitual desires of their souls before him, that all the saints, as well as themselves, may share abundantly out of the fulness of Christ, Ps. xc. 14; and that they keep themselves "in the love of God, looking for the mercy of our Lord Jesus Christ unto eternal life," Jude ver. 21.

Q. 40. What is the duty of Christians, after they have received the sacrament of the Lord's supper?

A. It is "seriously to consider how they have behaved themselves therein, and with what success; if they find quickening and comfort, to bless God for it, beg the continuance of it, watch against relapses, fulfil their vows, and encourage themselves to a frequent attendance on that ordinance."*

Q. 41. What is it to fulfil our vows?

A. It is to set about the practice of all commanded duty, according to our engagements, Ps. cxvi. 16, 18; and at the same time depend upon the grace and furniture that is in Christ Jesus for the right performance of it, Phil. iv. 13.

Q. 42. What if Christians can find no present benefit by their attendance on this ordinance?

A. Then they are "more exactly to review their preparation for, and carriage at the sacrament; in both which, if they can approve themselves to God, and their own consciences, they are to wait for the fruit of it in due time." †

Q. 43. What if they have failed in their preparation for, and carriage at the sacrament?

A. Then "they are to be humbled, and attend upon it afterward, with more care and diligence." ‡

Q. 44. "Wherein do the sacraments of baptism and the Lord's supper agree?"

A. "In that the author of both is God; the spiritual part of both is Christ and his benefits; both are seals of the same covenant;—and to be continued in the church of Christ until his second coming." §

Q. 45. In what do they differ?

A. In that baptism is to be administered but once, with water, to be a sign and seal of our regeneration and ingrafting into Christ, and that even to infants: whereas the Lord's supper is to be administered often, in the elements of bread and wine, to represent and exhibit Christ as spiritual nourishment to the soul, and to confirm our continuance and growth in him, and that only to such as are of years and ability to examine themselves." ||

---

* Larger Catechism, Question 175. † Ibid. ‡ Ibid.
§ Ibid. Quest. 176. || Ibid. 177.

OF THE NATURE OF PRAYER.

QUEST. 98. *What is prayer?*

ANS. Prayer is an offering up of our desires to God for things agreeable to his will, in the name of Christ with confession of our sins, and thankful acknowledgment of his mercies.

Q. 1. " Are we to pray to God only?"
A. "God only being to be believed in, and worshipped with religious worship, prayer, which is a special part thereof, is to be made by all to him alone, and to none other." *

Q. 2. Why is prayer to be made by all to God alone, and to none other?
A. Because "God only is able to search the hearts, hear the requests, pardon the sins, and fulfil the desires of all."†

Q. 3. May we not direct our prayers to any of the persons of the adorable Trinity?
A. To be sure we may: for the Three-one God being the sole object of religious worship, whichever of the three persons we address, the other two are understood as included, 2 Cor. xiii. 14.

Q. 4. Why may we not pray to angels, or saints departed?
A. Because it would be gross idolatry, they being but mere creatures; nor can they supply the wants, nor remove the miseries which sin has brought upon us.

Q. 5. Do we pray to God to inform him of what he knew not before?
A. Not at all: for from eternity he knew all the thoughts that ever should pass through our minds in time, Ps. cxxxix. 2, 4.

Q. 6. Do we pray to him that we may alter his mind, or incline him to any thing which he was formerly unwilling to grant?
A. No: for with him is no variableness, neither shadow of turning, James i. 17; but we pray to him, that we may obtain what we know and believe he is willing to confer, 1 John v. 14: " This is the confidence that we have in him, that if we ask any thing according to his will, he heareth us."

Q. 7. What are the several parts of prayer mentioned in this answer?
A. They are these *three;* petition, confession, and thanksgiving.

Q. 8. In which of these does prayer properly consist?
A. In *petition*, or supplication.

* Larger Catechism, Quest. 179.   † Ibid.

Q. 9. How does the answer describe our petitions, or supplications?

A. It describes them to be [an offering up of our desires to God.]

Q. 10. Why are our petitions called [our desires?]

A. Because the words of our mouth, without the desires of our heart, are nothing but empty sounds in the ears of God, Isa. xxix. 13: "This people draw near to me with their mouth,—but have removed their heart far from me."

Q. 11. Why must there be [an offering up] of our desires to God?

A. Because prayers are spiritual sacrifices, 1 Pet. ii. 5; and all sacrifices were appointed to be offered to God only, 2 Kings xvii. 35, 36.

Q. 12. From whence flow the desires of the heart?

A. From a sense of need: we cannot have any earnest desire after that, with the want of which we are no way affected; for, "the full soul loatheth a honey comb," Prov. xxvii. 7.

Q. 13. For what [things] ought we to offer up our desires to God?

A. [For things agreeable to his will.]

Q. 14. What [will] of God are we to have our eye upon, when we ask any thing from him?

A. Not upon his secret, but his revealed will, Deut. xxix. 29.

Q. 15. How shall we know, if what we ask be agreeable to his revealed will?

A. If we ask what he has promised, we are sure it is agreeable to his revealed will to confer it, because the promise is to us, Acts ii. 39.

Q. 16. Are we straitened, or narrowed, in our requests, when we are confined to the promise as the subject-matter of them?

A. By no means; for the promise contains infinitely more than we are able to ask or think, Eph. iii. 20.

Q. 17. May we ask temporal mercies at the hand of God?

A. Yes: because they are promised, so far as we have any real need of them, Ps. xxxiv. 10. Isa. xxxiii. 16.

Q. 18. Whether ought temporal or spiritual mercies to have the preference in our requests?

A. Spiritual mercies ought to have the preference, Matt. vi. 33: "Seek ye *first* the kingdom of God, and his righteousness, and all these things shall be added unto you."

Q. 19. What is meant by the kingdom of God, and his righteousness?

A. The work of grace in the soul, and the surety

righteousness imputed, as the foundation of it, Rom. viii. 4.

Q. 20. Why are these to be sought in the first place?

A. Because absolutely necessary to salvation, Rom. v. 21.

Q. 21. In whose *name* are we to ask things agreeable to God's will?

A. [In the name of Christ.]

Q. 22. What is it to pray in the name of Christ?

A. It is, " in obedience to his command, and in confidence of his promise, to ask mercies for his sake?" *

Q. 23. Is the bare mentioning of Christ's name, a praying therein?

A. No; but a "drawing our encouragement to pray, and our boldness, strength, and hope of acceptance in prayer, from Christ and his mediation."†

Q. 24. "Why are we to pray in the name of Christ?"

A. "Because the sinfulness of man, and his distance from God, by reason thereof, is so great, as that we can have no access into his presence without a Mediator."‡

Q. 25. Is there any other Mediator but Christ, in whose name we may approach to God?

A. No: " there being none in heaven or earth appointed to, or fit for that glorious work but Christ alone, we are to pray in no other name but his only, Col. iii. 17.§

Q. 26. Can we, of ourselves, pray in a right manner?

A. No: unless the Spirit of supplication is poured upon us, (Zech. xii. 10,) to help our infirmities; for we know not what to pray for as we ought, Rom. viii. 26.

Q. 27. "How doth the Spirit help us to pray?

A. "——By enabling us to understand both for whom, and what, and how prayer is to be made?"‖

Q. 28. "For whom are we to pray?"

A. "For the whole church of Christ upon earth; for magistrates, and ministers; for ourselves, our brethren; yea, our enemies; and for all sorts of men living, or that shall live hereafter."¶

Q. 29. For what are we to pray, in behalf of the whole church of Christ upon earth?

A. That they all may be one in Christ, the glorious head, John xvii. 21; and that they may grow up unto him in all things, Eph. iv. 15, till they "all come in the unity of the faith, and knowledge of the Son of God, unto a perfect man, unto the measure of the stature of the fulness of Christ," verse 13.

Q. 30. For what should we pray with reference to magistrates?

---

* Larger Catechism, Quest. 180. †Ibid. ‡Ibid. Q 181. §Ibid.
‖ Larger Catechism, Quest. 182. ¶Ibid. Q. 183.

A. That they may not be "a terror to good works, but to the evil," Rom. xiii. 3; and that, under them, we may lead a quiet and peaceable life, in all godliness and honesty, 1 Tim. ii. 2.

Q. 31. For what should we pray in behalf of ministers?

A. That they may not shun to declare to their hearers the whole counsel of God, Acts xx. 27; and that they may "watch for their souls, as they that must give account," Heb. xiii. 17.

Q. 32. Can we be hearty in praying for others, if we neglect to pray for ourselves?

A. No; for if we are indifferent about the state of our own souls, it is impossible we can be concerned for others, any farther than our interest and affection bind us, Job xxvii. 10.

Q. 33. Who are our brethren for whom we are to pray?

A. They are not only our kindred, according to the flesh, but all the members of the visible church; yea, all our fellow-creatures, 1 John iv. 21.

Q. 34. For what are we to pray in behalf of our enemies?

A. That their hearts may be changed, their tempers softened, that however they have treated us, they may be made Christ's friends, and partakers of eternal salvation through him, Matt. v. 44, compared with Luke xxiii. 34.

Q. 35. If we are to pray for all sorts of men living, how may we pray about the Roman Antichrist?

A. Out of the love we should bear to our fellow-creatures, who are under the yoke and dominion of the Roman Antichrist, we ought to pray no otherwise about him, than that the Lord would soon "consume him with the Spirit of his mouth, and destroy him with the brightness of his coming," 2 Thess. ii. 8.

Q. 36. What do we mean, when we pray for those that shall live hereafter?

A. We hereby desire, that Christ's kingdom and interest may be propagated and advanced in the world, until his second coming, Ps. cii. 18. John xvii. 20.

Q. 37. For whom are we not to pray?

A. We are not to pray "for the dead, 2 Sam. xii. 23; nor for those that are known to have sinned the sin unto death, 1 John v. 16."*

Q. 38. Why should we not pray for the dead?

A. Because at death the state of every man and woman is unalterably fixed, Luke xvi. 22, 27.

Q. 39. How may those be known, who have sinned the sin unto death?

A. By their rejection of the gospel which they once professed to embrace; by their malice and envy against Christ, and the way of salvation through him; by their treating

* Larger Catechism, Quest. 183.

the convincing evidences of Christianity, and the peculiar doctrines of it, with blasphemy and contempt; and by their rooted hatred of all religion, and the professors of it.

Q. 40. Why are we not to pray for those, who are known to have sinned this sin?

A. Because the sin against the Holy Ghost is declared, in scripture, to be unpardonable, (Matt. xii. 31, 32;) in regard it is a wilful and blasphemous opposition to the testimony of the Spirit of God concerning Christ, as the only way of salvation, Luke xii. 10.*

Q. 41. "For what things are we to pray?"

A. "For all things tending to the glory of God, the welfare of the church, our own or others' good, but not for any thing that is unlawful." †

Q. 42. "How are we to pray?"

A. "We are to pray—with understanding, faith, sincerity, fervency, love, and perseverance." ‡

Q. 43. What is it to pray with understanding?

A. It is to have some knowledge of God, who is the object of prayer, Ps. lxv. 2; of our own necessities, which are the subject-matter of it, Ps. lx. 11; and of the promises, which are our encouragement in it, Num. xiv. 17—19.

Q. 44. What is it to pray in faith?

A. It is to believe that we receive the promised blessings we ask, because he has said, "What things soever ye desire, when ye pray, believe that ye receive them, and ye shall have them," Matt. xi. 24.

Q. 45. What is it to pray with sincerity and fervency?

A. It is to have the heart and affections earnestly intent upon what we are praying for, Ps. xvii. 1; "O Lord, attend unto my cry; give ear unto my prayer, that goeth not out of feigned lips."

Q. 46. What is that love to God, which should be exercised in prayer?

A. It is an ardent desire of his presence, Ps. xxvii. 9; and an unfeigned delight in him, as the most amiable and soul-satisfying object, Ps. lxxiii. 25.

Q. 47. What is it to pray with perseverance? Eph. vi. 18.

A. It is to continue instant in prayer, as the word is rendered, Rom. xii. 12; or, to bear up against all discouragements, and not to give over, though we have not a speedy answer or return, Matt. xv. 22—29.

Q. 48. Is there any difference between praying with perseverance, and praying always, or without ceasing? 1 Thess. v. 17.

A. The difference may lie in this, that to pray with per-

---

* See a further account of the sin against the Holy Ghost, Part I. On the head of Sin in General.
† Larger Catechism, Quest. 184.   ‡ Ibid. Quest. 185.

severance, is not to become weary of the duty, or desist from it, though we do not immediately obtain what we are praying for; but to pray always, or without ceasing, is to study to maintain a praying frame, Ps. lxxiii. 23, and not to neglect the seasons of prayer, as they recur, Ps. lxi. 2.

Q. 49. What are the several kinds of prayer mentioned in scripture?

A. They are commonly ranked under these three, namely, secret, private, and public prayer.

Q. 50. What is *secret* prayer?

A. It is the retirement of individuals, or single persons, from all company with others, for a time, that they may have free and familiar intercourse with God by themselves, Matt. vi. 6: "But thou, when thou prayest, enter into thy closet; and when thou hast shut thy door, pray to thy Father which is in secret."

Q. 51. Is secret prayer incumbent on every Christian?

A. Yes; because every Christian has his own particular wants to be supplied, Ps. lxx. 5; doubts to be solved, Isa. xxxviii. 14; and difficulties to be removed, 2 Cor. xii. 8, which none but God himself can do, Ps. xxxv. 10.

Q. 52. May there not be secret prayer even in company with others?

A. Yes; there may be what is ordinarily called *ejaculatory* prayer.

Q. 53. What is ejaculatory prayer?

A. It is a secret and sudden lifting up of the soul's desires to God, upon any emergency that may occur in providence.

Q. 54. How may we engage in this kind of prayer?

A. Either by a simple thought darted up to heaven, as it would seem Nehemiah did, chap. ii. 4; or by words uttered in the mind, yet so as the voice cannot be heard, as we read that Hannah did, 1 Sam. i. 13.

Q. 55. With what success have these ejaculatory breathings of the soul met?

A. They have met with very quick and happy returns, as in the instance of Moses, who, in the midst of the people's murmuring at the Red Sea, despatched his desires to heaven, in some short ejaculation, to which the Lord gave a present return, Ex. xiv. 15: "Wherefore criest thou unto me? speak unto the children of Israel, that they go forward." And the sons of Reuben, &c., when fighting with the Hagarites, 1 Chron. v. 20: "They cried to God in the battle, and he was entreated of them."

Q. 56. What is the usefulness of ejaculatory prayer?

A. It tends to maintain fellowship with God, without any interruption of our lawful callings, Ps. lxxiii. 23. It is also a mean to repel sudden temptations, 2 Cor. xii. 8, 9; and to dispose the heart for a more solemn performance of the stated duties of prayer and praise in the season of them, Ps. xlii. verses 6th and 8th compared.

Q. 57. What is *private* prayer?

A. It is prayer among a few Christians, met together for joining in that solemn exercise, Rom. xvi. 5.

Q. 58. How is it commonly distinguished?

A. Into family,* and social prayer.

Q. 59. What is social prayer?

A. It is to pray in a fellowship society of Christians, out of several families, intermixed with spiritual conference upon soul-edifying subjects; and that at such times as they mutually agree among themselves, Mal. iii. 16.

Q. 60. What is *public* prayer?

A. It is the solemn worshipping of God by the church, in her public assemblies, in which a pastor, or one authorized to preach the gospel, is always the mouth of the people to God, Acts xx. 36.

Q. 61. What is it to *join* in private or public prayer, where one is the mouth of the rest?

A. It is to offer up the desires that come from the mouth of the speaker, (for things agreeable to God's will,) as if uttered by ourselves.

Q. 62. What is incumbent on those who are the mouth of others in prayer to God?

A. They are called, to take very special care, that their prayers be regulated exactly by the revealed will of God; in which case all present will be encouraged to join in every part of the duty.

Q. 63. What is requisite for joining in prayer in a right manner?

A. It is highly requisite, in order to this, that there be close attention without wandering, Acts ii. 42: "And they continued steadfastly in—prayers;" that there be a lively faith, without doubting, James i. 6; and a series of ejaculation concurring with the words of God that may be spoken, 1 Chron. xvi. 36.

Q. 64. What is the *second part* of prayer mentioned in the answer?

A. It is [confession of our sins.]

Q. 65. Why is confession of sin mentioned as a part of prayer?

A. Because, being sinners, we cannot pray in faith for any promised mercy, without acknowledging our unworthiness of it; or that it is infinitely above our desert, Dan. ix. 18.

Q. 66. What then does the confession of sin necessarily suppose?

A. It supposes guilt, and deserved punishment on account of it, Ezra ix. 13.

* About family prayer, see on the head Of Sanctifying the Sabbath.

Q. 67. Why is confession of sin necessary in prayer?

A. Because we cannot be cordial and hearty in asking forgiveness of our sins, unless we are some way affected by a sense of them, Ps. xxv. 11.

Q. 68. For what end should we confess our sins in prayer?

A. That God may be justified, and have the glory of his judgments, as being all of them just and righteous, Ps. li. 4; and that we may be humbled, and disposed to receive undeserved favours with gratitude, Ps. xxxii. 5.

Q. 69. In what manner should we confess our sins?

A. With grief and hatred of them, Luke xviii. 13; and with full purpose (in the strength of grace) to forsake them, Job xxxiv. 32.

Q. 70. What is the *third part* of prayer mentioned in the answer?

A. It is a [thankful acknowledgment of his mercies.]

Q. 71. Are prayer and thanksgiving joined together in scripture?

A. Yes; Ps. cxvi. 17: "I will offer to thee the sacrifice of thanksgiving, and will call upon the name of the Lord."

Q. 72. What is the subject-matter of thankfulness?

A. It is [mercies,] or benefits, whether offered or received.

Q. 73. Why are the blessings we want called mercies?

A. Because having made ourselves miserable by sin, we are most unworthy and undeserving of them, Gen. xxxii. 10.

Q. 74. Why called [*his*] mercies?

A. Because God himself is the author of them, and they are his free gift to us, 1 Tim. vi. 17.

Q. 75. For what mercies ought we to be thankful?

A. Both for temporal and spiritual; common and special mercies, Ps. cxlv. 9.

Q. 76. What is the best evidence of thankfulness to God for his mercies of any kind?

A. It is to be thankful for Christ, his unspeakable gift, 2 Cor. ix. 15.

Q. 77. When ought we to make thankful acknowledgment to God for his mercies?

A. At all times, and on all occasions; there being no condition of life, but what has some mixture of mercy in it, Job xi. 6. Ps. ci. 1.

Q. 78. Is there ground of thankfulness under afflictions or chastisements?

A. "Though no chastening for the present—be joyous, but grievous; nevertheless" it is ground of thankfulness, if "afterward it yieldeth the peaceable fruit of righteousness," and "be for our profit, and that we may be partakers of his holiness," Heb. xii. 10, 11.

Q. 79. Why ought prayer to be joined with a thankful acknowledgment of God's mercies?

A. That the mercies we receive may be blessed to us in the use of them; and that we may not, by our ingratitude, provoke God to deny us the mercies we may ask for the future, Isa. i. 15.

Q. 80. How may we know if our prayers are accepted and heard?

A. If we have been helped to enlargement and importunity in prayer, and yet have attained to a holy submission to the will of God, as to the particular we were asking, it is a good evidence that he has heard the voice of our supplication, 1 Chron. xx. 12, 17.

Q. 81. How may we know whether mercies come to us in the course of common providence, or as an answer to prayer?

A. This may be known both from the manner, and from the time, in which mercies are received.

Q. 82. How may it appear from the manner in which mercies are received, that they are in answer to our prayers?

A. It may be known by these two signs; namely, if the mercy be granted speedily and unexpectedly, Isa. lxv. 24; and other mercies are conferred together with, and over and above that which we desired, 1 Kings iii. 12, 13.

Q. 83. How may it be known from the time in which mercies are received, that they are given in return of prayer?

A. If they are granted at the time when we need them most, or at the time when we are most earnest and importunate about them; as Peter's deliverance from prison was on the very night which Herod had determined should be his last; and likewise when the church was assembled to wrestle in prayer for him, Acts xii. 6, 7, 12.

Q. 84. Why does the Lord delay mercies, which he designs afterwards to confer?

A. He delays granting them, that we may be the more thankful for them when they come; and in the mean time to make us more assiduous and ardent supplicants for them, 2 Cor. xii. 8, 9.

QUEST. 99. *What rule hath God given for our direction in prayer?*

ANS. The whole word of God is of use to direct us in prayer; but the special rule of direction, is that form of prayer which Christ taught his disciples, commonly called *The Lord's Prayer.*

OF DIRECTION IN PRAYER.

Q. 1. Why do we need [direction] in prayer?

A. Because man is naturally a stranger, both to God and himself; being ignorant both of the glorious perfections of God, Rom. iii. 11; and of his own sins and wants, Rev. iii. 17.

Q. 2. From whence are we to take direction in prayer?

A. From [the whole word of God] which is [of use to direct us] therein.

Q. 3. Is every part of the word of equal use for our direction in prayer?

A. Though "all things in the scripture are not alike plain in themselves, nor alike clear unto all;" * yet there is no part of the word from whence an intelligent person in the due use of the ordinary means, may not gather something that may be proper matter either for petition, confession, or thanksgiving in prayer, 1 John v. 14.

Q. 4. Of what use in prayer, are the sins of which we read in scripture, that other churches before us have been guilty of, and the judgments which have been inflicted for the same?

A. They are of use to direct us to pray, that the Lord would keep his church and people, in the day in which we live, from running into the same snares, and thus exposing themselves to the same judgments, 1 Cor. x. 11.

Q. 5. Of what use in prayer are the doctrines of the word in general?

A. They are of use to instruct us in the principles of religion, or chain of divine truth; without some knowledge of which, it is impossible to pray to the edification, either of ourselves or others, Rom. x. 14.

Q. 6. Of what use is the doctrine of the blessed Trinity, in particular, for our direction in prayer?

A. It is of singular use, to point out the method in which we are to hope for the blessings we pray for; namely, from the Father, through Christ, by the Spirit, according to Eph. ii. 18: "Through him (that is, through Christ,) we have access by one Spirit unto the Father."

Q. 7. Of what use are the offices of Christ, for our direction in prayer?

A. They are of use to us to direct us to pray, that, of God he may be made unto us wisdom, as a prophet; righteousness, as a priest; sanctification, as a king; and complete redemption, as being all the three in one person, 1 Cor. i. 30.

Q. 8. Of what use are the promises for this end?

A. They contain the very matter of prayer; and the pleading of them by faith, as also the right manner in which the duty should be performed, James i. 6.

* Confession of Faith, chap. i. § 7

Q. 9. What is [the special rule of direction] for the duty of prayer?

A. It is [that form of prayer which Christ taught his disciples, commonly called, *The Lord's Prayer.*]

Q. 10. Why is this called [the special rule] of direction?

A. Because there is not any one portion of scripture, where the petitionary part of prayer is so comprehensively and methodically laid down, as in the Lord's prayer.

Q. 11. Could Christ use this prayer for himself?

A. No; he could not put up the fifth petition, Forgive us our debts; because he had no sins of his own to forgive, being separate from sinners, Heb. vii. 26.

Q. 12. Why then is it [commonly called the *Lord's Prayer?*]

A. Because it was dictated by him to his disciples, in answer to their request, Luke xi. 1: "Lord, teach us to pray, as John also taught his disciples."

Q. 13. Did Christ prescribe this prayer as a form, or as a pattern?

A. He prescribed it as a pattern, for direction in the duty of prayer, Matt. vi. 9: "After this *manner* pray ye."

Q. 14. What is the difference between a form and a pattern of prayer?

A. A form of prayer is a certain mode of expression, which must be used without the least variation; whereas a pattern is only a directory as to the matter, leaving the suppliant himself to clothe his desires with such words as are most adapted to his present circumstances.

Q. 15. Why then is the Lord's prayer called, in the answer, [*that form* of prayer which Christ taught his disciples?]

A. Because the words of this prayer, "may be used as a prayer" to God, equally with other scriptures, "so that it be done with understanding, faith, reverence, and other graces necessary to the right performance of the duty of prayer."*

Q. 16. How does it appear, that this prayer is not designed for a form to the precise words of which Christ's disciples and followers are to be tied strictly down, in all after ages?

A. This plainly appears, from its not containing expressly all the parts of prayer; and from its not being related by Matthew and Luke in the same manner.

Q. 17. What are those parts of prayer which are not expressly contained in the Lord's prayer?

A. They are the confession of our sins, and the thankful acknowledgment of God's mercies: neither of which are in express terms, but by consequence only, contained in the said prayer.

---

* Larger Catechism, Quest. 187.

Q. 18. From what part of this prayer may confession of sins be deduced?
A. From the fifth petition; for, when we pray, Forgive us our debts, we, by consequence, confess that we have debts to be forgiven.
Q. 19. How is a thankful acknowledgment of mercies included in the Lord's prayer?
A. When we pray, Hallowed be thy name, we, of consequence, make a thankful acknowledgment of all those known instances, in which God's name has been glorified; and when we pray, Give us this day our daily bread, we acknowledge the bounty of his providence, which has hitherto so kindly supplied our wants.
Q. 20. How do the evangelists, Matthew and Luke, differ, as to the manner in which they relate this prayer?
A. Though there be a perfect harmony between them, as to the sense or matter of the prayer; yet there is some difference as to the mode of expression, particularly in the fourth and fifth petitions.
Q. 21. How do they differ in the fourth petition?
A. Matthew has it, Give us this day our daily bread, chap. vi. 11; Luke, Give us day by day our daily bread, chap. xi. 3.
Q. 22. What is the meaning of "give us this day?"
A. It is a petition of what we want at present.
Q. 23. What is imported in "give us day by day?"
A. The expression imports, that the wants, which need to be supplied, will daily recur.
Q. 24. How do the two evangelists differ, as to their manner of expressing the fifth petition?
A. Matthew says, Forgive us our debts as we forgive our debtors, chap. vi. 12; Luke expresses it, Forgive us our sins, as we forgive every one that is indebted to us, chap. xi. 4.
Q. 25. How do they differ as to the conclusion?
A. Matthew has it; Luke leaves it out.
Q. 26. What is the argument from all this, against the Lord's prayer being designed for a set form?
A. The argument is, that if it had been designed for a set form, the two evangelists would have expressed it in the very same words, without the least variation.
Q. 27. What argument is there from the practice of the apostles against its being a set form?
A. That though several prayers of theirs are recorded in the New Testament, yet none of them use the express words of the Lord's prayer.
Q. 28. Would it not seem that this prayer is commanded to be used as a form, from our Lord's prefixing these words to it: When ye pray, *say*, Our Father, &c.? Luke xi. 2.

A. No more can be intended by this expression in Luke, When ye pray, *say*, than what is meant in the parallel place, Matt. vi. 9: *After this manner* pray ye; namely, to use the Lord's prayer as a directory; otherwise, Luke's form, and not Matthew's, should be followed.

Q. 29. May none, at any rate, use set forms, however sound?

A. If set forms are sound, or agreeable to the will of God, they may be used by children, or such as are weak in knowledge, till they acquire some insight in the principles of religion; and then they ought to be laid aside, and extemporary prayer practised and improved.

Q. 30. But may not they, who are weak in knowledge, read sound forms as their prayers to God?

A. No; they ought to repeat them, because the committing of them to memory will tend to imprint the matter of them more deeply on the mind, than the bare reading can possibly do: besides, there is not the least shadow of an example in scripture, for reading prayers to God on any account whatsoever.

Q. 31. Why is the continued practice of set forms unwarrantable?

A. Because the case and circumstances of the church in general, and every member of it, in particular, are so exceedingly various, that it is impossible any set form can correspond to them. Moreover, the continued practice of a set form, as it encourages sloth, so is an overlooking the aid of the Spirit, whose office it is to help our infirmities, when we know not what we should pray for as we ought, Rom. viii. 26.

Q. 32. " Of how many parts does the Lord's prayer consist?"

A. The Lord's prayer consists of three parts, a "preface, petitions, and a conclusion."*

QUEST. 100. *What doth the preface of the Lord's prayer teach us?*

ANS. The preface of the Lord's prayer (which is, *Our Father which art in heaven*,) teacheth us, to draw near to God with all holy reverence and confidence, as children to a Father, able and ready to help us; and that we should pray with and for others.

Q. 1. In what words is the [preface] of the Lord's prayer contained?

* Larger Catechism, Quest. 188.

A. It is contained in these words, [Our Father which art in heaven.]

Q. 2. What is the end and design of this preface?

A. It is to give us a directory how to invoke or address the true object of all religious worship.

Q. 3. What is it to invoke or address God in prayer?

A. It is, in a believing and reverential manner, to make mention of some of his names, titles, or attributes, in a suitableness to the nature of the duty in which we are engaged: as in 1 Kings viii. 23. Dan. ix. 4.

Q. 4. Whom do we invoke, or call upon, when we address the [*Father*.]

A. We invoke the *Three-one God;* because though each person of the Trinity be the object of worship, 2 Cor. xiii. 14; yet when any of these adorable persons is addressed, we are, in our minds, to include the other two; in as much as the very same divine nature and essence is in them all, 1 Chron. xxix. 10.

Q. 5. Why are we directed to address the Three-one God as a Father?

A. To teach us, that the object of true and acceptable worship is a reconciled God, Ps. cxxx. 4.

Q. 6. In what respect is God called a Father, with reference to men?

A. He is called a Father, with reference to them, either in respect of creation, external covenant-relation, or the grace of adoption.

Q. 7. To whom is he a Father in respect of creation?

A. In this respect he is a Father to all mankind in general, Mal. ii. 10.

Q. 8. To whom is he a Father in respect of external covenant relation?

A. To all the members of the visible church, or such as profess the true religion, and their children, 2 Cor. vi. 18.

Q. 9. To whom is he a Father in respect of the grace of adoption?

A. To believers only, or such as are "the children of God by faith in Christ Jesus," Gal. iii. 26.

Q. 10. May not every one who hears the gospel warrantably cry to God, My Father, according to Jer. iii. 4?

A. No doubt but it is their duty to do so, upon the call and command of God; but none will actually do it in faith, but they into whose hearts "God hath sent forth the Spirit of his Son," Gal. iv. 6.

Q. 11. What are we taught, when we are directed to invoke God in prayer, by the title of Father?

A. We are hereby taught, [to draw near to God—as children to a Father.]

Q. 12. In what manner should God's children draw near to him as their Father?

A. [With all holy reverence and confidence.]

Q. 13. Why called [holy reverence?]

A. To distinguish it from that dutiful regard and respect which children owe to their parents by the dictates of nature's light.

Q. 14. In what consists the nature of this [holy reverence?]

A. It consists in a most profound inward esteem of God, as a Father, accompanied with "other child-like dispositions,"* becoming that relation, Isa. lxiv. 9.

Q. 15. What are these other child-like dispositions, which accompany the reverence with which God's children approach him?

A. Among others, there are patience under his rebukes, Mic. vii. 9; obedience to his commands, Acts ix. 6; and a fervent zeal for his honour and glory, Mal. i. 6.

Q. 16. What is that [confidence] which God's children have in him as their Father?

A. It is that entire trust they repose in him, as [able and ready to help] them.

Q. 17. Whence are they persuaded of his ability and readiness to help them?

A. From his all-sufficiency, Luke xi. 13, and boundless liberality, Ps. lxxxiv. 11, as laid out in the promise for their benefit.

Q. 18. What help does he afford them?

A. Such a help as to do *all*; "for it is God that worketh in us, both to will and to do of his good pleasure," Phil. ii. 13.

Q. 19. Why are we directed to address our Father [*in heaven?*]

A. To teach us to draw near to him with "heavenly affections, Lam. iii. 41, and due apprehension of his sovereign power, majesty, and gracious condescension, Isa. lxiii. 15, 16." †

Q. 20. What does the consideration of his being in heaven more particularly teach us?

A. It teaches us from whence to expect our blessings and benefits, and likewise the manner in which we ought to address God for them.

Q. 21. From whence are we to expect our blessings?

A. From above, James i. 17, because they are in heavenly places, Eph. i. 3.

Q. 22. Why are our blessings said to be in heavenly places?

A. Because their original is from thence, and there will the full enjoyment of them at last be, Ps. xvi. 11.

Q. 23. What does the consideration of God's being in heaven teach us, with reference to the manner in which we ought to address him for our blessings?

---

* Larger Catechism, Quest. 189.   † Ibid.

A. It teaches us to be modest, humble, and cautious, in our conceptions of, and applications to him; as being a God of such inconceivable greatness, and glorious majesty, Eccl. v. 2: " Be not rash with thy mouth, and let not thine heart be hasty to utter any thing before God; for God is in heaven, and thou upon earth, therefore let thy words be few."

Q. 24. To whom does the relative pronoun [our,] in the preface, refer?

A. It refers both to ourselves and others.

Q. 25. What is the import of it as it refers to ourselves?

A. When we are directed to say [our Father,] it imports the faith and confidence we are warranted to express in him, as standing in such an amiable relation.

Q. 26. Upon what grounds are we warranted to express our faith and confidence in him, as standing in the amiable relation of our Father?

A. Upon the ground of his being the God and Father of our Lord Jesus Christ, Eph. i. 3; and upon the ground of our new-covenant Head calling him " my Father," in the name of all his spiritual seed, Ps. lxxxix. 26: He shall cry unto me, Thou art *my Father*.

Q. 27. What do these words, our Father, import, as they have a respect to others?

A. They import [that we should pray with and for others.]

Q. 28. What is it to pray [with] others?

A. It is to be the mouth of others to God, or to join with them in family or social worship

Q. 29. What is it to pray [for] others?

A. It is to express our concern about them, or our sympathy with them before God, as sincerely and ingenuously, as we would do with reference to ourselves, were we in the same circumstances, Ps. xxxv. 13.

Q. 30. Who are these [others] for whom we should pray?

A. We should pray for all men, 1 Tim. ii. 1; yea, for them which despitefully use us and persecute us, Matt. v. 44; but especially for all saints, Eph. vi. 18.

Q. 31. Why have all the saints a special claim to our prayers?

A. Because they are the special favourites of heaven, John xv. 9, and therefore the very butt of the keenest resentment of hell, 1 Pet. v. 8.

QUEST. 101. *What do we pray for in the first petition?*

ANS. In the first petition, (which is, *Hallowed be thy*

name,) we pray, That God would enable us, and others, to glorify him in all that whereby he maketh himself known and that he would dispose all things to his own glory.

Q. 1. What is the meaning of the word [petition?]
A. It signifies asking or desiring any thing.
Q. 2. How many petitions are there in the Lord's prayer?
A. There are six.
Q. 3. In what order are these six petitions ranged?
A. The first three bear a more immediate respect to God; and the last three to ourselves.
Q. 4. What are we taught by this order of ranking the petitions?
A. We are thus taught, first to pray for what concerns the glory of God, as being the highest and most valuable end; and then for what respects our own advantage, as being only subordinate to it, Matt. vi. 33.
Q. 5. Which is the first of these petitions?
A. It is in these words, [Hallowed be thy name.]
Q. 6. What is signified by the [name] of God in this petition?
A. It is explained in the answer to be [all that whereby he maketh himself known.]
Q. 7. What is our duty with reference to this name of God?
A. It is to pray that it may be [hallowed.]
Q. 8. What is the meaning of the word *hallowed?*
A. It is explained in the answer to be the same with glorified: when we pray Hallowed be thy name, we pray, that God himself may be glorified.
Q. 9. By whom should we pray that God's name may be hallowed or glorified?
A. We should pray, that his name may be glorified by himself; and likewise that he [would enable us and others to glorify him.]
Q. 10. What do we mean, when we pray that God's name may be glorified by himself?
A. We mean, that he would be pleased daily to demonstrate it more and more to the world, to be what it really is, most holy and most glorious, so as to excite that adoration and esteem which is due to him: for, says he, "I will be sanctified in them that come nigh to me, and before all the people will I be glorified," Lev. x. 3.
Q. 11. Where does he thus demonstrate the glory of his own name?
A. In his word; and by his works both of creation and providence, particularly by the glorious device of redemption.

OF THE FIRST PETITION.

Q. 12. What do we acknowledge, when we pray that God would enable us and others to glorify him?

A. We thus acknowledge "the utter inability and indisposition that is in ourselves and all men, to honour God aright, 2 Cor. iii. 5."*

Q. 13. What is requisite in order to our honouring God aright?

A. In order to this, it is requisite that we diligently attend to the several ways, by which God [maketh himself known,] such as his attributes, ordinances, word, and works; and see if we are studying to glorify him in all these.

Q. 14. How do we glorify him in his attributes or perfections?

A. When we think or speak of them with becoming reverence, and endeavour to exercise suitable acts of faith upon them; such as, admiring his wisdom, depending on his power, and trusting to his faithfulness, that he will do as he has said.

Q. 15. How do we glorify him in his ordinances?

A. When we attend upon them, and improve them for our spiritual nourishment and growth in grace, Ps. lxxxiv. 10.

Q. 16. How do we glorify him in his word?

A. When we believe it as the record of God, John xx. 31.

Q. 17. How do we glorify him in his work of creation?

A. When we apprehend and admire his eternal power and Godhead, as shining in it, Rom. i. 20.

Q. 18. How do we glorify him in his works of providence?

A. When we have a grateful sense of his mercies, Gen. xxxii. 10; and tremble at his judgments, Ps. cxix. 120.

Q. 19. How do we honour him in his glorious device of redemption?

A. When we receive and rest upon Christ alone for salvation, as he is offered to us in the gospel, Acts xv. 11.

Q. 20. What do we mean, when we pray that God would enable [others] to glorify him, as well as ourselves?

A. We thus, in effect, pray, that the earth may be full of the knowledge of the Lord, as the waters cover the sea, Isa. xi. 9; that so from the uttermost parts of the earth may be heard songs, even glory to the righteous, chap. xxiv. 16.

Q. 21. What are those things we should pray God would prevent and remove, that his name may be glorified?

A. We should pray, "that he would prevent and remove atheism, ignorance, idolatry, and whatever is dishonourable to him." †

* Larger Catechism, Quest. 190.   † Ibid.

Q. 22. What should we pray God would do, in the course of his providence, for glorifying his own name?
A. [That he would dispose all things to his own glory.]
Q. 23. How does God dispose all things to his own glory?
A. By bringing a revenue of glory to himself, even out of those things that seem most opposite to it, Isa. xliii. 20.
Q. 24. What are these seemingly opposite things, out of which God brings a revenue of glory to himself?
A. Among others, there are persecutions and the falls of believers.
Q. 25. How does he bring a revenue of glory to himself out of persecutions?
A. By overruling them to the furtherance of the gospel, Acts xi. 19—21.
Q. 26. How does he bring glory to himself out of the falls of believers?
A. By overruling their falls and miscarriages, in such a manner, as that they are thus made more humble, watchful, and circumspect, for the future, Ps. li. 3.

QUEST. 102. *What do we pray for in the second petition?*

ANS. In the second petition, (which is, *Thy kingdom come*,) we pray, That Satan's kingdom may be destroyed; and that the kingdom of grace may be advanced, ourselves and others brought into it, and kept in it; and that the kingdom of glory may be hastened.

Q. 1. How many fold is God's [kingdom] in this world?
A. *Twofold;* namely, his general, essential, or providential kingdom; and his special kingdom.
Q. 2. What is his general kingdom?
A. It is the absolute power and sovereignty which he exercises over all things in heaven, earth, and hell, for the purposes of his own glory, Ps. ciii. 19: "His kingdom ruleth over all."
Q. 3. What is his special kingdom?
A. It is the government and care which he exercises in and over his church and people, as a society distinct from the rest of the world, Ps. lix. 13: "God ruleth in Jacob unto the ends of the earth."
Q. 4. Into whose hands is the management of God's special kingdom committed?
A. Into the hands of Christ as Mediator, Ps. ii. 6.
Q. 5. How is this kingdom, as committed into his hands, usually called?

A. His mediatory, or donative kingdom.
Q. 6. Why called his mediatory kingdom?
A. Because he holds it as Mediator, Luke xxii. 29.
Q. 7. Why called his donative kingdom?
A. Because it is given him of the Father as a reward of his meritorious obedience and sufferings, Matt. xxviii. 18; and to distinguish it from his essential kingdom.
Q. 8. May his essential kingdom be said to be given him?
A. By no means; because it is natural to him, as God equal with the Father, and can no more be given him than his divine nature and personality can.
Q. 9. For what are we directed to pray in this petition, with reference to God's kingdom in general?
A. That it may *come:* [Thy kingdom come.]
Q. 10. In what sense may we pray for the coming of his essential kingdom?
A. Only in this sense, that he would more and more demonstrate his supreme power and sovereignty over all things, and that the same may be more and more acknowledged by the children of men, Ps. lxxxiii. 18.
Q. 11. Would it be warrantable for us to pray, that he would govern the world, or actually exercise his supreme power?
A. It would be no more warrantable to pray for this, than to pray that he would be an infinite Sovereign, which he cannot but be; and act agreeably to his nature, which he cannot but do.
Q. 12. Whether is it the coming of God's general or special kingdom that is chiefly intended in the answer?
A. It is the coming of his special kingdom of grace here, and of glory hereafter.
Q. 13. Are the kingdoms of grace and glory different kingdoms?
A. They are not so much different kingdoms, as different *states* in the same kingdom: according to the common maxim, Grace is glory begun, and glory is grace consummated, or in perfection.
Q. 14. How may the kingdom of grace in this world be viewed?
A. Either as to outward dispensation, or inward operation.
Q. 15. What is it as to outward dispensation?
A. It is just the preaching of the gospel, Mark i. 14: "Jesus came, preaching the gospel of the kingdom of God."
Q. 16. What is it as to inward operation?
A. It is the work of saving grace in the soul, Luke xvii. 21: "Behold, the kingdom of God is within you."
Q. 17. Why called [the kingdom of grace?]

A. Because the gathering of sinners into this kingdom, for their salvation, is of grace, both as to the means and end, Eph. ii. 8.

Q. 18. What do we pray for with reference to the kingdom of grace, when we say, Thy kingdom come?

A. We do not pray that it may be erected as a new thing in the world, but that it may be [advanced] in it.

Q. 19. Why should we not pray, that Christ's kingdom of grace may be erected or set up as a new thing in the world?

A. Because this would be, in effect, to deny that Christ had ever a church upon this earth; whereas, it is most certain, that ever since the first promise, he has always had a church in it, and will have it to the end of time, Isa. lix. 21.

Q. 20. But is it not our duty to pray, that the kingdom of grace may be set up in those parts of the world where it is not at present?

A. To be sure it is; for we should pray, "That the word of the Lord may have free course and be glorified," 2 Thess. iii. 1; and that the earth may "be full of the knowledge of the Lord, as the waters cover the sea," Isa. xi. 9; which is the same with praying, That the kingdom of grace may be advanced.

Q. 21. For what should we pray as pre-requisite to the advancing of the kingdom of grace?

A. In order to this, we should pray, [That Satan's kingdom may be destroyed.]

Q. 22. What is the meaning of the name *Satan?*

A. It is a Hebrew word, signifying an adversary; as, indeed, the devil is an implacable adversary, burning with hatred and enmity both against God, and therefore called his enemy, Matt. xiii. 25, and against man, 1 Pet. v. 8: Your adversary the devil, as a roaring lion, walketh about, seeking whom he may devour.

Q. 23. What do you understand by [Satan's kingdom?]

A. That power and dominion which he usurps over mankind sinners, who are by nature lawful captives, Isa. xlix. 24, 25.

Q. 24. If sinners of mankind are by nature lawful captives, how can Satan's dominion over them be said to be usurped?

A. Though they be justly delivered into his hands, as a jailor, yet he has no right to rule over them as a prince.

Q. 25. Do they not voluntarily subject themselves to his dominion?

A. Yes; and this is both their sin and their judgment John viii. 44.

Q. 26 What is the principal seat of Satan's kingdom?

A. The *heart* of every man and woman by nature, Eph. ii. 2.

Q. 27. What is the foundation and bulwark of this kingdom?

A. *Sin*, both original and actual, Eph. ii. 3.

Q. 28. For what should we pray, with reference to this kingdom of Satan?

A. That it [may be destroyed.]

Q. 29. Why should we pray for the destruction of this kingdom?

A. Because the work of grace cannot take place, nor succeed in the soul, except upon the ruins of Satan's interest in it, Luke xi. 21, 22.

Q. 30. How then is Satan's kingdom destroyed in the world?

A. By the advancement of the kingdom of grace in it.

Q. 31. When may the kingdom of grace be said to be [advanced?]

A. When [ourselves and others are brought into it, and kept in it.]

Q. 32. How are we and others [brought] into this kingdom?

A. By the gracious influences of the Spirit of God, accompanying the dispensation of the gospel with irresistible power, Ps. cx. 2, 3.

Q. 33. How are we and others [kept in it?]

A. By continued emanations of grace out of the fulness of Christ, by which the principle of grace is quickened, strengthened, and preserved, Hos. xiv. 5.

Q. 34. For what should we pray, as the means of bringing into this kingdom?

A. We should pray, "that the gospel may be propagated throughout the world, the Jews called, the fulness of the Gentiles brought in; that the ordinances of Christ may be purely dispensed, and made effectual to the converting of those that are yet in their sins." *

Q. 35. For what should we pray as means of being kept in it?

A. That the same ordinances may be effectual to the "confirming, comforting, and building up of those that are already converted." †

Q. 36. Can any subject of this kingdom ever apostatize from it?

A. No; they are "kept by the power of God, through faith unto salvation," 1 Pet. i. 5.

Q. 37. Why then should we pray to be kept in it?

A. Because perseverance, being a promised privilege, should, on that account, be prayed for, Ps. cxix. 28. "Strengthen thou me, according to thy word."

* Larger Catechism, Quest. 191.   † Ibid.

Q. 38. What security have the saints that they shall be kept in this kingdom?

A. They have the stability of the promise, Jer. xxxii. 40; the efficacy of Christ's obedience to the death in their stead, Eph. v. 25—27; the prevalency of his intercession, John xvii. 24; and the inhabitation of his Spirit, Rom. viii. 11, for their security in this matter.

Q. 39. What is [the kingdom of glory?]

A. It is that state of inconceivable happiness and bliss into which the saints shall be brought after death, John xiv. 2, 3.

Q. 40. In what will the [glory] of this kingdom consist?

A. In a perfect conformity to, and the immediate and uninterrupted vision and fruition of God through all eternity, 1 John iii. 2.

Q. 41. When will the kingdom of glory come in the full manifestation of it?

A. At the second coming of Christ to judgment, Matt. xxv. 31, 34.

Q. 42. For what are we to pray, with reference to this kingdom?

A. That it [may be hastened.]

Q. 43. When we pray that it may be [hastened,] do we mean, that the set time for the second coming of Christ may be anticipated, or come sooner than the moment fixed for it in infinite wisdom?

A. No; we wish it no sooner; but only express our ardent "desire to depart, and to be with Christ; which is far better" than to be here always, Phil. i. 23.

Q. 44. Why do the saints so earnestly desire to be with Christ in glory?

A. That an eternal period may be put to all their sinning, and to every thing that has a tendency to detract from the glory of his kingdom, and the happiness of his subjects: wherefore, as he saith, Surely, I come quickly; so they pray, Amen, even so, come, Lord Jesus, Rev. xxii. 20.

QUEST. 103 *What do we pray for in the third petition?*

ANS. In the third petition, (which is, *thy will be done on earth, as it is in heaven,*) we pray, that God, by his grace, would make us both able and willing to know, obey, and submit to his will in all things, as the angels do in heaven.

OF THE THIRD PETITION. 235

Q. 1. How many fold is the [will] of God?
A. *Twofold;* his will of purpose, or disposing will; and his will of precept, or revealed will.

Q. 2. What is his will of purpose, or disposing will?
A. It is what he himself purposes to be done, as the final determination of the event of things, Isa. xlvi. 10: "My counsel shall stand, and I will do all my pleasure."

Q. 3. How is this will commonly designated?
A. It is termed his will of providence, because he infallibly brings it about, or accomplishes it, in the course of his adorable providence, Ps. cxxxv. 6.

Q. 4. What is God's will of precept, or his revealed will?
A. It is the rule of our duty, prescribing what he would have us to do, or not to do, Matt. xxvi. 39: "O my Father, if it be possible, let this cup pass from me: nevertheless, not as I will, but as thou wilt."

Q. 5. Whether is it God's will of purpose or precept that is meant in this petition?
A. Both are included, but chiefly his will of precept.

Q. 6. When we say, "Thy will be done," for what do we pray with reference to God's will of purpose?
A. We pray, [that God, by his grace, would make us able and willing—to submit] to it, and acquiesce in it, so soon as it is discovered or made known to us, Acts xxi. 14: "And when he would not be persuaded, we ceased, saying, The will of the Lord be done."

Q. 7. What does our praying for submission to God's will of purpose or providence, necessarily imply in it?
A. It implies that we are "by nature—prone to repine and murmur against his providence,"* especially in afflictive dispensations, Num. xiv. 2.

Q. 8. When do we submit to afflictive dispensations?
A. When we justify God in them, Dan. ix. 7; and acknowledge that he "hath punished us less than our iniquities deserve," Ezra ix. 13.

Q. 9. For what do we pray, when we pray that God's will of precept may be done?
A. We pray that God, by his grace, would make us able and willing [to know and obey] the same.

Q. 10. Why do we pray that God would [make us able and willing] to know and obey his revealed will?
A. Because, "by nature, we and all men, are not only utterly unable and unwilling to know and do the will of God; but prone to rebel against his word,—and wholly inclined to do the will of the flesh, and of the devil." †

Q. 11. Why do we pray that God would make us able and willing [by his grace?]
A. Because it is wholly of his free love and sovereign

---

* Larger Catechism, Quest. 192. † Ibid.

grace, that he works in us either to will or to do, Phil. ii. 13: "It is God which worketh in you, both to will and to do of his good pleasure."

Q. 12. For what do we pray, when we pray that God would make us able and willing to [know] his revealed will?

A. We pray, that, by his Spirit, he would take away our natural blindness, and open our understanding, that we may understand the scriptures, Luke xxiv. 45.

Q. 13. For what do we pray, when we pray that God would make us able and willing to [obey] his will?

A. We pray, that he would remove the weakness, indisposedness, and perverseness of our hearts; and, by his grace, incline us to set about, and keep up the practice of every commanded duty, in the strength of that grace which is secured in the promise, Ezek. xxxvi. 27: "I will cause you to walk in my statutes;" 2 Cor. xii. 9: "And he said unto me, My grace is sufficient for thee; for my strength is made perfect in weakness."

Q. 14. Why is knowing the will of God mentioned before the obeying of it?

A. Because there can be no true and acceptable obedience, but what flows from that saving knowledge which is inseparable from the faith of God's operation, John xiii. 17: "If ye know these things, happy are ye if ye do them."

Q. 15. Where should we desire that the will of God may be done?

A. We should desire that it may [be done on earth,] by all persons, and in all places on it, Ps. cl. 6.

Q. 16. In what things should we pray that the will of God may be done on earth?

A. We should pray that it may be done in [all things,] Ps. cxix. 6.

Q. 17. Why in *all things?*

A. Because we may be quite sure, that God's will, both of precept and providence, is perfectly, or in every respect, equal, and just, Ezek. xviii. 25.

Q. 18. Whom should we resemble in our obedience?

A. The holy angels: we should study to do the will of God [as the angels do in heaven.]

Q. 19. Can we know and obey the will of God as perfectly on earth, as the angels do in heaven?

A. No: but we should copy after them, as to the manner of their obedience.

Q. 20. What is it to copy after them as to the manner of their obedience?

A. It is to essay obedience "with the like humility, cheerfulness, faithfulness, diligence, zeal, sincerity, and constancy, as the angels do in heaven." *

* Larger Catechism Q. 192.

Quest. 104. *What do we pray for in the fourth petition?*

Ans. In the fourth petition, (which is, *Give us this day our daily bread,*) we pray, That of God's free gift, we may receive a competent portion of the good things of this life, and enjoy his blessing with them.

Q. 1 What does our Catechism mean by [bread] in this petition?
A. It explains it to be [the good things of this life.]
Q. 2. What do you understand by the good things of this life?
A. Not only meat and drink; but clothes to cover us, houses to shelter us, sleep to refresh us, and the like; which are called things needful to the body, James ii. 16.
Q. 3. May not spiritual mercies, or food to our souls, be intended by the bread here mentioned?
A. No: the petition respects temporal mercies, or the good things of the present life.
Q. 4. How do you prove, that the good things of this life, and not spiritual mercies, are intended in this petition?
A. From the completeness, and compendiousness of the Lord's prayer; for, it cannot be supposed, that, in a prayer so complete, the good things of this life would be quite omitted; or, that in a prayer so compendious, spiritual mercies would, without necessity, be repeated in this petition, when the other petitions are so full of them.
Q. 5. Why are these good things called by the general name of *bread?*
A. Because, though bread be the most common, yet it is the most useful and necessary support of natural life; and therefore called the staff, or stay of bread, Isa. iii. 1.
Q. 6. Why called [daily] bread?
A. Both because our need of the supports of nature recurs daily; and likewise to teach us contentment with our present allowance in providence, Phil. iv. 11.
Q. 7. For what quantity of daily bread, or of the good things of this life, may we lawfully pray?
A. For a [competent portion] of them.
Q. 8. What is meant by a competent portion?
A. Such a measure of temporal comforts, as our necessities may require, or will tend to our good, Prov. xxx. 8: "Give me neither poverty nor riches: feed me with food convenient for me."
Q. 9. What is imported in our praying, that God would [give] us this competent portion?
A. It imports our desire to receive it [of God's free gift.]

OF THE FOURTH PETITION.

Q. 10. What do we acknowledge, when we pray to receive temporal comforts of God's free gift?

A. We thereby acknowledge, that in Adam, and by our own sin, we have forfeited our rights to all the outward blessings of this life, and deserve to be wholly deprived of them by God."*

Q. 11. How does it appear that we have, by sin, forfeited our right to outward blessings?

A. It appears from this, that we have thereby forfeited our life itself, Gen. ii. 17; and, therefore, by necessary consequence, all the supports of it, Jer. v. 25.

Q. 12. Why do we say, [Give us *this* day?]

A. Because if God shall be pleased to afford us the necessary supplies of each day, when it comes, we ought not to be anxiously solicitous about to-morrow, Matt. vi. 34.

Q. 13. May we not lawfully pray for what respects the future condition of ourselves, or families, in this world?

A. Yes; if God shall continue us, or them, in life, then, in this case, we may lawfully beg of him, that neither we, nor they, may ever be destitute of what is necessary for our glorifying God, in the respective stations, in which he has, or may place us while in it, Gen. xxviii. 20—22.

Q. 14. Does God's giving us our daily bread, exclude the use of means for the obtaining of it?

A. No: for, "if any provide not for his own, and specially for those of his own house, he hath denied the faith, and is worse than an infidel," 1 Tim. v. 8.

Q. 15. May we not then ascribe our daily bread to our own diligence and industry?

A. No: because it is God who gives us ability to pursue our respective callings, and it is he who succeeds our lawful endeavours in them, Deut. viii. 17, 18: "Thou shalt remember the Lord thy God; for it is he that giveth thee power to get wealth."

Q. 16. Why do we say, Give us [our] daily bread? why do we call it *ours*?

A. Because whatever measure or proportion of outward blessings, God in his providence, thinks fit we should receive, is properly *ours*, whether it be more or less, 1 Tim. vi. 8: "Having food and raiment, let us therewith be content."

Q. 17. Since both the godly and the wicked have their daily provision from God, what difference is there as to the manner in which the one and the other hold their outward comforts?

A. There is a wide difference as to the manner in which the godly and the wicked hold their outward comforts, whether we consider their respective right and title; their present enjoyment; or their future expectation.

* Larger Catechism Q. 193.

Q. 18. What is the difference as to their respective right and title?

A. The wicked have only a civil and common right; but the godly have, besides this, a spiritual and covenant right also, 1 Tim. iv. 8.

Q. 19. What is the difference as to their present enjoyment?

A. The godly have God's blessing on what they presently enjoy; but the wicked his curse. In this respect, "a little that a righteous man hath, is better than the riches of many wicked," Ps. xxxvii. 16.

Q. 20. What is the difference as to their future expectation?

A. The godly have the good things of this world, as pledges of the far better things of another; but the wicked have them as their whole pay; for they have their portion in this life, Ps. xvii. 14.

Q. 21. For what should we pray in order to have the comfortable use of the good things of this life, which God may confer upon us?

A. That we may [enjoy his blessing with them.]

Q. 22. Why is the blessing of God necessary to all our outward comforts?

A. Because without this none of them could reach the end for which they are used: our food could not nourish us, nor our clothes warm us, nor medicines, however skilfully applied, give any relief from our ailments, Job xx. 22, 23.

Q. 23. Will God's blessing make the meanest fare answer the end of comfortable nourishment?

A. Yes; as is evident from the example of Daniel, and the other three children of the captivity, who desired to be proved ten days, with no better cheer than pulse and water: "And at the end of ten days, their countenances appeared fairer and fatter in flesh, than all the children which did eat the portion of the king's meat," Dan. i. 12, 15.

Q. 24. Why do we pray in the plural number; Give us?

A. To express a concern for the good things of this life to the rest of our fellow-creatures, as well as to ourselves, 1 Kings viii. 35—40.

QUEST. 105. *What do we pray for in the fifth petition?*

ANS. In the fifth petition, (which is, *And forgive us our debts, as we forgive our debtors,*) we pray That

God, for Christ's sake, would freely pardon all our sins; which we are the rather encouraged to ask, because, by his grace, we are enabled, from the heart, to forgive others.

Q. 1. Why is this petition connected with the former, by the copulative conjunction [and?]
A. To teach us, that we can have no outward comfort with God's blessing, unless our sins are pardoned, and our persons accepted in Christ, 1 Cor. iii. 22, 23.

Q. 2. What are we to understand by [debts] in this petition?
A. By debts we are to understand our *sins*, whether original or actual, of omission or commission, Luke xi. 4.

Q. 3. Why are these called debts?
A. Because of the debt of punishment we owe to the justice of God, on account of them, Rom. vi. 23: "The wages of sin is death."

Q. 4. Can we pay any part of this debt to the justice of God?
A. No; "neither we, nor any other creature, can make the least satisfaction for it, Ps. cxxx. 3;"* or pay the least farthing of it, Matt. xviii. 25.

Q. 5. What other debt are we naturally owing, besides the debt of punishment as transgressors?
A. We likewise owe a debt of obedience to the law as a covenant; in which we are also utterly insolvent; "being unto every good work reprobate," Tit. i. 16.

Q. 6. What are we to pray for with reference to our sins or debts?
A. [That God, for Christ's sake, would freely pardon them all.]

Q. 7. Whose prerogative is it to pardon?
A. It is *God's* only, Micah vii. 18.

Q. 8. From what spring or fountain in God does pardon flow?
A. From his own gracious nature, Ps. lxxxvi. 5, and sovereign will, Ex. xxxiii. 19.

Q. 9. What is it for God to [pardon?]
A. It is to "acquit us both from the guilt and punishment of sin, Rom. iii. 26."†

Q. 10. For whose sake does he pardon?
A. Only [for Christ's sake.]

Q. 11. What is it for God to pardon for Christ's sake?
A. It is to vent his pardoning grace "through the obedience and satisfaction of Christ, apprehended and applied by faith, Rom. iii. 25."‡

---

* Larger Catechism, Quest. 194.   † Ibid.   ‡ Ibid.

Q. 12. Could God pardon sin, without any respect to the obedience and satisfaction of Christ?

A. No; because justice behoved to be satisfied; for, "without shedding of blood is no remission," Heb. ix. 22.

Q. 13. What is the extent of pardoning grace?

A. It extends to [all our sins,] Ps. ciii. 3.

Q. 14. In what manner should we expect that God will pardon all our sins?

A. We should expect that he will do it [freely,] for his own name's sake, Ps. xxv. 11.

Q. 15. How can God be said to pardon our sins freely, when he does it on account of the surety righteousness imputed to us?

A. God's accepting of Christ as our Surety, and his fulfilling all righteousness in our room, were both of them acts of rich, free, and sovereign grace, Ps. lxxxix. 19. Luke xii. 50. Though the pardon of our sins be of debt to Christ, yet it is free to us, Eph. i. 7.

Q. 16. When a believer prays for the forgiveness of his daily sins, does he pray for a new and formal pardon of them?

A. Whatever may be the believer's practice as to this matter, at some times, through the prevalence of darkness and unbelief; yet it is certain, that the pardon of sin, in justification, is one perfect act, completed at once, and never needs to be repeated, Micah vii. 19: "Thou wilt cast all their sins into the depths of the sea."

Q. 17. If daily sins are already forgiven in justification, in so far as the not imputing of them is secured in it; why is the believer here directed to pray for the pardon of them?

A. As the evidences of pardon may be frequently eclipsed, and fatherly displeasure incurred, by our daily failings; it is therefore our duty to pray, that God's fatherly displeasure may be removed, and the joy of his salvation restored, by his "giving us daily more and more assurance of forgiveness, Ps. li. 8—10, 12."*

Q. 18. Upon what ground may we be encouraged to ask and expect from God, the intimation of the pardon of our daily sins and failings?

A. Because, by his grace, we are enabled, from the heart, to forgive others.

Q. 19. What is it we are to forgive others?

A. Personal injuries; or injuries as committed against ourselves, Matt. xviii. 15.

Q. 20. Have personal injuries an offence done to God in them?

A. They certainly have; and it is our duty to pray that God would forgive it, Ps. xxxv. 13.

* Larger Catechism, Quest. 194.

Q. 21. In what manner should we forgive personal injuries?

A. We should do it [from the heart.]

Q. 22. What is it to forgive our fellow-creatures from the heart?

A. It is not only to lay aside all resentment against them; but to wish and do them all offices of kindness that lie in our power, as if they had never done us any injury, Matt. v. 44.

Q. 23. Have we naturally such a disposition in us?

A. No; God enables us to do it [by his grace.]

Q. 24. To what are we naturally inclined, with reference to personal injuries?

A. We are naturally inclined to harbour hatred and malice in our hearts on account of them, and to revenge them if we can; as was the case with Esau against his brother Jacob, Gen. xxvii. 41.

Q. 25. What should excite us to the duty of forgiving personal injuries?

A. The examples of this disposition recorded in scripture for our imitation; such as, the example of Joseph, Gen. l. 17, 21; of Stephen, Acts vii. 60; and of our Lord himself, Luke xxiii. 34.

Q. 26. Can it ever be dishonourable to forgive a personal injury?

A. No; it is a man's glory to pass over a transgression, Prov. xix. 11.

Q. 27. Can forgiving the person infer an approbation of his crime?

A. No; we may forgive the person, and yet charge his sin close home upon his conscience, as Joseph did to his brethren, Gen. xlv. 4, and l. 20.

Q. 28. What if forgiveness imbolden the offender in the like injuries for the future?

A. The fear of this should not be an excuse for omitting the present duty of forgiving; because we should leave events to the Lord.

Q. 29. When we say, Forgive us our debts, as we forgive our debtors; do we mean to state a comparison between our forgiving others, and God's forgiving us?

A. No: there is an infinite disproportion between the one and the other; the injuries our fellow-creatures do us are but few and small, in comparison of the innumerable and aggravated crimes we are guilty of against God, Matt. xviii. verses 24th and 28th compared.

Q. 30. Can we consistently with the scope of this petition, make our forgiveness of others, the ground and reason of God's forgiving us?

A. No; for this would be to put our forgiveness of others

OF THE SIXTH PETITION.

In the room of Christ's righteousness, on the account of which alone it is that God forgives us.

Q. 31. What then, is the true meaning of these words [as we forgive our debtors?]

A. The meaning is, that we take encouragement to hope, that God will forgive us the sins of our daily walk, from this evidence, or "testimony in ourselves, that we, from the heart, forgive others their offences, Matt. vi. 14, 15. If ye forgive men their trespasses, your heavenly Father will also forgive you; but if ye forgive not men their trespasses, neither will your heavenly Father forgive your trespasses." *

Q. 32. What may we learn from the verses just now quoted, for illustrating the meaning of this petition?

A. We may learn this from them, as the meaning of it, that our forgiving others, may be an evidence of God's forgiving us: and that our being of an implacable and unrelenting disposition towards our fellow-creatures, who have injured us, is a sad sign, that our own sins are not forgiven us of God, Matt. xviii. 35.

QUEST. 106. *What do we pray for in the sixth petition?*

Ans. In the sixth petition, (which is, *And lead us not into temptation, but deliver us from evil,*) we pray, That God would either keep us from being tempted to sin, or support and deliver us when we are tempted.

Q. 1. What does this petition necessarily suppose?

A. It supposes, "that the most wise, righteous, and gracious God, for divers holy and just ends, may so order things, that we may be assaulted, foiled, and, for a time, led captive by temptations, 2 Chron. xxxiii. 31." †

Q. 2. How many ways may God be said to [lead] a person [into temptation,] and yet not be the author of sin?

A. Two ways, objectively and permissively.

Q. 3. How may he be said to lead into temptation objectively?

A. When his providential dispensations, which, in themselves, are holy, just, and good, do offer, or lay before us occasions for sin.

Q. 4. May these occasions be called incitements or motives to sin?

A. No; only our corrupt hearts abuse or pervert them

* Larger Catechism, Quest. 194.   † Ibid. Q. 195.

to this end; thus, David was envious when he saw the prosperity of the wicked, Ps. lxxiii. 3.

Q. 5. When may God be said to lead his people into temptation permissively?

A. When he suffers them to be assaulted by the tempter, and, at the same time, withholds those aids of grace, which would prevent their compliance with the temptation, as in the case of David's numbering the people, 2 Sam. xxiv. 1, compared with 1 Chron. xxi. 1.

Q. 6. What is the [evil] from which we pray to be delivered, and the temptations we pray against in this petition?

A. The evil of [sin,] and temptations to sin.

Q. 7. What is it to be [tempted to sin?]

A. It is to be strongly solicited, instigated, and enticed to it, Prov. vii. 16—24.

Q. 8. Can God be the author or efficient of such instigations and allurements?

A. By no means; "For God cannot be tempted with evil, neither tempteth he any man," James i. 13.

Q. 9. Why then does he permit them to take place?

A. That he may direct and over-rule them to the purposes of his own glory; as in the instance of Peter, Luke xxii. 31, 32: "The Lord said, Simon, Simon, behold, Satan hath desired to have you, that he may sift you as wheat; but I have prayed for thee that thy faith fail not."

Q. 10. From whence lo all temptations to sin spring, or take their rise?

A. All of them flow from "Satan, 1 Chron. xxi. 1; the world, Luke xxi. 34; and the flesh, which are ready powerfully to draw us aside and insnare us, James i. 14."*

Q. 11. Are we liable to be drawn aside and insnared by enemies, after we are in a state of grace?

A. Yes: "even after the pardon of our sins, by reason of our corruption, Gal. v. 17, weakness, and want of watchfulness, Matt. xxvi. 41, we are both subject to be tempted, and forward to expose ourselves unto temptations, ver. 69—72." †

Q. 12. Are we able to resist temptations when assaulted with them?

A. No; we are, "of ourselves, unable and unwilling to resist them, to recover out of them, and to improve them, Rom. vii. 23, 24." ‡

Q. 13. How is Satan denominated in scripture, with reference to temptations?

A. He is called, by way of eminence, *the tempter*, Matt. v. 3.

Q. 14. Why is he so called?

A. Because of his strong and violent instigation and solicitation to sin, Acts v. 3.

* Larger Catechism, Quest. 195. † Ibid. ‡ Ibid

Q. 15. When did he begin this trade of tempting?

A. He began it in Paradise, Gen. iii. 1, 4, 5; and has been making his assaults upon all ranks of mankind ever since, 1 Pet. v. 8.

Q. 16. Can Satan force and compel the will to yield to his temptations?

A. No; otherwise all his temptations would be irresistible.

Q. 17. How do you know that they are not irresistible?

A. Because the saints are exhorted to resist them, James iv. 7; and have actually been enabled, by grace, to do it, 2 Cor. xii. 8, 9.

Q. 18. How many are the ways by which Satan manages his temptations?

A. Two ways chiefly, either in a way of *subtlety*, using wiles and devices; hence called that old serpent which deceiveth the whole world, Rev. xx. 2, compared with chap. xii. 9; or in a way of *furious assault*, throwing his fiery darts, Eph. vi. 16. In both which respects he is called, in the Greek tongue, *Apollyon*; that is, a destroyer, Rev. ix. 11.

Q. 19. Why called a destroyer?

A. Because he aims at nothing less than the eternal ruin and destruction of all mankind, 1 Pet. v. 8: "Your adversary the devil, as a roaring lion, walketh about seeking whom he may devour."

Q. 20. What are some of those chief wiles and stratagems in which he displays his *subtlety*?

A. He makes choice of the most advantageous seasons for tempting; he employs the fittest instruments for carrying on his designs; and sometimes gilds over the foulest sins with the fairest names.

Q. 21. What are these advantageous seasons for tempting, of which Satan makes choice?

A. When a person is under sore affliction and distress, Job ii. 9; when the object is present that will enforce the temptation, 2 Sam. xi. 2, 4; and after some remarkable manifestation of divine love, 2 Cor. xii. 2, 7.

Q. 22. Who are the instruments he employs for carrying on his temptations?

A. Men of the greatest power and policy, 1 Kings xii. 26—30; and sometimes men of reputed piety and godliness. thus he employed the old prophet to seduce the man of God with a lie, 1 Kings xiii. 18.

Q. 23. What are these fair names, under which Satan wants to make the vilest sins pass among men?

A. He allures to covetousness, under the name of frugality, Eccl. iv. 8; to profuseness, under the specious title of generosity, chap. v. 13, 14; he tempts to drunkenness, under the disguise of good fellowship, Prov. xxiii. 29, 30;

and to neutrality and indifference in religion, under the colour of a prudent and peaceable spirit, Acts xviii. 14, 15, 17.

Q. 24. What are those temptations, which Satan endeavours to throw in upon the soul, in the way of *furious assaults*?

A. They are his temptations to blasphemous and atheistical thoughts.

Q. 25. What is his plot by injecting these horrid suggestions?

A. Either to beget unbecoming thoughts of God, or to disturb, vex, and distract the Christian?

Q. 26. Does he ever gain his design, in begetting unbecoming thoughts of God, in the minds of any of God's children?

A. Yes; as would appear by their speaking sometimes very unadvisedly with their lips, Ps. lxxvii. 8, 9: Is his mercy clean gone for ever? doth his promise fail for ever more? hath God forgotten to be gracious?

Q. 27. Are the saints suffered to continue long in such sentiments?

A. No; for as such words are far from their stated judgment, and only flow from their lips in the hour of temptation; so the Lord, by his grace, will soon make them change their speech, as in the words immediately following: "And I said, this is mine infirmity; but I will remember the years of the right hand of the Most High," Ps. lxxvii. 10.

Q. 28. Do blasphemous and atheistical thoughts ever take their rise in our own hearts?

A. Frequently they do; as our Lord testifies, Matt. xv. 19: "Out of the heart proceed—blasphemies."

Q. 29. When may we charge ourselves with such thoughts, as arising in our hearts?

A. When we make no resistance, but give way to them; contrary to the command of God: "Resist the devil, and he will flee from you," James iv. 7.

Q. 30. Can the saints of God distinguish between blasphemous and atheistical thoughts, suggested by Satan, and those that arise in their own hearts?

A. Yes, they can, in some measure; otherwise they would frequently be deprived of the comfortable use of those consolations that are allowed them in the word.

Q. 31. How may they know the one from the other?

A. If they are violent and sudden, coming in like a flash of lightning upon the mind, Matt. xvi. 22, 23; if their souls tremble at such thoughts, and oppose them with the utmost abhorrence, Ps. lxxiii. 15: and if nothing is more grievous than to be assaulted with them, ver. 21, 22; then they may conclude, that they are rather to be charged on Satan than themselves.

Q. 32. What are the extremes, to which Satan labours to drive sinners by his temptations?

A. Either to presumption or despair.

Q. 33. What is *presumption?*

A. It is a confident hope of the favour of God, and of obtaining eternal life, without any sufficient foundation to support it, like the foolish virgins, Matt. xxv. 11, 12.

Q. 34. What is Satan's conduct with reference to presumption?

A. He does all he can to foster and cherish it, and is sure to give it no disturbance, Luke xi. 21: "When a strong man armed keepeth his palace, his goods are in peace."

Q. 35. What is *despair?*

A. It is the melancholy apprehension of a person's case as being quite hopeless, and of there being no help for him in God, Jer. ii. 25.

Q. 36. By what artifices does Satan labour to drive persons to this deplorable extreme?

A. By suggesting that their sins are too many, and too heinously aggravated to be pardoned; that the time of forgiveness is past; or that they have been guilty of the sin against the Holy Ghost.

Q. 37. Is it possible that our sins can be more numerous and more heinously aggravated, than that they can be pardoned?

A. No: because no bounds or limits can be set to the infinite mercy of God, as vented through the meritorious obedience and satisfaction of Jesus; "for, he will abundantly pardon," (margin, " he will multiply to pardon," Isa. lv. 7;) and he declares, that though our " sins be as scarlet, or red like crimson, they shall be white as snow, and as wool," Isa. i. 18.

Q. 38. Can any be certain in this life, that the time of forgiveness is past as to them, or that their day of grace is over?

A. No; because while the gospel continues to be published to them, it is their unquestionable duty to believe the report made in it, concerning salvation for them in Christ, without diving into the secret counsels of God, 1 John v. 11: " This is the record, that God hath given to us eternal life; and this life is in his Son."

Q. 39. How may a person know if he is not guilty of the sin against the Holy Ghost?

A. If he is deeply concerned and perplexed about this matter, and has an habitual desire after salvation by grace, he may be verily assured he is not guilty of this: for " they that be whole need not a physician, but they that are sick," Matt. ix. 12.

Q. 40. What is the second spring of our temptations above mentioned?

A. The *world*, Mark iv. 19.

Q. 41. What are the things of the world which give rise to temptations?

A. Both the good things and the bad things of it.

Q. 42. What are the good things of the world, which may prove a snare and occasion to sin?

A. The profits, pleasures, and preferments of the world, when trusted to, and rested in, Matt. xiii. 22.

Q. 43. For what should we pray, in order to be delivered from such temptations?

A. That God would incline our hearts unto his "testimonies and not to covetousness," Ps. cxix. 36, and that he would set our "affections on things above, not on things on the earth," Col. iii. 2.

Q. 44. What are the evil things of this world, which may prove temptations?

A. The outward troubles and afflictions we meet with in it, John xvi. 33: "In the world ye shall have tribulation."

Q. 45. Is God the author of all outward afflictions?

A. Yes; Amos iii. 6: "Shall there be evil in a city and the Lord hath not done it?" Though men may indeed have an instrumental and sinful hand in their own troubles and distresses; Jer. ii. 17: "Hast thou not procured this unto thyself, in that thou hast forsaken the Lord thy God?"

Q. 46. When do afflictions prove temptations?

A. When we either "despise the chastening of the Lord,' or "faint when we are rebuked of him," Heb. xii. 5.

Q. 47. For what should we pray when visited with afflictions?

A. That when the Lord is pleased to chasten us, it may be for our profit, that we may be partakers of his holiness, Heb. xii. 10.

Q. 48. What is the third spring or fountain of our temptations?

A. The *flesh*, Gal. v. 17.

Q. 49. What is meant by the flesh?

A. Our corrupt and depraved nature, Rom. vii. 8: "They that are in the flesh cannot please God."

Q. 50. How is the flesh, or corrupt nature, the spring of temptation?

A. As it entices to it, James i. 14, and is the inlet to temptations from Satan and the world, Jer. xvii. 9.

Q. 51. How should we pray against such temptations as have their rise from corrupt nature?

A. That God would not only restrain the pernicious tendency of our natural dispositions, Ps. xix. 13, but likewise fortify our souls, by the powerful influence of his grace, against all these evils, to which we are naturally addicted, Eph. iii. 16.

Q. 52. May we pray absolutely against temptations?
A. No; but we may put an alternative into God's hand with reference to them.

Q. 53. What alternative may be put into God's hand with reference to temptations?
A. That he [would either keep us from being tempted to sin, or support and deliver us when we are tempted.]

Q. 54. What do we mean, when we pray, [that God would keep us from being tempted to sin?]
A. We mean by it, that, since the event of a temptation, with respect to us, is so dangerous and uncertain, if God has not some gracious ends to answer by it, he would rather be pleased, by his providence, to prevent the temptation, than suffer us to fall into it, Ps. xix. 13.

Q. 55. What do we mean, when we pray, that God would [support and deliver us when we are tempted?]
A. We thus express our desire, "that, if tempted, we may, by his Spirit, be powerfully enabled to stand in the hour of temptation, Eph. iii. 16; or, if fallen, raised again and recovered out of it, Ps. li. 12, and have a sanctified use and improvement thereof, 1 Pet. v. 8."*

Q. 56. How does the Lord enable his people to stand in the hour of temptation?
A. By making his grace sufficient for them, and perfecting his strength in their weakness, 2 Cor. xii. 9.

Q. 57. How does he raise and recover them out of temptation, when fallen into it?
A. By discovering the corrupt and natural bias of their heart toward the temptation; humbling them on account of it, and the offence done to God by their compliance; and by quickening their faith, to draw virtue from the righteousness of the Surety, for a fresh intimation of pardon, Ps. li. 4, 5, 7.

Q. 58. When have they a sanctified use and improvement of temptations?
A. When they are made more circumspect, watchful, and dependent on Christ for the future, as being sensible of their inability to resist the least temptation without him; for he has said, Without me ye can do nothing, John xv. 5.

Q. 59. What should be our habitual scope, and general end, in offering up this petition, "Lead us not into temptation, but deliver us from evil?"
A. Our aim and end in it, should be, "that our sanctification and salvation may be perfected, 2 Cor. xiii. 9; Satan trodden under our feet, Rom. xvi. 20; and we fully freed from sin, temptation, and all evil for ever, 1 Thess. v. 23." †

---

* Larger Catechism, Quest. 195. † Ibid.

QUEST. 107. *What doth the conclusion of the Lord' Prayer teach us?*

ANS. The conclusion of the Lord's Prayer, (which is, *For thine is the kingdom, and the power, and the glory, for ever, Amen,*) teacheth us to take our encouragement in prayer from God only, and in our prayers to praise him, ascribing kingdom, power, and glory to him. And, in testimony of our desire and assurance to be heard, we say, AMEN.

Q. 1. What does the particle [for] which ushers in the conclusion of the Lord's prayer, teach us?
A. It " teacheth us to enforce our petitions with arguments, Rom. xv. 30."*

Q. 2. From whence are these arguments to be taken?
A. "Not from any worthiness in ourselves, or in any other creature, but from God, Dan. ix. 19." †

Q. 3. What argument, for instance, may we fetch from God, to enforce our petitions?
A. That "mercy and truth have met together; righteousness and peace have kissed each other," Ps. lxxxv. 10.

Q. 4. What force is there in this argument?
A. A very great force, namely, that all the perfections and excellencies of the divine nature, harmoniously agree in conferring all promised blessings upon sinners of mankind, on account of the meritorious obedience, and satisfaction of Christ imputed to them, 1 Cor. iii. 22, 23: "All things are yours, and ye are Christ's."

Q. 5. For what end should we use arguments with God in prayer?
A. Not to prevail with him to grant what he does not see fit for us; but to quicken our own faith, and encourage our hope, to expect the good things of the promise which we want, in his own time and way, Dan. ix. 18.

Q. 6. Why should we essay [in our prayers to praise him?]
A. Because praise glorifies God, Ps. l. 23, and engages him to hear our prayers, Ps. lxviii. 5, 6.

Q. 7. What way should we praise him in our prayers?
A. By [ascribing kingdom, power, and glory to him.]

Q. 8. What is meant by [kingdom, power, and glory?]
A. "Eternal sovereignty, omnipotency, and glorious excellency," as appertaining "to God alone," 1 Chron. xxix. 10—14.‡

* Larger Catechism, Quest. 196.   † Ibid.   ‡ Ibid.

Q. 9. What [kingdom] do we ascribe to God as his?
A. The kingdom of nature, as God Creator; and the kingdom of grace, as God Redeemer.

Q. 10. What encouragement may we take in prayer, from the kingdoms both of nature and grace being his?
A. That we shall want nothing that is good for us, either as we are his creatures, Ps. cxlv. 16, or his children, Matt. vii. 11.

Q. 11. Why do we ascribe [power] to God, as well as kingdom?
A. Because, without power, his sovereignty could not be maintained, or his kingdom managed, Ps. lxvi. 3, 7.

Q. 12. What encouragement may we take in prayer, from the power being his?
A. That no difficulty whatever shall hinder the accomplishment of the promise, Rom. iv. 21.

Q. 13. What do we mean by ascribing [glory] to him?
A. We thus acknowledge, that he is possessed of all those excellencies, which render him glorious in the eyes of men and angels; and that the praise and honour of every thing that is great and excellent, or has a tendency to raise our esteem and admiration, is due to him, Ps. lxxviii. 4.

Q. 14. What encouragement may we take in prayer, from the glory being his?
A. That the accomplishment of his glorious purposes, and performance of his gracious promises, will bring in a revenue of glory and praise to him, Ps. xlv. 17.

Q. 15. How long will the kingdom, power, and glory be his?
A. [For ever,] without intermission through eternity. Ex. xv. 18.

Q. 16. What is the difference, in this respect, between God and all earthly kings and potentates whatsoever?
A. Their kingdom, power, and glory, are only of a short duration, Ps. lxxxii. 6, 7; whereas the God with whom we have to do changes not, but is ever the same, James i. 17.

Q. 17. Why do we say [Amen] in our prayers?
A. We should do it [in testimony of our desire, and assurance to be heard.]

Q. 18. How may we know we say [Amen] in testimony of our desire?
A. When "by faith we are imboldened to plead with God, that he would—fulfil our requests, 2 Chron. xx. 6, 11."*

Q. 19. What does the word signify, when we say it in testimony of our desire?
A. In this view it properly signifies, So be it, or so let it be.

* Larger Catechism Q. 196.

Q. 20. When do we say Amen in testimony of our [assurance to be heard?]

A. When " by faith we are imboldened—quietly to rely upon him that he will fulfil our requests, 2 Chron. xiv. 11."*

Q. 21. What does the word signify, when we say it in testimony of our assurance to be heard?

A. In this sense it denotes, So it is; or, so it shall be.

Q. 22. In which of these views is the word, Amen, to be understood in the conclusion of this prayer?

A. It is to be understood as signifying both; namely, as including a testimony of our desire, and likewise an assurance of being heard.

Q. 23. How does this appear?

A. Because there cannot be a desire of any promised blessing in faith, but there must be some measure of assurance that it will be granted in God's time and order, Ps. x. 17.

* Larger Catechism, Quest. 196.

CONTENTS OF THE FIRST PART.

	Page		Page
The Preface,	3	Of the second part, *viz.* his in-	
Advertisement,	7	tercession,	133
Of man's chief end,	9	Of Christ as a king,	136
Of the holy scriptures,	14	Of Christ's humiliation,	142
Of the scope of the scriptures,	21	1. In his incarnation and birth,	142
Of the nature and perfections of		2. In his life,	143
God in general,	24	(1.) In being made under the	
Of God's { Infinity,	27	law,	143
Eternity,	29	(2.) In undergoing the mise-	
Unchangeableness,	30	ries of this life,	144
Being,	31	(3.) In enduring the wrath	
Wisdom,	31	of God,	144
Power,	34	3. In his death,	145
Holiness,	35	4. In what passed on him after	
Justice,	36	his death,	146
Goodness,	39	Of Christ's exaltation,	147
Truth,	41	1. In his rising again from the	
Of the unity of God,	43	dead,	148
Of the Holy Trinity,	45	2. In his ascending up into	
Of the divine decrees,	51	heaven,	151
Of the execution of God's decrees,	57	3. In his sitting at the right	
Of the creation in general,	58	hand of God the Father,	153
Of the creation of man,	61	4. In his coming to judge the	
Of providence,	65	world at the last day,	155
Of the covenant of works,	71	Of the application of redemption,	162
Of *Adam's* fall,	76	Of union with Christ,	164
Of sin in general,	80	Of effectual calling,	168
Of the first sin in particular,	83	Of benefits in this life,	173
Of our fall in *Adam*,	85	Of justification,	175
Of man's state by the fall,	88	Of adoption,	182
Of the sinfulness of man's natu-		Of sanctification,	186
ral state,	89	Of the benefits that accompany	
Of the misery of man's natural		or flow from justification, adop-	
state,	95	tion, and sanctification,	193
Of the covenant of grace,	100	1. Of assurance,	193
Of the only Redeemer,	114	2. Of peace of conscience,	195
Of Christ's incarnation,	118	3. Of joy in the Holy Ghost,	196
Of Christ's offices in general,	122	4. Of increase of grace,	197
Of Christ as a prophet,	126	5. Of perseverance,	200
Of Christ as a priest,	129	Of benefits at death,	202
Of the first part of Christ's priest-		Of benefits at the resurrection,	206
ly office. *viz.* his satisfaction,	130		

THE

CONTENTS OF THE SECOND PART.

	Page		Page
The Preface,	3	1. Of the duties required in the seventh commandment,	110
Of man's duty to God,	7		
Of the laws of God,	9	2. Of the sins forbidden in the seventh commandment,	112
1. Of the moral law,	9		
2. Of the ceremonial law,	13	Of the eighth commandment,	117
3. Of the judicial law,	20	1. Of the duties required in the eighth commandment,	118
Of the ten commandments,	21		
Of the sum of the ten commandments,	26	2. Of the sins forbidden in the eighth commandment,	120
Of the preface to the commandments,	29	Of the ninth commandment,	124
Of the first commandment,	35	1. Of the duties required in the ninth commandment,	124
1. Of the duties required in the first commandment,	36	2. Of the sins forbidden in the ninth commandment,	127
2. Of the sins forbidden in the first commandment,	40	Of the tenth commandment,	131
3. Of the words [before me] in the first commandment,	46	1. Of the duties required in the tenth commandment,	131
Of the second commandment,	48	2. Of the sins forbidden in the tenth commandment,	134
1. Of the duties required in the second commandment,	49	Of man's inability to keep the law perfectly,	137
2. Of the sins forbidden in the second commandment,	52	Of sin in its aggravations,	140
		Of the desert of sin,	144
3. Of the reasons annexed to the second commandment,	57	Of the means of salvation in general,	146
Of the third commandment,	61	Of faith in Jesus Christ,	149
1. Of the duties required in the third commandment,	61	Of repentance unto life,	158
2. Of the sins forbidden in the third commandment,	70	Of Christ's ordinances in general,	164
3. Of the reasons annexed to the third commandment,	73	Of the word in particular as made effectual to salvation,	167
Of the fourth commandment,	75	Of the manner of reading and hearing the word,	174
1. Of the duties required in the fourth commandment,	76	Of the sacraments as effectual means of salvation,	176
2. Of the change of the Sabbath,	81	Of the nature of sacraments in general,	178
3. Of sanctifying the Sabbath,	86	Of the number of the sacraments,	182
4. Of the sins forbidden in the fourth commandment,	92	Of the nature of baptism,	185
		Of the subjects of baptism,	191
5. Of the reasons annexed to the fourth commandment,	93	Of the Lord's supper,	197
Of the fifth commandment,	96	Of the worthy receiving of the Lord's supper,	206
1. Of the duties required in the fifth commandment,	96	Of the nature of prayer,	212
		Of direction in prayer,	220
2. Of the sins forbidden in the fifth commandment,	100	Of the preface of the Lord's prayer,	224
3. Of the reason annexed to the fifth commandment,	101	Of the first petition,	227
		Of the second petition,	230
Of the sixth commandment,	103	Of the third petition,	234
1. Of the duties required in the sixth commandment,	103	Of the fourth petition,	237
		Of the fifth petition,	239
2. Of the sins forbidden in the sixth commandment,	105	Of the sixth petition,	243
Of the seventh commandment,	109	Of the conclusion of the Lord's prayer,	2

INDEX

OF THE

PRINCIPAL TOPICS CONTAINED IN BOTH PARTS OF THIS CATECHISM.

After the numeral letters, I. or II., signifying the first or second Part, the first figure stands for the page, and the second for the number of the question in that page.

Ib. [*ibidem*] signifies the same part and page that is last mentioned; and then the figure stands for the number of the question in the last mentioned page.

The part is not mentioned oftener than once under the same word; only the page, and the number of the question therein.

A

AARON's rod that budded, what it signified, II. 18. 73.

Adam, four reasons why the man and the woman were so called, I. 63. 20. A covenant head to all his posterity, proved by two arguments, 86. 10. His posterity *in him*, when he first sinned, two ways, 87. 18.

Adoption, the proper meaning of it, I. 182. 1. General adoption, what 183. 4; special, what, *ib.* 6.

Adultery, what, II. 116. 28. The aggravations of it, *ib.* 31.

Agency, the peculiar agency of each person of the Trinity, in the formation of the body of Christ, I. 121. 22.

Aggravations; four sources, from whence sins receive their aggravations, II. 141. 9—30.

Altar, brazen, what typified by it, II. 16. 57; of incense, what it typified, 17. 64.

Amen, what it properly signifies, II. 251. 17—21.

Appearances; ten bodily appearances of Christ, after his resurrection, I. 149. 16.

Apocrypha, four reasons why it ought not to be received as a part of the canon of scripture, I. 21. 50.

Apostle, why Christ so called, I. 126. 4.

Arguments, nine of them, for convincing infidels that the scriptures are the word of God, I. 15. 9.

Ark in the tabernacle and temple, what was within it, II. 18. 70.

Ascension of Christ, three ends of it, I. 153. 49.

Assurance; difference between the assurance of faith, and the assurance of sense, I. 194. 8. Assurance of God's love, attainable, proved by two arguments, *ib.* 12. Three evidences of it, 195. 17. The difference between it and presumption, *ib.* 18.

Atheist; no such thing in the world, as a direct speculative Atheist, proved, II. 41. 8—11.

Attributes of God not distinct from God himself, I. 26. 22; nor from one another, *ib.* 23

B

Baptism, the proper signification of the word, II. 185. 1. When Christ appointed it as a sacrament of the New Testament, *ib.* 3. Difference between the baptism of John and the baptism dispensed by the apostles, after Christ's ascension, 186. 6, 8. Proved, that it is rightly administered by sprinkling, 187. 15. Analogy between the sign in baptism and the thing signified, 187. 19. The ends and uses of baptism, 188. 27—35. The efficacy of it, wherein it consists, 191. 47. Why but once administered, 193. 12.

Baptize, why did not Christ baptize any himself, II. 186. 11.

Blasphemy, what, II. 70. 3. The aggravations of it, *ib.* 4.

Blasphemous thoughts, three ways whereby to know when they are suggested by Satan, II. 246, 31.

Blood of Jesus, why called the blood of sprinkling, I. 133. 43.

Body that Christ had, a true and real body, proved, I. 120. 17. Why Christ's body was not created immediately out of nothing, *ib.* 19.

Bodies; four properties of the bodies of the saints, at the resurrection, explained, I. 209. 19—23.

Bondage; a twofold right that Christ had to be our Redeemer from spiritual bondage, II. 34. 32.

Books; four books will be opened at the day of judgment, I. 158. 94, &c.

Brazen Altar: See Altar.

C

Cain, why not put to death for the murder of his brother, II. 108. 22.

Candlestick, what it signified, II. 16. 62.

Chastity, what, II. 110. 1. Three ways whereby to preserve our own chastity, 110. 3.

Cherubims of glory, what represented by them, II. 19. 82. What was signified by the posture of their faces, *ib.* 86.

Children; six duties incumbent upon them to their parents, II. 98. 20.

Christ; why he is not the cause of election, I. 101. 7. Why called the *last Adam,* 102. 26. As a prophet, hath revealed the will of God two ways, 127, 12, &c. As a surety made under the moral law, 143, 12; and that as a covenant of works, proved, *ib.* 14. How Christ is offered, and to be received, in three particulars, II. 153. 46—56.

Circumcision, when first instituted, II. 182. 2. The spiritual meaning of it, 183. 4.

Cleansing; the difference between cleansing by the blood, and cleansing by the Spirit of Christ, in two particulars, II. 187. 17.

Concurrence; God's immediate concurrence with every action of the creature, proved, I. 67. 20. How he concurs with the sinful actions of men, without sin, *ib.* 21.

Confession, a part of prayer, II. 222. 17.

Connexion between the preface and the first commandment, II. 35. 6.

Contentment with our own condition, what, II. 132. 6. Four cross dispensations, under which it is required, *ib.* 10—14.

Corruption of the whole nature, what, I. 91. 19. Wherein doth it appear, *ib.* 20. How proved from scripture, 92. 22. Four inward evidences of the universal corruption of nature, *ib.* 24.

Covenant of grace, why so called, I. 102. 18. How made with Christ 103. 27. Why made with him as the head, 104. 40. The proper condition of it, what, 106. 59. Difference between the covenant of grace, and covenant of works, illustrated in nine particulars, 112. 111—120. The principal part of the Sinai transaction, though the covenant of works was most conspicuous, II. 24. 26.

Covetousness, what, II. 134. 2.

D

Death; how it may be proved, that the precise moment ot every one's death is fixed in the decree, I. 54. 24. The difference between the death of believers and that of the wicked, in five particulars, 98. 28.

Death of Christ, what about it should be remembered in the supper, in three particulars, II. 201. 33—36. Four ways whereby we should show forth his death in that sacrament, *ib.* 37—41.

Debts, why sins are so called, II. 240. 3.

Decrees; why God's eternal purpose is called his decrees in the plural number, I. 52. 5. The absurdity of conditional decrees, 53. 13. How the decree is permissive, and efficacious at the same time, 55. 30.

Delighting in the glory of God, whether it is to be reckoned our chief end, I. 13. 46.

Deliverance of Israel out of Egypt, represents our spiritual redemption, in four particulars, II. 32. 23.

Despair, what, II. 247. 35. Three ways whereby Satan labours to drive persons to despair, *ib.* 36—39.

Dipping, not necessary in baptism, II 187. 14, 15.

Discipline of Christ's kingdom, what, I. 140. 41.

Discontentment, with our own estate, what, II. 134. 6. The aggravations of this sin, *ib.* 7.

Disposition; the difference between a federal, and a testamentary disposition, I. 111. 100.

Divorce, the grounds upon which it may be obtained, II. 114, 18

Duelling, the sin of it, II. 107. 17

E

Election, what, I. 55. 38.

End; men make themselves their own end and happiness in three instances, II. 42. 21.

Eternity; the difference between God's eternity, and the eternity of angels, and the souls of men, I. 29. 6

Eutychians, their error, I. 116. 28.

Exaltation of Christ, what, I. 147. 1.

Excellency, the incomparable excellency of the scriptures, in four articles, I. 21. 51.

Extent of the grant that God makes of himself to us, illustrated in nine particulars, II. 30. 11.

F

Faith, the place it has in the covenant of grace, I. 108. 74. What right it gives to the promise, 109. 84; the difference between saving and justifying faith, 181. 59. How connected with salvation, II. 148. 20. Four kinds of faith mentioned in scripture, 149. 1—9. The appropriating persuasion, in the nature of faith, necessary to answer the gospel offer, what, 155. 58. Why this appropriating persuasion is necessary to the nature of saving faith, *ib.* 59. Three evidences of a strong faith, 156. 64. Three evidences of the weakness of faith, *ib.* 65. Three marks of a true faith, however weak, *ib.* 66. Three ways in which faith views its objects, 157. 74—77. What is it for the worthy receivers of the sacrament of the supper, to partake of the body and blood of Christ by faith, 205. 66. Four ways how we may know if we have that faith which feeds on Christ in the word and sacrament, 208. 20.

Fasting; religious fasting, what, II. 51. 22. Three arguments, proving it to be of divine appointment, *ib.* 24. The occurrences which call for it, *ib.* 27.

Father, proved to be God, I. 49. 23. Not properly the fountain of the Deity, *ib.* 29. Three respects in which God is called Father with reference to men, II. 225. 6—9.

Fatherly chastisements, why they may not be called a penalty in the covenant of grace, I. 109. 88.

Flesh, what meant by it, II. 248. 49. How it is the spring of temptation, *ih* 50.

Freedom of will, since the fall, what, I. 78. 21.

G

Glorifying God, why set before the enjoying of him, I. 13. 44. Glorifying God, what, II. 39. 31. How we glorify him in his attributes, ordinances, word, and works, 229. 13—19.

Glory; God's essential glory, what, I. 10. 8. His declarative glory what, 10. 9. Four similitudes whereunto the future glory of believers is compared 204. 22.

God; how does it appear from scripture and reason, that there can be but one only, I. 43. 1, 2. Why said to be living, 44. 15. Why called true, *ib.* 16.

Godhead, the meaning of the word, I. 46. 8.

Golden pot, that had manna, what it signified, II. 18. 72.

Goodness of God, what, I. 39. 1. His absolute goodness, what, *ib.* 3; his relative, what, *ib.* 4. How his goodness is manifested in the contrivance of redemption, 40. 13; how in the execution of it, *ib.* 14.

Gospel-offer, the faith of it, what, I. 169. 14.

Gospel precepts, the absurdity of making faith and repentance new gospel precepts, II. 38. 26, 27.

Growth; believers grow four ways, I. 199. 12, &c. Four evidences of growth in grace, *ib.* 18.

H

High priest, a type of Christ, in two respects, II. 13. 35.

Holiness of God, what, I. 35. 1. How it appears in every thing pertaining to God, *ib.* 6, &c.

Holy Ghost, five arguments, proving that he proceedeth from the Son, as well as from the Father, I. 48. 19. His supreme Deity proved by four arguments, 50. 36.

Holy resting on the Sabbath, what, II. 88. 19.

Human nature of Christ, why it never subsisted by itself, I. 118. 3. Difference between the human nature, and a human person, 119. 7.

Humiliation of Christ, what it was, I. 142. 1.

I & J

Idea; an imaginary idea of Christ as man, no way helpful to the faith of his being God-man, I. 122. 30.

Illumination, saving; four distinguishing properties of it, I. 172. 40.

Image of God, wherein it consists, I. 64. 25.

Immanuel, the import of the name, I. 116. 25, &c.

Immensity, what, I. 28. 4.

Immortality of the soul proved by four arguments, I. 63. 17.

Imputation of Adam's first sin to his posterity; proved by two scripture-arguments, I. 86. 10.

Incomprehensibility of God, what, I. 28. 3.

Infants; the right that the infants of such as are members of the visible church have to baptism, proved at great length, and objections answered, II. 194 to 196. 25 to 44.

Infinite, what it is for God to be so, I. 27. 1.

Intercession of Christ, the nature of it described, I. 134. 51. The grounds of its perpetuity, 135. 64; difference between the intercession of Christ and the intercession of the Spirit, 136. 69.

Joy in the Holy Ghost, four seasons of it, I. 197. 5. Four evidences of it, *ib.* 9.

Journey, Sabbath day's, what, II. 88. 13.

Judge, four qualities of the Judge at the last day, I. 156. 82.

Judgment, that there will be a general judgment proved, I. 155. 69. &c.

Justice of God, what, I. 36. 1.

Justice, legislative, what, 37. 6; distributive, what, *ib.* 9; vindictive, essential to God, proved by four arguments, 38. 22.

Justification and sanctification connected in six respects, I. 187. 7.— The difference between them, in twelve particulars, *ib.* 9 to 21.
Justify, what it is to justify a person, I. 175. 3.

K

Kingdom, the twofold kingdom of Christ, essential, and mediatorial, explained, I. 138. 17 to 20.
Kingdom of God and his righteousness, what meant by the expression, II. 213. 19. God's kingdom of grace, why so called, 231. 17. What this kingdom of grace is as to outward dispensation, *ib.* 155; what as to inward operation, 16.
Kingdom of glory, what, 234. 39.
Knowledge, God's. How does it appear that God has a certain knowledge of contingent actions, I. 32. 9. How does he know things only possible, *ib.* 10. How does he know things future, *ib.* 11.
Knowledge, man's saving knowledge of God, wherein it consists, I. 26. 19, &c. Four evidences of it, II. 37. 16. Three ways how we may know if the measure of knowledge we have attained, be of a saving kind, 208. 16.

Last day, why the day of judgment is so called, I. 156. 76.
Law, natural, what, II. 9. 2. Some general principles of the law of nature, mentioned, 10. 7. Difference between the law of nature, and the moral law, *ib.* 11. Whether is the moral law of immutable obligation, 11 16. How is it a schoolmaster to bring to Christ, 12. 26. How Christ sweetens it to his subjects, I. 140. 36.
Lie, what is the formal nature of it, II. 127. 3. How it is aggravated, *ib.* 4. Three sorts of it, and each of them described, 128. 8 to 18.
Light, why is God so called, I. 25. 10.
Long life, three things that tend to make it happy and comfortable, II 102. 7.
Lotting, what, II. 68. 63, 66. Why only to be used in cases of absolute necessity, 67. 69.
Love, why God is said to be love, I. 25. 11. Three marks of supreme love to God, II. 27. 14. Three ways how to know if our love to Christ be sincere and unfeigned, 208. 24.
Lust, six remedies against all incentives to it, II. 117. 39.

M

Man, how he ought to glorify God, I. 10. 12.
Marriage, why instituted before the fall, I. 62. 11. Three ends of its institution, II. 111. 13.
Matter and form of an action, the difference between them illustrated by an example, I. 68. 23.
Mediator, why is he God and man in one person, I. 118. 40.
Melchisedek, order of, what, I. 130. 11. Why is Christ called a priest after this order, *ib.* 13.
Mercy, four kinds of mercy which God shows them that love him, II 60. 30.
Mercy-seat, what signified by it, II. 19. 80.
Messiah, Christ proved to be the true Messiah, I. 114. 6, &c.
Ministers, six duties incumbent upon them to their people, II. 99. 26.
Miracle, what is the true notion of it, I. 69. 38.
Morality of the fourth commandment, wherein it consists, II. 78. 24.
Murderers to be punished with death, II. 107. 10.

N

Name, the former and present name of the adopted children of God, in three particulars, I. 184. 22. How a good name may be obtained, II. 125. 11 How it ought to be maintained, 126. 15.

Names, three sorts of names, whereby God conveys the knowledge of himself to us, II. 62. 7.
Nature, Christ's human nature not represented in the first Adam, I. 87. 22; but legally derived, *ib.* 23.
Necessity of a further revelation than nature's light illustrated by five reasons, I. 16. 16.
Nestorians, their error, I. 116. 29.

O

Oath, the definition of it, II. 63. 17. The definition explained, *ib.* 18 to 21. The three qualifications of it, *ib.* 22 to 27. The obligation thereof, 66. 47 to 54.
Oaths, distinguished into assertory and promissory, both of which are illustrated, II. 65. 33 to 44.
Obedience, Christ's active and passive obedience described, I. 179. 40 and 41. Difference between the obedience due to God and to lawful superiors, II. 8. 11. Three qualities of acceptable obedience, *ib.* 14. Four reasons why the obedience of believers is called new obedience, 162. 42 to 48. Three ways how to know if our obedience is indeed new obedience, 209. 26.
Offices of Christ, not the proper fountain of the promises, I. 124. 23.
Order of doctrine laid down in the standards of the church of Scotland, illustrated, I. 22. 4 to 18.
Ordinances, nine religious ordinances mentioned from the Larger Catechism, and explained II. 165. 6 to 22.
Ordination, by presbyters, without a diocesan bishop, proved lawful and valid, II. 192. 2.
Original sin, proved to be damning, I. 94. 39. The evidences of it, antecedent to the commission of any actual transgression, *ib.* 40.

P

Parents, five duties incumbent on them to their children, II. 98. 19.
Passover, when first instituted, II. 183. 6. Why so called, *ib.* 7. What were the significant ceremonies in that sacrament, *ib.* 10 to 16.
Peace, three things to mar the peace of believers, I. 196. 8.
People, five duties incumbent upon them to their ministers, II. 99. 26.
Perfection not attainable by the saints in this life, proved by three arguments, II. 138. 12 and 13.
Perfections of God, why called attributes, I. 27. 24. How distinguished, *ib.* 25, &c.
Perjury, what, II. 70. 7. The aggravations of it, 71. 11.
Perseverance of the saints, six infallible securities for it, I. 200. 3. See also, II. 178. 38.
Person in the Godhead, what is meant by it; I. 46. 9. Four arguments, proving that there are three persons in the Godhead, 47. 13.
Pictures, or images of Christ, why to be abhorred, II. 53. 9, 10.
Polygamy, what, II. 113. 8. How God has testified his displeasure against it, even in the godly, 114. 15.
Portion, what meant by a competent portion of the good things of this life, II. 237. 8. Three differences as to the manner in which the godly and the wicked hold their outward comforts, 238. 17 to 20.
Power of God, what, I. 34. 1. How manifested in creation, *ib.* 5. How in providence, *ib.* 6. How in redemption, *ib.* 7.
Pray; what it is to pray in Christ's name, II. 214. 22. For whom are we to pray, in eight particulars, *ib.* 28 to 36. How are we to pray, in six particulars, 216. 42 to 49.
Prayer to be made to God only, II. 212. 1. Four reasons of it, *ib.* 2. Three kinds of prayer, secret, private, and public, explained, 217. 50 to 62. Two reasons for confessing sins in prayer, 219. 68. How may we know that our prayers are heard, 220. 80. Two ways whereby we may know

if mercies come to us in the course of common providence, or as an answer of prayer, *ib.* 81 to 84. *Lord's prayer,* why called the special rule of direction in prayer, 222. 10. Proved by two arguments, that it is not designed for a mere form, to the precise words whereof we are strictly tied down, *ib.* 16 to 28.
    Predestinated, what, I. 55. 35.
    Present, how God is present with his church on earth, I. 28. 8. How he is present in heaven, *ib.* 9. How in hell, *ib.* 10.
    Presumption, what, II. 187. 33.
    Priest, what, I. 129. 1.
    Privileges; five privileges of God's children, 1. 185. 25, &c.
    Probation, state of, when applicable to man, I. 76. 8.
    Promise of eternal life, what, I. 108. 79 to 81.
    Property; difference between a personal and an essential property, I 48. 20.
    Providence, divine, proved by five arguments, from reason, I. 65. 3 Extends to the smallest, as well as to the greatest of the creatures, 66. 7 How conversant about good actions, *ib.* 12. How about sinful ones, two ways, *ib.* 13.
    Providences of God, how to be observed, I. 69. 43.
    Punishment of loss in hell, set forth in four particulars, I. 99. 36; of sense, described from some scripture expressions, *ib.* 37. Both proved to be eternal, *ib.* 38. Eternity of punishment, whence it arises, *ib.* 40.

R

    Record of God, a ground of faith to all the hearers of the gospel, proved, I. 42. 12.
    Redemption, covenant of redemption, not a distinct covenant from that of grace, proved, I. 105. 50 to 58.
    Regeneration, why called a creation, II. 172. 46. Why a resurrection, *ib.* 47.
    Repentance, whether a transient action, or an abiding principle, II. 158. 3, 4. Flows from faith, 159. 16. The formal nature of evangelical repentance, 161. 25 to 31. Two differences between gospel and legal repentance, 163. 48. Seven evidences of true repentance, *ib.* 50 to 57. Three special seasons for the exercise of it in the Lord's people, 164. 60. Three ways how we may know if our repentance be genuine, or of a right kind, 208. 22.
    Reprobation, what, I. 56. 40.
    Resurrection of Christ proved, I. 148. 9 to 16. The necessity of it in three respects, 150. 23, &c. The general resurrection of the dead, proved by two arguments, both of which are explained at large, 207. 2 to 8. Difference between the resurrection of the godly, and the wicked, 209. 17.
    Righteousness of Christ, wherein it consists, I. 106. 60 to 71.
    Rule; how men make themselves their own rule, in three instances, II. 42. 20.

S

    Sabbath, when first instituted, II. 81. 1. The first day of the week proved to be the Christian Sabbath, of divine institution, by five arguments, each of which is illustrated, 83. 19 to 34.
    Sacrament, the two parts of it explained, II. 179. 7 to 16. The form of a sacrament, wherein it consists, 181. 26 to 29.
    Sacramental elements in the supper, described; II. 198. 10 to 15. The sacramental actions explained, 199. 16 to 27 The end of these sacramental elements and actions unfolded, 200. 28, 32. Who ought to be

kept from the Lord's supper, 210. 34—36. Four things wherein baptism and the Lord's supper agree, 211. 44. Four things wherein they differ *ib.* 45.

Saints; the reason why saints in heaven cannot be intercessors, II. 55. 22.

Samson, whether guilty of self-murder, II. 106. 6.

Sanctification, habitual and actual, how they differ, I. 190. 33. Sanctification useful and necessary in ten respects, 192. 45. Six marks of it, *ib.* 51. Four motives thereto, *ib.* 52.

Satan, his policy in enticing our first parents to eat the forbidden fruit in five instances, I. 84. 9. The way how to distinguish his suggestions from the dictates of the Spirit of God, II. 45. 47.

Satisfaction to justice necessary, I. 132. 30 to 33. Three reasons why it was demanded from Christ, *ib.* 34.

School of affliction, what learned at it, I. 128. 26.

Scriptures, why called a testament, I. 17. 23. A three-fold use of them, II. 168. 5. The manner of reading them, in three particulars, *ib.* 8 to 11.

Self, what is it for man to deny himself, II. 45. 39 to 42.

Show-bread, what meant by it, II. 17. 63.

Similitudes; to explain the doctrine of the Trinity by similitudes, proved to be unlawful, I. 50. 38.

Sin; that there is such a thing as sin in the world, proved by four arguments, I. 80. 2. Why called want of conformity to the law, 81. 9. Why a transgression of it, *ib.* 10. First sin, the nature of it, in six particulars, 84. 11, &c. The aggravations of it, in six instances, 85. 19.

Sin against the Holy Ghost, what, I. 82. 20. &c. Four evidences whereby a person may know he is not guilty of it, *ib.* 26. Four ways whereby it may be known that persons are guilty of it, II. 215. 39.

Sinai-covenant, opened, I. 105. 54, and II. 22. 14 to 26.

Sinfulness of an action, wherein it properly consists, I. 67. 22.

Son; Christ the Son proved to be truly and properly the supreme God, by four arguments, I. 49. 30, &c.

Son of God, the danger of asserting that Christ is so called, merely with respect to his mediatory office, I. 116. 20.

Sonship, Christ's, distinguished from his office, I. *ib.* 22.

Spirit, why is God so called, I. 25. 12.

State, five scripture characters of the state of sin and misery into which man has fallen, I. 89. 8.

Subjects, five duties incumbent upon them to their magistrates, II. 98. 23.

Supper, why this sacrament is called a supper, and why the Lord's supper, II. 197, 1, 2.

Surety, in what sense Christ is so, for his spiritual seed, I. 104. 38.

T

Tables of the covenant, and ark of the covenant, why so called, II. 18. 77.

Tables of the law, what was signified by their being written on both sides, II. 22. 7, 8.

Testament; the New Testament excels the Old, in five instances, I. 18. 32, &c.

Testament, Christ's, what time made, I. 111. 103. Who are the legatees, *ib.* 105. Who is the executor, *ib.* 106.

Temptation; two ways whereby God may be said to lead a person into temptation, and yet not be the author of sin, II. 244. 2. How he recovers his people out of temptation, 249. 57.

Tempter, why is Satan so called, II. 244. 13, 14. Two ways whereby he manages his temptations, enlarged upon, 245. 18 to 27.

Thoughts, the proper remedy and antidote against sinful ones, II. 140. 26.

Titles, four of them that are ascribed to God as the God of nature, II. 62. 10; and six that belong to him as the God of grace, *ib.* 11. His New Testament titles, what, 61. 12.

Transubstantiation, what, II. 203. 51. The absurdity of it in four particulars, *ib.* 52, to 56. The difference between it and consubstantiation, 204. 57.

Trinity of persons, proved from the Old Testament, I. 45. 3. from the New, 46. 7.

Truth of God, what, I. 41. 1. Wherein manifested, 42. 7.

U

Unchangeable, what is meant by God's being so, I. 30. 1. How proved from scripture and reason, *ib.* 2. and 3.

Unction of Christ, what, I. 124. 15.

Union with Christ, five properties of it, I. 166. 22, &c. The two bonds of it, 167. 29 to 34. Four resemblances of it, 168. 37.

Unition, what, I. 166. 18.

V

Venial, what do the Papists mean by venial sins, II. 145. 9. No sins venial in their sense, *ib.* 10.

Virgin; why was Christ born of a virgin, I. 121. 23.

Virgin Mary, proved to be a sinner as well as others, I. 121. 26.

Vow, the nature of it, II. 67. 55—Difference between an oath and a vow, *ib.* 56. The subject matter of vows. *ib.* 57.

W

Want of original righteousness, what, I. 91. 12.

War, when lawful, II. 107. 12

Wealth, six ways whereby our neighbour's wealth may be unjustly hindered, and each of them explained, II. 121. 9 to 38.

Will of God, twofold, and both of them unfolded II. 235. 1 to 4.

Will of man in a state of innocence, whether indifferent to good and evil, I. 64. 29.

Wisdom, how does the wisdom of God appear in creation, I. 33. 15. How in providence, *ib.* 16. How in redemption, *ib.* 17.

Witness, why is Christ so called, I. 126. 5.

Witness-bearing; five sorts of persons, who may be guilty of bearing false witness against their neighbour, in public judicature; and the manner how they may be so, II. 130. 26 to 32.

Word of God, why committed to writing, I. 17. 19. The manner in which it ought to be preached, in six particulars, II. 169. 15 to 22. Four metaphors whereunto the efficacy of the word is compared in scripture, 172. 49 to 53. Four effects of receiving the word with faith, 175. 13. Three things implied in laying it up in our hearts, 176. 18. Three evidences of our laying it up there, *ib.* 19.

Works of necessity on the Sabbath, what, II. 90. 36; instances of them, *ib.* 37.

World; five things in the world, which men naturally incline to idolize, II. 45. 44. Two things in it which give rise to temptations, 248. 41 to 47.

Worship; how are we to worship God inwardly in our hearts, in six particulars, II. 39. 36. How outwardly in our lives, in five duties, 40. 37.

Worship, family, what, II. 89. 25; proved to be a duty, from scripture precept, *ib.* 27; and from scripture example, *ib.* 28.

Z

Zeal, what it is for God to have zeal for his worship, II. 58. 12; **two** ways whereby he manifests his zeal for his own worship, *ib.* 13 to 34.

P. S.—If the reader would be pleased, now and then, to peruse this Index, he would readily at every time, meet with some article or other that would induce him to consult the book itself, till he were gradually led on to a tolerable acquaintance with the whole; which was indeed my principal design, in the composing this alphabetical summary of the contents.

JAMES FISHER.

GLASGOW, Nov. 25 1765.

THE END.

www.ingramcontent.com/pod-product-compliance
Lightning Source LLC
Chambersburg PA
CBHW071136300426
44113CB00009B/992